The UK Space
Resources, Environment and the Future

The UK Space
Resources, Environment and the Future
Second Edition

Edited by
J.W. House
Halford Mackinder Professor of Geography,
University of Oxford

Weidenfeld and Nicolson

London

Reprinted 1975
Second Edition 1977

ISBN 0 297 77356 9 cased
ISBN 0 297 77357 7 paperback.

Weidenfeld and Nicolson
11 St John's Hill, London SW11 1XA

Text set in 10/11pt IBM Press Roman,
printed by photolithography, and bound in
Great Britain at The Pitman Press, Bath

Contributors

Chapter 1
J. W. House, *M.A. (Oxon.)*
Halford Mackinder Professor of Geography, University of Oxford

Chapter 2
R. Lawton, *M.A. (Liverpool)*
Professor of Geography, University of Liverpool

Chapter 3
L. W. Hanna, *M.Sc. Ph.D. (Belfast)*
Senior Lecturer in Geography, University of Newcastle upon Tyne

Chapter 4
G. Humphrys, *B.A. (Bristol), M.A. (McGill), Ph.D. (Wales)*
Senior Lecturer in Geography, University College of Swansea

Chapter 5
N. R. Elliott, *B.A., Ph.D. (Dunelm)*
Senior Lecturer in Geography, University of Edinburgh

and

B. Fullerton, *M.A. (London)*
Senior Lecturer in Geography, University of Newcastle upon Tyne

Chapter 6
D. R. Diamond, *M.A. (Oxon.), M.Sc. (Northwestern)*
Reader in Regional Planning, London School of Economics and Political Science

Chapter 7
The Contributors

Contents

Contents

5   TRANSPORT   360

        N. R. ELLIOTT and B. FULLERTON

I   Introduction: Some Theoretical and Empirical Background (NRE and 360
        BF)
I.1   Transport Systems   360
I.2   Transport Development, 1950–75   361
I.3   Transport Policies   363

II   Inland Transport between Cities and Regions (BF)   369

II.1   Traffic Flows   369
II.2   Trunk Road Development   373
II.3   The Modernization of the Railway System   377

III   Local Transport (BF)   386

III.1   The Coordination of Urban Transport Systems   387
III.2   The Changing Pattern of Rural Transport   391

IV   Air Transport   395

IV.1   Traffic   395
IV.2   The Location and Development of Airports   398

V   Seaports and Water Transport (NRE)   400

V.1   The Hierarchy of Seaports   400
V.2   Seaports and Cargo-handling   409
V.3   Seaports and Industry   415
V.4   The Changing Status and Function of Seaports   419
V.5   Inland Waterways   424

VI   Retrospect and Prospect (NRE and BF)   426

VI.1   The Transport Revolution   426
VI.2   Pipeline Development   429
VI.3   Complementary or Competitive Transport Media?   431
VI.4   The Rationalization of the Ports   435

Figures

Chapter 3

Chapter 4

Figures 1.14, 2.6, 2.8, 2.9, 2.13, 2.21, 2.22 and 3.2 are reproduced by kind permission of the Controller of Her Majesty's Stationery Office.

Tables

Page

Chapter 5

Page

Preface

In the 1970s the UK stands critically poised in several respects. One generation on from the Second World War her international role and status have by now been painfully but not finally adjusted and will need further redefinition in our early years in the EEC. At home fundamental issues of our economy, society and polity need to be re-examined, in the light of a now slowly rising national population, the great debate on the merits and prospects in economic growth, the environmental question, the pursuit of greater social justice and regional equilibrium, and not least the pressures for political devolution.

This book seeks to contribute to the need for a national stock-taking, an evaluation of resources, both natural and human. It does so through a geographical interpretation, to be set distinctively alongside those by economists, sociologists or political scientists. To the common concern the geographer adds his perspective on the UK space, a sensitivity to the differences, trends and problems arising from the characteristics of people and places. These are set within the context of post-war changes and the shifting framework of key policies and decisions, both public and private. The interpretation covers the constituent parts of the UK, and much of the material is focused at the level of the economic planning region or the sub-nation. This is increasingly a valid scale for planning and also for the expression of a rising sense of provincially-based regionalism within the complex urban society of the UK. The exposition is by review of the essentials, highlighting of the trends, survey of policies and assessment of their spatial effects. This is in other words a set of considered judgements rather than the opening of new research frontiers, towards which the full bibliographies to each chapter provide an essential indication.

With desire for devolution such a potent force and with the importance of regional planning at last recognized, it seemed right to start from the regional perspective (ch. 1). This reflects the essential and striking diversities of people and resources, of heritage, problems and aspirations at work in the UK today. In one sense these are focused through the regional planning mechanism and the formulation of strategies for the remaining years of this century.

The people themselves come next (ch. 2), their distribution, structure, trends and the spatial implications of demographic change. Since the management of patterns of employment has played such a key role in public policy in the post-war UK, this links people and their work, with mobility between residence and work-place a most sensitive indicator of change and, at the same time, of the effects of urbanization. A proper evaluation of the UK environment is overdue (ch. 3) and has often been neglected in planning and policy-making in the past. The key questions concern land, its use and potential, the resources offered in turn by climate, soils and vegetation. The total environment implies many management and conservation problems, illustrated by water, forests and all the implications of environment for those living in our towns and cities.

In an urban industrial society in the throes of rapid technological change the range and cost of alternative energy sources vies with the manufacturing and services sector in critical importance in economic growth and transformation (ch. 4). Mobility through the diverse media of the transport network (ch. 5) is a key to the practicability and profitability of redeploying people or productive resources. The spatial potential unlocked by technological change in the transport fields bids fair to outrival all others before the end of the century.

The ambition of the book is to review spatially the tides, currents and trends of economic, social and political change in the post-war UK. Carrying an important part of the message, the line drawings are a valuable contribution by cartographers in the Geography Departments at Edinburgh, Liverpool, Newcastle upon Tyne and Swansea.

The help of all those who have kindly typed the manuscript or checked proofs is also gratefully acknowledged.

University of Newcastle upon Tyne   J W HOUSE
January 1973

Preface to the Second Edition

The past four years have been a time of almost unparalleled change in the UK. The national economy has moved from phases of slow growth and stagnation into a deepening recession. Unemployment has been contained short of massive proportions only by heavy and increasing public expenditure. New problem industries have emerged, notably car manufacturing, and hitherto more prosperous regions, such as the W Midlands or C London, have been adversely affected. Evidence from the 1971 census and subsequent further downward trends in the birth-rate have diminished longer-term population prospects. Major infra-structural decisions have been reached not to proceed with the Channel Tunnel, the Third London Airport (Foulness) and the Maplin seaport.

On the brighter side the UK membership of the enlarged EEC has been confirmed by referendum, and the dramatically rapid opening-up of the North Sea oil and natural gas resources promises major relief to an ailing national economy during the 1980s. This relief will be the more welcome after the traumatic upheavals of the 1974–5 oil crisis. The reform of local government throughout the UK in 1973 (N Ireland) and 1974 (England, Wales and Scotland) proved but a preliminary to wider claims for devolution of powers, for the satisfaction of nations, if not for regions in the national space.

The second edition takes stock of these most recent developments and attempts to assess the kaleidoscope of change in resources, society and sub-region. Some consideration is given to theories and models which may help to explain change, and also to the political forces which increasingly disturb and distort an economic and social interpretation of events. An additional chapter, on the Urban System (ch. 6), completes the systematic coverage of the resources, environment and the future of the UK Space.

Thanks are once again due to all those who prepared diagrams, including now the cartographers at Oxford and the LSE, typed the manuscript or corrected proofs. Particular thanks are due to Miss D J Wood-Mallock.

University of Oxford   J W HOUSE
February 1977

1

Regions and the System

I THE UK IN THE POST-WAR WORLD

I.1 General Assessment

By tradition geographical interpretation starts logically from the characteristics, location and pattern of all resources, including people, and studies their changes over time, using both systematic (or sector) and regional methods of analysis. Standard texts (Dury 1968; Smith 1949; Stamp and Beaver 1971; Watson and Sissons 1964) have favoured a long perspective in time, with a preferred objective of explaining the present in terms of the past. Less ambitious and more selective in conventional terms, this chapter adds a further dimension: concern for the future. It starts by reviewing the major economic and social changes differentiating the UK space since the end of the Second World War. It then seeks to evaluate the manifold and diverse forces affecting, and affected in their turn by the conditions of the UK space, the impact but also the resultant modification of policies, both public and private, relating to regions, areas and localities. After this preliminary context the greater part of the chapter attempts to look ahead, with an assessment and critique of the strategy proposals for each of the eight economic planning regions of England, together with those for Wales, Scotland and N Ireland, in the light of their present problems, current trends and the declared intentions of policy-makers. This can only be an interim stocktaking, since regional strategies are neither fully nor uniformly elaborated as yet, and scarcely inter-related, whilst inter-regional relationships, flows and accounts, remain imperfectly understood. Furthermore, no comprehensive regional policy has yet been advanced by any post-war British government and there has been continuing reluctance in official circles to see the spatial dimension in its rightful perspective in economic, social or even physical planning. Finally, the economic planning regions and the national units, upon which this interpretation necessarily rests at this time, though not altogether satisfactory units, are hopefully the basis upon which more comprehensive regional planning, and even a measure of political devolution will develop during the next decade.

Observers of the post-war UK are likely to agree that economic and social growth have both been substantial since 1945, though slower and perhaps more fitful than among our European neighbours, that profound and on the whole beneficial structural changes have taken place in British economy and society, and that in this transformation successive governments have been substantially, continuously, even increasingly involved. External influences have often imposed powerful constraints on growth, in volume and direction, but the UK has emerged as a wealthy country with rising living standards, in spite of persistent and persisting inability to sustain economic growth without unacceptable inflation. The indicators are clear: a gross national product (GNP) of £94,095 millions in 1975, representing almost one-third rise in real terms even since 1960; put differently, gross domestic product (GDP) at constant factor cost, a general barometer of economic growth, of 60.7 in 1951 (100 in 1970), and 109.1 in 1975. In the late 1960s the government was habitually the biggest spender in the economy, at 38 per cent of GNP. By the mid-1970s this figure had risen to over 50 per cent. Alternatively expressed, non-marketed expenditure as a ratio of marketed output had risen from 44 per cent in 1961 to 61 per cent in 1974. Little wonder that Rostow spoke of the stage of high mass consumption society being reached in Britain already in the late 1940s, whilst others referred to a consumer-oriented society emerging in the 1950s, with virtual satiation in consumer durables reached for an increasing number of citizens during the following decade.

Yet progress has been uneven, in time and space, as well as between social and economic groups throughout the UK, with important, at times disturbing, implications for the development of the regions. As an accompaniment to monetary and fiscal policies to restrain demand, Keynesian policies to minimize the effects of the trade cycle, intermittent and on the whole unsuccessful action on prices and incomes, together with direct action on the balance of payments, governments sought to mitigate the effects of change upon the economically and socially less-favoured classes and regions. Criteria such as unemployment level, rate of new job provision, real income per capita or new factory floor-space occupied, illustrate both fluctuations throughout the UK economy, but also its regional variations. In particular there were persistent differentials between the more affluent and the less affluent regions, to the continuing social as well as economic disadvantage of the latter. Elaborated later, these differences have been diminished in degree rather than in kind by the measures referred to in section III of this chapter.

The sum total of public and private achievements, development and change in the UK space since the war has also been the result of a complex balance involving internal changes, both planned for and unexpected, and externalities, particularly those arising from repercussions of the international trading and monetary system. Among the more formative internal changes have been those due to new technologies, leading to structural changes in the composition of the employed population, with decline in some sectors not quite matched by new job provision elsewhere; the rise of the services economy; the emergence of the conglomerate, the large firm and the large factory; automation of processes, in both industry and communications; and proliferation of consumer demand. In policy terms the burgeoning of the mixed (state-private enterprise) economy has been paralleled by the growth of the welfare state, with priorities for full employment and an intermittently growing public social concern, not least in the housing sector, slum clearance and universal provision of basic amenities.

These internal changes, involving at times painful adjustments, regionally and locally as well as nationally, were in part the inevitable outcome of economic growth and transformation, but also the product of the changed and diminished political and economic role and status of the UK in the post-war world. The Empire had become the Commonwealth, former Dominions and Colonies independent; despite its world currency status sterling showed built-in weaknesses; the balance of payments remained characteristically adverse and competition from other industrial trading nations became pronounced. On balance, to our disadvantage, these changes were somewhat mollified by the growth of international economic cooperation. Perhaps most significantly, a reinterpretation of the geographical position of the UK saw a

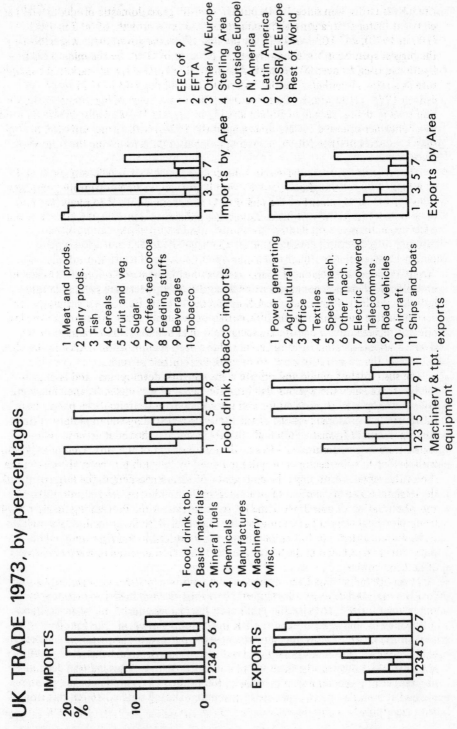

Figure 1.1   Trade, UK, 1973

shifting balance among policy perspectives: with limited horizons, self-contained and insular, facing the North Sea lands and Europe; or world-wide, the open-seas policy towards the Commonwealth, the N Atlantic basin and the trading world. During the 1970s it has become increasingly clear that the economic destiny of the UK is inseparable from that of the EEC.

I.2 Economy and Society

Table 1.1 shows the basic economic and social changes during the post-war period, by the use of selected indicators, a brief commentary upon which must suffice. The UK continues to be, and to suffer from being, a highly urbanized country with a population (fifth in density in the world) still rising, albeit on a decreasing tempo, with implications for congestion, overcrowding, matching of jobs with the numbers entering employment, and so forth (DoE 1971). The concentration of the population in seven conurbations, all with tendencies to decay at the core and growth on the fringes, illustrates a peculiarly British variant of an international problem; in addition, north country conurbations have for some decades tended to stagnate, whilst in London, the W Midlands and the Pennine towns the influx of immigrants implanted the social problem of racial minorities during the early 1960s (ch. 2). The quarter of the UK population classified as living in rural districts is somewhat illusory since many of these are almost urban in character, as on parts of the coalfields; nevertheless the truly rural population, perhaps 6 per cent in all, faces difficult problems through the rundown of employment in agriculture, the decaying social and transport provision in outlying areas, and recreational pressures from the town upon land in the countryside. The perceptible rise in the aged conceals the welfare problem likely to escalate during the last decades of this century, whilst the quasi-stability in numbers of the young will alarm some but comfort those who believe in a move towards 'zero population growth'. Alarming to all, surely, is the proportion still living in less prosperous areas, a product of differentially more rapid growth by natural increase, in spite of traditional outmigration, and compounded by an immobility nurtured by local community bias and, perhaps, fear of the unknown elsewhere.

The value of gross industrial output clearly accelerated during the 1960s, even taking inflation into account, whilst the index of power consumed tells a similar story. The working population (ch. 2.IV), however, has not increased in like ratio: male employment is even slightly down, the effect of both rising unemployment and structural change, but in some contrast the sharp rise in female employment, and in activity rate, indicates something of a 'petticoat' industrial revolution; the rise is indeed as marked in manufacturing as in the understandably more female preserve of service industries. There has been an improvement in real income per capita during the past decade, even allowing for changing price levels, with earnings growing somewhat faster than prices; in particular, the real income of the younger manually unskilled increased more rapidly than that of non-manual employees. The growth in the volume and proportion of unemployed, and the more severe incidence of this problem in the development areas, is both dramatic, tragic and all too well-known. Overall, however, the post-war period has seen an improvement in general living standards, indicated by an increase in the volume of domestic consumption per capita of something like 2 per cent per annum. During the mid-1970s this trend faded perceptibly.

TABLE 1.1

Post-war Economic and Social Change, UK, 1951–75

	1951	1961	1970	1975
Home-based population (million)	50.2	52.7	55.3	55.9
Dwellers in: 7 major conurbations (%);				
1975–7 metropolitan cos.	36.9	35.1	31.9	41.5
rural districts (%)	20.0	20.2	22.1	23.0
The young, 0–14 years (%)	24.1	23.4	23.4	23.3
old, 65+ years (%)	10.9	11.7	12.2	14.0
Affluent Britain: SE, E and W Midlands (%)	44.9	45.9	46.4	46.1
Poorer Britain: North, Scotland, Wales and				
Ulster (%)	24.1	23.7	22.9	22.5
Working population (million): male	15.9	16.7	16.4	16.1
female	7.3	8.5	9.2	9.7
Workers (%) in: agriculture, mining	9.0	7.2	3.5	3.3
manufacturing	39.3	37.2	38.9	33.0
services, incl. construction	51.7	55.6	57.6	63.7
Median income before tax (£), inflation accounting	320	620	1170	–
Average weekly earnings, male manual workers (£)	8.30	14.99	23.78	59.58[+]
Activity rates (%): male	87.2	86.8	81.0	80.8
(GB) female, all	34.7	37.4	42.7	
, single	21.7	29.7		
Registered unemployed (100,000), mid-year estimates	2.1	3.0	7.6	8.6
Gross industrial output (£1,000 million):				
(market prices) all industries	18.7	25.4	46.3	–
manufactures	15.9	20.7	36.9	83.7
Energy consumed (million tonne coal equivalent)	224	263	328	–
Large industrial establishments (% employment with				
> 1,000 workers)	33.7	34.9 (1963)	–	–
Rail track (1,000 km)	85.1	78.5	50.8	46.4
Goods transport (1,000 million tonne km)	No inf.	63.8	83.3	133.3
Road vehicles with current licence (million)	4.7	10.1	15.3	17.5
Housing completed (1,000)	201	303	362	322
University students (1,000)	103	135	251	274
Offences known to the police (1,000):				
1975 England & Wales	615	925	1,748	2,105
Juvenile delinquency (1,000 found guilty)	87	127	133	–
% Total public expenditure on:				
social security	12.1	15.8	18.1	17.8
NHS	8.4	9.0	9.7	10.5
education	6.8	9.8	12.0	13.7
housing	6.9	5.4	5.6	8.6

[+]£65.1 April 1976, for all males

Source: *Annual Abstracts of Statistics; Regional Statistics*, (HMSO)

Properly the subject matter of chs. 2 and 4, table 1.2 gives a preliminary indication of the principal shifts in industrial production since the mid-1950s, identifying
the six principal lead and lag sectors (1954–75), in terms of *output by value*.

TABLE 1.2

Post-war Change in Industrial Production, UK, 1954–75

Index change, ± national mean, 6 ranked lead and lag sectors (1954–75), output by value

> 5 per cent over national mean	1954–60	1960–7	1963–70	1970–5
Chemicals	+24.9	+38.2	+33.8	+12.1
Electrical engineering	+24.2	+26.4	+24.4	+12.3
Other manufactures	+14.0	+21.3	+21.5	+2.1
Gas, water, electricity	+12.8	+23.0	+19.7	+19.4
Glass, etc.	–	+15.3	+11.1	+19.8
Mechanical engineering	–	+16.2	+10.8	+1.1
>5 per cent below national mean				
Mining and quarrying	–31.2	–47.9	–45.8	–14.7
Shipbuilding	–28.4	–59.5	–38.0	+2.4
Leather, etc	–31.1	–44.2	–31.2	–8.5
Clothing/footwear	–	–10.9	–21.0	+9.8
Timber/furniture	–17.1	–9.1	–10.5	+9.2
Metals	–	–15.5	–9.3	–22.4

Source: Central Statistical Office (CSO) data

Contemporary with economic changes the face of *society* has altered: class divisions have become blurred and earning power has to some extent replaced life style or habits as the prime means of class differentiation; in particular, manual/non-manual differences are much less identifiable than in the early post-war years. The housing stock (ch. 2.III. 4; table 2.19) has visibly improved, with 3.2 millions re-housed since the war, mainly by slum clearance programmes; yet in 1975, 33 per cent of houses were still pre-1919, 22 per cent were built between 1919 and 1944, and 45 per cent were post-war. Of the 20.4 million dwellings in December 1975, half were owner-occupied and almost one-third were rented from local authorities. Drudgery for the housewife has been greatly reduced and ownership of consumer durables has become remarkably widespread; moreover, standards of nutrition are now high and still rising.

Educational provision (ch. 2.III.5) has greatly increased and the university popu-lation has almost trebled since 1951. 81 per cent of manual workers take an annual holiday of more than three weeks, compared to the 2 per cent who did so in 1961. Sensitivity to environmental problems, their management and improvement, became a watchword of the late 1960s, although for the under-privileged minorities the quality of life, expressed in urban ghettoes, inadequate housing, congestion, noise and squalor, has deteriorated further. This in spite of the increasing proportion of public expenditure seen to be devoted to housing, social security, the health service and education. On the distaff side the poor have become poorer and society to that extent more polarized; the figures for the increase in juvenile delinquency and in offences known to the police speak for themselves.

A final factor of change since the war has been the increased potential for mobility, and this in spite of the manifest decline in the rail network and the with-drawal of public bus services in outlying areas. The boom in road vehicles with current licences stands out in table 1.1, whilst infra-structure improvement in the creation of motorways, a better trunk road network and internal air routes are other striking features (ch. 5). Commuting has become a way of life for hundreds of thousands, perception and mental images of space have widened and there has been a rising demand for more personal space and access to more public recreational space. Inter-regional gross migration flows (ch. 2.II.5) have been building up, though net balances are still small in comparison with gross residential populations for most regions. The paradox of immobility preferences in less privileged areas has already been commented upon, perhaps a surprising tribute to the strength of communities, even in an age of greater movement potential. The facilities for greater mobility and the technological changes in transport are the subject-matter of ch. 5.

I.3 Land

Change and flux in economy and society inevitably have repercussions on the land, its use and misuse (Best 1959; Best and Coppock 1962; Stamp 1962; Champion 1974). Of the 24.0 million ha of UK land (1970) the 2.0 million ha built upon are the most valuable, congested (ch. 5), and in striking contrast to no less than 6.7 million ha under rough grazings. With a population density over 309 per km², expected to rise to perhaps 386 per km² by the year 2000, and a loss of farmland running at about 16,100 ha per annum in the period 1960–70 it is not surprising that there is widespread concern for conservation and careful husbanding of land (table 1.3). With agriculture doubling its output since the war whilst using no more labour and even suffering a reduction of the improved land surface, this concern may at first sight seem misplaced. That it is not so is well indicated by the mounting pressures for alternative or multiple uses of land and the uniquely high priority rightly given to land-use allocation in post-war economic and social planning in the UK, though the very high rate of increase in land values during the 1960s threatens to imperil these achievements.

Potential land-use conflicts, severe in the urban cores (Fordham 1974) around the business district perimeter, where town meets country, and in major estuarine tracts, are spreading to even the remoter rural areas, where there may be a need to harmonize farming, forestry, tourism, water policies and access for the townsman. With perhaps the most sophisticated town and country planning mechanism in operation anywhere the UK (ch. 6.IV) still lacks the comprehensive inter-related central policies for space allocations at the *regional* level, with appropriate priorities

TABLE 1.3

Land-use Change, UK, 1950–2000

1,000 ha	1950	1965	1950–65 change	% change pa	est. 2000	1965–2000 est. ch.	% change pa
Agricultural	20,254	19,623	−631	−0.2	18,122	−1,502	−0.2
Forest	1,532	1,816	+284	+1.2	2,617	+800	+1.2
Urban	1,773	2,043	+270	+1.0	2,745	+702	+1.0
Other	532	608	+76	+0.9	608	0	0
Total land	24,092	24,092	0	0	24,092	0	0

Source: A. G. Champion (1973)

assigned to what have all too often seemed to be conflicting strands of public policies.

Chapter 3.I surveys land use and land classification. Chapter 6.II.2 discusses the patterning and structure of urban land use.

I.4   Decisions and Policies

Because governments now spend the most sizeable part of GNP it is logical to give precedence to public policy objectives as these affect the UK space. Certainly the spatial perspective in UK policy-making is the least developed, hitherto poorly-esteemed and neglected, though almost all economic and social policies necessarily have, and have had, a spatial outcome, not infrequently without clearly defined spatial intentions. Among the principal public policy objectives since the war, which have had important spatial implications, the following might be listed:

(a) *maximization of sustained national economic growth without an unacceptable level of inflation*, success in which continues to prove elusive. The role of regional or spatial policies in meeting this objective is contested but it seems clear that successive inflationary bouts have been escalated by the scarcities of land and labour in affluent areas, with differentially higher costs there, whilst untapped or under-utilized resources continue to characterize the North, Wales, Scotland and N Ireland. The diminishing of this contrast in living standards and opportunities would thus contribute to the goals of social justice and, as the ill-fated *National Plan* (1964) recognized, might also have added significantly to the solution of national economic growth with least inflation.

(b) *balance as between the regions*, sometimes referred to as 'the need to rectify imbalance' and interpreted to refer to equality of living environment, adequacy and choice of employment, equitable dissemination of growth, prosperity and the full realization of economic potential. This objective logically relates to that above but, in view of the disparity of resources, both human and natural, the uneven way in which these have been developed through time, and the varied regional legacies of problems which have resulted, true equalization seems to be totally impracticable; a reduction in the present growing inequality, on the other hand, seems both feasible and desirable.

The objective of regional balance and equilibrium is the opposite of centre-periphery polarization, to whose diminution so much thinking on regional policy in France was devoted during the 1960s. It may also be related to the search for greater political devolution (ch. 1.IV.2), the accommodation, or even the neutralization of regionalist or nationalist sentiments, which gained widespread momentum during the past decade.

(c) *social justice*, including the full employment policy, relief of unemployment (Dixon and Thirlwall 1975) and improvement of the activity rate, spread of welfare particularly to the lower-paid and under-privileged, income and wealth redistribution, equality of access to education, health and housing opportunities. Problems of racial minority groups are particularly pressing.

(d) *improvement in the balance of payments*, to provide the basis for and re-inforcement of economic growth in the UK, and to strengthen participation in world economy, society and polity.

(e) increasingly since the late 1960s, the consciousness of the imperative need for *conservation* of scarce national assets in the landscape and townscape heritage and the safeguarding of threatened aspects of the quality of life.

Among this amalgam of policies, whose mix and priorities varied with the political complexion of governments, deliberate priority for coordinated action at regional, area or locality level remained rare, though economic first aid policies have matured into the latest, more constructive growth promotion and aid programmes for the assisted areas since 1974. The block grant financing for local authorities has increasing, if still inadequate, regard for local problems and needs, whilst acceptance of regional priorities may be detected in a rising number of key central decisions on communications, major new industrial projects or the decentralization of some government or nationalized industry establishments. It is only during the past decade, however, that governments have shown effective concern for longer-term and coherent analysis, forecasting and strategy formulation at the regional level. This has coincided with, but in large measure also stimulated, the flow of research by social scientists and geographers, being joined by regional economists, sociologists and political scientists; and the development of relevant analytical techniques, which had been lacking hitherto. (Chisholm and Manners 1971; House 1973).

As yet regional analysis, forecasting and programming is scarcely beyond its infancy in the UK and, not least, the complex nature of development itself remains imperfectly understood. Policies by central or local government must be examined alongside the decision-taking of countless entrepreneurs, firms and corporations, whilst the actions and intentions of multifarious groups and key individuals may also need to be taken into account. All or some of these non-public actions may work in directions or at a tempo contrary to the intentions of public policy. Through the complex interactions which result the UK space is further differentiated, the characteristics of regions or sub-systems evolve and change, their interrelationships are modified. It is difficult indeed to measure, much less predict, the spatial outcome of public policies and they are in turn variously susceptible to change by events, constraints of the times, new political controls or management thinking. Such process of change has accelerated during the post-war years, threatening even basic interpretations of the regional economic and social geography of the UK. The next step must thus be to look at the changing identity, and the role of the variegated and variously-defined regions making up the national space (Manners et al 1972).

II   REGIONS: IDENTITY, SIGNIFICANCE AND FUNCTIONS

II.1   A Perspective on Regions

To many Americans the notion of a regional breakdown of so small a unit as the UK might seem absurd, even for the purposes of an analysis, much less as the basis for more effective overall planning. To many citizens of the UK, on the other hand, if the evidence of the Redcliffe-Maud Report (Roy. Commn on Local Government in England 1969) is to be accepted, even the provincial level of regionalism is an unfamiliar, perhaps unwelcome extension of their concept of home area, which is characteristically and parochially expressed as a parish or an urban ward. For some economists regional identities are impediments to more effective use of national resources and space, but for most geographers, at least until recently, regions in their infinite diversity have been both a key tool of analysis and the prime means

of interpreting the use of resources and space. More importantly, the spatial organization of economy and society expresses itself in discernible and inter-related, if
complex, entities, whilst in a practical sense governments, both central and local,
work through networks of units, not always the same territorial entities for all purposes, and by this means help to reinforce the identities of particular areas.

Though few today are likely to accept that the UK space may be unambiguously
divided into universal-type regions, which will command widespread acceptance,
there is likely to be greater coincidence of views on the first-stage, or national/pro-
vincial level of identity. In reviewing regions, the many types, their utility and validity, may first be considered briefly; then the region-forming or disintegrating forces;
the flows and inter-regional linkages, of which presently so little is ascertainable; the
hierarchy, network or sub-system aspects of regions; and, finally, the significance of
regions within the organization of the national space. All this is an essential prelude
to a consideration of the current de facto regions, the eight economic planning
regions of England, together with Wales, Scotland and N Ireland, their differentiation, problems and prospects. The criteria for regional identity included: some dominant or inter-related set of attributes; utility in terms of economy, efficiency or
convenience; administrative role, popular recognition or representation; and, in a
practical sense, the extent to which the area identified may serve effectively as the
territorial basis for understanding or promoting economic and social advancement.

II.2 Types of Region

Given a potential infinity of regions, in scale level or characteristics, some priority
ordering is necessary. Conventionally, geographers have identified sets of systematic
regions, starting with those derived from the physical environment, followed by
those with historical, economic, social or politically dominant attributes. Thereafter
regrouping of regions to multi-factor identities in space has been the prelude to a
regionalization of the total UK space as near universal in character as possible. The
weaknesses of such an approach are allegedly that subjectivity creeps in early, there
is unacceptable abstraction from reality in the process, and that the end-product
risks being no more than academic, and may have neither practical utility, nor
reflect the long-felt territorial loyalties of the people.

It cannot be gainsaid that the traditional divisions of the UK space into uplands
and lowlands, with as complex a differentiation according to geological history,
morphological character and present surface or drainage characteristics, as in any
area of comparable size in the world, remain an essential prelude to further regional
differentiation. Likewise climatic, soil and vegetation characteristics diversify the
physiographic units, are as fundamental as ever to an understanding of land quality
and potential, and establish a framework for the range, flexibility and profitability
of its uses (fig. 3.1). Yet even in an increasingly environmentally-conscious age the
physical nature of the UK is likely to take second place, in official eyes, to regionalization derived from economic, social or political attributes, in so far as these may
be adequately disentangled and individually calibrated.

Determination of priorities as between economic, social or political regional nets
is likely to vary with the analyst, and the purpose. It involves basically a choice between dominant or spatially inter-related forms of production, incomes, consumption or marketing in the case of economic issues; the spatial structure of society,
regional, urban and local life styles, class, mobility or social pathology among social

criteria; effective political voice, democratic representation, national and sub-national recognition, or efficiency of government, in political terms (Robertson 1965; House 1969). All such factors tend to be inextricably inter-related and it may be that the nearest approach to collective identity is that of regional units with a common problem-mix, a related social or cultural identity and a sufficiently coherent and forceful political voice to seek redress or to power improvements.

From a planning point of view, since the war there has been some priority for identifying and studying urban regions (Wise 1966; Grieve and Robertson 1964; Senior 1966), or town-country relationships expressed in space, with special emphasis on circulation or activity spaces; mobility evidence, including journey to work, shopping, entertainments and so forth, affords the prime data. The provincial level of region has consistently been favoured by geographers, (Fawcett 1919; Gilbert 1939) but has variably and rarely found an echo in local government reform proposals (ch. 1.IV.3).

II.3   Region-forming/Region-disintegrating Forces

The seemingly well-defined, if not entirely static, regions beloved of geographers in this and other European countries earlier in this century, are more difficult to sustain these days. If planning is to work in the direction of fulfilling regionalist aspirations in economy, society or polity it is important to interpret, guide and work with the forces for change, not all of which are likely to be within planning control and many of which are at times in conflict with each other. Regional identities by some criteria are dissolving, but in others being steadily reinforced; overall the possibility exists for fashioning and developing new kinds of identity suited to a wider range of aspirations during the remaining decades of this century.

Among the balance of forces operating on the differentiation of regions at the present the centrifugal or disintegrating tendencies may be thought by some to be in the ascendant, though very unevenly over the UK space. Moreover the process has very far to go before identities are lost. Such fluidity of change is not new, but has been greatly accelerated in recent times, by: concentration of decision-taking, both political and economic, at or near the metropolis; economies of scale in production, concentrating upon fewer, larger, more nodal sites, whether these be for factories, farms, ports or profitable rail lines; urbanization, trending persistently towards larger-scale units, concentration within national growth areas and away from the less privileged regions or, within those regions, away from the sparsely settled hinterlands. These urbanizing tendencies (ch. 6) have been counteracted, but only partially, by suburban and commuting spread and sprawl; the basic contrast of polarization from larger regional tracts remains (Wibberley 1954). Rising inter-regional mobility of population, culminating in the peak net southward flows in the depression years of the early 1930s supplies the most dramatic evidence, offset but only in limited measure by the regional aid policies of successive governments to the present time.

Less apparent than the mass flows of people in search of betterment but equally indicative of some loss of regional differentiation is the spread of common urban life styles and aspirations, matched by consumer demand, and the uniformity fostered by advertising and the media. Yet against the dictates of such standardization or gravity model economics there has been a marked, perhaps rising reaction. Apart from the Royal Commission evidence that people think in terms of a very localized, not to say parochial 'home area', there is mounting and widespread evidence of a built-in reluctance to migrate in search of opportunity, even though greater means of mobility and better knowledge of the market make this possible. The strength of Welsh, Scottish or Ulster feelings on the matter of political devolution from Whitehall is a nationalist expression, weighted by sizeable populations, resources and problems, which finds echoes in less dramatic but equally heartfelt ways in the less privileged regions of England. Indeed the forceful presentation of regional needs through the economic planning councils is an indication of such feelings. Furthermore, to some extent the greater mobility of the townsmen, allied with aspirations of the countryman, is reducing urban-rural distinctions and the gradient in living standards and attitudes between the two milieux. To the extent that policies of economic balance between the regions progress, the provincial metropoli can help stabilize their hinterlands and act as the political, economic or social foci of either freshly-defined or reinforced regional identities.

It is appropriate to add that effective regional planning may be the most powerful of forces for stabilizing and developing new forms of regionalism. To be effective such planning needs to be applied to base populations and resources of adequate, even optimal size. Currently a population of around three millions is thought desirable for regional economic planning, whilst one of not less than 250,000 persons is thought preferable for any first-tier local government unit in the future. Likewise for New Towns target populations have been progressively revised upwards to 250,000 and beyond for the latest generation (ch. 2.IV.6, ch.6.IV.1). The need to bear these norms in mind implies a large measure of compromise in any redefinition of regions for the UK space, not only in terms of scale, or as between possibly conflicting economic, social or political purposes, but also in respect of regions and their national context.

II.4   Flows and Linkages

The study of these cardinal region-forming and disintegrating forces has hitherto been greatly limited by lack of adequate data, and the absence of a sufficient framework of inter-regional accounts (Woodward and Bowers 1970; Brown 1972). These shortcomings have led some to interpret regions as more clear-cut or self-contained than is justifiable. This failing leads through directly into current regional economic planning, where the strategies for individual regions often inadequately take into account proposals for even adjacent regions, and in sum total do not add up to a coherent national strategy for space.

Migration of population, both in gross flows and in the net interchange over a period of time, is probably the most useful general purpose indicator of regional differences in job prospects and living environment (ch. 2). Though net flows may be only a small proportion of total resident population there is a trend towards increased gross mobility as an outcome of rising affluence. If the assisted areas are to build up their populations, they will need to do this by attracting residents of other areas as well as by seeking to retain more of their own citizens.

Flows of passenger or freight traffic by the various transport media, including the interchange of telecommunications, further indicate both the state of interregional linkages, but also the sinews upon which further growth is likely to be generated (ch. 5). The traditional importance of the radial network of roads and railways based upon London has been reinforced in the motorway and air ages. The lack of adequate alternative axial routeways not only gave rise, between the wars, to the great industrial belt or axial zone (Hobson 1951; Baker and Gilbert 1944) from Yorkshire—Lancashire through the Midlands to the metropolis, but has also ensured that the national economic skeleton has changed so little since that time. The completion of the M4 London—S Wales, M62 Lancashire—Yorkshire and M8 Clyde—Forth motorways is, however, creating potentially powerful cross-flows. Recent work (Chisholm 1971) indicates that freight rate costs are not such a significant charge on production in a wide diversity of manufacturing that plants are tied to a restricted range of locations. That there is so little voluntary movement of plants and firms, least of all to the assisted areas, has much to do with the immobilities engendered by earlier location decisions, allied with strong adverse perceptions of the risks or inconvenience that added distance might create.

In spite of considerable advances in regional economics in recent years the formulation of *model frameworks* for inter-regional accounts or transaction flows remains a subject fraught with conceptual difficulties and lacking in adequate data sources (Brown 1972; Richardson 1969; Stilwell 1972). An interesting practical step (Brown 1972, 72 et seq) has been to define the degree of 'openness' of regions, that is the relationship between the trade external to the region and the regional GDP. The measure is imprecise and the relationship is apt to be distorted by variable areas or population size of regions, each of which tends to increase the volume of intra-regional compared to inter-regional or international trading. Nevertheless, 'openness' is a vital concept when the principles of regional policies are under review. To the extent that regions are open and thus more effectively interlinked it is increasingly likely that nationally-based policies for economic growth and its diffusion will be successful, rather than individual regional variations of such policies. In reality the trade/GDP ratio highlights strongly the categories of UK economic region (table 1.4): the peripheral or development regions have a lesser degree of openness, though it is in all cases greater than for comparable sovereign states of equal size; the intermediate regions, the regions of mixed trends and the growth regions have more varied degrees of greater openness. The most 'open' region is the E Midlands, athwart the major national communications arteries, followed by E Anglia, almost an economic dependency of the SE. The SE itself ranks low in openness, sharing bottom place with Scotland, though differentiated by being almost at the opposite end of the spectrum of quantum GDP. In other words, the SE has a very high intra-regional trade, as well as high ranking in inter-regional and international trading flows.

Clearly the study of both flows and linkages between regions, of people, commodities, wealth and investment, should have a high priority among operational planners and social scientists. Of these topics that of linkages is likely to prove the most difficult, but on a correct evaluation of essential economic and social linkages between regions (Archibald 1967), not only at the analysis stage but, more formatively, at the subsequent stages of monitoring and management of regional change, ultimately rests the entire regional planning process.

II.5   Regional Context

The interpretation of flows and linkages leads logically to the identification of scale order relationships between units within the framework of the UK space. Techniques for the analysis of these relationships are still in active evolution and most work so

far has been confined to urban hierarchies (ch. 6.III.2) and to circulation space.
Somewhat surprisingly, there is no substantive analytical work on regions and their
component sub-regions. Officialdom still creates units for administrative purposes,
on occasion almost arbitrarily, and then studies their characteristics and problems,
rather than the more creative reverse process.

Early work on the urban hierarchy by Smailes (1944, 1946, 1947) during the
immediate post-war years identified indicators of the economic and social status of
settlements, mapping their hinterlands and describing the resultant hierarchy of
inter-relationships. This was followed up by Green (1949, 1950, 1952) in pioneer-
ing work on the pattern of urban hinterlands through an analysis of public bus
services, again a useful general-purpose barometer of individual and collective needs
for circulation space. Carruthers (1957, 1962) studied service centres in Greater
London and in England and Wales, establishing a more sophisticated urban hierarchy.
Moser and Scott (1961) made a comprehensive statistical analysis of British towns,
and more recently Hall (1971, 1973) has made a novel interpretation of city regions
and standard metropolitan labour areas.

A clearer understanding of the way in which units of various types relate to one
another and nest within units of larger size, to make up a network or hierarchy, or
a functioning sub-system within the UK space, is obviously very important in
regional planning. Yet there is little indication that this type of research is being
given adequate priority. For the lack of such knowledge many sub-regional plans
necessarily have to be formulated for ill-defined units, and the outcome risks lacking
wider context or applicability.

II.6   Some Theoretical Considerations

The past few decades have seen the rapid development of regional science and a
spatial perspective previously lacking in economics. New theories and models have
been formulated (Wilson 1974), others adapted to the study of patterns, flows, networks and inter-relationships in space. In particular, the regional and sub-regional
levels of interpretation have been emphasized, but applications in regional planning
or resource management have lagged behind.

The objectives of regional theory are clear: to model regional behaviour at the
intra- and inter-regional scales, and that for several purposes. First, to analyse
changes in space with a view to fuller understanding of the dynamics of the situation, and thus to contribute to judgements upon change. Secondly, to enable con-
ditional predictions to be made, within many practical constraints upon a clear,
longer-term view of alternative futures. Thirdly, to contribute to the planning, programming and monitoring of change, and thus to a more effective spatial allocation
of public, and for that matter, private investment.

The theories most commonly drawn upon are those concerned with determination of regional incomes, inter-regional income exchange, regional growth and
regional policy- or decision-making. The fundamentals of these theories are derived
from economics, at both the macro (national/regional) and the micro (firm, city,
human group) scales. To avoid confusion among geographers it is important to
realize that an economist's use of the term 'region', whether homogeneous or nodal,
is in essence a space-less or point connotation. The transposition to the geographer's
finite and variegated patterning of space is not too difficult, but there evaporates a
good deal of theoretical elegance in the process.

Useful theories include those concerned with regional growth (Brown 1972, 84): the supply-based interpretation of the neoclassical production function; demand-related theories, once more than one product is being considered, with industrial functions taken as given and different; and the Harrod-Domar macro-economic model based upon the concept of a closed economy. Export-base theory, with its extensions in the evolution of multiplier effects, analyses the relationship between regional prosperity and levels of regional export activity (Brook and Hay 1974). This leads on to more complex input—output analysis, based upon as complete as possible a matrix of spatial transactions and accounts. The more complex the analysis the more the deficiencies of the regional or sub-regional data base become quickly apparent in the UK, and the more the computational problems mount with a sharp marginal upturn at each stage of expanding the relevant model.

The relationship between the course of growth and change, and the relevant policy objectives is bridged either by classical equilibrium theories or cumulative causation theories such as those of Myrdal (1957) or Hirschman (1958). In classical economic theory factor flows between regions are considerable, but through time work in the direction of an equalization of conditions and the elimination of differences between regions. In the cumulative causation model, on the other hand, it is postulated by Myrdal, but opposed by Hirschman, that regions become less equal with time. In the centre-periphery concept, essentially a gravity model formulation of considerable complexity, the centre (prosperous region, metropolis, central place) enjoys cumulative advantages, generates capital and attracts labour from the periphery. As in classical theory the equalizing return flows of capital seeking cheaper investment opportunities, and the improvement of labour supply by outmigration from the poorer region are admitted. These are the beneficial 'spread' effects, but according to Myrdal they are more than offset by the adverse 'backwash' effects, through the further cumulative impoverishment of the poorer region in terms of labour, investment, or entrepreneurial skills; conversely, the more prosperous region continues to attract capital, wages rise and inflation is promoted. The truth of regional differences in the UK since the war lies more with the implications of the Myrdal view of the cumulative causation model than with the neoclassical equilibrium model.

In reality, regional theories and their applications through models currently represent an imperfect art. An adequate data base is only slowly being created; the complexity of models even on a two-region basis are considerable, and the inputs are often restricted to trade variables or inter-industry transactions. The problems of incorporating time into the models is formidable, whilst the cross-correlation between econometric sectoral (Renton 1974) and spatial models poses very serious problems. The formulation of planning models is a further operational dimension and perhaps the most difficult of all to achieve, and once achieved, to sustain and up-date for the purposes of monitoring and feedback.

Decision-models based upon linear programming, with certain constraints built in, are thus very partial and necessarily somewhat abstract at the present time. The formulation of an optimal allocation of activities among regions is an even more theoretical construct, with or without a transport cost variable built in to the equilibrium analysis or the traditional input—output models (Saigal 1965). In addition to the work of Brown (1972) mentioned above, some important practical achievements include the structural model of the Welsh economy (Nevin 1966), based on an input—output analysis of inter-industry flows, with some capacity to afford con-ditional predictions. The *Strategic Plan for the SE* (SE Jt Planning Team 1970) studied ten potential employment-population distributions for that region, but it proved possible to model and investigate fully only two of these spatial strategies. The *Strategic Plan for the North West* (DoE 1974), however, did not take such methodology further, and the preferred spatial options seem to have been based as much on judgement as upon the objective findings of the modelled processes of change. The latest E Anglia strategy (E Anglia Reg. Strategy Team 1974) employed simulation techniques for the study of population, employment and resource potential, but stopped far short of attempting a full-scale regional model. Finally, the sub-regional models for Leicester and Leicestershire (Leicester Cy Coun. and CC 1969), Coventry–Solihull–Warwickshire (Coventry C Coun. 1971), and Nottinghamshire and Derbyshire (Notts–Derby Sub-regional Planning Unit 1969) illustrate more deliberately spatial options for the allocation of population and employment growth.

It may be that the next decade will produce an effective range of complex operational regional models and that these will become standard in each planning region or local authority, to match the existing national econometric models in the universities of Cambridge, London (LSE) and Southampton (Renton 1974). It is at least as likely that such models will remain beyond immediate reach and, furthermore, it may well be that in the efficiency-equity 'trade-off' in regional planning the demands for greater social and spatial justice will produce some powerful political inputs to disturb the symmetry and elegance of even the existing models.

II.7 Development Concepts

Wide subscription to a doctrine of promoting greater regional balance implies that there are undesirable (or politically inconvenient) inequalities, even distortions in the UK space, which might be reduced or removed by effective public action through urban and regional planning (McCrone 1969). A simple centre-periphery model (e.g. fig. 4.14) is inappropriate to explain the differentiation of these islands, but there are nevertheless markedly differing economic and social conditions and problems between the regions. There is sufficient concentration of affluence in the Midlands and the South East to provide a sharp and coherent contrast to the less favoured regions in the North, Wales, Scotland and in N Ireland, at the opposite end of the scale. Characteristically the less favoured areas are located on the outer margins of the UK space but they also have common problems arising from an industrial structure related to the use of coal, steam-power and the establishment of a range of traditional nineteenth-century manufactures. These have been increasingly affected during this century by competition from other products or from new centres of production in other countries. The tribulations of coal-mining, the heavy metallurgical industries or textiles lie at the heart of problems of industrial restructuring in the assisted areas of the UK, but in what proportion their regional problems are an outcome of unfavourable location as against outdated or narrow industrial structure remains a matter for conjecture. Both conditions illustrate marginality (House 1966) and point up the need to overcome a dual adversity, a task which cannot but be made more problematical as the UK develops within Europe and its outer areas may risk becoming even more peripheral within a European context (ch. 1, pp. 32–3).

Doubt might well be cast on the reality of creating ultimate balance or equilibrium

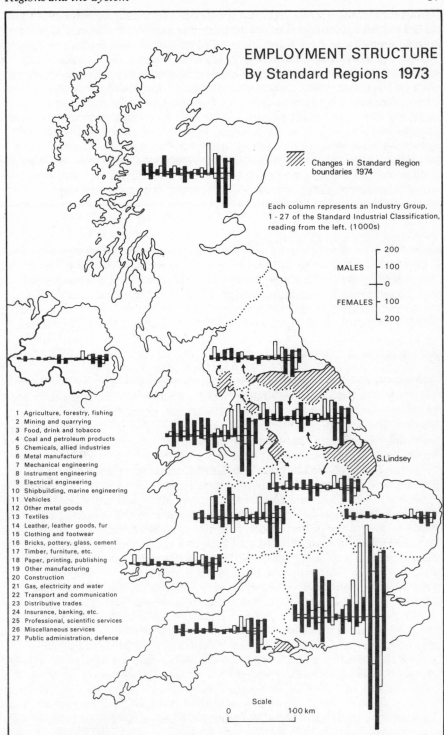

Figure 1.2   Employment structure, UK, 1973

between the economic regions of the UK, if such a state is to mean effective equalization of job opportunity, living standards, environmental conditions. The fundamental diversities of the UK preclude such an achievement, no matter the aggregate cost to public funds or the distortion of logical investment decisions which may prove acceptable. An intermediate, realizable and worthwhile target, however, is to move towards the earliest possible achievement of self-sustaining economic growth in the less favoured regions, adjusting, by any necessary public action, growth pressures in other regions of the UK space in the interim. A firmer economic base might thereby be implanted and developed in the assisted areas, their resources of manpower, land and social capital more fully utilized. With a growth-oriented strategy the assisted areas might then move to a more competitive status within the EEC as well as within the UK. This would build upon the most logical economic growth localities and employment sectors, whilst accepting, even programming for decline in the least favoured places (House 1976).

II.8   Economic Health and Deprivation

Figures 1.2, 1.3 and 1.4 taken together permit an introductory visual assessment of the essential characteristics and problems of the economic planning regions of the UK. These economic planning regions correspond broadly to the major provincial or sub-national entities which have emerged over the post-war years as a reasonable compromise for the first-stage breakdown of the UK space. Their boundaries and detailed composition may be criticized, most of all around the fluid northern borderlands of the SE, but they contain the core territories and are similar in number to those in most schemes for first-stage breakdown by geographers. In any event they are the regions for which economic planning councils and boards have been responsible since the mid-1960s and for which formulation of regional strategies has been actively, if variously, prosecuted. Whatever the criticisms of the units as the optimal first-stage regions there is a sense in which they are generating and consolidating their identity, through their continuing use for policy-making and its applications. For regional boundary changes 1974 see p. 43.

Figure 1.2 shows the volume and structure of employment and allows quick assessment of the relationship between regional space and the quantum of its labour force, the absolute numbers in any industry group in any one region and its relative importance compared with other regions, the degree of diversification and, in particular, a comparison of the numbers in service industries (orders XX–XXVII, 1968 Standard Industrial Classification) with those in manufacturing or extractive occupations. It further graphically illustrates the proportionate and absolute importance of male and female contributions to the labour force in each region. In essence the contrast, more fully developed later, between *four zones* is hinted at: the least-favoured or development regions: the North and Scotland, Wales and Ulster (Self 1965); the less-favoured or intermediate regions: Yorks. and Humberside, the NW; the zones of mixed trends: the SW and E Anglia; and the hitherto more affluent, diversified and balanced growth regions of the E and W Midlands and the SE.

This categorization is reinforced by consideration of the evidence in fig. 1.3. The indicators of economic health and deprivation, mapped as deviations from the national mean, have been chosen and grouped to give a representative impression of the essential contrasts; certain indicators were not available for N Ireland. The combination of a high proportion in fast-decline industries, as defined by job reduction

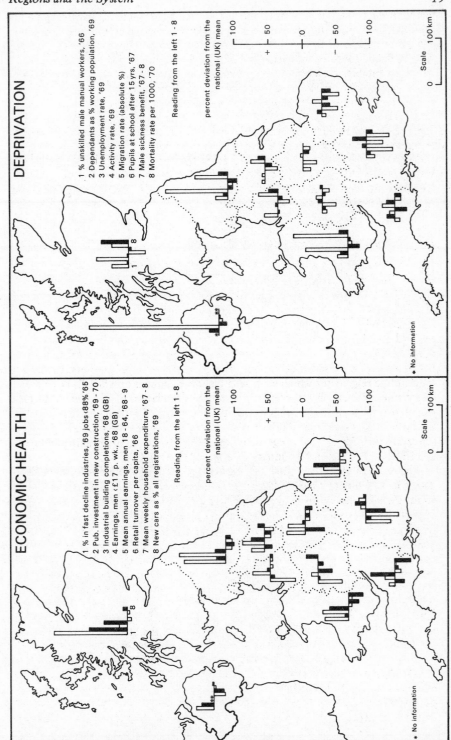

Figure 1.3   Economic health and deprivation, UK, 1960s

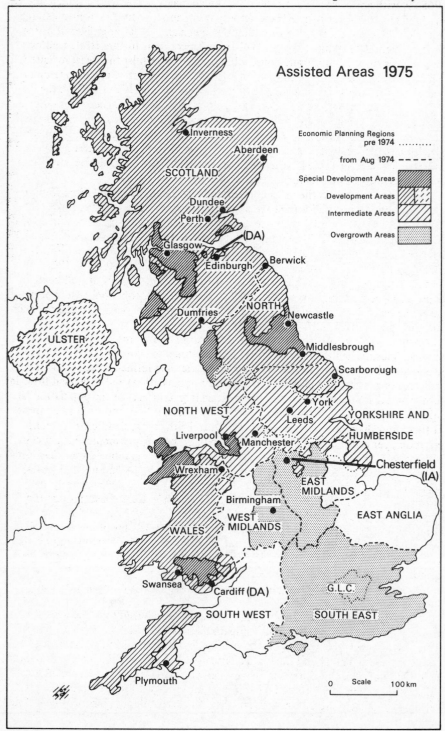

Figure 1.4   Assisted Areas, UK, 1975

1965–9, with an above average ratio of unskilled male manual workers, high unemployment and lower than average activity rates, and a high ratio of men earning less than £17 per week in 1968 or with lower mean annual earnings, identifies the same problem development regions. This adverse picture is further reinforced by the evidence on retail turnover, household expenditure, whilst the social malaise is equally highlighted by the outmigration rate, the low ratio of pupils staying on at school after fifteen years, the volume of male sickness benefit and, finally, the higher mortality rates. The situation in the three most affluent areas is not quite a mirror image, though positive and favourable aspects emerge on almost all counts. Remedial action by government is shown by the above-average public investment in new construction in the assisted areas and the volume of industrial building completions there in a recent year, in comparison with the markedly negative indications on both counts for the SE.

Since the early 1970s the measurement and assessment of *spatial disparities in social conditions and well-being* have emerged as a major research field for geographers in the UK. Studies have been at different scale levels: the national/regional (Coates and Rawstron 1971; Knox 1974, 1975), and the intra-urban. Such research has been powerfully motivated by social concern and has been directed towards more committed and more effective policy-making by public authority. Research methods have sought social indicators to define degree and extent of well-being or deprivation. A great mass of data has had to be processed, commonly using principal components or factor analysis, to bring to light the key groupings of social variables and their distribution through the national space.

Coates and Rawstron interpreted the distributional patterns of employment, income, housing, health and education. Knox defined ten constituents of level of living, including housing, health and education. He then refined these to a set of indicants (e.g. university places as one indicant of education) and expressed these in turn as variables, measured on an interval scale (e.g. that part of the population 'at risk' for any indicant). Fifty-three variables were established, and from an analysis of these four diagnostic variables were found to be the most significant: persons per room; per cent households without fixed bath; per cent unemployed; per cent persons over sixty years. The distributional pattern of the combined four diagnostic variables (Knox 1975, 39) showed a clear correspondence, in England and Wales, between high deprivation and the development areas (table 1.4); conversely the most favoured conditions occur in a broad belt from the Kent coast through the Home Counties to the Midlands. Inner urban areas, especially central London (Eversley 1973), and the heart of the conurbations were islands of low levels of living. Less expected perhaps were the unfavourable scores for Norfolk and much of Lancashire, whilst Yorkshire N Riding and Westmorland stood out when compared with the greater deprivation around them.

Chapter 2, sections III.3, 4 and 5 discuss social structure, housing, personal incomes and education achievement.

Figure 1.4 shows the pattern of assisted areas 1975, referred to in the next section and analysed in ch. 4 in terms of the impact on manufactures and services. Suffice it for the moment to comment on the striking, but not surprising, coincidence between the assisted areas and those already seen to be suffering the most pronounced economic and social hardships. In the assisted areas, the special development areas (SDAs), created in 1967, form a hard core of localities with severe problems, set within development areas (DAs) covering the North, Scotland, most of Wales, Ulster and much of Cornwall. The intermediate areas (1969) are well represented in the economic planning regions on the southern or eastern borders of the development areas.

III PUBLIC POLICIES ON THE REGIONS

III.1 An Outline Assessment

General public policy objectives with spatial implications were mentioned in ch. 1.I.4. Since the war the need for such policies has varied with the state of the national economy and both the policy mix and the extent of its enforcement have shifted according to the economic, social and political objectives of successive governments. (Needleman 1965; Wilson 1964, 1965; McCrone 1969, 1972; Moore and Rhodes 1973; Chisholm 1974). Nevertheless there has been a general political consensus on the continuing importance of full employment, industrial location policy, regional aid, the extension of welfare through the social services, population redistribution measures, the improvement of both the national infrastructure, particularly communications and housing, the total living environment and the need for local government reform. Priorities within all these policies have characteristically been given to distressed or development areas or districts, under a wide range of changing definitions and locations through time. Political differences between the parties have related to the extent of public involvement, the balance between inducements and controls, the definition, range and degree of enforcement of particular policies. Such policies for the UK space have required a planning mechanism, in the economic and social fields, and in physical terms for town and country, of great diversity and complexity, more wide-ranging in its nature than for any other western country. Yet the region came late into planning and even today there is no more than a set of policy objectives for the eleven economic planning regions of the UK, with approved strategic plans for the SE (1970) the W Midlands (1974) and the NW (1974). The interim verdict must be that though public policies have proliferated they have rarely been consistently applied for long enough and have been insufficiently related, with a particular gap between the objectives and achievements respectively of physical, economic and social aspects of planning, at either national or regional level. Cumulatively, however, the effects have been considerable in terms of industry, both manufacturing and services; other key economic sectors, including coal, electricity, gas, oil and natural gas; communications, rail, road, air, ports and telecommunications; the conurbations, cities and towns; and on definition of local government units or functions, and the status of the national groups within the UK. At times governments have acted directly through particular policies and institutions, but almost as frequently influence has been indirect, often hard to trace. For this and other reasons it is difficult here to make more than a general assessment of the impact of such policies on the UK space; that collectively and cumulatively these effects have been significant, even dramatic, there can be no doubt.

Shift and share analysis (Richardson 1969, 344) is a useful method of assessing the variable spatial impact of regional policy. Though usually applied to employment data the method can be used for investment, productivity, income or population, among other variables for calibrating economic progress. The share component measures the proportion each region (or sub-region) has of the factors of the national economy, whilst the shift records over time the difference between actual regional change and that which would have resulted had the region grown at national average rates.

III.2 Pre-1939 and Wartime

The mounting depression and severe unemployment of the early 1930s led to government intervention in S Wales, NE England, Cumberland and Clydeside, designated special areas under the 1934 Act of that name. Though powers were few and the effects very limited, only 4 per cent of factories established in GB 1934–8 going to the special areas, the pre-war years saw the introduction of trading estates, with powers to build and lease factories. Policy was directed towards relief of unemployment *in situ* but, uniquely for regional policy in the UK, there was also some attempt at planned inter-regional transfer and resettlement; however only 30,000 families were moved in six years, at high cost, and the experiment was never repeated.

Rearmament and the upturn of the trade cycle achieved much more than the special areas policy, though unemployment relief has remained in the forefront among objectives ever since. In 1940 the *Royal Commission on the Distribution of the Industrial Population* (Barlow Report) drew attention to the marked disparity in economic growth trends, in favour of the South East and the Midlands (the axial zone) and at the expense of the North, Wales and Scotland. The report called for national action on distribution of industry and population, recommended decentralization from congested urban areas, the redevelopment of older regions and the introduction of balance and diversification into their regional economies. Creation of garden cities and satellite towns was proposed, together with the expansion of rural towns. These far-reaching recommendations necessitated a new central organization for planning and in 1943 the Ministry of Town and Country Planning was born. A further view by the Commission was that there should be strategic dispersal of industries, to avoid the risks inherent in major vulnerable concentrations. This objective was in fact considerably furthered during the war through the policies of the Board of Trade, creating large ordnance factories and influencing the location of much new engineering, aircraft and vehicle production towards the peripheral and less exposed industrial regions of the north and west. Some of the major ordnance factories were available for conversion to trading (industrial) estates after the war, as at Aycliffe and Spennymoor in the North East, or Hirwaun and Bridgend in S Wales. Furthermore a pool of skilled labour, especially women, had been created in the special areas, capable of retraining for post-war industry, management had had the experience of operating successfully in the areas and their general communications had been improved. By 1945 unemployment in the special areas had fallen to the record low level of 1.5 per cent.

III.3 Post-war to 1960
(for references to all Acts see 'Public General Acts', p. 516)

Almost equally formative in changes in the UK space during this period were the *Distribution of Industry Act* (1945) and the *Town and Country Planning Act* (1947). Though the former was responsible for industrial location controls and inducements, and was vigorously prosecuted in the early post-war years, whilst the latter was concerned with development control, monitoring and programming changes in land use, the two objectives overlapped. Until 1954 there was also government control of building through a system of licences.

The development areas designated under the 1945 Act were more extensive, covering a population of 6.5 millions (13.5 per cent of the nation), in comparison with the 4 million people in the pre-war special areas. In territorial terms they were extensions of the special areas, to include major towns which had previously been excluded. As the agent for location policy the Board of Trade had powers to build factories and buy land, make loans to trading estate companies, finance basic public services, make loans and grants to firms and to reclaim derelict land. In addition, under the 1947 *Town and Country Planning Act* all applications to build factories or factory extensions of 465 m^2 or more had to have an industrial development certificate (IDC) issued by the BoT. In issuing such certificates the Board sought to ensure the 'proper' distribution of industry, a loose and flexible objective, but one which was used, with varying insistence, diminishing through the 1950s to the advantage of the development areas (DAs). As far as a common objective can be established it seems to have been the need to diversify the industrial structure of the DAs by the introduction and stimulation of new growth elements. A geographical outcome of this policy was a threefold division of the UK into: 'overgrowth' areas, mainly in the Midlands and SE England, in which manufacturing growth was discouraged; the DAs; and the remainder of the UK, commonly referred to as 'grey' areas in which neither encouragement nor discouragement was officially applied to those seeking industrial growth. Northern Ireland had similar legislation and effectively, though not in name, DA status. Further DAs were later added to the original four: Wigan and St Helens (1946); Merseyside, and parts of the Scottish Highlands (1949; NE Lancashire (1953).

In the years 1945–51 the DA policy showed dramatic results, no less than two-thirds of all recorded moves in manufacturing going to development areas. There was at that time plenty of mobile industry seeking new or additional factory space, the inducements in the DAs were substantial, not least in the availability of modern or converted wartime factories for rental, plus a skilled or semi-skilled labour force on the spot. In the two years to June 1947 233 tenants occupied rented DA factories, employing 50,000, whilst 301 new or extended factories in the areas provided only 20,000 new jobs during the same period. The early momentum was soon lost, however, and between 1948 and 1952 only 1,096 IDCs were granted for factory space in DAs, compared with 1,069 in London and the SE, and 808 in Greater Birmingham. Priority for exporters, many of whom sought to expand existing operations or develop new capacity in the more affluent areas, coupled with declining unemployment in the DAs, led to the relaxation of regional policy on industrial location. As an indication of this no 'advance factories', the spearhead of economic aid to the dispersed, less attractive sites in DAs, were built in the entire period 1947–59. Additionally, during the 1950s, the New Towns created under the 1946 Act were beginning to develop as powerful magnets for some of the light industries which might otherwise have been persuaded to move to DA sites.

The nationalization of the rail services, electricity generation and supply, the gas and coal industries, together with the alternating public and private control of the steel industry, permitted unusual coherence of central decisions, forward planning and rationalization of these key sectors. Although the collective outcome of decisions in these and other infra-structural sectors such as roads and ports, might thus have reinforced the regional and spatial policy objectives on industrial location or use of the land, the opportunities were not fully taken. Indeed rationalization in the sense of taking high cost or less profitable production units or links out of the industrial or communications networks threatened to have a precisely contrary effect. It is of course possible to argue that such a coordinated overview of spatial decision-taking would have been foreign to any post-war political climate in the UK, a verdict somewhat confirmed in due course by the demise of the ill-fated National Plan of 1964. The lack of such inter-related policy-making in the 1950s, in part the result of the independence rather than interdependence in the formulation and prosecution of policies by individual Ministries, was undoubtedly costly and frustrating to any thoughts of coherent regional planning. Concurrently the development plans by the counties and boroughs under the 1947 Act were being conceived and implemented without proper national context or allocation of resources, somewhat independent even of adjacent areas, and there continued that bugbear of planning in the UK, the lack of adequate inter-relationship between economic, social and land use aspects of planning policies concerned with space.

During the later 1950s, however, economic conditions deteriorated, unemployment rose again, becoming particularly severe in localized pockets, and official thoughts turned once again to the need for a more effective spatial, if still not a regional policy. The DA policy had been largely allowed to lapse and was revived, somewhat in piecemeal form, in amended legislation in 1958 (*Distribution of Industry, Industrial Finance Act*), recognizing the special needs of the pockets of more severe unemployment within the larger, but virtually defunct development areas. The decline in the fortunes of coal from 1957 onwards (ch. 4.I.2) foreshadowed the emergence of many problem localities where pits closed in rising numbers during the following decade. The steel industry similarly felt a recession and the capital goods industries, whose post-war revival had so effectively buttressed the economies of the major development areas, showed disturbing tendencies to instability and down-turn once more. The *Cotton Industry Act* (1959) involved public funds in a major reorganization and re-equipment operation for one of Britain's traditional staple industries, a practice which was to become characteristic and widespread during the 1970s.

III.4 1960–72

During the 1960s public policies on the UK space widened, became more coherent and inter-related, with emergence for the first time of regional economic planning. There was recognition that although relief of unemployment and social justice remained the priority objectives for the least favoured areas, and that this may lead at times to inefficient public investments in 'lame ducks' or localities, there was a more fundamental need, on a continuing basis, to examine, plan, programme and monitor the economic and social change in the major regions of the UK. To do this effectively required not only the appropriate planning mechanisms at national and regional level, but also implied that all major investment decisions, even by private entrepreneurs, needed to be reviewed and approved since they were likely to have regional or local repercussions, multiplier or 'spin-off' effects. The point that the social costs of the development of firms or industry are often borne by the community was well taken, justifying close and prior review of the locational intentions of any leader firm or key industry. Similarly, the role and significance of key decisions on major infrastructural improvements, such as roads, harbours, airports, housing or office space were now more fully understood and could be, though regrettably not always were, taken into account in the context of regional development. In short, the regional development process is nowadays more comprehensively studied, its ingredients more fully appraised and the relationships between manufacturing and services, in particular, more effectively understood. Belatedly, but importantly, the necessity of bringing local government units and functions more into line with the requirements of the times was also appreciated. Finally, the reducing of inequalities over the UK space is thought likely not only thereby to satisfy demands for fuller and more diverse employment, social justice, regionalist aspirations or the wish for improved living environments in less favoured areas, but also in its own right to make a significant contribution to overall national development. After UK entry into the EEC the future course of regional policy and the full implications of incorporating the national space into the European land-sea space must for the time being remain somewhat uncertain (House 1976).

Policies on industrial location have varied over the past decade. Under the *Local Employment Acts* (1960 and 1963) the spatially-coherent development areas were abandoned in favour of more rapidly changing and highly localized development districts, identified initially by an unemployment level double the national average over a period of six months; in time 4.5 per cent became a general yardstick for this, and imminent unemployment was also accepted as a justification for the scheduling of districts. Some of the grant and loan powers of the Board of Trade were extended, Industrial Estates Corporations were established for England, Wales and Scotland (though some estates now fall outside the scheduled districts) and the IDC system was widened to include conversion of non-industrial buildings. Yet the policy was negative: the scheduled districts were fragmented and transitory, being descheduled when the employment situation rose above the statutory unemployment threshold; and the districts variously included rural areas, localities of mining decline, or coastal holiday resorts with off-season unemployment, outmigration and lack of alternative work. In 1961 12.5 per cent of the national population was covered by Development Districts, in 1963 7.2 per cent, in 1966 16.8 per cent. Scheduling bore no relation to a district's potential for development, indeed often the converse was true, and competition between districts, as for example between Merseyside and Snowdonia, was very uneven. Industrialists lacked confidence in the continuity of scheduling, the growth potential and the adequacy and skills of any labour force available in or near these pockets of heavy unemployment. Nevertheless in the period 1960–8 (BoT 1968) no less than £269 million were spent under the *Local Employment Acts* and an estimated 428,000 jobs created.

1963 was a very formative year in the emergence of regional planning, first with the production of White Papers on C Scotland (SED 1963) and NE England (BoT 1963). These recognized that economic first aid to a dispersed and changing set of limited locations would not solve even the basic problems of development districts, and might well be at the expense of the economic health of wider regions, that larger and more coherent regions would need to be designated and that within these the concentration of public investment at *growth points* or *growth zones* would be the most effective means of promoting regional development. Infrastructure was to have a high priority in regional programmes for the two areas, the living environment should be improved, but diversification of the industrial structure and relief of unemployment remained enduring priorities.

In quite different spheres 1963 also saw the creation of the government-sponsored Location of Offices Bureau, part of the policy of persuading office development to move out of C London (1,976 firms and 139, 326 jobs moved in 1963—76 but mostly to other locations within the SE) (Rhodes and Khan 1971; LOB 1972), the Beeching Report on the rail system (MoT 1963) and the *Water Resources Act* of the same year. All contributed to the new thinking on how to achieve economic growth by fuller use of resources, balanced development for all economic regions and the recognition that such development might increasingly come from redistribution of services as much as from changes in location of new manufacturing. Nevertheless in several key decisions in the early 1960s the government showed itself alive to the need to influence location of new car assembly plants (at Linwood and Bathgate in Central Scotland, or three plants on Merseyside), aluminium smelters (Invergordon, Lynemouth in Northumberland, and Anglesey) or major greenfield steel plants (Ravenscraig on Clydeside and Newport—Llanwern in S Wales).

There followed quickly the creation under the short-lived Department of Economic Affairs of the eight economic planning regions of England (1965), each with its Council of lay members and its Board comprising senior representatives of the relevant Ministries at regional level (Turnbull 1967). The Councils and Boards have outlived their parent and, although consultative and advisory, have come to represent effectively the regional interest upwards to central government, downwards to their constituent local authorities. They have counterparts in the Welsh Office, the Scottish Development Department and until recently in the Economic Council for N Ireland. The greater part of section 1.IV is concerned with examining the economic and social problems faced at regional level, the strategies and courses of action recommended and the impacts of the first decade of even this rudimentary beginning of true regional planning. Outline or interim strategies have been published for all regions, but only the SE (SE Joint Planning Team 1970), the NW (DOE 1974) and the W Midlands (1974) have reached the stage of a definitive strategy, accepted by the government as the framework for future structure planning in those regions under the *Town and Country Planning Act* (1968). In 1974 the E Anglian EPC published its definitive strategy, (E Anglia Regional Strategy Team 1974), and that for Yorkshire and Humberside came out in spring 1976 (Yorks. and Humberside EPC 1976).

Meanwhile control over the location of services as well as manufacturing continued to be the spearhead of policies for regional balance, relief of unemployment or social justice in less favoured areas. The introduction of Selective Employment Tax (1965) had a differential effect on the regions; in the development areas, with an already lower ratio in service occupations the effect was less than in more affluent areas. In 1966 a new *Industrial Development Act* abolished development districts and re-created coherent development areas, covering virtually all the N Region, large parts of SW England and virtually all Scotland and Wales; N Ireland had similar status, but under its own legislation. These were the largest and most coherent development areas hitherto, with 40 per cent of the UK space and 20 per cent of the UK population. There has since been some conflict of interest between those favouring an economic growth and investment concentration policy for these areas, and others who continued to stress the merits of discriminatory, at times dispersing policies of relief to unemployment in or as near as possible to the localities afflicted.

The 'teeth' of the location policies were strengthened, the threshold for IDC exemptions was raised with industrial development in the Midlands and SE more positively restricted, but financial inducements to industrialists to move to development areas were also increased: grants were made towards building costs, loans made available at low rates of interest and rent-free accommodation provided in some cases. Investment grants were provided in development areas at double the national rate, no longer limited in relation to jobs created, and in 1967 a Regional Employment Premium (doubled in 1974, but cancelled in 1977) was introduced, helping to reduce labour costs there. In the same years localized special development areas (SDAs) were defined within development areas, largely in response to the severe local unemployment being created by coal-mining rundown. The SDAs enjoyed additional advantages of higher grants on new buildings, rent-free government factories for periods up to five years and assistance to cover operating costs. These measures led to a sharp rise in industrial moves to the development areas and in jobs created there: in 1966—7 over 30 per cent of industrial building approvals in Britain were for the scheduled areas compared with only 13 per cent in 1961—2. For the years 1963—70 Moore and Rhodes (1973) estimated that an additional 150,000 jobs had been created by stronger regional policies, excluding shipbuilding and metals. Manufacturing investment in the DAs was probably 30 per cent higher than it would otherwise have been.

In 1970—1 policies on industrial location were revised and investment grants were replaced by depreciation allowances on plant and machinery. In development areas a system of free depreciation was introduced and assistance under the *Local Employment Act* was strengthened. The general feeling in the areas was that the new measures would diminish the inflow of mobile industry, particularly the capital-intensive projects, and that it would be important to make the inducements to immigrant firms equally available to established industry.

The very success of the 1966 measures led to marked reaction in the regions bordering the development areas, whose problems were neither so wide-ranging nor so severe, least of all in the fashionable indicator of unemployment levels, and yet whose economic growth rates were scarcely more favourable. This led to an investigation into the problems of the so-called 'grey' or 'intermediate areas' (Sec. State Economic Affairs 1969). The main conclusion reached was that such areas were diverse in character, strongly represented in Yorks. and Humberside, in the NW, in certain coalfields of the Midlands, on the borders of Wales, at Plymouth and at Edinburgh—Leith. There was some evidence that parts of these areas were suffering economically from being within the shadow of adjacent development areas and were receiving few benefits in return. Though the recommendations of the Hunt Committee for the scheduling of wide intermediate areas were not accepted by the government of the time (1969), and incidentally a proposal to deschedule Merseyside as a development area was refused, an intermediate level of regional aid was granted to more restricted scheduled intermediate areas. In the *White Paper* (DTI 1972) a wider definition of intermediate areas was proposed embracing most of Yorks. and Humberside, together with the NW (outside Merseyside), Wrexham, the south-east borders of Wales, the Plymouth hinterland and Edinburgh—Leith; to this list of scheduled areas parts of Derbyshire, N Lincolnshire and Nottinghamshire were added later. The UK thus now had no less than *five gradations* of economic and social aid to scheduled areas, on a descending scale of priorities and an ascending scale of interdictions, as follows: special development areas; development areas; intermediate areas; non-scheduled areas; overgrowth areas. Such sophistication is ideal for allocation and channelling of growth when the national growth momentum is high and sustained. It is somewhat illusory in the slow, fitful growth situation more characteristic of national economic trends in the UK during the decade 1960–70.

In support of the policies on new or expanded manufacturing location the Location of Offices Bureau policy was strengthened during 1965 and had notable success in influencing intra-regional dispersal within the SE or within the W Midlands. In spite of steady growth in modern office accommodation and lower rentals in the DAs, however, it was the planned dispersal of government rather than private offices which had the most marked effect on the inflow of such service jobs to the North, Scotland or Wales. Government-sponsored moves accounted for about 3,000 per annum in the 1960s, whilst during the early 1970s some 41 per cent of government jobs planned for dispersal were to go to the Development Areas (Hardman Report, Civil Service Dept. 1973). The current (1976) Civil Service dispersal programme involves the movement of 31,000 people out of London by the mid 1980s.

In terms of infrastructure regional allocations in the later 1960s came to reflect more effectively the needs and priorities of regional development, though it is less clear that the motorway programme had this intended effect. The growth of widespread and mounting concern for conservation of both urban and rural environment also played its part in the eventual negative decision on the third London airport and in discussions on the proposed London Motorway Box.

Feasibility studies, 1969–71, probed the possibilities of fast economic and population growth in Humberside, Tayside and Severnside for later in the century (Campbell and Lyddon 1970; Central Unit for Environmental Planning 1963, 1971), though specifically without intended detriment to the priorities for the development areas up to 1981. The government has since decided that none of the fast-growth areas will be needed, and that controlled growth in existing urban areas or New Towns will cope with the extra population by the end of the century. For the extensive agricultural and recreational components of the UK space the 1966 *Agriculture Act* and the 1968 *Countryside Act* were especially formative, whilst the 1968 and 1971 *Town and Country Planning Acts* instituted a more flexible planning system with better integration between economic and social planning at national level, reflected through the economic regional strategies, and physical or land use planning at the level of a new pattern of local government units. The regional strategies, once approved in definitive form by the government, are to provide the framework for the flexible structure plans of the constituent local authorities.

III.5 Post-1972

The *Industry Acts* (Publ. Gen. Acts 1972 and 1975) substantially increased the inducements for firms to move to or develop within the assisted areas, at the same time cancelling the need for IDCs in all SDAs and DAs. Regional development grants were instituted to stimulate expansion or modernization of industry, payable to both native and incoming firms, and it was no longer necessary for the new investment to provide additional employment. Grants in SDAs were 22 per cent for plant and machinery, and for new buildings and works. DAs received 20 per cent for plant and machinery, and the same 20 per cent grant for new buildings and works enjoyed by other assisted areas. Investment grants to be phased out amounted

TABLE 1.4

Regional Development Grants, 1975–6

£ million	Plant and Machinery	Buildings
England		
SDAs	100.3	28.5
DAs	134.2	27.5
IAs		32.9
DLCA⁺		1.1
Scotland	98.5	
Wales	47.0	

⁺Derelict Land Clearance Area (N Midlands)
Source: Sec. State Industry (1976)

to £71 million: £46.5 million for ships, and £21 million for plant and machinery (1975–6).

Under section 7 (*Industry Act 1972*) regional selective financial assistance could be provided for improving employment prospects, by new job provision or by safeguarding existing jobs. For Scotland (December 1975) and Wales (January 1976) these powers were transferred to Development Agencies set up to promote industrial growth, provide factories and industrial estates, improve infra-structure, clear derelict land and, in particular, promote indigenous manufacturing by small Welsh or Scottish companies. Under section 1 the National Enterprise Board (NEB), with regional offices in Liverpool and Newcastle, was created to promote growth and restructuring at the level of firms and industries. From 1972 to December 1976 £214 million were paid under section 7 (31 per cent in Scotland, 24 per cent in the NW, and 20 per cent in Wales). 43,000 new jobs were provided and 20,000 safeguarded in five years.

Under section 8 selective financial assistance was to be available for modernizing, rationalizing, or restructuring particular firms or industries (ch. 4, p. 342). The clothing, ferrous foundry, machine tool, motor vehicle and wool textile industries were early beneficiaries.

Loans and grants made under the *Local Employment Act* (1972) were steadily run down as the new policy developed. Yet the administration of government-built factories continued (table 1.5). Furthermore, the advance factory programme grew

TABLE 1.5

Government-sponsored Factories, DAs and IAs (31 March 1976)

	North	SW	Mersey-side	Scotland (to Dec. 75)	Wales (to Jan. 76)	IAs England	IAs Wales	TOTAL
Factory space								
(1,000 m²)	18,156	319	2,140	21,658	17,670	1,550	200	61,963
Tenants	365	15	25	434	400	25	4	1,268
Employment M	25,052	719	2,577	45,364	26,916	1,981	556	106,165
F	24,552	853	3,225	31,006	20,885	1,310	202	82,033
Total	49,604	1,572	5,802	79,370	47,801	3,291	758	188,198

Source: Sec. State Industry (1976)

rapidly; on 1 January 1976 there were 636 advance factories in operation, covering 1,024,980 m^2.

In August 1974 Merseyside and parts of the NW Wales became SDAs; Edinburgh and Cardiff were included in the DAs; and Chesterfield became an IA. From this time the assisted areas have included 43 per cent of the national labour force. IDC exemption limits were lowered from 930 to 465 m^2 in the SE (excluding the Isle of Wight) and from 1,395 to 930 m^2 in other non-assisted areas. The limit was continued at 1,395 m^2 in the assisted areas, and in 1976 was raised to the same threshold for the W Midlands, a rapidly emerging problem region in unemployment terms.

In April 1977 further SDAs (p. 54) were created in Scotland, DAs on Humberside and at Shotton (N Wales), whilst parts of N Yorkshire were downgraded to IA status.

The regional debate There has been a long-continuing and unresolved argument on the merits and demerits of regional policy in its implications for national economic growth (Robertson 1965; McCrone 1969; Moore and Rhodes 1973 and 1976; Cameron 1974; Chisholm 1974; Diamond 1974; Sant 1975; Holland 1976; Buck and Atkins 1976). One school of thought, reinforced by DEA thinking at the time of the abortive National Plan of 1964, sees sound economic merit in a strong regional policy. Whilst there are under-utilized resources of labour, land and plant in the assisted areas it will be in the overall national interest to bring these more fully into use, rather than add to the already inflationary pressures by allowing growth in the congested (non-assisted) areas. Furthermore, social capital will be more effectively used thereby and workers will no longer be compelled to migrate in search of employment or betterment. In spite of the seemingly peripheral location of assisted areas it has not been established that spatial variations in transport costs are likely to be constraints upon such a regional policy, and indeed it is further argued that there are no significant variations in profitability in similar operations according to region (Chisholm 1974, 223). Finally, branch plants in the assisted areas have generally performed well and in more recent times have not fulfilled dire predictions of vulnerability to closure at the first whiff of depression.

The counter-arguments rest upon the proposition that preferential regional policies may well have been at the expense of aggregate national growth momentum (Chisholm 1974). Furthermore, if regional policies are to be continued as a form of social and spatial justice 'a faster rate of national growth is a necessary precondition' (Sec. State Trade and Industry, 1972, 1). To achieve such national growth must be the first priority, and since 1945 it has proved to be remarkably elusive. In seeing the regional problem as but the more severe variant of a national problem it is national remedies which must be sought: freedom of choice for firms to locate and to develop *in situ* wherever that may be; promotion of retraining, redeployment and greater mobility of labour, both sectorally and spatially; more flexible use of housing policy to promote expansion in the more logical economic growth points or zones. Much growth takes place outside regional policy in any case and it should not be artificially constrained. Expansion of service industries is linked particularly to variations in regional affluence, and this cannot readily and logically be diffused by regional policies. Even the creation of major provincial city service centres, on the French model of *métropoles d'équilibre*, will take considerable time and may be impracticable in the face of centripetal market forces. Finally, the effects of interdiction through refusal of IDCs in the non-assisted areas may have frustrated growth potential. Similarly, the constraints of Office Development Permits (ODPs) in Greater London have greatly contributed to inflationary rentals and distorted the market pattern. Certainly, the central area of London during the 1970s has generated major social and employment problems (Eversley 1973). These are often common in all major city centres and underline the need for an inner city variant of spatial aid policies hitherto conceived primarily in regional scale terms. During 1976 indeed there was a firm Ministerial commitment to rejuvenating city centres and other 'inner urban land', at the expense if necessary of continuing dispersal policies to new towns or overspill areas.

Some EEC implications There is much to hope for but also something to fear in the prospects for Britain's regions within the EEC of the Nine (House 1976). Economic opinion is divided upon the gains and losses and the time over which these may become evident. Nevin (1972) took the optimistic view that 'peripheral regions in the UK may enjoy a marginal profit after entry to the EEC' but he felt that this would be 'largely as a result of increased growth momentum in the national economy'. In this view he appeared to be siding with those who see the regional problem as capable of alleviation only within a national context. He was careful to stress that existing British regional policy should not be weakened in the interim and foresaw that the government might have to take additional protective measures for the assisted areas, as other national governments had already consistently done. Brown (1972) was less sanguine and thought that the development areas would 'presumably suffer more (in Europe) from positions peripheral to their market areas than they do now'. He thought that the regional problem in the EEC would continue to grow especially since international factor movements did not have the built-in economic stabilizers which national governments can provide for their regions.

Keeble (1976, 281) took a more optimistic view, encouraged by the vigour of industrial growth in the UK assisted areas after 1965. British firms would no longer need to locate in Europe to avoid tariffs; assisted areas suffered no significant transport cost disadvantage; and in world trading terms ports in peripheral regions should be equally competitive. Furthermore, common language would attract European plants of US firms rather to the UK; the available labour in the assisted areas was a unique asset; EEC regional policy would supplement the assisted areas policy; and, additionally, the general momentum of EEC growth would diffuse to even the peripheral areas of the UK. Against these optimistic points must be set: the lack of equally competitive transport organization, by road or rail, in the peripheral areas, and the quoting of 'special' rates for more isolated firms of sub-regions; the lack of regular cargo liner sailings and the limited development of container bases; the need to break bulk or transfer transport media by sea passage to Europe and the time factor involved as a marginal extra; the continuing perceptions of cost disadvantage by many industrialists in respect of assisted area location; the lack of skills, adaptability and productivity among those to be drawn from the unemployed; unemployment or even activity rates no reliable indicator of labour availability or quality.

Planners in the assisted areas (Northern EPC 1972, Welsh Council 1971, Yorks. and Humberside EPC 1972) have emphasized that the impact of EEC membership will be neither dramatic, for good or ill, nor quickly felt. On the contrary the impact will be highly selective, upon particular industry groups, or even individual firms, rather than upon regional economies as a whole, and its effects will often be indirect. For example, in the Northern Region it was estimated that almost one-half the labour force would be scarcely affected, one-quarter should benefit, and one-quarter would suffer adverse effects.

On 1 January 1975 the EEC (Commn. of the European Communities 1975) introduced, for three years in the first instance, new categories for permitted aid by member states. In addition, there was to be established a *Regional Development Fund* which would supplement rather than supplant nationally-based regional aids, and whose contributions would be administered by national governments. Only Ulster came into the highest category for aid, in which the maximum intensity of existing state aids was to be permitted; the EEC Commission was to be notified of all proposed aids with more than 35 per cent net grant equivalent. The British DAs and SDAs fell within the second category with a 30 per cent net grant ceiling to be achieved after three years. By implication Britain's intermediate areas were classed with non-assisted areas and limited to a 20 per cent net grant ceiling 1975–8 (House 1976).

IV NEW PATTERNS FOR DEMOCRACY

IV.1 The Political Variable
(for references to all Acts, see 'Public General Acts', p. 516)

In giving primacy in explanation and accommodation to economic or administrative principles of efficiency or convenience, studies of regional conditions have traditionally discounted political forces and processes. Planners at all levels have been similarly neglectful or perfunctory, on many occasions, in ignoring or underestimating the need for effective public participation in, and acceptance of, proposals for change. It has, however, become dramatically apparent that both politicians and the people they represent are today concerned to be more fully and directly involved in all decisions affecting popular well-being, expectations and aspirations, whether these be well-founded or not. The pursuit of social justice has also come to have an important spatial dimension, in the clamour for the redress of deprivation or perceived wrongs, and the demand for greater identity, self-expression and direct control over decision-making and destiny. Political ferment occurs at different territorial scales, from the national pressures for devolution of government to N Ireland, Scotland and Wales, to the claims of English regionalists; or the sturdy political pressures from interest groups in either town or countryside. Such ferment is channelled in the first instance through voting, in whose changing patterns and structures there are intriguing geographical variations (Busteed 1975). Secondly, the legislative programmes of governments seek to adjust the delicate balance of powers, functions, or territorial units, but satisfaction with any particular outcome is all too elusive and equilibrium remains unstable. Likewise in planning, the encouragement of public participation has been tardy (Commn. on Public Participation in Planning 1969) and not without many pitfalls, in another aspect of the search for a new balance between equity and operational efficiency. Such a search inevitably ends in a compromise between the general and the particular interests involved. If the nature of the compromise is to represent an improvement it must give the greatest satisfaction to the wish for decentralization of power with the least dislocation to the overall affairs of the nation. Such a desirable state of affairs is difficult enough to formulate, even more so to enact.

The complex skein of wishes for decentralization may be rationalized along a spectrum from local government reform, with modest claims for redistribution of powers, functions and units, to more far-reaching demands for increasing degrees of autonomy for constituent nations of the UK. In more extreme forms the nationalist aspirations in Scotland, and perhaps in N Ireland also, are for national status within a UK federation or even ultimately sovereign independence. It is convenient to assess the case and the provision for devolution, at the level of the nations, separately from the recently enacted and completed local government reform in all four nations of the UK.

IV.2 Devolution

Before discussing the proposals for devolution it is important to appreciate the existing differences between Scotland, Wales and N Ireland in terms of the extent of devolved powers, the varied dates of such devolution and the contrasting historical, social, cultural and economic background to claims for further devolution. Since these great differences do exist it is unlikely that a similar prescription for devolution will be equally applicable or acceptable to all three nations at the present time.

   Scotland has had a Secretary of State since 1885, and from 1939 the Scottish Office has been the focus for a wide measure of administrative devolution (H of C 1974). As a member of the UK government the Secretary of State has a major responsibility for formulation and execution of policy on agriculture and fisheries; education; local government and environmental services; social work, health and housing; roads and certain aspects of shipping and road transport. He is also responsible for a range of other functions from police and fire services to sport and tourism. The UK government administrative functions are carried out in five Scottish Departments based in Edinburgh. For most of the subjects there is separate legislation, a right preserved under the *Act of Union* of 1707, handled by the Scottish Grand Committee (all 71 Scottish MPs). The Secretary of State also has a major role in the planning and development of the Scottish economy.

   The first Minister for *Welsh* affairs was appointed in 1951 and most important measures of devolution took place between 1964 and 1975, the former being the date of creation of the first Secretary of State for Wales and the Welsh Office. The Welsh Office now has responsibility for housing, health, the social services, primary and secondary education, child care, town and country planning, forestry and agriculture. The Secretary of State has a general responsibility for economic development and for the coordination of government action to promote welfare in Wales. Welsh interests are further represented by the 36 Welsh MPs who sit on the Welsh Grand Committee, a forum for discussion and debate, rather than for decision.

   The devolution of powers to the parliament and government of *N Ireland* (*Government of Ireland Act 1920*) had been very substantial and had continued until the dissolution of the Stormont parliament in March 1972. A bicameral parliament had been set up (52 members of a House of Commons, plus 26 members of a Senate) with considerable internal powers over economic and social affairs, but limited in its authority to tax or retain customs revenue; the armed forces and international matters were also reserved to the UK government. In the *Ireland Act* (1949), passed when the Irish Free State resolved to become a republic and secede from the Commonwealth, the rights of the N Ireland parliament to be concerned in all decisions on future change of UK membership were defined and safeguarded.

Pressures for change Though there is a long and intricate background to the wishes for fuller expression of national identity and aspirations in Scotland, Wales and N Ireland, there has been a remarkable and widespread upsurge of feeling and of positive demands for political powers during the years 1965–75, demands furthermore which are not likely readily to be satisfied, if at all. All that can be attempted here is a brief assessment of the rising tide of nationalism and of the ingredients which have fuelled its discontents. In all three cases there are powerful reasons for arguing that on most economic and social counts (fig. 1.3) they are clearly, and perhaps increasingly under-privileged by comparison with other regions of the UK (see also table 1.4). In the case of the Scots, in particular, it is argued that over-centralized control from Westminster, or rather Whitehall, has steadily aggravated an unsatisfactory situation. Furthermore, not only might Scotland prosper more fully had she but control over her own economic destiny, but the potential of the North Sea oil 'bonanza' off her shores could and should be used initially, and perhaps entirely, for Scottish and not for UK benefit. The economic arguments for or against Scotland's benefits from greater political autonomy are not entirely conclusive if oil resources are not taken into account (Cairncross 1954; McCrone 1969; Scottish Council 1974; Mackay and Mackay 1974). Whether in international law or equity the Continental shelf oil resources are or should be Scottish, or belong to the UK is open to some debate, but probably not to political negotiation.

In neither the Welsh nor the N Ireland case for devolution are the economic arguments for benefit so powerfully advanced. Nevertheless the desire for greater decision-taking powers over their own economic destiny is fervently sought. Wales is with difficulty to be regarded as a coherent national economy (Thomas 1962), whilst the dependence of N Ireland on its UK neighbours is as inevitable as it is clear-cut.

Behind the economic arguments, whether to oppose perceived 'neo-colonialist' policies of the UK government, to achieve economic independence, or to promote greater self-sufficiency there are other less tangible, but equally powerful ingredients of national consciousness and identity. A Scottish identity is well-founded over centuries of history, reinforced by distinctive cultural traits, but only to a small degree related to language; Gaelic today is habitually spoken only in small and diminishing areas of the NW and the Islands. A sense of a distinctive past allied with rising discontent with an under-privileged present create a powerful ferment for nationalist politics. In the 1974 UK elections the Scottish National Party strengthened its support, and in October won eleven seats at Westminster. As yet there is less support for SNP in the great Strathclyde conurbation, whose economic and social problems are likely to continue to dominate in Scotland's future prospects as they have done in the past. The 1974 White Paper found opinion in Scotland still divided: the majority favoured devolution of powers to a directly elected Scottish assembly with real authority; the minority preferred further administrative devolution; overwhelmingly, outside the SNP, there was support for the preservation of the essential political and economic unity of the UK.

In Wales there is an even stronger cultural basis to the wish for devolution (Philip 1975). Though independence ceased as far back as 1535 and fewer institutional traits have persisted than in Scotland, the Welsh language remains a major factor in cultural cohesion and political will. Indeed there is some correlation between the strength of the Plaid Cymru vote and the proportion of those who in the 1971 census claimed to speak both Welsh and English, at least in Carmarthen, Caernarvon and Merioneth where the party won seats in October 1974. On the other hand, the correlation fails in Anglesey and in Cardigan. The nationalist vote in Wales, at little over 11 per cent, is much weaker than in Scotland and even fell back slightly between the February and October 1974 elections. Nevertheless, the sense of Welshness is strong, even in areas with predominantly English-speaking populations.

Pressures by the majority group in N Ireland, as measured by the *Ulster Constitutional Convention* (H of C 1975), are still directed to restoration of something like the rule of the Stormont Parliament, prorogued in 1972; between March 1972 and the last day of 1973 the province was under direct rule from Westminster. Under the *Northern Ireland Constitution Act* (1973) the principles of power-sharing and partnership between the traditional Unionist majority and the SDLP minority were to be fostered, but on 29 May 1974 the N Ireland Assembly (78 members elected by proportional representation) was also prorogued and the functions of the executive were taken over by the Secretary of State. The *N Ireland Act* (1974) established an Ulster Constitutional Convention. Three basic realities were to be observed: power-sharing and partnership; the outcome should be acceptable to the people of the UK as a whole; and the special relationship with the Republic of Ireland must be taken into account. In November 1975 the Convention reported but opinion was very deeply divided, the majority (UUUC, United Unionist Ulster Convention) continuing to favour a devolved regional parliament similar to that created under the *Government of Ireland Act* (1920). Direct rule continues.

The *White Paper* (H of C 1974) proposed separate Scottish and Welsh assemblies. Scotland would get a law-making assembly with a cabinet-type government and a chief executive. Wales would have an executive assembly at Cardiff without powers to make laws. Both countries would send the same number of MPs to Westminster as at present and the assemblies would have powers over local government, health, personal social services, schools, housing, roads, environment and many aspects of physical planning. The assemblies (Scotland 142 members, Wales 72, two for each existing parliamentary constituency) would get block grants from Westminster to pay for the services they control and the UK government would have over-riding authority in case of disputes. North Sea oil revenues would continue to go to the UK Exchequer.

The proposals for devolution to Scotland and Wales were incorporated in the *Scotland and Wales Bill* (1976). A growing sense of unease about the implications for England of this measure led to a consultative document (Office of the Lord Pres. of the Council 1976), which ruled out not only the creation of an English Assembly but also a series of assemblies with regional powers. It indicated that English fears of disadvantage in regional policy benefits would prove groundless since powers over assisted areas would be reserved to the UK government. Likewise, infra-structure investments forming part of a national network would not be devolved from the centre, and furthermore there would continue to be direct control over the allocation of block funds and capital expenditure.

Even the possibility of limited devolution to regional bodies, whether executive or advisory, was approached with ultra-caution: local government reform had only just been completed; health and water authorities had scarcely settled in; it was not clear that either more democratic participation or greater efficiency would ensue from the creation of any kind of regional institution. The number of regions and their boundaries might also pose controversial problems.

In December 1976 it was decided to hold referenda in Scotland and Wales to test public reaction to the Devolution Bill, but during 1977 the Bill was withdrawn.

IV.3 Local Government Reform

In a democratic society it is not surprising to find that local government units are diverse in size, character and resources, that many were established early and there has been persistent reluctance to accept change in either boundaries or in functions. For the more limited purposes for which they were designed the counties or boroughs served well enough and many have had a continued existence since early times. The *Local Government Acts* of 1888 and 1894 confirmed the existence of many such units but it is universally accepted that during the present century the pattern of units has proved increasingly unsatisfactory, not least because their functions have been increased; major changes in economy and society have taken place and the relationships between central and local government have become more complex. Nevertheless there remains even today a widespread feeling that in local government the least change is the best change, and it is equally clear that in defining and seeking acceptance of any new pattern of units or redistribution of functions the British penchant for compromise is always needed (Smith 1964—5; Freeman 1968). Compromise is needed in several respects: for example, on the balance of powers and the extent of devolution from the centre to the constituent nations, regions, cities, counties or districts; on the size of units for various kinds of function and the pattern and nesting of such units within a nation-wide administrative hierarchy, particularly having regard for the important relationships between town and hinterland. The 'viability of local democracy' has more than once been a priority principle in official reports on local government reform. The difficulty is to preserve this without doing violence to the economy, efficiency, convenience or choice which people have come to expect in an increasingly mobile and sophisticated urban society. With the grafting of a wide range of planning functions on to local government since the 1947 Act and the rise of regional planning in the 1960s the search for new patterns became increasingly urgent.

Successive attempts at local government reform since the war foundered less at the stage of principle than when new boundaries or new units were proposed to take the place of counties, boroughs or districts, in whose 'iconography' so many have believed for so long (Gilbert 1939, 1948; Thomas 1952; Mackintosh 1968). Yet the need for reform became steadily more pressing and the advantages to be derived more clearly seen in post-war years. This led finally to major investigations into the question, in the late 1960s, in all the national units of the UK (RC Local Govt. England 1969; RC Local Govt. Greater London 1960; RC Local Govt. Scotland 1969; Welsh Office 1970; Govt. N Ireland 1967, 1969, 1970), enquiries made the more urgent by a rising tide of regionalism in England and a renewed sense of national identity, even of grievance in Scotland, Wales and N Ireland. During the same period the *Royal Commn. on the Constitution* (see Kilbrandon Report, 1973) was set up to provide an essential link in the problem of redistributing powers between centre, the nations and the regions.

England

Unfortunately, water supply and demand (ch. 3.III.2) and the hospital service (ch. 4.IV.5) are organized regionally on quite different principles. The *Redcliffe-*

Maud Report (*Royal Commn. on Local Govt. In England 1969*) was voluminous, innovating and controversial, surely the most substantively researched document ever likely to appear on local government reform. Even here there were two clearly conflicting schools of thought represented respectively in the majority report and in the memorandum of dissent by Senior, both limited by their terms of reference, to report 'within existing functions' of local government. The majority report proposed 61 new local government areas, each covering town and country; in 58 of them, termed unitary areas, none less in size than 250,000, none larger than 1,000,000 people, a single authority would group all personal and social services with no lower second tier, whilst in the other three, the metropolitan areas around Birmingham, Liverpool and Manchester, as already for London (1960), there was to be a second tier of metropolitan districts. Counties and boroughs were to disappear and the economic planning regions to be replaced by provinces, each with a provincial council of undefined powers. The memorandum of dissent declined to accept the unitary area principle, seeing in it a violation of both the facts of social geography and the principles of democracy, which required more local ties than the large unitary authorities might permit. A two-tier system was preferred by Senior, based on city-regions, with directly-elected authorities, and a second order of town districts, below which there should be common councils at community level.

The proposals aroused discussion and controversy in academic (James, House, Hall 1970; D. Thomas et al 1969) and political circles. There was general agreement among geographers on the importance of the provincial level in any new patterns for planning or democracy, but a division of opinion on the merits of the unitary as compared with the two-tier systems, and a good deal of criticism about the nature of specific units or boundaries. In the author's view the unitary principle had much to recommend it, in its cleaner break with the past, the designation of units large enough for effective planning, the coherence of functions intended and the possibility of capitalizing upon the rising mobility and enlarging space perceptions of the population. Such a fresh system of units would have required new concepts of community, but offered the prospect of abandoning the parochialisms, which for so long have bedevilled planning in the UK, even as high as the level of large towns or counties.

Though the substance of the majority report proposals were acceptable to the government of the day they did not find the same favour with its successor. The proposals forming the basis of the *Local Government Act* (1972), operational from 1 April 1974, recognized two forms of authority, counties and districts, with a two-tier metropolitan-type structure for Merseyside, SE Lancashire—NE Cheshire (SELNEC), the W Midlands, W Yorkshire, S Yorkshire and the Tyne-Wear area. These metropolitan authorities had boundaries which most commentators have regarded as too tightly-drawn, thus infringing the city-hinterland principle, and relying perforce for their effectiveness upon the right planning decisions being taken at the strategic regional level. The pattern of local government areas adopted is seen on fig. 1.5, which brings out clearly the considerable disparity in size and rateable value per capita among the first-order units, and underlines the point that together with the problems arising from economic restructuring and unfavourable location the development areas had poorer, and at times larger, local government units for the most part. During the passage of the legislation through Parliament amendments to the units were vigorously pressed, as on Teesside (Cleveland County), Herefordshire—Worcestershire and the north-eastern borders of Essex. Larger cities which

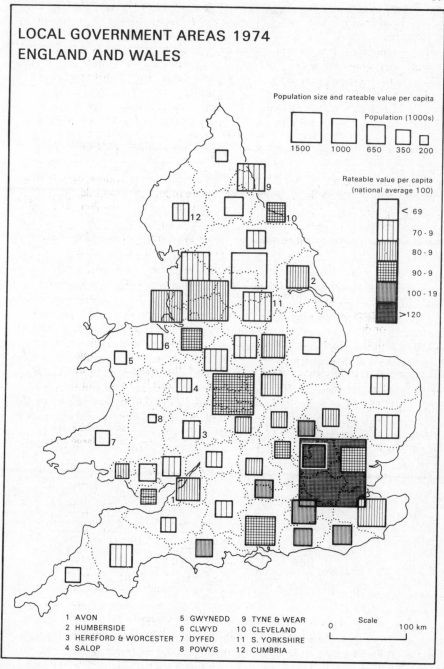

Figure 1.5   Local Government areas, England and Wales, 1974

became county districts under the new scheme campaigned strongly and with success for greater devolution of planning powers to the second-tier authorities. The definition and longer-term revision of second-tier units was undertaken by the Local Government Boundary Commission for England. The districts correspond as far as possible with pre-existing county districts, lie within or close to the preferred population range of 75,000 to 100,000, and are claimed to be acceptable in large measure to the local populations concerned.

Scotland

The *Wheatley Commission* (Royal Commn. on Local Govt. in Scotland 1969 rejected the unitary principle as unworkable for Scotland, believing that a single-tier solution would result neither in efficient planning and administration of the major services, nor in satisfactory democratic representation. On the other hand the regional level was already a reality in the regions of Scotland adopted for planning purposes, and Scotland itself had a measure of economic and social powers devolved from Whitehall. The second-tier in Scotland might best be represented by 37 'shires' and a third level, if required, could be made up of 'localities', typically a small town plus hinterland; of these there might be between 100 and 250 according to the criteria for definition. In the event the Commission settled for the 37 shires for local services and allocated personal services to the region; community councils were recommended for the localities. The *White Paper* (Scottish Office 1971) accepted the Wheatley proposals in principle, but changed the pattern of units, first by abandoning attempts at uniformity throughout Scotland and, secondly, by increasing the number of the new authorities.

Under the *Local Government (Scotland) Act* (1973) 430 Authorities (4 cities, 21 large burghs, 176 small burghs, 33 counties and 196 districts) were replaced by 65 Authorities (9 regions, 53 districts and 3 all-purpose island councils). The new units were a more deliberate attempt to establish logical economic and social entities in both city region and countryside. 9 regions were defined (fig. 1.7) rather than the 7 regions of the Wheatley Report; Fife was re-established and the identity of the Borders was accepted. There is great size variation among the regions. Strathclyde has half the population of Scotland and the greatest concentration of urban economic and social problems. The Highlands, on the other hand, have only 8 per cent of the population spread over a vast rural hinterland. The Scottish regions now have strategic planning, transportation, education and some social responsibilities. The districts have housing and local planning powers, but there is divided authority over social provision. Water and drainage are local government functions, at regional level in Scotland, unlike England. Furthermore, community councils have been established as forums of social opinion in each community, and there is to be a regional report on planning for each new region, as a basis for corporate policy-making.

Wales

Local government reform in Wales has created 8 county councils, 5 of which bear historic Welsh names (fig. 1.5), and 36 district councils to replace 13 counties, 4 county boroughs and 164 district councils. Most of the new county councils have populations over 200,000 but Powys has no more than 100,000 spread over 500,000 ha of rural territory. Glamorgan has been split into three rather than two, to avoid the creation of an E Glamorgan which would have had over 900,000 people. The two-tier system is similar in division of functions to that intended for England, with the county councils responsible for highways and traffic, education and personal social services, and district councils for housing, refuse collection, public cleansing, clean air and the prevention of nuisances. Town and country planning is shared between county and district councils.

The lack of uniformity in size, by area or population, of the new local government units for both Scotland and Wales recognizes that in remote rural or mountainous areas there is justification for special treatment. Furthermore the diversity reflects traditional community ties and loyalties and thus gives expression to the over-riding principle of 'preserving or fostering a viable local democracy'.

Northern Ireland

The first UK nation to complete local government reorganization is N Ireland. Since the creation of the Stormont Parliament in 1922 local government had been carried on through 73 directly-elected units, 27 of them with populations of less than 10,000. These units had the characteristic two-tier structure of counties and county boroughs, with dependent urban or rural districts. The local government franchise has been restricted, and generally thought to be biased against minority groups. There have also been persisting complaints about the effects of gerrymandering at the time the boundaries were originally established. Reform proposals in 1969 favoured a reduction from 73 to 17 single-tier local government units, with strengthening of the powers of Stormont as a central upper tier of authority. The principle behind the definition of the new units was alleged to be town-hinterland relationships, or everyday circulation spaces; with the exception of Fermanagh there was a clean break with previous territorial units.

The proposals encountered widespread opposition and in 1970 new proposals emerged from an independent review body. These confirmed that the local government functions of Stormont should be increased, to include all 'regional' services, whilst 'district' services should be devolved to twenty-six districts, each based on a town with its immediate hinterland; Londonderry and Belfast were to remain county boroughs but with transfer of some powers to Stormont. Johnson (1970) believed that the increase of powers to an upper tier provincial authority might well be justified, in terms of the area, size of population, rateable value when the province is compared with larger English county or city authorities.

On 1 April 1973 the twenty-six District Councils, elected by proportional representation, became responsible for local environmental services. Regional services came directly under the Ministry of Development, whilst Area Boards administered locally education, public libraries, health and personal services. Belfast (291,239 people) and Londonderry (50,018) are the largest districts, but have no additional powers.

V ECONOMIC PLANNING REGIONS AND NATIONS

V.1 Regional Strategies

The formulation of regional strategies was one of the principal tasks entrusted to the eight Regional Economic Planning Councils of England, together with the comparable bodies for Scotland, Wales and Ulster, at their inception in 1965. Strategy has been formulated in three stages and thus far only those for the SE (SE Jt. Plan-

ning Team 1970), the W Midlands (1975) and the NW (DoE 1974) have been completed, and approved in principle by the Minister. The characteristic first stage was
an assessment of the problems facing the region, followed by recommended courses
of action, and priority targets for 1981. At the second stage preferred spatial allocations are specifically mentioned in some strategies, but by no means equally emphasized in all. The third and definitive stage is a tripartite exercise involving central
government, economic planning council and board, and the constituent local
planning authorities, leading to a 'strategic plan'.

Presentation of regional strategies in the UK is thus far uneven in several respects:
stage reached; emphasis on space allocations; degree of regional initiative; extent of
cooperation and agreement between economic planning council and local authorities.
In reality the process is a continuing one since councils are responsible for advising
Ministers on the regional implications of national policies and, at the same time, are
constantly pressing regional needs and priorities upon central government. Regional
conditions and problems are never static and even after the final stage of an agreed
strategic plan it is necessary to set up a monitoring and feedback system, to test and
modify the plan as it is implemented. When approved by the Minister the regional
strategic plan becomes the framework within which the structure plans of the local
authorities must be fitted, as provided for in the *Town and Country Planning Act*
(1968).

TABLE 1.6

Economic Planning Regions and Nations, UK 1975

	Popn. 1975 (million)	% growth 1961−75	Density 1975 per km²	% in Metropolitan counties	Employment change 1963−73 fast growth[1]	fast decline[2]	% GDP as % popn. (national = 100)
Development							
Northern	3.12	0.4	45	24	27	14	89
Scotland	5.20	0.4	66	47	30	12	95
Wales	2.76	4.9	133	−	32	11	82
N Ireland	1.53	7.7	109	−	34	19	74
Intermediate							
Yorks. and Humberside	4.89	4.6	317	36	28	15	93
NW	6.57	2.6	900	53	28	10	95
Mixed trends							
SW	4.23	14.0	178	−	32	9	95
E Anglia	1.78	19.5	142	−	28	10	93
'Growth'							
E Midlands	3.72	11.9	239	−	25	20	95
W Midlands	5.17	8.7	398	46	32	5	99
SE	16.93	5.3	622	42	32	4	116

1963 = 100
[1] > 100 Metal goods; timber; other manufs.; financial, professional, scientific services; catering
and hotels; national and local government.
[2] < 85 Agriculture; mining and quarrying; shipbuilding; textiles; leather; clothing.

Source: Reg. statistics HMSO; Dept. of Employment

Structure plans are: (a) to state and justify the authority's policies and proposals for the development and use of land, (b) to interpret regional and national policies in terms of physical and environmental planning, and (c) to provide the framework and statutory basis for local plans.

In practice, delay in preparation and approval of third-stage definitive strategies has meant that formulation of structure plans has gone ahead in a measure independently. Even so, many structure plans have been delayed and local plans have often been drawn up and put into effect lacking context in a wider framework. In the SE, for example, the *Greater London Development Plan* (1969) was submitted one year ahead of the Strategic Plan for the SE. Late in 1975 the structure plan for the GLC had still not been approved and in its absence London boroughs have been proposing local plans almost independently.

For discussion of urban planning mechanisms see ch. 6, section IV.

In considering current regional strategy proposals in the UK it is convenient to group the regions as in table 1.6.

For each region there is a review and evaluation of current problems, the policies proposed and the strategy put forward. Since this is a geographical interpretation there is particular regard for the spatial implications and intentions expressed in regional strategies. To illustrate some of the key trends of economic and social change, and the strategies proposed, there is a diagrammatic map for each region (fig. 1.6 to 1.14 inclusive). These maps are not uniform, reflecting the diversity of the strategies themselves, and are not intended to be comprehensive. Rather they attempt to guide the reader by indicating some of the formative elements in the strategy for each region. A more comprehensive cartographical overview is provided in the regional planning atlases of the Department of the Environment.

On 1 April 1974, when local government reform was implemented in England, there were the following changes in the economic planning (standard) regions:

to N Region	from NW Region, Furness and Barrow	107,030 (1971)
	Yorks. and Humberside, Sedbergh	3,680
to Yorks and Humberside	from Northern Region, former N Riding (less Cleveland Co.)	266,800
	E Midlands	1,670
to NW Region	from Yorks. and Humberside, Bowland, Earby, Barnoldswick	20,480
	Saddleworth	20,550
to E Midlands Region	from Yorks. and Humberside, S Lindsey	167,050
	NW, Tintwhistle	1,480
to SW	from SE, Dorset	364,300
	part Hampshire (Bournemouth, Poole)	188,240

V.2 The Development Regions

Of the four regions identified as 'development regions' three (Scotland, Wales and N Ireland) have a national identity and already enjoy a measure of political devolution. Only the Northern Region of England lacks this degree of independence in regional decision-taking. All four are characterized by certain common problems, though their incidence and mix vary, and there are differences too in the policies adopted and the extent of their success. The problems include: higher and persistent unemployment rates; a narrow industrial base, with a higher ratio of fast decline industries, not adequately compensated for by new post-war growth elements; lower median incomes; persistent out-migration, particularly of the young and more able; peripheral location in the UK space, and according to some (Brown 1972) even more marginal in an enlarged Common Market economy; and a less favourable living environment for the majority, especially in the cities. The development regions, on the other hand, have been, and continue to be, the main beneficiaries of the regional and industrial location policies by successive governments discussed in ch. 1.III.

Northern England (fig. 1.6)
For 1974 changes in regional boundaries see above. In the nature, range and severity of its economic and social problems the Northern Region is a microcosm of all the development regions (Bowden 1965; House 1969). For this reason, perhaps, it has consistently been used as a pilot-area for application of government location policies, from the *1934 Special Areas Act* to the present day. Much of the earlier legislation was remedial in character, with relief of unemployment as a perennially high priority. In the *1963 White Paper* (Sec. Trade & Industry 1963), however, for the first time the emphasis was firmly laid on economic growth by diversification, improvement of the infrastructure and the living environment and, most significantly, on the concentration of future public investment into a designated 'growth zone'. These more comprehensive objectives were followed up and codified in the first-stage strategy document, entitled *Challenge of the Changing North* (NEPC 1966). Three years later an *Outline Strategy for the North* was published (NEPC 1969), one of only a small number of second-stage strategies to have as strong a spatial as a sector perspective in its recommendations. Perhaps for this reason the sub-regional proposals did not find favour with the local planning authorities and the document was looked upon by the optimists as falling short of legitimate regional aspirations. Others regarded the diagnosis and recommendations as both realistic and practical, a view shared by the government of the day. The third stage of definitive strategy took place in 1973–76 (NRST 1976). In the meantime the Economic Planning Council has kept under review the basic problems of the region, publishing reports on key sectors, such as housing, education and ports (NEPC 1969, 1970, 1971). The local authority-sponsored North of England Development Council has concurrently undertaken successfully the major task of promoting the NE and aiding more official efforts to attract industry and improve regional living conditions.

It is fair to ask how far all these reports and all this activity has solved, or mitigated the basic problems affecting the N Region. The verdict must be more cautious than commendatory. For all the fluctuations in unemployment levels in the UK since the war the N Region level has obstinately remained between one and a half and twice the national figure and it is difficult to envisage secular, long-term improvement based on present policies (1975). Industrial restructuring has made significant progress: the growth-decline mix in employment has improved markedly (1947–66 definitions, fast growth sector: 38 per cent of jobs 1947, 51 per cent in 1966; fast decline sector: an improvement from 34 to 21 per cent over the same period). From 1963–73 (table 1.4) a different range of growth and decline indus-

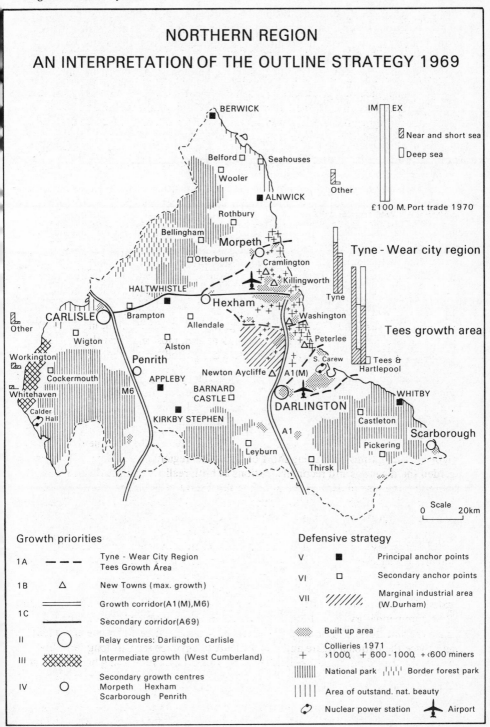

NORTHERN REGION
AN INTERPRETATION OF THE OUTLINE STRATEGY 1969

BERWICK

Belford   Seahouses
Wooler
ALNWICK
Rothbury
Bellingham
Morpeth
Otterburn
Cramlington
Killingworth
HALTWHISTLE
Hexham   Tyne
CARLISLE   Brampton   Washington
Other   Allendale
Wigton
Workington   Alston   Peterlee
Penrith   S. Carew
Cockermouth   APPLEBY   Newton Aycliffe   A1(M)
Whitehaven   M6   BARNARD   Tees & Hartlepool
Calder   CASTLE   WHITBY
Hall   KIRKBY STEPHEN   DARLINGTON   Castleton
A1   Scarborough
Leyburn   Pickering
Thirsk

IM [ ] EX

▨ Near and short sea
▯ Deep sea
Other
£100 M. Port trade 1970

Tyne - Wear city region

Tees growth area

Scale
0 ————— 20km

Growth priorities

1A	– – –	Tyne - Wear City Region Tees Growth Area
1B	△	New Towns (max. growth)
1C	═══	Growth corridor(A1(M),M6)
	───	Secondary corridor(A69)
II	◯	Relay centres: Darlington Carlisle
III	▩	Intermediate growth (West Cumberland)
IV	◯	Secondary growth centres Morpeth Hexham Scarborough Penrith

Defensive strategy

V	■	Principal anchor points
VI	□	Secondary anchor points
VII	⁄⁄⁄⁄	Marginal industrial area (W.Durham)
	░	Built up area
	+	Collieries 1971 ›1000, ✛ 600 - 1000, ✛ ‹600 miners
	‖‖‖	National park ¦¦¦ Border forest park
	‖‖	Area of outstand. nat. beauty
	⟳	Nuclear power station ✈ Airport

Figure 1.6   Northern Region

tries was identified. By these definitions the N Region has further improved its
relative position. Diversification and job choice have both increased, with a significant number of industrial moves into the region coming from the South East,
followed by moves from Yorks. and Humberside, the adjacent economic planning
region, and then the affluent W Midlands. The employment of 94,157 in some 388
firms on 75 'industrial estates' and sites financed by government (October 1975),
together with the sanctioning of 387 'advance factories' for the North (1959–74)
indicates the scale of direct government aid. In support, IDC approvals were given,
1960–70 inclusive, for 4.3 million m² of new factory space in the region. Out-
migration, a persistent ebb-tide from the North, has been perceptibly slowed, but it
is too early to ascribe this to the working of regional policies (House 1964–72).

On the debit side, however, high unemployment seems to be endemic. The problem has certainly been aggravated by the dramatic downturn in the region's basic
industries during the 1960s. Overall between 1960 and 1970 some 138,000 jobs
were lost, and they were mostly male jobs, in only five industries: coal-mining,
agriculture, shipbuilding, steel and transport. In spite of the build-up of alternative
employment, by 1970 there were 80,000 fewer male jobs than ten years earlier.
Prospective further substantial male job loss during the 1970s, the result of continuing rundown in basic industries and also the mounting effects of automation, means
that industrial restructuring will continue to be the most critical problem in the N
Region. This necessitates the continuance of strong, even stronger regional policies
and a growth-orientated, streamlined strategy for taking the region to the end of the
century. Judged by IDC approvals 1968–71, N Region had an unfavourable share
of national approvals, which fell from 14.8 to 6.6 per cent, whilst that for the SE
rose from 11.2 to 29.4 per cent.

Diversification is not solely a matter for manufacturing employment. The services
economy in the North has traditionally been under-represented (Fullerton 1960,
1966) and government incentives to its growth were lacking until 1973. Within the
first two years of the 1973 scheme only seven applications had been made, involving
about 500 jobs. The limited extent to which offices have been persuaded to move
from the London region or the W Midlands to the development areas has already
been commented upon. 3,000 government clerical jobs were created in the North
1963–70 but the scale of such growth is clearly insufficient to aid economic restructuring in a significant way. The importance of research and development projects in building up the newer image of the North has constantly been stressed, and
the need for government to decentralize major establishments to the development
areas during the next decade. The *Hardman Report* (Civil Service Dept. 1973) proposed 3,287 more government jobs for the North.

If the N Region was to become fully competitive it also required both improved
communications of all types and a modernized living environment. The M6, A1(M)
and the Durham motorway, the Inter-City and Freightliner rail services (with the
west coast electrification now extended to Glasgow), the regional airports at Newcastle (Woolsington) and Teesside, and the port facilities, such as Teesport or the
Tyne ferry-terminal, contributed to the transport network. The up-dating of the
housing stock to a present state that is comparable with that of other regions, the
improvements of educational facilities and achievements, the range of entertainment
and recreation provision all helped towards the objectives of a better living
environment.

The sector objectives were elaborated in the *Outline Strategy* (Northern EPC

1969, but it also stressed the need for a spatially-defined and inter-related growth hierarchy of settlements and sub-regions. Appropriate defensive elements were proposed for areas likely to be adversely affected by general decline or by concentration elsewhere. Figure 1.6 tentatively completes the hierarchy which was put forward only in broad outline in the 1969 document. Furthermore it allocates priorities, stressing the cardinal importance of the two major areas of growth potential, the Tyne–Wear city region and the Teesside growth area. The Tyne–Wear conurbation has 40 per cent of the regional population, a manufacturing structure with over-representation of decline sectors (including the coalfield hinterland) and a concentration of service population. In the early post-war years a new and diversified industrial base was implanted, especially on the industrial estates, and this gives a better prospect of short-term growth to 1981 from established firms than on Teesside. Teesside has the twin pillars of industrial strength, iron and steel with associated fabricating industries and chemicals, with a strong and growing relationship to the local post-war oil refineries. With greater prosperity in its basic industries Teesside had less diversification through industrial estates. However during the 1960s there were programmes for the rationalization of plants and further redundancies caused by technological change in the steel industry, whilst the chemical industry continued to increase its output substantially but without adding to its labour force. With the oil refineries also capital-intensive but with small contribution to new jobs, Teesside unemployment rose and remedial government action has followed. In contrast to the Tyne the estuarine lands of the Tees offer large tracts for industrial and port development. Among major prospects for the area is the 6 million ingot tonnes 'brownfield' steel development growing alongside the new Redcar ore terminal.

A successful regional strategy for the North must get the sums and the spatial allocations right, as between Tyne–Wear and Tees. The Teesplan (MHLG 1969) forecast potential for accommodating +220,000 people by 1991 and +422,000 by AD 2001 and the Tyne–Wear Plan (Voorhees 1972) revealed sizeable capacity for future growth and concentration. Without being able to programme sub-regional allocation of growth, except in broad and indirect terms, it is important for planners in the North to see Tyne–Wear and Tees as inter-related cores for a regional industrial growth complex. Presently they are less inter-related economically than might be the case.

Both Tyne–Wear and Teesside conurbations are embedded within a major coalfield which has been undergoing dramatic rundown in employment since the late 1950s (1951, 156,000 mining jobs; 1961, 118,000; 1976 only 36,600). The impact at community level of the many pits which have closed has been severe, though many of the redundant men have been re-employed at other pits. The New Towns, at Peterlee, Newton Aycliffe and Washington together with the county council developments at Cramlington and Killingworth have implanted growth and a new living environment in the coalfield. The SDA policy since 1967 has also helped in the provision of new jobs in or near the mining settlements. Yet as pits close it is accepted that districts may lose their *raison d'être* and both regrouping and decline by out-migration of people may be the logical answer, as it seems to be for W Durham.

As a small-scale microcosm of the problems of the N Region, W Cumberland faces continued restructuring with the prospective closing down of coalmining and the cessation of steel-making at Workington in June 1974. Redundancies have been offset by introduction of new jobs under government location policies, and by a remarkable community spirit of enterprise. However, W Cumberland was designated for only an intermediate level of growth and it was felt in 1969 that Carlisle had the better long-term potential of land and location, to act as a 'relay' centre to build up employment and diffuse growth over a wide hinterland.

A sub-regional study (Taylor 1972) surprisingly reported otherwise and interpreted the problems and potentials of W Cumberland as different in both degree and kind from those of Carlisle. It is nevertheless likely that the best future prospect lies in the development of an integrated Carlisle–W Cumberland economic axis, to the benefit of both partners.

Other novel elements in the Outline Strategy were the proposals for corridor growth at nodes, along the main south–north motorways and rail links, east and west of the Pennines. The corridor concept through Durham aroused memories of earlier thinking on a prospective Tyne–Tees linear city. For the vast rural hinterland it was accepted that growth at the most logical centres in conurbation or cities would increase gradients in living standards, to the disadvantage of the countryside, and lead to accelerated rural depopulation. To stabilize the rural areas and indeed to build up jobs in both industry and services, to support the primary agricultural population, rural 'anchor point' settlements were to be designated. Figure 1.6 shows a suggested pattern for these, with principal and secondary centres. The *Outline Strategy* (Northern EPC 1969) was indicative, a discussion basis, and was lacking in precision as to space allocations, timings or priorities. 1973–76 a N Region Strategy Team, commissioned by central government, regional planning council and local authorities, worked upon a strategic plan. The main themes of the plan were published in 1976 (NRST 1976). Compared with other definitive third-stage strategies, that for the North is characterized by the emphasis upon economic and social sector recommendations, together with a package of principles for spatial allocation of growth. These latter are to be elaborated at a later stage, in conjunction with the parallel work being undertaken on structure plans.

The sector objectives included: rapid movement to self-sustaining economic growth, in the long term, without the need for special government assistance; greater variety of choice in employment; greater equity in distribution of benefits; improvement and protection of the environment. Industry within the region should be given particular stimulus to growth, and in time less reliance on 'mobile' industry should be envisaged. SDA status should be limited, since it affords few additional benefits, but assistance should be more selectively concentrated.

Spatial options were: continuance of present policies; urban rehabilitation; concentration; growth zones; and market forces. For rural areas market forces, centralization or balanced development were posed as alternative courses for policy. It was decided after consultation that no single alternative would be appropriate for the region, and also that different choices, or combinations of choices, would be appropriate in different parts of the region – as in 1969 a judicious political conclusion.

Scotland (fig. 1.7)

Between 1961 and 1971 employment in Scotland fell by 75,000 and the population failed to grow. The basic regional development problems of Scotland thus have much in common with those of N England, but there are differences of significance, both in degree and in kind. The differences in degree arise from the greater territorial size and population of Scotland, a more marked degree of concentration of that

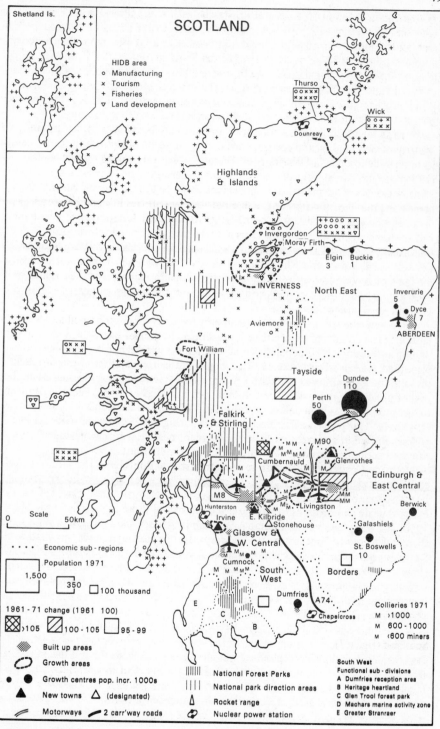

Figure 1.7   Scotland

population in the industrial Central Lowlands, with a vast thinly-peopled rural hinterland, and an even more peripheral location in respect of the major economic growth areas of the Midlands and SE England. Differences in kind arise from the degree of autonomy exercised by representatives of the Scottish nation, the distinctive problems posed by slow population growth, the need to decongest and distribute massive overspill from the Clydeside conurbation, the sharp contrast offered by major rural problem areas, and a particular sequence of stages in regional planning. The massive potential of North Sea oil is a further differentiator.

Perhaps the most important factor of all lies in the economic, social and political identity of Scotland, giving coherence and purpose to its planning and strengthening its independent voice in UK affairs. This identity was referred to by Cairncross (1954), speaking of the Border as 'not a barrier between two economic systems but a line between two segments of a single economy'. He further added 'yet the segment lying north of the Border is a distinct society with a unity and cohesion of its own', and he was in no doubt that the Scottish economy functioned as a unit and had an independent momentum. Later writers have confirmed this diagnosis (McCrone 1965, 1969; Johnston et al 1971; Mackay and Mackay 1974; Scottish Council 1974; Moore and Rhodes 1974; Firn 1975), which is indeed derived from the facts of geography, with the concentrated urban population of C Scotland well away from the southern borders and 160 km from the nearest industrial region of England, on Tyneside.

Already in the special areas programme of the early 1930s Scotland had a Secretary of State, compared with only commissioners in other areas. This degree of continuing autonomy and independence in economic and social decision-taking or planning has been advantageous in two ways: clearer formulation of the problems, through the availability of Scottish statistics, and coherence in the design or application of policies. It is possible for Scotland, but not as yet for the regions of England, to measure national income and to calibrate and monitor economic change more effectively. This proved particularly valuable during the 1960s when UK regional policies shifted in emphasis from unemployment relief towards achievement of balanced economic growth.

McCrone (1969) believed that gross domestic product (GDP), the sum of values added in all production pursuits in the economy, provides the most accurate indicator of Scotland's economic progress. Changes in the Scottish GDP since 1961 indicate that living standards in Scotland fell relative to those in the UK in the late 1950s and early 1960s, and although Scottish GDP per capita increased more rapidly than that of the UK in the 1960s, this was probably due in large part to a fall in the Scottish proportion of the UK population. Johnston et al (1971) derived the gloomy prediction from post-war trends in Scotland that she is 'in some danger of reverting to the position of poor relation of England and Wales as existed for some time in the past'.

During the early 1970s the Scottish GDP per capita continued to rise appreciably, as a percentage of UK, from 91.3 in 1970 to 93.6 in 1974. In reality, the economic situation in Scotland in the mid-1970s has not been as unfavourable as in other DAs. Unemployment levels had been reduced from 1.7 times the UK level (1973) to 1.3 (1975–6), the lowest ratio recorded since 1954. Out-migration continued, except for a small net gain 1973–4, but at a rate only half that of the early 1960s. North Sea oil activity has helped by creating, directly or indirectly, 40,000 jobs.

Scotland has faced the same industrial restructuring problems as other development regions in post-war years, but her legacy from past industrial revolutions had been more unfavourable than most. Moreover the resulting secular unemployment in declining industries such as coal-mining, mechanical engineering, or ship-building was highly concentrated in and around Clydeside and in Lanarkshire, affecting the economic health of sizeable, congested populations. The nature and course of industrial restructuring in a DA has already been treated under N England and only specifically Scottish features need touching upon. Ship-building was uniquely hard hit (1959, 73,000 jobs; 1973, 43,900), culminating in the failure of Upper Clyde shipbuilders; the Dundee jute industry passed through particularly difficult times, whilst employment in the primary industries fell sharply (agriculture, forestry and fishing: 1959, 104,000 and 1975, 48,800; mining and quarrying: from 102,000 in 1959 to 36,000 in 1975. On the credit side the electronics industry had a sharp rise from 11,000 to 25,000 jobs in the period 1961–75 and United States investment in Scotland has been striking (89 manufacturing companies in 1969, employing 73,000). Furthermore, in striking contrast to the overall decline of 102,000 manufacturing jobs 1964–75, mostly for males, there had been an increase of no less than 44,000 in professional and scientific services, and 14,000 in insurance, banking and finance. These new jobs, however, employed mainly women.

Yet the overall verdict must be similar to that for N England: the massive rundown in male jobs in basic industries has not been fully compensated for by the growth of new forms of employment and the situation would have looked even more dramatic had there not been a marked rise in jobs for women in manufacturing. Rates of growth in service employment have lagged behind UK levels and, as in N England, there is the same clamour for more research and development units, more head offices, and a more forceful decentralization of central government establishments, to add to the Savings Bank already established in Glasgow. In 1975 the government announced that 6,000 Ministry of Defence and 1,000 Ministry of Overseas Development jobs would be transferred to Glasgow within ten years; the headquarters of the British National Oil Corporation was also located there.

Regional planning had an early start in Scotland and its effectiveness has proved a valuable aid both to economic development policies generally, and to the formulation of sub-regional proposals within an overall Scottish programme. The *Clyde Valley Regional Plan* (Abercrombie and Matthews 1946) appeared at a time when the government was particularly active in steering industry under the *Distribution of Industry Act* (1945). Though undue concentration of such industrial moves into Clydeside helped to diversify industry there it was at the expense of balance in the Central Lowlands or indeed over Scotland as a whole. Scottish economists and planners were early alive to the need for balanced distribution of growth and equally emphatic in both the Cairncross Committee (1952) and the Toothill Report (1961) that this objective would not be realized by the 'worst-first' policy of priority for relief of unemployment where it was most severe. Indeed Toothill spoke deliberately of the need to build up industrial complexes and centres which offered the best prospect of becoming zones of growth. This found an echo in the White Paper of the following year (SDD 1963), which designated nine growth areas (fig. 1.7). These included the then four New Towns of C Scotland, together with Irvine (later designated a New Town) and the Grangemouth/Falkirk area, both the latter with considerable potential for both industrial and housing development. Other growth areas were older industrial tracts like N Lanarkshire, Central Fife, the Lothians around Livingston and the Vale of Leven, which had land and labour but where social capital was rundown.

Though the *Industrial Development Act* (1966) defined the greater part of Scotland as a development area and thus temporarily annulled the 'growth area' concept, the philosophy of concentrating growth at designated nuclei, has proved remarkably persistent, cropping up in all the later sub-regional studies. Since Scotland was the proving ground it is interesting to note the comments of Cameron and Reid (1966). They concluded that from an industrial location point of view C Scotland was too small and well-developed for small growth areas to have particular advantages in terms of external economies. Their view was that the growth areas were really the means of integrating various strands of economic and social policy, with an emphasis on potential for substantial population growth. From the White Paper, however, it is clear that the growth areas were to be the most ready and effective channel for attracting industrial investment and creating locally new living environments, the benefits of which would be diffused through their labour hinterlands and would indeed link up with the development proposed in the main centres of Glasgow and Edinburgh.

Equally innovating, the publication of a plan for expansion of the Scottish economy 1965–70 (Scottish Office 1966) sought to speed up the evolution of a modern industrial structure in Scotland, to make the fullest use of manpower and to cut the net out-migration rate from 40,000 per annum in the 1960s to only 10,000 per annum by 1980. It provided a planning framework both in sectoral terms and in respect of sub-regional patterns of growth and expansion. Between 1965 and 1971 initial strategies had been prepared for seven of the eight planning regions of Scotland (McGuiness 1968, Self et al 1967) and two major transportation studies had been achieved, for Greater Glasgow and Perth. Physical planning, so active in English regions during the same period, lagged behind sub-regional plan formulation in Scotland. This put Scotland in a better position to develop structure plans within a set of existing sub-regional strategies and within the overall context of a short-term Scottish Plan.

In the strategies the regional development problems of Scotland emerged as of three types: those of the peripheral rural regions, sizeable, diverse but over-dependent on primary industries and with severe infra-structural deficiencies, notably in public transport; the decaying industrial tracts in need of diversification, rehabilitation and an improvement in living environment; and thirdly, the problems of an over-developed, congested conurbation on Clydeside. It is the last, with an almost stagnant population of about two millions, which uniquely dominated the Scottish planning scene and has overshadowed all other sub-regions there since the war.

Decisions on the future shape, structure and size of **Clydeside** have been and remain the key to the prospects for dispersal of population and the dissemination of growth throughout Scotland (Minay 1965). With the preparation of the last of the regional strategies, the *West Central Scotland Plan* (Study Team 1971), the dimensions and prospects for the Clydeside economy have become clearer. For the moment the short-term problems there are only too tragically apparent, and it seems uncertain if economic growth can be generated on the scale necessary to permit the massive redistribution of people and work which many think desirable. The dilemma may be posed thus: Clydeside is too congested and its industrial structure cannot adequately be transformed within its borders, yet the large-scale redistribution of overspill population has not been adequately matched by attraction of industry out of the Clydeside habitat. The overspill plan for Glasgow envisages a movement of no less than 200,000 more out of the city by 1980, the latest phase of a trend which had seen the population of the city fall by 183,000 between 1951 and 1970. No fewer than 54 local authorities have overspill agreements with Glasgow, plus the five New Towns, but planned overspill for the 66 schemes over long distances has been difficult to achieve. Most industrial firms leaving Clydeside have preferred sites within 48 km, whilst the 'growth areas' of C Scotland had by 1965 attracted no less than 60 per cent of overspill families and three-quarters of industrial moves to over-spill areas. The government expectation back in 1963 was that the growth areas would absorb 300,000 by 1981. In 1972 a further New Town was designated at Stonehouse (Lanarkshire) with a target population of 70,000 to assist in this pro-cess of decentralization, but during 1976 this New Town project was abandoned. West Central Scotland (Strathclyde) continues to have the unfavourable hall-marks of two-thirds of Scots unemployment and a continuing net population loss.

The risk that the solution to Clydeside's problems would be at the expense of the rest of C Scotland seemed to have been diminished by the possibility of creating a major fast-growth sub-region based on Tayside (Campbell and Lyddon 1970), the open end of industrial Scotland, and also by the vigour of other sub-regional plan-ning proposals. (Robertson, Johnson-Marshall and Matthew 1966, 1968). The Tay-side proposals established that an additional 300,000 could be settled in that sub-region by the year 2001, two-thirds of them into the Dundee and Perth areas, though for the first ten years there would have to be a vigorous programme of re-habilitation allied with growth. With the prospective population of Scotland by the end of the century now estimated at $+\frac{1}{2}$ million, rather than the two millions earlier anticipated, the full potential of Tayside may not be required.

One of the most intriguing prospects for revitalization of the role of C Scotland is the Oceanspan proposal (1970) for creating a land-bridge with rapid transit systems between the Atlantic and the North Sea. Vital to the concept is the develop-ment of Hunterston on the Clyde as the prime site for an integrated complex, on 903 ha zoned for industry by the government in 1970–1 (ch. 5.V.3). Presently only a deep-water port and an iron ore unloading terminal have been sanctioned, the latter already under construction. There is a logical case for at least one oil refinery, a major steel-works, smaller pipe and beam mills, a pipe-coating yard, and a fabricating yard for North Sea concrete platforms (Nicoll 1973). Permission for an oil refinery has been refused, as it had been earlier for the Murco proposal for a refinery at Bishopton (near Glasgow).

The problems of **Scottish marginal regions** bring out a contrast between the High-lands and Islands, with NE Scotland, on the one hand, and the Border and South West on the other. The case for the diversion of investment to the Highlands and Islands, in the face of overall Scottish priorities is not universally accepted, and indeed there are those who argue that even north of the Central Lowlands there is a better case for investing in the modernized agrarian structure, manufacturing base and growth prospects of NE Scotland (Mackay and Buxton 1965; Gaskin 1968). Certainly the *Gaskin Report* cautiously confirmed the 'substantial assets for further development' in the North East, but saw an important ingredient in the solution of the problems of that region in the redistribution of overspill from the Aberdeen city region to two main growth zones: the lower Don valley and, on a smaller scale, the lowlands of Banffshire and W Morayshire.

Redevelopment and growth in the Highlands and Islands is almost an 'act of faith' for many Scots (Thomson and Grimble 1968) and it is impossible to ignore the substantial achievements of the Development Board created for that region in 1965. These have been equally impressive whether one considers the many disseminated improvements in fisheries, tourism, manufacturing and land development, or the larger-scale proposals to create growth areas: on the Moray Firth (HIDB 1968), in the Wick—Thurso region or around Lochaber (Fort William). Increasingly a policy of concentration and urbanization seems called for (Turnock 1970) and the eastern littoral is likely to prove a powerful magnet for major new developments. Already the aluminium reduction works at Invergordon is in full production and the early stages of 'spin-off' from adjacent North Sea oil exploration are being felt.(ch. 4.I.3).

By contrast the strategy proposals for the C Borders (SDD 1968) and the South West (SDD 1970) must be interpreted, in the first place, as programmes for arresting decline and out-migration. By the careful promotion of a regional community as an inter-related and regrouped pattern of small towns, with St Boswells and Berwick as growth centres, the Borders plan seeks to exploit intermediate location of the area, whilst seeking new industries and developing Galashiels as a commercial centre. The strategy for the South West is couched more in sectoral terms with proposals for new job creation and relief of unemployment, attraction of industry and improvement of communications. The tourist plan for Galloway (Scottish Tourist Board 1968) touches on one of the most promising prospects, with detailed proposals for the sub-regions shown on fig. 1.7.

The mid-1970s A recent survey of the Scottish economy (Nicoll 1973) carries an encouraging message. The industrial restructuring is well under way; great natural resources of oil, natural gas, deep water, and strategic location relative to the EEC are in process of being realized. 19,000 direct jobs have been provided by oil-related operations (April 1975) and with indirect jobs the total is probably around 40,000. There is a general drift of labour north-eastwards, and substantial public investments are being made in roads, harbours, housing, drilling rig and platform sites, There is a major planning problem to avoid the worst effects of a massive boom, appreciation of whose full commercial importance dates only from 1971.

Nicoll postulates the need for a new growth axis NE—SW from Aberdeen to Ayr, with growth nodes to be sited along it. This will complement the existing E—W Central Lowlands belt. Elsewhere there should be a positive concentration policy, with growth only at carefully chosen nodal points. Glasgow would continue to decline, perhaps to 650,000; major growth would occur in Hunterston—Irvine—Kilmarnock. Edinburgh would continue to develop in services and commerce, and Galashiels was seen as a modest growth-point in the Borders. The SW would change little, though tourism would develop further and there might be a long-term prospect for a Solway city. Tayside had the growth potential mentioned earlier and would be likely to absorb surplus growth from the lower Forth. Oil operations would ensure a prosperous, but ill-balanced growth in the NE and North. The population of 90,000 in the Moray and Cromarty Firths might well double by the end of the century. Oil rig supply bases, deep-sea platform-fabricating sites, pipeline landfalls are all in progress, affecting points as far afield as the Shetlands, Orkney, Lewis and the remoter NW (Hutcheson and Hogg 1975). In 1977 Lanark, Cumnock, Kilbirnie, Dundee and Arbroath became SDAs.

Wales (fig. 1.8)
By comparison with Scotland, Wales is smaller, lacking in economic coherence, and its three economic sub-regions are ever more inter-dependent with areas of the

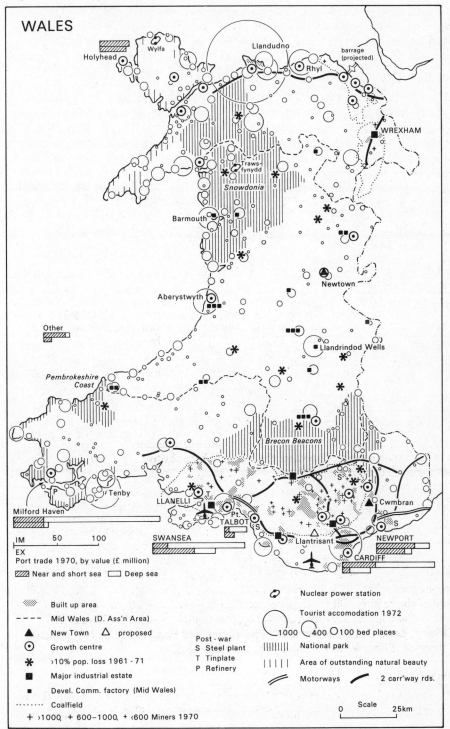

Figure 1.8   Wales

English economy. As a senior Welsh geographer put it (Bowen 1957), 'we certainly cannot accept that what is now Wales in a political sense represents a unity of any kind', though he was quick to point out the cultural identity of a smaller Welsh heartland redoubt. Yet, paradoxically, there is a strong, mounting feeling for greater political devolution than present institutions afford. The Welsh Council (1968) is responsible for economic strategy proposals, and there are many institutions at national level to reinforce the Welsh cultural personality (Lloyd and Thomason 1963). On the whole, however, Wales lacks the degree of self-sufficiency or economic independence (Nevin, Rose and Round 1966) appropriate to Scotland and in reality until recently the devolution of economic, social or political decision-taking had been more apparent than real. A realistic estimate is perhaps that UK policies have been tempered in Wales 'to suit the particular circumstances' as the Treasury has put it. At times this may have led to the reducing of economic growth rates or prospects, to preserve Welshness and avoid damaging effects on society or community. The truth is that, like all development regions, Wales is a net recipient of funds from the rest of the UK (Tomkins 1971). In respect of central government finance in Wales in 1968 there was a deficit of 20 per cent, when comparing receipts with expenditure (total public expenditure in Wales: 1963–4, £326 million; 1973–4, £1,213 million). Finally, Wales has been even more closely bound into the English economy by the strategy of communications in post-war years, by ties of capital flows and by the establishment of branch plants of English companies in the principality. Nevertheless the creation of a Welsh Development Agency (1976) and proposals for political devolution to a Welsh Assembly promise to give Wales what she has notably lacked – a controlling voice in her internal affairs.

Wales passed through the characteristic stages of the development area life-cycle from the early 1930s, but her geographical layout, particularly the constraints imposed by relief, and disposition of resources, conditioned a distinctive degree of response. The extent of concentration in mining areas like the Rhondda was unparalleled and subsequent readjustment the more agonizing. From over 215,000 coal-mining jobs in the valleys in 1921 the figure fell to 92,000 in 1958, 52,000 in 1970 and 31,000 in 1976. Iron and steel, and tinplate manufactures grew rapidly in the nineteenth century but during the 1920s–30s suffered dramatic changes in location and in technology. The industrial specialization was high, the industrial base narrow and, because it was smaller in scale, proved more difficult to diversify. Wartime brought munitions factories, chemical, aluminium and vehicles plants, helped retrain labour and brought women into the factories, encouraged journeys to work, and led to closer economic ties with England.

Post-war benefits under successive government policies were substantial. Out-migration from Wales was first slowed down and then reversed (1946–57, net loss of 17 per 10,000; 1961–70, +19 per 10,000, 1971–4, +9.7 per 10,000). Comparable figures for Scotland over the first two periods were –70 and –68 per 10,000; and for N Ireland, –67 and –47 per 10,000. Rates of industrial investment were high in the 1950s and early 1960s, partly the result of major capital-intensive projects in basic industries such as the Llanwern integrated steel-making plant. Diversification had played its part in the growth of new industrial and service jobs, but the limited size of the total labour force imposed constraints on the tempo of the process. Most of the new employment was located off the S Wales coalfield though nearly half the population continued to live there amidst industrial dereliction and an outworn social fabric. Between 1958 and 1968 employment in Welsh manufacturing grew 18.7 per cent, five times the UK rate, although Wales had a working population only one-tenth that of London. Moreover new manufacturing jobs replaced 91 per cent of the jobs lost in mining and quarrying (cf 18 per cent in N England, 26 per cent in Scotland). Though Scotland made the running in foreign investments in her industry in the 1950s Wales bids fair to lead in this respect in the 1970s (Thomas 1970, Davies and Thomas 1976). Between 1969–73 Welsh manufacturing employment rose by 2 per cent, whilst that in the UK declined by 3 per cent; 1973–5 both declined by 4 per cent.

Yet **regional planning** had been disappointing (Hagger and Davies 1961) to the time of the *1967 White Paper* (Sec. State Wales 1967) which defined spatial objectives only secondarily to those for economic and social sectors. Furthermore the proposals were as for three scarcely related economic sub-regions: S Wales, Mid-Wales and N Wales. This strong sub-regional level of strategic thinking has still to be incorporated effectively into a Welsh national context. Yet the basic problems are nation-wide: economic restructuring, especially jobs for men; improvement of external and internal accessibility, and the need for a coherent geographical overview (Manners 1968). The problems of S Wales (Humphrys 1972) tend to overshadow the Welsh scene as did those of the C Lowlands in Scotland. With some two-thirds of the Welsh population living within 56 km of Bridgend the economic restructuring, settlement regrouping and environmental rehabilitation are concentrated in this major industrial and urban area. The 1967 White Paper proposed to concentrate efforts to attract new industry along improved east–west communications linking up towns at the mouths of the mining valleys where these debouched on to the coastal plain. The valleys would then conserve their communities, journeys to work would develop down the valleys and the environment would be renewed; the Heads of the Valleys road would also attract some industries.

Several growth-points were defined, including importantly the New Towns of Llantrisant, designated in 1972, and Cwmbran (1949). Llantrisant, already the site of part of the Royal Mint, was to help reduce out-migration and to attract industry. It was to grow from its present population of 25,000 to 70,000–75,000 by 1991, and by natural increase to 90,000 by the year 2001, but in 1974 the Secretary of State decided not to proceed with this New Town. Cwmbran is to regroup population from the Monmouthshire valleys (31 March 1975 population 43,500; target 55,000). Other growth centres are to be seen on fig. 1.8, notably those at Bridgend, Kenfis (Port Talbot), Landore–Morriston (Swansea) and Fforestfach. As capital of the principality Cardiff is to reinforce its commercial, administrative and educational function. Its scheduling as a DA in August 1974 further improved its industrial prospects.

There are however potential spatial growth pressures not taken adequately into account. Proposals to develop Severnside as a coherent sub-region must stimulate growth in the Newport sub-region. The M4 motorway will powerfully extend economic linkages of S Wales with Greater London, to match those along the M5 to the W Midlands. The delay in granting the Newport area 'intermediate' status (1969) meant a lack of growth momentum, and the tendency to think of the south-east coastal tract as a perimeter area of Wales rather than an economic bridge seems endemic in planning circles. On the other hand current studies on Milford Haven (45,000 population in 1970), which refined 28 per cent of UK throughput of crude oil in 1973, indicate a further and major hidden growth potential. But is there likely to be sufficient population in Wales to provide for all these developments?

The problems of **Mid-Wales** (Welsh Office 1964; Welsh Council 1971; Development Commn. 1972) are almost an exact antithesis to those of the South, as are those of the Highlands to those of Central Scotland. But, unlike the Highlands, Mid-Wales lacks a comprehensive development organization, and Welsh social and economic problems, though smaller in scale, require more sensitive planning. Depopulation down to threshold levels is the key issue, with political as well as social and economic undertones, but the numbers leaving are few in total. Unemployment and under-employment are both endemic but the numbers in any one place are often not sufficient to attract an industrialist. The largest town is Aberystwyth (11,000) and the New Town commenced in Montgomeryshire in 1970 has an objective of raising the population from 5,500 to only 11,000–12,000 in 1981. Sceptics feel that the New Town proposal is rather to serve overspill needs of the English Midlands, but to achieve its target will necessitate a careful policy of attracting small firms. In any case repopulation of Mid-Wales is likely to be necessary if the area is to prosper in the longer term, and this will be singularly difficult to achieve.

The objectives of Welsh rural strategy are to establish a firmer economic base by restructuring agriculture in commercially viable units, whilst maintaining the family farm (though a Rural Development Board was declined), building up forestry, using water resources more to the advantage of Wales, conserving the landscape heritage, developing tourism and attracting industry to small country towns. Basic to all is the underpinning of Welsh rural society as a way of life (Houston and Jenkins 1965). Figure 1.8 shows the sparse and fragmented tourist capacity in hotels in Mid-Wales, in striking contrast to the north coast. It also indicates the pattern of small rural growth-points to which small firms are to be attracted. The work of the Industrial Development Association and the Development Commission has had notable successes (thirty factories in ten years, with 64,500 m^2 of new floor space). In 1970 it was estimated that return to the Exchequer had been 23 per cent on public capital invested. By these means a self-sustaining economic base may be created, but it will be a delicate task, and the developing of both internal and external communications will be a key factor.

North Wales, recognized since August 1974 as having SDA status, is to have a similar concentration of growth at selected centres. Several of these are tourist centres, with a rising population including those coming for retirement. Introduction of industry to balance seasonal unemployment is proposed. Portmadoc is to serve as a centre for regrouping population in an area of high unemployment, whilst the Holyhead–Anglesey area with an aluminium smelter and nuclear power station has a unique growth potential. Late in 1975, however, the aluminium smelter was producing at only 60 per cent of its 100,000 tonne capacity and had been losing money for some time. Finally, in NE Wales there is a microcosm of S Wales problems in coal and steel. Now that the *Dee Estuary Scheme* (MHLG 1967; Sec. State Environment 1971) has shown a crossing to be both feasible and viable the development potential of the Flintshire coast for water storage, recreation and industrial expansion has been greatly enhanced. It is estimated that the present Deeside population could be increased from 109,000 to 320,000. In 1977 (April) Shotton became a DA.

Northern Ireland (fig. 1.9)
Until the prorogation of the Stormont parliament in 1972 N Ireland had on balance benefited from its degree of political and economic autonomy. Had the province been a self-financing unit, providing all its own services, locally generated revenue

in 1967–8 would have been £110 million per annum below requirements (cf
Scotland's calculated deficit in the same period £276 million, though with a population 3.5 times that of Ulster) (Simpson 1971). In 1974–5 the UK Exchequer
contribution to N Ireland was £205 million, 27 per cent of total local revenue. The
Stormont Parliament had exercised powers over agricultural and industrial development and was also responsible for both physical and economic planning. On the
other hand it is possible to argue that with direct ministerial control from
Whitehall more substantial public investment might have been forthcoming, and the
impact on the fundamental economic problems of the province that much greater.

In common with other development regions N Ireland has a problem mix
compounded of economic structure and location, but there are distinctive features.
The total population is scarcely more than one-third that of the Scottish Lowlands,
no less than two-thirds being concentrated within 48 km of Belfast. The spatial
imbalance which has resulted reflects sharp differences in living standards and
economic potential within the province. The overall average annual income is only
75 per cent that of the UK, but in the rural areas it is even lower. Post-war
unemployment in N Ireland has usually been the most severe for any of the
economic planning regions; since 1963 it has never fallen below 5.9 per cent, and
during 1975 stood at 8.1 per cent (9.4 per cent for males). Fig. 1.9 shows the
sizeable, mainly Catholic, rural areas which had more than 9 per cent unemployment throughout 1974. There is moreover much concealed rural under-employment,
incomes are low and economic prospects have traditionally been poor. The flows of
population within Ulster 1961–6 (fig. 1.9) indicated the gravitational pull of
Greater Belfast but, perhaps surprisingly, also the small scale of movement out of
the least privileged rural areas. This may have been the result of strong rural community ties as much as the uncertain job prospects at that time in the larger towns,
in which declining industries have long been strongly represented.

The problems arising from economic structure and internal location within
Northern Ireland were early seen to be inter-related and it was recognized that
solutions might be the more difficult to achieve in view of the peripheral, and overseas position of Ulster within the UK space (Isles and Cuthbert 1957). The *Wilson
Report* (Govt. N Ireland 1965) clearly formulated the need to promote economic
expansion and to do so both by an orderly planning of physical development,
involving major spatial redistribution of growth in the longer-term, and also by
direct attacks on the problem of unemployment through effective restructuring of
the economy. From a rather different standpoint, that of the planning problems
facing Greater Belfast, the *Regional Survey and Plan* (Matthew 1964) reached
similar conclusions, though the study area was too restricted to take into account
the problems of outlying areas of the province. In order to check imbalance being
further reinforced in Greater Belfast a major effort to reverse the process was to
be initiated: growth in Belfast was to be limited, a New Town created at Craigavon
(Portadown–Lurgan) and further population and industrial growth to be dispersed,
as much as possible to fifteen designated centres. Just as the Wilson Report
recognized the important arguments for spatial redistribution of growth and
opportunity so did the Greater Belfast Plan accept also that to achieve such an
objective a 50 per cent stepping up of the industrial growth rate 1956–61 would be
required. The case in favour of limiting the growth of Belfast was not only that of
economic and social justice to outlying towns and villages. It was also that unless
the population within the Belfast stopline could be limited to 600,000 instead of

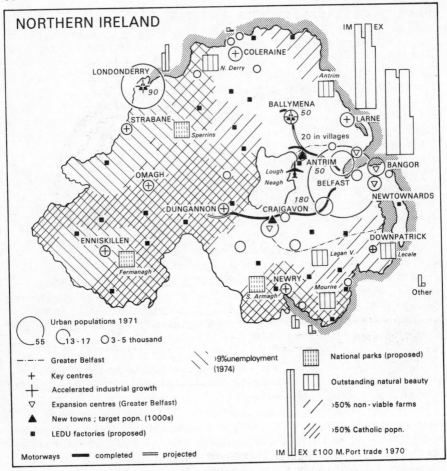

Figure 1.9   (a) N Ireland

the 800,000 it might reach by 1984 unless planning intervened, the redevelopment and economic growth of the city would be made unacceptably difficult.

In the 1970 *Development Programme* (Govt. N Ireland 1970) the sectoral and spatial objectives were consolidated within a coherent programme for investment and planned growth. Priority targets were to be the reduction of unemployment and the raising of living standards, both seen as relevant to eradicating the root causes of unrest within the Ulster community. It is appropriate to look briefly at the physical development strategy agreed upon and, secondly, at the stage reached in economic restructuring (N Ireland Economic Council 1969).

The concept of **Growth Areas** formulated in both the 1963 and 1965 studies is accepted as the basis for a regional and economic strategy, and there is to be a co-ordination of all public sectors to achieve such concentration at centres of accelerated industrial growth (Londonderry and Ballymena) and at eight key centres (fig. 1.9). The New Town developments at Craigavon, Antrim–Ballymena and

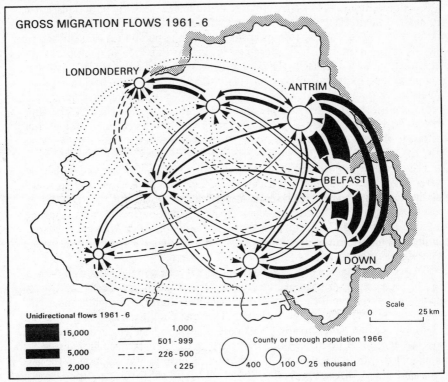

1.9(b)   Gross migration flows, 1961–6

Londonderry are the spearhead of such disseminated growth. Within seven years of
the Development Commission taking over at Craigavon the population had been
built-up by 10,000 and stood at 57,000 (1975) in relation to a perhaps too
ambitious target of 108,000 by the mid-1980s. There were 33 factories with 4,500
jobs and a further 46 factories were under construction. Antrim–Ballymena, one
of the most prosperous localities in the UK, had attracted leader firms, in Michelin
and British Enkalon, whilst Londonderry was programmed to rise from 70,000 to
90,000 people by the mid-1980s; the basis for such growth will come from jobs
provided on the industrial estates recently established at Maydown and Springtown
(March 1968).

The intention is that both industrial and services growth at the designated
centres will diffuse benefits over a wider rural hinterland, in which the main
problem is a declining labour force (1948, 103,000; 1971, 52,000) with few
alternative jobs (N Ireland, Min. of Agriculture 1970). To underpin this policy,
having regard to the lower rate of car ownership and decay of public transport in
rural areas, a micro-level programme for dispersal of small industrial plants is in
progress under the Local Enterprise Development Unit (LEDU) programme. The
pattern of initial LEDU investment can be seen on fig. 1.9a, with advance factories
(300m^2) and nursery workshop combines (four units, each of 59m^2) suited to a
wide range of small industries. By the end of 1974, 4,500 jobs had been provided
in LEDU factories.

Greater Belfast poses a major urban redevelopment problem, with replacement of much of the housing stock and decongestion as key issues (Building Design Partnership 1972). The expansion centres to which population is to be moved from the city are seen on fig. 1.9. The strategy for Belfast thus rests upon improvement of its attractiveness for industry, the modernizing of a sub-standard living environment and promotion of growth at the capital city of Ulster. The attractiveness of the outer Belfast commuting area is shown by a 73 per cent population increase 1951–69, in comparison with only 18 per cent in five other towns in Ulster in the same period. Under resettlement legislation grants are payable to persons moving from Belfast to the receiving areas, and since 1974 to all who settle in Craigavon from any part of N Ireland.

The centre of Londonderry has suffered severely from violence and destruction. Nevertheless, plans for creation of new shops and offices are under way, as well as for the zoning of land for open space. Minor industries are being moved when possible to estates on the city perimeter; a substantial Courtaulds factory opened at Campsie during 1975. Hotel provision is not only replacing what has been lost during civil unrest, but is also to help establish Londonderry as a tourist centre for the town and hinterland.

Between 1945 and 1974 72,000 new industrial jobs were created, over 44 per cent of total employment in manufacturing. Diversification has been a keynote, including electronic and electrical goods, man-made fibres, automobile and aero-engine components, and rubber products. The textile industry (35,500 employed 1975) has become more broadly based and resilient, and the engineering sector is now less dependent upon declining staple products. There is indeed impressive industrial growth momentum at the present time in spite of disruption in the economic life of Ulster. From mid-1969 to mid-1972, 151 manufacturing firms had been disrupted by civil unrest, but only 10 closed, with the loss of 621 jobs.

A look ahead In the *Regional Physical Development Strategy, 1975–95* (N Ireland Dept. Housing, Local Govt. and Planning 1975) the slower population growth forecast (1.53 million 1975 to 1.70 million 1995) was acknowledged. Mobility patterns had been diminished as the result of civil disorder in the province. Too little had been done to redevelop Belfast, though the stopline policy had been successful, and perhaps too much economic growth had taken place in small towns and villages, rather than in the designated growth centres. To solve the endemic unemployment problem, with several severe localized pockets and an overall high level, much resettlement was needed and an increased journey to work for many would have to be envisaged.

Six spatial strategies were formulated and tested, from concentration to dispersal and from managed to *laissez-faire*. One was the continuance of the sixteen growth and key centres policy (fig. 1.9); another, concentration on Belfast and Londonderry; a third, a linear Belfast city; the fourth was a district town level of dispersal; the fifth, complete diffusion of growth; and sixth, polarization on Belfast by accepting market forces. Of these the strategy for an eighteen-district town network was preferred, after testing all models both by quantitative evaluation and by consultations. Thus rural and small town populations might be stabilized within the same general area. The Belfast stopline is to be held, except perhaps in the south-west, and a decline to 550,000 by 1995 envisaged. There will be greater emphasis on the development of Antrim (to 50,000); Londonderry will be programmed for 100,000 people by 1995, and it is intended that Craigavon NT will reach its intended target population by the end of the century.

Following local government reorganization in 1973 the New Town corporations in N Ireland were dissolved and their functions transferred to district councils.

V.3 The Intermediate Regions

There is some generalization involved in identifying as intermediate regions the whole of Yorks. and Humberside, and the NW. Though both economic planning regions were scheduled in 1972 for Intermediate Area benefits, extending the previous fragmentary zoning after the decisions on the 1969 Hunt Report, the NW also includes the Merseyside development area (1949) now an SDA (1974). Further, as fig. 1.4 shows, there are intermediate areas elsewhere in the UK, notably in the SW, the eastern periphery of Wales (less Cardiff and part of N Wales, DAs since August 1974), and in the Chesterfield area (1974); N Lincolnshire, and the High Peak (1972).

Nevertheless the two trans-Pennine economic planning regions most fully represent the problems of the intermediate areas and have very substantial populations living in sizeable, well-established towns and cities. Employment is sluggish or falling, though unemployment since the war has rarely been high enough for development area status to be conferred; the only exceptions to this, apart from Merseyside, were the short-term scheduling of parts of SE (1946) and NE Lancashire (1953). Regional incomes have been rising more slowly, and the industrial structure has been weighted with slow growth or decline sectors. Out-migration has been a less severe problem than in the development areas, though it has been ever-present. Furthermore the intermediate regions had a major legacy from the Industrial Revolution in their townscapes and there was a serious problem of dereliction. To meet all these problems, in aggregate at times scarcely less severe than those of the development areas, there was no special locational aid from successive governments. It was only in 1969 that a lesser scale of aid became available and then only for strictly localized areas. The 1972 extension of inter-mediate status to virtually all of the Yorks. and Humberside, and NW regions permitted for the first time a coordinated thrust towards economic as well as social or physical objectives in their regional development.

Both regions are less than 320 km from London, linked by the direct motorway network and fast Inter-city rail services. They are thus subjected to greater locational pulls from the Midlands and SE than are the development areas; in return they may hope to offer less disadvantageous freight hauls to incoming industry, in respect of service to national markets. In 1977 Hull and Grimsby became DAs.

Yorks. and Humberside (fig. 1.10)

This economic planning region changed its boundaries after local government reform in 1974, gaining the former N Riding, less Cleveland County, and losing South Lindsey (to the E Midlands), Saddleworth and Bowland (to the NW) and Sedbergh (to the Northern region). For details on population involved see p 43.

Fawcett (1919) spoke of Yorkshire as a 'microcosm of England'. The same might be said for the regional development problem posed today for the entire economic planning region. It lacks homogeneity or coherence, and there have persisted clear differences of emphasis as between alternative strategies for growth

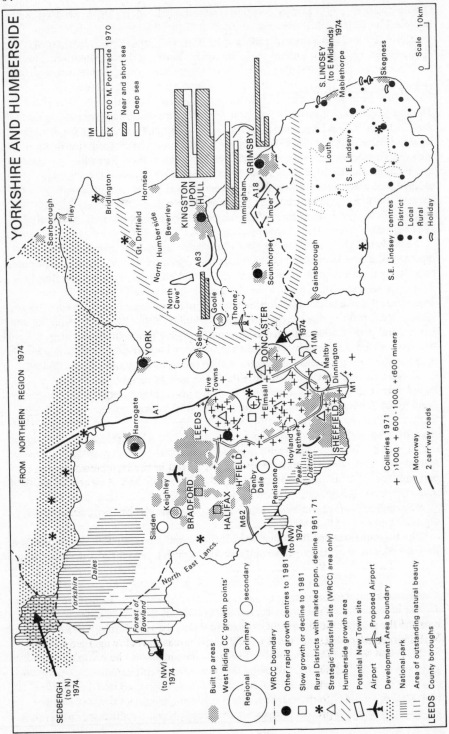

Figure 1.10   Yorkshire and Humberside

and development. Broadly speaking, the planning region may be differentiated into *western, central and eastern zones*, each with distinctive characteristics and problems. Within the *Pennines* and their fringe zone west of the A1(M) are concentrated $3\frac{1}{2}$ millions, no less than 75 per cent of the regional population. This is an urban-industrial zone with major cities and smaller, specialized industrial towns, the home of the woollen and worsted industries, engineering, and other sectors which have been stagnant or declining in employment since the war. It is also a zone with a relatively low population growth and serious environmental difficulties, notably so in the smaller, specialized woollen towns in the more remote Pennine valleys. In the south, around Sheffield–Rotherham, concentration on the steel industry and its specialized product range means too narrow an employment base and poses particular problems of economic vulnerability, with an even more pronounced counterpart around the integrated steel plants at Scunthorpe to the east. In the W Riding conurbation the problems are thus those of a massive slow growth or declining urban and industrial complex, without obvious means of achieving an industrial transformation.

The *central zone* includes the most productive localities of the Yorkshire coalfield, flanking the major north-south arteries of the A1(M) and the main east coast rail link, and set within a rural hinterland. Since the late 1950s there has been a sharp rundown in mining jobs, even in this prosperous coalfield. The exciting prospects for the new Selby coalfield will not radically transform this basic employment problem. The development problem is that of regrouping mining and agricultural populations and finding alternative work within daily travelling distance, to absorb those displaced by redundancies. In meeting this problem the nodal location on the national communications network should prove a major asset.

The problem in the third zone, *Humberside*, is of a different order. The north bank, around Hull, has had a limited port-based industrial structure and has suffered from relative isolation within the UK space. There are also physical planning problems, particularly those of urban redevelopment and conservation of high-grade agricultural land. On the south bank industry has grown rapidly since the 1950s, but many plants have been capital-intensive rather than providing great numbers of new jobs. There is, however, ample land in the Humberside region to accommodate both population and industry. This potential was clearly established in the Feasibility Study (CUEP 1969), to which reference is made later, but the government has decided against such massive growth, though giving consent to a Humber bridge, to be completed in 1978.

The fundamental problem for Yorks. and Humberside is then to decide on broad **spatial allocations and priorities for growth** as between the major zones, for both the shorter-term (to 1984) and to the end of the century. Strongly-held convictions in cities and Ridings have not made the tasks of formulating and gaining acceptance of a coherent strategy any easier. Nor is the task lightened by the difficulties of forecasting the tempo and nature of economic growth which may be expected. Whilst most of the region enjoys only Intermediate status the transferred part of the former N Riding retained its DA status. In 1977 several areas were downgraded to IAs.

The *1966 Review* (Yorks. and H. EPC 1966) emphasized the complexity and diversity of the region and underlined the varied needs and problems of each sub-region. The 'collective regional action and new sense of coherence' then called for have since been slow to materialize. Basic to the arguments of the review is the proposition that the problems of each sub-region should be mitigated largely *in situ* and there are no proposals for intra-regional transfers of population, or selective investment in areas where economic growth might be most readily induced. The defence may well have been that mobile industry would be difficult to attract, without greater government incentives, that existing industry had prospects for regeneration and this would have to take place on existing sites, and that with the outlook for only very modest additions to the labour force by the mid-1980s no dramatic intra-regional transfers were either practicable or desirable. The insistence that future development should be concentrated mainly on existing centres of population, that existing industries should power such development, and that the need to improve the general urban environment in the Pennines was paramount, has persisted in economic planning council thinking. So too has the early emphasis on sub-regional analysis (Yorks. and H. EPC 1968, 1969, A, B) and the lack of an adequately inter-related overall framework. For example, in the Halifax and Calder Valley study the recommendation is made for growth at the mouths of the valleys and along the M62, a micro-strategy similar to that for S Wales, but this sub-regional solution is not set within any wider regional context.

In the *Hunt Report* (Sec. State Economic Affairs 1969) on the intermediate areas a clear difference of opinion arose on prescription for the future development of Yorks. and Humberside. The majority view was that growth centres should be selected and a strategy of selective investment for them pursued. Industrial estates at strategic points, capable of drawing in labour from a wider hinterland, would play the role they had already had in development areas. Concentration on growth centres should not be at the expense of other parts of the region and, indeed, no inherent conflict of interests was envisaged. In the same Report A J Brown laid stress on the scale of the large urban concentrations and the importance of channelling growth to these, even after the needs of any growth centres had been met. He further saw the coalfield as the one location in Yorks. and Humberside where a growth centre might be justified. To him the growth centre concept was appropriate only when the entire pattern of settlement was being changed, as in the regrouping of agricultural or mining populations, or when substantial moves from congested cities were being made through overspill schemes. Growth centres would contribute less to the problems of a massive slow-growth industrial and urban complex.

The division of views on strategy surfaced again in the *Development Plan Review* of the W Riding CC (1969, 1971), which admittedly did not have responsibility for the problems of its included county boroughs. The strategy proposals therein were for the longer-term, to the year 2001, and were firmly based on the designation of growth points and, indeed, an even greater emphasis upon such selective investment as the future population for the region seemed likely to be lower than in earlier forecasts. The pattern of suggested growth points, at regional, primary and secondary levels is seen on fig. 1.10; the selection of Doncaster confirmed the potential already identified in the EPC sub-regional study. The pattern of growth points was carefully chosen to exploit under-utilized resources of land or labour, capitalize in other cases upon favourable location, and on other occasions lead to environmental improvement. In addition, a series of strategic industrial sites, each of over 40 ha, (fig. 1.10) and major sites (not less than 18 ha) were proposed. All but one lay within what had since 1970 been scheduled as in intermediate area. Furthermore no less than fifty-one key villages were selected for expansion.

The Regional Strategy (Yorks. and H. EPC 1970) confirmed the basic recommendation of the 1966 Review and suggested that in view of the longer time-scale of the WRCC Development Plan (2001 rather than the year 1984) there was no fundamental conflict between the different perspectives on strategy. The regional strategy re-emphasized that growth should follow the broad pattern of existing settlement, that the larger towns had the better and more diversified growth prospects, particularly for attraction of service industries, but that growth should also be disseminated throughout the urban system at all levels. For Bradford, Huddersfield and Halifax the current adverse trends were to be stabilized, with some increase at Huddersfield, whilst in the longer-term Leeds was recommended as a major growth area of employment and population. Urgent provision of new jobs for men was prescribed for Greater Doncaster, Barnsley, the Five Towns (Castleford, Knottingley, Pontefract, Featherstone and Normanton) and Wakefield, with some decline in population in the central coalfield. For Sheffield and Rotherham the economy was to be diversified and the possibility kept open for accommodating regional population growth in the longer-term. The strengthening of the economic base and improvement of the environment were priorities for Humberside, whilst conservation or modest development were envisaged for country areas and market towns.

Apart from the degree of emphasis upon growth in the industrial—urban complex of the Pennines as against the coalfield, through which passes the north-south communications corridor, there are two other fundamental uncertainties. Can the industrial structure be regenerated or transformed to serve the priorities of regional planning adequately, and what might have been the effects of a government decision to press ahead with Humberside as a fast-growth estuarine industrial region? The Economic Planning Council remains cautious and exploratory on the first issue (Yorks. and H. EPC 1972). Brown (1970) had already drawn attention to the sharp structural changes in employment which had taken place prior to 1965. Though these had not been cumulative as in the development areas, nevertheless 1965 marked a threshold after which unemployment began to rise differentially and income per capita began a decline relative to other regions. The EPC recognized these problems and indeed reviewed the 1965—70 continuation of the trends. Among further declines in employment were listed: coal-mining, —30,000 jobs; wool textiles, —31,000, though future decrease was thought likely to be small (Atkins 1969); metal manufactures, —14,000; construction, —26,000; the distributive trades, —26,000. On the other hand, some service industries had shown a rapid increase, e.g. professional and scientific services, +41,000 jobs. Unfortunately declines were taking place in areas different from those with growth in employment and, moreover, there were skills and training of a different order required in any attempt to balance growth with decline. Projection of trends identified further declines, requiring up to 35,000 new jobs in the coalfield by 1975, a considerable problem arising from redundancies in the steel industry, to say nothing of the implications of further automation or EEC membership (Yorks. and H. EPC 1972 B). The attraction of new industry had unfortunately proved minimal. For the period 1945—65 only 24,500 male jobs came from all manufacturing moves into the region. Moreover, even under intermediate area stimulus the rate of new job provision was inadequate to replace losses. The conclusion was drawn that in the short-term the inducements for industrialists had to be maximized within the region. This would seem to strengthen the case for designation and selective investment in an inter-related hierarchy of growth points as soon as practicable.

The problem posed by the future development of **Humberside** is longer-term and national in the first instance but its regional implications are profound. Had the government accepted the case for rapid estuarine growth on Humberside between now and the end of the century a safeguard would have already been built-in to protect the development areas up to 1981, but no such protection had been vouchsafed for adjacent areas of Yorks. and Humberside. In national and local terms (Lewis and Jones 1970, Craig, Evans and Showler 1970) the case for Humberside development remains strong, potentially dramatic. A case for between an additional 320,000 or 720,000 people by the year 2001 can be substantiated, with alternative growth and urban location strategies, including New Town development at Limber or North Cave (fig. 1.10). It was anticipated that major growth would take place by spontaneous mass movements from the 1980s onwards, but that in the short-term industry and people might be attracted more from the Midlands and the SE, partly by planned overspill. The impact of such major developments, had they been acceptable to government, upon the massive slow-growth industrial and urban complex in the Pennines, to say nothing of general strategic balance within Yorks. and Humberside, would have posed extraordinary problems, even within an enhanced European future.

The *1975 Regional Strategy Review* (Yorks. and H. EPC 1976), considered the implications of a slow-growth economy at a time of national recession. In some respects the region was more favoured than at the time of the 1970 review; the net out-migration had fallen from about 14,000 per annum (1966–71) to less than 1,000 (1971–4); the communications pattern had improved, with virtual completion of the M62, and a start had been made on the Humber Bridge. UK entry to the EEC bid fair to favour the Humberside ports, even though the government had decided against the MIDAS concept there. At the newly discovered Selby coalfield there was the prospect of 8 million tonnes of coal per annum by the mid-1980s and 4,000 mining jobs. At Scunthorpe the Anchor scheme had been commissioned by the BSC in 1973.

Certainly other developments had been markedly unfavourable. The woollen industry had gone into recession with a loss of 40 per cent of jobs, 1970–5, necessitating the special aid of the wool textile scheme (1973) to improve the structure and assist much-needed investment; closures and short-time working affected also the clothing industry. Engineering employment had held up well, but little restructuring had taken place; services had grown slightly faster than the national average since 1971, but from a lower proportionate base level. In steel employment was down by one-fifth, 1971–5, and under the BSC ten-year strategy (1973) further redundancies were to be expected. Employment in coal-mining, on the other hand, had fallen less than anticipated (1967, 93,000; 1975, 65,700), and output from the Yorkshire pits was to be expanded (33 million tonnes 1974, 45 mt 1985).

Sectoral priorities in the review stressed the over-riding need to develop productive industry, then to complete essential communications, and only thereafter to focus upon environmental problems. Among environmental problems pride of place was to be given to housing, followed by water and sewerage, air pollution, health, education, derelict land, river pollution, in that order of importance. It was strongly asserted that regional policies should increasingly be concerned with reducing out-migration, improving the quality of life, and raising average incomes, rather than being excessively preoccupied with unemployment levels.

The review considered in detail the prospects for each economic sub-region. In N Yorkshire the problems of agriculture dominated, but coastal resorts had severe seasonal unemployment and the need for modest provision of industry. Growth prospects for Thirsk, Northallerton and York seemed promising; that at Selby would necessarily bring environmental problems in its wake. In West Yorkshire the diverse industrial and commercial base of Leeds offered the best prospects; those at Bradford were clouded by recession in woollen textiles. Overall job prospects in the West were better than forecast in 1970 and there had been both lower out-migration and little rise in unemployment. The potential of the motorway network as a growth generator was particularly stressed. In S Yorkshire, Barnsley and Doncaster had sound growth prospects, but not sufficient to solve problems such as those of the Dearne Valley. A strong case could be made for Sheffield as a major service centre, as manufacturing jobs declined in traditional industries. Humberside had a vulnerable economy, but with chemicals, petroleum refining and steel the potential was seen as considerable, the more so within a European future.

The North West (fig. 1.11)
In April 1974 this region lost Furness and gained two areas from Yorks. and Humberside. The problems of the NW (Smith 1969; Nuttall and Batty 1970) arise initially from the very size of the regional population, its concentration between the Ribble and the Mersey (5.9 millions), a low population growth-rate, and the scale of industrial transformation and rundown which have taken place in cotton, coal and engineering since the war. Though there has been some replacement of jobs by growth industries, especially so in services, the region is still characterized by a low level of autonomous economic growth. In common with Yorks. and Humberside the urban-industrial problem is most serious in the traditional single-industry towns in the Pennines, but in the NW the decline of employment in cotton textiles has been more profound and its sub-regional effects more traumatic. Furthermore, the presence of major conurbations on Merseyside (1.2 millions) and at Greater Manchester (2.3 millions) in lowland Lancashire, each until 1974 controlled by independent planning authorities, has weighted the restructuring problem and coloured policies for development and change. Merseyside has been consistently scheduled as a DA since 1946 (SDA since August 1974), to its great advantage, and has acted as an engine of economic growth in the North West (DEA 1965). The only other DA has been Furness, on the borders of the Northern Region, and transferred to that region in 1974. Manchester, on the other hand, failed to attract the same scale of new industrial investment but has built up service employment. Both conurbations need substantial and continuing overspill schemes to permit redevelopment and decrease congestion, and there is a major problem of priorities as between the sub-regions for the distribution of such population and employment. Nowhere in Britain is the range of possible regional development options greater: dissemination of growth and sub-regional balance; perimeter additions to one or both conurbations; major developments at the New Towns, including the Central Lancashire New Town (CLNT); balance between growth in the Ribble Belt (CLNT and NE Lancashire) and the Mersey Belt, particularly in the sub-region between the conurbations; concentration of growth in areas most attractive to industry or remedial measures in problem sub-regions. Nowhere in Britain has there been such a slow growth momentum, in population or employment, in relation to the scale of problems to be faced, and scarcely anywhere else

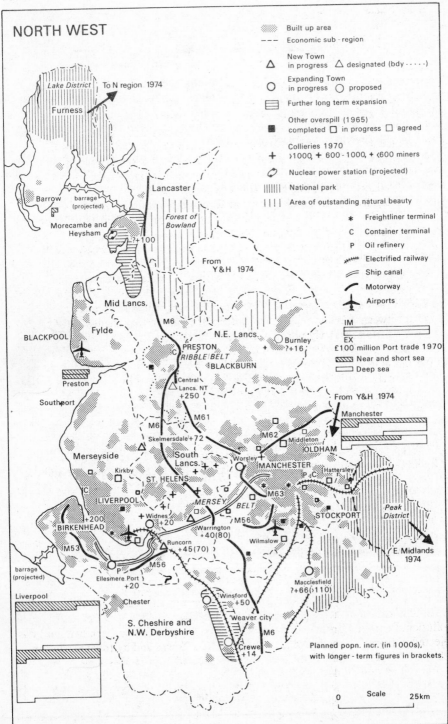

Figure 1.11   North West

has the fragmentation of planning authorities made coherent policies so difficult to achieve. On the other hand, the growth of the motorway network, the completion of main-line electrification on the west coast route, and developments in the ports are creating a new dimension in regional economic potential within the UK system.

The *North West Study* (DEA 1965) stressed the twin objectives of better living conditions and the need to stimulate economic growth. The problem of housing obsolescence was placed in the forefront, and has remained a major preoccupation (N West EPC 1970). The forward projections for the regional population were then more sizeable (+800,000 to 930,000 by 1981), even though out-migration was assumed to continue. Overspill schemes for intra-regional redistribution (fig. 1.11) were numerous but for the most part small and separately negotiated by the con-urbation local authorities. The New Town designated at Skelmersdale, together with proposals for similar developments at Runcorn, Warrington and Leyland-Chorley were also to accommodate overspill, and it was not anticipated that other overspill schemes would be required, certainly not before the last decades of the century. The problem industrial areas within the Pennines were scarcely touched upon.

A counterpart study for *Merseyside* (DEA 1965; Lawton and Cunningham 1970) noted the youthful population and a high natural increase rate. Though there had been a net migration loss of 72,000, nevertheless the population had risen by 117,000 between 1951 and 1964. The industrial economy was changing during the same period from narrowly port-based to a greater diversification linked to the hinterland of the NW. Yet industrial transformation had not been sufficient to off-set job loss in port-based industries and still meet the needs of an increased labour force. Unemployment has persisted, particularly for young persons, and justified the scheduling of Merseyside as a Development Area as far back as 1949.

The *1966 Strategy* (NW EPC) optimistically proposed to reduce net out-migration and contemplated a population increase of one million by 1981. Two growth areas were proposed: in N Lancashire and S Cheshire; but the green belts around the conurbations were to remain inviolate and there was to be no in-filling in the intervening Mersey Belt. The industrial problem areas of Rossendale and the NE were considered in the context of the effects of the *Cotton Industry Act* (1959) which had achieved massive rationalization and reduction of both capacity and employment in that industry. Yet NE Lancashire had been descheduled under the 1960 Local Employment Act and the prospects of attracting sufficient new industrial growth correspondingly reduced.

The *Strategy II* (NW EPC 1968) had less regard for allocations of population growth, whose target figure for 1981 had now fallen to +750,000, but much greater emphasis upon the need for industrial location efficiency, buttressed by effective action on transport, housing and schools. The environment was to be improved by urban renewal and attacks on the problems of derelict land (N West EPC 1971) and pollution. Peripheral growth of the conurbations by inroads into green-belt land was rejected in favour of continued growth at the New Towns and by town expansion schemes. Increased journeys to work were anticipated both to these new develop-ments and to industrial sites within the marginal problem localities in Rossendale, the NE and the Pennine fringe. The early development of the CLNT was firmly supported and the urgency of local government reform seen as necessary if a coordinated strategy was to be achieved.

In its proposal, not accepted by the government, to deschedule Merseyside as a development area, the *Hunt Report* (Sec. State Economic Affairs, 1969, 159) brought into the open one of the principal strategic issues, the role of the conurbations in regional economic growth, and particularly the extent of distortions in the growth which development area scheduling may have introduced. It was argued that in the two years 1966–8 Merseyside had attracted 5,350 jobs by industrial moves from neighbouring areas (27 per cent of all new jobs created by moves), probably mostly from Manchester. In its perimeter industrial estates with their major housing developments, the green-field industrial sites capable of taking motor vehicle plants, the nearby New Towns of Skelmersdale and Runcorn and the overspill town of Winsford, Merseyside represented the major North West growth complex. It was for this reason that descheduling was proposed, but opposed by Brown (Sec. State Economic Affairs 1969, 159). Brown argued that the high natural increase and immigration, leading to perhaps an additional 200,000 people within twenty years, required continued government support policies for creating new employment. If the area was to be descheduled it did not follow that the same industrial growth would be available for other sites in the North West. In the event development area status was retained and in August 1974 SDA status was conferred. NE Lancashire was designated an intermediate area in 1970, a status extended to the entire North West in 1972.

The Central Lancashire New Town (MHLG 1967), intended to build-up to a population of no less than 430,000 by 1991, from the present 250,000 in the designated area, has clearly the potential to act as a counter-magnet to the two principal conurbations, and also as a major growth centre to underpin the industrial economy and help stabilize the population of the entire Ribble belt. Indeed it is intended deliberately to relive growth pressures in the Merseyside– Manchester axis, to act as a base for concentrating large immigrant growth industries, and to provide an attractive environment and modern living conditions. There must be some uncertainty about the prospects of attracting sufficient mobile large-scale industry in time, some doubt about the potential adverse effects upon NE Lancashire, and some regrets that the designated area did not extend further south, to help relieve unemployment problems in the area north of Wigan. To clarify the possible effects upon NE Lancashire an Impact Study (Matthew et al 1968) was commissioned, to be followed by a project study for a fast road link to the NE. The Impact Study argued that the needs of the NE were for improved communications, south towards Manchester as well as along the Ribble valley, rehabilitation and urban renewal. It was felt that the effects of CLNT would on balance be favourable. Out-migration from the towns of NE Lancashire might rise by 10,000–15,000 over the twenty-year period 1971–91, but would probably rise to double that figure had the New Town not been introduced. The effects would increase after 1981 in a period of faster CLNT growth but there would be closer economic and social linkages with existing towns from Blackburn eastwards.

The options in the North West remain open. Much will depend on national economic growth rates, in an area lacking in sufficient indigenous momentum. If growth is fast and sustained the CLNT can be vigorously prosecuted and a Ribble Belt economy regenerated. At the same time the Mersey Belt can gain momentum, with maximum growth in towns and overspill centres. On the most favourable outlook for growth major developments may be required in the Lancaster area and South Cheshire (Weaver City) by the end of the century. The conurbations are likely to be restructured but not to grow on any hypothesis for the region. On a slow-growth hypothesis agonizing choices between alternatives will be needed, not least for the many smaller or remote industrial towns, whose problems have been neglected in most policies to date.

The *Strategic Plan for the North West* (DoE 1974) was formulated before economic recession became pronounced. Its attitude to growth could thus be more catholic and there was a proper regard for quality of life in its proposals (Powell 1974). Between 1966 and 1973, however, the pattern of employment was changing rapidly, with a fall of 8 per cent in total number of jobs, 25 per cent in engineering, and 35 per cent in textiles; growth elements were scarce, though professional and scientific services rose by 26 per cent. The plan aimed to optimize job distribution rather than to maximize growth and its proposed patterning of change was not limited to the most likely growth areas.

The method of evaluating options (Activity Allocation Model) seems to have involved a blend of measurement with judgement. The first cycle of evaluation established weighted objectives within a goals achievement matrix; the second moved from preferred emphases of policy to preferred spatial patterns of employment, degree of population displacement, and assessment of land release required for new development. The third cycle produced the recommended physical pattern to 1991.

The spatial patterns tested varied from concentration to dispersal (Mersey belt; CLNT—Ribble belt; Weaver city; peripheral growth around conurbations; Lancaster—Morecambe; Deeside). Concentration was favoured: greater job choice; access to urban facilities; level and costs of provision; benefits of public transport; better treatment of the underprivileged. Disadvantages were seen as more a matter of urban form and structure rather than those of sheer weight of numbers. It was determined that the best prospects for regional employment growth lay in existing centres of industry and commerce. This favoured the Mersey belt within which also the greatest environmental problems were to be found.

The recommendation was that job growth should thus be greatest in S Lancashire, especially around the three New Towns and to the north and east of the Merseyside and SELNEC conurbations, in each of which there should be maximum job retention. Corridor growth in the directions of Bolton, Bury and Tyldesley—Westhoughton would focus this outward growth, and southwards only the Macclesfield corridor should be developed. There should be careful management of the rates of job creation, fast in S Lancashire, much slower in S Cheshire. Overall the displacement of population should be moderate rather than high.

The price of such a priority for the Mersey belt necessarily implies slower rates of growth elsewhere. The CLNT will grow more slowly in the short-term, but make a major contribution to growth in the 1980s and 1990s. The *Hardman Report* (Office of the Lord Pres. of the Council 1973) recommended dispersal of 3,000 civil service jobs from London to the CLNT. For NE Lancashire, the Fylde and Furness (now part of Northern Region), existing policy restraints were to continue. At first sight this seems to imply a harsh policy towards marginal areas of all types and it seems that many former single industry textile towns are going to face difficult problems of readjustment. The degree of mismatch between population growth locations and economic potential further indicates that mobility will need to be high at a time of recession and retrenchment.

The SPNW was vigorously attacked by the *Lancashire County Co.* (1974), for its degree of pessimism, its alleged unjustified and untested change of direction in major planning policy, and for its preferred strategy of concentration on the Mersey belt. It was argued that such a concentration policy would add seriously to environmental problems, that it was incompatible with an objective of improving the quality of life, and that in any event the policy had not been costed. Furthermore, the creation of growth corridors would consume valuable open land and there would be peripheral accretion around the conurbations as a result.

In the view of Lancashire CC economic growth should be promoted where it had the greatest possibility of success, but the search for quality of life should always be an important qualification on purely economic strategies. The CLNT was seen as the best prospect for growth upon land already allocated, and the SPNW report was accused of over-estimating the growth intended there. It should have been +120,000 people between 1971 and 1991, and not +210,000 as indicated in SPNW. A further condemnation of the SPNW was that it did not have a basic transportation policy in mind, particularly ignoring rail, and that it did not provide a realistic, flexible and balanced view of the future.

It might be countered that every local authority is always likely to demand more growth for its own area and its own people. If this is so, then all overall regional strategies are going to be rejected by at least some constituent local authorities. Faced with this situation an alternative policy for strategy formulation might be to concentrate, at regional level, entirely on a background economic and social framework, leaving spatial allocation perhaps to the structure plan level. This would of course devalue the regional strategic level and might well result in division of growth available among the strongest political contenders.

During 1976 industrial plant closures at Skelmersdale created one of the most serious unemployment 'black spots' in the North West, at a New Town which had been the focus of a crash programme of growth during the previous ten years. As national urban policy began to shift to priorities for rejuvenating run-down city centres and other 'inner urban land', the target for in-migrants at CLNT during the Development Plan period was also reduced from 100,000 to 23,000 (1977).

V.4   Regions of Mixed Trends

The South West and E Anglia economic planning regions do not fall into any clear category, though they share certain common features. Neither has coherence, least of all the SW, and indeed each has four distinctive sub-regions. As a result there are built-in conflicting economic and social trends, and a marked territoriality between urban and rural interests. Both are identified by the lowest population densities among UK economic planning regions, but nevertheless there are strong pressures for growth and development in parts of both the SW (Severnside, Swindon) and E Anglia (New Town and town expansion schemes). In both regions the influence of the metropolis is increasingly felt and is spreading; this too adds to the problems of developing a regional sense of purpose.

The South West
In April 1974 the SW gained Dorset and part of Hampshire from the SE (population 1971, 552,540). The *Draft Strategy for the South West* (S West EPC 1967) accepted from the outset that very different treatment would be required for each of its *four component sub-regions* (fig. 1.12). Indeed, in view of the distinctive

economic and social problems of each, the strength of county-based loyalties, the lack of a clear capital for the region and the extent of outside, particularly metropolitan, influences, it is not surprising that a coherent and universally agreed strategy has not yet emerged. Furthermore, each of the four sub-regions is further differentiated internally, which adds to the problems of the regional planner. Nine sub-regions were identified in 1967 and thirty economic planning areas in 1974.

The strategic issues facing *Bristol and Severnside* are those arising from strong population and economic growth pressures, with the need to define priorities for proper physical planning of future growth, to avoid congestion and loss of amenity and to balance development of manufacturing with that of services, with least detriment to the environment. Linkages through the motorway and port network have set the region more firmly within a national context, as containing one of the most impressive prospects for fast growth during the latter part of this century. The influence of Greater London has spread along the M4, beyond the planned expansion centre of Swindon (+28,000 overspill population by 1970); the motorway has also linked Severnside more effectively with S Wales.

Even growth industries have their problems, however, and for example some of the 20,000 direct jobs on Concorde airframes and engines in the SW might be threatened unless sales for the aircraft improve markedly. The Concorde project has led to about £15 million per annum investment at Filton, Patchway, Fairford and at dispersed centres through the south-western counties. Similarly, though further port development at Bristol may prove to be an income generator it is less likely to provide many new jobs. Tertiary employment, particularly in the office sector, may offer better prospects. Though Bristol is only eighth in size among UK urban areas the city is already the fourth largest office centre outside London.

The *central sub-region* lacks focus, is strongly rural in character and has limited growth potential in its market towns and at selected south coast resorts. It is subjected to strong growth influences from Bristol—Severnside to the north and, to a lesser extent, from the metropolis. These are indeed likely to increase with the extension of the M5 through Somerset to Exeter (1976) and by double-carriageway road to Plymouth by 1980. The southern and western sub-regions comprise *Devon and Cornwall*, with a fringe area of north-western Somerset (fig. 1.12). The problems here are, first, those of establishing and maintaining viability for an economy with agriculture and the holiday trades as its basis, and thereafter of promoting growth by the introduction of a balance of industry. With remoteness and economic inaccessibility underlying weaknesses (Caesar 1949) the improvement of communications is a vital priority. Official recognition of the problems of Devon and Cornwall came with the scheduling of several localities under DATAC (Development Areas Treasury Advisory Committee) or development district legislation between 1958 and 1966. In 1966 much of Cornwall became a development area, and during 1970 Plymouth was granted intermediate area status, followed by Okehampton and Tavistock in 1971.

Pressures for growth on **Severnside**, in either the short- or long-term, are unlikely to benefit Devon and Cornwall, and may indeed prejudice any kind of balanced development in the rural or outer areas of the SW. Present trends of growth on Severnside are among the most substantial in the UK and the verdict of the Severnside study (CUEP 1971) was that the potential for population growth by the end of the century was double that expected from projection of even the present buoyant trends. The industrial employment mix is diverse and contains powerful growth elements (Walker 1965; Britton 1967), as in the aircraft and airspace, engineering, paper and printing industries of the Bristol area; the high level of mechanical and instrument engineering in N Gloucestershire; and the iron and steel industry in Monmouthshire—Ross.

There has been a steady net in-migration to Severnside since the war, the product of economic opportunity and attractive environment. Furthermore, the building of the Severn bridge and linkages along the M4 and M5 have strengthened the infrastructure for a coherent Severnside region, with close attachment to the SE, the Midlands and S Wales. Today, for example, Bristol (Parkway) is within 1 hr 35 mins of London by non-stop fast rail service and the 1976 introduction of the Advanced Passenger Train (APT) has reduced this still further. The feasibility study forecast continuing growth tendencies sufficient to attract a net inward flow of about 7,000 people a year, which if sustained, together with natural increase, would add 450,000 to the population by 1991 (650,000 by the year 2001). This might be stimulated to a maximum potential for an additional population of 600,000 by 1991 (one million by 2001). The allocation of such massive potential growth was distributed to several major sites: 200,000 to 300,000 to Bristol—Bath by 1991, if there can be major development at the Frampton Cotterell site; 150,000 to 250,000 in North Gloucestershire, possibly involving a New Town on the west bank; and 100,000 to 150,000 people in Monmouthshire—Ross, representing almost the maximum physical capacity of that area. The preferred strategy was thus for a major centre of industrial and population growth associated with existing urban development in each of three areas, posing a testing problem of harnessing and channelling growth, without suffering the dangers that could accompany excessive size.

Devon and Cornwall The problems of the outer sub-regions of the SW could scarcely be more different: to promote rather than restrain growth, and to do so from a narrow agricultural—tourism base; to create better accessibility rather than channel growth arising from an ultra-modern communications net; to attract industry and reduce unemployment rather than avoid 'over-heating' arising from rapid economic growth; to create many small centres of growth rather than major urban growth concentrations.

The *1966 Strategy* (S West EPC 1967) stressed the importance of strengthening agriculture and horticulture, whilst accepting that employment in these sectors would continue to fall, by amalgamation of holdings, increase in gross output per holding and more effective marketing. Tourism was seen as a major but vulnerable growth industry, which might be inter-related with other elements of the rural or coastal economy, but one whose prospects could not alone carry Devon and Cornwall to prosperity (MHLG 1970). Farming and tourism would provide the base from which self-sustaining economic growth might be promoted by the introduction of manufacturing and its location at selected regional or local growth centres (fig. 1.12). Plymouth was recommended as a major centre for growth and potential for the two growth triangles, Exeter—Honiton—Taunton and Truro—Camborne—Falmouth, was specifically indicated. Indigenous population growth might be inadequate to provide sufficient labour at the growth centres and the prospects for self-supporting growth would be enhanced by planned overspill location of immigrants from Greater London.

At present population growth comes disproportionately from the influx of retired persons, whilst younger people continue to leave Devon and Cornwall in search of work. The multiplier effect of retired people on the local economy might

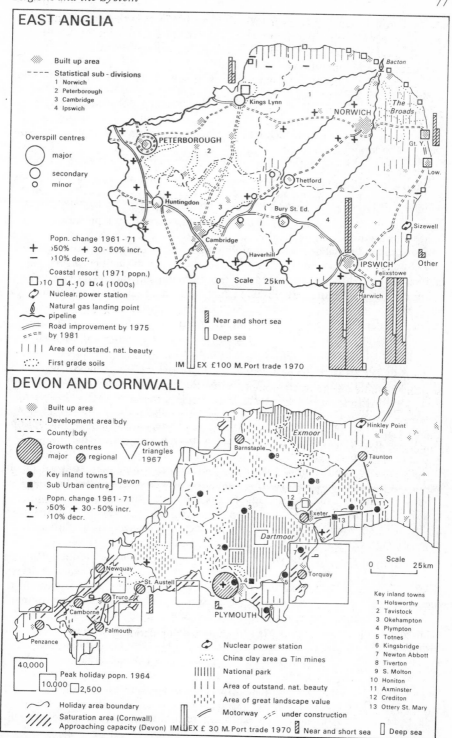

Figure 1.12   East Anglia; Devon and Cornwall

be as much as the equivalent of one service job equivalent per retired household compared to £1,500 as the public cost of creating one new job in manufacturing, but the manufacturing job is likely to be the more stable long-term investment.

During the period 1966—70 Devon CC carried out feasibility studies for several growth centres, the Cornwall Council investigated the proposals for West Cornwall (Cornwall CC 1970) and the economic planning council published the Plymouth area study (SW EPC 1969). Neither county council accepted that the growth triangles should have precedence for investment, or indeed that population or employment should be channelled into such areas. Furthermore the proposal that Greater London overspill should contribute to the build-up was strongly resented locally and, indeed, in 1968 the GLC announced that no further town development schemes would be accepted for the time being. In Devon and Cornwall the strategy is rather for smaller-scale and inter-related growth points, with redistribution of population from larger towns like Exeter or Plymouth into an immediate hinterland. As in Wales there is a strong sentiment for promoting development from indigenous resources and population.

Studies in industrial development at Plymouth and in Devon and Cornwall (Braithwaite 1968; Spooner 1972, 1974) have shown the difficulties of generating and maintaining sufficient momentum without government aid and, even with it, the problems of attracting new developments on the necessary scale and with adequate growth prospects. There is some expectation that EEC entry will help rather than damage the SW. Early favourable indications include: a roll on/roll off service Plymouth—Roscoff (Brittany); a possible container outport at Falmouth; and a potential increase in tourism from Europe.

The *1974 Strategic Settlement Pattern* (SW EPC 1974) reformulated the principle of securing economic growth to match population growth, consistent with consideration for the environment. Interestingly, the process of hypothesizing and testing alternative spatial strategies was held to be inapplicable for the SW, in view of the limited economic interaction between the sub-regions. Regional-scale options for influencing population flows were thus regarded as very limited and the principle of redeploying or inter-relating growth was firmly rejected. The role of the EPC was seen to be that of counselling, but neither costing nor dating a regional pattern of population allocation. The population proposed for most of the thirty economic planning areas, each broadly homogeneous in economy and environment, was that likely to occur by extrapolation of existing trends. Capacity to move against the trends was thought to be very limited, even though half the anticipated population growth was estimated to be by net in-migration.

Pressures for growth, perhaps overall by one-third in population terms by the end of the century, were seen to be very uneven. For Bristol—Bath the feasibility (CUEP 1971) for +300,000 in that sub-region by 1991 was confirmed, even though the government is now firmly against special stimulus for Severnside. The possibilities of S Gloucestershire for major growth were assessed as good, and other planning areas where population growth was to be stimulated beyond that expected were at S Swindon (raised from +80,000 to +120,000 by 2001), Taunton—Bridgwater, Poole—Bournemouth (+50,000 on trend projection), N Devon and Plymouth. West Cornwall, at a delicate stage of economic transition, was to be looked at cohesively and a growth-point policy established. The major population growth was thus to be along and flanking the motorway axis from Gloucester to Exeter with detached nodes towards the peripheries of the region. In all other planning areas population growth was to be restrained to the minimum practicable.

The most interesting features distinguishing this 1974 document are: the long-time scale (to 2001), the stress upon marginal influencing of population location without a thoroughgoing analysis of employment potential, and the extreme compartmentalization of what is proposed.

East Anglia (fig. 1.12)

Difficult to establish in the first place, the identity of this region risks being increasingly submerged by metropolitan influences expressed through the communications network and the pattern of New and overspill towns. The Outer Metropolitan Area bounds the region on the south and London lies only 193 km from the furthest point of the Norfolk coast. The location of E Anglia has traditionally been interpreted as oblique to the main axis of national economic life and its identity has been built-up as one of the foremost agricultural regions in the UK, somewhat isolated by poor communications, but with a degree of coherence from the inter-linking of sub-regions based on Norwich, Peterborough, Cambridge and Ipswich. The economic planning council came into being later than others (1966) and it seems clear that in official circles E Anglia had hitherto been something of a statistical abstraction.

The *East Anglia Study* (E Anglia EPC 1968) recognized the problem of consolidating an identity for a region lacking homogeneity and subject to strong external influences from the south. The regional development problem is compounded of conflicting trends. On the one hand, the size of population is small (1.78 millions in 1975) and the overall density is low, whilst the traditional economic structure has been developed from an agrarian base. Manufacturing is poorly developed, with many small firms in food and fish processing, and light engineering. Labour has a restricted range of skills and average incomes are lower than for any UK region other than Scotland; furthermore, there have been persistent but highly localized unemployment 'black spots' in coastal and rural Norfolk. Not only is the internal road system inadequate but rural transport, both road and rail, has declined markedly. Housing, education and health standards have been lower than those of the nation. Not surprisingly, rural depopulation has proved to be a characteristic feature.

On the other hand the total population of E Anglia has shown the fastest regional growth rate since 1951 and this is likely to be sustained until 1981 at the least. This growth has been generated from the South East with the influx of size-able London overspill population. In the study it was estimated that from 1966 to 1981 between 85,000 and 114,000 additional males would be seeking jobs, three-quarters of them at the New Town of Peterborough or in overspill areas. The distribution of overspill schemes is seen on figs. 1.12 and 2.22. Under the *Town Development Act (1952)* ten local authorities made overspill agreements with what is now the GLC and it is estimated that a total capacity, 1966—81, for about 250,000 people might be made available in E Anglia. This would represent a maximum and no further overspill agreements have been entered into by the GLC since 1968.

The strategy problem facing the E Anglian Council was to draw up a plan which would strengthen the regional economy and benefit from the London-inspired growth momentum, without at the same time becoming no more than a peripheral extension of the SE. Indigenous growth was likely to have been small and hard to realize, since the region had never had development area status and only intermittently and in piecemeal fashion aid under the 1960 and 1963 *Local Employment Acts*. Additionally, office development had been restricted, in principle, and firms could not be attracted, under overspill arrangements, from the adjacent OMA.

A strategy for concentration of development along radial growth corridors from the SE: to Peterborough (A1(M)), or to Ipswich (A12) and thence to Norwich, was rejected as damaging to the coherence of E Anglia. Transverse growth corridors seemed unlikely to be realized, although a Haven Ports—Cambridge—Northampton axis was developing in the 1960s, and there might result a loss of sub-regional balance. Nor did a major New Town growth in Breckland seem in the interests of the region and the proposed scale of such a development, at Thetford, also threatened amenity.

The proposed strategy envisaged the build-up of the *four city regions*, each with a dispersed hinterland of about 24 km radius. Norwich, Peterborough, Cambridge and Ipswich were nodally located, though large parts of the hinterland of the first three lay outside the E Anglian planning region. Second-order urban regions were to be based on King's Lynn, Great Yarmouth—Lowestoft and Bury St Edmunds, and it was intended to select smaller scale rural growth-points. In commenting on the proposed strategy the government agreed that there was no reason to concentrate development in any one part of the region, but rejected any notion of uniform sub-regional growth. Sub-regional studies were to be undertaken to identify areas with the greatest growth potential. Office development controls were lifted and firms from the OMA would be permitted to move to New or expanding towns. The rural growth-point strategy was acceptable and some IDC relaxation might be expected.

The prospects for the *four sub-regions* are uneven and differential growth might disturb or distort any coherent strategy for E Anglia. Norwich (160,000 in the city; 500,000 in sub-region) typifies the regional problem, in its diverse industrial structure (food processing, shoes, engineering) with few growth elements, the less prosperous hinterland (including small coastal resorts) and the least adequate intra-regional and long-distance communications. Peterborough, on the other hand, is a New Town with major expansion programmed (MHLG 1966). The 1965 population of 78,000 might be built up to 172,000 by 1981 if a planned intake of 70,000 is achieved, but clearly such a growth rate implies problems in scale and timing of job provision, even though there is growth potential in the local industries of mechanical and electrical engineering. The Fenland peat basin hinterland of Peterborough typifies the agrarian problem of the vulnerability of high grade horticulture with its associated food-processing industries. Within this hinterland King's Lynn is programmed to grow to 55,000 by 1981, with a strong influx of overspill population.

The Cambridge sub-region (DoE 1974) poses the problem of conserving the special qualities of a university town under strong economic growth pressures. The 1952 Cambridgeshire Development Plan proposed to stabilize the town population at 100,000, with an encircling green belt, and to distribute a further 25,000 people over the immediate hinterland. The 1968 Study recommended a greater build-up at the technological scientific complex of Cambridge, but the government wished to keep its options open. The 1974 Report advanced the case for a new urban centre immediately south of Cambridge central area, to preserve that city's special qualities. The government decided not to go ahead with the Ipswich New Town proposal outlined in the 1967 South East Study but the town has strong growth potential based on its relationship to Greater London and the nearby Haven Ports—Colchester growth area.

The *Strategic Choice Report* (DoE 1974) is conceptually in strong contrast to that for the SW, published in the same year. The exceptional growth pressures upon E Anglia, accelerating and particularly heavy over the years to 1985, were seen as a great opportunity to redress imbalances sub-regionally and at different levels in the urban hierarchy. Manipulation of the immigrant streams under a selective growth and location policy would be the means, and the merits of diversity and continuity with the past would be secured by flexible small-scale units of provision. The effective solution to the longer-term problems of E Anglia should not be sacrificed by short-term maximum growth policies, which might in fact heighten existing spatial imbalances through the sheer speed of development.

External pressures for growth would be expressed centrifugally from Outer London in zones of diminishing intensity across the western and southern sub-regions of E Anglia. Policy should be directed to building up the four sub-regional centres (Norwich, Cambridge, Peterborough and Ipswich) but there should also be a deliberate attempt to stimulate greater growth proportionately in the northern and eastern sub-regions. A small-towns policy should be fostered to diffuse growth and to assist in evening out growth and change. Such an inter-related policy of selecting growth, sub-regionally and within the urban network, is in sharp contrast to what is proposed for the SW economic planning region (SW EPC 1974).

V.5   The 'Growth' Regions

As far back as the *Barlow Report* (Royal Commission 1940) the growth potential of the Midlands—SE axis had been recognized. Indeed during the inter-war period it was the reception area for the so-called 'drift to the south'. It had and still has the cardinal advantages of location on the rail and motorway network, access to the major gateway ports, and has long had the sites preferred for a wide range of twentieth-century growth industries. The living environment, for the most part, has escaped the worst of the Industrial Revolution heritage. With all these assets, confirmed by agglomeration, the economies of scale, the creation of an ever larger market in the rising population, it is entirely justifiable to speak of 'growth regions'. Yet the term is not applicable in all parts of the regions and in the late 1960s there have emerged ominous signs of unemployment locally above the national average, even in such hitherto prosperous cities as Coventry and Birmingham. Within a coherent growth zone encompassing large parts of all three regions it is somewhat arbitrary to treat each separately. In the present state of regional planning and the formulation of strategies, however, the intentions of each economic planning council must be taken into account. They will be found to be different and, it may be thought, still insufficiently inter-related.

The East Midlands (fig. 1.13)
In April 1974 this region gained S Lindsey (167,050) from Yorks. and Humberside, and Tintwhistle from the NW. The first two reports by the E Midlands Economic Planning Council in the 1960s struck a confident note. The most recent report (E Midlands EPC 1976) is more sober and cautious. The region lies in the heartland of England, nodally located astride four major national communications arteries: the M1 and A1(M), and the east coast and the electrified Euston—Manchester—Glasgow

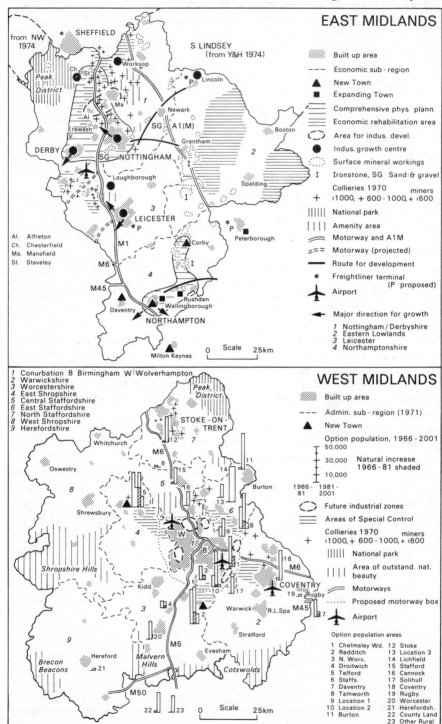

EAST MIDLANDS

from NW 1974
SHEFFIELD
Worksop
Ch. St.
Peak District
Al Ma
Erewash V.
DERBY
SG NOTTINGHAM
Loughborough
LEICESTER
*P
M1
M6
M45
Daventry
NORTHAMPTON
Milton Keynes

S. LINDSEY (from Y&H 1974)
Lincoln
Newark
SG A1(M)
Grantham
Boston
Spalding
Corby
Peterborough
Rushden
Wellingborough

Al.   Alfreton
Ch.   Chesterfield
Ma. Mansfield
St.   Staveley

1
2
3
4

Built up area
Economic sub - region
New Town
Expanding Town
Comprehensive phys. plann.
Economic rehabilitation area
Area for indus. devel.
Indus. growth centre
Surface mineral workings
Ironstone, SG Sand & gravel
Collieries 1970   miners
>1000, + 600 - 1000, + <600
National park
Amenity area
Motorway and A1M
Motorway (projected)
Route for development
Freightliner terminal
                          (P proposed)
Airport

Major direction for growth
1 Nottingham / Derbyshire
2 Eastern Lowlands
3 Leicester
4 Northamptonshire

Scale 25km

WEST MIDLANDS

1 Conurbation B Birmingham W Wolverhampton
2 Warwickshire
3 Worcestershire
4 East Shropshire
5 Central Staffordshire
6 East Staffordshire
7 North Staffordshire
8 West Shropshire
9 Herefordshire

Peak District
STOKE - ON - TRENT
Whitchurch
M6
Oswestry
Shrewsbury
Shropshire Hills
Kidd.
Hereford
Brecon Beacons
Malvern Hills
M50
Burton
COVENTRY
Rugby
Warwick   R.L.Spa   M45
Stratford
Evesham
Cotswolds
M5

Built up area
Admin. sub - region (1971)
New Town
Option population, 1966 - 2001
50,000
30,000   Natural increase
              1966 - 81 shaded
10,000
1966 -   1981 -
81   2001
Future industrial zones
Areas of Special Control
Collieries 1970   miners
>1000, + 600 - 1000, + <600
National park
Area of outstand. nat. beauty
Motorways
Proposed motorway box
Airport

Option population areas
1 Chelmsley Wd.   12 Stoke
2 Redditch   13 Location 3
3 N. Worc.   14 Lichfield
4 Droitwich   15 Stafford
5 Telford   16 Cannock
6 Staffs.   17 Solihull
7 Daventry   18 Coventry
8 Tamworth   19 Rugby
9 Location 1   20 Worcester
10 Location 2   21 Herefordsh.
11 Burton   22 County Land
                            23 Other Rural

Figure 1.13   The Midlands

rail links. It is equally well-connected to the national power systems, and has the most striking regional concentration of thermal electricity generation. The industrial structure has strong representation of key national growth industries, in engineering and electrical products, and its industrial cities are sufficiently close-knit to permit linkages and economies of scale to develop. The strong population growth trend is a stimulus to further economic development, and regional unemployment levels have been consistently below the national average. Unlike the W Midlands or the SE, the E Midlands has no single massive and congested conurbation to dominate its development strategy. Not least among its many assets are reserves of space for industrial and urban development, or redeployment of people and work. It includes, furthermore, one of the most prosperous agricultural areas of Europe. Provided its economy remains vigorous and well-balanced, on which serious doubts surfaced in the mid-1970s, the region should make a growing contribution to national prosperity and may well accommodate a significantly larger share of the UK population by the end of the century.

On the other hand the region is somewhat lacking in coherence, not only by virtue of its internal diversity, but also because there are powerful and independent economic influences just beyond its borders. The metropolitan influence is strongly felt in the Northampton sub-region, only 96 km from London, and its growth potential has also to be measured against that of nearby Milton Keynes or Peterborough. The influence of Sheffield penetrates southwards to Chesterfield, whilst Greater Birmingham is a powerful magnet to the south-west of the region. In many ways the divided state of Lincolnshire is the most vexatious of all. Until the transfer of S Lindsey to the E Midlands in 1974, Lincoln remained very much a border town. Today, with the building of the Humber bridge it will be more closely linked with Humberside. In the face of these many conflicting pulls around the perimeter the E Midlands has sought a corporate identity with the creation of many regional bodies and the strengthening of others. Nevertheless the city-based loyalties are strong and local government reform, establishing fewer, larger units, is likely to prove a valuable precursor to more effective regional planning.

Diversity in the E Midlands economy has overall been a force for stability, but not all parts of the region are prosperous or have equal prospects. There are declining coalfield settlements in both the Erewash valley and in Leicestershire and a general sub-regional employment restructuring problem in many parts of the E Midlands coalfield. The decrease in agricultural jobs has led to unemployment and out-migration, particularly in the Eastern Lowlands sub-region, whilst job loss in traditional industries, such as hosiery or footwear, affects the fortunes of specialized towns outside the main Nottingham—Derby—Leicester manufacturing belt. However the regional planners are confident that, with the intermediate area status granted to the most seriously affected localities in 1969 and extended both in 1972 (N Lincolnshire, High Peak) and 1974 (Chesterfield) (fig. 1.4) the E Midlands has sufficient growth momentum to take care of most of these problems within its borders. There is, however, likely to be some difficulty in phasing employment growth in newer industries, such as electrical goods or light engineering, with redundancies in declining industries, and in creating the new jobs within daily travelling distance of the old. In particular, there is the prospect of large redundancies in the Nottinghamshire coalfield; but the area of most rapid employment growth is to be in the Northampton sub-region. Here there will be competition with the overspill population scheduled to come from the Greater

London area.

The population growth momentum of the E Midlands is due to accelerate to 3.87 million by 1981 and 4.0 million by 1986. Already between 1961 and 1970 some 6,000 net migrants were being added annually (1971—73 +7,000 per annum), and natural increase rates in a population with a youthful age structure were high. On the most optimistic estimates net in-migration will rise to 15,000 per annum up to 1981, with no allowance made for the likely effects of immigration from overseas. The population capacities for growth by 1981 are high in all sub-regions: Northampton +200,000, with a strong in-migration of overspill population; Leicester +115,000; Nottingham—Derby +355,000, and the Eastern Lowlands +60,000. There are likely to be two powerful constraints, however, arising from the massive public investment which would be required to effect such dramatic changes, and the uncertainty as to the volume and intentions of mobile industries in a period during which development areas have been assured of a continuing priority for government locational aid. Nevertheless, 1970—5, the E Midlands population rose by 7.5 per cent.

The prospects for growth in *employment* are the most impressive in engineering and the electrical industries, though a shadow has recently passed over the prospects for aero-engine manufacture. Engineering in particular is extremely diverse and there are many growth firms, both large and small. Such an industrial group is polygamous in its linkages but generally capable of being persuaded to locate in the interests of regional planning. Chemical manufactures are under-represented, with only one firm making man-made fibres. The textile and footwear industries, with more than one-fifth of all jobs, were in deep recession in the mid-1970s, with further closures and rationalization likely. It is however rather to the possibilities of fast growth in services that attention has been turning recently (Burrows and Town 1971). Hitherto the ratio in service jobs has been below the national average (45 per cent, E Midlands; 55.2 per cent, national 1973), but it has been estimated that by 1981 perhaps one-quarter of the regional labour force may be in office employment. Rejuvenation of areas with declining industries, though, will still be dependent on attracting mobile manufacturing units, the base upon which service and office jobs can develop. The proposed pattern of physical development includes concentration of some of the growth originating in Derby or Nottingham into the Alfreton—Mansfield area, and part of that from Sheffield into the Chesterfield—Worksop area; the continued expansion of Leicester as a free-standing town and Loughborough as a technological centre; the creation of a new industrial sub-region around Northampton; and a readiness to encourage small developments in Newark, Grantham and possibly other Lincolnshire towns as a base for later expansion.

The **Northampton sub-region** is likely to show the most dramatic growth during the next decade (MHLG 1966 A and B) principally as the result of overspill schemes from the SE and W Midlands. At Northampton the target of the Development Corporation is for expansion from 124,000 to between 213,000 and 222,000 by 1981; at Corby NT from 43,000 to 87,000 by 1989 and 105,000 by 1998; at Wellingborough from 31,860 to 91,000 by 1981; and at Daventry from 6,690 to 36,600 during the same period. Growth is expressed in population terms rather than in rate of prospective job expansion. With the limited range of mobile industry nationally and the built-in problems of decline in the footwear industry, which employs 40 per cent of those in manufacturing and is dominant at Wellingborough and Kettering, there is also clearly going to be a difficult restructuring problem. The targets for Corby are the only figures to have firm Ministerial approval as yet, but there also is a need for diversification in an over-specialized steel town, with an inadequate range of jobs for both men and women.

The **Leicester sub-region** may well contain one million people by the end of the century. During the period 1951–66 employment rose sharply, in spite of contractions in agriculture, the hosiery and footwear industries, and a stringent policy on the release of IDCs. Growth came mostly from the establishment of new industries such as light engineering, electronics and some of the distributive trades, the latter strongly influenced by the northward extension of the M1. The sub-regional plan (Leicester City Co. and County Co. 1969) recommended concentration of expected growth in and around Greater Leicester, with emphasis on suburban locations. It also proposed the development of two growth corridors, a more substantial one to the north-west, linking up with and diffusing growth towards the declining coalfield, and a lesser corridor towards the south-west.

Nottingham and **Derby** are the complementary industrial poles of their sub-region, which includes half the population and many of the more serious problems of the E Midlands. Nottingham has the more diverse economy, with emphasis on lighter consumer goods, including textiles and tobacco; Derby is a centre for capital goods, with half its manufacturing employment in vehicles, 8 per cent in textiles and 7 per cent in engineering. Northwards there stretches a compact mining and industrial zone, linking in the north with the outskirts of Sheffield. Within this zone the western portion, in the Erewash and Rother valleys, has the more difficult problems of landscape and settlement renewal, restructuring of employment and stabilization of communities in an area where coal mining and industrial decline have been endemic. Further east the collieries are larger but mining decline has spread and there is a need for balanced employment to be brought in for settlements which are scattered, shapeless, and often deficient in basic amentities. Prospects for this area are strengthened by its location astride the M1 routeway and the London–Leeds rail line.

The *Nottinghamshire–Derbyshire sub-regional study* (1969) ambitiously recommended a major growth zone for the Mansfield–Alfreton area, with new city forms and a population which might rise to at least 260,000 by 1986 and maybe 350,000 by the end of the century. The functions of Nottingham and Derby were to develop in complementary fashion, whilst other growth points were recommended for West Hallam, west of Ilkeston (for some growth from Derby or Nottingham), and between Staveley and Renishaw.

As in so many economic planning regions the **E Lowlands is** a somewhat neglected rural counterpart to the urban-industrial complex in the west. The local economy is based on agriculture, particularly so along the eastern coastal area where the local market town economy has been undermined by reductions in manpower. The *E Lowlands sub-regional study* (Fennell 1971) distinguishes this more rural zone as having sparse population, low density of small or dispersed settlements, low rateable values and small-scale local finances. Depopulation has been continuing, but the Holland CC has worked out an ingenious and inter-related pattern of rural growth points for stabilizing the rural economy (Holland CC 1970). A transitional zone in the western half of the lowlands comes under the influence of towns either on its periphery or outside the E Midlands. The Economic Planning Council speaks cautiously of growth possibilities at Grantham, Newark and Retford along the main communications axis, but higher priorities are likely to be conferred elsewhere. The expansion of Peterborough and the major estuarine growth potential on south Humberside also cast their shadows.

The latest economic review (E Midlands EPC 1976) expressed concern at an unemployment percentage which had risen to the national average, and was more severe in localities such as Alfreton, Corby, Leicester and Newark. Nevertheless, the capacity of agriculture to expand under a more favourable economic climate was confidently assessed, but attention was drawn to the need for further rationalization in the textile industry. The prospects for steel-making at Corby were considered secure at least until the early 1980s, but it was engineering industries which had the greatest potential for growth. It was argued that the E Midlands had suffered because its problems were not recognized under assisted areas policy, dominated by the unemployment indicator, and that competition from assisted areas was constraining recovery in the region.

West Midlands (fig. 1.13)

In the general nature of their regional development problems the W Midlands have certain features in common with the SE. Both have traditionally been areas of faster and, until recently, stable economic growth, with lower than average unemployment and a persistent attraction for migrants from other areas of the UK or from overseas. Each has at its heart a major conurbation, Birmingham–Black Country and Greater London respectively. With rather more than 40 per cent of the regional population in the statutory conurbation in each case (Birmingham–Black Country, 45 per cent; Greater London 42 per cent, 1974) the problems of these great city clusters dominate those of the region, and tend to take precedence, some would say excessively so, in the formulation of regional strategies. Furthermore the W Midlands has shared with the SE a nodal location on the main axes of economic growth in the UK since the early 1930s, later confirmed by the development of the motorway network and the electrification of the main railway route north-west from Euston. In both cases the conurbations and their hinterlands are so bound into the national economy, and provide so much of its growth momentum and potential, that it is vital that the strategies for both regions should develop from a framework of national rather than regional growth priorities. Policies for each of these growth regions should seek to maximize their contribution to the solution of regional problems elsewhere in the UK, but without detriment to their own prospects and with adequate priority for meeting their own difficult internal problems of redistributing a growing volume of people and work. The complicated balancing act implied by what seem at first sight conflicting objectives can be interpreted through successive phases of post-war government location policies, but the overall interim verdict must be that the compromise achieved thus far has indeed benefited the development areas, but now begins to threaten the vital growth momentum in the Midlands and the SE and their potential for powering major inter-regional shifts of economic growth between now and the end of the century.

There are, however, significant differences in scale, industrial and services structure, location and overseas role as between the W Midlands and the SE. The W Midlands with 5.17 million people (1975) has less than one-third the population of the SE, and the Birmingham–Black Country conurbation, 2.3 millions in 1971, is only one-third the size of Greater London. The W Midlands and the SE share an economic structure with diverse fast-growth sectors but the composition is essentially different: W Midlands, 45 per cent in manufacturing, 44 per cent in services (1973), the SE 28 per cent and 66 per cent respectively. The national and international role of Greater London needs no emphasizing, but it contrasts with a greater dependence on manufacturing, and indeed on a narrower range of industries in the W Midlands. Not only has Greater London long been the seat of national decision-taking, but it has also had an economic structure less vulnerable to the growth restriction on manufacturing industry which has been the fundament of government location policies for the two regions since the war.

Growth axes Two issues are thus peculiarly important for effective regional planning in the W Midlands: the extent to which economic, and particularly industrial growth generated in the region can be used to regional rather than national advantage; and the growth pressures likely to be generated along the communications axes passing through the region. A correct assessment on both will determine the degree of success of both the sector and the spatial regional strategies published in 1971 (W Midlands EPC 1971, W Midlands Regional Study 1971). The north-west to south-east axis is dominant at present and confirmed by the M1–M6 line and the Euston–Manchester–Glasgow electrification scheme; any major growth on Deeside would weight this axis westwards. The north-east to south-west axis may in the longer-term have no less significant effects, if there are ever to be fast-growth estuarine developments on Humberside and/or on Severnside. The 1971 strategy also refers to a U-shaped axis from Merseyside through the W Midlands and northwards to Sheffield, encompassing urban centres with common problems and constraints, which might be relieved by a coherent policy for growth. The effect of nodal position in relation to these axes has been to generate growth and to channel it along corridors radiating from the conurbation, whilst reducing travel times and permitting greater mobility and flexibility in strategic proposals.

Economic growth potential As always the problems and potential for growth are concerned with people and work. The W Midlands have long had a natural increase rate above the average, a youthful population with a strong representation of young adults, and an overall net in-migration balance. 1961–70 the population rose by 5 per cent and there was an average net in-migration of 6,000 persons per annum; gross migration flows were considerably more, some 100,000 passing across the region's boundaries between 1961 and 1966 alone, some 250,000 leaving and 210,000 entering the region 1966–71. This was double the rate of net loss 1961–6 and represented a considerable rise in gross mobility. From 1971–3 the rate of population growth slowed markedly to +0.25 per cent per annum whilst migration ran at a net loss of 2,000 persons per annum. The 1973 OPCS projection envisaged a net out-migration rising to 12,000 per annum for 1975–6 and as high as −14,000 per annum thereafter. From 1966–71 78,000 immigrants from abroad entered the region, 59 per cent settling in the conurbation, where serious problems of stress and deprivation were already apparent among the immigrant community. Even with the reduced longer-term population targets for the end of the century the W Midlands are likely to have 6.4 millions, with 40 per cent of the growth coming before 1981.

The scale and problem implied by such a growth-rate is underlined by the fact that much of it will be generated within the conurbation, which already has major problems of congestion and continuing renewal. As in London a conurbation containment policy has been advocated since the early post-war years (Wise 1972; DEA 1965; W Midlands EPC 1967; Coventry CC et al 1971) but this has already resulted

in a major overspill issue which will become more dramatic between now and the
end of the century. Thus far relief by overspill redistribution has indeed been
modest, only 25,000 being moved by planned overspill between 1945 and 1965. The
estimated overspill population to be relocated between 1966 and the end of the
century is no less than 867,000, some 154,000 being moves between sub-regions
outside the conurbation. The sheer scale of such redistribution is staggering; the
fine tuning needed to redistribute work, of the right variety, to the right places at
the right time, is no less problematical. It is indeed the relative immobility of workplaces allied with outward dispersal of Birmingham—Black Country residences, that
explains the sharp rise in commuting to work, no less than 58 per cent of movements using the private car (1966, 83,500; 1981, estimated 190,000; 2001,
estimated 330,000). The impracticability of accommodating such a massive
journey to work is a determining imperative in any strategy formulation.

The economic prosperity of the W Midlands rests essentially upon four manufacturing sectors: engineering and electrical goods, £486 million net output 1968;
vehicles, £426 million; metal goods, £309 million; and metal manufactures, £263
million. Together these provided 70 per cent of the net output in all manufacturing,
and the region has long been distinctive for its pattern of close and proliferating
industrial linkages. This has made manufacturers reluctant to develop new capacity
outside the region, or indeed in many cases even outside the conurbation. 1961—71
employment in metal-using industries fell by 5 per cent, in pottery manufacture by
17 per cent; jobs in professional and scientific services rose by 50 per cent over the
same period. The extent of sub-regional specialization by industry is well-known
and introduces further rigidities: the conurbation, with metal-using industries,
motor vehicle manufacture, electrical engineering, metal manufacture and small
metal fabrication; the Coventry belt, with motor vehicles, electrical and mechanical
engineering and aerospace industries; N Staffordshire, with pottery manufacture,
engineering and electrical goods. Immobility tends to be underpinned by the
localization of skilled labour and, for all these reasons, industrial moves have been
fewer than desirable to fulfil regional planning objectives. Between 1960 and 1965
only 1,000 per annum went to other sub-regions, though it is expected that 29,000
manufacturing and 37,000 service jobs might be moved out between 1967 and
1981. Restructuring of industry is continuing within the conurbation but newer
kinds of employment tend to grow rather in areas where decline is reducing labour
in traditional employment. The greatest pressures for growth are on the conurbation rim and it is there that the 1971 strategy envisages regrouped major industrial
zones.

The *1971 strategy* appeared in two separate studies: an economic appraisal from
the regional Economic Planning Council and a more general strategy from the local
authorities' planning consortium. The Planning Council study makes a strong case
for greater regional powers to promote economic growth and greater autonomy for
local industrialists to choose their locations. It also emphasizes that the economic
health of the conurbation is the most vital regional issue and that this should have
at least parity in shared economic growth with other sub-regions, New Towns or
expanded towns, for the remainder of this century. The argument is that the
advantages of agglomeration, the linkages and the growth prospects are greater in
the conurbation and that industry cannot easily be made more mobile without
unacceptable economic loss.

This thinking contrasts with that for Greater London or indeed even with that of the 1970 strategic plan for the SE, where decentralization and the development of powerful counter-magnets on the perimeter of the region are a major strategic proposal. The limited decentralization desirable from Birmingham and the Black Country is, however, a continuing theme in W Midlands regional planning since the war. Certainly the rezoning of industry in the five 'comprehensive redevelopment areas' of central Birmingham, or the clearance of dereliction in the Black Country are both impressive achievements, and the preservation of a green belt around the conurbation is no less so. On the other hand, the limited success in building up the New Towns at Telford (1968 in its present form) and Redditch (1964) and the small scale of overspill redistribution thus far make the 1971 plan seem remarkably ambitious.

The 1971 local authorities' study is exceptionally thoroughgoing. It defines an option population of 1,021,000 by the year 2001 which will need to be located in relation to the basic growth which is to be expected anyway. Fig. 1.13 shows the proposed allocation of the option population to twenty-three localities, differentiating the growth allocated for 1966–81 and that for 1981–2001. No less than 87 per cent of the growth is allocated to the 'central urban complex', a zone larger than the present conurbation and bounded by Stafford–Worcester–Telford-conurbation –Coventry. The locational pulls of the north-west to south east axis are admitted and the schemes already committed, e.g. at Chelmsley Wood, are reinforced by growth just outside the conurbation at locations 1 and 2. These developments will function as part of the conurbation in the early years due to limited employment mobility, but later will link with more distant sites. The Lichfield–Burton zone and growth in the Coventry belt are logical responses to economic development pressures, but there is no coordinated growth point policy for outer settlements or sub-regions. The study sees the urban fabric of the W Midlands as too closely-knit to permit islands of growth to develop independently.

The strategy is thus very conurbation-orientated, identifying there the nodal points for longer-term economic growth, even admitting the shorter-term and continuing problem of renewal, restructuring and elimination of pockets of serious deprivation. Around the central city activities there will be new industrial zones on the conurbation rim, flanked by service industry growth corridors from Solihull to Redditch on the south and Sutton Coldfield to Lichfield on the north.

Critique of the 1971 strategy documents has pointed out the absence of policies for the N Staffs sub-region or for the rural economies of the western and southern sub-regions. The impression is that what is good for the conurbation must be good for the W Midlands, just as what is good for the W Midlands must surely be in the national interest.

The *Monitoring document* (Jt. Monitoring Steering Gp. 1975) emphasized the importance of qualifying national policy for regions according to particular regional circumstances. In April 1975 the unemployment level in the W Midlands rose to equal the national level (4.6 per cent) for the first time. The troubles of major employers, including British Leyland, Chrysler (UK) and their component suppliers, highlighted a generally deteriorating situation, particularly so for male employment (Wood 1976).

The South East (fig. 1.14)
In April 1974 Dorset and part of Hampshire (total 1971 population 552,540) were transferred to the South West region. With almost one-third of the UK

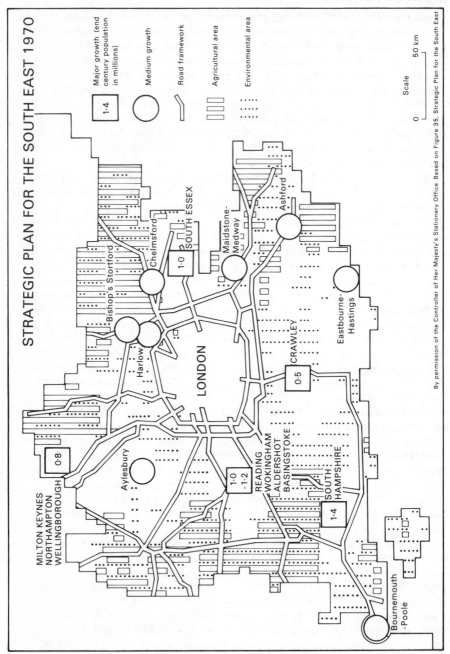

Figure 1.14   South East: Strategic Plan, 1970

population (1975 16.93 millions), the greatest concentration of fast-growth services and manufacturing, and the most favoured nodal location at the hub of radial communications network within the UK, facing Europe and overseas, it is not surprising that the SE is uniquely important in British regional planning. The basic issue is the extent to which Greater London is to be permitted to make its distinctive and vital contribution to the national economy, with least detriment and indeed maximum stimulus to policies of regional balance or social justice for other parts of the UK. Allied with this is the question of how, if at all, the growth pressures throughout the South East may or should be controlled or channelled, and how far the growth of Greater London should be restrained, not only in the interests of its citizens, but also those of the region and the nation.

There has been no unanimity of view on these matters. As far back as 1940 the *Barlow Report* (R. Commission 1940) spoke of 'the continued drift of the industrial population to London and the Home Counties as a social, economic and strategic problem demanding attention'. Between 1921 and 1951 there had been a 30 per cent growth in employment in Greater London compared with only 19 per cent nationally. The role of London had grown steadily, nationally and internationally, and there was fast growth in a wide range of manufacturing and services. The arguments against longer-term continuing growth concerned: physical and mental health, on both of which counts London came out well; overcrowding and poor housing, but slum clearance and urban renewal had greatly decreased this problem; air pollution and environmental hazards; the social costs of congestion, traffic and journey to work; strategic aspects of the vulnerability of large population concentrations; and wider issues, such as the promotion of regional balance in the UK or the rising strength of provincial regionalism (Hall 1963). Many of these issues are town planning problems, though indissolubly inter-linked with wider regional questions.

The *Greater London Plan* (Abercrombie 1945) set London within its regional context and ambitiously sought: first, to plan for a stabilized population of ten millions in the plan area; secondly, to reduce urban sprawl by establishing a green belt; thirdly, to reduce net residential density in London by a massive overspill programme to relocate some 750,000 from the LCC area and a further 500,000 from areas outside, to a ring of New Towns and expanded towns beyond the green belt. The plan was approved in 1947, with raised population targets, but several basic assumptions proved to be false. Employment was not effectively controlled by restrictions on new industries in the London area; indeed no less than 52 per cent of all new employment growth in the UK, 1952–8, took place in the SE and 32 per cent in London. Much of the manufacturing growth was in the outer urban ring whilst the inner ring lost jobs heavily; central London attracted much of the growth in services, and there was a massive increase in commuting, especially to office employment. Secondly, the overspill movement fell short of expectations: in 1946–61 the New Towns took 235,000 but not all came from London and many who did so commuted back to work; the expanded towns took only 28,000 through overspill schemes in the same period. Thus the interdiction policy on growth in London and the SE largely failed. The government did not press restrictions for fear of damaging national economic growth or the export trade. Many central services could not effectively be decentralized and, overall, the growth pressures had been much greater than anticipated. In particular, there had been an unexpected surge in the national birth-rate in the mid-1950s and a sharp influx of immigrants from overseas.

In the early 1960s a more rigorous restriction policy came through the *Local Employment Acts*, but the growth in service jobs continued largely unchecked, since only *new* office space was controlled. Growth was especially fast in technological services, design and development, and in new manufactures, such as light engineering, vehicles or electronics. Indeed economic growth generally was more rapid and structural than the plan process could accommodate. Between 1948 and 1959 and LCC had licensed no less than 5.3 million m^2 of new office space. There had been some movement out by manufacturing firms (−80,000 jobs, 1960–4) but these jobs were more than replaced by the growth in construction (+28,000) and services (+169,000) in the same period. The Outer Metropolitan Area beyond the GLC boundaries but within 64 km of London, increased in population by 40 per cent 1951–66, the product of the first generation of New Towns, the strong immigration from other parts of the UK and its own youthful age structure. The Outer South East began to grow more rapidly during the 1960s and regional planning has since become increasingly concerned with allocations of growth, in population and employment, as between the concentric zones around Greater London.

The *South East Study* (MHLG 1964) proposed a second generation of New Towns and major town expansions in the region, proposals which envisaged some very large concentrations of people and work between 80 and 160 km out from C London. Such major growth might create cities in their own right to act as a series of counter-magnets to the continuing attractions of agglomeration around Greater London. From 1965 office development throughout the metropolitan region was brought under official control, whilst in the following year creation of the SE Economic Planning Council strengthened the regional voice against that of Greater London.

The *South East Strategy* (SE EPC 1967) had similar policies, but added new priorities: the urban renewal of London; redesign of the transport system, with corridors and orbital roads; stimulus to the large new city regions, to act as counter-magnets to the metropolis; and protection of the countryside. If London was to be more efficient its growth should be restricted to not more than eight millions, whilst the remainder of the SE region should be able to absorb into employment not only its own natural increase, but also most of London's continuing overspill and, additionally, a much reduced immigration from other parts of the UK. Overspill movement by 1981 was estimated at about one million, to be accompanied by decentralization of work. For the first time overspill was programmed outside the regional boundaries: 500,000 to E Anglia and the E Midlands; internally, 200,000 to the OMA, and 300,000 to the OSE.

A more coherent spatial strategy was postulated by the proposals for radial growth along corridors linking Greater London with the counter-magnet cities. Within the corridors urban growth was to be concentrated in a few localities, and each corridor had parallel major and minor axes. Industrial investment was to be concentrated when possible into medium- and large-scale firms and commuting to London was to be reduced. Rural land was to be conserved, extending the concept underlying the green belt to all parts of the SE.

The 1967 Strategy thus sought to solve the problems inherent in prospective growth of population of four millions by the end of the century, through spatial allocation within the economic orbit, but not altogether within the boundaries of the SE. Such redeployment of growth was to improve the efficiency of the region, both nationally and internationally, but the effects upon the prospects for less-favoured regions were left uncertain. In short, the strategy of 1967 recognized that growth pressures in the SE were too great to be effectively countermanded, and that economic growth had displaced welfare as the fundament of regional policy.

The *Strategic Plan for the South East* (SE Jt. Planning Team 1970), with its reports of studies (DoE 1971), was the first definitive tripartite regional planning study, the product of central government, regional planning council and board, and local authorities. The strategy (fig. 1.14) was primarily concerned with the period after 1981, by which time the regional population was likely to be 18.6 million (+1.5 million), up to the year 2001 (estimated population 21.5 millions, +4.5 millions). By 1981 the Greater London population was likely to be 7.3 millions, that of the OMA 6.2 millions and the OSE 5.2 millions. In other words, there would be a decline in Greater London, a slower growth in the OMA and faster growth in the OSE.

A main feature of the 1971 strategy was confirmation of development at a limited number of major growth areas at varying distances from London, using existing or planned urban settlements as bases for growth. The far-sighted corridor concept was abandoned in favour of a more flexible strategy, to allocate growth both within and outside the London metropolitan region, according to the changing needs of the times. With slow growth, the three designated areas: Reading–Wokingham–Aldershot–Basingstoke; South Essex; and the Crawley area, were likely to absorb a higher proportion. If faster growth, then the South Hampshire (Buchanan 1966) or Milton Keynes–Northampton–Wellingborough schemes might be accelerated, so that these self-contained counter-magnet cities might play their role earlier and more substantially.

Additional flexibility in the plan was to come from the expansion of a number of medium-sized employment centres, which might be used to relieve unacceptable pressures in the major growth areas or compensate for failure to achieve desired rates of growth. Such smaller centres would also assist in the restructuring of the metropolitan region. Greater London was to 'accommodate the maximum number of residents consistent with the achievement of improved housing conditions and improved environmental standards at reasonable cost'. It was further intended to ensure that commuting did not increase further and this meant phasing the outward movement of jobs with that of population. Hitherto there had been optimism on this point, in contrast to the views for Birmingham and the Black Country. Tentative estimates were for 15,000–20,000 mobile jobs a year in manufacturing and a similar number in services needed to phase in with population growth in areas selected for substantial population growth. The consultants' advice was that all parts of the SE were acceptable to industrialists, provided labour was available and the environment reasonable. The strategy would succeed or fail on the ability to adjust job relocation with population redistribution. Its novelty lay in the flexible approach, even if the preferred development pattern was less imaginative and more permissive than the 1967 Strategy.

Greater London Published about the same time as the SPSE the *Greater London Development Plan, GLDP* (GLC 1969) was the prototype structure plan for what is certainly the most complex and large-scale planning unit in the UK. Its recommendations were subjected to a most searching critique in the *Panel of Inquiry (Layfield Report*, DoE 1973A), many, but not all, of whose criticisms were accepted by the government of the day (DoE 1973B). The problem of planning a major

conurbation within the context of its economic region is one common to five other
regions of the UK (table 1.6). The case of Greater London (1975 population 7.11
millions) within the SE (16.93 millions) is exceptional, however, both in scale and
and in the multifarious national and international roles played by the capital city.
To safeguard these vital roles by planning for a suitable level of growth, and its
allocation either within the conurbation or as between Greater London and the rest
of the SE is a difficult conceptual and management problem. The problem is greatly
aggravated by the lack of economic planning powers at GLC level, by the strength
of market forces generally in relation to limited powers of planning control on
allocations, and, thirdly, by the pressing and growing social problems within
Greater London.

The social problems of Greater London concern housing (quantity, quality and
cost), imbalance both structurally and spatially between labour supply and demand,
persistent localized pockets of severe unemployment (more than 7 per cent, 1975,
in some inner urban wards) and social deprivation, traffic congestion, and the
deteriorating general urban environment. Both the structural changes in employment
(table 1.7) and the net demographic changes (table 1.9) in Greater London have

TABLE 1.7

Greater London Employment Change, 1961–71, by Major Sectors

(in '000s)	GB	GLC Total	Manufs.	Professional & Scientific	Other services	Construc- tion
1961	22,373	4,664	1,604	975	1,780	305
1971	22,026	4,264	1,201	1,173	1,671	219
%	−1.5	−8.6	−25.1	+20.3	−6.1	−28.2

Source: London, Population and Employment, GLC 1975

been dramatic in recent times. On the other hand, the issue of ODPs was greatly
relaxed for Greater London 1966–81 (table 1.8).

TABLE 1.8

Greater London, ODPs 1966 and 1971

('000 m^2 floor space)

	London Central	Rest	OMA	Other SE	Total SE
1966	51.3	73.7	119.0	14.9	259.0
1971	605.1	539.1	442.8	454.2	2,021.3

Source: GLC 1975

The GLC Strategy is to provide for a more equal geographical spread of
employment opportunity, with a balanced structure of industry, commerce and
services to match the skills available in each area. Secondly, a determined attack
on the social polarization developing within Greater London is being made through

TABLE 1.9

SE Region: Population Change, 1951–73, by Economic Sub-regions

(average annual change in '000s)

	Natural change 1951–61	1961–71	1971–3	Migration 1951–61	1961–71	1971–3
Greater London	+33.3	+44.9	+17.8	–61.0	–98.2	–106.8
OMA	+24.2	+41.4	+28.1	+77.5	+43.8	+ 16.2
OSE	+ 8.9	+13.5	+ 3.4	+27.3	+50.6	+ 55.4
South East	+66.4	+99.6	+49.3	+43.8	– 3.7	– 35.2

Source: Annual Abstract of Regional Statistics 1974

housing policies as well as job provision. This task is made the more difficult as jobs in manufacturing decline and there is a steady net outflow of lower middle class and skilled workers from both Inner (ILEA) and Outer London. The prospective danger is that further social polarization will create an even larger elite in the central area, a greater commuting flow of office workers and professional people from the GLC periphery and beyond and a more marked concentration of low-paid unskilled workers and socially deprived households in an expanding, intervening belt. The GLC might then be unable to solve its mounting welfare problem and, for this reason among others, would wish to see a larger population retained and tertiary growth stimulated at twenty-two strategic (shopping) centres plus six *major* strategic centres, together with Brent Cross (fig. 6.6b). There is a paradox in that to create more congenial living conditions in Greater London fewer people should live there, but on the other hand without an enhanced employment base and a greater representation of medium- and higher-income groups the welfare problem will not be solved and community life will not improve. If the overspill areas were prepared — which has not hitherto been the case — to accept a balanced proportion of the aged, the poor and the unfortunate, the problem might be solved. If only the more able, the more skilled and the better paid continue to be attracted away the problem becomes steadily worse. In January 1976 the GLC ended its policy of dispersing population and jobs to areas outside the capital, declined to enter into any further 'overspill' agreements (ch. 2.IV.6) and sought to renegotiate a reduction in those already in force.

The Panel of Inquiry (*Layfield Report*, DoE 1973B) did not accept that the rate of decline in the GLC population should be slowed down, and argued that the imbalances in labour supply and demand were but transitional in their implications. This meant accepting 1981 population targets in the 6.3 to 6.8 million range rather than the 7.0 to 7.3 million advocated for that date by the GLC. Thus 30.000 per annum and not the 20,000 per annum proposed by the GLDP (1969) should be the planned overspill target. The ODP system was thought to be inappropriate and it was recommended that IDCs should be more freely available to firms which wished to move within London. The GLC policy for strategic growth centres was endorsed, but refined by the designation of four of the six major strategic centres as deliberate employment and not simply tertiary growth points, and the acceptance of all others as more local shopping and service centres. The need for an integrated GLC transport strategy was strongly underlined.

The government view (DoE 1973B) was that Greater London's population should be allowed to decline further, and that the rate of continuing decrease in employment as well as in population was of benefit both to those who leave and those who stay. The concentration policy for industries and offices was endorsed, but the recommendation to relax the IDC system was not acceptable, nor should powers over ODPs be transferred to the GLC. In May 1977 the ODP policy was relaxed.

Crucial to the effective spatial redeployment of population in the SE by 1991 are the volume of mobile jobs, and the nature and strength of public industrial location policies. It has been estimated (Stewart 1971) that 30,000—40,000 mobile jobs per annum will be needed for the SE, 1981—91, but that only 20,000 are likely to be available. The SPSE Team (1970) emphasized the need for maximum short- and medium-distance moves, since flows of more than 80 km would potentially conflict with assisted areas policy; yet longer-distance moves, e.g. to South Hampshire or South Essex would also be needed. The SE EPC would prefer more development at greater distances from London but, on balance, the *Strategic Plan* (SE Jt. Planning Team 1970), in principle at least, sees inter-regional (Assisted Areas) and intra-regional (South East) policies on industrial employment as complementary, and the spatial restructuring of the SE and the GLC area in particular as important and difficult objectives in their own right.

The *1976 Review* of the SPSE (SE Jt. Planning Team) took account of the now expected static population forecast for 1991, increasing migration of people and businesses out of London, and the general effect of economic recession. The problems of London were the centrepiece of the Review: bad housing; a significant proportion of the homeless; extensive areas of dereliction; pockets of high unemployment and low income; congested roads and inadequate public transport services; and high costs for land, housing, rents, rates and labour. The principle of five major and six medium-growth areas outside Greater London was confirmed, but the rates of growth in such urban clusters would need to be contingent upon what happened in London. For the first time since the *Abercrombie Plan* (1944) the need to restrain rather than promote the flow of people and industry out of London became a prime objective for the regional planners. Indeed it was argued that planning policies for London should be changed to encourage industrial development. IDCs and ODPs should be abolished for those wishing to develop in London. Indeed in 1977 the Location of Offices Bureau was instructed to be more flexible in its policies.

V.6   A Final Note

The review of regional strategies indicates the diversity of policy mixes, the different stages of preparation and indeed varied degrees of forcefulness in presentation and advocacy. None of the strategies published thus far has been fully costed, all lack adequate context of national priorities, and there is a conspicuous absence of sufficient liaison between adjacent economic planning boards and councils in the formulation of what at times appear to be mutually conflicting proposals. Furthermore, it is only since 1969 that published strategies have quantified and weighed alternative options. The techniques have been lacking until recently and it must be said that, even today, when a preferred strategy is advanced it tends to bear the hallmarks of political compromise.

Yet the strategy documents illustrate the growing potential of corporate regionalism, a sense of economic, social or political identity at less than UK but more than local authority level. Just as governments in the future need to set a more adequate framework for spatial, economic and social affairs nationally, with more coherent regional priorities, so too these priorities will need increasingly to take account of the legitimate aspirations of the component nations and provinces of the UK space to a fuller, more prosperous life and a better living environment.

FURTHER READING

ALDCROFT, D H and FEARON, P (1969) *Economic Growth in Twentieth-Century Britain*, London

BECKERMAN, W et al (1965) 'The British Economy in 1975', *Natn. Inst. Soc. and Econ. Res., Econ. and Soc. Stud., 23*, Cambridge

CHISHOLM, M D I (ed) (1972) *Resources for Britain's Future*, Harmondsworth

LIVINGSTONE, J M (1974) *The British Economy in Theory and Practice*, London

LONDON and CAMBRIDGE ECON. SERV. (1973) *The British Economy, Key Statistics, 1900–66*, Cambridge

PREST, A R (1970) *The UK Economy: a Manual of Applied Economics*, London

YOUNGSON, A J (1968) *Britain's Economic Growth, 1920–66*, London

REFERENCES

All references to political change are to be found in section IV; regional references are under section V

General, and Sections I–III

ARCHIBALD, G C (1967) 'Regional Multiplier Effects in the UK', *Oxford Econ. Pap., 19*, 1, 22–45

BAKER, J N L and GILBERT, E W (1944) 'The Doctrine of an Axial Belt in England', *Geogrl. J., 103*, 49–71

BEST, R H (1959) *The Major Land Uses in Britain*, Wye College, Ashford

BEST, RH and COPPOCK, J T (1962) *The Changing Uses of Land in Britain*, London

BoT (Board of Trade) (1968) *Local Employment Acts 1960 to 1966: 8th Annual Report*, HMSO

BROOK, C and HAY, A (1974) 'Export Base Theory and the Growth and Decline of Regions', unit 4 in *Reg. Analysis and Devel., 2*, Open Univ.

BROWN, A J (1972) *The Framework of Regional Economics in the UK*, Cambridge

BUCK, T W and ATKINS, M H (1976) 'The Impact of British Regional Policies on Employment Growth', *Oxford Econ. Pap., 28*, 118–32

CAMERON, G C (1974) 'Regional Economic Policy in the UK', in SANT, M (ed) *Regional Policy and Regional Planning for Europe*, Farnborough

CARRUTHERS, W I (1957) 'A Classification of Service Centres in England and Wales', *Geogrl. J., 123*, 371–85
                (1962) 'Service Centres in Greater London', *Tn. Plann. Rev., 22*, 4, 345–56

CHAMPION, A G (1974) 'An Estimate of the Changing Extent and Distribution of Urban Land in England and Wales, 1959–70', *Centre for Environ. Stud., Res. Pap. 10*

CHISHOLM, M D I (1971) 'Freight Costs, Industrial Location and Regional Development', ch. 8 in CHISHOLM, M and MANNERS, G (eds) *Spatial Policy Problems of the British Economy*, Cambridge, 213–44

(1974) 'Regional Policies for the 1970s', *Geogrl. J., 140, 2,* 215–44

(1976) 'Regional Growth Policies in an Era of Slow Population Growth and Higher Unemployment', *Reg. Stud., 10,* 201–13

CHISHOLM, M D I and MANNERS, G (eds) (1971) *Spatial Policy Problems of the British Economy*, Cambridge

CHISHOLM, M D I and OEPPEN, J (1973) *The Changing Pattern of Employment. Regional Specialisation and Localisation in Britain*, London

CIVIL SERVICE DEPT (1973) *Dispersal of Government Work from London* (Hardman Report), Cmnd 5322 HMSO

COATES, B E and RAWSTRON, E M (1967) 'Regional Income and Planning, 1964–5', *Geogr., 52,* 393–402

(1971) *Regional Variations in Britain*, London

COMMN. EUROPEAN COMMUNITIES (1975) *General Regional Aid Systems*, COM (75) 77, Brussels

COMMN. PUBLIC PARTICIPATION IN PLANNING (1969) *People and Planning* (Skeffington Report), HMSO

DoE (Dept of Environment) (1971) *Long Term Population Distribution in GB*, HMSO

D T I (Dept Trade and Industry) (1972) *Industrial and Regional Development*, Cmnd 4942, HMSO

DIAMOND, D R (1974) 'The Long-Term Aim of Regional Policy' in SANT, M (ed) *Regional Policy and Planning for Europe*, Farnborough, 217–23

DIXON, R J and THIRLWALL, A P (1975) *Regional Growth and Unemployment in the UK*, London

DURY, G H (1968) *The British Isles: a Systematic and Regional Geography*, London

FAWCETT, C B (1919) *Provinces of England and Wales*, revised by East, W G and Wooldridge, S W (1961), London

FORDHAM, R C (1974) 'Measurement of Urban Land Use', *Univ. Cambridge, Dept. Land Econ., Occ. Pap. 1*

GREEN, F H W (1950) 'Urban Hinterlands in England and Wales. An Analysis of Bus Services', *Geogrl. J., 116,* 64–88

(1952) 'Bus Services as an Index to Changing Urban Hinterlands', *Tn. Plann. Rev., 22, 4,* 345–56

GRIEVE, R and ROBERTSON, D J (1964) 'The City and the Region', *Univ. Glasgow, Soc. & Econ. Stud., Occ. Pap. 2*

HALL, P G (1971) 'Spatial Structures of Metropolitan England and Wales', ch. 5 in CHISHOLM, M and MANNERS, G (eds) *Spatial Policy Problems of the British Economy*, Cambridge, 96–125

HALL, P G, GRACEY, H, DREWETT, R and THOMAS, R (1973) *The Containment of Urban England*, London, 2 vols

HALLETT, G, RANDALL, P and WEST, E G (1973) 'Regional Policy for Ever?', Readings *II Inst. Econ. Affairs*

HART, P E and MACBEAN, A I (1961) 'Regional Differences in Productivity, Profitability and Growth', *Scott. J. Pol. Econ., 8*, 1–11

HEMMING, M F W (1963) 'The Regional Problem', *Natn. Inst. Econ. Rev., 25,* 40–57

HIRSCHMAN, A O (1958) *The Strategy of Economic Development*, New Haven

HOBSON, A C (1951) 'The Great Industrial Belt', *Econ. J., 51,* 562–76

HOLLAND, S (1976) *Capital versus the Regions*, London

HOUSE, J W (1966) 'Margins in Regional Geography: an Illustration from Northern England' in HOUSE, J W (ed) *Northern Geographical Essays*, Newcastle upon Tyne, 139–56

　　　　(1969) 'Future Trends of Regionalism in Britain', *Br. J. Marketing, 3,* 176–82

　　　　(1973) 'Geographers, Decision-takers, and Policy Makers', in CHISHOLM, M and RODGERS, B (eds) *Essays in Human Geography*, London, 272–305

　　　　(1976) 'UK Marginal Regions in the Context of EEC Policies', ch. 11 in LEE, R and OGDEN, P E (eds) *Economy and Society in the EEC: Spatial Perspectives*, Farnborough, 194–216

KEEBLE, D (1976) *Industrial Location and Planning in the UK*, London

KNOX, P L (1974) 'Spatial Variations in Level of Living in England and Wales in 1961', *Trans. Inst. Br. Geogr., 62*, 1–24

　　　　(1975) 'Social Well-being: a Spatial Perspective', *Theory and Practice in Geography*, Oxford

LOCATION OF OFFICES BUREAU (1972) *Annual Report 1971–2*, London

McCRONE, R G L (1969) *Regional Policy in Britain*, London

　　　　(1972) 'The Location of Economic Activity in the UK', *Urban Stud., 9*, 369–75

MANNERS, G et al (1972) *Regional Development in Britain*, Chichester

MINIST. OF TRANSPORT (1963) *The Reshaping of British Railways* (Beeching Report), HMSO

MOORE, B C and RHODES, J (1973) 'Evaluating the Effects of British Regional Economic Policy', *Econ. J., 83*, 329, 87–110

　　　　(1974) 'Regional Policy and the Scottish Economy', *Scott. J. Pol. Econ., XXI, 3,* 215–35

　　　　(1976) 'Regional Economic Policy and the Movement of Manufacturing Firms to the Development Areas', *Economica, 43,* 17–31

MOSELEY, M J (1974) *Growth Centres in Spatial Planning*, Oxford

MOSER, C A and SCOTT, W (1961) *British Towns: a Statistical Study of their Social and Economic Differences*, Edinburgh

MYRDAL, G (1957) *Economic Theory and Underdeveloped Regions*, London

NATN. INST. SOC. and ECON. RES. (1963) 'The Regional Problem', *Natn. Inst. Econ. Rev., 25*, 40–57

NEEDLEMAN, L (1965) 'What are we to do about the Regional Problem?', *Lloyds Bank Rev., 75*, 45–58

NEVIN, E T (1972) 'Europe and the Regions', *Three Banks Rev., 94*, 54–78

O'SULLIVAN, P (1971) 'Forecasting inter-regional freight flows in GB' in

CHISHOLM, M et al *Regional forecasting*, London, 443–50
PUBL. GEN. ACTS See list p. 516
RENTON, G A (1974) *Modelling the Economy*, London
RHODES, J and KHAN, A (1971) 'Office Dispersal and Regional Policy', *Univ. Cambridge, Dept. Applied Econ., Occ. Pap., 30*
RICHARDSON, H W (1969) *Regional Economics*, London
ROBERTSON, D J (1965) 'A Nation of Regions?', *Urban Stud., 2*, 121–36
ROY. COMMN. LOCAL
ROY. COMMN. LOCAL GOVT. IN ENGLAND 1966–9 (1969) (Redcliffe-Maud) *Report*, Cmnd 4040 HMSO, 3 vols.
SAIGAL, J C (1965) *The Choice of Sectors and Regions*, Rotterdam
SEC. STATE ECONOMIC AFFAIRS (1969) *The Intermediate Areas*, (Hunt Report) Cmnd 3998, HMSO
SEC. STATE INDUSTRY (1975) *Industry Act 1972, Annual Rep. for Year ended 31 Mar. 1975*, HMSO
SEC. STATE TRADE and INDUSTRY (1972) *Industrial and Regional Development*, Cmnd 4942 HMSO
SELF, P (1965) 'North versus South', *Tn. Ctry. Plann., 33*, 330–6
SENIOR, D (ed) (1966) *The Regional City*, London
SMAILES, A E (1944) 'The Urban Hierarchy in England and Wales', *Geogr., 29*, 41–51
            (1946) 'The Urban Mesh of England and Wales', *Trans. Inst. Brit. Geogr., 11*, 87–101
            (1947) 'The Analysis and Delimitation of Urban Fields', *Geogr., 32*, 151–61
SMITH, W (1949) *An Economic Geography of GB*, London
STAMP, L D (1962) *The Land of Britain: its Use and Misuse*, London
STAMP, L D and BEAVER, S H (1971) *The British Isles: a Geographic and Economic Survey*, London
STILWELL, F J B (1972) *Regional Economic Policy*, London
TURNBULL, P (1967) 'Regional Economic Planning Councils and Boards', *J. Tn. Plann. Inst., London, 53*, 41–9
WATSON, J W and SISSONS, J B (eds) (1964) *The British Isles: a Systematic Geography*, Edinburgh
WIBBERLEY, G P (1954) 'Some Aspects of Problem Areas in Britain', *Geogrl. J., 120*, 43–61
WILKINSON, R K and RAINNIE, G F (1970) 'Criteria for Regional Policy', *Tn. Plann. Rev., 41*, 207–22
WILSON, A G (1974) *Urban and Regional Models in Geography and Planning*, London
WILSON, T (1964) 'Policies for Regional Development', *Univ. Glasgow, Soc. and Econ. Stud., Occ. Pap., 3*
            (ed) (1965) *Papers on Regional Development*, Oxford
WISE, M J (1966) 'The City Region', *Advmt. Sci., 22*, 104, 571–88
WOODWARD, V H and BOWERS, J (1970) 'Regional Social Accounts for the United Kingdom', *NIESR Reg. Rep. I*, Cambridge

Section IV New Patterns for Democracy

BUSTEED, M R (1975) 'Geography and Voting Behaviour', *Theory and Practice in Geography*, Oxford

FREEMAN, T W (1968) *Geography and Regional Administration*, London

GILBERT, E W (1939) 'Practical Regionalism in England and Wales', *Geogrl. J.*, *94*, 29–44

(1948) 'Boundaries of Local Government Areas', *Geogrl. J.*, *111*, 172–206

GOVT. N. IRELAND (1967) *The Reshaping of Local Government: Statement of Aims*, Cmnd 517 Belfast HMSO

(1969) *The Reshaping of Local Government: Further Proposals*, Cmnd 530 Belfast HMSO

HOUSE OF COMMONS (1974) *Democracy and Devolution – Proposals for Scotland and Wales*, Cmnd 5732 HMSO

(1975) *Our Changing Democracy: Devolution to Scotland and Wales*, Cmnd 6348 HMSO. Supplementary Statement, Cmnd 6585

JAMES, J R, HOUSE, J W and HALL, P G (1970) 'Local Government Reform in England', *Geogrl. J.*, *136*, 1, 1–23

JOHNSON, J H (1970) 'Reorganisation of Local Government in Northern Ireland', *Area*, *4*, 17–21

LOCAL GOVT. BOUNDARY COMMN. FOR ENGLAND – DESIGNATE (1972) *Memorandum on Draft Proposals for New Districts in the English Non-Metropolitan Counties proposed in the Local Government Bill*, HMSO

MACKINTOSH, J P (1968) *The Devolution of Power*, Harmondsworth

OFFICE OF LORD PRES. OF COUNCIL (1976) *Devolution: the English Dimension*, HMSO

PHILIP, A B (1975) *The Welsh Question*, Univ. Wales

PUBL. GEN. ACTS See list p. 516

REV. BODY ON LOCAL GOVT. IN N. IRELAND (1970) *Report*, Cmnd 546 Belfast HMSO

ROY. COMMN. CONSTITUTION 1969–73 (1973) (Kilbrandon) *Report*, Cmnd 5460 HMSO

ROY. COMMN. DISTRIBUTION INDUSTRIAL POPUL. (1940) (Barlow) *Report*, Cmnd 6513 HMSO

ROY. COMMN. LOCAL GOVT. IN ENGLAND 1966–9 (1969) (Redcliffe-Maud) *Report*, Cmnd 4040 HMSO, 3 vols

ROY. COMMN. LOCAL GOVT. IN GREATER LONDON 1957–60 (1960) *Report*, Cmnd 1164 HMSO

ROY. COMMN. LOCAL GOVT. IN SCOTLAND (1969) (Wheatley Commn.), *Report*, Cmnd 4150 Edinburgh HMSO, 2 vols

SCOTT. OFF. (1971) *Reform of Local Government in Scotland*, Cmnd 4583 Edinburgh HMSO

SEC. STATE ENVIRONMENT (1971) *Local Government in England. Government Proposals for Reorganisation*, Cmnd 4584 HMSO

SEC. STATE LOCAL GOVT. AND REGIONAL PLANN. (1970) *Reform of Local Government in England*, Cmnd 4276 HMSO

SEC. STATE N IRELAND (1973) *Northern Ireland Constitutional Proposals*, Cmnd 5259 HMSO

SEC. STATE SCOTLAND (1971) *Reform of Local Government in Scotland*, Cmnd 4583 Edinburgh HMSO
SMITH, B C (1964–5) *Regionalism in England*, London, 3 vols
THOMAS, D et al (1969) 'The Redcliffe-Maud Report: Royal Commission on Local Government in England, 1966–9', *Area, 4*, 1–20
THOMAS, J G (1952) 'Local Government Areas in Wales', *Geogr.*, *37*, 9–18
WELSH OFFICE (1970) *The Reform of Local Government in Wales. Consultative Document*, Cardiff HMSO

Section V Economic Planning Regions and Nations

Northern Region

BOWDEN, P J (1965) 'Regional Problems and Policies in the North East of England', in WILSON, T (ed) *Papers on Regional Development*, Oxford, 20–39
FULLERTON, B (1960) 'The Pattern of Service Industries in North-East England', *Univ. Newcastle upon Tyne, Dept. Geogr., Res. Ser. 3*
          (1966) 'Geographical Inertia in the Service Industries: an example from Northern England' in HOUSE, J W (ed) *Northern Geographical Essays*, Newcastle upon Tyne, 157–77
HOUSE, J W (ed) (1964–72) *Papers on Migration and Mobility in Northern England, 1–11*, Univ. Newcastle upon Tyne, Dept. Geogr.
HOUSE, J W (1969) *Industrial Britain: the North East*, Newton Abbot
MINIST. HOUSING and LOCAL GOVT. (1969) *Teesside Survey and Plan. Final Report to the Steering Committee.* Vol I, Policies and Proposals, HMSO: vol II (1971), Analysis (2 parts), DoE, HMSO
NORTHERN EPC (1966) *Challenge of the Changing North*, HMSO
          (1969) *An Outline Strategy for the North*, Newcastle upon Tyne
          (1969) *Regional Ports Survey*, Newcastle upon Tyne
          (1970) *Report on Education*, Part 1, Newcastle upon Tyne
          (1971) *Report on Housing Needs for the Northern Region*, Newcastle upon Tyne
          (1972) *The Northern Region and the Common Market*, Newcastle upon Tyne
N REGION STRATEGY TEAM (1976) *Main Themes of the Strategic Plan*, 3rd Interim Rep., Newcastle upon Tyne
SEC. STATE TRADE, INDUSTRY and REGIONAL DEVELOPMENT (1963) *The North East: a Programme for Regional Development and Growth*, Cmnd 2206 HMSO
TAYLOR, R S (1972) *Carlisle and West Cumberland Sub-Region, A Social and Economic Study*, London
VOORHEES, A M et al (1972) *Tyne-Wear Plan*, Newcastle upon Tyne

Scotland

ABERCROMBIE, P and MATTHEW, R H (1946) *Clyde Valley Regional Plan*, HMSO
CAIRNCROSS, A K (1952) *Local Development in Scotland*, Edinburgh
CAIRNCROSS, A K (ed) (1954) *The Scottish Economy*, Cambridge
CAMERON, G C and REID, G L (1966) 'Scottish Economic Planning and the Attraction of Industry', *Univ. Glasgow, Soc. and Econ. Stud., Occ. Pap. 6*

CAMPBELL, A D and LYDDON, W D C (1970) *Tayside: Potential for Development*, Edinburgh HMSO

FIRN, J R (1975) 'External Control and Regional Development: the Case of Scotland', *Environ. & Plann.*, 7, 393–414

GASKIN, M (1968) *Survey of the Economy and Development Potential of North East Scotland*, Edinburgh HMSO

HIGHLANDS and ISLANDS DEV BD (1968) *The Moray Firth. A Plan for Growth in a Subregion of the Scottish Highlands* (Jack Holmes Planning Group), Glasgow

HUTCHESON, M A and HOGG, A (1975) *Scotland and Oil*, Edinburgh

JOHNSTON, T L, BUXTON, N K and MAIR, D (1971) *Structure and Growth of the Scottish Economy*, London

McCRONE, G (1965) *Scotland's Economic Progress, 1951–60: a Study in Regional Accounting*, London

(1969) *Scotland's Future: the Economics of Nationalism*, Oxford

McGUINESS, J H (1968) 'Regional Economic Development, Progress in Scotland', *J. Tn Plann. Inst., London*, 54, 103–11

MACKAY, D I and BUXTON, N K (1965) 'The North of Scotland Economy: a Case for Redevelopment', *Scott. J. Pol. Econ.*, 13, 23–49

MACKAY, D I and MACKAY, G A (1974) *Scotland: a Growth Economy*, Edinburgh

MINAY, C L W (1965) 'Town Development and Regional Planning in Scotland', *J. Tn Plann. Inst., London*, 51, 13–19

MOORE, B and RHODES, J (1974) 'Regional Policy and the Scottish Economy', *Scott. J. Pol. Econ.*, 21, 215–35

NICOLL, R E (1966) 'The Physical Implications of the White Paper on the Scottish Economy, 1965–70', *J. Tn Plann. Inst., London*, 52, 314–8

(chairman) (1973) *A Future for Scotland*, Scottish Council, Edinburgh

ROBERTSON, D J, JOHNSON-MARSHALL, P E A and MATTHEW, Sir R H (1966) *Lothians: Regional Survey and Plan*, Edinburgh HMSO, 2 vols
(1968) *Grangemouth/Falkirk Regional Survey and Plan*, Edinburgh HMSO, 2 vols

SCOTT. COUN. (1968) *Lochaber Study*, Edinburgh
(1970) *Oceanspan I: a Maritime-based Development Strategy for a European Scotland, 1970–2000*, Edinburgh

SCOTT. COUN. RES. INST. (1974) *Economic Development and Devolution*, Edinburgh

SCOTT. DEV. DEPT. (1963) *Central Scotland: a Programme for Development and Growth*, Cmnd 2188 Edinburgh HMSO
(1968) *The Central Borders: a Plan for Expansion*, Edinburgh HMSO, 2 vols
(1970) *A Strategy for South-West Scotland*, Edinburgh HMSO

SCOTT. OFF. (1966) *The Scottish Economy, 1965 to 1970: a Plan for Expansion*, Cmnd 2864 Edinburgh HMSO

SCOTT. TOURIST BD. (1968) *Galloway Project*, Strathclyde Univ.

SELF, P et al (1967) 'Scotland: Planning and Economic Development', *Tn. Ctry. Plann.*, 35, 265–325

STUDY TEAM (1971) *West Central Scotland Plan*, Stage A, Draft Report, HMSO

THOMSON, D C and GRIMBLE, I (1968) *The Future of the Highlands*, London
TOOTHILL, J N (1961) *Inquiry into the Scottish Economy*, Scottish Council
(Dev. & Ind.), Edinburgh
TURNOCK, D (1970) *Patterns of Highland Development*, London

Wales

BOWEN, E G (ed) (1957) *Wales: a Physical, Historical and Regional Geography*,
London
DAVIES, G and THOMAS, I (1976) *Overseas Investment in Wales – The Welcome
Invasion*
DEV. COMMN. (1972) *Mid Wales: An Assessment of the Impact of the Develop-
ment Commission Factory Programme*, HMSO
HAGGER, D F and DAVIES, H W E (1961) 'Regional Planning in South Wales',
Advmt. Sci., *18*, 65–73
HOUSTON, E and JENKINS, R (1965) *The Heartland: A Plan for Mid Wales*,
London
HUMPHRYS, G (1972) *Industrial Britain: South Wales*, Newton Abbot
LLOYD, M G and THOMASON, G F (1963) *Welsh Society in Transition*, Coun.
Soc. Serv. Wales & Mon.
MANNERS, G (1968) 'Wales: The Way Ahead', *J. Tn Plann. Inst., London*, *54*,
67–9
MIN. HOUSING and LOCAL GOVT. (1967) *Dee Crossing Study, Phase 1*, HMSO
NEVIN, E, ROSE, A R and ROUND, J I (1966) 'The Structure of the Welsh
Economy', *Welsh Econ. Stud.*, *4*, Univ. Wales
ROY. COMMN. CONSTITUTION (1973) 'Survey of the Welsh Economy', *Res. Pap.
8*, HMSO
SEC. STATE ENVIRONMENT, WALES et al (1971) *Dee Estuary Scheme, Phase 2*,
HMSO, 2 vols
SEC. STATE WALES (1967) *Wales: The Way Ahead*, Cmnd 3334 Cardiff HMSO
THOMAS, B (1962) *The Welsh Economy in Transition*, Cardiff
       (1970) 'Economic and Social Planning in Wales', *J. Tn. Plann. Inst.,
London*, *56*, 262–3
TOMKINS, C R (1971) *Income and Expenditure Accounts for Wales, 1965–8*,
Welsh Coun.
WELSH COUN. (1971) *A Strategy for Rural Wales*, HMSO, Cardiff
       (1971) *Wales and the Common Market*, Cardiff
WELSH OFF. (1964) *Depopulation in Mid Wales*, HMSO

N Ireland

BUILDING DESIGN PARTNERSHIP (1972) *Belfast Urban Area Plan*, London
GOVT. N IRELAND (1965) *Economic Development in N Ireland* (Wilson Report),
Cmnd 479 Belfast HMSO
       (1970) *N Ireland Development Programme 1970–5*, Belfast
HMSO
       (1970) *N Ireland Development Programme 1970–5*, *Govern-
ment Statement*, Cmnd 547 Belfast HMSO
GREEN, F H W (1949) 'Town and Country in N Ireland', *Geogr.*, *34*, 89–95
HOUSE OF COMMONS (1975) *N Ireland Constitutional Convention*, HMSO
ISLES, K S and CUTHBERT, N (1957) *An Economic Survey of N Ireland*, Belfast
HMSO

J MUNCE PARTNERSHIP (1968) *Londonderry Area Plan*, Belfast & Londonderry
MATTHEW, R H (1964) *Belfast Regional Survey and Plan*, Belfast HMSO, 2 vols
N IRELAND, DEPT. HOUSING, LOCAL GOVT. and PLANNING (1975) *Regional Development Strategy, 1975–95*, Belfast HMSO
N IRELAND ECON. COUN. (1969) *Area Development in N Ireland*, Belfast
N IRELAND MINIST. AGRIC. (1970) *The Changing Structure of Agriculture*, Belfast HMSO
SIMPSON, J V (1971) 'Regional Analysis: the Northern Ireland Experience', *Irish Econ. & Soc. Rev.*, 2, 507–29

Yorks. and Humberside
ATKINS, W S and PARTNERS (1969) *The Strategic Future of the Wool Textile Industry*. Econ. Dev. Comm. Wool Ind., HMSO
BROWN, M B (1970) 'The Concept of Employment Opportunity with Special Reference to Yorks. and Humberside', *Yorks. Bull. Econ. & Soc. Res.*, 22, 2, 65–100
CENT. UNIT ENVIRONMENTAL PLANN. (1969) *Humberside: a Feasibility Study*, HMSO
CTY COUN. W RIDING YORKS. (1969) *The County Strategy*, Wakefield
(1971) *The County Strategy for Development*, Wakefield
CRAIG, J, EVANS, E W and SHOWLER, B (1970) 'Humberside: Employment and Migration', *Yorks. Bull. Econ. & Soc. Res.*, 22, 2, 123–42
LEWIS, P and JONES, P N (1970) *Industrial Britain: The Humberside Region*, Newton Abbot
YORKS. and HUMBERSIDE EPC (1966) *A Review of Yorkshire and Humberside*, HMSO
(1968) *Halifax and Calder Valley* HMSO
(1969A) *Doncaster: an Area Study*, HMSO
(1969B) *Huddersfield and Colne Valley*, HMSO
(1970) *Yorkshire and Humberside Regional Strategy*, HMSO
(1972A) *Growth Industries in the Region*, Leeds
(1972B) *Implications of UK Entry into the Common Market for the Yorkshire and Humberside Region*, Leeds
(1976) *Regional Strategy Review 1975. The Next Ten Years*, Leeds

The North West
DEPT. ECON. AFFAIRS (1965) *The North West: a Regional Study*, HMSO
(1965) *The Problems of Merseyside*, HMSO
DoE (1974) *Strategic Plan for the North West*, HMSO
LANCS. CC (1974) *Observations on the Strategic Plan for the North West*, Preston
LAWTON, R and CUNNINGHAM, C M (eds) (1970) *Merseyside: Social and Economic Studies*, London
MATTHEW, R H et al (1968) *Central Lancashire New Town Proposal. Impact on North East Lancashire*, HMSO
MINIST. HOUSING and LOCAL GOVT. (1967) *Central Lancashire. Study for a City*, HMSO

_____
_____

NORTH WEST EPC (1966) *An Economic Planning Strategy for the North West Region*, Strategy I, HMSO
　　　　　　(1968) *The North West in the Seventies*, Strategy II, Manchester
　　　　　　(1970) *Housing in the North West Region*, Manchester
　　　　　　(1971) *Derelict Land in the North West*, Manchester
NUTTALL, T and BATTY, M F (1970) 'The North West – Problem Area for Regional Planning', *Tn Plann. Rev.*, *41*, 372–82
POWELL, A G (1974) 'Regional Policy and Sub-regional Planning in the NW', in SANT, M E (ed) *Regional Policy and Planning in Europe*, Farnborough, 157–70
SMITH, D M (1969) *Industrial Britain: The North West*, Newton Abbot

The South West
BRAITHWAITE, J L (1968) 'The Post-War Industrial Development of Plymouth: and Example of National Industrial Location Policy', *Trans. Inst. Br. Geogr.*, *45*, 34–50
BRITTON, J N H (1967) *Regional Analysis and Economic Geography. A Case Study of Manufacturing in the Bristol Region*, London
CAESAR, A A L (1949) 'Devon and Cornwall', in DAYSH, G H J (ed) *Studies in Regional Planning*, London, 197–223
CENT. UNIT ENVIRONMENTAL PLANN. (1971) *Severnside: A Feasibility Study*, HMSO
CORNWALL, CC (1970) *West Cornwall Study*, Truro
DEVON CC (1966–70) *Feasibility Studies*, Barnstaple, Exeter and District, Honiton, South Brent and Ivybridge, Tiverton–Sampford Peverell
MINIST. HOUSING and LOCAL GOVT (1970) *The Holiday Industry of Devon and Cornwall*, HMSO
SOUTH WEST EPC (1967) *A Region with a Future: A Draft Strategy for the South West*, HMSO
　　　　　　(1969) *Plymouth Area Study*, Bristol
　　　　　　(1974) *A Strategic Settlement Pattern for the South West*, HMSO
SPOONER, D J (1972) 'Industrial Movement and Rural Periphery: the Case of Devon and Cornwall', *Reg. Stud.*, *6*, 2, 197–215
　　　　　　(1974) 'Some Qualitative Aspects of Industrial Movement in a Problem Region of the UK', *Tn Plann. Rev.*, *45*, 63–83
WALKER, F (1965) 'Economic Growth on Severnside', *Trans. Inst. Br. Geogr.*, *37*, 1–13

E Anglia
DoE (1974) *A Study of the Cambridge Sub-region*, Parts I and II, HMSO
E ANGLIA CONSULTATIVE COMMN. (1969) *East Anglia: A Regional Appraisal*, Bury St Edmunds
E ANGLIA EPC (1968) *East Anglia. A Study*, HMSO
E ANGLIA REG. STRATEGY TEAM (1974) *Strategic Choice for East Anglia*, HMSO
MINIST. HOUSING and LOCAL GOVT. (1966) *Expansion of Peterborough*, HMSO

SANT, M E C and MOSELEY, M J (1976) *Industrial Britain: East Anglia*, Newton Abbot

E Midlands
BURROWS, M and TOWN, S (1971) *Office Services in the East Midlands: An Economic and Sociological Study*, Nottingham, 2 vols
E MIDLANDS EPC (1966) *The East Midlands Study*, HMSO
                 (1969) *Opportunity in the East Midlands*, HMSO
                 (1976) *A Forward Economic Look*, Nottingham
FENNELL, K R (1971) *The Eastern Lowlands Subregional Study*, Kesteven Cty. Plann. Dept.
GIBSON, M and PULLEN, M (1971) *Retail Patterns in the E Midlands, 1961–81*, Leicester
HOLLAND, CC (1970) *Rural Policy Structure*, Boston
LEICS. CY COUN. and LEICS. CC (1969) *Leicester and Leicestershire Subregional Planning Study*, Glenfield
MINIST. HOUSING and LOCAL GOVT. (1966A) *Expansion of Northampton*, HMSO
                           (1966B) *Northampton, Bedford, North Bucks Study*, HMSO
NOTTS–DERBYS. SUBREG. PLANN. UNIT (1969) *Notts. and Derbyshire Subregional Study*, Alfreton

W Midlands
COVENTRY CY COUN. et al (1971) *Coventry–Solihull–Warwickshire: A Strategy for the Sub-region*
DEPT. ECON. AFFAIRS (1965) *The W Midlands: A Regional Study*, HMSO
JT MONITORING STEERING GROUP (1975) *A Developing Strategy for the W Midlands*, DoE, Birmingham
W MIDLANDS EPC (1967) *The W Midlands: Patterns of Growth*, HMSO
                  (1971) *The W Midlands: An Economic Appraisal*, HMSO
W MIDLANDS REG. STUDY (1971) *A Developing Strategy for the W Midlands*, WMRS
WISE, M J (1972) 'The Birmingham–Black Country Conurbation in its Regional Setting', *Geogr.*, 57, 89–104
WOOD, P (1976) *Industrial Britain: The W Midlands*, Newton Abbot

South East
ABERCROMBIE, P (1945) *Greater London Plan 1944*, HMSO
COLIN BUCHANAN and PARTNERS (1966) *South Hampshire Study*, HMSO, 3 vols
DoE (1971) South East Joint Planning Studies. vol. I: *Population and Employment*; vol. II: *Social and Economic Aspects*; vol. V: *Report of Economic Consultants Ltd.*, HMSO
       (1973A) *Greater London Development Plan. Report of the Panel of Inquiry* (Layfield Rep.), HMSO, 2 vols.
       (1973B) *Greater London Development Plan, Statement by Rt Hon Geoffrey Rippon*, HMSO
EVERSLEY, D E C (1973) 'Problems of Social Planning in Inner London': in

DONNISON, D V and EVERSLEY, D E C (eds) *London, Urban Patterns, Problems and Policies,* London

GLC (1969) *Greater London Development Plan*, London

HALL, P G (1963) *London 2000*, London

MILTON KEYNES DEV. CORPN. (1970) *The Plan for Milton Keynes*, Bletchley, 2 vols

MIN. HOUSING and LOCAL GOVT. (1964) *The South East Study, 1961–81*, HMSO

SOUTH EAST EPC (1967) *A Strategy for the South East*, HMSO
          (1971) *Views on the Strategic Plan for the South East*, London

SE JOINT PLANN. TEAM (1970) *Strategic Plan for the South East*, HMSO
          (1976) *Strategy for the South East: 1976 Review*, DoE

STEWART, J M W (1971) 'Planning and South East England', *Area, 3*, 267–70

2

People and Work

I   INTRODUCTION

1   General Context

In a mature industrial society and long-settled land such as the UK, the population
map mirrors environmental, economic and social contrasts and changes in these
over both time and space. The population distribution map (fig. 2.1) therefore
reveals much of earlier origin as well as more recent trends and forces. Many consequences are still with us from nineteenth-century industrial and urban growth,
when population was concentrated by a coal-based, steam-powered and railway-
linked economy, and from eighteenth- and nineteenth-century agrarian reform,
which resulted in much increased output per unit of land and of manpower, and
led to a declining agricultural labour force. Thus, powerful and long-established
economic and social forces underlie long-standing population trends: losses from
the countryside; a continuing move to urban areas; a progressive focusing on
London and the major provincial cities. These pose some of the greatest problems in
population and regional planning for the present and the immediate future. To these
long-established forces have been added variants of specifically twentieth-century
origin. More mobile, technologically-based and assembly-line industries which
demand access to labour and markets rather than to power or raw materials have
broken the dominance of the nineteenth-century industrial regions and drawn
population south-eastwards to Greater London and the Midlands. The growing
significance of services and commercial activities in the economy have focused a
large and increasing section of employment on the conurbations. Increasingly, mass
transit systems and greatly augmented car ownership have markedly increased
mobility, permitting increasing separation of home and workplace and accentuating
the growth of city regions, within which dispersal of housing areas and concentration of jobs are pulling in different directions. Thus, while in the true countryside
population has continued to decline, in a growing rural—urban fringe around *all*
large cities population has increased rapidly, both through private house-building
and, especially since the Second World War, through local authority estates and
overspill agreements.

Such trends reflect not only the process of urbanization (ch. 6), which has been
such a prominent feature of the UK since early Victorian times, but also the recent
and present inter- and intra-regional mobility which is reshaping its real social
regions. Population change, in turn, is basic to many aspects of present and future
economic, social, political and administrative organization.

A population of some 56 millions living on only 24.4 million ha much of which
is unsuitable for cultivation or settlement, especially in highland Britain, creates
densities of population second in Europe only to the Netherlands and among the

highest in the world. The position is more severe in England and Wales, as Best (1972) has shown. At the beginning of this century only 5 per cent of the land surface was in urban land use but during the inter-war sprawl of towns loss of farmland reached levels of over 25,000 ha per year. Better planning controls since the war have seen this loss reduced to an average 15,800 ha per year. Even so, the built-up area of England and Wales had increased from 5 per cent of the total area in 1900 to 10 per cent in 1950 (UK, 1950: 7.3 per cent) and, despite the reduced rate of consumption of land, to over 11 per cent at present (UK, 1965: 8.5 per cent). At current rates of conversion the proportion of land in urban use in England and Wales could rise to some 15–16 per cent by the end of the century, though for the UK as a whole (11.3 per cent in 2000 AD) the long-term prospect is somewhat less daunting (table 1.3) (DoE 1971). Moreover, it has been pointed out by Best and Champion (1970) that during the 1960s urban growth was greatest around the midland and northern conurbations and, in general, did not correspond closely with the pattern of population change. New house-building for existing population has been the dominant force in urban growth since 1951.

Improvements in housing and urban amenities in sub-standard regions have contributed very considerably to urban demands for land. Pressure on land for communications, water supplies and recreation, already considerable, will increase, together with demands for industrial sites. It has been increasingly urged that we should not add to the pressures arising from existing population by further population increases, even though in many parts of the UK there may be room for more population growth.

The economic value of a numerous and growing population depends on its ability to release greater productive power than its demands on resources generate. During the post-war years there was a relative decline of population in the productive age groups – a product of the low inter-war fertility rates – and shortage of labour led to acute pressure of demand for both skilled and unskilled workers. This contributed to the considerable influx of immigrants in the late 1950s and early 1960s (ch. 2.II.6) and to the general feeling that population growth was no bad thing. The combined effects in the 1970s of severe economic problems and the growth of the potential work force has led to a renewed feeling that the UK cannot provide for a large population, a fact reflected in the recent rapid decline in births.

1.2   Recent Demographic Trends: Some Basic Factors

Following upon the toll of the First World War on the young men of Britain and its consequent effect on marriage-rates, the economic depression of the early 1930s contributed to the continuing fall in fertility. The crude birth-rate in the UK, which had reached a peak of 35 per 1,000 in the early 1870s, declined gradually to 1914 and fell rapidly in the inter-war years. The idea of the smaller family spread through all sections of society and fertility fell below replacement level in the 1930s. Although population continued to increase slowly, supported by a net gain by migration, the long-term prospects for population growth were poor. A continuing decline in death-rate contributed to a slowly growing, but ageing, population (table 2.1). Hence, the population predictions of the 1930s, almost without exception, were of future decline. The most optimistic forecast of the *Report of the Royal*

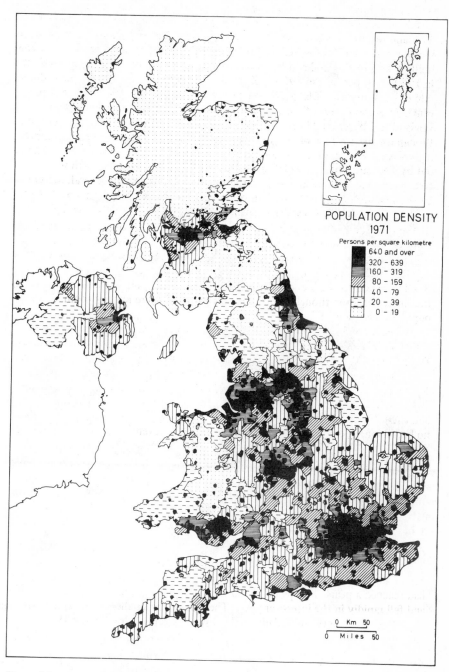

Figure 2.1   Population density, UK, 1971

Commission on Population (1949) for GB was of a population of 52 million by the end of the century; the least optimistic assumption placed it as low as 41 million.

Three sets of forces have rendered these predictions invalid in the post-1945 period. First, *birth-rates increased* markedly in the baby boom of the immediate post-war years when crude birth-rates reached an average of 18 per 1000 in 1946–50. Despite considerable fluctuations in birth-rate, involving a fall in the early 1950s, birth-rates generally remained above those of the inter-war years until 1972 (fig. 2.2; table 2.1). General fertility also increased due to earlier and more universal marriage. In GB the average age of first marriage for women, at 25.5 years in the 1920s and 1930s, fell to less than 25.0 after 1945, and continued to fall in the 1960s to its present level of 22.6 years. Moreover the proportion of women aged 15–49 with experience of marriage increased in England and Wales from 529 per 1000 in 1931 to 700 in 1961, and was 698 in 1969; the equivalent figures for Scotland are 483, 677 and 697.

All these factors are reflected in the growth of the average number of children per marriage in Britain from the low level of 2.05 for marriages in 1936, to 2.23 for 1951, to an estimated 2.50 for 1961, but falling for those married in the late 1960s to some 2.45 and perhaps as low as 2.20 for those of the mid-1970s. These changes were enough to create post-war growth and projected future growth. Yet, if the 1960s level of about five children born to every two families *were* to be reduced slightly to some nine children for every four families the population in the year 2000 would be 6 to 7 million less than the 1969 estimate, whilst a reduction in births of one child in three families would eventually stabilize population numbers. It is, as yet, too early to judge the longer-term impact of the recent decline in birth-rate from the second post-war peak of 1964 (table 2.1). Birth-rates have fallen from a second post-war peak of 18.6 in 1964 to 12.5 per thousand in 1975, well below the level even of the mid-1930s. If the families born to the generation of the post-war baby boom fall to below 2.00, as suggested by recent birth trends, this could lead to a further downward revision of future population totals. Indeed, if the provisional net reproduction rate of 0.89 calculated for 1974, were to continue, it would lead to a *declining* future population. (Pearce 1975.)

While increased fertility has greatly increased the numbers and proportion of young dependants, continuing improvements in health and standards of living have been reflected in a slow *lowering of mortality*. Although due in part to an ageing population structure, crude death-rates have fallen but slowly, from 12.7 per 1000 in 1921, to between 11 and 12 in the 1960s and 1970s (fig. 2.2). Expectation of life has increased steadily, especially for women, and is reflected in the increased proportion of retired people in the population (table 2.5). A second factor in continuing population growth, this is also one reason for the increased dependency ratios which have been a feature of the post-war years.

A third factor in population growth since the 1930s has been the general gains, on balance, from *overseas migration*. In contrast to the losses from migration sustained during the nineteenth and early-twentieth centuries, during the 1930s and 1940s a slowing down of emigration and increased immigration, much of it of refugees from Europe, combined to reverse the UK's long-standing net loss from migration. Moreover from the mid-1950s a new wave of immigration from the New Commonwealth countries has contributed to a considerable continuing inward movement which produced a net gain due to migration of 20,000 in the civilian population 1951–61 and of 113,000 in 1961–6 (table 2.2). This was slowed down

TABLE 2.1

Birth, Death and Marriage Rates UK, 1901–74

	1901	1911	1921	1931	1951	1961	1966	1967	1969	1971	1973	1974
Births per 1,000	28.6	24.6	23.1	16.3	15.8	17.8	17.9	17.5	16.6	16.2	13.9	13.2
Fertility rates per 1,000 women 15–44	114.9	99.1	91.5	66.5	73.0	90.1	91.1	88.4	85.9	84.4	72.0	67.1
Percentage illegitimate births	4.2	4.7	4.9	4.8	4.9	5.8	7.7	8.2	8.4	8.2	8.4	8.7
Deaths per 1,000	17.3	14.1	12.7	12.2	12.6	12.0	11.8	11.2	11.9	11.6	12.0	11.9
Male deaths/1,000	18	15	14	13	13	13	12	13	12	13	12	12
Female deaths/1,000	16	13	12	12	12	11	11	11	11	11	12	11.6
Average age of first marriage												
male	27.2	27.3	27.6	27.4	26.8	25.6	24.9	24.8	24.7	24.6	24.8	24.8
female	25.6	25.6	25.5	25.5	24.6	23.3	22.7	22.7	22.5	22.6	22.7	22.6
Percentage women ever married: 20–24	—	24.0	27.0	25.5	47.3	57.4	58.2	58.2	57.1	59.0	59.2	NA
25–29	—	55.8	58.2	58.4	77.5	84.3	85.5	85.5	85.7	85.8	86.0	
40–44	—	81.6	81.6	81.4	85.3	90.1	91.3	91.3	91.7	91.9	92.6	

Source: Social Trends 5, (1974), and *Popul. Trends 3* (1976) *Registrars' General Quarterly Returns 1974*
Birth and death rates calculated on the basis of the revised mid-year estimates for 1971. NA = not available

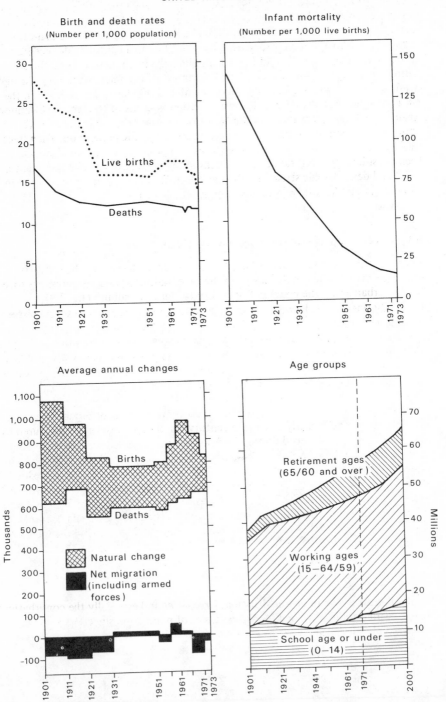

UNITED KINGDOM

Birth and death rates
(Number per 1,000 population)

Infant mortality
(Number per 1,000 live births)

Live births

Deaths

Average annual changes

Age groups

Births

Deaths

Natural change

Net migration
(including armed
forces)

Thousands

Retirement ages
(65/60 and over)

Working ages
(15-64/59)

School age or under
(0-14)

Millions

Figure 2.2   UK vital trends, components of population growth (1961–73), and age structure
(1901–2001)

by the *1962 Commonwealth Immigrants Act* (Publ. Gen. Act 1962) and nearly arrested by the *1968 Act* (Publ. Gen. Act 1968), though the influx of dependants of previous migrants has continued to generate considerable immigration. Nevertheless, increasing control of immigration and deteriorating economic conditions, especially in terms of labour surpluses, have resulted in a considerable recent loss by migration (see table 2.2). In the decade since the introduction of the International Passenger Survey (IPS) in 1964, a sample of the migrants passing through major sea and air ports, a net migration loss of 452,000 has been recorded in the UK (Davis and Walker, 1975). However, continuing gains of foreign and Commonwealth migrants, especially from the New Commonwealth, and losses of UK nationals have led to continuing diversification of the UK population. The effects of this distinctive, if short-lived, process on the composition of the population have been considerable. In certain areas overseas immigrants have become dominant in social and demographic structure, though it is difficult at this stage to judge their longer-term effects upon population trends (ch. 2.II.6).

1.3   General Population Trends, Rural and Urban

Since 1945 the dominant trends have been those characteristic of the last fifty years: the drift to the South East from the older industrial regions; movement from rural to urban areas; the counterflow from city centre to suburb (fig. 2.3). Especially since 1961, however, some significant variations on these themes have become apparent (fig. 2.4). In particular, the large cities and conurbations of the North have all experienced marked losses, while other conurbations throughout the UK have experienced losses similar to those of adjacent areas (tables 2.3 and 2.4).

The *rural areas* of the UK had been characterized by population losses throughout the Victorian period. After the mid-nineteenth century all types of farming areas experienced population decline as outward migration exceeded natural increase. Despite the slowing down of such excessive draining of population from the countryside in the early twentieth century, rural depopulation, as measured by net outmigration, continued during the inter-war years, especially from the more remote areas. In the post-Second World War period, despite the reversal of aggregate losses from the rural areas in England and Wales and in N Ireland, and their slowing down in Scotland, depopulation of the remoter rural areas continued. Most of the rural districts which have increased their population have done so by overspill into administrative rural districts from adjacent towns. The balance of gain in rural districts must chiefly be seen as a response to suburban dispersal and the increase of commuting or of movement by people on retirement. In Scotland, where such changes are mainly limited to Central Scotland or a few small growth-points such as those near Fort William, Inverness and the Moray Firth, rural depopulation continues (table 2.3).

In contrast to the inter-war situation, *large cities* and especially the conurbations have experienced marked and increasing losses of population since 1945. In the more closely-settled areas of the UK many large urban authorities are losing population to suburbs in adjacent local authority areas, often to rural districts. Accompanied by loss of rateable value and, often, by increasing social segregation of centre and periphery in essentially inter-dependent urban regions, this process is reflected in the growth of population in the smaller urban areas, many of which are

TABLE 2.2

Components of Population Change, UK, 1901–74

(1,000s)	Census enumerated 1901–11		1911–21		1921–31		1931–51	
Population at start of period	38,237		42,082		44,027		46,038	
Average ann. change	Total	%	Total	%	Total	%	Total	%
Births	1,091	2.85	975	2.32	824	1.87	785	1.71
Deaths	624	1.63	689	1.64	555	1.26	598	1.30
Net natural change	467	1.22	286	0.68	268	0.61	188	0.41
Net Migration — Civilian / Armed Forces	−82	−0.21	−92	−0.22	−67	−0.15	+22	+0.05
Total av. ann. change	385	1.01	195	0.46	201	0.46	213	0.47

Mid-year estimates 1951–6		1956–61		1961–6		1966–71		1972–4	
50,290		51,184		52,816		54,654		55,610	
Total	%	Total	%	Total	%	Total	%	Total	%
797	1.58	880	1.72	988	1.87	938	1.72	780	1.40
583	1.16	603	1.18	633	1.20	645	1.18	668	1.20
214	0.43	277	0.54	355	0.67	293	0.54	112	0.20
−48 } +13	−0.07	+30 } +20	+0.10	+12 } +1	+0.02	−18	−0.03	−26	−0.05
179	0.36	327	0.64	368	0.69	275	0.50	86	0.15

Source: Soc. Trends 1 (1970), 'Population and Environment' Table 10 (p. 53) and *Registrar General's Estimates* (for 1969–71). *Popn. Trends 3* (1976), table 3, p. 28. *Soc. Trends* 3 (1972) estimates net migration for 1961–7 as −33,000 (Civil) and −15,000 (Armed Forces).

suburban satellites of the large cities. In all parts of the UK small towns are in the fastest-growing group of settlements.

Cumulatively, the result has been to shift the balance of regional growth within the UK. During the nineteenth century the most rapidly growing regions included northern England and the industrial areas of C Scotland and S Wales. But since the First World War, the Northern, Yorks. and Humberside, and NW regions of England together with Wales and Scotland have suffered a relative fall in population, while

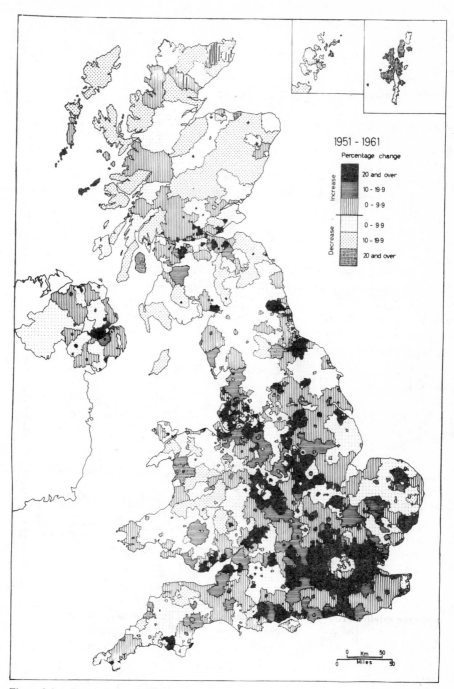

Figure 2.3   Population change, UK, 1951–61

TABLE 2.3

Population Changes in Urban and Rural Areas, UK, 1951–71

	Total population (1,000s) 1951	1961	Percentage % change 1951–61	Total 1971	Percentage % change 1961–71
England and Wales	43,758.9	46,104.5	5.2	48,593.7	5.3
Conurbations	16,794.4	16,741.9	– 3.4	15,928.0	– 4.8
Urban areas					
over 100,000	6,279.2	6,640.4	5.8	6,754.1	1.7
50–100,000	4,423.1	5,008.7	13.2	5,392.2	7.5
under 50,000	8,067.7	8,759.7	8.5	9,961.2	13.7
Rural districts	8,193.4	8,953.9	9.3	10,568.3	18.0
Scotland	5,096.7	5,179.3	1.6	5,227.7	0.9
Conurbation	1,763.7	1,807.8	2.7	1,731.0	– 4.2
Other cities and large burghs	1,315.6	1,441.9	9.6	1,491.8	3.5
Small burghs	793.4	866.6	9.2	994.8	14.8
Districts or County	1,223.7	1,065.4	–11.9	1,018.4	– 4.4
N Ireland	1,370.9	1,425.0	3.9	1,527.6	6.8
County boroughs	493.8	469.6	– 4.9	412.0	–12.3
Other urban areas	256.4	300.4	17.2	429.9	43.2
Rural districts	620.7	655.0	5.5	685.7	4.7
UK	50,255.2	52,708.9	4.9	55,346.6	5.0
Conurbations	18,558.1	18,549.7	– 0.5	17,659.0	– 4.8
Large urban areas	8,092.6	8,551.9	5.7	8,657.9	1.4
Other urban areas	13,540.6	14,935.4	10.3	16,768.1	12.3
Rural districts	10,037.8	10,674.3	6.3	12,272.4	15.0

Source: Census of 1951, 1961 and 1971
Because of the different basis of classification in Scotland, figures for urban and rural areas have had to be adjusted and do not exactly equal the total.

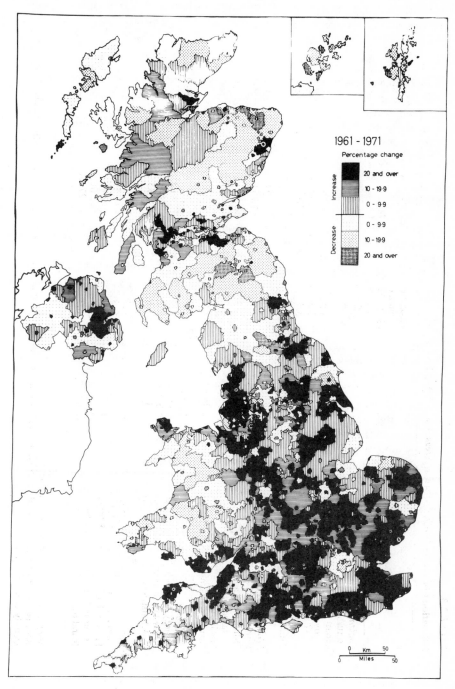

Figure 2.4   Population change, UK, 1961–71

the Midlands and South East have increased their relative share of population and are expected to continue to do so up to the end of the century.

1.4   Effects on Population Structure

These changing distributions reflect changing economic forces, but the demographic results of changes in natural and migrational components of population trends also carry considerable economic and social implications at both national and regional levels. The declining birth-rate and falling mortality of the early twentieth century caused a considerable increase in the elderly (over 60 years), both numerically and as a proportion of the total population (table 2.5). In 1911 the 60+ age-group formed 9.2 per cent of the total population, but by 1941 it was estimated at 13.9 and, in 1971, 18.6 per cent. The increase in older dependants was offset between the wars by falling birth-rates; the proportion of those under 15 years fell from 30.8 per cent in 1911 to 21 per cent in 1941. Hence, the dependency ratio (conventionally measured by the proportion of those aged 0–14 years and of retirement age, here reckoned as 60 years and above, as related to the 15–59 age group) which was 61.5 in 1911 had dropped to 53.9 in 1941. By 1970, because of generally higher birth-rates since 1945 and increased expectation of life among older people, the dependency ratio was 70.8. While from 1941 to 1971 the under-15s increased by 34 per cent and the over-60s by 53 per cent, the main workforce increased by a meagre 2 per cent. Hence, in the 1950s and 1960s we experienced a relative decline in the workforce, though the actual numbers of the population or working age increased slightly. During the 1970s the dependency ratio fell to 67.0 in 1975, and is expected to fall to 63.0 in 1981. Though raising of the school-leaving age to sixteen in 1973 offset the rise in numbers of the workforce, they will now rise again into the 1980s (Davis 1976) and, secondly, with some slight upward fluctuation in the 1980s, on the evidence of recent trends the numbers will fall further in the last years of the century.

This stagnation in the potential workforce in the 1950s and 1960s was offset by drawing more women into gainful employment, a trend accelerated by two World Wars and by changing attitudes to the role of women in society and their potential role in professional, commercial and industrial life. These changes are reflected in the increase in the proportion of women in employment, especially during and since the Second World War, though there are considerable regional variations in female activity rates (fig. 2.14).

One of the factors in 'full employment' since 1945 has been the coincidence of labour shortage, due to changing population structure, with a generally expanding economy. These were also basic factors attracting immigrant labour to the UK in the 1950s and early 1960s. A relatively stagnant economy coupled with increasing economy in the use of labour in the face of rapidly rising labour costs has now changed this situation in a period of rising numbers of people of working age. It is reflected in increases in unemployment, a fall in activity rates and a decline in the immigration of workers though not yet of dependants.

Sex structure   From the 1920s to the 1940s the catastrophic casualties of the First World War, reflected in the relatively high ratios of women to men (table 2.7), were a factor contributing to reduced fertility between the wars. Since the Second World War much improved ante- and post-natal care has resulted in a marked increase in

TABLE 2.4

Components of Population Change, UK Regions, 1951–71

(1,000s) Region	1951–61			1961–6			1966
	1951	average annual change natural	migration	1961	average annual change natural	migration	
Northern	3,127	19.3	− 8.0	3,246	20.7	− 7.1	3,314
Yorks. & Humberside	4,509	19.5	− 9.6	4,631	28.1	− 1.0	4,767
North West	6,417	23.5	−12.4	6,545	38.0	− 5.7	6,713
E Midlands	2,896	15.8	+ 3.9	3,108	23.4	+ 8.7	3,266
W Midlands	4,426	27.6	+ 4.7	4,761	41.1	+ 7.1	4,999
South East	15,216	66.4	+43.8	16,346	110.2	+20.8	17,006
Greater London	8,206	33.3	−61.1	7,977	52.3	−82.7	7,832
OMA	3,509	24.2	+77.5	4,521	43.5	+54.8	5,013
OSE	3,502	8.9	+27.3	3,848	14.5	+48.7	4,161
E Anglia	1,388	6.5	+ 2.7	1,489	8.7	+11.9	1,582
South West	3,247	10.5	+ 9.9	3,436	16.9	+24.8	3,635
Wales	2,589	8.4	− 4.9	2,635	11.5	+ 1.9	2,704
Scotland	5,103	33.9	−28.2	5,184	38.7	−38.8	5,191
N Ireland	1,373	14.6	− 8.9	1,427	17.4	− 6.9	1,478
UK	50,291	246.0	− 7.0	52,807	354.6	+15.7	54,654

Table 2.4 continued

| (1,000s) Region | 1966–71 average annual change | | 1971 | Total changes, 1951–71 | | | | | |
	natural	migration		Total No.	%	Natural No.	%	Net migration (+) No.	%
Northern	14	− 9	3,293	166	5.3	367	11.7	− 151	− 4.8
Yorks. & Humberside	25	− 12	4,811	302	6.7	461	10.3	− 161	− 3.6
North West	30	− 13	6,747	330	5.1	575	9.0	− 218	− 3.4
E Midlands	21	+ 6	3,390	494	17.1	380	13.1	+ 112	+ 3.9
W Midlands	38	− 1	5,121	695	15.7	672	15.1	+ 78	+ 1.8
South East	89	− 28	17,289	2,073	13.5	1,660	10.9	+ 502	+ 3.3
Greater London	37	−112	7,441	−765	−9.3	779	9.5	−1,585	−19.3
OMA	39	+ 34	5,345	1,836	52.3	655	18.7	+1,219	+34.8
OSE	12	+ 51	4,502	1,000	28.5	222	6.3	+ 772	+22.1
E Anglia	8	+ 15	1,686	298	21.5	149	10.7	+ 162	+11.6
South West	13	+ 20	3,792	545	16.8	255	7.9	+ 323	+ 8.9
Wales	8	− 1	2,723	134	5.2	182	7.1	− 44	− 1.7
Scotland	33	− 34	5,230	126	2.5	698	13.7	− 646	−12.7
N Ireland	17	− 6	1,534	163	11.9	318	23.1	− 156	−11.4
UK	296	− 63	55,605	5,317	10.6	5,717	11.4	− 306	− 0.6

(+) excludes Armed Forces, hence the totals do not always sum. Cf. Champion (1976), table II, but his basis of calculation differs

Sources: Eversley (1971): Abstract of Regional Statistics (1971); Long-term Population Distribution in G.B.: A Study (1971);
Registrar General's Revised Estimates . . . Regions (1975)
Figures are derived from Registrar General's Mid-year Estimates of Home Populations.

the surplus of male births. (There is a tendency in all mammals for a greater conception of males and a higher proportion of males at birth, but this has been offset in the UK by higher male mortality at all ages.) Despite higher male mortality at all ages, especially in later life, the imbalances of the sexes in the inter-war years in the UK is now much reduced. Current estimates show that men outnumber women in all age-groups up to 44 years in England and Wales and up to 19 years in Scotland and N Ireland where the lower age of male deficits is due largely to differential migration.

A very notable feature of changing age and sex structure is the increasing dominance of women in later age-groups. Among the over-60s the ratio of men to women is about 1:1.4 but among the over-70s it is 1:1.8 and 1:2.6 for the over-80s. As Thompson (1970, 27) states: 'The problem of caring for the increasing number of very elderly people is very much that of caring for an increasing proportion of elderly women.'

1.5 Population Composition and the Workforce

In a *Select Committee report* for 1970–1 (House of Commons 1971) it was noted that, after a post-war phase of increased dependency-rates perpetuated by the proposal to raise the school-leaving age to 16 in 1973, the working population would increase from 1974. Compared with the period 1941–69, when the population of working age increased by a mere 4 per cent, and with an estimated decrease of some 1 per cent 1969–73 there is likely to be an increase of 10 per cent in the population of working age by the end of the century.

This will be both an opportunity and a challenge. Any increased labour force may contribute to increased output, quite apart from increases in productivity per unit of manpower. Thus the changing demographic structure is of considerable potential economic significance. Similarly the changing employment situation in the 1950s and 1960s is partly related to a changing manpower situation. The present labour surpluses are a product of increased supply, especially in the younger age-groups, at a time of economic recession and increasing economy in the use of manpower in a high-wage economy. There should be no parallel bottleneck of labour shortage in the 1970s to that which hampered the economy in the 1950s and 1960s and generated a demand for immigrants to fill the gap in home labour supplies. Nevertheless varying regional demands for labour and changing skills and demands for these will no doubt involve continuing labour mobility leading to further population migration.

1.6 Population Trends and Social Provision

Provided that increased manpower can be put to work, some of the burden of dependency which has fallen upon a relatively static working-age population during recent times may be eased. Post-war increases in children and old people have placed heavy pressures upon the whole range of social services, such as education, health, social and family benefits, and also upon housing. For example, the boom in births of 1945–7 led to a 30 per cent increase in school intake in 1950–2 which reached the universities and colleges in the Robbins boom period of 1963–5. Similarly the upward trend of births of the period 1955–64, which produced a second post-war increase of 29 per cent in school entries, has exerted a more

TABLE 2.5

Age Distribution, UK, 1911–2001

Age group	Total popn. (millions) Census enumeration			Projections*		Per cent of total popn. Census			Projections		Percentage changes		
	1911	1941	1971	1981	2001	1911	1941	1971	1981	2001	1911–41	1941–71	1971–2001
0–14	13.0	10.1	13.5	(12.0)	(13.3)	30.8	21.0	24.1	(21.3)	(22.4)	− 22.3	+33.7	−1.5
15–59	25.7	31.4	32.1	33.1	35.2	61.1	65.1	57.2	58.8	59.2	+ 22.2	+ 2.2	+9.7
60 and over	3.4	6.8	10.4	11.2	10.9	8.2	13.9	18.6	19.9	18.4	+100.0	+53.0	+4.8
All ages	42.1	48.3	56.0	56.3	59.4	100.1	100.0	99.9	100.0	100.0	+ 14.8	+15.9	+5.9

*The projections are those of 1973; bracketed figures are estimates including those as yet unborn

Source: Soc. Trends, 1 (1970) and 3 (1972) and Census 1971, *Preliminary Reports* (HMSO); *Registrar General's Quarterly Returns*, 31 March 1974; Registrar General, *Popn. Projections*.

gradual, but increasing, pressure on educational facilities, youth services, etc., which has yet to work its way through. However, the fall in births, 1970–5, is reflected in the sharp fall in the estimates of teachers needed for the late 1970s and 1980s.

Meanwhile, increased longevity is requiring the provision of more special services for the elderly. These fall unequally on the community both in regional terms (fig. 2.10), as between urban and rural areas, or between older-established and more recently formed communities. The general tendency to an ageing population since the First World War has not been offset by increased births since 1945. Taking 1969 as base year, the index of rates of change in the older age-groups has shown a marked upward trend which is expected to continue, especially among the aged, calling for much greater provision of special homes, hospitals and other services than is yet available (table 2.6).

TABLE 2.6

Older Age-groups, UK, 1941–2001, as a ratio of 1969 (= 100)

		Actual (1)				Estimated (2)		
		1941	1951	1961	1969	1981	1991	2001
All retire-								
ment ages	Total	65	78	89	100	108	109	107
	M	71	84	89	100	113	116	112
	F	65	78	89	100	106	107	102
85 and over	Total	35	53	81	100	120	155	170
	M	32	50	77	100	104	138	151
	F	35	53	81	100	126	161	177

Source: (1) *Soc. Trends, 1*, (1970), Table VIII, p. 29;
(2) OPCS, *Population Projections 4*, 1973–2013 (1974)

II   POPULATION DISTRIBUTION AND TRENDS

II.1   Intra-regional Contrasts

With an average of 0.92 persons per acre (2.27 persons per ha) the UK is one of the most densely populated areas of the world. Moreover there are very wide variations, ranging from the extremely crowded inner-residential areas of the large towns, with densities of over 24 per ha rising to over 123 per ha, to thinly populated rural areas of under 0.25 per ha and extensive, uninhabited moorlands which cover much of upland Britain (fig. 2.1). The key to the intensity of occupation lies in an unusually high degree of urbanization (ch. 6). In 1911, after over a century of rapid urban growth, 78 per cent of the population of England and Wales lived in urban districts and perhaps as many as nine-tenths were 'urbanized'. Similarly in Scotland population numbers were dominated by the large towns and industrial districts cf C Scotland. Even in N Ireland, where Belfast is the only large industrial city, about one-half of the population were urban-dwellers.

The proportion of *urban-dwellers*, narrowly defined as those who live under urban administrations, is still at about the level of fifty years ago according to the 1971 census: 77.7 per cent in the UK; 78.3 per cent in England and Wales; 81.5

per cent in Scotland; and 55.1 per cent in N Ireland. Many large towns, Greater London included, reached their peak population before the First World War, however, and have since maintained growth by outward movement to suburban satellites. Even where land has been available within the city boundaries for new housing, slum clearance and lower density house-building has led to large net losses of population by migration and, since the Second World War, a fall in total numbers of people in the majority of the large cities of the UK.

Although some 33 per cent of the population of England and Wales today lives in the 6 *conurbations* officially designated in the 1951 Census (Greater London, Merseyside, SE Lancashire (now SELNEC), Tyneside, W Yorkshire, and the W Midlands) this proportion has fallen from the 38 per cent of 1951 and there has been a fall of 725,000 in the conurbation population, 1961–71. There has been a similar reduction from 35 to 33 per cent in the population of Scotland who live in the central Clydeside conurbation, due to a fall in the total since 1961.

TABLE 2.7

Female:Male Ratios, UK, 1911–2001

Census of population

Total in millions	1911 Total M	F	F per 100M	1921 Total M	F	F per 100M	1931 Total M	F	F per 100M
England and Wales	17.45	18.62	106.8	18.01	19.81	109.6	19.13	20.82	108.8
Scotland	2.31	2.45	106.2	2.35	2.53	108.0	2.33	2.52	108.3
N Ireland	0.60	0.65	105.9	0.61	0.65	106.2	0.60	0.64	106.7
UK	20.36	21.72	106.7	20.97	22.99	109.5	22.06	23.98	108.7

Source: Censuses; Registrar General's Estimates (1973 base)

This relative loss of population from the conurbations is paralleled in most large towns over 100,000 inhabitants; 1961–71 these grew more slowly than small towns, both relatively and absolutely (table 2.3). In England and Wales during that period their growth was only one-third of the national average (Champion 1976, 412–3). Yet in terms of the urban regions the loss is illusory. Reduced densities in the inner areas are the result of clearance either for commercial and other redevelopment, or for housing renewal at much lower densities, even where high-rise apartments have been built. However, compared with the very high intensity of occupation in nineteenth-century housing areas and due to enhanced standards of space for amenities such as schools and open spaces, even such intensive redevelopment does not usually absorb more than half the pre-existing population. The people displaced do not usually 'leave' the city but are rehoused on the periphery, often in adjacent local authority areas, many of which are still designated as 'rural districts'. Thus the moderately-high density areas have extended their bounds around the cities and there has been some evening-out of the population gradient between city centre and periphery. While less marked than in the inter-war years, the physical expansion of towns continues (ch. 6.I.3). Hall et al (1973) identified

100 labour centres which form the core of labour areas, jointly making up Standard Metropolitan Labour Areas (SMLAs). In these there was general and progressive decentralization of population 1951–66, a tendency which Champion (1976) has shown is continuing and extending to outer city areas beyond the SMLAs.

Fears have been expressed of megalopolitan tendencies in the corridor from Greater London to NW England and W Yorkshire, which contains about 51 per cent of the population of England and Wales, though Best (1972) argues that this danger lies some distance into the future. Moreover this is only one aspect of a general problem of concentration. Another eleven urban tracts in the UK, each with over one-quarter of a million people, together with the conurbations, add up to some 60 per cent of the UK population (Smailes 1961). Of the rest, only some two million, less than 5 per cent of the population, in England and Wales live over 16 km from a major city. Hence the activities of a large part of the workforce focus upon the major urbanized areas (ch. 2.IV.5).

Population densities within purely *rural areas* continue to decline, despite more than a century and a half of outward migration from the countryside (figs. 2.3 and 2.4). Indeed within the remoter areas of highland Britain a mere 1 per cent of the

Table 2.7 (cont.)

1951			1971			1981 (est.)			2001 (est.)		
Total		F per 100M	Total		F per 100M			F per 100M			F per 100M
M	F		M	F		M	F		M	F	
21.02	22.74	108.2	23.62	24.98	105.8	24.17	25.40	105.1	25.72	26.69	103.8
2.43	2.66	109.2	2.52	2.71	107.5	2.51	2.67	106.4	2.57	2.69	104.7
0.67	0.70	105.3	0.75	0.78	103.8	0.77	0.79	102.6	0.86	0.87	101.2
24.12	26.10	108.3	26.89	28.47	105.9	27.44	28.86	105.2	29.14	30.23	103.7

country's population lives on over one-third of its land area. In such thinly-peopled areas, there is a progressively ageing structure, many places experience excess of deaths over births, and, slowly but surely, such places are dying in demographic as well as in economic and social terms. Lack of basic amenities, including transport, difficulty of access to schools and other services, suggests that in much of central Wales and the Scottish Highlands and Islands further depopulation is likely except in more accessible recreational areas. Even where farming prospers and supports a range of active professional and service functions in local market towns, population decline or stagnation often continues. Increased food output has been achieved by greater productivity, much of it by increased mechanization. The farm labour-force has declined to less than half its 1945 total, while amalgamations continue to reduce the number of farms. Indeed, the UK now has only 3 per cent of its working population engaged in agriculture, though the area of tillage and stock numbers alike are considerably above inter-war levels (Coppock 1972, 36).

Although, at first glance, the fall in aggregate rural population has abated and even been reversed in many parts of England and Wales, in central and eastern Scotland, and in N Ireland, such a trend is frequently illusory. Increasing population and higher densities in the rural areas of the UK are mostly the result of dispersal of town-dwellers beyond urban administrative limits or, in certain favoured seaside and country districts, are due to the inward movement of population to live in

retirement. Dispersal into adjacent rural areas is no longer confined to the private
housing sector. Increasingly since the 1950s, local authority housing estates and
overspill agreements have moved outside urban boundaries into rural districts,
enlarging commuter hinterlands and extending the real city regions. In this sense
the urbanized areas within England and Wales have tended to coalesce (fig. 2.1)
and the same process is going on in Scotland and in N Ireland, principally around
Belfast (ch. 6.III).

II.2   Regional Components of Population Change

Within the basic pattern of population distribution and change, there are considerable contrasts in regional trends. Moreover, despite the persistence of trends
characteristic of the last fifty years — rural decline, urban overspill and the drift
south-east — there have been recent shifts in the scale and intensity of population
movements which presage future change. During the first half of the twentieth
century the major population growth was concentrated into three standard Regions
(as at present defined): the South East, and the W and E Midlands. The redistribution of the late eighteenth and nineteenth centuries had been partially reversed. The
SE Region increased its share rapidly and the Midlands Regions more gradually. In
the older industrial areas higher birth-rates were offset by massive out-migration.
During the depression years of the 1930s unemployment rates in the Midlands and
SE were often only half the national average while in the depressed industrial
areas of S Wales, Scotland and Northern England they were well above average
(ch. 1.III.2). Between 1921–51 the SE Region gained nearly 1.2 million people
by migration, the Midlands Region over 300,000 between 1931–51 and the SW
Region rather fewer over the same period. In contrast, between 1921–51, the net
migration losses of Northern England were 912,000, Wales 434,000 and Scotland
675,000. N Ireland's losses, a continuance of nineteenth-century rural-urban
movement to Britain, were somewhat abated in the stagnant UK industrial
economy of the inter-war period; against an increase of 23,000 in population from
1926–37 must be offset an estimated net migration loss of 70,000 during the same
period.

One of the aims of post-war planning has been to diminish the continuing drain
of population from the so-called depressed areas of the inter-war period. The extent
to which planning policy has succeeded in this may be judged, in part, from
population trends, not least rates of net migration. Between 1951 and 1961 the
South East's population increased by 1.13 million with a net migration gain of
438,000; the adjoining Regions, E Anglia and the South West, which received overspill from and growth associated with the SE had increases of 111,000 and 189,000
respectively (table 2.4). The other regions of population growth, the W and E
Midlands, which increased by 335,000 and 212,000 respectively, also had considerable migration gains. All other areas of the UK experienced losses by migration
between 1951 and 1961, which were substantial in some cases, as, for example,
from Scotland and the North West.

Despite vigorous attempts in the 1960s to attract industry to the development
areas and to control the supply of new jobs in the growth regions (chs. 1 and 4)
these population trends have persisted. Thus, since 1966, the SE Region has lost
population by migration, essentially due to massive losses from Greater London,
whose population decreased by 540,000 from 1961–71. These mainly went to the

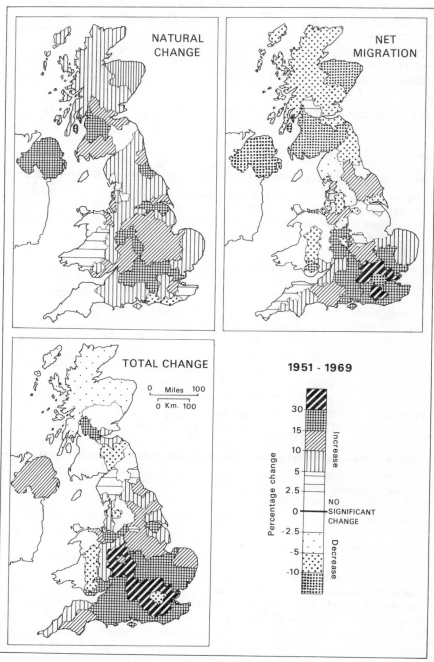

Figure 2.5   Natural, migration and total population change, economic planning sub-regions, 1951–69

adjacent regions of E Anglia and the SW. In the Midlands, however, there has
recently been a significant slowing down in the growth rate of the E Midlands. This
last case apart, however, the ratio of regional to national population trends reflects
the same essential features as those of the 1950s, though relative recovery of
population growth, and corresponding reduction of outward movement, in N
Ireland, Scotland, Wales and Yorks. and Humberside is interesting. On balance, we
must agree with the verdict of Eversley (1971) that, although regional policies have
not succeeded in arresting population losses from areas of long-standing decline,
'Without government policies the situation would be far worse' and it may well be
that some levelling out of regional rates of change may be expected in the future.

II.3   Sub-regional Patterns of Change

While regional trends pick out the main features of population change since the war,
they are on too broad a scale to permit accurate assessment of the relationship
between components of population change involving considerable intra-regional
contrasts, such as between urban and rural areas or between urban core and
periphery; furthermore, both natural and migrational components must be considered. Areas of high natural growth, such as the coalfields of NE England and
S Wales, or the Merseyside sub-region, have traditionally exported surpluses arising
from high birth-rates. Many rural areas still have a higher natural growth than they
can support. Thus a certain level of migration must always be expected at both
regional and sub-regional level as a regulator of population growth; but when such
migration seriously affects population and social structure, especially by continuously draining away the younger and more talented sections of the population,
it may create serious problems.

From the Registrar General's mid-year population estimates and census tabula-
tions for sixty-three planning sub-regions in England and Wales and twenty-two in
Scotland it is possible to analyse components of population change in fair detail
(SDD 1972, DoE 1971) (figs. 2.5 and 2.6).

Total change   The pattern of total population change at sub-regional level between
1951–69 (fig. 2.5) underlines those features already analysed, drawing particular
attention to the contrasts between decrease in the remote rural areas, the stagnation
or decline in such old industrial regions as the S Wales coalfield, and the W Yorkshire and E Lancashire textile districts. The fall in Greater London's total
population is typical of the inner areas of conurbations and has also occurred in all
other conurban sub-regions, during the 1960s and 1970s. Indeed the combined
population decline of Greater London and the central CBs of the five other English
conurbations, 1961–71, was 952,024, while in the more extensive conurbations
themselves the population fell by 724,557.

Natural change   Some of the features of total change are quite closely related to
natural change, i.e. the balance between births and deaths. High-growth areas in SE
England and the Midlands are marked by above-average natural increase, except in
inner urban areas. But many areas of slow overall growth or even of decline have
relatively high rates of natural increase: such are the Glasgow region and industrial
NE England, while in N Ireland the moderate total increase since 1951 is considerably below the rate of natural growth. Much of rural Scotland has a moderate

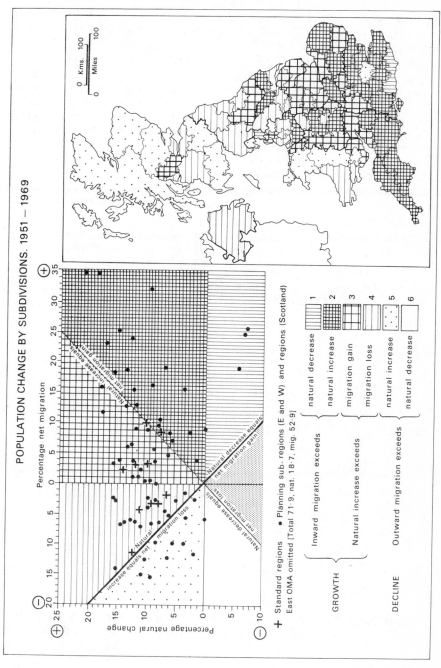

Figure 2.6   Components of population change, UK economic planning sub-regions, 1951–69

level of natural increase, but overall population stagnation or decline. In contrast, the south coast of England, an area of generally high total increase of population has little or no natural increase or may actually show a natural decrease, as in the Sussex coast sub-region. While certain of these contrasts are due to differences in age structure, they also imply considerable variations in migration.

Net migration Even at sub-regional level net migration conceals a good deal of inter- and intra-regional mobility which can only be fully analysed from information on changes of residence first collected in the 1961 census. Net migration figures reflect the resultants of more complex patterns of inward and outward movements and are often regarded as a good indicator of the relative power of 'push' and 'pull' forces acting upon population at a regional level. The pattern in fig. 2.5 is a remarkably concise commentary on the continuing pull of population to the more prosperous economy and attractive social image of the south-eastern quadrant of Britain. Apart from migration losses from the Greater London and W Midlands conurbation sub-regions, much of which has been due to outward movement to adjacent areas in a process of intra-regional overspill of housing and population, with corresponding increases in commuting, this quadrant was one wholly of migration gain. This growth now extends into the SW and Bristol–Severn areas, and into E Anglia, both of which have had higher migration gains in the 1960s than the inner metropolitan sub-regions (table 2.4). In part such increases have been due to retirement migration to rural or seaside areas, especially in the South West and along the south coast.

Components of population change These often complex inter-relationships can be conveniently summarized by combining in a single diagram the natural component of change (on the vertical axis) and the migrational component (horizontal axis) (fig. 2.6). Of the resultant eight possible type-areas of population change only six were represented in the 1951–69 period. In most areas there was growth in total population (types 1–4). In a very few cases, confined to the retirement areas of the Fylde, Morecambe–Lancaster, the Sussex and N Wales coasts, natural losses were more than compensated for by net migration gain, leading to population increase (type 1). In contrast, areas where natural increase exceeded migration loss (type 4) include most of the conurbations and older industrial areas, together with less remote rural areas of S Wales, Northern England and Southern Scotland which, either by retaining sufficient of their natural increase or by attracting migrants from adjacent areas, have increased in population over the post-war period.

Fastest growth occurs generally in areas of both natural and migrational increase (types 2 and 3). Natural increase predominates over migrational gain (type 3) in much of the E Midlands, peripheral areas of the W Midlands and the north-western parts of the Outer Metropolitan Area. Apart from the growth area of Bristol, the Severn estuary and the Welsh border, influenced by overspill from the W Midlands, such growth patterns are virtually absent from the rest of the UK. However, rural N Yorkshire and the Falkirk–Stirling area, both of which have been affected by outward movement from adjacent urban regions, show this type of trend. The latter has received much of the overspill from the central Clydeside conurbation and east-central Scotland.

The major areas of attraction for population are picked out by retention of natural increase together with a larger element of growth due to net migration (type 2). This type of growth accounts for very large increases in population in most of the inner and outer metropolitan areas. Much of southern and the whole of south-western England now shares these characteristics, due to considerable recent gains by migration, a trait shared with much of E Anglia, where a good deal of recent in-movement is associated with the effects of overspill agreements with Greater London (fig. 2.22). Similar features have occurred in the outer sub-regions of the W Midlands but, apart from the suburban commuter belts of north Cheshire (with links to Manchester and Merseyside) and of mid-Yorkshire (with links to Leeds—Bradford and Hull), this 'healthy' type of population trend is absent from the rest of the UK.

The remaining areas fall into two categories of population loss. In one area, NE Lancashire, a long-continuing net outward migration is combined with a slight natural decrease (type 6), due largely to the region's ageing population structure, the only example of natural losses outside the 'retirement' areas. Yet there are a number of areas where net outmigration exceeds natural gain to produce a fall in total population (type 5). These occur in two distinct types of area. The first includes Greater London where, as in all central city areas, population is moving out. In two nineteenth-century industrial areas, Furness and the north-eastern parts of the S Wales coalfield, both long-standing industrial decline and an ageing population contribute to population losses. The second type of area of population loss is confined to the remote rural areas including most of southern and highland Scotland, and Mid and North Wales. Here longstanding out-movement has created an aged population with a low rate of natural growth and stagnating or slowly declining populations.

II.4 Vital Trends

The broad components of population change reviewed in section II.3 of this chapter are resultants of three basic factors in population dynamics: births, deaths and migration. Variations in the fertility, mortality and morbidity of the population reflect economic and social conditions; they are also the outcome of present population structures and are determinants of future population trends and structure. Thus, vital and migrational differences are basic elements in explaining and planning for economic and social problems at both national and regional levels.

Birth-rates The rapid decline of birth-rate in all social classes and all regions of the UK was one of the most remarkable demographic features of the early twentieth century and the inter-war years. While the reduction in family size was general, significant variations in fertility and family size remain between social classes and are found between the various parts of the UK. Glass and Grebenik (1954) showed that higher fertility persisted among wives of manual workers, despite the general decrease in family size. The tendency to a somewhat larger average family since 1945 has been more marked among professional and managerial classes, changing slightly the progression of high social class/small family to low social class/large family which was characteristic up to the Second World War.

The 1961 census revealed that between couples of equivalent age of marriage, e.g. those married between ages 20—24, the average size for *all* durations of marriage among manual workers was higher than among non-manual workers.

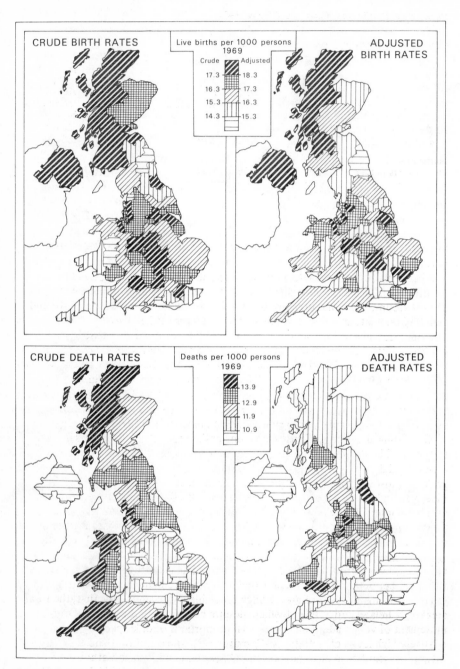

Figure 2.7   Birth- and death-rates, UK economic planning sub-regions, 1969

TABLE 2.8

Variations in Family Size, England and Wales, 1961

Children per marriage

| Class | manual workers | | | non-manual workers | | |
	V unskilled	IV semi-skilled	III M skilled	I professional	II employers and managers	III N intermediate
All durations of marriage	2.55	2.16	1.92	2.10	1.82	1.64
Married for up to 5 years	1.74	1.47	1.36	1.69	1.34	1.29

Source: Census (1961)

Even among those married for less than five years in 1962, these differentials were found (table 2.8).

However, the differential fertility between social classes has narrowed. According to Glass and Grebenik (1954): 'The ratio of fertility of manual to non-manual groups, which has been around 1.4:1.0 for the marriages of the 1920s and early 1930s, fell to less than 1.2:1.0 for the marriages of the 1940s.'

However, while fertility among semi- and unskilled workers has tended to stabilize at relatively low levels, that for employers and professional workers has tended to rise since 1945. The *Population Investigation Committee's* national survey of Britain (1967–8) observed little difference between social classes in the proportion of recently married couples adopting birth control methods and noted that the gap between manual and non-manual groups had narrowed considerably over the previous twenty years (House of Commons 1971, 189).

Geographical patterns of birth-rates substantiate the social differences in fertility within all cities. For example, on Merseyside, traditionally an area of relatively high fertility, the fertility-rates are clearly zoned from high rates, 75 per cent above national rates, in the central and inner residential areas of Liverpool and Bootle CBs, through moderate levels 50–75 per cent above national average in intermediate areas, including much inter-war corporation and some private residential areas, to low values 20–25 per cent above national average, in outer areas of recent corporation and private housing estates (Pickett 1970, 92–7).

Despite the general evening-out of birth-rates during the 1960s, crude regional birth-rates ranged from 12.1 to 23.6 per thousand in 1969 (fig. 2.7), as compared with 16.3 per 1000 for England and Wales, 17.4 for Scotland and 21.4 for N Ireland. Two major types of area of high crude birth-rate stand out: first, the rural areas of N Ireland and Scotland which, despite heavy and long-continued out-movement of young adults and quite high proportions of older people, have relatively high levels of fertility. As Compton (1976) has shown, there are considerable disparities in birth-rate between Protestant and Roman Catholic communities in N Ireland, the Catholic birth-rate being over one-third higher, a fact reflected in regional patterns of fertility and natural change. Secondly, in industrial regions in C Scotland and the axial belt from London to S Lancashire and

W Yorkshire manual worker groups and younger population structures both seem
to lead to rather higher birth-rates. In contrast, lower crude birth-rates are associated
with the rural regions of Wales and N and S England, and, not surprisingly, with
many of the retirement areas of N Wales, Southern and SW England. Thus, while in
the past higher birth-rates prevailed in the north and west of Britain (especially
Scotland and N Ireland), by the mid-1960s this differential had to some extent
been ironed out. Indeed, the fall in birth-rate since 1969 to 13.0 per 1,000 for
England and Wales, 13.4 for Scotland, and 18.8 for N Ireland in 1974 (UK 13.2)
seems to have affected the North relatively more than the Midlands and South.

However, crude birth-rates are affected by the age structure of the population
and the Registrar General's adjusted rates allowing for this show the regional
position more clearly. High rates still characterize N Ireland and the Highlands and
Islands of Scotland. The highest adjusted birth-rates in England and Wales and S
Scotland tend to occur in the suburban and peripheral areas of the large cities and
industrial areas, though this is less marked in SE England. Adjusted rates narrow
the overall range of birth-rates and certain rural areas, for example in N Wales, SW
England and N Yorkshire, achieve moderate or above-average birth-rates when age
structure and the small number of total births are taken into account.

Death-rates The patterns of mortality in the UK, though offering many parallels,
are in certain respects more clear-cut than those of fertility. General mortality-rates
and those from many specific diseases are well above average in large urban
authority areas and much below average in rural districts. There is also a general
regional gradient from relatively high death-rates in north-western Britain to
relatively low rates in south-eastern Britain in areas of equivalent character,
whether urban or rural.

Some of the highest death-rates in the UK are found in association with poor
environments and higher-than-average incidence of social and economic problems.
Many such conditions occur in the large nineteenth-century industrial towns and,
in turn, within all urban areas there is still a marked gradient between unhealthy
inner areas and the suburbs, partly due to environmental conditions, partly to
social and demographic characteristics. The average risk of death in Salford, one of
the highest mortality areas, was 33 per cent higher than in Bournemouth, one of
the lowest, in 1969, according to adjusted death-rates. Similarly wide contrasts
occur between inner urban areas and the outer suburbs, as witness the Merseyside
comparison between a 1969 adjusted death-rate of 16.19 per thousand for Bootle,
and the much lower rates for the middle-class suburban areas, e.g. 10.71 in Wirral
UD or 7.16 for Formby UD.

Many contrasts are, however, generic rather than regional in character. Clearly,
different social classes have very different mortality experience (table 2.9). Despite
the reduction of mortality differentials in all social classes, due doubtless to the
progressively better health, dietary and housing conditions of the lower classes, a
considerable range remains, involving many factors, social, environmental and, perhaps, genetic. Among indices of class differentials in mortality experience, infant
mortality, regarded as a sensitive measure, was 2 to 2.5 times higher among children
of socio-economic class V parents than of class I (table 2.10). In 1973, on the basis
of data for Scotland, it was twice as great among social class V as in class I in the
1960s (stillbirths 16.2 and 7.4 per 1,000 respectively). Factors quoted include the
higher incidence of premature births, linked to the earlier age of child-bearing

TABLE 2.9

Male Standardized Mortality rates by Socio-economic Class, England and Wales, 1921–72
(England and Wales = 100)

Class	1921–3 (age 20–64)	1930–2	1949–53	1959–63 (age 15–64)	1970–72
I	82	90	86	76	77
II	94	94	92	81	81
III	95	97	101	100	104
IV	101	102	104	103	113
V	125	111	118	143	137

Class I = professional
       II = employers and managers
       III = intermediate and junior non-manual (N); skilled manual (M)
       IV = semi-skilled manual
       V = unskilled manual
Source: Social Trends 6 (1975), Table 7.1, 26

among working-class mothers, more closely-spaced pregnancies, poorer ante- and post-natal care, and greater risk and poorer treatment of infection in children such as bronchitis and gastro-enteritis, all of which are often coupled with poor and overcrowded housing conditions.

The pattern of crude death-rates by planning sub-regions (fig. 2.7) is misleading in that areas with a high proportion of old people are bound to have a higher relative number of deaths than those with a more youthful population. This is reflected to some extent in the high rates for NW Scotland, N and SW Wales, SW and Southern England; when adjusted for age-structure, these relatively high rates are modified in most cases.

Above-average adjusted death-rates pick out C Scotland, especially the Glasgow region, the industrial NE of England, a belt from S Lancashire through W Yorkshire to Humberside, and the S Wales coalfield. The W Midlands have generally modest rates, though mortality is higher in the Potteries and the W Midlands conurbation. In general, the rural Midlands and the Welsh border, E Anglia, SE and SW England have low or moderate rates, though the higher figures for Greater London underline the less healthy and poorer social conditions of inner urban areas.

The regional patterns of general mortality and of morbidity of particular diseases have been fully mapped and analysed by Howe (1970), whose maps, using

TABLE 2.10

Infant Mortality, England and Wales, 1964–5

| Infant deaths per 1,000 live births | Socio-economic classes | | |
	I and II	III	IV and V
Neonatal	9.2	11.8	13.2
Post-natal	3.5	5.4	7.6

Source: Kelsall (1967), 49

standardized mortality-rates, support the more general picture given in fig. 2.7. He observes that in the 320 administrative units mapped, 53 areas had very high male mortality ratios of which only 4 were in the London area, the rest being in northern and western Britain with the Glasgow and S Lancashire areas having the greatest concentration of high rates. While the pattern of female mortality differs in detail it is similar to that for men, though there is a rather less marked concentration of high rates in Greater London, NE England, S Lancashire and S Wales.

Infant Mortality One of the most telling demographic indicators of social and environmental conditions and, indeed, of overall living standards, is the rate of infant mortality. Not only are there marked class differences in its national incidence (table 2.10), but there are pronounced regional differences (Coates and Rawstron 1971, 227–35). In the majority of local authority areas in SE, Eastern, Southern, SW and Midland England infant mortality rates are relatively low. The greatest incidence of high infant mortality occurs in Wales, NW and N England and Yorkshire, and in particular in C Scotland and N Ireland. Despite the fall in infant mortality in the UK since 1945, in continuance of a marked downward trend since the mid-Victorian period (fig. 2.2), which has reduced rates from around 31 per 1,000 in 1917 to about 16.3 per 1,000 in 1974 in England and Wales (19 per 1,000 in Scotland and 22.1 per 1,000 in N Ireland), significant regional variations persist. For example, whereas the infant mortality rates in the central Clydeside conurbation in 1969 were 24.2 per 1,000 they ranged from 19.8 to 14.0 in the Scottish New Towns; similarly, there was considerable variation at sub-regional level in England and Wales, the highest (24 per 1,000) being experienced in the SE Lancashire and NE Cheshire (SELNEC) and Merseyside conurbations and in the central and eastern S Wales valleys, while in the Essex sub-region the rate was only 13 per 1,000. Such regional variations exist. In 1974, in England and Wales, all the regions north of the Severn-Wash line, with exception of the E Midlands, had above average rates of infant mortality, while E Anglia, the SE and the SW were below.

Ironically, those areas with the poorest mortality and health records are frequently those with the poorest medical and health services. Despite the overall improvement in provision under the National Health Acts of 1946–8, the National Health and Social Services have not yet succeeded in levelling out substantial regional inequalities. Thus the average number of patients on general practitioners' lists tend to be higher in industrial towns in the North than in towns of the Midlands and South, and the list bigger in poor inner-city residential areas than in the middle-class suburbs (Coates and Rawstron 1971, 188). There is a strong case for positive discrimination in *favour* of such areas in the provision of social services.

II.5 Migration

After a flurry of movement in the early war years involving 19 per cent of the population of England in non-local moves in 1940 (7.5 million) this mobility had dropped to 7.4 per cent by 1950 (3.2 million moves). According to the figures of residential mobility, gathered by the sample census of 1966, the percentage of movers respectively over one and five years had fallen to 4.7 and 4.8; moreover, only 29 per cent of the non-local moves involved distances of over 64 km. Thus, though the total volume of migration is likely to increase, there will be much greater growth of short-distance movement, strengthening the ties between cities

TABLE 2.11

Regional Mobility, GB, 1970–1 and 1966–71

	Migrants 1970–1 (1,000s)			Migrants 1966–71 (1,000s)		
Regions	(1) Total from local region	(2)	$\frac{2}{1}\%$	(4) Total from local region	(5)	$\frac{5}{4}\%$
Northern	349.5	299.2	86(84)	1,112.7	947.4	85(85)
Yorks. & Humberside	505.3	422.5	86(86)	1,577.8	1,363.0	86(86)
North West	697.5	607.3	87(88)	2,135.6	1,865.1	87(89)
E Midlands	339.8	271.3	80(81)	1,015.8	821.7	81(83)
W Midlands	536.5	454.2	85(85)	1,650.3	1,400.5	85(86)
E Anglia	170.4	131.7	77(76)	479.7	374.2	78(80)
South East	2,004.7	1,773.7	89(89)	5,698.6	5,029.7	89(90)
South West	413.5	326.2	79(81)	1,167.6	931.2	80(82)
Wales	245.4	204.4	83(84)	765.7	642.5	85(85)
Scotland	606.1	546.1	90(N.A.)	1,810.3	1,643.8	91(N.A.)

The tabulations are on a 10% sample base. Comparative figures for 1966 are given in brackets in columns 3 and 6: 'local' refers to the number of migrants not moving outside the region in which they were enumerated.

The figures for Scotland are not comparable with those for the less extensive English regions.

Source: Census 1971 Great Britain Migration Tables Part I

and their hinterlands and leading to a much greater volume of daily journeys to work, to school, to shop and to share in all city services.

Inter-regional migration Though of considerable importance to regional variations in population growth, net migration conceals both the volume and patterns of movement which are difficult to study from British census sources before 1961, when information concerning changes in residence were first collected. However, unlike many European countries the UK has no system of continuous registration of personal or residential mobility, though for wartime and early post-war years the National Register could be used for this purpose (Newton and Jeffrey, 1951). Contrasts in migration between town and country or between inner and outer zones or urban regions are part of a mobility continuum which involves not only inter- and intra-regional residential migration but also considerable personal mobility in all sections of the community. Up to 1961 the only census source of information on migration flows was derived from birth-place statistics which do not permit direct study of movement over specific time periods. In its 10 per cent sample the 1961 census enquired about change of address over the year prior to the enumeration. The 1966 and 1971 censuses extended the question to include change of residence over a five-year, as well as a one-year, period prior to the census (table 2.11). These data permit analysis of in-, out- and gross migration in varying regional detail down to local authority areas and may be cross-tabulated by age, sex, occupational group, etc.

Net inter-regional mobility The relatively small net balance of migration in all regions in both 1960–1 and 1965–6 concealed considerable in- and out-movements;

indeed gross migration usually exceeded net by over 10 to 1 and for many regions
was a good deal higher (table 2.12). It is not easy to summarize inter-regional
movements, even at the very general level of the UK economic planning regions,
since it is difficult to link these various components to the population at risk. The
scale, direction and balance of the migration streams are much what one would
expect from general population trends. Net balances are small, mostly under 5 per
1,000 of the resident population, but gross migration indices for population aged one
year and over exceed 40 per 1,000 in some areas (table 2.12). The greatest mobility
rates in 1960–1 occurred in E Anglia and the SW region, followed by the E and W
Midlands. Though by far the greatest numbers moved into and from the SE region,
its gross migration rates were relatively small, especially in Greater London. Many
regions had very similar degrees of movement and very small differences between
inward and outward rates of migration as shown by modest net balances. Such
features well exemplify the dictum that every migration flow produces a counterflow. Hence, the differentials in migration rates between such regions as the NW,
Yorks. and Humberside, and Wales differ little from 'healthy' growth areas of the
W Midlands or even the SE.

In 1965–6 migration rates confirmed the attraction of E Anglia, the SW and the
E Midlands. The most sluggish were those for the NW and Scotland and, in terms of
migration rates, Greater London, despite the latter's large volume of both in- and
out-movement. The migration rates to the development areas were generally higher
than in 1960–1; in particular, the inward balance of movement to Wales suggests
that development area policies in the 1960s were beginning to make an impact on
population trends. Scotland's very low rate of inward migration and considerable
net loss remained, however.

It is not possible to show the complexity of inter-regional movements on a single
map, but the balance of migration of population aged over one year for the period
1961–6 gives a graphic picture of both the essential mechanism and the resultants
of such movements (fig. 2.8). The inset map of net migration rates and the actual
net flows are a clear commentary upon the drift south-east. Inter-regional movement
is seen to be not so much a direct transfer from areas of loss to areas of gain but
rather a 'shunting' movement culminating in the transfer of considerable numbers
of people to only four major regions: E Anglia, the E Midlands, the SW and the
Outer South East (OSE). The latter is involved in a second major determinant of
post-war migration, the movement from inner London which is now spreading from
Greater London to the Outer Metropolitan Area (OMA) and the OSE. This involves
rehousing of people from these areas of the SE in a second generation of New
Towns and overspill schemes mainly located in the three adjacent planning regions
(table 1.7).

Those regions which gained population by residential migration in the 1960s
all reflect the same basic features. The SW gained from all other regions over the
period 1961–6, not only from gains by outward movement from the metropolitan
area but also to its own attractions in the Bristol–Severnside growth area and in the
rural and coastal retirement areas of Devon and Cornwall (Law and Warnes, 1976),
a fact reflected in the age structure of the migration (table 2.14). However by
1965–6 over 90 per cent of the region's gains were from the SE, W Midlands and
NW. E Anglia gained from all other regions except the SW and, perhaps surprisingly,
Wales, though this inter-action was on a very small scale. The E Midlands similarly
gained from all regions, except E Anglia and the SW, to both of which there were

TABLE 2.12

Inter-regional migration, GB, 1960–1 and 1965–6

Planning region	All ages above one year (1,000s)						Net balance of working age 15–59			Migration rates of resident population (per 1,000)							
	1960–1			1965–6			1965–6			1960–1				1965–6			
	in	out	net	in	out	net	male	female	total	in	out	gross	net	in	out	gross	net
Northern	35.9	45.6	−9.7	45.3	48.1	−2.8	−0.8	−1.2	−2.0	11.0	14.0	25.0	−3.0	13.6	14.5	28.1	−0.9
Yorks. and Humberside	53.4	60.8	−7.4	66.4	66.0	+0.4	+1.0	−0.8	+0.2	11.5	13.1	24.6	−1.6	13.9	13.8	27.7	+0.1
North West	61.9	68.9	−7.0	70.5	72.9	−2.4	−0.4	−2.2	−2.6	9.4	10.5	19.9	−1.1	10.5	10.9	21.4	−0.4
E Midlands	55.9	48.6	+7.3	67.4	55.6	+11.7	+4.3	+3.3	+7.6	18.0	15.7	33.7	+2.4	20.6	17.0	37.7	+3.6
W Midlands	63.5	61.4	+2.0	66.0	70.5	−4.5	−0.3	−3.0	−3.3	13.4	12.9	26.3	+0.4	13.2	14.1	27.3	−0.9
South East	173.3	153.2	+20.2	174.6	194.8	−20.1	−3.8	−0.7	−4.5	10.7	9.4	20.1	+1.2	10.3	11.4	21.7	−1.2
Greater London				60.7	78.7	−18.0	−3.1	−1.9	−5.0					7.8	10.1	17.9	−2.3
OMA	61.7	59.7	+2.1	52.0	60.1	−8.1	−1.9	−1.8	−3.7	7.6	9.9	17.5	−2.3	10.4	12.0	22.4	−1.6
Rest	111.6	93.5	+18.1	61.9	55.9	+5.9	+1.2	+3.1	+4.3	16.1	14.5	30.6	+1.5	14.9	13.4	28.3	+1.5
E Anglia	35.0	30.8	+4.2	48.1	36.1	+12.0	+3.0	+3.9	+6.9	23.8	20.9	44.7	+2.9	30.4	22.8	53.3	+7.6
South West	87.0	67.7	+19.3	93.2	72.6	+20.7	+4.1	+6.3	+10.3	25.5	19.8	45.4	+5.7	25.6	20.0	45.6	+5.7
Wales	33.9	38.7	−4.8	36.7	36.0	+0.7	−0.5	−0.3	−0.8	12.8	14.6	27.5	−1.8	13.6	13.3	26.9	+0.3
Scotland	27.4	51.6	−24.2	37.0	52.7	−15.7	−6.6	−5.3	−11.9	5.3	10.0	15.3	−4.7	7.1	10.1	17.2	−3.0
GB	627.1	627.1	—	705.2	705.2	—	—	—	—	—	—	—	—	—	—	—	—

Source: Long Term Population Distribution, GB: A Study (HMSO, 1971), Appendix 2, Tables 1a and 1e

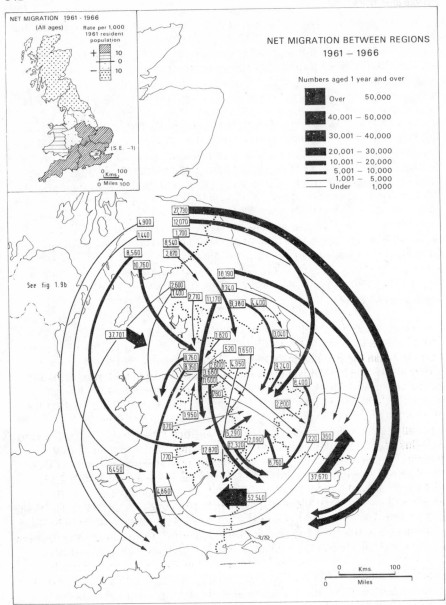

Figure 2.8   Net inter-regional migration, UK, 1961—6

small net losses. The SE epitomizes many of the features of both intra- and inter-regional movement. While there were large net losses from the Greater London sub-region to the OSE and adjacent regions, it attracted large numbers in the 15—24 age-group, a feature also found in the OMA. Residential dispersal from the centre to the periphery is seen in the gain in all age-groups of the OSE sub-region which is comparable in this respect to E Anglia and the SW (see also table 1.7).

All other regions suffered a net loss of population by migration, though this did not occur in every age-group. The W Midlands' losses were mainly to adjacent regions, the NW and E Midlands, and to the 'gain' areas of E Anglia and the SW; but it gained from all other regions. The NW gained from other regions of the north of England, from Scotland and the W Midlands, but lost to all other regions; while Wales gained from the NW, and the North, Scotland and E Anglia. Those with the weakest attraction in this phase were Yorks. and Humberside, which lost to all regions except the North and Scotland; the North, which lost to all save Scotland, and Scotland, which lost population to every other region and in every age-group. As Champion (1976) has shown, these tendencies have persisted in the last decade. Scotland, the three regions of northern England, the W Midlands and SE have all continued to lose population by migration. The only regions of consistent gain are the E Midlands, E Anglia and the SW, though Wales – having staunched the outflow which has characterized it for much of the century – actually had a small gain by migration in 1966–71, a gain due in part to retirement migration to N Wales. Within all regions, however, a factor of increasing importance in population redis-tribution is the movement of people out of the inner areas of large cities, a factor which is now giving cause for considerable concern in relation to age structure (section III.2), housing and social structure (sections III.3 and III.4) and employment (section IV.4).

Age-selective migration Population migration is highly age-selective. All recent studies of migration in the UK confirm the tendency of young Britons to be more migratory than the population as a whole. There is a strong movement of school-leavers and people in their late teens and early twenties from both rural areas and stagnating industrial regions of limited employment opportunities. In areas of residential development accessible to large towns, rural out-migration is offset by inmigration of young families. But the inner residential areas of the cities, especially London, are generally a zone of population loss, offset in certain cases by an influx of overseas immigrants and of single young people, including many students. Cumulatively, such differences contribute to striking contrasts between the age structure of migrants and that of the population as a whole (table 2.13). The 15–24 age-group is by far the most mobile with migration-rates in 1970–1 35 per cent above that of the next most mobile 10-year group, 25–34 years. On the limited evidence of the 1960–1 and 1970–1 data, migration rates seem to be rising more quickly in the 15–24 age-group than in any other. Inasmuch as there has been a considerable increase in the number of people in full-time higher education, a proportion of this may be ascribed to temporary migration but there is much evidence to support the belief that such migration leads to permanent movement away from home, especially in the case of those moving from rural areas or depressed industrial regions.

Such age-selective migration is reflected both in the structure of the migration itself and in the age structure of both sender and receiver areas. The clear-cut losses of 1960–1 in virtually all age-groups from the three northern regions of England and from Scotland and Wales, had been ameliorated by 1965–6 (fig. 2.9). By 1970–1 the trend to loss was reasserting itself in the NW and in Yorks. and Humberside. Scotland alone showed a net migration loss in every age-group through-out the period and this was quite severe for the young and mature age-groups of 15–44 years, representing a substantial draining of vigorous, working-age popula-

TABLE 2.13

Age Structure of Inter-regional Migrants and Total Population, GB, 1961 and 1971

| | Per cent of age-group | | | | All ages |
	1–14	15–24	25–44	45+	1+
Population 1961	22	13	27	38	100
Migrants 1960–1	23	23	35	19	100
Population 1971	22	15	24	39	100
Migrants 1970–1	24	27	30	19	100

Source: Census 1961; Census 1971

tion of both sexes from the region. This loss of the active, youthful population persisted in the NW and for Wales, despite a general slowing down of the migration flow in the mid-1960s; indeed in the NW there was an increase of one-third in the net loss from the 15–24 group between 1960–1 and 1965–6 and from 1966–71 the losses from this region were double what they had been in 1961–6. The population situation of Yorks. and Humberside, encouraging in the mid-1960s in that loss in all three younger age-groups (0–44 years) was arrested, reverted to the former pattern of high losses in the younger age-groups by 1970–1. But in the W Midlands there was a reversal of the modest gains in the younger age-groups by the mid-1960s, though the losses in the 15–24 groups were mainly female. The 1971 census confirmed the change in this region's fortunes by showing an increased net loss of population in all age-groups, 1970–6 (fig. 2.9), a trend confirmed by table 2.14.

In contrast, the regions of gain not only added considerable numbers of population but, apart from the SW, had their greatest gains among the under-45s. It is clear that E Anglia and the SW in particular, and the E Midlands to an extent, were closely linked with the SE in an age-selective redistribution of population. In the SW the growing dominance of migration by the age-groups over 45 is reflected in the fact that by 1965–6 over one-third of the net migration gain was in the over-60 'retirement' groups which came mainly from the SE, W Midlands and NW. E Anglia is mainly a recipient of family migration from Greater London, reflected in the large net gains in the 25–44 and 0–14 groups and the smaller gains of 15–24-year-olds.

The key to much selective redistribution lies in the SE region. Despite a striking reversal of migration balance between 1961 and 1966, there was still a considerable gain in the 15–24 age-group, the migrants coming from all regions of the UK and from overseas. However, by 1965–6 major out-movement had developed in all other age-groups with a considerable overspill movement of young families to E Anglia (the 0–44 year group). That to the SW was dominated by the over-45s, and the over-60s were very important, especially women. These trends had intensified by 1970–1.

Within the SE gross movements have been almost as large as the gross movements with all other regions (e.g. 304,000 as compared with 370,000 in 1965–6). This massive dispersal of families from the centre of Greater London and the OMA to the periphery (the OSE) involves two distinct types of mover: first, a residential migration of ages 1–14 and 25+; secondly, retirement migration of the over 60s to

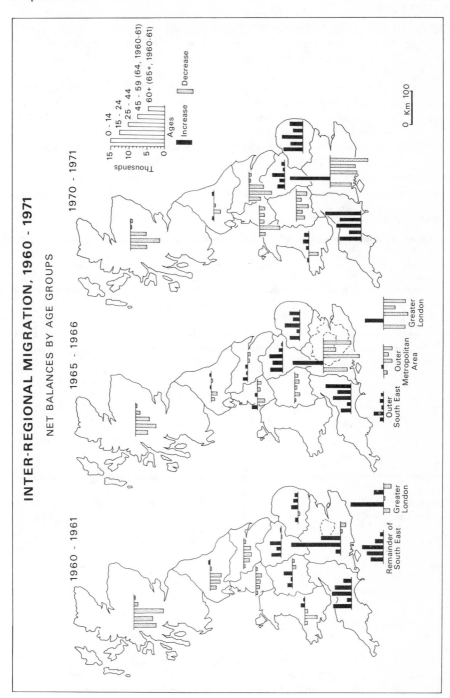

Figure 2.9   Inter-regional migration by age-groups, GB economic planning regions, 1960–71

the south coast in particular, reflected in the fact that one-third of the flow from Greater London to the OSE in 1965–6 was of those over 60 years.

The effects on population structure may be derived from the relationship between the regional net migration balance and the gross movements in each age-group (table 2.14).

Two aspects of migration have shaped trends in the distribution and structure of population since 1945. First, fluctuations in *net overseas migration* have had considerable impact at both national and local level. Secondly, *differential inter-regional movement*, the net resultants of which explain much of the regional variations in population growth, is of considerable importance in its effects on regional structure and future population trends. Though in demographic terms both have much in common, their social impact is very different: thus each will be discussed in turn.

TABLE 2.14

Regional Migration Gain or Loss 1961–71, by Major Age-groups, GB (net balances by age group in 1,000s)

Region	5–14	15–24	25–44	45–59	60+	All ages 5+
A. *1961–6*						
Northern	−12.1	−14.5	−20.3	−6.0	+1.7	−51.2
Yorks. and Humberside	−1.8	−6.3	−8.2	−4.2	−4.8	−25.2
North West	−1.4	−9.5	−7.2	−4.6	−5.8	−28.5
E Midlands	+6.8	+2.8	+16.8	+3.4	+1.8	+31.6
W Midlands	−0.2	−6.1	−1.9	−8.1	−8.3	−24.6
E Anglia	+8.4	+3.7	+14.8	+8.3	+12.5	+47.7
South East	−14.8	+34.0	−18.0	−13.0	−32.8	−44.6
South West	+13.6	+6.1	+25.2	+21.5	+29.7	+96.1
Wales	+1.5	−10.3	−1.2	+2.7	+6.0	−1.2
B. *1966–71*						
Northern	−5.2	−15.3	−8.1	−0.7	+2.3	−27.0
Yorks. and Humberside	−5.0	−17.7	−15.9	−3.8	−2.3	−44.7
North West	−1.9	−20.5	−5.3	−5.9	−8.9	−42.4
E Midlands	+6.7	+3.0	+16.9	+2.0	+0.7	+29.3
W Midlands	−5.0	−7.3	−10.1	−9.3	−11.2	−43.0
E Anglia	+12.4	+9.5	+22.7	+10.9	+16.4	+71.8
South East	−15.8	+47.3	−24.9	−23.6	−47.6	−64.6
South West	+12.5	+11.4	+23.1	+24.5	+42.3	+113.9
Wales	+1.3	−10.3	+1.6	+6.0	+8.3	+6.8

Source: Champion (1976), table IV

II.6 Immigration from Overseas

General review Despite its importance, precise information on the scale and regional impact of immigration is limited. Immigration statistics leave many gaps, while census data on immigration are defective in a number of ways. British census tables of birth-place before 1971 show nothing of the date of movement and give nationality but not ethnic origins. Moreover, the census probably under-enumerated the overseas-born in both 1961 and, especially, in the 10 per cent sample census of

1966. Furthermore, it was difficult to distinguish persons born overseas of British parents. The questions in the 1971 census concerning place of birth, nationality and place of birth of parents and year of first entry into Britain of overseas-born have provided the basis for a fuller and more accurate picture of immigration from census sources.

There have been three phases in post-war immigration to the UK. Between 1945–55 renewed emigration to the Dominions led to slight net migration losses, despite a considerable gain of European refugees, especially those of Polish origin. Nevertheless, during this period England and Wales gained by migration, not least because of continuing immigration from Eire (table 2.2). After 1955, immigration from the New Commonwealth increased considerably, leading to a relatively large net inward movement of 479,000 in 1958–62. Rising labour demands, especially in the early 1960s, had much to do with this influx which produced net gains of 45,000 in 1958. This rose to 172,000 in the peak year of 1961, leading to restriction of movement under the *Commonwealth Immigrants Act* of 1962 (Publ. Gen. Act 1962). This Act created a graded system of employment vouchers which immigrants were required to hold to obtain entry: 'A' vouchers were issued to those who had jobs to come to, 'B' vouchers were for those with particular needed skills or qualifications (such as nurses or doctors), and 'C' vouchers were issued to unskilled workers. Preference was given from the outset to A and B categories. C vouchers were officially discontinued from 1965, and the policy of selective recruitment of highly-qualified persons was confirmed by new regulations in 1968.

The 1962 Act allowed dependants of immigrants already in the country freedom of entry, though this was tightened up under the *1968 Commonwealth Immigrants Act* (Publ. Gen. Act 1968). Since 1962, therefore, the emphasis has shifted from the immigration of workers to their families and dependants: thus, in 1969 of 36,557 Commonwealth immigrants 29,459 were dependants. In 1968 250,000 dependants were estimated to be eligible for entry into the UK, mostly from India and Pakistan (Eversley and Sukdeo 1969). A further group of coloured Commonwealth immigrants are the holders of British passports, mainly East Africans of Asian origin, the estimates of whom vary considerably: for example, estimates of the potential numbers involved in recent expulsions from Uganda vary from 23,000 to over 50,000 against the 26,000 who had arrived in Britain around the expiry of the expulsion deadline in November 1972.

In relation to the total population of the UK, the increase of immigrants, more particularly of coloured Commonwealth immigrants, is not large (table 2.15); but it has led to considerable changes in the characteristics of the overseas-born population of the UK since 1945 and, in some localities, has had very marked social and demographic consequences. As compared with about 1 per cent overseas born in 1931 (perhaps 1.5 per cent allowing for those whose birth-place was not stated), the increase in GB to 1,053,200 (2.1 per cent) in 1951, 1,507,600 (2.9 per cent) by 1961, to 1,876,300 (3.5 per cent) by 1966 and to 3,100,000 (5.8 per cent) by 1971 represents a considerable change. In 1966 less than half the 1.88 million people of overseas birth in Britain were coloured (852,750), a figure which was estimated to be 1,030,000 by 1971; it is around these figures that most of the debate on immigration has focused. It is difficult to estimate precisely the numbers of coloured population, since this also involves children born to immigrants in the UK. It has been suggested that 543,000 children should be added to the 943,000 people from the New Commonwealth recorded in the 1971 census. Such figures indicate a total of about 1.49 million of New Commonwealth birth in GB in 1971 (2.7 per cent of total population) and about 1.74 millions in mid-1974 (3.2 per cent of the total). (Rose *et al* 1969.)

Distribution

The problem is not primarily one of overall numbers of immigrants, but rather of their proportionate distribution. Like most immigrant communities, past and present, coloured immigrants tend to concentrate in relatively few areas. In 1951 the greater part of the overseas-born population of the UK lived in London and SE England, though at that time these were chiefly European-born. Since that time the overseas-born have increased much more rapidly than the population as a whole and have become even more concentrated in distribution. While the SE planning region (including Greater London) was by far the main focus of coloured immigrants, considerable increases had taken place in the W Midlands and, especially of Indians and Pakistanis, in the NW, Yorks. and Humberside, and the E Midlands (table 2.16). By 1971 these proportions remained much the same. While the percentage of New Commonwealth immigrants in the conurbations had fallen slightly, it had done so at about the same rate as the total population.

TABLE 2.15

Estimated Population of Major Immigrant Groups, England and Wales, 1966–86, in 1,000s

Area of origin	1966 Born overseas	1966 Born in UK	1966 Total	1971	1981	1986 Low fertility estimate	1986 High fertility estimate
India	180.4	43.2	223.6	377	579	768	890
Pakistan	109.6	10.1	119.7	211	306	408	485
Ceylon	12.9	3.2	16.1	NA	NA	NA	NA
Jamaica	188.1	85.7	273.8	343	411	474	529
Other Caribbean	129.8	50.5	180.3	229	293	341	375
W Africa (former Br.)	43.1	7.6	50.7	68	80	83	94
Far East	47.0	13.0	60.0	NA	NA	NA	NA
Total	710.9	213.3	924.2	1,228	1,669	2,074	2,373

NA = Not available
The estimates exclude Indians and Pakistanis of British origin.
For 1971 and 1981 the estimates are based on low fertility assumptions.
Source: Rose *et al* (1969) *Colour and Citizenship*, tables 10.2 and 30.1

By far the greater proportion and the highest densities of coloured immigrants are to be found in the inner areas of the major cities, particularly metropolitan boroughs and the W Midlands conurbation. Every local authority with over 5 per cent coloured population in 1966 was in Greater London (Coates and Rawstron 1971, 122–73). The highest rates of increase between 1961 and 1966 were found in a few areas of Greater London and the evidence from the 1971 census indicates that this has continued. The degree of concentration is becoming even more marked at the local level. In 1966, 16,7700 (5.6 per cent) of the population of

Ealing was from New Commonwealth countries, but in Northcote Ward 31 per cent of the population was coloured (Deakin *et al* 1970). Even with such a high proportion of immigrants and the widespread belief that this was a predominantly Indian area, half the households surveyed were European. While Glass (1960, 41) argued that these concentrations do not yet constitute ghettos, the continuing inflow and considerable concentration of coloured immigrants into a few parts of the inner city *is* a matter for serious concern. Thus the Southall district of Ealing, with a population of about 70,000 in 1976, now has an immigrant population of 20,000–30,000, most of whom belong to Sikh families from the N Punjab, as compared with only 2,000 Commonwealth immigrants in 1961, 1,600 of whom were Indian-born. It has been suggested that other parts of the Borough of Ealing are developing marked concentrations of immigrants, for example Acton Town, but some parts of the Borough have scarcely any immigrants (Dalton and Seaman 1973); such sharp spatial contrast within a town is typical of this problem. Studies of mainly West Indian working-class areas of Birmingham show that over half the enumeration districts of the CB had no West Indians, while 30 per cent of this group was concentrated into wards in which they formed over 15 per cent of the total population (Jones 1967). At such a stage of assimilation this is, perhaps, to be expected; historical parallels may be seen in the segregation of Irish immigrants in the Mid-nineteenth century and of Jewish immigrants from Eastern Europe in the late-nineteenth century. But difficulties arising from colour and custom, aggravated by housing shortages and problems of education, are unlikely to lead to rapid acceptance by or assimilation into the community at large.

Structure and trends in immigrant populations Immigration is highly age-selective, particularly in the early stages when it is dominated by young persons, especially men. Dependants usually follow to give a more normal age and sex structure to the immigrant community. In the case of the Commonwealth immigration of the late 1950s and 1960s this process is still in train, with consequent effects on the demographic and social structure and fertility patterns.

A large-scale survey of Irish, and Old and New Commonwealth immigrants in 1961 showed that 75 per cent were men, 62 per cent were between 18 and 34, and 83 per cent under 45, as compared with 62 per cent in the population at large; only half the men were married as compared with 73 per cent of the population over 19 years in England and Wales (Krausz 1971, 45, 146). These characteristics were still apparent in the remarkably low proportions of over-45s and the predominance of mature adults of 25–44 in the early 1960s. The effects of immigrant births and the arrival of dependants in the mid- and late-1960s are apparent in the changes between 1966 and 1971 (table 2.17). While the female:male ratios are low, especially among Pakistani (39:100 in 1971) and, to a lesser extent, Indian and W African groups, a trend towards normality may be seen in lower sex ratios among the 1961–6 arrivals and especially among those coming between 1966 and 1971. The considerable number of dependants is leading to a further balancing of the population structure. The large number of women among West Indian immigrants to London in the 1960s is reflected in the very low male:female ratios of the period.

The impact of a mainly young immigrant population can be seen in the above-average 0–14 age-group and in a high rate of natural increase. It is difficult to compare the fertility of immigrants with British rates, since most immigrant families are still in the process of formation. 1961 census data suggest that for

TABLE 2.16

Main New Commonwealth Immigrant Groups, England and Wales, 1966 and 1971

	(1) India 1966*	1971	(2) Pakistan 1966	1971	(3) West Indies 1966	1971	Total of 1–3 1966	1971	Total population 1966	1971
Total (1,000s) in England and Wales	163.8	313.4	73.1	135.7	267.9	301.4	504.9	750.5	47,135.5	48,602.9
Percentage in Conurbations										
Tyneside	0.9	0.6	0.8	0.6	0.1	0.1	0.5	0.4	1.8	1.7
W Yorks.	5.6	5.1	17.3	16.1	3.1	3.4	6.0	6.4	3.6	3.6
SELNEC	3.7	4.0	7.0	9.1	4.0	3.5	4.3	4.7	5.1	4.9
Merseyside	0.9	0.7	0.6	0.3	0.6	0.5	0.7	0.5	2.8	2.6
W Midlands	14.9	14.3	19.3	17.0	13.4	13.1	14.7	14.3	5.0	4.9
Greater London	33.9	34.2	22.0	22.1	56.7	55.4	44.3	40.5	16.3	15.2
Total	60.0	58.9	67.0	65.2	77.9	76.0	70.5	66.8	34.6	32.9
Rest of England and Wales	40.0	41.1	32.9	34.8	22.1	24.0	29.5	33.2	65.4	67.1
Scotland		9.2		3.8		1.6		14.6		

* excluding White Indians

Source: Sample Census 1966 and Census 1971

marriages of comparable duration immigrant fertility is, at present, higher than among native-born English; but the highest rates were among Irish women (40 per cent above the English rates) while those for coloured immigrant women were 20 per cent above native-born (Thompson 1969). There is some evidence that the differential is lower among completed immigrant families and not significantly different from British-born people of comparable social class. Much has been made of a survey 1969–73 by the Ministry of Health and Social Security showing that 11.5 per cent of all births in England and Wales were to foreign-born mothers but, of the 11.5 per cent, 2.9 per cent were to Irish mothers and 2.9 per cent to other white immigrants, leaving 5.7 per cent of births to coloured immigrants. True, in areas of high concentration of immigrants much higher figures obtained; e.g. in Lambeth and Brent (1969), 1 in 3 births were to mothers from the New Commonwealth; in some parts of the Midlands similarly high proportions were found, e.g. 1 in 4.5 in Wolverhampton and 1 in 6 in Birmingham and Leicester, while in Huddersfield the figure was 1 in 5. How long these proportions will persist depends partly on age structure. In 1971, however, as compared with the 5.6 per cent of the British population who are of New Commonwealth origin (1.49 millions) 3.7 per cent were aged 15–19, 4.0 per cent 10–14, 4.7 per cent 5–9 and 6.6 per cent under 5.

With many immigrant women in the younger, child-bearing ages, such crude statistics can be very misleading. Limited calculations of fertility rates among immigrant families suggest that they 'are larger by about one-third than those of the English population' (Krausz 1971, 49: Moser 1972, 20–30). Studies by the OPCS, based on data showing the country of birth of parents of new babies, data collected since 1969, indicate that in 1974 6.2 per cent of all births in GB were to parents one or both of whom were of New Commonwealth origin. As compared with an estimated 4.5 per cent in 1966 and 5.9 in 1971. With a youthful population, death-rates among the New Commonwealth population in GB are low and the natural increase considerably higher than that for the population of UK origin. Natural increase rates for immigrants have thus been high over the past decade, compared with the rest of the GB population: 4.1 per cent in 1966–7 as compared with 0.7, but falling to 3.4 as against 0.5 in 1970–1 and 2.4 as against 0.12 in 1973–4 (OPCS, 1975).

On the basis of such evidence, while admitting that the proportion will increase, it is difficult to justify some of the wild forecasts of future coloured population. Using 'high fertility' assumptions, Rose *et al* (1969) suggested that the numbers in England and Wales are unlikely to exceed 2.37 million by 1986 (4.5 per cent of the estimated total population), perhaps 3.5 million (6 per cent) by the end of the century – far below the 4.5–7.0 million quoted in some quarters. A 'low fertility' estimate is likely to give some 2.5–3.0 million by the end of the century and finds some support in the downward trend in fertility with length of stay in Britain found among New Commonwealth immigrants.

II.7 Differential Inter-regional Movement

Two further aspects of population migration in the UK deserve special mention: rural-urban movements and differential migration according to socio-economic groups. Though the massive flood-tide of rural migration of the nineteenth century has since abated, there are still considerable losses from many rural areas. The

TABLE 2.17

Age and Sex Structure (percentage) among Selected Groups of Commonwealth Immigrants, GB, 1966 and 1965–71

Age	India (1) 1966	India (2) 1965–71	Pakistan 1966	Pakistan 1965–71	Jamaica 1966	Jamaica 1965–71	Rest of Caribbean 1966	Rest of Caribbean 1965–71	Former British W Africa 1966	Former British W Africa 1965–71	Cyprus 1966	Cyprus 1965–71	Total Popn. 1966–7	Total Popn. 1971
0–14	33	21	24	32	40	36	39	40	23	37	35	42	23	24
15–24	16	28	15	38	11	39	12	40	16	37	18	33	14	14
25–44	40	38	51	26	41	22	41	16	59	25	34	18	25	24
45+	11	14	10	3	8	4	8	4	2	2	13	7	38	38
Males per 1,000 1966 Females 1971	1,479	1,193	4,231	1,568	1,066	1,004*	1,026		1,614	1,205†	1,191	1,165	940	944
M:F 1961–6 arrivals (1)	1,373		3,541		733		809		1,452		1,016			
1965–71 arrivals (2)		891		1,465		679		715		1,095		922		

OPCS (1975), table 2, gives similar estimates
* West Indies as a whole
† Africa as a whole
Sources: (1) Rose *et al* (1969) and (2) *Census* 1971

aggregate population of rural districts is actually increasing (table 2.3) due to urban overspill, whilst areas within commuting distance of town jobs are enabled to retain natural increase. A second factor in growing rural populations, notably in coastal areas, is retirement migration, an important aspect of growth in N Wales, the OSE, the SW, and in parts of E Anglia, N Lancashire, Yorkshire and the Lake District (Law and Warnes 1976). In contrast to these more accessible areas, the remoter country districts, especially the hard core areas of depopulation in upland Britain, continue to lose population on a considerable scale (Wibberley 1954).

Rural population loss is markedly greater among youthful than among mature age-groups (DoE 1971 89–131). Limited opportunities for jobs and higher education in rural areas force young people to leave home. Though facilities for primary and secondary education are generally good in the countryside, in some remote areas of Wales and especially of Scotland, closure of schools is one factor in continuing family migration. Higher education or instruction for the professions or skilled trades requires a move to town. Hence, country districts tend to be 'denuded of people of superior abilities' (Musgrove 1963, 3). Once gone, they seldom return. Jones (1965) has shown for C Wales that 'over half the distant migrants were taking their first job after leaving school or college', many of them in large cities such as Liverpool or Birmingham, with the main flow to London and the South East. An official enquiry (MHLG 1964) noted that such selective out-migration ' . . . must influence adversely the quality of the community'.

A similarly long-established draining of population from rural Scotland, especially from the remoter parts of the Highlands and Islands, continues and indeed is the cause of actual or threatened depopulation (Turnock 1969; Caird 1972). The extent of such migration from Scotland 'increases with education attainment': the rate of migration of highly qualified persons is some two and a half times that of the population of Scotland in the same age group (MacKay 1969, 209).

Detailed studies of Northern England have indicated that while all young people in rural areas are mobile, school-leavers were especially so (House, Thomas, and Willis 1968). Though they went mainly to adjacent towns, the next most important flow was a long-distance movement to London and the SE. In some cases family migration resulted from the wish to give children a better chance of a career without them having to leave home.

These examples may be multiplied from other parts of the UK. As population in remoter rural areas contracts, educational opportunities there tend to narrow and the gap in opportunity between urban and rural areas is likely to continue to widen, thereby increasing the flow of able young people from the countryside. The less skilled remain, though the girls tend to be more mobile. Farm families also tend to be less migratory, in contrast to the nineteenth-century situation when many farm labourers left the countryside.

Varying social and economic opportunities are also key factors in the pattern and scale of both inter-regional and intra-urban migration. The growing concentration of higher services upon a relatively few major cities has increased socio-economic differentials between regions in the post-war period, leading to increased differential mobility of highly qualified manpower. Few investigations have been made of this aspect of migration, but the general relationship between levels of education and inter-regional movement have been observed in the context of manpower and employment (Roberts and Smith 1960). Friedlander and Roshier

(1966, 57) have observed that '. . . in general, the higher occupational (and education) groups were found to be more mobile and this differential increased with distance moved'. Recently, a detailed study of professional and managerial manpower showed that the greater opportunities for upward social mobility have led to a pronounced movement of these groups to the major cities, especially to Greater London (Waugh 1969). Conversely, the progressive decrease in the proportion of high-status jobs in both rural and declining industrial regions high-lights the contrasts in this type of inter-regional migration. The migratory elite, as they have been described, are more mobile both in terms of distance moved and as a proportion of their age-group. Whereas 70 per cent of manual household heads had *not* moved house in the five years previous to the *General Household Survey* (1972), 50 per cent of professional and non-manual heads had done so. Moreover, the latter group made more frequent moves.

Much present-day migration in the UK is local or intra-regional. Short-distance movements, often primarily changes of residence mainly for social reasons, account for 80 per cent of the moves, nine-tenths of which are under 16 km (Harris 1966). Movements of this kind are mainly within urban regions and take two forms: first, the displacement of working-class families from rented accommodation in the residential areas affected by slum clearance, who move to peripheral local authority housing or, more recently, farther afield to New Towns or overspill areas; secondly, a large outward migration to private residential areas, often in adjacent rural districts, of managerial and professional classes and certain types of skilled workers. Such people rise professionally and socially through a series of higher positions, moving residence within the community in which they live. This 'spiralist society', as it has been called' thus produces 'a characteristic combination of social and spatial mobility' (Watson 1964).

This process of peripheral migration from the inner areas of large cities is exemplified in a study of migration on Merseyside (Lawton and Cunningham 1970, ch. 5). Internal migration between and within local authorities on Merseyside has increased with the rapid sprawl of the conurbation in the twentieth century. Move-ment within the region has increased considerably since 1950, a fact underlined since 1966 by the development of the New Towns of Skelmersdale and Runcorn. Indeed between 1961 and 1971 the population of Liverpool CB fell by 138,916, a decrease of 19.9 per cent, almost the same percentage loss as experienced by Manchester and paralleled by some of the inner London boroughs. On Merseyside movement to the outer conurbation extended into adjacent areas of south-central Lancashire and N Wales. This is symptomatic of a national trend towards residential decentralization in all large cities (Champion 1976). One aspect is the decline in both the inner core of the city and, more recently, in the outer city ring, both of which are losing population to the outer city region; another aspect is the problem of the adjustment of all classes of society to changing residential patterns through more complex commuting links (Hall 1971; Johnson, Salt and Wood, 1974).

Most of the residential migration to the peripheral areas up to 1966 was of professional and managerial groups. For example, population of the rapidly growing Merseyside suburb of Formby UD leapt from the 12 per cent increase of 1951–6 to a staggering 100 per cent in 1961–71. Already in 1966 the population structure was mainly young: 31 per cent were between 25–44 years as compared with Liverpool's 24 per cent, and 28 per cent under 15 years (Liverpool 25 per cent). Formby is a predominantly middle-class area with 39 per cent in the social classes 1 and 2

(Liverpool 10 per cent). One-quarter of the population had changed address in 1965–6 and of a sample social survey conducted in 1968 (Pickett 1970, 133) nearly one-half of the movers had come from the Merseyside conurbation, over one-quarter from Liverpool itself. This is endorsed by the survey finding that 49.5 per cent of the whole sample but 58.9 per cent of the migrant heads of households travelled to work in the inner areas of the conurbation. These findings are supported in a wider context by a research study on migration between major centres and their surrounding areas carried out by the *Redcliffe-Maud Commission* (R. Commn. 1969, III, 39–56), which showed a strong positive correlation between migration loss from county boroughs and low indices of men over 15 in professional and managerial classes and of males 25–44 as a proportion of all males of 15 and over. Taking England outside Greater London as = 100, the indices were:

TABLE 2.18

Mobility of Professional and Managerial Workers, England, 1961–6

	% net migration 1961–6	Proportion managerial and professional		Proportion of males 25–44 to males 15+	
		1961	1966	1961	1966
All CBs	−3.19	79	78	100	97
CBs with migration losses (61 out of 78)	−4.10	74	73	101	98

Source: Royal Commission on Local Government in England (1969), vol. III, appendix 3, table 1, 48–9

In a more detailed study of fourteen towns it was shown that the migration loss of men aged 25–44 in the professional and managerial classes was roughly twice that of losses among all males over 15 years (table 2.18) (Roy. Commn. 1969, III, 43–5).

While there is some compensatory in-migration to city centres, as observed in Greater London, this does little if anything to offset the loss of the more prosperous and vigorous sections of the population. Indeed many of the vacated residences are occupied by poor people including, in many areas, a large proportion of overseas immigrants. Thus the four county boroughs of inner Merseyside included 23,820 (2.3 per cent) Irish-born and 14,330 (1.3 per cent) from overseas. In Liverpool most of the New Commonwealth immigrants were concentrated into three central wards and in the 1960s this influx has increasingly focused in one, Granby Ward, which also has high indices of virtually all criteria of social decay.

III POPULATION STRUCTURE

Contrasts and changes in natural and migrational trends result from and influence population structure. In the UK differential migration as between different age groups and between men and women is an important factor in regional differences in population structure and future population trends alike.

III.1 Sex Ratios

Due to the better survival rates of male children and the diminishing importance of
the 'lost generation' of men killed during the First World War, the pronounced
imbalance between the sexes of the 1921–51 period has been progressively modified
since the war (table 2.7). There are, however, considerable regional variations from
the 1971 UK figure of 105.5 females per 100 males. In broad regional terms (fig.
2.10) this average is exceeded only in rural Wales, southern and much of eastern
Scotland, SW England, Greater London and the OMA and NW England. At the higher
level of definition of administrative county and county borough (fig. 2.11), the main
factors involved in these differences become more apparent.

In 1971 the majority of rural areas had a below-average ratio of women to men.
The long-standing tendency for women to be more migratory than men and the
more restricted job opportunities for women in rural areas both contribute to this
situation. The lowest female:male ratios are found in parts of N Ireland and the
Scottish Highlands, but most of the rural areas from the Welsh border to the
Fenland counties also have relatively low ratios. Women dominate the population
structure of retirement areas, in which resorts and spas have notably high ratios: due
to their greater longevity, there are very large proportions of elderly women in such
areas. This accounts for such ratios as 122 in Peebles and Pitlochry, 126 in
Torbay, 128 in Bournemouth, 133 in Eastbourne and 123 in Southport.

In addition, above-average female:male ratios are found first in Greater London
and, secondly, in textile districts such as the NW and the Scottish Border country.
A recent detailed study of the Scottish Border counties (Soulsby 1972) has shown
that differential migration and occupational structure account for considerable
variations in sex ratios at local as well as at regional level, in which a sharp upswing
in the proportion of women in the population in the later nineteenth century was
due to female employment in the textile industry. Though much less pronounced
than in the past, due to the absolute and relative decline of jobs in the cotton
mills, some of E Lancashire textile towns, for example Blackburn and Burnley
(108), have above-average ratios, though the Lowry-like image of shawled and
beclogged women clattering over cobblestones to work in the spinning mills is now
a picture from the past, as the below-average ratios for many SE Lancashire mill
towns show. In a very different context, the majority of Greater London boroughs
have high proportions of women, though the highest ratios tend to be found in west
London. This tendency for higher proportions of women is indeed typical of the
inner residential areas of many large towns.

Apart from the male-dominant rural areas, districts with below average sex
ratios, and hence relatively more men than average, tend to be associated with
heavy industrial areas. Some of the lower ratios are found in coalfield areas of
south-east Wales (e.g. 104.8 in Glamorgan AC) and NE England (e.g. Durham AC,
102.6). The lowest tend to be in the heavy industrial districts such as the W
Midlands, where Wolverhampton, Walsall and West Bromwich all have ratios of
around 101, or S Yorkshire, where the Barnsley and Rotherham ratios are
102.

III.2 Age Structure

The general increase in numbers in both young and older age-groups since 1945
has already been shown to underlie continuing population growth in the UK

(table 2.5). The increased birth-rate of the early 1960s brought the proportion of under-15s to 24.3 per cent in 1971, comparable with the 24.1 per cent of 1931. Meanwhile, population of retirement age has greatly increased to an estimated 16.0 per cent for 1971 as compared with 9.6 per cent in 1931. However, very considerable spatial variations in age structure exist and were analysed in some detail for local authority areas by Dewdney (1968). In his study of four age-groups 0–14, 15–44, 45–64 and 65+, Dewdney stressed two aspects: first, the distribution of different age-groups; secondly, the age-structure within the various local authorities or regions in which, he observes, the various age-groups are complementary, so that 'Quite different mechanisms of population growth and movement may give rise to similar results as far as the age composition of a particular area is concerned' (Dewdney 1968, 9).

The essential features of Dewdney's detailed analysis are reflected at the more general of UK economic planning sub-regions for 1971 (fig. 2.10). Above-average proportions of young people (0–14 years) may result from a variety of causes. High birth-rates explain the relatively large proportion of young people in much of rural Scotland and N Ireland. In both areas fertility is relatively high, despite long-standing out-migration, and a continuing migrational loss of young adults increases the relative importance of other age-groups. High birth-rates also explain the high proportions of under-15s in certain industrial regions, including C Scotland, NE and NW England, and Yorks. and Humberside. A growing tendency to outward migration of young families from inner residential areas to the periphery of the large towns tends progressively to increase the proportion of children in the population of many parts of the major city regions, notably in the outer metropolitan areas.

The 15–59 group is a rather large one which tends to conceal differences between the more mobile 15–44 and more stable 45–59 year age-groups. Dewdney's analysis showed that relatively high proportions of the younger adult population were found in areas of economic growth and in-migration, and tended to be prominent in the conurbations and large industrial areas, though residential over-spill has reduced the proportion of this group in the inner metropolitan areas, as may be seen in the 1971 map (fig. 2.10). In contrast, the 45–59 group has many different tendencies. The inner areas of large cities have considerable numbers of small households made up of parents over 45 whose families are grown up and have left home. Elsewhere, in declining industrial areas of long-standing out-migration, the older mature population has above-average representation, but the broad 15–59 age-group conceals the deficiency of younger adults in the population.

In rural areas of Wales, Scotland and E England, along the south coast of England and in the SW, there is a considerable representation of over-60s, arising from two frequently inter-related factors. Prolonged out-migration of young adults often leads eventually to a deficiency of births, thus creating a predominantly elderly population, as in much of rural Wales and the Scottish Highlands. Indeed this situation is sometimes found in industrial areas, notably in the small industrial towns of NE Lancashire. In the resort areas, of the south coast of England and N Wales for example, the reasons for very large proportions of over-60s are more positive and, as has been shown previously, involve a considerable in-migration of people of retirement age.

Without a very carefully integrated analysis of age–sex structure, area by area, it is difficult to summarize the regional inter-relationships of these various age-

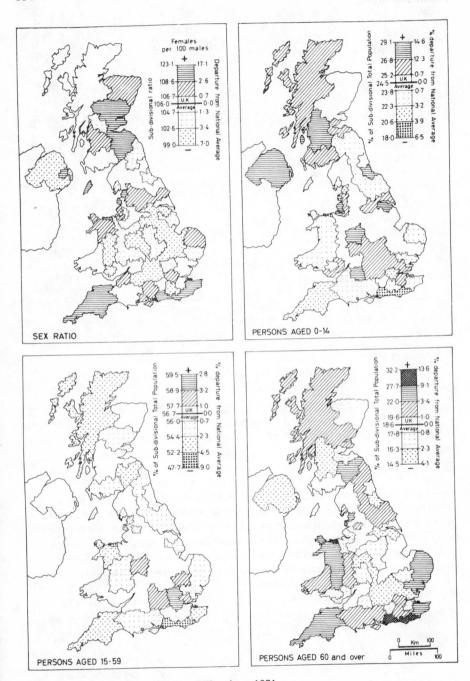

Figure 2.10   Age and sex structure, UK regions, 1971

group patterns. However, certain broad groupings emerge. In N Ireland, high birth-
rates are reflected in the large proportion of under-15s but the deficiencies in the
other age-groups reflect long-standing out-migration. Much of rural Scotland shares
the characteristic of relatively high proportions of children but in areas of marked
depopulation in the Highlands and Southern Scotland this is associated with large
proportions in the over-60 group and a deficiency in the 15–59s, especially due to
large outmigration of younger adults. The Central Valley of Scotland, in contrast,
like many English industrial regions has a high proportion of both children and
young adults; above-average proportions of over-60s in the Scottish industrial
sub-regions are found only in the Fife coalfield.

In England and Wales there is a generally clear distinction between the rural
areas, with below-average under-15 and 15–44 age-groups and above-average shares
of the elderly which become very pronounced in retirement areas, and the urban
and industrial areas. The urban regions are more complex with many contrasting
structural features which are not apparent at sub-regional level. Intra-regional
migration tends to produce a series of zones within the city region. The central
areas have relatively few young and old, and are often dominated locally by young
adults, as in parts of central London. The older residential areas of the inner city·
are frequently dominated by mature adults and elderly people, with younger families
and children depleted by outward movement to the suburbs. The peripheral areas
complement the inner city and are dominated by families at an active stage of
formation, with above-average proportions of children and young adults, though
in the outer areas the 45–59 age-groups are dominant, as for example in the outer
metropolitan region.

All these situations are dynamic, and age structures reflect economic and
social change, especially in the progressive extension of urban-based population
into rural areas. Thus the implications of present and projected age structures are of
considerable significance to both physical and social planning on a regional basis, as
well as on a national basis (section I.4).

III.3 Social Structure

Experience of fertility, mortality and migration varies regionally to produce
differences in age and sex structure. Many of these demographic contrasts are due,
in part, to differing social structure. Hence, an analysis of population trends must
take account of differing social structures at both regional and local level (Knox
1974). Moreover, social contrasts are themselves often a resultant of aspects of
population dynamics; thus selective migration varies not only with age and sex but
also with education, skills and job mobility.

Socio-economic indices The analysis of social structure is hampered by the lack of
any one generally agreed or readily measured criterion. British population censuses
have collected information on occupations in some detail since 1841. In association
with the fertility analysis of the 1911 census the Registrar General adopted a
system of social groups and classes based on occupation which has led to the present
socio-economic classification (Booth 1886; Marsh 1965): a discussion of social
class composition and contrasts in family, household, demographic, social and
economic characteristics between classes is in *Social Trends* (CSO 1975, 10–32).

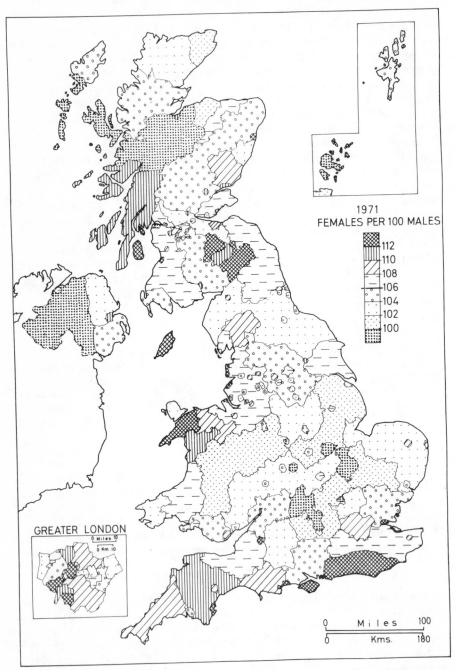

1971
FEMALES PER 100 MALES

112
110
108
106
104
102
100

GREATER LONDON

Figure 2.11   Sex ratios, UK, 1971

Such classifications are very valuable, especially in cross-tabulations with other population data, but they raise a number of problems of comparison, especially as between 'middle-ranking' manual and non-manual occupations.

Hence they are often used in association with other socio-economic information. Since **housing** is one of the biggest investments made by a family, it may be expected that the quality and spaciousness of dwellings will reflect household income and may, therefore, be a useful surrogate of living standards and social class. A number of housing variables concerning type of tenure, intensity of occupation and amenities have been used with considerable effectiveness by social geographers and sociologists in defining the social areas of towns (Moser and Scott 1961; Gittus 1964; Robson 1969). Moreover, the characteristics of housing and the relationship of residential trends to employment are of direct interest in relation to many aspects of daily mobility and of the structure and development of urban regions (ch. 6.II).

Educational qualifications have become increasingly important in the modern UK for professional, business and technical skills; hence educational achievement is increasingly valuable as a measure of social class. From 1951 there has been increasing information on educational achievement in British censuses which now provide data on the terminal age of education, scientific and technological qualifications (1961 census), higher educational qualifications (1966 census) and, in the 1971 census, school-leaving qualifications. In addition the Department of Education and Science issues annually the six-volume *Statistics of Education* which includes much information on the educational provision by local authorities, the proportions of various age groups in full-time education, qualifications of school-leavers and the like.

Personal income is one of the best indices of social class but is not available in any detail for the UK. Some aggregate data on personal incomes are published by the Inland Revenue, tabulated for counties. Since 1965 these have been used as the basis of figures published in the annual *Regional Abstract of Statistics*. From these data it is possible to analyse, in broad terms, the distribution and trends in personal incomes (Coates and Rawstron 1971, ch. 2).

While each individually is of value in social analysis, such criteria may be combined with demographic variables through the use of multivariate statistical techniques, such as principal components analysis, to delineate spatial variations in social structure more fully. Work of this kind has been pioneered for British towns by Moser and Scott (1961) and Armen (1972). Such studies are of particular value in distinguishing the differing character of social areas within cities, in which demographic, social and economic conditions are often closely inter-related and in which an understanding of population distribution and trends is inseparable from social geography.

III.4 Housing and Households

Of the UK's 20 million dwellings (1975) 45 per cent have been built since 1945 but 33 per cent are pre-1920 in date. Half the dwellings are owner-occupied, about one-third rented from local authorities or public corporations and the rest mainly rented from private landlords (tables 2.19 and 6.2). Although the number of dwellings now roughly equals the number of households there are still housing shortages in the conurbations and industrial areas, especially in inner city areas.

The large inter-war building and slum clearance programme added nearly four million dwellings to the housing stock of England and Wales, about 30 per cent of which were built by local authorities. Yet this very large increase only slightly exceeded the rate of growth of households; indeed 1901–39 the number of dwellings built lagged slightly behind the increase in families. Hence, if essential slum clearance is taken into account, there was an estimated deficit of housing in 1939 of over half-a-million homes in England and Wales alone (Cullingworth 1960).

Moreover, at that time conditions of *overcrowding* were still widespread, though the yardstick of $1\frac{1}{2}$ persons per room was generous by nineteenth-century standards. The virtual cessation of building during the Second World War and the damage to and loss of property by bombing, which affected one in three of all dwellings in England and Wales, both contributed to a general post-war housing shortage in the UK, which was particularly acute in the large cities. Despite the building of nearly three-quarters of a million homes in Britain between 1946 and 1950 (Holmans 1970), there was a shortage of over one million dwellings at the time of the 1951 census, when the ratio of households to dwellings was 1.056 for GB.

Since 1951, the situation has improved considerably, though the continuing high rate of formation of new households, due to high marriage rates and a falling average age of marriage, together with immigration and inter-regional migration to certain areas of rapid population growth, has caused regional shortages of housing to persist. Estimates of formation of new households due to marriage *less* losses due to deaths, together with a falling demand from immigrant households suggest that there may be some reduction of demand for new homes from about 145,000 per year in 1970 to some 120,000 per year in the mid-1970s, rising to 130,000 per year around 1981.

A further considerable post-war demand for additional housing has come from *slum clearance*. Some 992,000 houses were 'demolished or closed' in England and Wales from 1955–71 and 250,000 in Scotland, and 2.25 million people have been rehoused since the mid-1950s, but 2.1 million unfit dwellings remain (DoE 1971, 48). In addition to clearance, an average of 80,000 houses per year were improved in England and Wales, 1965–71, under various sections of the *Housing Acts* (of 1957, 1961 and 1969) and the *Public Health Acts*. In an attempt to upgrade the 4.5 million dwellings in England and Wales and 200,000 in Scotland which lack amenities or are in poor repair, though structurally sound (MHLG 1966; SDD 1968), an average of 307,000 improvement grants per year were made in Great Britain in 1970–4 (DoE 1974, 38).

Although the number of slums in England and Wales was reduced from the 1.8 million dwellings estimated as unfit in 1967 to around 1.35 million by 1970 (Holmans 1970, 38), a considerable number of pre-1919 houses remains in all regions of Britain (table 2.19). While the estimated net increase in households of some 145,000 per year for 1970 and perhaps 120,000–130,000 per year in the 1970s may not now be realized, the rate of slum clearance of about 100,000 per year has fallen to 79,000 pa 1970–4 and we may still need to build 250,000–300,300,000 new houses per year in the foreseeable future. If, in addition, a reserve of at least 3.5 per cent is to be created to allow for vacancies required by movements of households, the need for new dwellings in the UK may still be 345,000–390,000 per year up to 1981; of these perhaps 55–65 per cent will be owner-occupied and 32–40 per cent provided by local authorities (Holmans 1970, 33–42; DoE 1964, tables 32 and 33). Such a rate of house-building (345,000–390,000 per year, as

Figure 2.12   Housing and social characteristics, Merseyside, 1966 (see p. 169)

compared with 306,000 completions in Britain in 1972–4) is well below the maximum annual completions in Britain of 414,000 dwellings reached in 1968 (426,000 in the UK). It would give Britain a housing stock of 21.1 million dwellings in 1981 as compared with an estimated 19.7 million households, a much healthier position than at present (table 2.19).

Inter-regional housing contrasts   There are considerable regional differences in the relative supply of housing in relation to households and population, in the degree of overcrowding, in the characteristics of housing tenure and in the amenity of housing. These partly reflect population trends over a considerable period, partly relate to pressures of recent population movements, and partly reflect broad social and economic contrasts between regions. Most of these features also reflect two distinctive and sometimes pronounced intra-regional contrasts between rural and urban areas and, secondly, more marked contrasts between inner and outer residential areas of large cities.

Tenure   One of the characteristics of housing in the UK since 1920 has been the increasing importance of local authority housing (table 2.19). Inter-war corporation

TABLE 2.19

Dwelling Stock, UK, 1974

	Number of dwellings (millions)	Tenure of dwellings (percentages)			Age of dwellings (percentages)			
			Rented from					
					Pre-1891	1891 to 1918	1919 to 1944	Post-1944
		Owner-occupied	Local authority[1]	Private owner[2]				
Standard regions								
Northern	1.14	44	40	16	15	17	22	64
Yorks. and Humberside	1.79	52	32	16	17	17	24	42
E Midlands	1.35	55	28	17	18	14	22	46
E Anglia	0.66	55	26	19	25	9	17	49
South East:	6.10	54	26	20	17	15	26	42
Greater London	2.63	46	28	26	30	9	31	30
Rest of region	3.47	60	24	16	15	11	22	52
South West	1.55	61	22	17	24	12	19	45
W Midlands	1.80	54	33	13	14	13	26	47
North West	2.37	57	29	14	20	16	24	40
England	16.76	54	29	17	18	15	24	43
Wales	1.00	58	28	14	25	20	15	40
Scotland	1.87	33	54	13	15	18	19	48
G Britain	19.63	52	31	17	18	15	23	44
N Ireland	0.47	48	37	15	13[3]	21[4]	16	50
U Kingdom	20.10	52	31	17	33		23	44

[1] or New Town
[2] including 'other tenures'
[3] pre-1870
[4] 1870–1919
Source: DoE (1974)

housing estates became a distinctive element in the British townscape and gave birth to almost exclusively working-class residential suburbs which were marked by many problems of social adjustment to the new environment. During the 1920s and 1930s much early Victorian housing, mainly privately-rented, was being cleared from city centre slums. While most of the surplus population from these grossly over-crowded areas was decanted to the new local authority estates, a considerable amount of housing renewal, mostly through blocks of flats, was also leading to social and visual changes in the inner city.

Since 1945 these trends towards replacement of slums by local authority housing have continued, leading to a shortage of rented property in the private sector, in great contrast to the nineteenth century or even the inter-war situation. From 1950 to 1970 the total housing stock increased at an average annual rate of 1.57 per cent per year. New building in the private sector (mainly for purchase) increased by 1.2 per cent per year and in the public sector at 1.0 per cent per year. While owner-occupied dwellings grew at the rate of 1.8 per cent per year and local authority and New Town property at 1.1 per cent per year, the privately-rented housing stock has *decreased* continuously at an average of 1.2 per cent per year. Thus, the proportion

TABLE 2.20

Permanent Dwellings Completed, UK, 1945–73

	Average annual completion of permanent dwellings (1,000s)					
	England	Wales	Scotland	N Ireland	GB	UK
1945–50	115	7	15	3.6	137	141
1951–5	237	13	33	7.3	284	291
1956–60	248	12	30	6.0	290	297
1961–5	284	16	31	8.5	331	340
1966–70	325	18	41	11.4	384	395
1971–3	272	15	34	12.1	321	333
Total 1945–73	6,978	380	873	224	8,230	8,454
Annual av. 1945–73	240	13	30	7.7	284	291

Source: Housing Statistics GB, 23 (1971) and *26* (1974)

of owner-occupied dwellings has increased from 20 per cent in 1950 to 42 per cent in 1960 and 52 per cent in 1974; property rented from local authorities and New Town corporations has grown over the same period from 18 per cent to 27 per cent and now to 31 per cent; privately-owned property has fallen from 45 to 26 and now to 13 per cent (table 2.19). This betokens a social revolution of considerable proportions.

While the proportions of housing in different tenures varies regionally, owner-occupied houses provide the majority of the stock in all regions except Scotland and, to a lesser extent in Greater London and some other conurbations. A high level of owner-occupation is the hallmark of rural and many suburban areas, though the further extension of peripheral local authority housing estates is changing this situation. Many areas of the inner city and of the older industrial regions have lower proportions of owner-occupation. In very broad regional terms this situation is reflected in the above-average proportion of owner-occupied property in the south-eastern quadrant of Britain from the Midlands to the south and east coasts (Greater London excepted) and in Wales, and in the below-average proportion in the industrial north and in C Scotland. In detail, as Storrie (1968) has shown, there are contrasts; for example the high percentage of owner-occupied houses in the textile towns of E Lancashire.

Privately-rented dwellings dominated the housing stock up to the mid-1950s, especially in the large cities and industrial towns. Slum clearance and the gradual decline of the small-scale property owner (Cullingworth 1963), who was most affected by rent control, have led to a rapid reduction in this sector of the housing market; between the *Rent Acts* of 1957 and 1965 there was a fall of one million in such properties (one-quarter of their total). Rural areas have been less affected by this, so that the proportion of privately-rented dwellings is above-average in many rural areas, especially of N and SW England, of Wales and of N Ireland.

As privately-rented property has declined, so local authority rentings have increased, especially in the urban areas. The proportion of such property is most marked in those regions of greatest housing need, especially in those areas where local administrations, often Labour-controlled councils, have invested heavily in housing as one of the most vital social services. Hence, C Scotland, industrial NE

England, S Yorkshire, the Black Country and much of the S Wales coalfield stand out on a detailed map of local authority tenure (Storrie 1968, fig. 10). More recently, local authority overspill to peripheral areas such as New Towns and over-spill areas (figs. 2.21 and 2.22) have led to rapid increases in such tenures around all city regions. Thus, the major contrasts are intra- rather than inter-regional, apart from the considerably above-average values for Scotland, N England and the W Midlands (table 2.19). As may be expected in predominantly owner-occupied areas, such as the OSE, SW England and E Anglia, the proportion of local authority houses is relatively low.

Amenities Housing quality provides a useful measure of the general social characteristics of the population. Amenity is a complex notion involving a wide range of factors influencing property valuations, such as: state of repair; freedom from damp; adequate lighting, heating and ventilation; water supplies; cooking facilities; sanitary arrangements; and food storage. The most easily comparable data are those collected in censuses concerning water supply, bathroom and sanitary facilities. In the 1966 and 1971 censuses the exclusive use of a hot-water supply and fixed bath and WC were regarded as evidence of adequate amenities from this viewpoint. The lack of sewerage in rural areas tends to dramatize relatively poor levels of amenity in the countryside. At the regional level there is a perceptible gradient between the low level of amenities in most inner city areas rising to very high levels in all suburbs (private and local authority), and falling to lower levels in the rural hinterlands (Humphrys 1968). Growing affluence, slum clearance and increasing standards in all housing sectors are rapidly ironing out regional differences in housing quality as judged by such limited criteria, though relatively high proportions of housing without those basic amenities, especially that of a fixed bath, persist in Greater London, the conurbations and older industrial regions of Scotland, Wales and N England; many rural areas also have relatively low levels of amenity (table 2.21).

Overcrowding Many studies of conditions in cities have shown that one of the more useful criteria of social structure is some measure of overcrowding. Though appropriate standards vary over time and between social classes, the number of persons per room is generally regarded as an acceptable measure of overcrowding (Clarke 1960). The currently accepted index of overcrowding in the UK is the proportion of households at an occupancy rate of over 1.5 persons per room, though in the Britain of the 1970s 1 per room might be a better yardstick. The highest proportions of overcrowding are in N Ireland and Scotland, where smaller dwellings and the larger average size of household, together with poor economic and social conditions, are responsible. Similar, though less extreme, conditions are reflected in the higher rates of overcrowding in parts of the industrial North and Midlands, especially in the conurbations, and in Greater London. The proportion of households at over $1\frac{1}{2}$ persons per room is now low, and the major contrasts are intra-regional, with a general emphasis on greater overcrowding in rural areas, especially of western and northern Britain and N Ireland, and in the inner-city areas. City slums still have considerable levels of overcrowding, especially among immigrant communities, where subdivision of housing and 'Rachmanite' exploitation of tenants by private landlords have been a reproach to both national and local administrations in post-war Britain.

Studies of immigrants' housing in the Greater London and W Midlands conurbations have shown very high densities of occupation, high proportions of sharing of dwellings, very low proportions of local authority housing and very high proportions of rented furnished accommodation among all immigrant groups (table 2.22). Moreover, there has been little overall improvement in the situation since the early 1960s, though more enlightened policy concerning local authority accommodation in some areas is beginning to make an impact. Nevertheless the view that 1961–6 '. . . has been one of improvement for English residents of these boroughs' (of inner London) while '. . . the coloured immigrants were being left even further behind as the general level of housing amenity has risen' (Deakin 1970, 72) is unfortunately largely true today.

In general, better control of rented housing, slum clearance and local authority building have led to the reduction in the proportion of homeless and overcrowded families in the 1960s, though many black spots exist and the UK is still some way from solving its shortage of housing. One-third of Britain's housing stock is pre-1919 in age, a situation which is general in nearly all regions (table 2.19): we are clearly far from satisfactory housing standards for all. Thus, despite half-a-million demolitions 1955–65, the remaining number of houses classed as unfit was almost unchanged. In the less fortunate areas the proportion of sub-standard property was very much higher: as compared with 12 per cent unfit houses in England and Wales in 1967, the SE's proportion was only 6 per cent, while the North, Yorks. and Humberside and NW regions had 15 per cent (Sec. State Econ. Affairs 1969, 29). Such regional inequalities point to fundamental contrasts in the social geography of modern Britain, and it is in such deprived areas where environmental and social needs are greatest that the house improvement schemes of the late 1960s have made the greatest impact. Of the 1.27 million improvement grants approved in GB, 1971–4, 0.83 million were in the development areas. There remain, however, massive problems of social deprivation in the inner areas of all large towns, the solution to which lies in a much more widely-based and more integrated programme of redevelopment than can be achieved through housing policy alone (ch. 2.III.5).

Households During the twentieth century separate households have tended to increase at a faster rate than population in the UK. In part due to decreasing family size, in part to increased mobility of population leading to break-up of two-generation adult households, it also reflects a considerable social revolution, that of a separate home for each individual family unit of parents and children. In England and Wales, for example, the rate of household formation in the inter-war period was three times that of the increase in population (Lawton 1963A). Post-war increases in marriage-rates and the reduction in the average age of marriage, together with increasing expectation of life, have accentuated these tendencies since we must now cater for separate homes for three generations: elderly people; mature married couples with children; and young married couples or single persons. Each requires a home of a different type and location, a fact underlying the considerable level of intra-regional residential migration which reflects changing needs during the family cycle. Thus since 1951 households have continued to grow at over twice the rate of the growth of population throughout the UK (table 2.23).

The regional structure of household size reflects both demographic and social trends. Intra-regional contrasts are often of greater significance than inter-regional

People and Work

TABLE 2.21

Regional Indices of Housing and Households, GB, 1971

Regions and conurbations	TOTAL (1,000s)			PERCENTAGE HOUSEHOLDS	
	Persons	House-holds (Hh)	Occupied dwellings (Dw)	At $> 1\frac{1}{2}$ persons per room	Without all three amenities
NORTHERN	3,296	1,100	1,115	1.6	18.3
Tyneside con.	805	277	280	2.3	19.5
Rest.	2,491	823	835	1.3	17.9
YORKS. & HUMBER-SIDE	4,799	1,650	1,664	1.2	17.7
West Yorks con.	1,728	605	609	1.7	15.8
Rest	3,071	1,045	1,055	0.9	18.7
NORTH WEST	6,743	2,273	2,279	1.3	20.0
SELNEC con.	2,393	827	829	1.5	21.8
Merseyside con.	1,267	405	403	1.9	21.3
Rest	3,083	1,040	1,047	0.9	18.0
E MIDLANDS	3,390	1,145	1,151	0.9	19.6
W MIDLANDS	5,110	1,677	1,680	1.6	16.4
W Mids. con.	2,372	781	778	2.2	17.6
Rest	2,738	896	903	1.0	15.4
E ANGLIA	1,669	569	578	0.5	17.8
SOUTH EAST	17,230	5,915	5,790	1.8	17.3
Greater London	7,452	2,652	2,501	2.9	24.3
OMA	5,307	1,717	1,726	0.8	10.1
OSE	4,471	1,546	1,563	0.8	13.3
SOUTH WEST	3,781	1,280	1,286	0.7	14.2
WALES	2,731	901	912	0.8	22.5
SCOTLAND	5,229	1,686	1,717	6.5	13.7
C. Clyde con.	1,728	547	553	10.7	16.8
Rest	3,501	1,139	1,164	4.4	12.2

Source: Census 1971, Household Tables

differences. The average household remains much larger in N Ireland than elsewhere in the UK, due to higher fertility, and is somewhat higher in Scotland than in England and Wales (table 2.23). The lowest figures of average size of household are generally found in areas where there are high proportions of young adults (especially in single-person households) or of elderly people. Thus central residential areas of cities frequently have small households, as for example in Greater London, mainly because of the large numbers of young people living in flats. At the other end of the scale retirement areas, such as the South West, or areas of long-standing out-migration, both rural (eg rural Wales) and industrial (eg W Yorkshire and much of E Lancashire), have above-average numbers of one- or two-person households of pensionable age.

The relationship of such indices, which may be elaborated by other aspects of household size and composition, are best illustrated from a specific case, that of *Merseyside* (Lawton 1970, 33–4). Post-1945 clearing of housing in the inner areas has led to growth of both large-scale corporation housing estates and private residential developments in the intermediate and, more recently, peripheral areas

Table 2.21 (cont.)

Regions and conurbations	TENURE (% HOUSEHOLDS)			PERCENTAGE HOUSEHOLDS		
	Owner-occupied	Rented from LA or New Town	Privately rented	1- or 2-person hhds with person(s) of pensionable age	Car owning 1 car	2+ cars
NORTHERN	41.0	38.6	20.4	26.5	36.8	5.8
Tyneside con.	31.7	43.6	24.7	27.6	30.3	3.8
Rest	44.0	36.9	19.1	26.0	38.9	6.5
YORKS AND HUMBER-SIDE	48.6	32.1	19.3	27.7	37.5	6.3
West Yorks con.	52.6	30.8	16.6	29.1	34.6	5.5
Rest	46.3	32.9	20.8	26.9	39.2	6.8
NORTH WEST	53.8	27.9	19.3	27.4	38.5	7.0
SELNEC con.	51.4	29.7	18.7	27.5	35.8	6.3
Merseyside	40.5	33.5	26.0	25.9	34.8	6.0
Rest	61.0	24.3	14.7	28.0	42.2	7.9
E MIDLANDS	51.1	28.9	20.0	26.0	44.1	8.7
W MIDLANDS	50.7	33.5	15.8	23.7	44.2	9.8
W Mids. con.	46.3	39.7	14.0	24.1	40.5	8.2
Rest	55.0	28.1	16.9	23.3	47.6	11.0
E ANGLIA	51.1	27.0	21.9	28.3	49.4	11.2
SOUTH EAST	50.9	24.3	24.8	26.5	44.2	10.2
Greater London	43.4	25.0	31.6	25.8	38.5	7.8
OMA	57.0	26.6	16.4	22.7	51.1	14.5
OSE	57.1	20.6	22.3	31.9	46.4	10.2
SOUTH WEST	56.8	23.4	19.8	29.5	49.2	11.1
WALES	54.0	28.9	17.1	26.7	44.1	8.5
SCOTLAND	29.3	53.5	17.2	25.9	36.5	5.9
C Clydes con.	24.9	59.2	15.9	24.0	28.9	4.1
Rest	31.1	50.6	18.3	26.7	40.1	6.7

of the conurbation. Moreover, the character of the larger terraced and villa housing of former middle-class areas of the later nineteenth century has changed with subdivision into flats. In general, though the proportions of overcrowding as measured by the number of persons per room has considerably declined, it is still relatively high by national standards (table 2.24).

In a principal components analysis for census enumeration districts of the 1961 census, components related to intensity of occupation, household amenities, shared dwellings and multi-dwelling buildings (type III dwellings) accounted for 68 per cent of the variation between the variables analysed (Gittus 1964). Figures related specifically to single criteria diagnostic of those components are mapped for wards from the 1966 census, together with a simple grouping of all four indices in what is, in effect, a map of social areas derived from housing criteria (fig. 2.12). Of the sixteen possible groupings in a 4 x 4 matrix, using a simple positive or negative deviation from the Merseyside average, seven are dominant and the few cases in the other nine types can be linked to these. The inner area is dominated by working-class districts (types 1–3). Type 1 has low standards of amenity and moderately

TABLE 2.22

Housing Tenure of Coloured Immigrants and English: Greater London and W Midlands Conurbations, 1966

| Area | Owner-occupiers | | From local authority | | Renting Private unfurnished | | Private furnished | |
	Coloured immigrants	English	Coloured immigrants	English	Coloured immigrants	English	Coloured immigrants	English
Greater London	32.6	38.9	4.2	22.3	18.1	29.0	43.6	7.3
W Midlands conurbation	59.4	41.1	7.7	39.1	9.4	14.6	21.2	2.6

Source: Rose *et al*, p. 133

TABLE 2.23

Population, Dwellings and Households, UK, 1951–71 (in 1,000s)

	Total population	per cent change	Total house-holds	per cent change	Total dwellings	per cent change	Persons per household	Households per dwelling	Per cent >1½ persons per room
England and Wales									
1951	43,758		13,118		12,389		3.53	1.056	8.8
1961	46,005	5.3	14,890	13.5	14,646	18.2	3.09	1.017	5.3
1971	48,750	6.0	16,509	10.9	16,455	12.4	2.96	1.003	2.9
Scotland									
1951	5,096		1,436		1,424		3.54	1.008	35.2
1961	5,179	4.8	1,609	12.0	1,627	14.2	3.22	0.989	22.4
1971	5,229	1.0	1,686	4.8	1,717	5.5	3.13	0.982	12.6
N Ireland									
1951	1,371		338		343		4.05	0.985	25.5
1961	1,425	3.9	373	10.3	387	12.8	3.82	0.964	5.6
1971	1,528	7.2	415	11.3	413	6.7	3.08	1.005	

The totals are for all households (present or not) and all dwellings (occupied and vacant)
Source: Censuses of England and Wales, of Scotland (1951, 1961, 1971) and of N Ireland (1951, 1961, 1971)

high proportions of shared dwellings, though because of a high proportion of small households (many of pensionable age) some areas (type 3) are distinctive in being less overcrowded. The classic combination, for poor social areas, of high intensity of occupation, below-average amenities and a good deal of sharing is, in the redevelopment areas of the centre, now found together with high proportions of multi-dwellings in high-rise flats (type 2). In certain sectors of formerly high-class villa and large terrace property (the middle-class merchants' suburbs of mid-Victorian Merseyside) high proportions of shared buildings and multi-dwellings pick out the young middle-class family areas of the inner conurbation.

Groups 5–7 are the post-1920 suburbs of which type 7, low on measures of congestion and high in amenity, largely occupy the middle-class commuter belts of the Wirral and along the rail routes to Southport and Ormskirk, and much of south Liverpool, though they are less dominant here than formerly. Types 5 and 6 are more complex, with high persons-per-room indices indicating large families on corporation overspill estates, with considerable numbers of high-rise flats found in parts of south Liverpool, and in Huyton and Kirkby.

The 'social space' pattern of the city is discussed in ch. 6.II.2.

III.5 Educational Achievement and Personal Incomes

Indices of housing and the like are closely related to other social criteria, such as those based on educational achievement and income, which are often more directly indicative of social status and of social and economic health or deprivation (fig. 1.3). The better-educated and qualified part of the population are more mobile, both geographically and socially, and the patterns of their mobility reflect regional and intra-regional opportunities.

Public expenditure on **education** has increased from 2.2 per cent of GNP after the Second World War to 6.6 per cent at present; meanwhile the size of the school age-groups has greatly increased, from 7.0 million in 1951 to 8.8 in 1971 and to 11.1 in 1974, while the numbers in full-time higher education have leapt from only 100,000 in 1951–2 to 482,300 in 1972–3. Of the estimated 10.1 million of school-age in the mid-1980s almost certainly a higher proportion will stay on into the sixth form and go on to higher education, though not as many perhaps as were expected in the late 1960s.

However, there has been no general levelling-up of opportunities in education, even in the public sector. The varying investment in education by local authorities as well as by individual families, points to the diversity in regional opportunities, which in turn reflect levels of prosperity as well as differing choices in the allocation of resources. One important criterion of educational opportunity is the proportion of those who stay on to 16 (the O-level group) or to 18 years (the A-level group). The proportions of pupils staying on after the compulsory age are highest in the SE, Wales and N Ireland (table 2.25). 18+ leavers show less striking variations, but the Welsh tradition of higher education stands out, while the SE and Yorks. and Humberside are also above average. Some of the industrial regions, for example the N Region and the W Midlands, are below average. Whilst many rural districts have below-average numbers of 18+ leavers E Anglia is the only economic planning region among the mainly rural areas which is below average. However, post-war censuses show that while the proportion of both girls and boys in full-time educa-

TABLE 2.24

Housing Indices, Merseyside, 1951–66

		Central 1951	1961	1966	Intermediate 1951	1961	1966	Peripheral 1951	1961	1966	Merseyside 1951	1961	1966
(Totals in 1,000s)													
Persons per household (present on census night)		3.58	3.41	3.26	3.63	3.49	3.42	3.51	3.19	3.02	3.58	3.34	3.15
Households in shared dwellings	Total	61.4	30.7	27.2	2.2	0.6	1.3	11.6	6.0	6.9	77.9	37.3	35.4
	%	16.6	7.6	6.6	4.1	0.8	1.2	12.1	5.5	6.1	14.6	6.3	5.6
% Households at: >1½ per room		8	5	2	4	3	1	7	2	1	8	4	2
at >1 person per room		21	15	9	14	13	7	20	10	5	20	13	8

Source: K. G. Pickett *Merseyside: Social and Economic Studies* (1970) pp. 86–8

tion up to the age of 17 was above average in rural areas, it fell sharply for boys in the 18+ group and was well below average for the 20–24 year group, though the proportion of girls in those age-groups in full-time education was above average.

Although no full-scale analysis of these inequalities has yet been made the general implications are known. The Report of the Committee on Higher Education (Min. of Education 1963), the Robbins Report, underlined the varying opportunities for high-school education, especially as between different social groups: in areas of generous provision and high social status 14.5 per cent of 17-year-olds were in school in 1960; in low status, low-provision areas, only 6.4 per cent had full-time schooling at that age. In regional terms, S and SE England had low proportions of people with a terminal age of education at 15 and under and much higher-than-average proportions of 15–19 and, especially, of those with a 20+ terminal age of education. In Scotland, the proportion of 15 year-old leavers was fairly high, especially in the industrial regions, but the proportion continuing in full-time education at 20+ is similar to that for England and Wales; in the crofting counties high proportions in this group echo the traditional Scottish emphasis on higher education.

These differences reflect both affluence and social class differentials but also involve the diversity in emphasis given to education by local authorities. In detail there are many puzzling differences in local authority provision for education, especially as between the former county boroughs. Coates and Rawstron (1971, ch. 10) have shown that not only does provision of private schooling directly reflect regional character and extent of affluence, but many similarities appear in the provision of sixth-form education. Private school places are well above average in all the counties of England south of a line from Suffolk to Gloucester, except Essex, Wiltshire, Somerset and Cornwall, and are important around Edinburgh. There is above-average sixth-form provision for Greater London, the South East and in Wales. Whilst there was some levelling-up in opportunities during the 1960s, in general there is still poorer provision in the county boroughs than in the administrative counties of England; the level of provision of sixth-form places is especially poor, especially for girls, in such industrial areas as Durham county, parts of the W and E Midlands and in some of the more rural areas, notably in E Anglia.

These features undoubtedly reflect considerable regional disparities in **personal incomes.** Though data available for study of incomes are limited, a number of studies by Coates and Rawstron (1971, ch. 10) have drawn attention to salient features of the distribution of personal incomes in the UK. Their analysis shows that in respect of tax on all types of income – schedule E (basic salaries and wages), schedule D (on fees) or on investment income – the SE quadrant of Britain is a favoured area. Levels of income are highest in Greater London and the SE, shading away west and north through average levels of income over most of the industrial quadrilateral of the Midlands to reach the lowest levels in the Scottish Highlands and Islands and in N Ireland. Moreover, during the 1960s the greatest improvement in incomes was largely within the South East, but outside Greater London; no doubt out-movement of higher income groups from the centre explains this. The lowest increases and the greatest relative declines in incomes were experienced in Scotland, much of N England and in N Ireland. By the mid-1960s the disparities in personal incomes ranged from an index of 72 in counties Londonderry and Tyrone to 108 in Hertfordshire (UK = 100). Between 1949–65 the best Scottish counties were all in C Scotland, but the highest index of 96 was reached only in West and

TABLE 2.25

School-leavers and Pupils at School beyond the Statutory Age, UK, 1967–73

REGION	Percentage leaving school at 15		Percentage leaving school at 15–17		18+		University		Going to Polys. Colleges of Education or other full-time education		Employment		% Pupils* remaining at school beyond 15 (State maintained schools only) 1964 at age		1972–3 at age	
	1967	1973	1967	1973	1967	1973	1967	1973	1967	1973	1967	1973	16	18	16	18
North	52	42	37	47	11	11	4	9	12	21	84	70	20	5	29	6
Yorks. and Humberside	49	40	38	48	13	12	6	8	14	22	81	70	22	6	30	7
North West	47	43	40	47	13	11	6	10	13	23	81	67	23	5	29	5
E Midlands	53	43	35	47	13	10	5	7	12	23	83	69	21	5	30	6
W Midlands	49	42	39	48	12	10	5	8	13	22	82	70	23	4	32	6
South East																
Greater London	31	34	52	53	17	13	7	8	10	17	83	75	33	6	41	8
Rest	35	38	48	50	16	12	7	9	16	25	78	66	–	–	–	–
E Anglia	47	44	42	47	12	9	4	8	16	28	79	64	21	4	29	5
South West	38	41	47	49	16	10	7	10	17	27	76	65	27	5	34	6
Wales	42	32	41	52	17	15	7	10	18	25	75	65	30	9	36	9
Scotland	30		61		9		12		5		83		23	3	33	3
Northern Ireland													14	5	35	12

*18 year-old pupils as compared to the 13 year-old group 5 years earlier; N Ireland figures are for all schools
For non-maintained (private) schools the respective percentages were 71 and 14 in 1964, and 75 and 15 in 1972–3
Source: Statistics of Education (1967 and 1973); *Social Trends 6* (1975)

Mid-lothian; in Ireland the best county, Antrim, had an average index of only 90.
Indeed only the SE and the W Midlands had an index of over 100. In 1973–4 as
compared with an average monthly household income in the UK of £54.7, the
range was from £43.8 in N Ireland to £62.4 in the OSE. Taking the UK as 100 the
SE took 116.2 per head of GDP, N Ireland 71.5, Northern Region 85.3 and Scotland
90.6.

It is not unrealistic to speak of continuing *poverty* within the UK, not only in
the poorer social classes but in poorer areas. While real wages have increased considerably since 1951, during which time the average weekly earnings of manual
workers have increased more than three-fold, many poorly-paid workers still
depend on various supplementary payments for support. One of those measured by
Coates and Rawstron, free school meals, shows that a similar gradient to that of
incomes exists in England and Wales, with low levels of claim in the SE quadrant
increasing westwards and northwards to reach peaks in N England and Mid- and
NW Wales. Once more, however, greater contrasts exist within urban areas. While
most of the county boroughs of N and NW England, Yorkshire and S Wales have
high proportions on free school meals, the proportions are greatest in the inner city.
Here they join forces with the various indices of social deprivation which have been
discussed in the context of 'levels of living' by Knox (1974) and in terms of housing
and social problems within cities by Kirby et al (1976). An early attempt at an
analysis of this kind was in the methods used to identify the priority areas designated
under the *Plowden Report* (Central Advisory Co. for Education 1969). The primary
schools selected for special assistance are almost wholly concentrated into central
city areas of low incomes, poor housing, high levels of social malaise and general
overcrowding; in Liverpool, for example, of 25 priority schools, 17 were located in
9 central wards out of the city's 40 wards. These were all areas with high proportions of poor housing and other census measures of low socio-economic status,
which lay within the inner zones defined in the 1951 census: zones 1 (the inner
core), 2a (the inner bye-law residential area) and 2b (in 1951 regarded as better-
class pre-1914 housing, but much deteriorated by the late 1960s). These wards also
had the highest incidence of various criteria of social malaise, according to a City
Planning Department survey of 1969, and the highest cumulative indices of social
deprivation which were matched only in two other wards, both in peripheral areas
of predominantly local authority housing (Flynn, Flynn, and Mellor 1972;
Holtermann 1975).

Social segregation in urban residential areas is treated in chapter 6, pp. 459–63.

IV THE WORKFORCE – DISTRIBUTION AND DAILY MOBILITY

While on a broad regional scale incomes reflect many of the demographic and social
contrasts within the UK, they are also closely related to considerable regional
contrasts in employment and unemployment.

IV.1 Size and Structure of the UK Workforce

Demographic structure determines the size of the potential workforce now and for
the future. The rapid increases in both under-15s and retirement age-groups in the
last thirty years will not be repeated over the next thirty when the greatest increases

TABLE 2.26

Economically Active Population UK, 1951–86

(1,000s) GB	Actual 1951	1961	1971	Projected 1976	1986
Economically active	22,610	23,811	25,103	25,164	26,659
male	15,649	16,071	15,917	15,833	16,330
female	6,961	7,740	9,186	9,331	10,329
married female	2,658	3,886	5,799	6,327	7,521
Activity rates					
male	87.6	86.0	81.4	80.4	78.5
female	34.7	37.4	42.7	43.5	46.0
married female	21.7	29.7	42.2	45.0	50.7
N IRELAND					
Total working	466	539	595		
male	295	365	394		
female	171	174	201		
Activity rates				NA	
male	62.3	63.2	64.2		
female	35.8	33.6	35.2		

Activity rates: economically active as percentage of total population aged 15 and over. Data for N Ireland not directly comparable with those for GB
NA = not available
Source: Social Trends, 5 (1974) and *Abstract of Regional Statistics*

will probably occur in the working age-groups, especially in the 15–44 year olds (table 2.5). Present dependency-rates (677 per 1,000 of working age in 1974) will fall to an estimated 630 by 1981, and to 623 per 1,000 by 2001. It is not easy to relate such age-structure trends to the available workforce, since this involves knowledge of factors influencing activity rates in the various sections of the population. The proportion of married women and elderly people at work varies with labour demand; the proportion of school-leavers going on to higher education, which has risen continuously and relatively rapidly in the 1960s, continues to do so, but at a much slower rate. In 1973, assuming a continuing increase of demand from labour and taking account of the raising of the school-leaving age to 16 in 1973, which led to a sharp apparent drop in the workforce for that year, the available workforce was expected to increase between 1974–85 by an estimated 6.4 per cent (4.7 for men and 9.2 per cent for women) (fig. 2.13). This presents a severe challenge in the context of an EEC area which in the past has had some regional shortages of labour, but which today has considerable problems of unemployment which will become even more serious if continuing recession makes it difficult to absorb the potential labour force. It also assumes a somewhat larger proportion of married women in the workforce than at present, which is in turn very much larger than in 1951 (table 2.26), though this is by no means certain.

IV.2 Factors Influencing Regional Trends in Employment

The capacity to absorb these increased numbers will depend on the state of the economy; at regional level this will be related to varying trends in employment

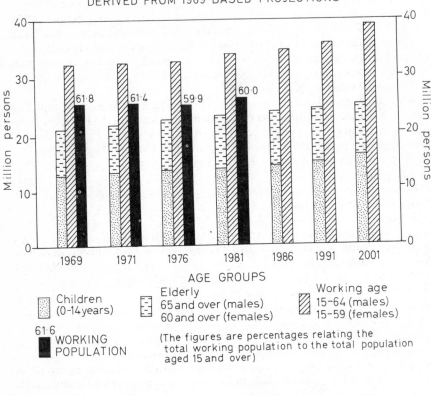

GREAT BRITAIN
WORKING AND DEPENDENT POPULATION
DERIVED FROM 1969-BASED PROJECTIONS

Children
(0-14years)

Elderly
65 and over (males)
60 and over (females)

Working age
15-64 (males)
15-59 (females)

61·6 WORKING
POPULATION

(The figures are percentages relating the
total working population to the total population
aged 15 and over)

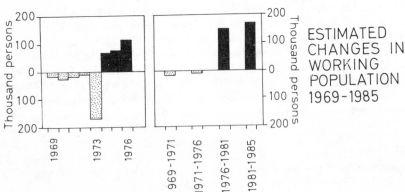

ESTIMATED
CHANGES IN
WORKING
POPULATION
1969-1985

Figure 2.13   Working and dependent population, GB, 1969–2001

(ch. 1) and population. Hence, if migration to the SE is to be contained, greater provision of employment will have to be made in the less prosperous regions of high unemployment and slow economic growth (ch. 1.V.1). Measures taken since the war have been partly successful in slowing down population losses from the poorer areas, but have been followed with varying rigour (ch. 1.V.2). Of a total of 870,000 jobs resulting from movements of manufacturing industry between 1945 and 1961, 427,000 were from Greater London, 98,000 from the rest of the SE and 62,000 from the Midlands, in all 687,000 (79 per cent of the total) from the prosperous regions (Howard 1968). Of these jobs only 231,000 (34 per cent) went to the less prosperous regions, 119,000 between 1945–51, a mere 28,000 from 1952–9 and 84,000 in 1960–5.

Moreover, for nearly twenty years after the Second World War no attempt was made to influence the distribution of employment in services (ch. 4.IV), the fastest-growing sector of employment since 1945 and that in which the SE is dominant, especially in administrative and managerial (Standard Industrial Classification – SIC – group 25) and professional and technical (SIC group 26) workers (fig. 1.2). Voluntary movement of offices from London was first encouraged by the Location of Offices Bureau, set up with government assistance in 1963. Initially few firms moved far from Greater London and the main beneficiaries were places like Croydon, whose new office complex led to a remarkable increase in jobs in the borough in the mid-1960s and which by the mid-1970s was itself largely saturated as an office centre, and the New Towns. Some government departments moved to development areas, e.g. the Post Office Savings Bank to Glasgow and the National GIRO to Bootle. Even after the *Control of Offices and Industrial Development Act* (Publ. Gen. Act 1965) brought office development under controls similar to those for manufacturing industry and restricted new office building within 65 km of C London, the policy had to be relaxed in the face of shortage of office accommodation in the SE. Moreover, only 1 per cent of office employers were willing to move to a development area in the period 1963–9, even to Merseyside where there was a surplus of good office accommodation (Manners et al 1972, 21). During the 1970s, office devolution policy, particularly in London, has experienced difficulties as the recession has slowed down expansion of office jobs. This has resulted in a surplus of office accommodation in most of the six centres around the GLC periphery scheduled for office development under the structure plan.

According to the *Hunt Report* (Sec. of State for Economic Affairs 1969, 14–15), the greater part of the 4 per cent growth in employment between 1961 and 1966 was due to a 6 per cent increase in the prosperous regions: in most of the development areas, Merseyside and the South West apart, there were small increases in total employment and a fall in industrial employment. Most indices of economic development in the less prosperous areas continue to compare unfavourably with national trends (table 2.27). In the 1960s the DAs fared badly in terms of unemployment, changes in employment, female activity rates and average male earnings and very badly in some of the sub-regions. Not surprisingly these facts were reflected in the total net migration figures for the regions (table 2.12), though the presence of other than economic factors influencing migration is apparent in the high levels of net immigration to the SW, an area of generally low earnings and some pockets of considerable unemployment, but of great environmental attraction, especially to older people. The general 1965–6 pattern of inter-regional mobility of working-age population shows the position very clearly (table 2.28). Considerable losses by

TABLE 2.27

GB. Some Regional Indices of Employment, Earnings and Net Migration, 1960s; Unemployment 1961–6, 1971, 1975

| | Sub-regional range (regional value in parentheses) Unemployment (%) | | | Employment change 1961–6 (%) | | Women at work | | Index of male earnings 1965–6 | Net inter-regional migration (All ages 5+) total (1,000s) 1966–71 | |
	1961–6*	1971	1975	Total	Male	% 1966	Changes in % 1961–6			%
Regions mainly in Development Areas										
Scotland	1/10(3.4)	3/9(5.6)	3/9(4.8)	+1/−5(+1)	−1/−7(−2)	28/44(40)	0/+3(+2)	90.6	–	+0.3
Wales	1/5 (2.7)	3/9(4.5)	6/13(5.2)	0/+13(+3)	−5/+12(−1)	22/38(30)	+1/+4(+3)	93.9	+6.8	−0.9
England	2/4 (3.1)	3/9(5.5)	5/11(5.6)	+1/+6(+2)	−4/+3(−1)	25/37(35)	+1/+3(+2)	92.2	−27.0	
Regions partly coinciding with Development Areas										
North West	1/4 (2.0)	3/17(3.7)	4/11(4.9)	−5/+5(+1)	−4/+4(0)	33/47(43)	−4/+1(0)	97.0	−42.2	−0.6
South West	1/4(1.7)	1/5(3.4)	4/8(4.5)	+3/+10(+6)	+1/+7(+4)	27/37(33)	+1/+3(+2)	92.7	+113.9	+2.9
Regions with no Development Areas										
Yorks. and Humberside	0/3(1.1)	2/9(3.7)	4/9(3.6)	0/+9(+3)	−3/+5(+2)	25/44(40)	−1/+4(+1)	94.5	−44.7	−0.9
E Anglia	0/3(1.4)	2/3(3.0)	3/4(3.4)	+13/+15(+13)	+11/+12(+11)	31/35(34)	+1/+4(+2)	91.5	+71.8	+4.6
E Midlands	0/2(1.0)	1/5(2.8)	2/6(3.3)	+4/+7(+6)	0/+5(+4)	36/47(40)	+1/+2(+2)	95.7	+29.3	+0.8
W Midlands	0/2(1.1)	2/7(2.9)	4/8(3.7)	+4/+10(+6)	+3/+9(+5)	33/50(44)	+1/+4(+1)	103.0	−43.0	−0.9
South East	0/3(0.9)	1/4(1.9)	2/7(2.6)	0/+11(+5)	−1/+17(+4)	28/55(44)	0/+4(+2)	109.5	−64.6	−0.4
GB	1–2	3–4	3–4	+4	+2	40	+2	100	0	0

*Regional averages for 1966 for South East, East Anglia, East Midlands, Yorks. and Humberside.
Source: The Intermediate Areas (1969), Appendices C and D; and *Department of Employment Gazette*, *83*, No. 9 (Sept. 1975); Census 1971 (1974); Champion (1976), table III.

TABLE 2.28

Net Inter-regional Flows of Working-age Migrants (15–59), GB, 1965–6 (100s)

		Net gain from (+) or loss (–) to										Total	
		North		Midlands		South		Wales		Scotland			
		M	F	M	F	M	F	M	F	M	F	M	F
North	M			–9.1		–5.0		–9.7		+22.1		–1.7	
	F				–9.5		–38.1		–9.8		+15.6		–41.8
Midlands	M	+9.1				+6.9		+6.3		+17.8		+40.1	
	F		+9.5				–22.9		+1.6		+14.8		+3.0
South	M	+5.0		–6.9				+7.0		+27.1		+32.2	
	F		+38.1		+22.9				+9.9		+24.3		+95.2
Wales	M	+9.7		–6.3		–7.0				–1.0		–4.6	
	F		+9.8		–1.6		–9.9				–1.3		–3.0
Scotland	M	–22.1		–17.8		–27.1		+1.0				–66.0	
	F		–15.6		–14.8		–24.3		+1.3				–53.4

'North' includes the Northern, Yorks. and Humberside and North West planning regions;
'Midlands' includes the East and West Midlands;
'South' includes the South East, East Anglia and the South West.
Source: Long Term Population Distribution in GB. A Study (HMSO 1971) Generalized from Appendix 2, Table 6

Scotland and the North and a small out-movement from Wales were transferred, though not directly, to the Midlands, where the main gains were of male workers, and the South, which had considerable gains of both men and, especially, of women. Much of this movement was of highly qualified professional and managerial workers. Waugh (1969) has shown that between 1961 and 1966 the North and West lost both population and 'a disproportionate share of talent and expertise'. This no longer went directly to the SE and W Midlands, and indeed the SW and E Anglia benefited most in the early 1960s. Yet the SE, which had in 1961 the greatest concentration of high-status socio-economic groups (groups 1–4), made the greatest gains in these groups 1961–6, Greater London apart, both in managerial and professional groups. Conversely, most rural counties showed a decline in such groups and in many of the depressed industrial areas, notably the coalfields of NE England and S Wales, the proportions of high status population were low despite an increase in commuter residents in the 1960s. Thus, regional contrasts in socio-economic status have continued to increase, with upward social mobility reinforcing the already strong position of the more prosperous regions, though the precise details of distribution are being reshaped with intra-regional changes in residence and workplace.

IV.3 Economically Active Population

Two aspects of employment are relevant to the analysis of social and economic health of the regions of the UK: the numbers and proportion of those in employment and of those out of work. Though complementary in many respects, they illustrate different facets of labour demand and supply, and of population structure as related to the actual and potential workforce.

Employed population The employed population is partly a function of age structure, partly of socio-economic factors, especially the proportions in full-time education beyond the compulsory age, and partly also of demand for labour. For example, opportunities of well-paid jobs for school-leavers may account for relatively low proportions of boys staying on at school in the W Midlands (table 2.25). The relatively high proportions of employed population in E Lancashire result from a long-standing tradition of women mill-workers; the much smaller percentage working population of coal-mining areas is by contrast, due to low proportions of women in the workforce, a response to a tradition of women staying in the home in an area of shift workers, as well as of lack of job-opportunities for girls. In many areas the reserve of labour among married women not at work offers one of the best ways of expanding the labour force in the short-term, often using part-time labour. Yet when demand for labour falls such women are often the first to be laid off; since they often are not in benefit and do not register as unemployed they may well in times of high unemployment represent a considerable measure of concealed unemployment. Workers of pensionable age, also often employed part-time, perform a similar role in the labour force.

Activity rates Thus, the proportion of persons in employment, as a percentage of the population over fifteen, as in table 2.26 and fig. 2.14, is a significant index of the varying intensity of economic activity and labour utilization. Figures derived from the 1971 *Census Advance Analysis* (OPCS 1972) for the administrative counties and county boroughs show clearly the higher proportions of the

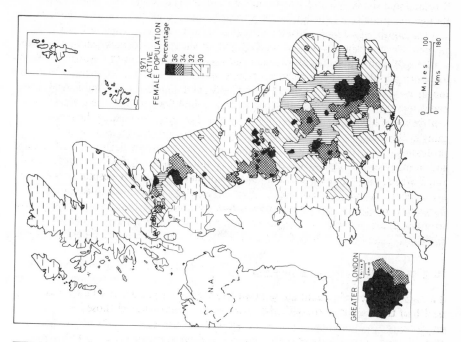

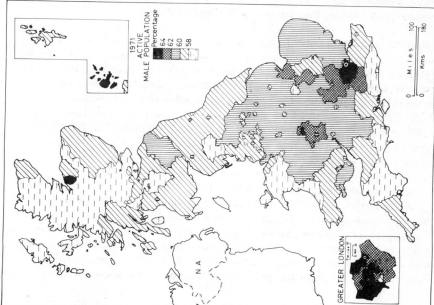

Figure 2.14   Economically active population, GB, 1971

economically-active, both men and women, in industrial and urban areas than in rural, though this is more pronounced for the male population. In part this is due to the more elderly population structure of rural areas but it also reflects the narrower range of job opportunities as well as economic activities. Where this is wider, as in the textile areas of the Scottish Border counties, activity rates are much higher.

The highest regional proportions of active male population are in Greater London and parts of the inner metropolitan area and in the Midlands (fig. 2.14). There is a general gradient of decreasing activity rates southwards and westwards, though there are exceptions as, for example, in the western parts of the Fenland counties, while the industrial areas of the north and west tend to have higher rates than the regional average (for example, S Wales), though the rates for C Scotland are low.

Female activity rates vary considerably at the regional level (table 2.27) and there are also considerable variations within regions, or even counties, as between employment exchange areas. The highest levels of female activity in 1966 were in SE England and W Midlands, also the regions with the highest local figures, though the NW was above the national average and the E Midlands, Yorks. and Humberside and, perhaps surprisingly, Scotland were at the national rate. There were, however, very considerable variations at sub-regional level. In 1969 the proportion of women over fifteen at work in GB was 40 per cent, but regional percentages varied from 22 to 45 per cent. Moreover, although rates of increase in female activity rates between 1961 and 1966 were at or above the national rate in some of these low-activity areas, these were insufficient to close the gap. However, this proportion has in national terms increased since the war. A recent survey (Britton 1975) shows that in England and Wales a major factor in the increase has been the considerable rise in the proportion of married women, especially older married women, at work. The percentage of the female labour force who are married has risen from 40 to 64 be-between 1951 and 1971, and the activity rate of married women, aged 45–59, from 22 to 54 per cent. While this partly reflects more universal marriage it is principally due to a shorter period of family formation. 85 per cent of families are now complete within ten years of marriage, with a return to work while children are still young.

In 1971, the highest female activity rates were clearly in the boroughs of the axial belt but, Lancashire apart, were mainly concentrated into Greater London and its surrounding metropolitan area and in the W and E Midlands (fig. 2.14). The highest Scottish rates were mainly in Glasgow, Edinburgh and other major towns and, apart from these, rates were low except in the Border textile districts. Wales, the SW, N and NE England tended to have low or very low female activity rates. This is a pattern which fits closely the differing intensity and patterns of labour demand in the prosperous and less prosperous regions, a pattern which a number of studies have shown to exist also at intra-regional level (Gordon 1970; Coates and Rawstron 1971, ch. 5). Moreover the trends in activity rates fit closely the regional rates of change in employment which between 1966 and 1975 declined more sharply in the less prosperous regions, especially so far as male employment was concerned, and where, apart from the NW, female activity rates are low (Manners et al 1972, 40–2; Prest 1970, ch. 5) (table 2.27).

The variations in female activity rates have been related to unemployment, degree of urbanization, and unfavourable industrial structure. Hence they suggest a considerable labour reserve locally and in certain regions, notably in 1966 in the

North, Yorks. and Humberside, Wales and the NW, but also in the SE. Assuming a 'norm' for female activity rates as some 8 per cent above the national average, estimates for 1961 suggested a female labour reserve of about 800,000 for the UK. This was a cautious estimate but one should remember that any such 'reserve' would include a high proportion of part-time workers. Taking account of the increasing proportions of women entering employment (table 2.26) this figure might now be greater, though at the time of the 1966 census a gross female labour reserve of only 300,000 was calculated by Gordon (1970). Taylor (1968) has shown that in the late 1960s there were still hidden female labour reserves but the trend of women to stay in employment longer after marriage and to return more quickly after child-bearing has considerably reduced this reservoir.

IV.4 Unemployment

Many local and regional indices of social inequality and of demographic, notably migrational, experience are related to varying regional rates of unemployment. Since the Second World War neither national nor regional rates of unemployment have reached the extremes of the inter-war period, but there remains a wide gap between rates in the more prosperous and less prosperous regions. Despite many efforts to diminish the uneven distribution of job opportunities, unemployment rates were above average in the development areas in the period 1961–8 when they had one-fifth of the working population, but over one-third of the unemployed, and experienced unemployment at up to two and a half times the national rate. Moreover, the North, SW, Wales, N Ireland, together with most of Scotland and the NW, traditionally had higher-than-average proportions of long-term unemployed, of unskilled workers and of out-of-work in the 18–44 age-group. Furthermore, these regions have tended to suffer bigger swings in cyclical unemployment. In such areas there is a great need for retraining of labour to attract new types of industry, for the level of provision of industrial retraining is generally much too low.

During the 1970s, however, other regions previously largely immune from high levels of unemployment have suffered, relatively and absolutely: for example, in the W Midlands unemployment rates have risen considerably, because of cyclical unemployment due to difficult and competitive conditions in the car trade, combined with structural weaknesses in the economy of the region, arising from its high level of dependence upon the motor car industries.

While much of the recent upsurge in unemployment in *all* regions of Britain is due to cyclical unemployment following a prolonged and severe downturn in economic activity, its increased severity as compared with other post-war cyclical fluctuations reflects structural imbalance in the national and in many regional economies. Such structural unemployment is deeper-rooted and likely to be more difficult to deal with, particularly through the existing framework of development area policy. It will demand investment in new industry, retooling of outdated plant and more extensive industrial retraining schemes which go beyond those at present provided even in DAs. Unless and until there is national recovery there will be little prospect of any region, whether in the DAs or the prosperous areas of the post-war period, reaching a better employment level.

One problem in many areas of high unemployment is the extent to which labour mobility may be impeded by housing problems, difficult journeys to work or other factors which tend to inhibit the decanting of surplus labour to jobs, locally or in other regions. Such frictional unemployment could be eased by more flexible housing policies for, as Johnson et al (1974) have recently shown, the migration of labour is considerably influenced by housing availability, and local authority tenants in particular often find it difficult to find accommodation if they should move to a new job. Conversely, people decanted from city centres to overspill estates or, in certain cases, to New Towns may often have to give up a job if the journey to work becomes difficult and do not always find secure alternative employment, as the recent experiences of closures of factories in Skelmersdale, near Liverpool, indicate.

At the core of much unemployment, however, lie the imbalances which arise from a rapidly changing technology in which new methods of production and of handling and retailing of goods are all seeking to economize in a period of rapidly rising labour costs. For example, the drastic reduction in the dock labour force on Merseyside is due not only to the relative decline of the port, but to the decasualization of dock labour in 1967 (following the recommendations of the *Devlin Report* on the Port Transport Industry, (Min. of Labour 1965) and to the revolution in handling of both bulk cargoes (through largely automated processes such as the bulk sugar terminal at Huskisson Dock, Liverpool) and of general cargo, much of which is now containerized and handled and moved by machines rather than, as in the past, by men (Lawton and Cunningham, 1970). Similarly, redundancy in the coal industry in the 1950s and 60s was a consequence of a number of factors including alternative fuels and exhaustion of resources but also of greater mechanization.

In such redundancies it is usually the older people who find it difficult to retrain or to find alternative employment. This is a problem which has spread in the 1970s to the tertiary sector as the recession and new technologies (for example, computer facilities) have affected business operations. As Prest (1970, 205–6) has shown, this age factor is a major problem in the reemployment of nearly one-quarter of unemployed men: in 1969 some 45 per cent of unemployed men were over forty-five. In the case of manual workers in particular, ill-health may add to this problem which is significant in social as much as economic terms.

Unemployment rates (excluding school-leavers) in GB have ranged between 1 per cent in the mid-1950s to 5.2 per cent (1975), while regional figures have ranged from as little as 0.4 per cent (W Midlands) and 2.2 per cent (Scotland) in 1955 to the 2.2 (SE) and 6.5 per cent (Scotland) in 1972 (fig. 2.15). Throughout, N Ireland's unemployment rate (7.9 in 1975) has been far above that for the UK as a whole. Intra-regional rates have had an even wider range. The *Hunt Report* (R. Commission 1969) showed that in 1961–6, a period of relatively low unemployment, rates reached 10 per cent in parts of the Scottish Highlands and Islands and in most regions of Britain there were local pockets of unemployment of two to three times the regional rate. Thus, though in August 1975 regional rates were below 5 per cent except in the North, Wales and N Ireland, the unemployment rate in the development areas as a whole was 7.5 per cent and the intermediate areas (5.5 per cent) also were above the average for GB (5.2 per cent). At the level of employment exchange areas (or groups of areas) unemployment rates ranged up to 11.9 per cent in Bargoed and 30.5 in Strabane while, on the other hand, in the SE there were still many areas with less than 2 per cent unemployed.

On the basis of data for DAs, intermediate areas and certain local areas an impression may be gained of the incidence of local unemployment in the early 1970s (fig. 2.16). High unemployment is found in many parts of N England, S Wales,

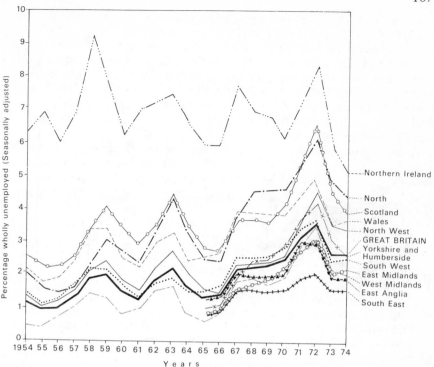

Figure 2.15   Regional unemployment, UK, 1954–72

Scotland and N Ireland, and in parts of the SW. Moreover, areas little affected by unemployment until recently now have above-average unemployment, especially of male workers. Thus Coventry and Birmingham now have over 7 per cent unemployed, including skilled workers in engineering and allied industries. The fall of jobs in manufacturing industry since 1970, the growing hard-core of unemployed among older men and the difficulties of both school-leavers and graduates in finding jobs underline the generality of the problem and emphasize the need for some regulation of regional distribution of employment in the servicing and commercial sector as part of government location policies.

Unemployment statistics alone do not show the full situation, since not all those who are out of work register as unemployed. The data on active population who were recorded in the 1971 census as 'not working' forms a useful basis of analysis at county and county borough level (fig. 2.17). The same marked regional differences appear, if anything more strongly, with high proportions of both men and women not in work in Scotland, N England and Wales and relatively low proportions in the Midlands and SE. The relatively high proportions of women not working in the Midlands, E Anglia and the SE suggest that there may well be much concealed unemployment or under-employment of women, though in certain areas seasonal unemployment may be involved, as for example in the resort areas of the Fylde, the Isle of Wight and SW England. Such seasonal unemployment tends to be dominant in the winter months; mid-year figures (for July) are thus more indicative

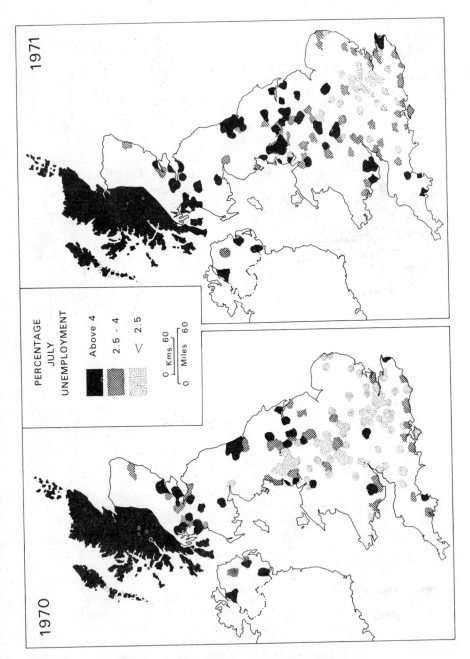

Figure 2.16   Some unemployment 'black spots', UK, 1970 and 1971

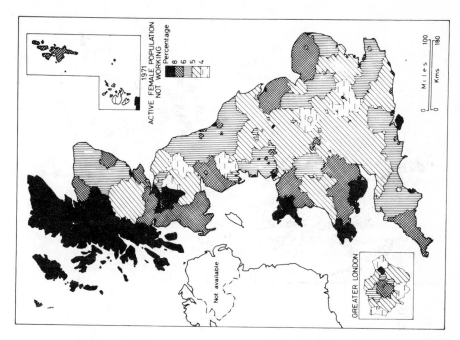

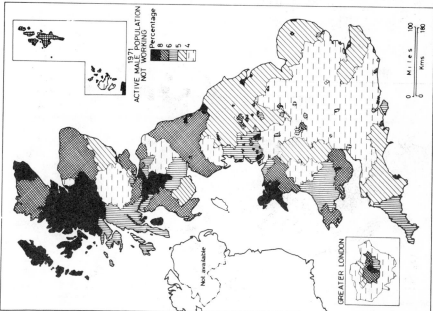

Figure 2.17   Active population not working, GB, 1971

of deep-seated trends (fig. 2.16). In rural areas the relatively higher proportions of active females not working suggests a reservoir of labour. Within all regions the 1971 census data suggest higher levels of unemployment in central city areas, especially in Greater London and the conurbations where there are higher proportions of both men and women out of work in the central boroughs than in the surrounding areas. This reflects the higher levels of unemployment among the semi- and unskilled groups among whom New Commonwealth immigrants are particularly adversely affected. Many of these people came to Britain in the late 1950s and 1960s to make up regional shortages of unskilled labour, but now find it difficult to get jobs in an economy which finds it increasingly difficult to absorb unskilled labour. From 1961 and 1966 census data Davison (1966, 89) showed that unemployment among New Commonwealth immigrants was above the 3.2 per cent average for English people, especially for Jamaicans (7.4 per cent), other West Indians (6.0 per cent), Pakistanis (5.4 per cent) and, to a lesser extent, Indians (4.4 per cent). These rates, for example for West Indians, correlate inversely with the low proportions in higher socio-economic groups and directly with high proportions in manual and unskilled groups. The *Census 1971, Advance Analysis* (OPCS 1972) shows that a higher proportion of New Commonwealth-born are out of employment as a percentage of all in this group than are in employment or in the total population (table 2.29). Moreover, all the main coloured immigrant groups have higher proportions out of employment than their total numbers would suggest and this is especially so in the case of West Indians.

It has been argued that these people find it hard to break out of this situation and to gain the educational and occupational skills which will permit them to rise in socio-economic status (Krausz 1971, ch. 4, 111–22: Deakin 1970, 72–82).

TABLE 2.29

Commonwealth Immigrants Employed and Out of Employment, UK, 1971

Born in	Population enumerated (1971)		Per cent of total		
	Total (1,000s)	% of GB	Employed	Out of employ- ment	Student and others in- active
UK	50,514	92.85	92.77	91.34	95,18
Irish Republic	721	1.34	1.87	2.83	0.82
Old Commonwealth	145	0.23	0.29	0.29	0.25
New Commonwealth	1,157	2.15	2.57	3.38	1.72
Foreign and not stated	1,077	2.00	2.28	2.01	1.68
Totals	53,826		23,560	1,355	28,469
India	323	0.60	0.75	0.87	0.46
Pakistan	139	0.26	0.32	0.38	0.20
West Indies	303	0.56	0.81	1.30	0.31
Cyprus	73	0.14	0.15	0.19	0.12
Africa	176	0.33	0.30	0.39	0.34

Source: Census 1971, Advance Analysis

Discrimination in employment and isolation within poor residential areas will only compound the problem. That this *is* now a problem can be seen in the statistics gathered since May 1971 on unemployed minority group workers. In May 1972 coloured workers formed 2.7 per cent of all unemployed in GB as compared with a total of 2.15 per cent New Commonwealth immigrants living in Britain at the time of the 1971 census, with rates of unemployment particularly high among West Indians and, to a lesser extent, among Pakistanis. Moreover, between November 1973 and May 1975, a period of generally rising unemployment, the workless among such groups increased by 156 per cent as against a 65 per cent increase among all unemployed. The increases have been most severe among younger people. An analysis of minority group unemployment by age (February 1975) showed that 31 per cent of men and 44 per cent of women without jobs were under twenty-five (Dept. of Employment 1975).

The problem of the immigrants, however, is but a special aspect of the more general problem of high unemployment as an aspect of social deprivation in the inner areas of our cities (Davidson, 1976, 108–17). This problem has been exacerbated by the fall in the number of jobs available in such areas following redevelopment of city centres and the movement out of industry under planning policies of the 1960s, a fall which has led to the loss of thousands of jobs and considerable rating revenue. The consequences are two-fold: those that remain in the inner areas tend to be the older or less-privileged and less well-educated and well-trained sections of the population to whom fewer jobs are open; secondly, housing policies have tended to increase the relative proportion of such groups of people within inner areas which have become increasingly dominated by local authority rented accommodation (often in high-rise flats) and the remaining, often old and poor-quality, private rented housing. There is real need for an urgent drive not only on unemployment but on the associated social and population problems of the inner city. The level of the problem may be judged from the situation on Merseyside. Here, in a region with persistently above-average rates of unemployment, there has been a considerable decline in the population of inner areas since 1951 and the region as a whole is losing families at a rate which could create 60,000 empty dwellings in the next decade. As compared with the 750,000 jobs and 15,000 jobless of 1966 there are now, in 1976, 100,000 fewer jobs and over 80,000 unemployed. If the money needed to bring back life to the area – estimated by the Merseyside County Planning Office as £4,500m over the next ten years – is to be forthcoming it may need to be diverted from proposed overspill and existing and projected New Town development (ch. 2.IV.6).

IV.5 Workplace and Residence

General features One of the most distinctive characteristics of population distribution in the modern UK is the increasing separation of workplace and residence. Successive censuses from 1921 have revealed a growing volume and intensity of daily travel to work. By 1961, 36 per cent of the economically-active population in England and Wales and 25 per cent in Scotland worked outside the local authority area in which they lived. Between 1921 and 1961 the numbers who travelled to work outside their area of residence in England and Wales increased by 115 per cent from 2.6 to 5.6 million as compared with a 29 per cent increase of

the working population. The *Redcliffe–Maud Report* (R. Commn. 1969, III, App.)
estimated that, excluding Greater London, daily travel to work was 70 per cent
higher in 1966 than in 1921, and showed that in all regions this increase had been
much greater than for the population as a whole. Taking 1921 values as 100, the
1966 index of daily out-movement ranged from 144 in the SE, already a
considerable commuter area in 1921, to 250 in E Anglia.

The rapid growth in both numbers and range of commuter journeys has been
especially marked since 1945. Two sets of forces are involved: first, concentration
of jobs, with an increasing range of labour recruitment from surrounding residential
areas; secondly, residential dispersal from the inner city to commuter suburbs
(Lawton 1967), a feature of post-war population mobility reflected in intra-urban
migration and commuting alike, and permitted by improvements in both public and
private transport. The causes have been conceptualized by Warnes (1972) as the
result of structural changes in industry and the economy, principally increases in
real incomes, decreasing hours of work, increasing size and concentration of
manufacturing units and a growth in employment in the tertiary sector; the latter
is mainly located in central city areas. These may lead to concentration of
employment in fewer units, focused in fewer locations, particularly in the urban
areas. Higher incomes, however, leave more money for increased travel costs which,
combined with a widening search for land for housing outside the city centres, has
led to dispersal of both private and local authority housing. Even where, as in the
case of London's New Towns and overspill agreements, the intention is to disperse
both homes and jobs, the outcome is usually an increase rather than a decrease of
both volume and distance of journey to work.

One of the features of recent changes in population has been a growth of
adventitious population resident in rural areas but working in the towns. The
growing extent of the dependence upon urban employment is seen in the
considerable increase in the proportion of people commuting from rural districts.
Between 1921 and 1966 daily out-movement of resident working population from
rural districts in England increased from 22 to 47 per cent as against 21 to 34 per
cent in all types of area (excluding Greater London), and rural commuter flow to
urban areas increased from 387,000 (14.2 per cent of the occupied resident population) in 1921 to nearly 1.5 million (37.4 per cent) in 1966. In over one-third of
rural districts in 1966, over 40 per cent of the active population travelled to work in
urban areas as against 3.5 per cent at this level in 1921; conversely, in 22 per
cent of rural districts of England in 1966 there was less than 20 per cent daily out-
movement as compared with 78 per cent of RDS in 1921 (Roy. Commn. 1969, III, App. 2

Working, residential and commuter population, 1951–71 The basic changes in
journey to work may, therefore, be focused on two aspects: first, on relative changes
in the residential and working population of the major cities of the UK; secondly,
on changes in daily movement to and from these major centres. Attention has been
focused here upon twenty-four metropolitan centres with a working population of
about 100,000 or over in 1971, though a number of such centres have had to be
excluded: West Ham (now part of the London Borough of Newham) and Wolverhampton because major boundary changes preclude comparison; the London
boroughs of Camden and Westminster, and Teesside and Warley because they are
essentially the creation of major local government changes in the 1960s. Moreover,

TABLE 2.30

Aspects of the Journey to Work, Major British Cities, 1951–71

		TOTAL POPULATION				DAILY MOVEMENT						JOB RATIO		
		Resident active		Working		IN			OUT				change	
		Total 1971	% change 1951–71	Total 1971	% change 1951–71	Total 1971	1951–61	1961–71	Total 1971	1951–61	1961–71	1971	1951–61	1961–71
City of London	(CL)(1)	3.55	− 1.1	340.46	+ 0.6	338.50	+15.6	−14.6	1.09	− 1.3	+43.4	9,590.4	+1,927	−7,664
Croydon	(Cr)	165.42	(+34.0)	134.79	(+39.1)	50.67	+46.0	(+20.8)	64.49	+ 7.1	(+15.7)	82.1	+ 5.6	1.0
Birmingham	(B)	501.37	−11.1	565.14	−11.8	163.20	+44.7	+15.4	47.21	+36.8	+14.5	112.7	+ 3.0	− 2.3
Bradford	(Bd)	140.15	− 6.6	140.14	−13.6	32.95	+26.8	+ 7.1	18.21	+10.6	+36.5	100.0	+ 0.5	− 8.6
Bristol	(Br)(1)	197.25	− 1.0	203.29	+17.8	53.59	+62.4	+38.4	25.83	+12.4	+ 1.7	103.1	+ 3.4	− 0.6
Cardiff	(Ca)(1)	126.92	(+ 4.5)	137.62	(+19.6)	35.99	+37.8	(+15.7)	10.28	+34.9	(−11.2)	108.4	+ 1.2	− 8.4
Coventry	(Co)(1)	161.74	(+27.1)	171.32	(+24.3)	41.48	+12.1	(+ 8.9)	17.26	+49.5	(−25.1)	105.9	+ 6.1	− 5.4
Derby	(De)	100.23	(−13.1)	107.83	(− 1.6)	23.72	+25.7	(+ 1.9)	7.44	+25.9	(+24.7)	107.6	+12.0	(+4.8)
Hull	(H)	130.67	+ 1.5	127.38	− 6.7	25.91	+28.4	+28.0	13.35	+29.1	+26.4	97.5	+ 3.3	− 5.1
Leeds	(Le)	233.62	− 7.6	244.78	− 9.1	57.78	+25.6	+37.3	22.19	+ 7.5	+19.7	104.8	+ 0.0	− 1.7
Leicester	(Lr)	140.55	− 4.9	171.98	+ 2.1	57.90	+68.3	+20.9	13.97	+32.4	+36.1	122.3	+ 8.8	− 0.5
Liverpool	(Li)	280.94	−22.8	312.31	−24.3	119.08	+22.3	+ 6.1	47.49	+ 4.4	+15.5	111.2	+ 0.7	− 2.9
Manchester	(M)	257.08	−28.3	321.48	−25.9	156.87	+23.4	− 7.6	56.98	− 0.5	− 9.6	125.1	+ 7.5	− 3.0
Newcastle	(Nc)	102.10	−24.3	148.02	−25.9	82.68	+25.1	+ 1.5	22.09	+10.4	− 1.3	145.0	− 6.0	+ 3.0
Nottingham	(No)	141.59	− 7.8	168.36	− 2.9	66.18	+25.0	+22.7	24.24	+ 6.4	− 1.7	118.9	+ 2.5	+ 3.4
Plymouth	(Pl)(1)	100.94	(− 1.4)	99.48	(−14.7)	13.24	+14.7	(+ 6.4)	4.97	+21.7	(+23.9)	95.7	+ 0.0	+13.9
Portsmouth	(Po)(1)	91.39	−10.1	103.90	− 2.3	33.34	+75.7	+43.8	9.61	−10.5	+27.8	113.7	+12.0	− 3.0
Sheffield	(Sh)	245.05	(− 5.2)	255.95	(+ 5.9)	48.70	+67.2	(+19.2)	15.79	+16.3	(+ 2.2)	104.4	+ 4.0	− 5.1
Southampton	(So)	98.45	+27.3	105.99	+29.3	31.95	+48.8	+43.8	13.83	+ 4.8	+31.2	107.7	+ 2.8	− 1.8
Stoke	(St)	134.27	− 6.4	141.98	−10.1	36.50	+26.2	+ 3.8	17.05	+10.1	+16.0	105.7	+ 0.3	− 4.7
Aberdeen	(A)	82.24	+ 6.2	80.37	+ 0.8	12.60	+21.0	+65.9	6.61	+43.7	+14.8	97.7	− 4.7	+ 0.5
Dundee	(D)	87.97	+ 5.0	85.40	− 1.9	10.74	+19.6	+62.0	3.28	− 7.5	+35.7	97.1	− 4.9	+ 1.9
Edinburgh	(Ed)	212.63	+ 1.3	222.54	+ 1.1	42.10	+50.2	+54.8	11.81	+ 7.4	+38.5	104.7	− 0.5	+ 0.4
Glasgow	(Gl)	410.96	−16.1	414.02	−19.5	116.89	+20.4	+16.8	55.21	+ 6.1	−11.7	100.7	− 4.1	+ 0.1

(1) Substantial boundary changes to Croydon, Cardiff, Coventry, Derby, Plymouth and Sheffield preclude comparison of 1971 with earlier figures: calculations for 1951–66 (cols. 2 and 4) and for 1961–66 (cols. 7 and 10) are substituted for 1951–71 and 1961–71 respectively, and are shown in parentheses, and are the job ratio change for Derby, 1961–66.

Source: Based on *Workplace Tables*, Censuses of 1951, 1961, 1966 (Sample Census) and 1971.

boundary changes in several towns since 1966 preclude direct comparison of certain trends to 1971 (table 2.30).

Between 1951–71 the residential population of the majority of such cities fell, by as much as one-fifth in some cases, though Cardiff, Coventry, Croydon, Plymouth, Southampton and Dundee had an estimated increase, and in Bradford, Leicester and Aberdeen there was little change (fig. 2.18). However, the rate of increase of working population, which up to 1961 had generally exceeded that of residential population or which had fallen at a lesser rate, declined and, in many cases, showed an absolute fall in the late-1960s. The fact that residential populations are still smaller than the numbers who work in the large cities reflects post-war spread of population into the suburbs, a process which continues with relatively little abatement. On the other hand, there have been significant changes in the distribution of workplaces. Up to the early-1960s a high proportion of jobs in the large urban areas were focused on a few areas, especially in metropolitan centres. The job ratio, an index of working population:resident active population x 100, still indicates a surplus of jobs in most such towns in 1971 (which mainly have ratios of over 100) (table 2.30). Up to 1966, however, all the cities studied, except Croydon, had a job surplus and in all except the City of London job ratios were higher than in 1951: moreover, with the exception of small downward trends between 1961–66 in Bradford, Bristol, Southampton and Stoke, job ratios were *increasing* up to 1966. But by 1971, there was a general fall in job ratios in the major towns reflecting a greater fall in their working populations, in the late-1960s, than in their residential populations. This suggests a flight to the suburbs of both homes and places of employment. Among the more marked reductions of job ratio, 1961–71, the City of London's trend reflects office dispersal from central London, while Plymouth has lost jobs in the town with the decline of its naval dockyards and has located much of its new industry outside the 1971 Borough boundary. In contrast, Croydon, which, until the 1950s, was predominantly a commuter suburb of Greater London with a low job ratio, greatly increased its job potential with the injection of 10,000 new office jobs in the mid-1960s, when it acquired 79 per cent of offices and nearly 60 per cent of office jobs decentralized from London between 1963 and 1968 (Daniels 1969). Yet even here, between 1966–71 job ratios fell as from the late 1960s office dispersal went further afield.

Analysis of trends in daily in- and out-movement (fig. 2.19) shows that in only one case, the City of London, did in-movement decline in 1951–71. In every other large city there were considerable increases in daily in-movement (36.0 per cent in aggregate) and these generally exceeded increases in daily out-movement (21.1 per cent in aggregate). This was changing, however, in the 1960s as job dispersal from the centre to the periphery of cities gained momentum, especially with the development of peripheral industrial estates and dispersal of some office jobs and many distributive industries to sites outside city boundaries. In Greater London, where 51 per cent of the employed population commutes, British Rail have suggested that between 1966 and 1973 the number of commuters fell by 8 per cent. However, increases both of in-commuting and out-commuting have generally greatly exceeded changes in the resident population between 1951–71 and, collectively, these trends have added to both the volume and complexity of cross-currents of commuting in and around large metropolitan centres.

Two forces are at work in job location, leading to greatly increased daily travel. In the tertiary sector of the economy, the sector of most rapid growth in employ-

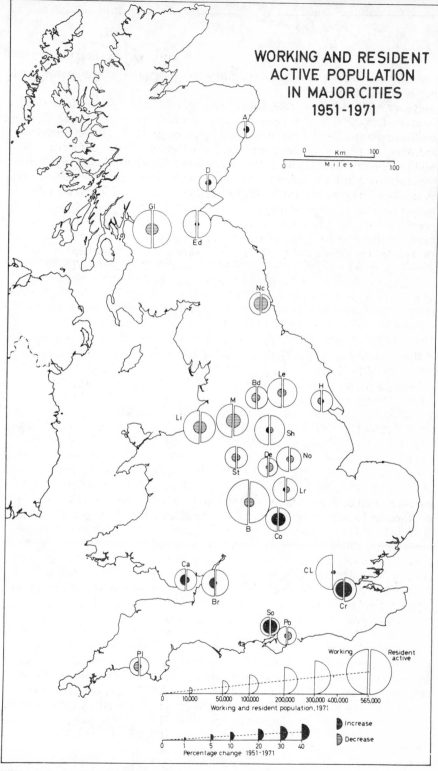

**WORKING AND RESIDENT
ACTIVE POPULATION
IN MAJOR CITIES
1951–1971**

Figure 2.18   Working and resident populations, major cities, GB, 1951–71

*Where the symbol for percentage change is larger than that of total population the latter is superimposed (in white) and percentage change appears as a black border.

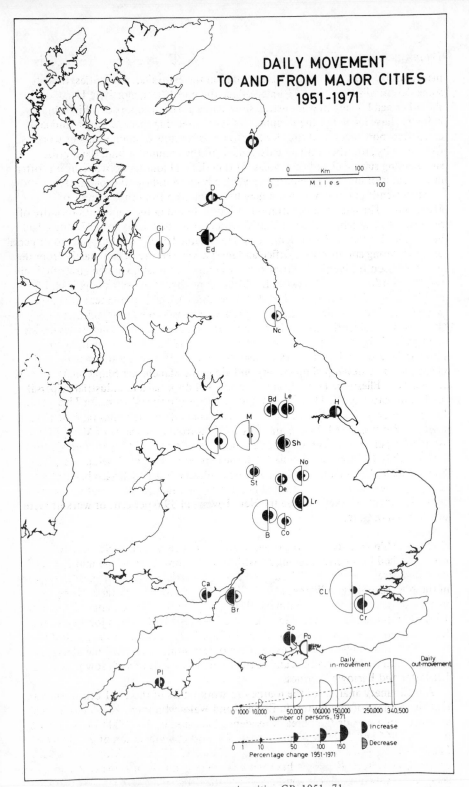

Figure 2.19   Daily in- and out-movement, major cities, GB, 1951–71

*Where the symbol for percentage change is larger than that of total population the latter is superimposed (in white) and percentage change appears as a black border.

ment, until recently most jobs were created in the central areas of cities, though some decentralization has taken place since the mid-1960s, mostly in London, On the other hand, many new industrial sites, and a greater proportion of jobs in industry, have moved to the periphery of towns, seeking space, cheaper land and easier transport access and thus leading to a reverse flow of commuting of workers from the city, together with an enlargement of the commuter hinterland into surrounding suburban and rural areas. This peripheral journey to work, as it is often described, is of increasing importance in all advanced industrial economies.

Such trends in journey to work may be epitomized from the example of *Merseyside*. The largest concentration of jobs is found in the conurbation centre of Merseyside to which, in 1961, 157,000 workers travelled daily. By 1971 there had been a massive fall in this movement to 93,000, due largely, one suspects, to dispersal of warehousing and industry. Office and service workers are drawn mainly from the suburbs of south Liverpool, Wirral and the commuter areas along the electrified railways to Southport and Ormskirk. Dockside employment in both shipping and industry, though much reduced, still attracts a considerable movement along the waterfront, much of it from the suburbs following widespread slum clearance in the dockside residential areas. Most of the newer labour-intensive industries drawn to Merseyside by development area policy since 1949 have gone to peripheral industrial estates and many 'port industries', such as oil-refining and petrochemicals, have developed up-estuary and along the Manchester Ship Canal, especially at Ellesmere Port. However, residential dispersal and industrial dispersal are not in harmony. Kirkby, for example, a post-war overspill town for Liverpool, has many new industries on its extensive industrial estates and a job ratio of 131.3 in 1971. But it drew 61.7 per cent of its workers from other parts of Merseyside, while 44.8 per cent of its resident active population travelled to work outside the town, mainly to Liverpool. Similarly, in the early stages of the development of Skelmersdale, Merseyside's first New Town, industry typically lagged behind residential development, as reflected in the 1971 job ratio of 87.0, but 43.6 per cent of residents worked outside the New Town and 39.6 per cent of workers were drawn from outside.

Commuter hinterlands The loss of population from central city areas has not been matched by a corresponding redistribution of jobs. Even where industry has been decentralized, it draws labour from wider hinterlands. Over the past fifty years in the NW, according to Warnes (1972, 325), journey to work distances have increased by an average of 0.8 km in 1921–51, 1 km in 1951–61 and 1.2 km in 1961–6, resulting in an overall increase of 50 per cent in the mean journey to work from 2.35 to 3.54 kms between 1921 and 1966. These increases were greatest and the commuting range most extensive in the outer suburban areas of the Merseyside and the SELNEC conurbations and in the rural hinterlands of such towns as Lancaster and Barrow-in-Furness.

A preliminary analysis of the journey to work tables of the 1971 census shows that the number of commuters in England and Wales who travel to work in a local authority area outside their area of residence increased by 309,000 (3.8 per cent) between 1966 and 1971 to 37 per cent of the working population of 22.7 million. In Scotland 33 per cent of the working population (3.17 m) were involved in such commuting. Despite this there has been a fall in commuting into the centre of most large cities, which is a direct consequence of the decline in employment in inner areas of large cities (ch. 2.IV.4). This decentralization of employment has followed in the wake of post-war decentralizing policies in housing. As Hall (1971 and 1973) has pointed out this has created a very complex commuting structure, with a number of tiers of journey to work which reflect the hierarchical structure of urban areas, and which contain complex two-way movements between city centre and periphery and considerable and often very complex sets of movements between peripheral centres of employment. Hall et al (1973) have described the growing complexity of commuting both between the 'core' and its surrounding 'ring' in one hundred Standard Metropolitan Labour Areas, defined in terms of the size and density of the labour force, and also with the 'outer city region' within Metropolitan Economic Labour Areas. Their analysis showed that, of 100 SMLAs, 68 were experiencing some decentralization in 1951–61, and 94 were doing so in 1961–66. In a subsequent analysis of 20 of these centres, Champion (1976) has shown that between 1961–71 *all* were showing a decline of population in the 'core' and acceleration in the 'ring'. Warnes (1975) showed that in 1921–66 in Liverpool and Manchester, population decentralized faster than employment, with a consequent tendency of commuting to increase, relatively, though the actual volume of movement into the city centre was beginning to decline as compared with the growth of employment around the conurbation fringes. While the strength of movement to the centre is tending to diminish, it is clear that over a lengthy time period such cities generate forces which are reflected in the organization of employment, population and commuting patterns in the metropolitan region and that these regions have a growing influence, both directly and indirectly, on population and employment.

Despite the concentration of journey to work on the major conurbations, rural commuting is also on the increase: in English counties such as N Yorkshire and Westmorland some 20 per cent of the working population are commuters and even in remote and thinly populated counties, such as Radnor, the level of daily journey to work is some 10 per cent or more of those employed.

The general increase in the extent and complexity of commuter hinterlands is not fully reflected in the volume and pattern of daily movement between towns and their surrounding territories in urbanized and rural areas alike (Lawton 1963B, 61–9; R. Commission, 1969, III, 25–6). The major foci, both in terms of their commuter demand and the range over which daily movement is drawn, are the large boroughs. The hinterlands of such cities, together with the City of London, are defined in terms of those local authorities which supplied over one hundred commuters (fig. 2.20). These cover the most populous regions of the UK, and also correspond broadly with the areas from which the greatest proportions of daily out-movement (over 40 per cent of the resident population) are recorded. The extent of these areas of high job-dependence has grown considerably in the last twenty years. In the North West Warnes suggests that, by the end of the century, the distance travelled to work could increase by as much as 50 per cent on the evidence of recent trends. From a number of recent studies it seems that longer-distance commuting is increasing most rapidly, a process aided by the wider availability of private transport. The major metropolitan areas increasingly dominate the social and economic life of all regions of the UK and are of fundamental significance to the inter-dependence of town and country as the various local government studies, including the *Redcliffe–Maud Report*, (R. Commn. 1969, III, App. 3, 39–47), showed in the 1960s. The Report showed that commuting and intra-regional migration are inter-dependent. In a detailed study of fourteen towns of varying size

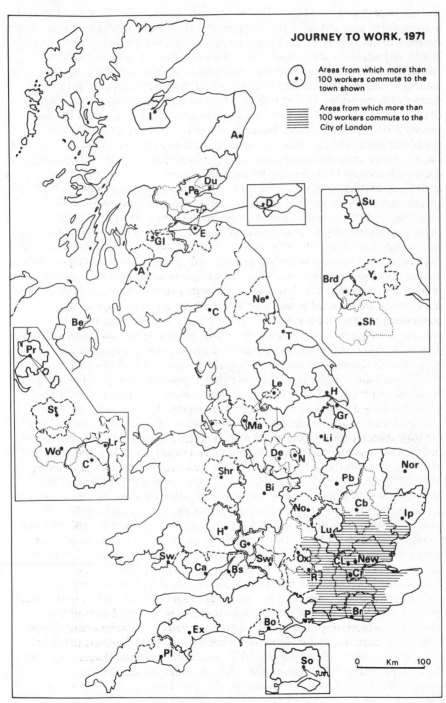

Figure 2.20   Journey-to-work hinterlands, UK, 1971

and character it was shown that all had lost population in the 15–44 age-group, especially among professional and managerial classes, but that the return daily flow among these groups was stronger than in the journey-to-work pattern as a whole. The towns analysed, ranging in population from 427,800 down to 32,800, were Bristol, Coventry, Nottingham, Leicester, Luton, Northampton, Norwich, York, Exeter, Doncaster, Colchester, Shrewsbury, Taunton and Canterbury. Intra-regional migrants who move to the rural fringes of large towns thus continue to be linked to them through the journey to work as well as for shopping and other services.

Such inter-dependence is not, however, confined to the hinterlands of large towns or industrial regions but may be found also in rural areas at much lower levels in the urban hierarchy. True, apart from rural Wales, parts of N and SW England, and Southern and Highland Scotland, there are few areas of the UK beyond commuting reach of the employment opportunities in large towns. Yet even in such areas a small town may exert a considerable influence on its region, attracting considerable numbers of workers from an extensive hinterland. For example, Aberystwyth, with important commercial, servicing and cultural functions, in which the University College of Wales plays an important part, had a job ratio of 143.2 in 1971. There are many other similar cases, notably in county towns, though quite small market centres may provide surrounding rural districts with a focus of jobs absorbing 20–40 per cent of their resident occupied population. In most 'rural' counties of England and Wales, therefore, the mean job ratio of municipal boroughs and urban districts is relatively high, while only Merioneth of the rural Welsh counties has a collective urban job ratio of under 100. Somerset's combined urban job ratio in 1971 was 106.4 with very high values in towns like Taunton (136.7) and Yeovil (158.9). Similar examples could be quoted from Hereford, south Lincolnshire, and W Suffolk, to mention only a few counties.

A particularly significant aspect of commuting is that associated with the conurbations. All have job ratios of over 100 and massively large daily movements of population into their industrial and service areas. In the period 1951–66 the numbers travelling to work in the five English provincial conurbations increased by 87.5 per cent. Out-movement also increased substantially, largely due to travel to peripheral industrial estates. Even from a simple analysis of areas contributing over 100 workers per day, the conurbation hinterlands appear very large, extending up to 32 km from the centre in the provincial conurbations and in the case of Greater London forming a vast region containing many complex cross-currents of daily movement of some 80 km in diameter. In all these regions, the level of commuting has greatly increased in the 1950s and 1960s and the greatest increases, for example in the NW conurbations and in Greater London, have been recorded from the outer areas, a response to the greater dispersal of homes than of jobs.

Not surprisingly a considerable part of the working day or, as it may more properly be regarded, of people's leisure time, is taken up by travel to work. The National Travel Survey (Dept. of the Environment) has shown that 28 per cent of work journeys in GB take thirty minutes or more and that 37 per cent are of over 8 km. While these figures are highest for Greater London (51 per cent and 47 per cent respectively) even in the SW similar journeys involve 16 per cent of people in half-hour journeys, 29 per cent of which are over 8 km (table 2.31). Rather surprisingly the National Travel Survey suggests that the percentage of journeys taking over thirty minutes fell in London from 62 per cent to 53 per cent between 1966 and 1973, and from 53 to 38 per cent in other major urban areas, though

TABLE 2.31

Journeys to work in GB, Time and Distance, 1973

Region of residence	% journeys to work taking (minutes)				% journeys to work of distance (miles)					
	Under 15	15–30	30–60	Over 60	Under 1	1–2	2–5	5–10	10–25	Over 25
North	35	37	23	5	3	14	42	27	13	1
Yorks. and Humberside	36	39	22	3	7	12	47	23	10	1
E Midlands	42	39	16	3	3	17	56	16	7	1
E Anglia	41	40	16	3	9	16	38	22	13	2
South East										
Greater London	23	26	36	15	3	12	38	25	20	2
Rest of South East	38	34	20	8	6	14	38	19	18	5
South West	55	29	14	2	14	15	42	17	11	1
W Midlands	33	40	24	3	3	15	46	25	10	1
North-West	38	35	24	3	5	14	46	24	10	1
Wales	42	38	18	2	7	14	54	13	10	2
Scotland	36	38	22	4	8	17	42	20	12	1
GB	37	35	23	5	6	14	43	22	13	2

Source: Soc. Trends (1974) 5, 106

TABLE 2.32

Journeys to work in GB, Time Taken 1966–73

	% journeys to work taking (minutes)							
	1966				1973			
	Under 15	15–30	30–60	Over 60	Under 15	15–30	30–60	Over 60
Major urban areas								
London	12	26	42	20	18	29	37	16
Other[1]	14	33	43	10	25	37	33	5
Other urban areas								
Population of:								
250,000–1,000,000	30	46	20	5	23	47	28	3
100,000–250,000	23	42	28	8	37	37	21	5
25,000–100,000	39	34	20	6	35	42	20	3
3,000–25,000	27	34	27	13	35	37	23	6
Non-urban areas	34	31	24	10	33	41	22	4
All areas	25	34	30	11	29	38	26	6

[1] Includes Birmingham, Glasgow, Liverpool and Manchester

Source: Soc. Trends (1975) 6

they have increased slightly in large provincial cities (table 2.32). Perhaps the reduction in journey times, not least in the rural areas, reflects the increased use of private cars in work travel. Indeed private transport now accounts for the vast majority of journeys, ranging from 62 per cent of *all* journeys in Greater London to 85.6 in E Anglia. Even so, a small sample taken in Reading in 1973 suggested that men involved in work travel spent, on average, 2.25 hours per day on it (Bullock et al 1974, 57, 179).

IV.6 New Towns and Overspill

An important aspect of population policy and distribution since 1945, and one of particular significance for the conurbations, has been the attempt to relieve congestion and to provide new homes and jobs through the building of New Towns and the development of overspill arrangements with existing towns (ch. 6.IV.1). Such planned decentralization is not unique, but the first post-war New Towns set up under the 1946 Act were a pioneer venture aimed at providing 'balanced communities of a manageable size, with improved living conditions, employment opportunities of sufficient range to ensure economic stability, besides full social services, including physical and cultural amenities' (Edwards 1964, 279).

The twenty-nine New Towns established in Britain and three in Northern Ireland to date (fig. 2.21), are at very varying stages of development. The British New Towns have already provided 218,000 new dwellings and absorbed a population of 862,000. The *first wave* of New Towns were largely provided for Greater London, some 40–48 km out, beyond the green belt. Initially mainly concerned with providing housing, they have increasingly developed their employment base, though many are still over-dependent on one or two large firms. Collectively, the 'first wave' London New Towns had a population of 493,000 at the end of 1974, of which some 372,000 was overspill, as compared with their planned capacity of 668,500 (table 2.33).

Relatively small in size and close to London, the largest (Basildon) is planned to reach 134,000. The counter-attraction of the conurbation and the relatively restricted number and range of job opportunities within the individual towns have necessitated a considerable degree of commuting, including a sizeable element of travel to work from the New Towns to C London. In 1961 only Bracknell, Stevenage and Welwyn had job ratios of over 100 and the levels of out-commuting ranged from 14.40 per cent, while 6.8 per cent of men and 3.7 per cent of women still travelled to work in the County of London. In 1966, 26 per cent of the active population worked outside the eight London New Towns and 29 per cent of their working populations were drawn from outside. Clearly the number and range of jobs was healthier in the 1960s, including more in the service and commercial sector but it would seem that even where the objectives include that of a 'balanced community' a considerable level of commuting is unavoidable in an economy in which more than one member of a household is in work and transport is relatively easy, in terms of cost and accessibility.

Similar problems have been encountered in the New Towns of other regions, though often in a more marked form. The *second wave* of New Towns of the 1960s, in the SE and elsewhere, have generally been focused on existing towns, farther from the major city and often with a considerable initial population of their own (table 2.33 and fig. 2.21). Their original target populations were much larger presenting a greater opportunity to develop a wider range of jobs and facilities and, since they are farther from the metropolis, giving the chance of becoming more independent than the first wave of New Towns. Such targets were much greater, up to 420,000 in the case of C Lancashire, and an addition of up to 210,000 population at Milton Keynes, perhaps the most ambitious New Town in the UK to date. In 1977 the government cut New Town targets.

While London has progressed much farther in its programme of New Town building, the case is paralleled in C Scotland where pressing problems of urban renewal, job provision and population overspill, especially from C Clydeside, led to the designation of five New Towns with a present population of 50,000. Glenrothes, the fifth Scottish New Town, was developed in a depressed mining area of Fife and has much in common with Peterlee and Washington in NE England. During 1972 Stonehouse was designated a further Scottish New Town but closed in 1976. The dual motives of overspill housing and job provision are present also in the New Town programme for the W Midlands and the NW, where, in both cases, the later developments are of greater size than the earlier. Wales so far has only one New Town at Cwmbran in south-east Wales, specifically for the problem area of the eastern coalfield. Llantrisant (fig. 1.8) was designated in 1972, but discontinued in 1974 (ch. 1.V.2, Wales). The recent development at Newtown (Montgomeryshire) is modest and designed to attract some industrial growth to Mid-Wales, perhaps from the W Midlands, rather than to take large-scale overspill. In N Ireland, Belfast and Londonderry, which alike present enormous problems of slums and unemployment, led to the designation of New Towns at Craigavon, Antrim–Ballymena, and Londonderry itself (fig. 1.9). In 1973, however, the N Ireland New Towns were dissolved and incorporated into the local government structure.

Despite the relative success of GB New Towns in terms of absorbing population **overspill** and attracting new jobs, the scale of development has been inadequate and additional overspill arrangements have been sought by many large cities to relieve pressing problems of housing and population. A variety of arrangements were made in England under the *Town Development Act* (Publ. Gen. Act 1952) and in Scotland under the *Housing and Town Development Act* (Publ. Gen Act 1957). Under these Acts an 'exporting' authority will negotiate with a 'receiving' authority for transfer of population, often bearing the cost of housing. Not all such housing is available for overspill, for firms moving to these towns often need accommodation for their labour force, but the schemes have been of material assistance to large towns in relieving pressure on their housing lists (Scargill 1968).

Of the nine British cities which have made overspill arrangements under these Acts, by far the biggest scheduled developments are for Greater London (a target of 93,049 dwellings), Glasgow (23,261 dwellings), Birmingham (21,011 dwellings) and Liverpool (18,526 dwellings). No less than sixty-seven schemes involving sixty 'receiver' towns exist in England and Wales. Under separate Scottish legislation Glasgow has sixty-six schemes scattered throughout virtually the whole of Scotland, ranging from a mere eight houses at Innerleithen to 4,725 in Renfrew county (fig. 2.22). In January 1976, however, the GLC ended its twenty-five-year-old policy of dispersing population and industry to areas outside the capital. The Council resolved not to enter into any more agreements with 'expanding towns' and to negotiate reductions in existing agreements wherever possible.

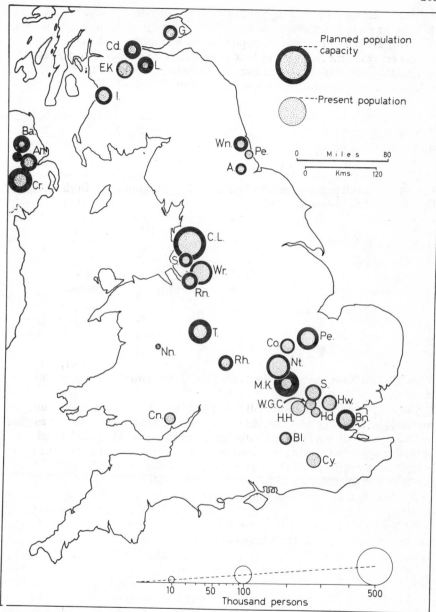

Figure 2.21   New Towns: actual and target populations, UK, 1971

Altogether fifty schemes are presently active, some of which are considerable developments of substantial benefit to the towns involved, since they frequently bring new economic activity. As with New Towns, the success of overspill schemes varies with the local and regional economic situation. Thus, Liverpool's overspill agreement with Ellesmere Port has made rather slow progress because of the con-

TABLE 2.33

New Towns and Overspill Schemes, UK, 1946–74

REGION (and New Towns) (with date of designation)	NEW TOWNS Population (1,000s)			OVERSPILL AGREEMENTS Dwellings (1,000s)				
	Original	Planned	31 Dec 1974	Towns	No. of Schemes	To be Built	Completed 31 Dec 73	Overspill Population 1968–81 (1,000s)
LONDON and SOUTH EAST: TOTAL	356.4	1,366.4	800.6	Greater London	32	93.0	50.9	181
First Wave Stevenage (1946); Crawley, Harlow, Hemel Hempstead (1947); Hatfield, Welwyn Garden City (1948); Basildon, Bracknell (1949)	98.4	668.5	493.2					
Second Wave Milton Keynes (1970); Peterborough (1967); Northampton (1968)	258.0	697.6	307.4					
MIDLANDS and SOUTH WEST: TOTAL	117.7	423.0	196.9	TOTAL	23	27.8	17.1	
First Wave Corby (1950)	15.7	83.0	53.0	Birmingham	15	21.0	10.3	48+
Second Wave Redditch (1964);	102.0	340.0	143.9	Wolverhampton	4	4.5	4.5	–
				Bristol	4	2.3	2.3	–
Telford (1968)				TOTAL	9	31.5	11.9	66
NORTH WEST: TOTAL	413.2	809.0	462.7	Liverpool	4	18.5	6.0	41
Second Wave Skelmersdale (1961);	413.2	809.0	462.7	Manchester	4	8.5	1.4	25
Runcorn (1964); Warrington (1968);				Salford	1	4.5	4.5	–

First Wave							
Aycliffe (1947);		133.0	90.5				
Peterlee (1948)	0.3	75.0	5.15				
Second Wave							
Washington (1964)	20.0	80.0	39.0	Newcastle 2	2.6	10.5	21
WALES: TOTAL	17.5	68.0	49.7				
First Wave							
Cwmbran (1949)	12.0	55.0	43.0				
Second Wave							
Newtown (1967); Llantrisant (1972, discontinued 1974)	5.5	13.0	6.7				
SCOTLAND: TOTAL	54.2	565.0	222.8				
First Wave							
East Kilbride (1947); Glenrothes (1948) Cumbernauld (1955)	6.5	275.0	142.5	Glasgow 66	23.3	9.6	—
Second Wave							
Livingston (1961); Irvine (1966);	40.7	220.0	72.5				
Stonehouse (1972, discontinued 1976)	7.0	70.0	8.0				
TOTAL GB	979.3	3,386.4	1,823.2	TOTAL GB 132	186.1	92.1	
NORTHERN IRELAND	320.0		179.8				
*Second Wave**							
Craigavon (1965);	108.0[1]		61.8				
Antrim–Ballymena (1966);	120.0		48.0	Merged into local govt. units, 1973			
Londonderry (1969)	100.0[2]		70.0				

Data on overspill population targets are incomplete

*Under *Planning Order (N Ireland) 1973* Development Commissions were dissolved and Ulster New Towns incorporated into local government structure

[1] by 2001

[2] by 1995

Sources: Long Term Population Distribution in GB: A Study (1971), tables 6.2 and 6.3; Manners, *Regional Development in Britain* tables 5A, B and C; Census 1971; Blake (1975) *Town and Country Planning, 43, 86–97*

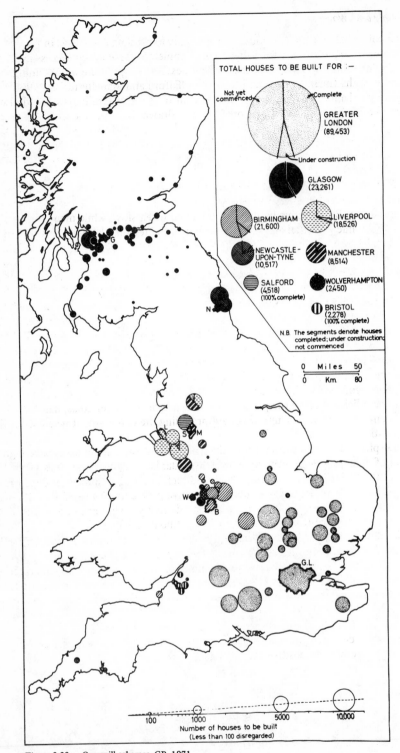

TOTAL HOUSES TO BE BUILT FOR :—

Not yet commenced — Complete

GREATER LONDON (89,453)

Under construction

GLASGOW (23,261)

BIRMINGHAM (21,600)

LIVERPOOL (18,526)

NEWCASTLE-UPON-TYNE (10,517)

MANCHESTER (8,514)

SALFORD (4518) (100% complete)

WOLVERHAMPTON (2450)

BRISTOL (2,278) (100% complete)

N.B. The segments denote houses completed; under construction; not commenced

Miles 0 50
Km. 0 80

Number of houses to be built
(Less than 100 disregarded)
100   1000   5000   10000

Figure 2.22   Overspill schemes, GB, 1971

siderable local demand for housing in a rapidly expanding economy. In the Worsley overspill scheme for Salford CB, completed in 1966, the success in providing homes was not matched with success in overspill families obtaining work locally, so that many commuted to work in Salford and Manchester. In 1966 Worsley had a job ratio of 81 and 58 per cent of its active residents worked elsewhere while 49 per cent of its workforce was drawn from outside the town, a situation not dissimilar from that in the earlier stages of the scheme (Rodgers 1959). Another overspill scheme for Liverpool, at Winsford, Cheshire, has been successful both in terms of rehousing Liverpool's population and gaining jobs for the local authority's industrial estate.

There is little doubt that New Towns and overspill schemes have cumulatively made a considerable impact in relieving housing and social problems in many British cities. But progress has been limited and often slow, while many aspects of their economic potential and its relationship to the regional labour market need careful thought (Manners et al 1972, 33–4). Over-rapid decentralization of housing and jobs from the inner areas of large cities has been, in the view of many, a factor contributing to an economic and social decline which now presents serious problems. An aspect of this, recently highlighted in a review of the *Strategic Plan for the South East* (SE Joint Planning Team, 1976), is that, in the context of the decline in birth-rate in the 1970s, population is not likely to grow from the present level of 17 million in the foreseeable future, in contrast to the 3 million increase still forecast in 1971. With population still moving out of C London at around 100,000 per year and housing policy still geared to overspill, both to New Towns and in private and public sector overspill, population is declining too rapidly in the inner areas. Moreover, continuing movement out of industrial and office jobs, due in part to positive policies limiting the provision of new jobs in the inner areas, has led to problems of financing the resources and providing the employment needed for their population.

Despite the general prosperity of the SE, many of these inner areas have high rates of unemployment, even by national standards, reaching as much as 10 to 12 per cent in such areas as Canning Town and high levels of all indices of deprivation (ch. 2.IV.4). As on Merseyside there are massive problems associated with the need to redevelop dockland and the inner industrial areas yet planning policy still inhibits active encouragement of industry to locate in the inner areas.

It may well be that in this situation much of the capital and planning controls devoted to dispersal of industry, houses and population to New Towns and overspill areas should be diverted to active programmes of renewal of inner city areas along lines that will enable them to retain and even attract both jobs and population. In so doing, one of the most pressing problems in modern Britain – the interlocking population, social and economic problems of the inner city – may receive more urgent attention at a time when public funds are severely limited. The recent government decision to divert funds from the New Towns to inner area development in the cities is a positive step in this direction.

REFERENCES

ARMEN, G (1972) 'A Classification of Cities and City Regions in England and Wales, 1966', *Reg. Stud.*, 6, 149–82

BEST, R H (1972) 'March of the Concrete Jungle: Urban Hazards in Britain', *Geogrl. Mag. Lond.*, *45*, 1, 47–51

BEST, R H and CHAMPION, A G (1970) 'Regional Conversions of Agricultural Land to Urban Use in England and Wales, 1945–67', *Trans. Inst. Br. Geogr.*, *49*, 15–32

BOOTH, C (1886) 'Occupations of the People of the UK', *Jl R. Statist. Soc.*, *XLIX*, 314–435

BRITTON, M (1975) 'Women at Work', *Popul. Trends*, *2*, 22–5

BULLOCK, N, et al (1974) 'Time Budgets and Models of Urban Activity', *Soc. Trends*, *5*, 45–63

CAIRD, J B (1972) 'Population Problems of the Islands of Scotland with Special Reference to the Uists', unpubl. paper presented to a symposium on Scottish Population Problems, *Inst. of Br. Geogr.* (Aberdeen meeting)

C. ADVISORY COUN. EDUCATION (ENGLAND) (1967) *Children and their Primary Schools*, HMSO

CHAMPION, A G (1976) 'Evolving Patterns of Population Distribution in England and Wales, 1951–71', *Trans. Inst. Br. Geogr., New Ser. 1*, 401–20

CLARKE, J I (1960) 'Persons per Room: an Index of Population Density', *Tijdschr. econ. soc. Geogr.*, *51*, 257–60

COATES, B E and RAWSTRON, E M (1971) *Regional Variations in Britain*, London

COMPTON, P A (1976) 'Religious Affiliation and Demographic Variability in N Ireland', *Trans. Inst. Br. Geogr., New Ser. 1*, 433–52

COPPOCK, J T (1972) 'Farming for an Urban Nation' in CHISHOLM, M (ed) *Resources for Britain's Future*, Harmondsworth, 36–49

CSO (1975) 'Social Commentary: Social Class', *Soc. Trends*, *6*, HMSO, 10–32

CULLINGWORTH, J B (1960) *Housing Needs and Planning Policy*, London
                               (1963) *Housing in Transition*, London

DALTON, M and SEAMAN, J A (1973) 'The Distribution of New Commonwealth Immigrants in the London Borough of Ealing, 1961–6', *Trans. Inst. Br. Geogr.*, *58*, 21–39

DANIELS, P W (1969) 'Office Decentralization from London – Policy and Practice', *Reg. Stud.*, *3*, 171–8

DAVIDSON, R N (1976) 'Social Deprivation: an Analysis of Intercensal Change' in KIRBY, A M et al 'Houses and People in the City', *Trans. Inst. Br. Geogr., New Ser. 1*, 108–17

DAVIS, N (1976) 'Britain's Changing Age Structure, 1931–2011', *Popul. Trends*, *3*, 14–17

DAVIS, N and WALKER, C (1975) 'Migrants Entering and Leaving the United Kingdom 1964–73', *Popul. Trends*, *1*, 2–5

DAVISON, R B (1966) *The Black British*, Oxford

DEAKIN, N (1970) *Colour, Citizenship and British Society*, London

DES *Statistics of Education*, annually, HMSO

DEPT. EMPLOYMENT Area Statistics of Unemployment, *Dept. Employment Gaz.*, HMSO
                               (1975) 'Unemployment among Workers from Racial Minority Groups', *Dept. Employment Gaz.*, *9*, 868–71

DoE (1971) *Long Term Population Distribution in GB: a Study*, HMSO

DoE, SCOTT. DEV. DEPT. WELSH OFF. (1964 and 1974) *Housing Statistics GB*, HMSO

DEWDNEY, J C (1968) 'Age Structure Maps of the British Isles', *Trans. Inst. Br. Geogr.*, *43*, 9–18

EDWARDS, K C (1964) 'The New Towns of Britain', *Geogr.*, *49*, 279–85

EVERSLEY, D E C (1971) 'Population Changes and Regional Policies since the War', *Reg. Stud.*, *5*, 221–8

EVERSLEY, D E C and SUKDEO, F (1969) 'The Dependants of the Coloured Commonwealth Population of England and Wales', *Inst. Race Relations, Spec. Ser.*, London

FLYNN, M, FLYNN, P and MELLOR, N (1972) 'Social Malaise Research: a Study in Liverpool', *Soc. Trends*, *3*, 42–52

FRIEDLANDER, D and ROSHIER, R J (1966) 'A Study of Internal Migration in England and Wales', *Popul. Stud.*, *20*, 45–59

GITTUS, E (1964) 'An Experiment in the Definition of Urban Sub-areas', *Trans. Bartlett Soc.*, Univ. Coll. London, *2*, 107–135

GLASS, D V and GREBENIK, E (1954) *The Trend and Pattern of Fertility in Great Britain*, London

GLASS, R (1960) *Newcomers: West Indians in London*, London

GORDON, I R (1970) 'Activity Rates: Regional and Sub-regional Differentials', *Reg. Stud.*, *4*, 411–24

HALL, P (1971) 'Spatial Structure of Metropolitan England and Wales', in CHISHOLM, M and MANNERS, G (eds) *Spatial Policy Problems of the British Economy*, Cambridge, 96–125

HALL, P et al (1973) *The Containment of Urban England*, London

HARRIS, A I (assisted by CLAUSEN, R) (1966) 'Labour Mobility in GB 1953–63', *Soc. Surv. Rep. SS 333*, Minist. Labour and Natn. Serv., HMSO

HOLMANS, A E (1970) 'A Forecast of Effective Demand for Housing in GB in the 1970s', *Soc. Trends*, *1*, 33–42

HOLTERMANN, S (1975) 'Areas of Urban Deprivation in GB', *Soc. Trends*, *6*, 33–47

HOUSE, J W, THOMAS, A D and WILLIS, K G (1968) 'Where did the School-leavers go?', *Pap. on Migration and Mobility, 7*, Dept. Geogr., Univ. Newcastle upon Tyne

HOUSE OF COMMONS (1971) *Population of the United Kingdom, 1st Rep. Select. Comm. Sci. and Technol.*, HMSO

HOWARD, R S (1968) *The Movement of Manufacturing Industry in the UK*, HMSO

HOWE, G M (1970) *National Atlas of Disease Mortality in the UK*, 2nd ed., London

HUMPHRYS, G (1968) 'Housing Quality' in HUNT, A J (ed) 'Population Maps of the British Isles 1961', *Trans. Inst. Br. Geogr.*, *43*, 31–6

INLAND REVENUE *Annual Reports of the Commissioners*, HMSO

JOHNSON, J H, SALT, J and WOOD, P A (1974) *Housing and the Migration of Labour in England and Wales*, Farnborough

JONES, H R (1965) 'Rural Migration in Central Wales', *Trans. Inst. Br. Geogr.*, *37*, 31–45

JONES, P N (1967) 'The Segregation of Immigrant Communities in the City of Birmingham 1961', *Univ. Hull Occ. Pap. in Geogr.*, 7

KELSALL, R K (1967) *The Social Structure of Modern Britain: Population*, London

KIRBY, A M et al (1976) 'Houses and People in the City', *Trans. Inst. Br. Geogr. New Ser. 1*, 2–122

KNOX, P L (1974) 'Spatial Variations in Level of Living in England and Wales in 1961', *Trans. Inst. Br. Geogr.*, *62*, 1–24

KRAUSZ, E (1971) *Ethnic Minorities in Britain*, London

LAW, C M and WARNES, A M (1976) 'The Changing Geography of the Elderly in England and Wales', *Trans. Inst. Br. Geogr., New Ser. 1*, 453–71

LAWTON, R (1963A) 'Recent Trends in Population and Housing in England and Wales', *Sociol. Rev.*, *11*, 303–21

(1963B) 'The Journey to Work in England and Wales: Forty Years of Change', *Tijdschr. econ. soc. Geogr.*, *34*, 61–9

(1967) 'The Journey to Work in Britain: Some Trends and Problems', *Reg. Stud.*, *2*, 27–40

(1970) 'Housing and Social Structure' in PATMORE, J A and HODGKISS, A G (eds) *Merseyside in Maps*, London, 33–4

LAWTON, R and CUNNINGHAM, C M (eds) (1970) *Merseyside: Social and Economic Studies*, London

MACKAY, D I (1969) *Geographical Mobility and the Brain Drain: a Case Study of Aberdeen University Graduates 1860–1960*, London

MANNERS, G et al (1972) *Regional Development in Britain*, London

MARSH, D C (1965) *The Changing Social Structure of England and Wales, 1871–1951*, 2nd ed, London

MINIST. EDUCATION (1963) *Report of the Committee on Higher Education* (Robbins Rep.), Cmnd 2154, HMSO

MINIST. HOUSING and LOCAL GOVT. (1964) *Report of the Committee on Depopulation in Mid-Wales*, HMSO

(1966) *Our Older Homes: A Call for Action*. Report of the Sub-Committee on Standards of Housing Fitness, HMSO

MINIST. LABOUR (1965) *Final Report of the Committee of Inquiry into certain matters concerning the Port Transport Industry* (Devlin Report), Cmnd 2734, HMSO

MOSER, C A (1972) 'Statistics about Immigrants: Objectives, Sources, Methods and Problems', *Soc. Trends*, *3*, 20–30

MOSER, C A and SCOTT, W (1961) *British Towns*, London

MUSGROVE, F (1963) *The Migratory Elite*, London

NEWTON, M P and JEFFREY, J R (1951) 'Internal Migration', *Stud. in Medical and Popul. Subjects*, *5*, HMSO

OPCS (1972) *Census 1971, England and Wales: Advance Analysis*, HMSO

(1975) 'Country of Birth and Colour, 1971–4', *Popul. Trends*, *2*, 2–8

PEARCE, D (1975) 'Births and Family Formation', *Popul. Trends*, *1*, 6–8

PEARCE, D and BRITTON, M (1977) *Popul. Trends*, 7, 9–14

PICKETT, K G (1970) 'Merseyside's Population and Social Structure' in LAWTON, R and CUNNINGHAM, C M (eds) *Merseyside: Social and Economic Studies*, London, 72–107

PREST, A R (ed) (1970) *The UK Economy: A Manual of Applied Economics*, London

PUBL. GEN. ACTS See list p. 516

ROBERTS, B C and SMITH, J H (eds) (1960) *Manpower Policy and Employment Trends*, London

ROBSON, B T (1969) *Urban Analysis*, Cambridge

RODGERS, H B (1959) 'Employment and the Journey to Work in an Overspill Community', *Sociol. Rev.*, 7, 213–29

ROSE, E J B *et al* (1969) *Colour and Citizenship*, Inst. Race Relations, London
R. COMMN. LOCAL GOVT. IN ENGLAND 1966–9 (1969) Vol III, *Research Appendices*, Cmnd 4040, HMSO
SCARGILL, D I (1968) 'The Expanded Town in England and Wales' in BECKINSALE, R P and HOUSTON, J M (eds) *Urbanization and its Problems. Essays presented to E W Gilbert*, Oxford, 119–42
SCOTT. DEV. DEPT. (1968) *The Older Houses in Scotland – A Plan for Action*, Cmnd 3598 Edinburgh HMSO
        (1972) *The Size and Distribution of Scotland's Population: Projections for Planning Purposes*, Edinburgh HMSO
SEC. STATE ECON. AFFAIRS (1969) *The Intermediate Areas*, Cmnd 3998 HMSO
SMAILES, A E (1961) 'The Urbanisation of Britain', *Problems of Appl. Geogr.: Polish Academy Sci. Geogr. Stud.*, Warsaw, *25*
SOULSBY, E M (1972) 'Changing Sex Ratios in the Scottish Border Counties', *Scott. Geogr. Mag.*, *88*, 5–18
SE JOINT PLANN. TEAM (1976) *Strategy for the South East: 1976 Review*, HMSO
STORRIE, M C (1968) 'Household Tenure' in HUNT, A J (ed) 'Population Maps of the British Isles 1961', *Trans. Inst. Br. Geogr.*, *43*, 25–60
TAYLOR, J (1968) 'Hidden Female Labour Reserves', *Reg. Stud.*, *2*, 221–31
THOMPSON, J (1969) 'Differential Fertility among Immigrants to England and Wales and some Implications for Population Projections', *Jl. of Biosocial Sci.*, Suppl. 1
        (1970) 'The Growth of Population to the End of the Century', *S Soc. Trends*, *1*, 21–32
TURNOCK, D (1969) 'Regional Development in the Crofting Counties', *Trans. Inst. Br. Geogr.*, *48*, 189–204
WARNES, A M (1972) 'Estimates of Journey to Work Distances from Census Statistics', *Reg. Stud.*, *6*, 315–26
        (1975) 'Commuting towards City Centres: a Study of Population and Employment Density Gradients in Liverpool and Manchester', *Trans. Inst. Br. Geogr.*, *64*, 77–96
WATSON, W (1964) 'Social Mobility and Social Class in Industrial Communities' in GLUCKMAN, M (ed) *Closed Systems and Open Minds: Limits of Naivety in Social Anthropology*, Edinburgh, London, 129–57
WAUGH, M (1969) 'The Changing Distribution of Professional and Managerial Manpower in England and Wales 1961–6', *Reg. Stud.*, *3*, 157–69
WIBBERLEY, G P (1954) 'Some Aspects of Problem Rural Areas in Britain', *Geogrl. J.*, *120*, 43–61

3

Environment and Land Use

I   LAND USE

I.1   Land Utilization Surveys

The first land utilization survey of Britain, directed by Stamp from 1930–47, was designed as a national inventory which could be used as a basis for land-use planning. To achieve national coverage in an acceptable length of time (the field survey was completed between 1931 and 1934) detail was not possible and the classification had to be simple enough to allow accurate mapping by volunteers, many of them school-children. Seven forms of land use, sub-divided, were mapped at the six-inch scale and subsequently plotted on one-inch maps. Between 1936 and 1948 one-inch sheets and county reports were published as they were completed. A summary of the work done in the survey and an analysis of the findings was published by Stamp (1947). The Geographical Association of N Ireland became interested in the survey in 1936 and by 1939 had completed a survey of N Ireland, using the same classification. Due to different farming methods and the amount of land of a marginal character in N Ireland some modifications were adopted; for example, all grassland whether rotation or permanent was grouped in one class. One-inch sheets were published by the Government of N Ireland between 1945 and 1951. A memoir was written for the Belfast sheet (Hill 1947), but a description and analysis for the whole of N Ireland was not published until 1963 (Symons 1963), which allowed the work of the original survey to be extended by considering trends up to 1953.

Stamp's land utilization survey proved invaluable in post-war planning, but rapid changes in agriculture and urban growth soon rendered it obsolete. A second survey was inaugurated in 1960 (Coleman 1961) and, in it, an attempt to map more detail. Factories were mapped according to industrial group and crops identified. The twelve types of vegetation proved too difficult for volunteer surveyors and this aspect of the mapping was undertaken by the Nature Conservancy to be published on 1:100,000 maps in *A Wildscape Atlas for England and Wales*. This scale will permit mapping communities of at least 2 ha in extent. The land use maps have been produced at the scale of 1:25,000 showing sixty-four categories grouped to give two levels of intensity: first, the old World divisions of the World Land Use Survey, but with transport, open spaces, derelict and unvegetated land added; secondly, sub-divisions were made by variations in tone and the overlay of symbols. For example, grassland was indicated in green with symbols and letters to show ley, infestation by rushes, scrub and bracken, etc. By 1968 all England and part of Wales had been completed in manuscript and by 1975 just over 100 sheets had been printed. Many of these are scattered widely, but there is a useful cover in the London area, S Wales, the Vale of York and NE England. The survey of Scotland is incomplete, but some sheets have been published.

I.2   Land Classification

On the assumption that land utilization in the years 1931–9 was a consequence of
the nature of the land, Stamp produced a classification which was used in many
planning reports (Abercrombie 1945; Watson and Abercrombie 1943; Thompson
1945). Although criticized by soil scientists because of its basis in use rather than
soil (Stamp 1947, 353), the Soil Survey could not meet the urgent need for a complete mapping cover. With rapidly expanding urban population, good agricultural
land needed delimitation if the country were to avoid serious losses of good land.
The Land Utilization Survey divided England, Wales and Scotland into 10 categories:
1–4 were of high agricultural value, 7–10 land of low agricultural value, and types
5–6 of intermediate quality (fig. 3.1). First-class arable land was considered to be
as valuable as first-class grassland, but would be defined by different physical conditions. In N Ireland land classification began in 1954 but was made difficult because
of lack of information apart from the land-use maps and only a few soil survey
maps. While the same principles of classification were applied, a scheme emerged
which was similar to that of the Dept of Agriculture of Scotland. However, the
field-by-field analysis carried out in Scotland could not be attempted in N Ireland
because of the smaller fields and the quantity of small farms which produced a
greater variation in management. The first-class land in N Ireland was that considered
suitable for all crops which the climate permitted and some of this would not have
been graded for first-class land in Scotland. All these classifications attempted an
assessment of short-term potential assuming reasonable drainage, fertilization, etc.
However, it is important to realize that herbicides and fertilizers have since led to
greater intensification of use and many of the lands classified as poor or very poor
have proved productive under forest.

The *Agricultural Land Service Research Group* (1962) attempted to improve on
these classifications by finding a classification which would have relevance at the
scale of the individual farm and yet be consistent in its grading throughout Britain.
Following the principle adopted by earlier surveys (NEDA 1950), physical characteristics of the land were considered most important, largely because of their per-
manence and the difficulty in altering them. The difficulty, clearly recognized by
the survey, is that it is impossible to evaluate the land without considering the uses
to which it might be put. Moreover, it was difficult to be objective in the absence
of a comprehensive soil survey, and data on local climates. The inter-relations between physical factors and land productivity being imperfectly known made the
choice of parameters often purely arbitrary. Five grades were chosen according to
the limitations imposed by physical factors and mapped at the 1:63,360 scale
(fig. 3.2). At the same time productivity, assuming standard management, was
estimated as a check for each area mapped. The great number of holdings within
any one physical group makes this a difficult exercise without considering farm
structure, equipment and location. Grade I is land with very minor or no physical
limitation to agricultural use, which because of climate, soil and slope conditions
occurs most readily on the lowlands of S and SE England. Limitations associated
with the soil will produce grade II, while more serious limitations of soil such as the
poor drainage of the Lias, Oxford and London Clays as well as the glacial drifts,
and slope and climate produce grade III classifications. Grade IV has severe limitations of soil, either wetness or low water-holding capacity, shallowness or stoniness.
The steepness, high rainfall and short growing season of the upland margins also will

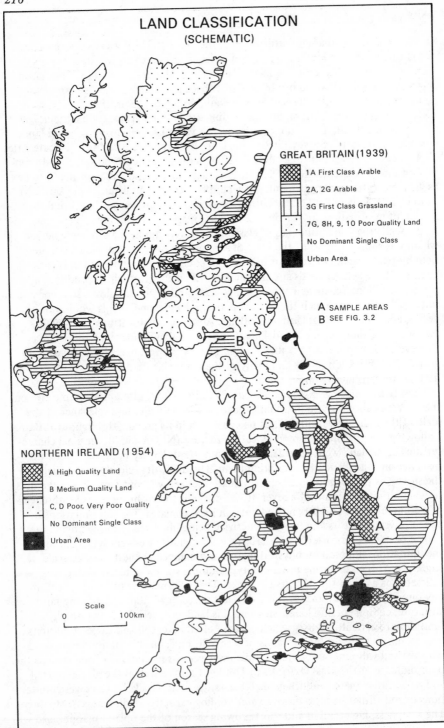

LAND CLASSIFICATION
(SCHEMATIC)

GREAT BRITAIN (1939)

1A First Class Arable

2A, 2G Arable

3G First Class Grassland

7G, 8H, 9, 10 Poor Quality Land

No Dominant Single Class

Urban Area

A SAMPLE AREAS
B SEE FIG. 3.2

NORTHERN IRELAND (1954)

A High Quality Land

B Medium Quality Land

C, D Poor, Very Poor Quality

No Dominant Single Class

Urban Area

Scale

0   100km

Figure 3.1   Schematic land classification, GB 1939, N Ireland 1954

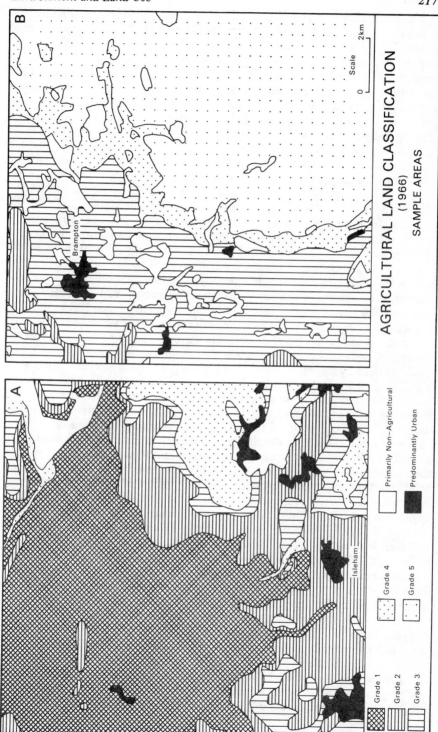

Figure 3.2   Agricultural land classification, sample areas, UK, 1966

put these areas into this grade. About 50 per cent of England and Wales is Grade V which is of little agricultural value because the limitations of soil, slope and climate are very severe. Thus flood plains of rivers, as well as much of the uplands above 300 m, are grouped in this class together with areas seriously affected by pollution either from the atmosphere or due to waste disposal. Insufficient information on the range of output per unit area for each of these five grades and the differences in type of farming within any one grade makes interpretation difficult. The survey gives merely an indication of the range of productivity for the dominant type of farming likely to occur within the physical class. It serves no more than to test the accordance between physical and economic gradings.

At the same time the Soil Survey of England and Wales and of Scotland produced a land-use Capability Classification with the aim of assisting planners and other land users. This is a cooperative effort between the Agricultural Development and Advisory Service, the Soil Survey of England and Wales, the Meteorological Office and the Agricultural Land Service. In 1972 these bodies jointly reviewed progress in land classification and its application within agriculture, advisory work, forestry, planning and multiple land use (MAFF 1974). Land-use capability has been described for the soil units in recent soil survey memoirs (Clayden 1971; Scale 1975) and for two areas one-inch land-use capability maps have been published with the memoirs (Thomasson 1971; Jarvis 1973). The classification (Bibby and Mackney 1969) was modified from that developed by the Soil Conservation Service of the US Department of Agriculture. The major modification is the omission of class 5 which relates to flat wet land. Thus seven classes range from land with minor or no limitations (I) to that with extremely severe limitations that cannot be rectified (V). These are sub-divided by the physical limitations which put them in this class. The system is firmly based on purely physical limitations and economic considerations are completely ignored. It does, however, attempt a more careful evaluation of the physical properties of the soil and draws upon the basic soil maps of this survey. Interpretation of the soil data depends on the more detailed studies of selected soils, which have been termed 'benchmark' soils. These studies cover four years and consider potential yields under normal rotation conditions in commercial farming. One of these studies in the Vale of Belvoir, Nottinghamshire and Leicestershire, was commenced in 1968 and involved six soil series. Soil profile analyses, together with meteorological observations, were related to problems of soil preparation, fertilizer application and crop yields. An attempt was also made to assess susceptibility to disease and physiological limitations at each site. This would have been an impossible task if applied universally, but the aim was to concentrate on key agricultural areas and apply the results to similar soils elsewhere. Information on crop responses exists and is accumulating in results of field experimental studies of crop response to nutrients, effect of crop variety, technique and management on crop yields, together with weed, pest and disease effects, as well as data provided for advisory work and a great body of farming experience. This classification involves both analysis, that is the individual components of the soil system, and synthesis, where the data is interpreted according to the classification. Thus the final classification is an appraisal of soil characteristics, crop yields and management and it is only the quantitative evaluation of the individual components which reduces its subjectivity. The proposal to use computers for future analysis and mapping will not improve the classification but of course will greatly facilitate its application.

II ENVIRONMENTAL FACTORS AND AGRICULTURAL LAND USE

II.1 Introduction

Land classifications have been largely concerned with agricultural land use and indeed most had the original aim of preserving the best agricultural land from urban use. The various classifications differ in their relative emphasis on physical characteristics and land use, but they all share the uncertain relationships which exist between land use and environment. Elements in the environment are measurable, though imperfectly, but the real problems lie in identifying those which limit productivity and the weighting given to each in the complex inter-relationships. This section deals with the measurement of these factors in the UK, the parameters derived from them and their relevance to land use and productivity. The opportunities for improving productivity by controlling the environment are also discussed, as well as the consequences of agricultural land-use polluting the environment.

II.2 Measurement of the Climatic Environment

Precipitation Precipitation comes mainly in the form of rain and an extensive network of about 6,500 rain gauges is in operation (Bleasdale 1965). Since the last century these gauges have been standard, that is 12.7 cm diameter with the rims 0.3 m above the ground. The accuracy of the readings varies from site to site. At Wallingford differences of up to 15 per cent in winter months were found between standard and ground level gauges, though this was reduced to less than 5 per cent in June and July. Greatest errors occur with high winds and small raindrop size, when turbulence diverts most of the rain away from the funnel of a standard gauge (Rodda 1970A). It is obvious that rainfall in the wetter areas of the west and upland areas is underestimated. The Institute of Hydrology has developed a grid to be used with ground-level gauges which largely removes the effect of turbulence. Recording rainfall in isolated mountain regions has proved difficult in the past, but automation is likely to overcome this. Experiments by the North of Scotland Electricity Board, using a rotating collecting funnel and thirty-two bottles, have reduced recording to monthly visits. Also at Glen Kingie a radio rain gauge transmits information powered by solar cell batteries, while at Achnesheen a telephonic gauge allows remote reading in units, tens or hundreds, depending on the frequency of the signals. Less progress has been made in measuring snow which is a significant proportion of precipitation in highland regions in winter. The interpolation of rainfall is made difficult by the fact that the effect of altitude varies with the synoptic situation and seasonally. In Scotland it has been shown that no satisfactory regression is possible for short periods (Smithson 1969). Point sampling by gauges has limited value when spatial variations in rainfall are required, and even if the rainfall for a crop or forest is required, gauging must be at the site. Radar readings related to gauge recordings may provide clearer patterns for these purposes.

Evaporation Evaporation, or the transfer of water from the earth's surface, includes the loss from water surfaces, the soil and that transpired by plants; however, loss from a vegetated surface is termed evapotranspiration. The measurement of evaporation by pans or tanks is made difficult by the effects of advection, so that under dry conditions the evaporation rate is much higher than over a large open water surface where advection effects are limited to the edges. Nevertheless at least twenty stations in the UK have tank data, sixteen of these recording data since 1956. This data is from standard evaporation tanks which are sunk in the ground, but the more recent class 'A' pan which is placed above ground level has been installed at many stations as well. The accuracy with which the water level in a tank will indicate evaporation losses depends to a large extent on the gauging of rainfall. Also in winter many pans and tanks cannot be used to record evaporation. It is usual, therefore, to use the summer half-year, April to September, which accounts for about 80 per cent of the annual total, to estimate the twelve-month total and by assuming a symmetrical curve in evaporation from January to December, redistribute the evaporation between the months to give a 'norm'. Calculations based on this method are published in *British Rainfall*. Using rainfall data and measured runoff it is possible by subtraction to estimate the amount evaporated or transferred from the surface. This has been calculated by the Meteorological Office for the period 1937–62 for fourteen catchment areas in England and Wales. Both tank data and catchment data indicate evaporation in excess of 51 cm in S England and less than 43 cm in the North. However it is impossible to construct an accurate map when each site may not be regionally representative as regards exposure.

Estimates of evapotranspiration using lysimeters have only recently been made in this country. By weighing a tank of soil and vegetation, irrigated lysimeters allow a measure of the loss by evaporation. Since irrigation ensures a constant supply of water to the plants the loss can be considered the potential. The Nature Conservancy has twenty-two stations with lysimeters but with only a short run of recordings (Green 1970A). However, they generally show a ratio of lysimeter potential evapotranspiration (PE) to tank evaporation of between 1 and 1.25.

Calculations by the Penman method (Penman 1948) avoid the error caused by condensation which results in higher tank evaporation readings in winter. However, for summer months which are most critical for land-use problems, Penman estimates of potential evapotranspiration accord fairly closely with the tank and lysimeter data (Penman 1950). The application of the Penman formula depends on the measurement of meteorological elements, temperature, humidity, radiation, wind and sunshine. The importance of potential evapotranspiration in irrigation, as well as in other problems, prompted the Ministry of Agriculture to publish a detailed description of the Penman method and tables of values for the British Isles (Min. of Agriculture 1967). Averages for the period 1950–64 were calculated or estimated for over one hundred stations. Interpolation beyond these stations depended on distance from the coast, where higher radiation increases the potential evaporation rate, and on altitude.

Height increases wind and relative humidity but decreases temperature and sunshine in a complex relationship. Observations have allowed an empirical correction during summer of 16 mm per 100 m in England and Wales and 20 mm per 100 m in Scotland and N Ireland. In winter these corrections become 12 and 6 mm respectively. These corrections have been used to derive values for: the coastal strip 8–16 km wide; for each county at the mean height; and at 365 m where appropriate. As these values are averages it is important to account for year-by-year deviations of the meteorological controls, of which the dominant in summer is radiation and in winter the saturation deficit. Since the weighting of these factors varies from place to place and month to month they have been published for each station. Thus for a summer month, deviation from average potential transpiration is x times the deviation from the average sunshine. The x factor varies between 0.14 and 0.38, the higher values occurring in June. The factors are generally lower in spring and autumn in the North than in the South but in mid-summer higher factors are needed for northern locations. These tables were prepared for use at any location in the British Isles (Min. of Agriculture 1967), but isoline maps would be unsatisfactory at a small scale although they have been constructed from this data by others. Figure 3.3 shows the pattern of potential evapotranspiration based on average county data. It is useful to reflect that potential evapotranspiration is a theoretical concept and refers to a green crop, completely covering the ground with an adequate supply of soil water at its roots. Variation in plant height and colour of the crop will influence the potential evapotranspiration. Also the supply of water to the roots will depend on the soil type and the rooting habit of the crop. Thus the application of these tables to agriculture and, in particular, irrigation control requires careful appraisal of the specific problem and location. Errors which exist in the Penman results, notably in summer, are often compensated by under-estimation of rainfall though it has been suggested that they could still lead to over-irrigation (Edwards 1970). However, since potential evapotranspiration rates change very slowly from place to place and changes from year to year are very small compared with rainfall, most irrigation planning can be based upon the averages for the area as derived from these tables. It is on this assumption that water balances have been calculated for long-term planning of irrigation and these are discussed in the next section.

Temperature   Temperature is given particular importance because of its obvious control over growth and in particular the length of the growing season. Maps of temperature have been based upon readings from the standard exposure of a Stevenson screen. Accumulated temperature is an attempt to integrate the excess or deficiency of these temperatures to a fixed datum. $6°C$ is used as a base because of its significance for the commencement and maintenance of growth. Maps of accumulated temperature above $6°C$ by Gregory (1954) were based upon mean monthly temperatures. More detailed calculations were made by Shellard (1959) for forty-nine stations in the UK, and he also calculated accumulated temperature below $21°C$, $15°C$ and $10°C$ because of its importance in heating engineering. More important, however, is his use of the standard deviation of temperature to allow for departures from the means which is a vital consideration when the mean temperature is at or near the base level. An attempt to produce a larger-scale map of more practical use has been made recently by Birse and Dry (1970) for Scotland. For this map the base was $5.6°C$ but the method was similar to that of Shellard. For each station the accumulated temperature was calculated at intervals of 100 m assuming a lapse rate of $0.6°C$ per 100 m. Thus contour lines could be used in drawing the isopleths, at intervals of 275 day degrees C, differentiating zones according to length of growing season. Using the same procedure accumulated deficiency in temperature below $0°C$ provided a measure of frost severity. This work on temperature was combined with calculations of moisture conditions and exposure on two maps at the scale of 1:625,000 giving the climate of sites to help in field surveys of soil and vegetation. It is of obvious value in agriculture, particularly in Scotland where relief imposes rapid changes in local climates. Local climates or mesoclimates which take into account the special circumstances of relief, exposure, aspect, soil and vegetation cover are clearly of more value in agroclimatology than the macroclimates (Hogg 1968) suggested by the long-term means from standard meteorological exposures. Mesoclimates can refer to areas less than 25 km^2 and can be mapped at 1:25,000

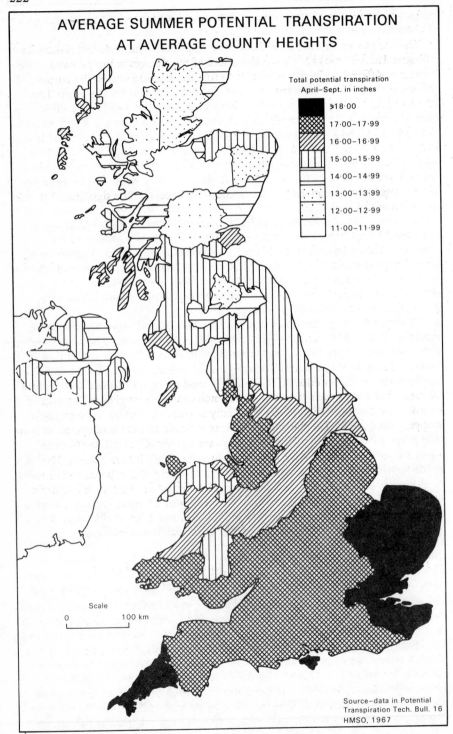

Figure 3.3   Average summer potential transpiration at average county heights, UK, 1967

scale, whereas macroclimates refer to areas over 258 km² and are mapped at 1:250,000 scale.

There is the assumption in all descriptive maps that conditions will remain unchanged. Lamb (1965) has shown the nature of the changes in the past and while there is insufficient evidence to be able to forecast climatic trends, the purpose of the study should determine the choice of the period of records. Elsewhere Lamb has cast doubts on the validity of the thirty-year norm for agroclimatic work. It is also difficult to relate screen temperatures to the conditions under which plants are growing. Soil temperatures have been recorded by agrometeorological stations since the 1920s. The nature of the surface, its colour and vegetation cover is therefore of importance. Most of the readings for depths less than 30 cm are taken only once per day and are therefore of limited value. Gloyne (1971) has attempted to map the 8°C average annual mean daily earth temperature because of its significance in the processes of soil formation.

Records of hours of bright sunshine and net radiation are available for many stations and both have been used in estimating potential evaporation by the Penman method. The relevance of these to agriculture depends very much on the aspect, exposure and slope of the particular site. The theoretical energy which would result from optimal insolation (Knoch 1963) together with the study of the effects on air temperature or soil temperature (Taylor 1964) is of importance particularly in relation to earliness of crops.

Wind speed is measured at the standard height of 10 m in open level country. Friction affects wind speed as high as 305 m and land-forms can obstruct or create their own circulations. Gloyne has suggested that wind will follow the surface if windward slopes are less than 40° and leeward slopes less than 11° which has obvious implications for shelter effects. The effect of wind speed is to reduce temperature extremes but wind speeds in excess of 40 kmph can dessicate plants. The map of exposure by Birse and Dry (1970) is the only attempt to consider topography in mapping wind speed. The thirty-four stations in Scotland were inadequate for mapping purposes and were supplemented by an assessment of the visible effect of exposure on broad-leaved trees and on common heather, *Calluna vulgaris*. The map shows five categories of exposure ranging from sheltered, 2.6 m per sec wind speed, to extremely exposed, 8.0 m per sec. The authors point out that the limits define exposure satisfactorily so long as other factors such as salt spray are not also having an effect on plant life. This shows one of the major problems of equating a single parameter with an effect when relationships are not fully understood.

II.3 Influence of Climate on Agricultural Land Use and Productivity

As in other developed countries assessment of land potential is important for decisions on the conflicting claims on the land, and displacement of agricultural enterprises by urban growth has called for reappraisal of other areas to which the farmers could move with hopes of success. Hogg (1966) quotes a survey of potential sites for horticulture in England which was prompted by the needs of displaced growers in the Lea Valley. To some extent the measurement of the climate described above has been prompted by a practical need so that the parameters have relevance to land-use problems. However, it is the derived values such as day degrees or evapotranspiration which are used. The relationships between climate and the crops which can be grown and their yields are complex. Even if these relationships are understood it is often impossible to apply these results beyond the limits of the experimental plots because of lack of data. In general agricultural surveys the climate can usually be expressed in macroclimatic terms and uncertainties only exist in marginal areas. Fruit growing has been a rewarding field of study, for growth of buds, leaf growth, fruit set and maturity can be correlated with microclimate. Attempts have been made at Long Ashton, Bristol, to relate fruit-tree microclimates to screen or standard exposures. Practical applications follow from detailed experimental work only if the knowledge can be applied to broader areas. The present network of stations is not nearly close enough and the validity of the principles used to apply the data from them needs verification. The Met. Office provides a frost-warning service and irrigation advice to farmers. This is mainly for high-value horticultural enterprises which can afford the cost of protection. The initial improvement in productivity due to irrigation or frost protection is undoubtedly large enough to pay for the exercise. It is, however, difficult to justify further improvements in relation to the cash returns. The methods used in frost prediction have had some value in planning the expansion of horticulture, particularly soft fruit-growing. Microclimatic readings over a short period are related to screen temperatures. The long-term screen records are used to predict the occurrence of the frost detected in the micro-study. Requests for irrigation advice based upon generalized water balance calculations are now largely met by *The Atlas of Long-term Irrigation Needs for England and Wales* (Hogg 1967). Practical agrometeorologists are forced to adopt subjective methods because of the lack of data and knowledge. However, the high-value horticulture is invariably in more favoured areas and the hazards can be estimated with some degree of certainty. A more recent area of study of relevance to land use has been the study of workdays, the climatic requirements depending very much on the type of work, whether it be sowing, weeding, harvesting, etc. So far most of this work has been done in grass farming where the distinction between dry days, when work is possible, and wet days, when it is not, is clear cut.

Farming activities are not equally sensitive to environmental conditions and in many cases changes in management can bring about more significant improvements. Also climate has more influence on crops than on livestock. There is little point in investigating the actual limits of growth for a particular crop, because economically it becomes impracticable long before this is reached as this depends on fluctuating prices as the changing margins of moorland in our uplands indicate. Thus present land use cannot help in identifying the degree of control imposed by environmental factors.

Water With the exception of their woody parts actively growing plants have 75—90 per cent water. Together with the fact that vast amounts of water must pass through the plant and evaporate from the leaf surface, this accounts for the importance of water in growth. Alfalfa requires over 431 kg of water to produce 0.45 kg dry matter. Drought affects agriculture in the UK to some extent and the degree depends very much on location. A broad view can be obtained from a simple subtraction of average potential transpiration from average rainfall, to give mean potential soil moisture deficit. This relates to crop distribution, the ratio of grass to crops and grass decreases at a constant rate from a mean potential soil moisture deficit of −150 mm to +100 mm; above this the proportion of grassland decreases more rapidly (Hogg 1965A). However, this is of limited value to agricultural planning as excess rainfall in winter could cancel out high deficits during the crop-growing season. There is a limit to the amount of water which can be held in storage in the soil and a great deal of the winter excess runs off the land in streams and is lost to plants. Detailed water balances can be made which will take these factors into account. Day-to-day balances will be most accurate though, for most purposes, five or ten-day or monthly periods will suffice. The water balance as developed by Thornthwaite (Thornthwaite and Mather 1955) must include some basic assumptions. Apart from the problem of estimating potential evapotranspiration which has been outlined above, the accuracy of the balance depends mainly on the limits of our knowledge of soil–plant–water relationships and inevitably any agroclimatic model using water balance data must be simplified for practical application. As a general principle crop water use is related to atmospheric conditions. A factor is frequently used to reduce Penman E_0 to potential evapotranspiration, in the UK about 0.6 in winter and 0.8 in summer months. For annual crops this factor should increase from a small fraction when the plant emerges, to the maximum when leaf area achieves full ground cover. However, wide spacing can reduce this maximum level. Actual evapotranspiration depends on the presence of water in this root zone. When the soil is fully charged with water it is said to be at field capacity. As the soil begins to dry the tension rises until it reaches permanent wilting point (16 atmospheres) when roots can no longer extract water. The water held between these extremes is termed available soil water (AW). Soil textures can alter the limits; field capacity can range from 4 cm per m for sand to 17–21 cm per m for clay loam. Permanent wilting point is more difficult to define and is probably a function of plant type as well as soil. Clarke (1971) quotes figures of available water in cm per m according to texture: sand and loamy sands 2–4, sandy loams 8, fine sandy loams 12.5–14.5, loams 16.6, clay loams 25 and clay 29. However rooting depth is probably of more importance than texture. The depth of root penetration depends on the plant, but generally it will be shallow when the water-table is high. Since roots do not extend into unaerated soil the plant is depending entirely on water from precipitation. If the water-table is kept constant by controlling drainage a significant part of the water used by plants can come from the ground-water; however for most farmland in the UK the water-table rises in wet periods causing roots to die back, and falls in dry weather permitting root extension.

Thornthwaite assumed that potential evapotranspiration (PE) only occurs at field capacity and the rate of actual evapotranspiration becomes a progressively small fraction of PE as the soil dries. Another school suggests that water is equally available until permanent wilting point is reached. Denmead and Shaw (1962) have shown that the critical level of soil water above which evapotranspiration occurs at this potential rate depends on atmospheric conditions. For example if the potential evapotranspiration is low (E_0 = 1 mm/d) the critical value is near permanent wilting point, so that plants will transpire at the potential rate until all other available water is removed. On the other hand, under high potential evaporation conditions (E_0 = 7 mm/d) the rate of evapotranspiration will decrease as soon as soil water falls below field capacity. Penman (1968) has suggested that water is equally available if we consider the root range only. Plants however do extract beyond this and movement of water to the root system would slow down transpiration rates and if potential evapotranspiration is high the actual rate could be a small fraction of this.

The concepts of field capacity and permanent wilting point are an over-simplification of the complex soil hydrological horizons. In the process of drying, water is removed from the surface horizons first and progressively each horizon follows a strict succession of phases ranging from total saturation to below permanent wilting point of physical dessication (Rode 1968). The process of soil-wetting is usually from above and the water content of each horizon is suddenly increased to the maximum.

Water balances For *The Atlas of Long-term Irrigation Needs for England and Wales* (Hogg 1967B) water balances were calculated for a twenty-year sample, 1930–49, for seventy-nine stations in England and Wales. These balances consider only growth periods between April and September and in calculations assume soil water to be at field capacity at the beginning of each period. Certainly in most areas of the UK the soil has its maximum water content at the end of the winter, but for periods beginning in June, July or August it is unlikely that conditions of field capacity will always occur. A half-monthly balance was considered frequent enough to show the effect of dry spells, though it was probably chosen to correspond with the maximum frequency with which irrigation can be satisfactorily applied. However in SE England heavy rain from summer thunderstorms can balance the total water needs of the fifteen-day period, and in many cases, obscure serious deficits. Since these balances include the application of irrigation water, when required, transpiration was considered to continue at the potential rate. Balances were calculated allowing maximum soil moisture deficit of 25 mm, 50 mm, 76 mm and 127 mm at any time. Since water from rainfall or irrigation enters the soil profile from the surface and percolates downwards, each of these calculations refers to soil water deficits within a surface layer whose available water capacity equals this. Thus the total need with a planned 127 mm deficit would apply to deep-rooting plants; in sandy loams this could be 1.5 m and in clay loams 0.6 m. Shallow-rooting plants where the planned deficit must be smaller, say 25 mm, require more frequent irrigation. Crops will undoubtedly respond to a situation where soil moisture deficits are kept at a minimum. However, it has been shown (Winter, Salter and Cox 1970) that the practice of restoring the soil to field capacity by irrigation whenever it reaches a certain deficit may not be economically sound. Because of the costs of irrigation, higher profits per acre can be obtained only by limited irrigation. Watering to achieve only 90 per cent maximum yield would appear to be the most efficient programme for grain crops, but for crops whose vegetative growth is harvested, irrigation for maximum yield would be the most efficient use of water (Fisher and Hagan 1965).

Grass may require irrigation any time between April and September, However, other crops have much shorter growth periods and irrigation may be required only for a short period of the growth cycle. Thus combinations of successive periods 2, 3, 4, 5 and 6 months have been calculated. For the 2.5 cm soil moisture deficit plan (SMD) all lowland England would require irrigation 17 years in 20, but a 12.7 cm SMD plan would require irrigation 8 years in 20 in the NE and over 14 in 20 in the SE. Using the 2.5 cm SMD plan the driest year in 20 would require 20 cm in the NE and 33 cm in the SE. The atlas is a good example of the application of a simplified water balance calculation to a practical problem. More detailed balances are possible for specific sites where more assumptions can be made appropriate to the crop and soil. For example, a crop of grass can be assumed to transpire at this potential rate as long as water is available in the top layers of soil, the first 5 cm AW. The second 5 cm AW will be used at one-half of the potential and the final 2.5 cm AW will be used at one-quarter of the potential. Water balances calculated in this way for growing seasons have agreed with actual field conditions (Min. Agriculture 1967, 17).

This method has the advantage that soil moisture conditions are estimated for each horizon in the soil rather than integrated in a single soil moisture deficit for the whole profile.

It has been shown that grass growth is sensitive to the first 7.5 cm AW and when this is removed growth practically ceases even though deeper roots may allow continued transpiration (Stiles and Garwood 1964). Nutrition is obviously a complicating factor and as this is concentrated within surface layers of soil, the presence of available water in these horizons is vital for growth. This is further supported by high correlations between hay yields and the actual transpiration during periods when deficits were less than 50 mm (Hurst 1964). Hurst calculated daily water balances for fifty stations in East Anglia in 1961 and counted the grass-growing days, that is days when the moisture deficit was 50 mm or less. Using empirical relationships with monthly water balances he mapped grass-growing days in England and Wales, and showed how these rough estimates correlated with milk production.

Irrigation and growth Most studies of the effects of water on growth have been concerned with the increased production brought about by irrigation. Fisher and Hagan (1965) review research on the effects of water stress on a variety of crops and distinguish them according to their economic yield: vegetative, e.g. in the case of grass; a carbohydrate storage organ, e.g. in sugar beet or potatoes; or a reproductive organ, e.g. grain crops and fruit. Correlations between actual evapotranspiration and yields have been shown for crops of lucerne (Davies and Tyler 1964) in Wales. However, such studies can only be of practical value if they can be used to forecast harvests, or on the basis of accurate seasonal forecasts of water stress permit an economic assessment of the yield improvement in relation to expenditure on irrigation. Outside the UK investments in weather protection have been assessed using simplified models of operating costs. Certainly where water for irrigation is limited its efficiency becomes important.

In the drier areas of SE England the effects of irrigation are likely to be most important. Vegetative production, as in the case of grass, is particularly sensitive to water supply. But Goode (1970) has shown that the cumulative effect of irrigation on fruit production can also be significant. This is because fruit production depends very much on plant vigour and, in the case of soft fruit, new growth becomes fruit-bearing in the following season. Over a period of 5 years irrigated bushes had 100 per cent more fruit than unwatered bushes. The cumulative effect of irrigation over ten years produced a 50 per cent increase in apple yields. Undoubtedly this is due to the prevention of a growth check when the soil dries out, but as well as this the absence of large soil water deficits reduces the need for an extensive root system, which would deplete the assimilates available for shoot growth and fruit production.

The growing season The studies of grass growth and fruit production in relation to water availability, described above, refer to the summer half-year, April to September, when temperature does not prevent growth. However, the influence of temperature and radiation on the beginning of the growing season and its length is obvious and their variation within the UK considerable. For early production the months January to April are most important. The South West of England has more than 139 day degrees C above 6°C in January and February (fig. 3.4). Radiation and sunshine in these months are noticeably higher in south coastal areas, while positive temperature anomaly associated with the Atlantic and the SW winds favours the western

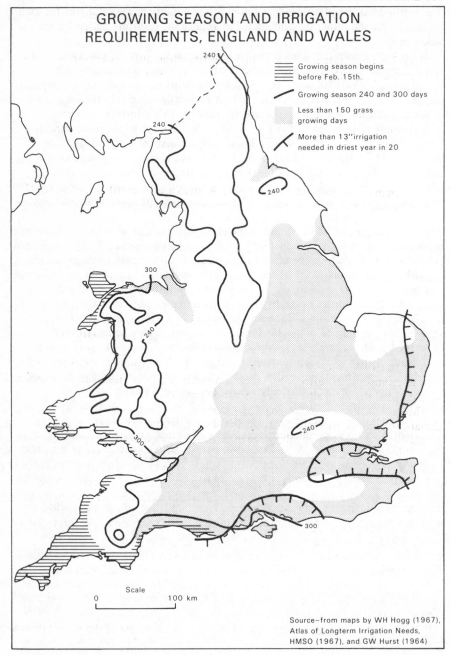

Figure 3.4   Growing season and irrigation requirements, England and Wales, 1964, 1967

coasts. In particular, maximum temperatures are raised in coastal areas of the SW, which is important for early growth. The beginning of the growing season has been taken as the average date on which mean screen temperature rises above 6°C (Hogg 1967A). Soil temperatures which will allow germination differ as between crops. Hogg assumed growth will commence when the 10 cm soil temperature at 0900 GMT remains above 6°C. However, soil type is a major factor controlling this parameter as has been demonstrated by the difference in 'earliness' between sand and peat areas in SW Lancashire (Taylor 1964).

The effects of **altitude** on the growing season are most obvious in the highland areas of the West and North. In Scotland there is an average of 1,375 day degrees C on the lowlands of the Moray Firth, Fife and Angus while the Highlands above 549 m have less than 825 day degrees C. However, light is as important as temperature in the growth of hill pastures (Grant 1969). Western areas benefit from the maritime influences, but in day degrees the differences between east and west coasts are not significant and inland from the east coast, higher summer temperatures tend to raise the accumulated temperature figure. In N Ireland equivalent day degree isotherms are believed to occur at generally higher elevations than in GB, although this is based on a very limited number of observations (Symons 1963, 86). The advantages of a westerly position are most apparent in the monthly accumulated temperatures of southern England where the effect extends from January to March; in March, Plymouth has 75 day degrees C above 6°C while Dungeness has only 46. The growing season decreases by ten days for every 79 m of altitude in the north of England, although such estimates can only be a general guide. Calculations of accumulated temperature at Chopwell Wood (250 m) in Durham suggest a growing season fifteen days shorter than at Tynemouth (30 m, ASL). Higher altitudes can have the compensating effect of increased moisture but grass yields can be diminished by 2 per cent per 30 m altitude, (Hunter and Grant 1971).

The date of the start of the growing season can be greatly influenced by microclimatic influences, particularly aspect and shelter. Within any region of the UK favoured areas may have an advantage in local markets with early crops of potatoes and vegetables. This is true of the coasts of Co Down in N Ireland and in Wigtown in SW Scotland. However, mapping of the average date of the start of the growing season (fig. 3.4) shows the considerable advantage enjoyed by the early growing areas of Anglesey, SW Wales, Cornwall, Devon, S Hampshire and the Isle of Wight. Even here, however, southerly aspect can increase radiation in the short days of January by as much as 50 per cent on a 10° slope, though the effect is reduced to only 15 per cent in April (Hogg 1967A, 90).

Frost is a hazard to early growing and is an important factor in location. Frost surveys by the Met. Office in horticultural areas, mainly in the SW, have been successful in delimiting areas of risk and expressing the probability of satisfactory crops or the increased production made possible by protecting from frost by sprinkling. Hogg (1970) describes how the feasibility of installing a frost prevention scheme on a Somerset farm can be calculated from an estimate of the probable duration of night frosts in April. In areas of light soils, irrigation equipment is often already installed to overcome summer deficits and can be used for frost protection in spring as well. Soil is usually kept moist when there is a frost risk, estimated by a grass minimum temperature below −2.2°C. Damage to a crop of early potatoes by a single night's frost, grass minimum of −3.9°C, at the end of May was averted by sprinkling. The unretarded crop was able to fetch high prices and the protection

probably saved the farmer about £3,000 (Hogg 1967A, 117). With reliable frost
warning it is possible to plant earlier without undue risk of failure. Frost is very
much a local problem for cold air drainage at night causes greater frequency of frost
in hollows and valley floors. Differences of 2.7–3.3°C in daily minimum temperatures have been reported within a few hundred acres in fruit-growing areas of S
England. On the assumption that downflow will cease on slight slopes, i.e. less than
2°, areas of frost liability in Somerset have been estimated from 1:25,000 topographical maps (Hogg 1965A). Together with air photographs, taken where shallow
radiation fogs occur, this approach could augment the few scattered meteorological
stations to provide maps of local climate with more immediate application than the
macroclimatic maps already discussed.

Exposure Work on the effects of shelter have suggested that yields of crops are
significantly improved if protected even from relatively light winds. Increase of 27
per cent in the yield of lettuces due to lath shelter have been reported (Hogg 1965A).
Sheltered valley sites can have wind speeds 20 per cent below more exposed neighbouring sites. This has an important effect on crop-growing since the power to
damage is proportional to the cube of the velocity. The frictional effect of trees,
hedgerows or artificial windbreaks are more important in that they can be modified.
Artificial windbreaks have the advantage of being immediately effective, whereas
trees are slow to establish themselves and compete with the crops for moisture and
nutrition. The shelter given by a windbreak depends on the width/height ratio as
well as the degree of permeability. If too wide, the wind on crossing the barrier
descends rapidly and the eddy zone to the lee is greatly reduced. If the break has an
edge inclined to the windward the wind is deflected upwards and little penetrates.
However for agriculture it is important to prevent stagnation of air which would
increase frost risk and for this reason permeability is favoured. Systems of narrow
parallel windbreaks can shelter wide areas if the distance between each belt is
twenty-six times the height of the windbreak (Caborn 1957). Studies by Hogg suggest that wind and evaporation are more affected by shelter in autumn and winter,
while temperature shows its greatest effects in summer. In this connection it is
worth mentioning that with increase in field size, hedgerows have been removed and
the effect is to increase exposure. The upslope valley winds induced by sun and
aspect are not so important in this climate, though near industrial areas they have
the damaging effect of carrying pollutants to agricultural areas.

Disease Since disease and pests have strong associations with weather and climate
they have a place in the complex crop-weather interaction. Penman (1962) has thus
described them as second-order effects. If the onset of the disease can be anticipated,
timely action, e.g. spraying against potato blight, can be done effectively. When the
potato plant is receptive to blight, i.e. when carbohydrate reserves are high, it will
occur only with suitable local weather conditions. Since the spores will only grow
on wet surfaces, attempts have been made to anticipate condensation on leaves. This
can be done by moisture meters or estimated from minimum temperature and
relative humidity readings (Grainger 1967). Work on black stem rust in wheat (Hogg
1967C) illustrates how the origin of the spores can be traced to countries in Europe.
A close connection was found between deposition of spores in SW England and
upper air trajectories from the south or south-east during spring and early summer.
However, epidemics only developed if humidities were high in June and July, and

temperatures high in July and August. Not enough is yet known about most diseases, their vectors and their relationships with the weather to be able to provide effective early warning systems.

The flexibility of land use Green (1970B) has discussed this question in relation to the water balance and suggests that the potential land use is rarely achieved because of social and economic considerations. Areas of excess water are less flexible than the deficient areas which can respond to irrigation under conditions of high radiation. Varieties of farm crops and farming systems are used because of their adaptability to the fluctuating seasonal conditions. Reliable long-term forecasts could allow greater flexibility, though the necessary information on the relationships between weather and the performance of different varieties will take some years to accumulate.

II.4 The Amelioration of Climate by Man

Some of the ways in which climate can be improved locally to benefit crop production have been touched upon in the preceding section. Apart from changing the plants' immediate environment by irrigation or shelter, completely artificial climates are created by glasshouses. It has already been suggested that improvements in production are possible if the prevailing conditions can be accurately anticipated, but it is also important to recognize that great improvement is possible by controlling growth to suit sub-optimal conditions.

Drought Generalized irrigation needs have been discussed in the previous section. Of the total acreage quoted by Prickett (1970) 50 per cent was in E and SE England (table 3.1). Heavy concentration of irrigation occurred in the early horticultural

TABLE 3.1

Area of Crops Irrigated during Droughts, England and Wales, 1967 (in ha)

Grass	33,321
Second early and main crop potatoes	17,596
First early potatoes	8,506
Vegetables	16,953
Sugar beet	12,753
Orchard fruit	3,981
Cereals	2,818
Small fruit	2,602
Hops	1,205
Other crops	4,509
Total	104,246

Source: C N Prickett (1970)

areas of SW England and Pembrokeshire, but even in the north considerable acreages had irrigation; for example, over 3,238 ha in Yorkshire and 400 ha in Northumberland. Irrigation is characteristically on land with good natural or artificial drainage, but there would be problems if drainage were poor or the soil unstable. Suitable water, for example not saline, is not equally available for irrigation. The cost of water and the need to provide storage to take advantage of low winter charges is reducing the practice of irrigation for low-value crops (O'Riordan 1970). Horticulture, particularly small fruit, is becoming a more important water user. Crops under glass are very heavy users of water, the irrigation needs of a glasshouse being equivalent to those of a herd of seventy to a hundred dairy cattle. Crops such as grass and potatoes require sufficient irrigation to maintain water at near field capacity, which ought not to be practised in successive years for it prevents the beneficial effects of cracking during drying out of heavy soils.

Emulsions sprayed on the soil surface can reduce evapotranspiration for up to two months. Soil water storage is improved if the surface soil is rough, encouraging the retention of water. Yields have been increased by arresting excessive drainage in sandy soils using asphalt barriers below the root zone. These devices, developed largely for arid climates, may have applications in high value crops and in soils hitherto unproductive.

Soil wetness For most of the UK wetness is more of a problem than drought. The large-scale drainage schemes in the Fenlands date back to the seventeenth century and illustrate the way in which the water-table in level alluvial areas can be controlled by engineering. They provide over 324,000 ha of the richest farmland in GB. Elsewhere drainage can be considered a major soil factor, since moderate drainage can increase yields by as much as 20 per cent (Coppock 1971, 45). It has been suggested that the failure of modern varieties of crops to reach full potential yield is due to defects in soil structure and drainage (Agricultural Advisory Unit 1970). Cereals are particularly susceptible to soil conditions which affect root development. Waterlogging excludes air and the anaerobic conditions cause roots to die back, leaving the crop more susceptible to drought later, but it has the effect also of limiting operations with machinery. If a soil is at field capacity or wetter, it usually has insufficient strength to hold machinery or livestock and is too plastic for ploughing or cultivation. Soil texture and structure is important but the smearing effect of ploughing wheels and treading can reduce porosity and cause surface ponding. The early work of Thornthwaite on the water balance was partly concerned with the ability of soil to bear weight. The date of the return to field capacity has been calculated from meteorological records (AAU 1970) for sites throughout England and Wales. These demonstrate the early return to field capacity in the western areas, but also show the advantage of light freely-drained soils and the considerable variation between wet and dry years at all sites. However, estimates based upon meteorological data can only be approximate, for no universal relationship exists between soil water tension and estimated soil water deficits. It is suggested that a more useful correlation may be found between interpolated soil shear strength and accumulated moisture deficit (Mil. Eng. Experim. Estab. 1969).

Extensive areas of farmland were underdrained prior to 1939, though many systems no longer function effectively and need replacement or improvement. Collapse or silting of old drains is common but more intensive use of this land can lead to puddling of surface soil which prevents water percolating to the underdrains. Removal of the old ditches associated with the small fields of Wales to create the large units of arable farming frequently necessitates new systems of drainage, though cultivation is in any case less flexible than grass in its soil water requirements. In the wetter areas of the west higher stocking rates increase the need for more drainage or subsoiling. Since 1966 there has been an annual increase of 10 per cent expenditure on drainage in the SW. Without improved drainage overstocking can lead to poaching of pastures and this is a feature of the intensive dairying area of Cheshire. Wetter than normal summers extend the dangers of poaching throughout the season, particularly in the low evaporation areas of the Pennine foothills. For cultivation in the wetter areas, drainage is usually the only way of ensuring enough work days. Even in the drier areas of the east, heavy soils are manageable only within a very narrow moisture range and only regular subsoiling and mole drainage can keep them in production. Among these difficult soils are the keuper marls, coal measure soils and boulder clays of the E Midlands, Oxford clay, London clay and the clays of the low Weald. However, drainage in many of these areas is not practicable because of their flatness and low elevations. Improvements in arterial drainage can make the drainage of low-lying areas feasible. For example, in N Ireland, since the 1947 Drainage Act, 1,449 km of main water courses have been altered in drainage schemes giving flood relief to 24,000 ha and, ultimately, affecting drainage of about one-quarter of the province. The danger of continual ploughing is to create sub-surface pans which seriously restrict the depth of rooting, and yields are greatly reduced. Intensive arable can cause serious structural changes. Continual cultivation of early potatoes in Pembrokeshire has led to clod formation in the soil which may limit future use.

Drainage of any kind brings improvements and the problem is usually the degree of water control required, which is often decided on the lines of cost. Since 1939 grants have increased areas under drainage by 80,000 ha in Yorkshire and Lancashire, 40,000 ha in the North, 57,000 ha in the W Midlands and 36,000 ha in Wales. However, it has been estimated that over 2.8 million ha or 26 per cent of the total farmland could be improved still further (AAU 1970, 33). Because of soil and relief and its intensive land use, eastern England has a very large area, 650,000 ha, which could be usefully drained and this is being improved at the rate of about 19,000 ha per annum.

Temperature and radiation Modifications of temperature are possible by using windbreaks or spraying to prevent frost, but major changes are possible by using glass and artificial heating. Hogg (1966) quotes heating periods for some horticultural crops which range from approximately four months for chrysanthemums to ten months for cucumbers. Heating requirements in terms of fuel have been estimated using accumulated temperatures below 15°C (Shellard 1959) and Hogg has calculated this for the heating periods of each crop (table 3.2). Assuming 10 degree days require 1 tonne of coal per 4,046 m^2 of glass he has estimated that 40–45 tons more

TABLE 3.2

Heating Requirements for Cultivated Plants, Selected UK Stations, 1966

| Crop | Heating period | Average number of day degrees below 15°C | | |
		Penzance	Weymouth	Cheltenham
Tomatoes	4 Nov–28 May	2,470	2,870	3,290
Cucumbers	4 Oct–4 July	2,780	3,180	3,700
Lettuce	11 Nov–27 Apr	2,190	2,585	2,975
Carnations	4 Nov–27 Apr	2,260	2,665	3,080
Chrysanthemums	27 Nov–28 Mar	1,710	2,015	2,325

Source: W H Hogg (1966)

coal is needed at Cheltenham for one acre of glasshouse tomatoes than at Weymouth, and there is a similar difference between Weymouth and Penzance.

II.5   Harmful Accidental Effects of Agricultural Activity

Farming activity can lead to damaging effects and this is more likely if there is a change in the type of farming or its intensity. The more obvious are effects on soil water conditions but equally serious are the structural changes which can reduce productivity and in many cases lead to soil erosion. Exposed flat lowlands of E England suffer from soil erosion by wind on the sandy soils; those with more than 35 per cent organic matter, such as Fenland soils, are particularly susceptible. High wind speed, in excess of 80 kmph is the main cause, and it is also related to soil moisture content. The methods of preparing seed beds for vegetables and the application of herbicides have recently aggravated the situation (Pollard and Miller 1968). Large-scale sugar beet growing which began in the 1930s is considered an important factor in the peat fens. The removal of hedges is thought to have contributed to the severe blowing of soil in the Vale of York in 1967 (Douglas 1970) but the decrease of hedgerows in areas of stable soils is not having any serious effect. Studies of sediment yields from catchments have not provided any conclusive evidence that there has been any general change in the rate of soil erosion and suggest that it is only serious locally. For control it is necessary to reduce windspeed, stabilize the soil and trap blowing soil. Windbreaks have a limited effect, especially if strong winds come from several directions. Strip-cropping and inter-row cropping can also reduce wind velocity and soil moisture can be retained better by reducing cultivations, creating rough soil surfaces or mulching. Only high-value cash crops warrant such expensive control measures.

The practice of growing grass leys and green manuring are declining in farming and the soil structure deteriorates due to reduced organic content. Inorganic fertilizers are preferred as the balance of nutrients can be easily controlled. There has been an increase of about 150 per cent in nitrogen application since 1957. However, organic fertilizers are important in the livestock areas of the UK. In 1969 farmyard manure was used on 23 per cent of the arable land of N England and Wales; the percentage was less elsewhere, but 36 per cent of the permanent pasture of Yorkshire and Lancashire was so treated. Inorganic fertilizers do confer benefits in that they encourage better root growth and thus improve soil structure and they give better vegetative growth which can be ploughed into the soil. Nitrogenous fertilizers have the effect of reducing the calcium in soil and thus increase its acidity. Damage to organisms by pesticides is less in soils with a high organic content. The most serious are the organochlorides which harm beneficial insects and persist in food chains, to appear ultimately in milk and meat (R. Comm. Environ. Pollution 1971). Use of the more persistent organochloride insecticides by agriculture in England and Wales fell from 460 tons in 1963 to 250 tons in 1972 (R. Comm. Environ. Pollution 1974). It has been suggested that these ecological effects are much less than those in lakes and seas. In Scottish fresh-water lochs agricultural runoff contributed more nitrates than phosphates and as much as 43 per cent of the nitrogen added as fertilizer is washed from the soil. The absence of any extensive algal blooms may be due to the low temperatures (Stewart, Tuckwell and May 1975). In the UK the contribution of agricultural chemicals to pollution of streams and rivers is very small. Mercury from fungicides used in bulb farming in the Fens is deposited in sediments within a few hundred yards of its entry to the streams so that the reason for the recent ten and twenty-fold increase in mercury levels in the rivers and in waters of the Wash is not yet certain. It has been suggested that future surveillance should use molluscs as monitors of mercury pollution (NERC 1976). Less than 9 per cent of the nitrogen in rivers can be attributed to run-off from agricultural land and sewage contributes a significant proportion of the phosphates in rivers.

III   WATER SUPPLY

III.1 Hydrology of Water Resources

Considering the demands by evaporation, the amount of rainfall and its seasonal distribution appears adequate, but the problem is really one of annual and monthly departures from the mean. For example, one month's runoff can be as low as 10 per cent of the mean for that month. The severe drought of the summer of 1959 emphasized the inadequacy of the existing water supply and prompted the government action which led to the *Water Resources Act* (Publ. Gen. Act 1963). Three important trends have aggravated the situation: the rise in population, increasing individual requirements due to rising living standards, and growing industrial needs, calling for action to plan water resources for the future.

It is difficult to define hydrological zones in the UK, because of the lack of co-incidence between the physiographic and climatic factors which control the hydrology. Slope is important to runoff, but its effectiveness depends on whether the rock is pervious or not. Potential evaporation is only closely related to runoff if the rainfall is always high enough to meet the atmospheric demand. In SE England actual evaporation often falls below the potential during periods of drought in summer. Granite uplands have a similar effect due to rapid drainage, which limits the amount of water which can be held in the soil and made available for evaporation. Because of the dependence of actual evaporation upon water storage, variability of rainfall is usually adopted as a guide to runoff characteristics. In eastern areas the summer months have more than 50 per cent of the annual total, while elsewhere summers are drier and in the SW summers have 38 per cent of annual total rainfall. High mountains have the highest runoff, exceeding 2,000 mm pa in the wettest areas, but in SE England the average annual runoff is 125 mm and in dry years it can fall to 25 mm. The coefficient of variation of rainfall in the SE is more than 16 per cent, so that rainfall would be less than 80 per cent of the average once in ten years. The River Greta in Cumberland reflects the runoff regime from a wet mountain area (fig. 3.5) with a minimum flow in May and June when rainfall is at its lowest. The Great Ouse, on the other hand, represents the drier SE and the minimum in September corresponds to the time of the greatest soil water deficit. The mountains of the north and west have average rainfalls of over 2,500 mm and these are areas of lowest evaporation; south-eastwards rainfall decreases to less than 500 mm in SE England and evaporation increases. Thus hydrometric areas can be roughly arranged in order of wetness. The Islands and Western Highlands of Scotland; the rest of Scotland, excepting the E Central area, N Ireland, NW England and Wales; the SW peninsula; E Central Scotland and NE England; Severn and Humber; and SE England, including the Wash. The minimum river flow becomes progressively later in the year as one moves from the wetter areas to the dry SE. The absence of any

AVERAGE MONTHLY AS % AVERAGE ANNUAL RUN OFF

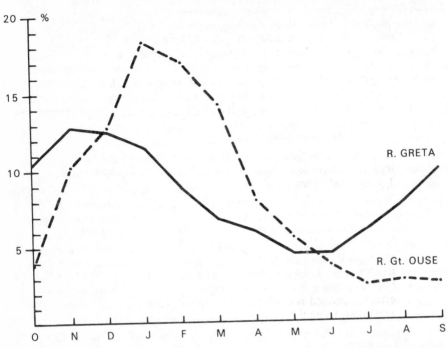

Figure 3.5   Monthly average as percentage annual average runoff, rivers Greta and Great Ouse

surplus in the SE has created a water supply problem. However, extensive aquifers, especially in chalk, absorb some winter surplus and help to augment summer flows. Winter storage in the form of snow is significant only in the Cairngorms area. Flooding is a feature of the wet mountains of the north and west, but the area most prone is the SW peninsula where storms have produced daily falls in excess of 150 mm on five occasions since 1920 (Rodda 1970B, 49). Since the rainfall in these mountain areas is orographic the heavy falls tend to be widespread. On the drier lowlands the heavy falls are associated with thunderstorms and the North Sea coast is the most prone; however, individual falls rarely exceed 125 mm. Land use is as important as rainfall and slope in influencing runoff and flooding. Flooding is not a major problem in the lower parts of UK rivers except on the low-lying east coast, where sinking of the North Sea basin has caused a rise in normal tides of about 77 ± 10 cm per century. Deep depressions over the N Atlantic can cause gales in the North Sea and when associated with abnormally high tides can cause serious flooding, as in 1953. Since 155 km[2] of the Thames floodplain are increasingly at flood risk a barrage is being designed for protection (Horner 1971).

Water storage The basic problem is one of storage to provide for times of deficit and to transfer water from areas of plenty to areas where it is scarce. The total requirements exceed the residual rainfall, which is the rainfall less the demands of evaporation and evapotranspiration. At the same time it is necessary to provide for the exceptional drought which may occur only once in a period of a hundred years.

Upland catchments have been the main suppliers of water for the urban areas of the UK because of their high rainfall and impervious rock, and also because of the short growing season and isolation which have restricted settlement. Until fairly recently there has been little organized resistance to the building of reservoirs (Gregory 1964A). Water supply can be considered as another way in which urban demands for space are threatening agricultural land. The total proposed expansion of water storage for 1981 is 27 km² which is small compared with the 202 km² lost annually to urban expansion. The benefits of increased water supply and increasing production by irrigation, could outweigh the loss of agricultural acreage. The SE has an annual residual rainfall of only 127 mm and every acre of urban settlement could demand as much as 700 mm (Speight 1968). Sites for storage in the SE would have to be on productive farmland and because of the nature of the topography wide shallow valleys would have to be drowned. The alternative is to impound upper streams and, without affecting existing settlement, four times the present storage could be obtained, only one-third of which would be required this century. The water from these reservoirs could regulate the flow of rivers and ensure a steady supply for abstraction downstream. While management is now possible in short and relatively clean rivers like the Dee, for longer rivers such as the Severn the time lag of several days for the release from a reservoir to be effective downstream means that more efficient weather forecasting for the basin would have to be developed. The quality of water in the Trent makes it unacceptable as a source of supply and doubts have been expressed as to whether the necessary standards could be attained at an acceptable cost. Using the Trent to recharge the Bunter sandstone would be similar in cost to water treatment and furthermore would require a larger area of land.

Storage in *impounded estuaries* or *maritime basins* is another possibility. Estuary storage has been considered for the Dee, Severn, Morecambe Bay, Solway and the Wash, as well as many smaller schemes in Wales and SE England. For most the cost is a major drawback, especially if the estuary is separated from demand areas by high mountains. The proposed Dee barrage (fig. 3.6) which would yield 1 Mm³ per day, little more than the expected yield of Kielder reservoir 0.95 Mm³ per day, would cost almost five times as much. Since estuaries are at lower elevations and have larger surface areas than upland reservoirs of similar capacity higher evaporation losses would make them less efficient. Salt-water intrusion may necessitate desalination adding further to the cost of estuary schemes, making them less attractive than any other alternative. The Solway barrage was suggested as a source of water for the Tyne, while Morecambe Bay was to serve Lancashire and by transfer across the Pennines, the W Riding conurbation. The Wash was to serve the water-scarce areas of SE England. Together Solway, Dee, Morecambe and Wash barrages could hold 1,818 Mm³ and meet all demands this century. Barrage schemes are difficult to evaluate because of the possible effects on silting and fisheries. Because the environmental impact cannot be easily predicted not more than two estuaries could be developed this century and, in fact, the preferred strategy suggested by the Water Resources Board (1973) includes only the Dee estuary for all development up to 2001 (fig. 3.6).

In Jersey and Guernsey, where the peak summer demands could not be met by surface reservoirs, desalination has been developed for public water supply. A desalination study in connection with the proposed Wash barrage scheme suggested

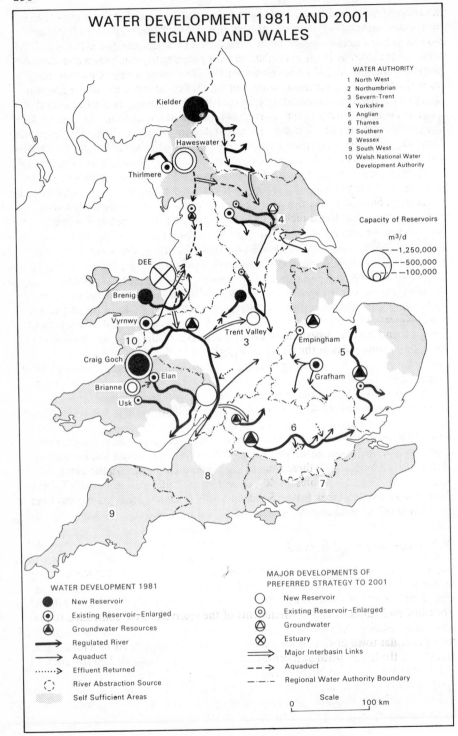

WATER DEVELOPMENT 1981 AND 2001
ENGLAND AND WALES

WATER AUTHORITY
1 North West
2 Northumbrian
3 Severn-Trent
4 Yorkshire
5 Anglian
6 Thames
7 Southern
8 Wessex
9 South West
10 Welsh National Water
Development Authority

Capacity of Reservoirs

m³/d

—1,250,000
—500,000
—100,000

WATER DEVELOPMENT 1981

● New Reservoir
◉ Existing Reservoir–Enlarged
◓ Groundwater Resources
→ Regulated River
→ Aquaduct
·····> Effluent Returned
⌇ River Abstraction Source
░ Self Sufficient Areas

MAJOR DEVELOPMENTS OF
PREFERRED STRATEGY TO 2001

○ New Reservoir
◎ Existing Reservoir–Enlarged
◓ Groundwater
⊗ Estuary
⇒ Major Interbasin Links
--→ Aquaduct
—·—·— Regional Water Authority Boundary

Scale
0   100 km

Figure 3.6   Water development proposals, England and Wales, 1981 and 2001

that it might be competitive by the end of the century in coastal areas of the SE, but it could not meet all the deficiency in the SE after 1981 as the cost, estimated in 1973 as £369 m in excess of other alternatives. (Water Resources Bd. 1973, 50), would be prohibitive. Plans to establish a pilot project at Ipswich were abandoned by the government in 1972 because the cost of developing desalination was rising faster than that of conventional sources of water. For inland areas, where rivers can be regulated, desalination could only be considered if it proves too difficult and costly to clean up grossly polluted rivers like the Trent. Apart from the cost of desalination, which includes rapid deterioration due to corrosion, the Water Resources Board suggested that objections on environmental grounds to the building of plants at the coast would be as strong as those which have already faced reservoir proposals.

Another alternative is to use *underground aquifers* for storage. In winter groundwater can give a high yield in the form of flow from springs but in summer pumping is necessary. Since the outcrops of these aquifers could receive only a limited amount of rainfall artificial recharge would be essential. The Thames Conservancy pilot scheme for recharging the chalk from 1967 to 1969 proved successful and it is now proposed to use this ground-water to augment the Thames. If the water used for charging contains effluent then treatment is necessary.

In N Lincolnshire up to 95 per cent of winter percolation could be abstracted in the following summer without causing encroachment of sea water. However, over-development of boreholes in the London Basin has already caused a serious decline in ground-water and any further development must be accompanied by recharging. The chalk and Jurassic limestone of the Thames basin could yield 700,000 m^3 per day and the same rocks in the Great Ouse basin 330,000 m^3 per day. The other major aquifer is the Bunter sandstone, mainly in the Midlands and on both flanks of the Pennines. The Vale of York sandstone could yield 135,000 m^3 per day to regulate the Yorkshire Ouse for abstraction to serve Humberside. The major difficulty with the Trassic rocks is that much of the ground-water is mineralized, which is true also of the coal measures, which have the added problem of pollution from toxic waste dumped in old mine workings. Shropshire has a large potential for ground-water from Trassic rocks, estimated at 225,000 m^3 per day, which will be used to augment the Severn. All of these sources have been incorporated in the plans for development (fig. 3.6). At present 40 per cent of the water in England and Wales is from ground-water sources, but in Scotland and N Ireland it accounts for less than 10 per cent of the total supply.

III.2 Water Supply and Demand

Rapid urban growth during the industrial revolution led to the development of nearby uplands as sources of water supply, and as demand increased more distant uplands in the North of England and Wales served the industrial belts of the Midlands, Yorkshire and Lancashire. The catchments of the reservoirs were controlled to preserve water quality. All major storage works built in the past 120 years were designed for a particular town or city, the main consideration being cost. As potential sites diminished the larger urban authorities had an advantage (Gregory 1964B, 270). Amalgamation of smaller boards was encouraged in the 1950s: in 1945 there were 1,100 water undertakings in England and Wales, but by 1966 these had been reduced to 286. In addition to statutory undertakings there are water companies operating under individual Acts of Parliament or Orders by the Minister. All undertakings in

Scotland are by local authorities which were reorganized into thirteen regional water boards by the *Water (Scotland) Act* (Publ. Gen. Act 1967). In N Ireland distribution of water is mainly in the hands of local authorities but grants towards water schemes are made under the *Water Supplies and Sewage Act (NI) 1945.*

Supply The Metropolitan Water Board is the largest water undertaking in the UK, supplying 1.67 Mm^3 per day to 6.25 million people. The effects of population concentration were first felt in the industrial areas. Grossly polluted rivers were no problem as long as new sources of water could be found in the uplands, which had been the case up to the Second World War. Subsequent population growth led to water demands which approached the limit of available supplies. Together with an increasing awareness of the recreational value of the uplands, this led to a new concept of water supply. Reservoirs were to be regulators for the rivers, maintaining the volume needed for abstraction in the lower reaches. Extraction of water can reduce the flow of fresh water so that salt-water invasions may increase upstream similar to the effect of the deepening of channels. However, the quality of water which depends on the volume of river flow and the treatment of effluent, needs to be assured and this is part of the cost of transporting water in this way. The Thames receives 0.81 Mm^3 of sewage effluent per day and 0.18 Mm^3 per day from industry, yet two-thirds of London's water, 1.36 Mm^3 per day, is abstracted from the river. Manchester and Liverpool have so dominated the water resources development of the Lake District and N Wales, respectively, that any further move for developing river resources is vigorously resisted. Yet Manchester maintains that industry demands high quality water supplies. The use of rivers as transporters provides the opportunity to economize, but also permits twice the yield obtainable if reservoirs were used for direct piped supply. It also has the advantage of permitting flood control and maintaining dry weather flow. To be most efficiently used, regulating reservoirs require management on a wider scale than hitherto possible and the *Water Resources Act* (Publ. Gen. Act 1963) was the first move towards this end; this Act applies only to England and Wales. So far, in Scotland and N Ireland pressures on water resources have not called for this kind of administrative machinery. In N Ireland management of water resources is under review, in anticipation of further industrial development.

Under the Act, twenty-nine River Authorities were created and the government appointed the Water Resources Board as an advisory body to plan and coordinate their efforts, by overseeing their proposals for meeting demand at seven-yearly intervals. Amenity and recreation are considered as well as water supply. The *Water Resources Board* (WRB) undertook three major studies of future demand and formulated strategies for the supply, which they reviewed in their final report (Water Resources Bd 1973). In April 1974 ten regional water authorities were created to take over the function of the river authorities, water undertakings and sewage disposal. The aim was to integrate the activities involved in river management (DoE 1973). The regions are large enough to plan successfully for water needs and pay for any necessary transfers, each having a twenty-year plan and a seven-year programme of investment. The overall national policy is now in the hands of the *National Water Council,* which is to announce its first broad strategy in 1978, based on long-term resource guidelines from the government (DoE 1974A).

It is more economical to meet the needs for several years ahead with one major scheme, rather than by a programme involving a succession of small schemes. By increasing a dam from 18 m to 33 m in height the capacity per unit cost is increased three times (Speight 1968). The amount of land flooded would be four and a half times greater, but since land costs are only 2.7 per cent of the total this is not likely to be relevant except for social and amenity considerations. There is a limit to the size, as the larger the storage capacity the longer it takes to refill after a drought. The rate of refill is also dependent on the locality. In NE England an impounded estuary would be drawn down 61 cm for six-month periods only twice in thirty-two years, while a pumped storage reservoir in SE England would have a similar draw down on six occasions, two of which would remain at this level for two years at a time (Rydz 1969).

The average rainfall of the UK is 900 mm and this produces an average of 460 mm runoff or 190 Mm³/d. The aggregate residual rainfall in the UK (0.068 Mm³ per annum, or 3,864 l per person per day in England and Wales) is much greater than is likely to be required by the community. The maximum possible yield in England and Wales is 185 Mm³ per day (Central Advisory Committee 1959); current abstractions are about 64 Mm³ per day. 48 Mm³ per day were abstracted in 1969 in England and Wales, 1.57 Mm³ per day in Scotland, and 0.45 Mm³ per day in N Ireland in 1955. N Ireland is already fully served by well-distributed uplands and the centrally-placed Lough Neagh, so that any supply problems are local and can be solved by normal development. Scotland is equally well-placed and the problem is one of distribution to the C Lowlands. The Loch Lomond and Loch Bradan Schemes will provide for all industrial and urban growth except in Fife. Apart from the administrative problems, the Southern uplands effectively separate Scotland from England and no water resources of Scotland have been developed for transfer to England.

Demands Demands for water have been increasing at the rate of 2.4 per cent per annum; in England and Wales demands from the public water supply increased from 8.9 Mm³ per day in 1955 to 14.1 Mm³ per day in 1971. This trend will continue and by the end of the century, due to a higher per capita demand and higher total population, could be between 26 and 28 Mm³ per day, but the net requirement may be much less if the siting of new industry and the treatment of effluent is advanced enough to allow increasing re-use of water. The new water authorities hope to improve forecasts of water demand by examining these uncertain factors (DoE 1974A). Table 3.3 is taken from estimates by Pugh (1963). Estimates of deficiencies

TABLE 3.3

Estimated Regional Water Supply, UK, 1990

	Estimated demand Mm³/d	Average net water available Mm³/d	Surplus resources thousand m³/head popn in 1990
N Ireland	.5	21.8	11.8
Scotland	2.9	227.5	33.1
N England	4.3	59.6	3.7
Wales and Midlands	2.5	57.8	5.8
SW England	.9	23.7	7.2
SE England	8.6	44.6	1.1
UK total	19.7	435.0	–

Source: Pugh (1963)

Environment and Land Use

TABLE 3.4

Estimates of Regional Water Deficiencies, Selected UK Regions, 1981 and 2001

	Public water supply '000 m³/d		Direct industrial and agriculture '000 m³/d		Total '000 m³/d	
	1981	2001	1981	2001	1981	2001
Wales and Midlands	495	3,080	195	645	690	3,725
North	1,155	3,535	80	405	1,235	3,940
SE Central Area	385	2,065	260	800	645	2,865
SE Outer	160	1,080	15	85	175	1,165
SW England	90	315	35	80	125	395

Source: WRB (1973)

have been made in the reports of the WRB which are summarized in table 3.4. If these estimates prove to be right then the area with the greatest future problem is the SE.

Additional supplies will be needed for: domestic purposes; industrial processes; and in agriculture, for cleaning as well as irrigation. Apart from these uses water is needed for: navigation, mainly in the Trent, Severn and Thames; amenity and recreation. However, if the rivers are to be used as a source for abstraction, regulating reservoirs will be needed to maintain flow in the upper courses and returned effluent will ensure sufficient volume in the lower reaches. Quality of the water is likely to affect fish before other forms of life. Total abstractions for public supply in 1971 were 14 Mm³d; by 1981 16.3 Mm³d will be needed and by 2001 26 Mm³. Industry which abstracted 42 Mm³d in 1971 will require 45 Mm³ in 1981 and 54 Mm³d in 2001. The total deficit in the country by 2001 will then be about 12 Mm³. This must be met by long-term planning.

Domestic Demand Domestic use in England and Wales amounts to 153 l per head per day. While in 1951 over one-third of houses in the UK had no fixed bath, today the figure is less than 10 per cent. Houses are being built at a rate of 350,000–450,000 per annum and all have modern facilities, yet 11 million pre-1939 houses require modernization or replacement. Washing machines, dishwashers, car washing, etc. are increasing and make demands upon the public supply. It is estimated that needs may rise to 450 l per head per day by the end of the century (WRB 1973, 30). The total demand by the year 2000 depends on the population forecast which in 1965 was 66 million but in 1971 this was reduced to 58 million and in 1972 to 55 million.

Industrial Demand The most important industrial use of water is for cooling which at present amounts to 23 per cent of the water abstracted (table 3.5) and the Central Electricity Generating Board uses a further 51 per cent for cooling. Assuming that industry will re-use water industrial demand for water will only be a small part of the future deficiency since the quantity consumed by industry is small compared with the amount it circulates.

Because of this recycling and the fact that the CEGB uses sea water (47 Mm³ per day sea water compared with 18.9 Mm³ per day fresh water) industrial expansion will demand only 20 per cent of the future development of water resources. Industry currently draws only 1.6 Mm³ per day of its water from boreholes, 5 Mm³ per

TABLE 3.5

Water Abstractions 1971 and Future Deficiencies

	Abstractions 1971	Deficiencies Mm^3/d 1981	2001
Public water supply	14	2.3	10.1
Direct industrial abstraction	28	0.6	2.0
Total	42	2.9	12.1

Source: WRB (1973)

day comes from public supply while 21.4 Mm^3 per day is abstracted from rivers and canals. The quality of returned effluent therefore is important for a continuation of re-use. Water abstracted for power generation is returned altered in temperature and a great volume is needed for circulation. This is called a direct cooling system, which for 2,000 MW output will circulate 0.27 Mm^3 per hour. A smaller volume, 40,000 m^3, is needed if cooling towers are used, since the same water can be constantly re-cycled, though about 1 per cent is lost by evaporation. This has the advantage of releasing heat to the atmosphere rather than the river. However, water is needed to flush the system to prevent salt concentration and thus in total up to 50 per cent of the water abstracted would be dissipated to the river. A 2,000 MW station at full output requires 0.13 Mm^3 per day of which 0.06 Mm^3 could be lost. The desirability of siting power stations near the areas of demand has become vital in the SE. Coal-field sites are not as favoured because of possible changes in sources of fuel, as well as distance from the demand areas, whilst coastal sites may be unacceptable for amenity reasons. Of the fresh water used by the CEGB 55 per cent comes from the Trent, and 40 per cent from the three rivers, Ouse, Mersey and Severn. New stations will be sited near the major water transfer networks or major sewage outfalls (Water Resources Bd. 1966). In 1971 the CEGB abstracted 18.9 Mm^3 per day from non-saline sources and only 0.9 Mm^3 per day was significantly altered in quality (WRB 1973, 32).

The extent to which returned industrial effluent can be re-used depends on the quality requirements. Sewage and saline water can be used for cooling but food industries require high standards. Effluents from food industries are usually of reasonable quality but those from engineering and chemical industries are often highly toxic and may even inhibit the biological processes used by sewage works. Re-use is essential to save substantial construction in meeting the industrial needs of the future. In estimates of needs up to the year 2000, the WRB in its report on the North (1970) has assumed repeated re-use of river water so that the increase in industrial effluents will offset the 1.36 Mm^3/d of new demands from industry. Industrial demand from public supply will rise from 4.6 Mm^3 per day in 1971 to 10.5 Mm^3 per day in the year 2001, and from rivers the 1971 consumption of 1.8 Mm^3 per day will rise to 5.7 Mm^3 per day by 2001. The steel industry currently uses approximately 37 tons of water to produce 1 ton of steel but if recycling is developed this could be reduced to 4 tons of water. This makes the estimating of future industrial needs more difficult than that for domestic needs, which relate to population numbers. In 1959 the *C Advisory Water Committee* estimated a 2.5 per cent per annum increase in demand. This was based on ten-year projections by a

TABLE 3.6

Authorized Abstractions of Water by Industry (excluding CEGB) and Agriculture, Selected
UK Regions, 1969

	Licences	Industry (1,000 m³/d)	Licences	Agriculture (1,000 m³/d)
North	2,857	10,250	4,883	170
Wales and Midlands	2,307	6,855	10,108	170
SE	2,480	3,835	11,007	485

Source: Water Resources Board (1971)

few sample industries, but a later report changed the figure to 5.2 per cent. In 1971
industry abstracted 9.4 Mm³ per day of which 7.0 Mm³ per day were returned without significant quality change. The *Water Resources Act* (Publ. Gen. Act 1963)
made it obligatory for industry to have a licence and pay a charge for private supply.
The maintenance of flow in rivers by regulating reservoirs and the use of sewage
effluent will increase the cost of abstraction and this may encourage industry to re-
use water internally by the treatment of effluent. Rees (1969) estimated 0.79 per
cent increase per annum for the future, but this figure could be altered by a change
in the cost of water.

   Agricultural demand Although agricultural demand is only a fraction of the total
demands by industry, the peak demand in the growing season is so high that this
was given consideration in the *Water Resources Act* (1963). The growth in demand
is closely related to the extension of mains supplies to rural areas. Rural Water
Supply and Sewerage Acts have made grants available for this purpose and areas of
low population have been able to get water at lower prices than if it were developed
privately. 350,000 farms in England and Wales now have mains supply, though water
required for cleaning and animals is a small proportion of the total demand. In
recent years spray irrigation, especially for potatoes, vegetables and fruit has increased and could be doubled by the end of the century, demanding 0.54 Mm³/d. In
SE England alone, the peak seasonal demand for spray irrigation in 1965 was 77
Mm³ and is expected to reach 159 Mm³ by the end of the century. Unlike water
used by industry most of this is transpired and is therefore lost to the rivers. There
is a need for storage on the farm to meet these and future demands and this might
be a serious disincentive for low-value crops. The WRB suggested that it would be
cheaper for farms to provide their own storage to meet their seasonal needs since
the intermittent demand would not justify conservation works (WRB 1973, 34).

   In 1963 there was enough equipment to irrigate 52,611 ha and this is increasing
at about 6,070 ha per annum. Most of this is in the south and east, particularly in
E Anglia. It pays to irrigate high-value crops in small areas in Pembrokeshire, Cornwall and in the lower Tees valley. However, it is unlikely to be economic in areas
with rainfall in excess of 890 mm. Future development is possible for large acreages
of low-value crops where large quantities of water are available cheaply. Because
they require less water small areas of high-value crops can more easily find a source
and because of high profits earned can pay for it. (Prickett 1970, 117.) About
607,000 ha in all could benefit from irrigation, which would need 13 Mm³ per day.

   The most common source of water for irrigation is from surface streams, but this
is difficult in the SE where many dry up in summer. Improvements in land drainage
have aggravated the situation by increasing the efficiency of catchment drainage.

Apart from irrigation, water is also needed for spraying, as a protection against frost, for stock, milk cooling, and cleaning. Only in areas where storage on the farm is not possible, thus requiring additional water, have agricultural needs been considered in the total estimate.

III.3 Strategies

After all local sources of water supply have been developed there will be a large deficiency in England and Wales as a whole. This is termed the strategic deficiency which can be met only by transfer between regions. This deficiency has been estimated at 9.5 Mm^3 per day in the year 2001. However, it depends on the accuracy of estimates of population increase and on the change in per capita consumption. Both are difficult to forecast and as a result estimates of deficiency vary (table 3.7).

TABLE 3.7

Strategic Water Deficiency in the year 2001

(Mm^3 per diem)	Local forecast	Alternative forecast
North	3.45 (±1.5)	3.20
Wales & Midlands	3.20 (±1.3)	2.40
SE & Central	2.85 (±1.2)	2.60
Total England & Wales	9.50 (±4.0)	8.20

Source: WRB (1973)

Strategies to meet these deficiencies were first outlined by the WRB in its short existence from 1963 to 1974, but will be continued in a national plan considered by the central water planning unit, advising both the government and the new regional water authorities.

The WRB produced three regional reports and a report for England and Wales assessing the probable demand for water up to the end of the century and possible programmes of development to meet these needs. The reports stress the importance of flexibility in long-term planning and the need for regular revision, which since 1974 has become the responsibility of the ten *Regional Water Authorities*. The North, Wales, the Midlands and the SE have special problems which emerge clearly from these detailed regional surveys. All three reports already show that developable resources exist in the UK to meet all foreseeable demands, but the problem is finding the optimal programme of development. The needs are to be met by regulation of rivers, by reservoirs, or ground water, and the combined use of resources. The three regions used to assess the needs and problems of water development are different from the ten regional water authorities set up in 1974; nevertheless they provide a useful framework for a national plan. The Welsh National Water Authority has extra-territorial jurisdiction over the Dee and Wye basins, the Severn-Trent Authority over the entire Severn system including that part within Wales.

In the *SE* the basic problem is lack of internal resources to meet future demands and development of surface storage would encroach upon valuable farmland. The report on the SE (WRB 1966) was most concerned with providing water for the very large deficiency zone within the SE requiring an additional 2.95 Mm^3/d by the year 2000. A combination of surface and underground storage including schemes like the

Chichester barrage, if acceptable, could provide more than the estimated needs at the end of the century. However, it is probably more realistic to assume that long-term schemes must include bulk imports from the west and north. For climatic reasons river regulation can be met only by ground water. Using ground water to augment summer flows and artificially recharging the aquifers in winter could yield as much as 0.56 Mm^3/d in the Ely-Ouse, equal to the internal needs of the Great Ouse area by 2001. The Thames could also be regulated, using ground-water from the chalk to meet all needs this century, provided it is possible to recharge the aquifer which is in places already overpumped and threatened by salt-water intrusions. Many of the rivers in the SE are only indirectly polluted and, if regulated and further deterioration prevented, can continue to be used for abstraction. Re-use of water in the SE is a significant aspect of the water-supply pattern. The Thames and Lee at present are supplying 1,750 m^3 per day but in the future could only be modestly increased to 2,300 m^3. Much greater demands will be made on other rivers, notably middle Severn, which will rise from 750 m^3 to 2,400 m^3 per day by 2001.

The Trent and many of the larger northern rivers are so grossly polluted as to preclude them as sources for public supply. There are of course in Wales and the North many clean rivers, like the Wye, whose obvious amenity and recreational value is likely to safeguard their purity and they will be used increasingly to transport water and for abstraction in the future. Remedial works will further improve the quality of rivers so that abstracting from the Tees will increase from 540 m^3 per day at present to 1,250 m^3 per day in 2001 and the Dee from 560 to 900 m^3 per day. Up to 1,250 m^3 per day will be abstracted from the Tyne when the river can be fully regulated by the Kielder reservoir.

Industries sited on the rivers of the *Midlands* and *North* use and re-use the river water. This is particularly so of the Trent which provides 55 per cent of all the river water used by the CEGB. Although the quality prevents its use for public supply it has sufficient dry weather flow to allow abstraction for industry. Further industrial demand can be partly met by recycling the increased effluent from the industries themselves. However, the industrial effluents may need treatment and because of the nature of the industries this is a greater problem than in the SE. Industry in the North requires more water than elsewhere in England and Wales and this explains the higher per capita consumption, 278 l per day compared to 254 l per day in SE England. However, the North requires less for agriculture since the greater part of the agricultural use is for spray irrigation.

Additional storage needed to regulate rivers for the *Wales* and *Midlands* regions can be found in the Welsh Valleys and Peak district. Public supply in Wales and the Midlands still finds 80 per cent of its water directly from upland reservoirs. Aqueducts carry 0.35 Mm^3 per day from the Elan reservoir on the Wye to Birmingham, 0.20 Mm^3 per day from the Vyrnwy, a tributary of the Severn, to Liverpool. Direct supplies from the Derwent, a tributary of the Trent, serve Sheffield, Derby, Nottingham and Leicester. But the Severn, which is regulated by the Clywedog reservoir, is a source for abstractions as far downstream as Gloucester. The dry-weather flow of the Trent is almost entirely effluent so that it cannot be used for direct supply.

The *WRB* was concerned with the immediate problem and has made proposals for development up to 1981. The urgent need can be met for the most part by reservoir enlargement for river regulation. For Wales and the Midlands, Craig Goch and Vyrnwy are to be enlarged to regulate the Severn, while the new reservoirs of Brenig and Carsington will serve the N Midlands and S Lancashire. A political argument has developed (1975) over the revenues for water exported from Wales. The Welsh Water Authority seeks to equalize water charges with those of the English neighbours. This is opposed by the Severn–Trent Authority, which is not prepared to pay more for water from Wales than Welsh abstractors would pay. If necessary, alternative sites for water storage in England might be sought, including Longden Marsh, near Tewkesbury.

In the *North* there is no shortage of resources as the region includes the Lake District, with the heaviest rainfall in England and Wales. The problem lies in the siting of storage reservoirs and the systems for transporting the water. The decision to develop the new reservoir at Kielder rather than a stepwise development of several smaller reservoirs serves the immediate future as well as the estimated longer-term demand. Kielder will regulate the Tyne and by pipeline across the divides also serve the Wear and Tees. The Ouse and its tributaries will be regulated by enlarging the existing reservoirs of Grunthwaite and Gouthwaite. Whilst it is possible to cost the loss of productivity of agricultural or forestry land, it is more difficult to estimate the value of amenity or to judge the demands from the environment of the often conflicting urban and rural users.

1981–2001 Assuming all the 1981 developments (fig. 3.6) take place, meeting further needs up to the end of the century will have to be met by more ambitious strategies involving major inter-basin links. If deficiencies were to be met by developing surface reservoirs for direct supply, forty-one reservoirs would be needed, of which twenty-five would be in national parks, and moreover they would require 9,100 km^2 compared with 59 km^2 needed to meet the demands by means of river regulation. However the use of rivers as transporters of water has problems especially in the North for, unlike the Midlands, it has no very large rivers and all its rivers are polluted to varying degrees. The S Tyne is suggested as a major transporter eastwards and the Swale southwards to the Yorkshire Ouse, thus helping to alleviate the supply problems posed by the potential development of a Humberside conurbation in an area where reservoir sites are difficult. To the west of the Pennines there is at present a major transfer south from the Lake District. This is to be augmented by the development of Haweswater which may be linked by pipeline to the Ouse.

The choice for development beyond 1981 is between regional self-sufficiency and major inter-regional transfers. Regional self-sufficiency is the least efficient as it requires eighteen additional reservoirs and the enlargement of six existing reservoirs. The cheapest solution lies in continuing to develop inland storage for river regulation which would require a further seven reservoirs and the enlargement of three existing reservoirs. Two of the new reservoirs would be in national parks and one of the enlargements would destroy a village, so that its effect on the environment would be considerable. While complete dependence on inland reservoirs can be ruled out on environmental grounds, equally the development of estuary storage in the Dee, Morecambe and the Wash is too costly. The preferred strategy involves a combination of estuaries and inland reservoirs. The development of further surface reservoirs is impossible in the SE though the preferred programme includes enlargements of reservoirs in the Wash basin. This ground-water development and the transfer of water from the Severn to the Thames is the preferred development for the SE until the end of the century.

III.4 Conservation

Water conservation has been defined as the

> 'preservation, control and development of water resources whether by storage, including natural ground storage, prevention of pollution, or other means, so as to ensure that adequate and reliable supplies of water are made available for all purposes in the most suitable and economical way whilst safeguarding legitimate interests'

(WRB 1966, 1970, 1971). The White Paper was followed by the *Water Resources Act* (Publ. Gen. Act 1963). In the UK the problem of water conservation lies in the last clause of the official definition, for the reconciliation of conflicting interests becomes more difficult with increasing population pressure. The present water storage provides only 10 per cent of the normal river flow in drought conditions which is insufficient to meet the demands for recreational pursuits. The part of the whole cycle of water use concerning people and recreation is of considerable importance in the management of water.

From 1963 to 1973 water management in England and Wales was controlled by two main categories: the water undertakings who supplied water, and the River Authorities who were concerned with the wider problems of water conservation and management of river basins (MHLG and MAFF 1962). At central government level these two categories were supervised by the Water Resources Board. The *Water Resources Act* (1963) did not, however, overcome the problem of the divided responsibilities for water supply, river management, water conservation, pollution control, sewerage and sewage disposal. The division of responsibility for industrial effluents between the sewerage and River Authorities, in particular, was a major problem. In 1974 the functions of the River Authorities, together with water supply and sewage disposal which were in the hands of some local authorities, were taken over by ten large multi-purpose authorities whose task was to manage rivers on an integrated systems basis (DoE 1973B). Planning at the national level, formerly in the hands of the WRB, became the responsibility of the DoE for water supply, water quality and recreation and the MAFF for land drainage, flood protection and fisheries. The large units could be more self-sufficient than the smaller River Authorities they replaced, but broader central planning will now be done by the National Water Council. In Scotland and N Ireland conservation problems have not yet warranted major reorganization, though *Regional Supply Boards* and a central body are being considered.

Landscaping, ecology and the requirements for leisure activities add a new dimension to the role of water authorities, who will now undertake surveys of potential demand for recreation. The public right of access to reservoirs provided in the 1963 Act has proved satisfactory but without any special provisions for parking or recreation. By the year 2000 a further 16,188 ha of reservoir water will be available and in addition the cleaning of many rivers and their regulation for satisfactory abstraction makes them attractive for recreation for a greatly increased number of users. Landscaping and planning for recreational and ecological interests demand a more direct involvement by water authorities in the multiple use of water. Whether these additional uses can be financed by participants or by the country at large has not yet been resolved.

Pressure on the land has led to more opposition to water storage proposals and the larger Water Authorities claim to be in a better position to consider conflicting demands and especially those of the community directly affected by water development. The changes in policy from direct supply to river regulation will avoid the construction of several new reservoirs. However, practical and less expensive schemes may have to be developed to meet national needs and the larger authorities will be in a better position to choose sites or use landscaping techniques to reduce the impact on the environment and rural communities. Attempts to make better use of present resources by waste prevention, re-use by industry, dual systems for potable and non-potable supplies have come to the fore. At present only one-third of water is metered and more information is needed on the use of the remaining two-thirds. Industry frequently uses water of high quality when lower quality would serve as well, but much research needs to be done on the quality of water required by all users as well as that required to maintain aquatic life. Also economies could be encouraged by metering, off-peak tariffs or rationing. Useful as these may be the additional 0.45 Mm/d required each year can only be met by surface reservoirs, estuary barrages, aqueduct systems, recirculation and complementary use of ground- and surface-water. The great deficiency in the *Water Resources Act* (1963) was that the River Authorities could not make a comprehensive management plan. The lack of a policy on the quality of river water seriously limited the effectiveness of any of the strategies outlined by the WRB. The regional Water Authorities have the advantage of control of industrial effluents, however, which was denied to the River Authorities. Water supply to industry and to the public must be safeguarded by control over effluent discharges. The building of a new sewage works to raise the quality of river water to permit abstraction may be the alternative to a new reservoir and has the added attraction of improving amenities. The cost of cleaning rivers like the Trent must be considered along with the amount of water made available for abstraction. However, to allow abstraction, the quality must be higher than the Royal Commission standard and the costs can only be met by a levy on all the users.

Costs of conservation Alternative schemes usually include combinations of upland storage, barrages and ground-water development. Evaluation must go beyond the costs of construction; it must also consider the treatment. For example, desalination is part of the cost of a marine barrage storage scheme. There are many other considerations, such as national parks, salmon fishing and flood control. In considering a scheme a decision must be made on whether or not the extra cost of the more expensive alternative is a fair price to pay for the preservation of an environmental factor. The WRB has approached this problem in terms of cost effectiveness, but unless a scheme is multi-purpose it is extremely difficult to weigh the desirable and undesirable effects of development. At present the primary concern is for water, recreation is secondary and flood control is only important if schemes are otherwise equal. These are only part of the analyses and are frequently based on inadequate information. The Nature Conservancy is now concerned with the construction of models to guide land use decisions in the uplands.

The WRB urged regional control because of the effect that water is likely to have on future industrial location more easily realized after reorganization in 1974 (DoE 1973B). Surplus can either be exported or used to attract industry, and the River Authorities can already exercise some control by issuing or refusing licences and by charging for private abstraction. In SE England some industrial concentrations are attracted to waterways or are located on aquifers. Rees (1969) has shown that availability of potable water is a major location factor for food, drink and some chemical industries, Plastics and chemicals also need a great volume of water for disposing of noxious effluent. As suitable sites for water abstraction become scarce, water may exercise greater control over distributions of industry.

IV FORESTS

IV.1 Afforestation

The *Forestry Act* (Publ. Gen. Act 1919) established the Forestry Commission with the task of replanting areas which had lost timber through decades of uncontrolled exploitation, so replenishing a seriously depleted resource. In 1975 the Commission had a total estate of 1.2 M ha, of which 0.8 M ha were planted in trees, and there were plans to plant a further 90,000 ha. Cheap land was inevitably land of poor agricultural value and for this reason the dominant land type for afforestation has been upland heaths and moors, accounting for 70 per cent of the total area in 1963 (Wardle 1966). Deciduous hardwoods, mainly in private forests, occur on the more productive soils of the lowlands, but the poorer soil and harsher climate of the uplands is better suited to the introduction of conifers which account for 90 per cent of all Forestry Commission woodland. The conifers have proved that they can be highly productive even on poor site conditions. The average growth rate of Sitka spruce and Douglas fir is more than three times that of oak and twice the growth rate of beech (Grayson 1967). Much of the planting has been in the more favoured parts of the uplands, though recent techniques have allowed the planting of peat bogs. There are still vast areas suitable for forestry so that the difficult areas, such as the exposed west coast of Scotland, may not be developed for extensive forests for some time. In 1950 the Forestry Commission's activity in Scotland came under the Secretary of State for Scotland, but its role has remained unchanged and much of the recent planting has been in the Highlands. Forestry in N Ireland has been the concern of the Ministry of Agriculture of the N Ireland government set up in 1922. By 1975 N Ireland had 65,900 ha in government forest, and it is planned to plant on average 570 ha per annum up to 1980.

The establishment of vast forests of conifers in what seemed to be the less productive uplands has raised one of the most difficult problems of land-use management. The profitability of forests depends to a very large extent on the nature of the site, the soil drainage and exposure in particular. Agriculture and especially sheep or cattle farming would not be so sensitive to environmental qualities and it would be difficult to decide on an optimum land-use pattern based on productivity alone. In any case this would entail a fragmentation of forest blocks which would be uneconomic and may not be compatible, for example, with the practice of the spring burning of grazing areas, which is a hazard to forests. Comparisons of productivity may be meaningless at another time when new techniques of either forest or agricultural management may be developed. A land survey has been carried out jointly by the Departments of Agriculture and Forestry in N Scotland, in which land suitable for forests is identified and, on the basis of its agricultural potential, is either earmarked for purchase by the Forestry Commission or retained for agriculture (McVean and Lockie 1969). Assessment of changes resulting from different agriculture and forestry policies have not been attempted in the UK (Grayson 1967).

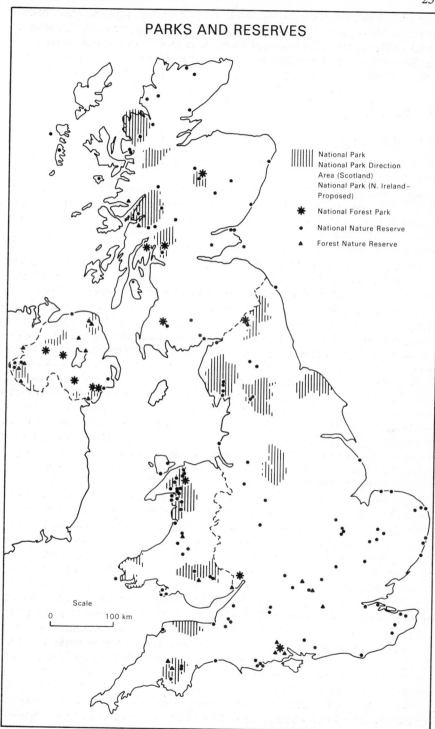

PARKS AND RESERVES

‖‖‖	National Park National Park Direction Area (Scotland) National Park (N. Ireland – Proposed)
✳	National Forest Park
●	National Nature Reserve
▲	Forest Nature Reserve

Scale

0   100 km

Figure 3.7   Parks and reserves, UK, 1972

Much afforestation by the Commission in the 1920s was on grazing lands, especially in the Highlands of Scotland. Whilst the presence of forest had the value of providing shelter for stock, the forests were largely planted on the lower slopes and effectively isolated the high grazings from the valley floors, thus reducing their value for stock farming. Technology has made it possible to plant over a wider range of conditions so that this serious conflict need not occur with new plantings.

Forestry Commission planting has been in large units, of which 55 per cent are over 400 ha in extent and the landscape effect is less pleasing than the fragmented pattern of small private woods and farmlands typical of the lowlands. However, attempts to landscape their estates and provide a valuable resource for recreation led the Forestry Commission to establish four large forest parks in Scotland, Snowdonia forest park in Wales, the Forest of Dean and Wye and the Border forest park in England. In 1975 the Forestry Commission had 347 picnic sites and 421 forest trails and was selecting sites for forest cabins to meet the demand for accommodation (Forestry Comm. 1975). The development of Kielder reservoir in the Border forest park and its potential for recreation has led to more specific landscape planning.

IV.2 Environmental Factors in the Productivity of Commercial Forests

The large-scale commercial forests established by the Forestry Commission since 1919 have been developed on low-value land, most of which was marginal for agriculture. In the 1950s forests were expanding at the rate of 16,000 ha per annum and most of this was on the rough grazing land of the uplands. Since 1966 annual planting has averaged 25,000 ha of which 17,000 ha were in Scotland (Forestry Comm. 1975). Although similar to agriculture in that trees are planted like a crop and harvested at the optimum stage of growth, forestry was forced to develop in areas of difficult conditions of climate and soil. Productivity has been improved through increasing knowledge of the relationships between growth and environment, and the development of technology to take advantage of this knowledge. The scale is also very different from agriculture, which makes the control of temperature and moisture in nurseries a more difficult task. The softwoods have predominated largely because of their rapid growth and their ability to survive in a wide range of conditions. Although Scots pine is the only native conifer, spruce is preferred for the upland plantations and, in the wetter areas of the west, sitka spruce predominates. Spruce and pine accounted for 80 per cent of post-war planting, lodgepole pine increasing in popularity to become second to sitka spruce (Forestry Comm. 1974).

The sitka spruce, a native of the wet Pacific coast of N America, grows well on the wet western mountains, but under dry conditions the tree becomes susceptible to attack by aphids. For this reason the low rainfall and the dry sandy soils of the Breckland in E Anglia and the Culbin Sands, Morayshire, have suited Scots and Corsican pine rather than spruce. In the Border forests, pine is also grown in the poorest deep peats, while the mid and upper slopes are exclusively in spruce (Pyatt 1966). Larch is usually planted on the areas of better soils, for example the bracken sites of the uplands, and was successfully planted on large private estates in Scotland in the late nineteenth century. For economic reasons broad-leafed trees, mainly beech and oak, are less important and are confined to the better soils; in 1975 they accounted for less than 1 per cent of total plantings (Forestry Comm. 1974).

Despite the generally poor conditions in the forested areas, elevation, topography and position influence the local climate and soil. Growth is dependent on the length of season, temperature and moisture. Since the growth rate in trees depends on the leaf area available, soil water deficits in winter can retard the new season's growth; girth and volume are increased from April onwards. The conditions for survival in the early years, such as freedom from dried-out surface soil, attacks by rabbits, grouse and deer and late frosts, are not needed once the trees are established, but they do succeed in eliminating forests from many areas unless they can be remedied, as by high fencing in the Highlands of Scotland, to protect seedlings from deer. The effects of environmental conditions on the growth of mature trees can be considerable. The average annual growth increment of 19 m³ per ha for Corsican pine in E Anglia was reduced by 30 per cent in a dry year (Rouse 1961). However, multivariate analysis suggests that winter temperature, sunshine, content of clay and stones in the soil, depth of the water table, soil depth, humus type, soil pH and phosphorus content are significant components in the growth of the species (Forestry Comm. 1968, 55). Once trees are established the environmental conditions can change, such as the improved soil water capacity due to the growth of root systems which can be substantial, even for shallow-rooting trees in peats (O'Hare 1972).

Interception of *precipitation* in forests is appreciable. Together with the direct evaporation from the soil, which may be as much as 10 per cent of the total, it forms an important part of the water balance. Conifers differ from deciduous trees in that they transpire and intercept precipitation throughout the year. In wetter areas the evaporation of intercepted water can be as much as that transpired by the trees. The deep-rooting habits of trees, which under conditions of free drainage are commonly 2 m, increase the available water capacity to 300–500 mm depending on soil type, which permits a long period of unrestricted evapotranspiration after the onset of drought. For this reason forests transpire more than grassland under the same conditions of potential evapotranspiration and the difference is greatest in SE England. Thinning reduces evapotranspiration; in one case, streamflow from a forest increased by 4.5 mm after clearing 10 per cent of the trees. This is only temporary as the branches of the remaining trees rapidly grow to fill up the spaces and the roots extend to occupy all of the soil volume (Rutter 1972; Holmes and Colville 1968).

Temperature is also important to growth, so that altitude and latitude are of significance. In the uplands, records of temperature are sparse and assumptions must be made on crude lapse rates which need not be constant from time to time nor apply without variation over a very wide area. The present tree line in the UK is not entirely determined by nature, but the upper level of potential growth must be based on physical conditions, which in upland areas are complex. In the Cairngorms it is probably about 690 m on sheltered slopes, but about 600 m on exposed sites (Pears 1972). While the physical limit can be defined broadly as a mean summer temperature of 10°C, the effects of temperature conditions on growth rates are more difficult to isolate.

Studies in Hampshire have shown that Douglas fir starts growth when the mean weekly average rises to 7°C and continues as long as this mean rises, but growth is checked with even a slight fall in this mean (Rouse 1961, 306). However, the mechanism is not understood and in any case is not likely to apply to all species.

Wind effectively excludes trees from the exposed western coasts, where the salt content accentuates its effects, whilst at high altitudes wind speed and temperature are inter-related. However, the dessicating effect of high wind velocity is more general. Areas in Scotland which have poor tree growth correspond with mean wind velocities of 4.4–6.2 m per sec (16–23 kmph) – though other factors complicate this general relationship in coastal areas and at high altitudes (Birse and Robertson 1970). On sites with mean wind velocities of about 27 kmph young seedlings of sitka spruce grew better than lodgepole pine but larch failed completely. (Forestry Comm. 1968, 38). The effect of strong winds on large plantations is to prevent the emergence of dominant trees and in the Border forests growth is generally restricted by exposure to the south-west and in more exposed sites the result may be rapidly tapering stems which would have limited commercial value (Fraser 1972). Wind is reduced by 10 per cent in a 3–4° hollow, by as much as 40 per cent at the base of a 7–12° lee slope, whilst a reduction of 75 per cent has been noted on a lee slope of 14° (Roberts 1972). Tatter flags are now used to estimate the effects of exposure prior to planting. Experiments in planting at exposed sites began in 1953 at Shetland and Orkney. While trees can grow at altitudes up to 610 m in C Wales and Scotland exposure on the Hebrides and northern islands can limit growth at sea level (Forestry Comm. 1974).

At one time forests were planted with little or no preparation of the *soil* but recent work in Inverness has shown that cultivation before planting can double the height of six-year-old Scots pine and lodgepole pine. The problem is often mechanical and is especially difficult on wet peat and soils with iron pans. Rapid growth on ploughed ridges, thought to be due to increased mineralization of nitrogen under thicker peat, may not be sustained, for the larger trees eventually feel the mineral deficiencies while smaller, less demanding trees will continue to grow. Phosphates have been successful in improving growth on heath and infertile peat soils and lodgepole pine has proved the best species for these soils (Forestry Comm. 1974).

Pollution, particularly of the air, may present problems, notably on urban and industrial sites which are to be planted in the rehabilitation of derelict land. Sulphur dioxide has caused discoloration of leaves and premature leaf fall in forests near Port Talbot (Jones 1972). Together with dust, which limits photosynthesis, this is thought to contribute to poor growth in sitka spruce, though some genetic variations have a degree of tolerance. Many parts of the Pennines have been dismissed as potential areas for afforestation because of their exposure to sulphur dioxide from Lancashire and the W Riding of Yorkshire (Forestry Comm. 1974).

As knowledge of the nature of environmental problems in forestry grows, it is possible to control the natural hazards and improve soil conditions by nutrients and drainage. Wind throw is a problem in exposed areas. The problem has become increasingly important as trees grow to heights of over 10 m, when they become more susceptible. Between 1961 and 1967, 970 ha suffered wind throw, half of this sitka spruce, mainly 30- to 40-year-old timber which had reached between 9–18 m in height. In years of strong winds, as in 1961 and 1962, great damage was done. Damage tends to occur during single severe storms. In January 1968 850,000 m^3 of timber was lost in C Scotland due to wind throw, during a 75 kmph westerly wind which persisted for six hours (Pyatt 1966, 41). Wind is reduced in passing over an extensive forest, and wind speeds in the tree tops of the Border forests are only 10 per cent of the speeds in open country. However, gaps for roads and firebreaks create higher speeds, due to turbulence, and the highest incidence of wind throw is around small clearings. The eddy effect is also obvious near the base of lee slopes. Wind throw can be reduced at forest margins by high pruning which increases permeability but the damage by wind throw in the UK does not justify extensive treatment of all forest margins. Improvements in rooting can be brought about by drainage and cultivation, particularly in compacted heathland and clay soils. It has been estimated that about 90 per cent of the Border area needs improvement, though deep rooting in peaty podsols requires breaking of the iron pan, which can only be done at planting (Wardle 1970). Drainage and cultivation can increase the critical height for winds of 75 kmph from 15–20 m. While shelter belts can effectively reduce wind speeds by 40 per cent for distances ten times the shelter height, this can only be of use in young forests. Established forests can benefit most from a margin inclined to the windward as this reduces the risk of turbulence (Caborn 1957). Losses due to wind blow are mainly the lost potential growth but the difficulty of recovering the fallen timber incurs additional expenditure. Felling before the timber reaches full height reduces the risk of windfall but the crop has not then realized its full potential. Forest management in the Border forests where the wind blow is a serious hazard has made use of simulated effects to decide on the optimum time for felling (Wardle 1970, 78).

Fire is less of a problem in the UK but its high incidence in spring is related to the dryness of the forest and surrounding vegetation. The risk can be reduced by using herbicides on undergrowth and models of the rate of the spread of fire by physical factors allow the planning of more effective windbreaks (Forestry Comm. 1974). Rouse (1961, 309) has devised an empirically-derived scale of fire risk which depends on the number of days after rain over 6 mm in twenty-four hours; temperatures above 15°C; wind speed and relative humidity. Fire risk can be reduced during these critical periods by forest management. Recent dry summers, notably 1974 and 1976, brought many fires but the area burned was comparatively small.

V   URBAN AND INDUSTRIAL LAND USE

V.1   Introduction

While the location of certain types of industry can be considered the product of economic history, the development of industry in the nineteenth century was to a large extent influenced by the coalfields. With the exception of Belfast heavy industry is concentrated on or near the coalfields. Twentieth-century growth of light industry has not favoured the northern coalfields, but rather lowland England (ch. 4.III.1). Since the 1950s the growth of urban land has been greatest in an axial zone from Lancashire through the Midlands to London, and the total demand for additional development may be of the order of 700,000 ha by the year 2000 (table 1.3). An estimated 1 per cent per annum of land in this area was lost to agricultural use from 1955–60 and the percentage of land in urban use in the SE is likely to reach 36 per cent by the end of the century. The area in urban and industrial use, estimated by Best at no more than 15 to 16 per cent of the land surface of England and Wales, will still be small compared with that in rural use (Best 1968). The effects of industrial activity range from the sprawling New Towns and industrial estates in the SE to the dereliction of the declining heavy industries and old mines in S Wales, the NE, C Scotland and on the flanks of the Pennines. While coalmining and heavy industry have left vast areas of derelict spoil heaps which present major problems of rehabilitation, surface mining and, in particular, gravel extraction have also made increasing demands upon the land. The annual consumption for these latter purposes was above 1,600 ha in 1967 which could increase to 3,200 ha by about 1980 (Beaver 1968). Modern power stations make heavy demands on land and because of the need for vast supplies of cooling water are sited on major rivers like the Trent or, in the case of nuclear-powered stations, at the coast (fig. 4.8). Petrochemical industries needing deep-water sites have formed vast complexes on the major estuaries. Through its effects on the atmosphere, the land surface, the rivers and the surrounding seas, industrial and urban land use has influenced the environment far beyond the area of land which it occupies. The most serious effect is that of pollution. The suggested control of pollution by planning buffer zones around major pollution sources would make further demands on land (Royal Comm. Pollution 1976A).

V.2 Pollution

Pollution occurs when man's activity adds substances to the environment which because of their properties or quantity constitute a danger to health and well-being. It is perhaps more useful to broaden the influence to systems in the environment rather than to man alone. It is difficult to define pollution scientifically since many of the substances causing pollution occur naturally. Carbon dioxide, for example, is essential to life, yet in high concentrations it contributes to chronic respiratory disease. Phosphates are also essential to the growth of vegetation yet the great increase in the use of detergents in this country has contributed possibly as much as 50 per cent of the phosphate content of streams and rivers causing enrichment or eutrophication. Some natural substances, such as lead and mercury, may be more damaging since they can accumulate in organisms and disturb biochemical processes and through food chains present a hazard to man very much greater than if the substances were diluted in the environment. Increasingly man-made substances such as the chlorinated hydrocarbons used in pesticides have been adding to the pollution problem. As industry increases in sophistication, the emission of effluents whose effects are not yet known will increase.

When an effect of pollution is suspected there are usually moves to control it. The inversion of temperature in London in the winter of 1952–3 had the disastrous effect of unusual accumulations of smoke and carbon dioxide (Bleasdale 1959). The deaths caused by the smog, some 3,000 to 4,000 in excess of a normal winter, led to the *Clean Air Acts* (Publ. Gen. Acts 1956 and 1968). In the same year, air pollution in E Lancashire caused lost production estimated at £2,600,000 (R. Commn. Environment and Pollution 1974). Toxic pollutants from some individual industries have led to action. For example, fumes from brickworks in the Midlands causing fluoride poisoning in cattle, lead smelting causing deaths of stock, fluorine in effluent from the aluminium smelters at Fort William contaminating pastures on the leeward side, have all led to the offending industries being required to clean their effluent. The effect of the pollutant depends very much on the toxicity, persistence, mobility and ease of control. These are all-important, for a highly toxic pollutant which breaks down quickly is less serious than a less toxic but more persistent pollutant. For this reason organophosphorous pesticides are preferred to organochlorides though they are equally toxic.

The stability of the environment is important but cannot be seen as a UK problem in isolation. Nicholson (1970) estimates that artificial ecosystems, which constitute most of the UK surface, account for only 10 per cent of the globe, the rest being natural or biologically-exploited natural ecosystems. All our pollutants finally reach the sea, carried by rivers, dumped by man or washed by rain from the air. The sea appears to be able to break down and recycle waste and so far the harmful effects seem to be localized. However, there may be no grounds for complacency in UK waters, as we share the North Sea with other highly-populated countries which use it as a sink. Equally, the almost enclosed waters of the Irish Sea may be particularly vulnerable in the future. The global atmosphere has shown an increase in carbon dioxide of 0.2 per cent per annum since 1958, largely as a result of fuel combustion. Stratosphere traffic, which must increase in the future, will continue to add water vapour and carbon dioxide. The possible climatic effect of this, together with the impact of sulphur dioxide which finds its way to the stratosphere where its life is prolonged, has not yet been assessed, but in air corridors with dense traffic a 60 per cent increase in water vapour is suspected, leading to more stratospheric cloud (Wilson 1970). Shipping and offshore drilling for oil in the North Sea add to the pollution of the seas. Indeed it has been estimated that approximately two million tons of oil enters the oceans annually.

V.3 Air Pollution

Atmospheric pollution is mainly the result of combustion of fossil fuel so that the main sources are the built-up areas. The UK climate has required fires in winter and the problem of pollution was recognized centuries ago in Edinburgh and London. The high concentration of pollutants in the cities was largely due to the back-to-back housing, narrow streets and an absence of open spaces which characterized the early growth of industrial cities. While industry was controlled to some extent from 1863 onwards the emission of household smoke, which constitutes some 85 per cent of total smoke emitted, remained unabated until the *Clean Air Acts* (Publ. Gen. Acts 1956, 1968). Sulphates and carbon monoxide are added to the atmosphere from the sea and the bacterial decomposition of organic debris adds ammonia and hydrogen to the atmosphere. Combustion can occur naturally as forest fires, whilst soil erosion from farmland in eastern England during dry springs adds dust to the air. There is no question of eliminating these natural pollutants but rather of finding the acceptable level; simple models have been devised to reduce ground level pollution to acceptable levels (MHLG 1967). There is still a need for some guidelines on air quality (R. Comm. Pollution 1976A). With exotic pollutants concentrations must not be allowed to exceed the toxic levels, at threshold limits of seven to eight hours a day. However, less is known about the effects on plants and it is likely that vigour may be adversely affected at lower concentrations than those actually causing damage, and the long-term effects on growth and yield of economic species should be the concern of future studies (Williams and Ricks 1975). It is difficult to measure pollution at low concentrations and therefore most of the evidence is of a crude nature and confined to the most obvious: sulphur, carbon dioxide, carbon monoxide, nitric oxide and particulate matter. The latter includes both larger particles of dust and grit with diameters exceeding 10 μm, which quickly settles, and the finer particles which may remain in suspension forming mist clouds and haze and thus obstructing radiation. The problems of measurement were reviewed by Ball (1971) who suggested the use of laser and low temperature infra-red spectroscopy for future work.

The effect of air pollution on *climate* is measurable. Dust in suspension obstructs solar radiation. Average monthly hours of bright sunshine in the winter months in C London (Kingsway) between 1958 and 1967 showed a 50 per cent increase over the thirty-year normal (Lawrence 1971) when little or no change was recorded in the suburbs. This increase took place during a period when global solar radiation levels were generally low. This trend has continued with increasing smoke control; 93 per cent of the area of London is now smoke-controlled. Maximum mean daily concentrations in C London, which exceeded 6,000 μg per m^3 (microgrammes per cubic metre) for smoke and 3,500 μg per m^3 sulphur dioxide in 1952 were reduced to 200 μg per m^3 for smoke and 1,200 μg per m^3 for sulphur dioxide in 1972 (DoE 1974B). The climatic effects were considerable, visibility increasing three times and December sunshine was increased by 70 per cent (GLC 1974). Because of its well-known 'greenhouse' effect of permitting incoming short-wave radiation while obstructing outgoing long-wave radiation, carbon dioxide influences temperature. This is more important on a global scale than within the UK, where the local effects of carbon dioxide concentration are probably counteracted by the reduced insolation caused by smoke and dust. For this reason neither temperature nor radiation change can be reliable indicators. However the global effects of carbon dioxide and damage to the protective ozone layer by fluro-carbons must be the concern of central government and could affect policies of controlling authorities in the UK.

Effects on *life forms* have been explored as possible indicators and the long-term effects on growth and yield of economic species is a matter of priority. The value of indicators depends on whether the effects are known and can be related to other species of resource value. While lichens can be correlated with sulphur dioxide concentrations it is not possible to extrapolate the effects on crops. (Edwards *et al* 1975). Any realistic emission controls must consider not only individual pollutants but interaction between them for in mixtures the dominant element may differ between species (Williams and Ricks 1975). Research on the damage to lichens by pollution from aluminium smelting and the search for reliable biological indicators of atmospheric pollutants is continuing (NERC 1976). Sulphur dioxide concentrations in Tyneside inhibit the epiphytic flora of ash trees (Gilbert 1971). Fallout on hillsides near Port Talbot is thought to be the reason for the local lichen desert and is considered a contributory factor in the poor growth of sitka spruce in the nearby Margam forest (Jones 1972, 154). The sensitivity of lichens to sulphur dioxide has also been used to map zones of air pollution levels (Hawkesworth 1971). Since they are based on frequency of species each locality must have a different scale; however, they provide a rapid qualitative assessment.

The National Air Pollution Survey began in 1961 and there are now over 1,200 sites where sulphur dioxide levels are recorded and smoke, dust and grit are measured either by filtering of air or rain water. This survey allows estimates of pollution within 5 per cent accuracy on a national scale and within 10 per cent on a regional scale. In 1975 twenty of these sites began sampling airborne sulphate particles and at another group of twenty sites a number of elements including heavy metals, oxides of nitrogen, oxidants and hydrocarbons are being sampled. Sulphur dioxide is produced mainly by the burning of coal. When this was the dominant fuel in the UK sulphur dioxide was a reliable guide to all gaseous pollution, but today there are other sources, such as high temperature furnaces, road traffic exhaust and jet exhaust at airports, all of which are increasing. Pollution at airports is difficult to assess, because of the inadequacy of measuring techniques, but it is assumed to be comparable to that of an industrial estate. In winter Heathrow receives as **much** pollution from W London as it generates and in summer the difference between the airport and its surrounds is slight (Robinson 1971). Nevertheless it is considered important to monitor nitrogen oxides and hydrocarbons at airports. Road traffic is a more serious problem. Average monthly measurements of carbon monoxide concentrations in busy streets in England and Wales show that for Manchester and Glasgow a total of sixty hours had more than 10 parts per million (ppm) but levels over 50 ppm averaged less than one minute in a monthly period, except for Cardiff with a total of ten minutes at this level (Reed and Trott 1971). Concentration of 50 ppm is considered the threshold for continuous exposure for eight hours day after day. Industrial furnaces contribute nitric oxide to the atmosphere, though as much as 50 per cent of the total concentration may be due to traffic. Nitric oxide has shown concentrations as high as 29.5 μg per m^3 at Islington (Min. of Technology 1965), but it changes chemically and can be washed from the air by rain. The mean concentration of lead estimated from UK emissions is 0.55 μg per m^3 which is small compared with 71 μg per m^3 mean concentration of smoke in urban areas. However high concentrations of lead are highly localized around smelters and traffic thoroughfares. Lead, largely from petrol exhaust, showed a mean concentration of 6.3 μg per m^3 in Fleet Street for the year 1971. Although these concentrations appear small, lead can accumulate in the body and continuous exposure over long periods could be harmful. Only a few yards from the busy thoroughfares these concentrations fall rapidly and become negligible at 45 m. Measurable levels of photochemically-produced ozone occurred in S England in July 1971 during anticyclonic conditions and at the same time oxidized sulphur dioxide in the form of sulphuric acid and sulphates were much higher than during windy or cloudy weather (Atkins, Cox and Eggleton 1972). This was supported by findings in London in 1972 and it is now possible to predict the weather conditions producing photochemical reactions. Photochemical pollution is not only an urban phenomena as it can be transported up to 1,000 km and on occasions emissions from Europe can contribute to photochemical pollution in the UK (Cox 1975). However, because of the topography and climate in the UK the serious photochemically-produced fogs in Los Angeles are not likely to occur. The regional distribution of smoke and sulphur di-

The regional distribution of smoke and sulphur dioxide in 1973—4 shown in table 3.8, shows higher concentrations of smoke in the north of England, about 70 μg per m^3 and much less in the south where the lowest was 34 μg per m^3 in the SW. However, sulphur dioxide concentration in the SE is comparable to the NW and North. The table reflects the balance between the industrial built-up areas, which are the major sources of pollution, and the open country and at the same time the degree of pollution control that has been achieved in the urban areas.

Control is vital because of damage by air pollution to health, living organisms and man-made structures. Control at the point of emissions is in the hands of the Alkali Inspectorate (Industrial Pollution Inspectorate, Scotland) and local authorities. This control is most effective for grit and dust. Monitoring of pollutants in the atmosphere is done by sampling, the density of the network depending on whether the control is to be for local or national purposes or to measure spread from a source. While complete control of emissions is the most effective it is not realistic and a balance must be made between the cost of control and the benefits it brings. The National Survey has shown the progress of control in the former 'black areas' of cities many of which are now cleaner than towns which were considered less polluted and therefore not needing urgent control. Planning authorities can prevent

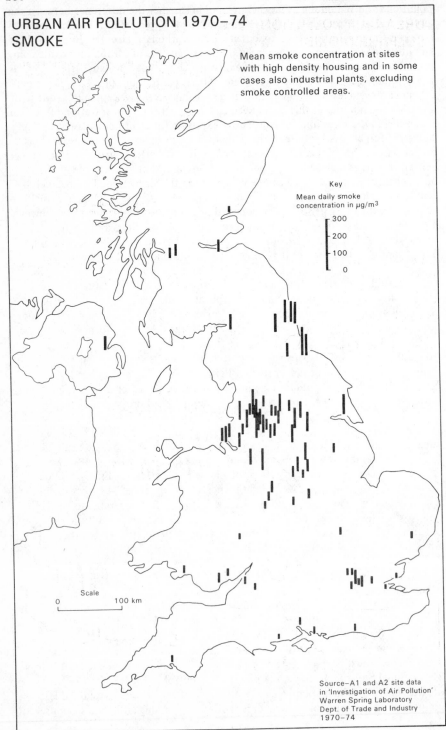

URBAN AIR POLLUTION 1970–74
SMOKE

Mean smoke concentration at sites
with high density housing and in some
cases also industrial plants, excluding
smoke controlled areas.

Key

Mean daily smoke
concentration in µg/m^3

300
200
100
0

Scale
0   100 km

Source–A1 and A2 site data
in 'Investigation of Air Pollution'
Warren Spring Laboratory
Dept. of Trade and Industry
1970–74

Figure 3.8   Urban air pollution, UK, 1970–4, smoke

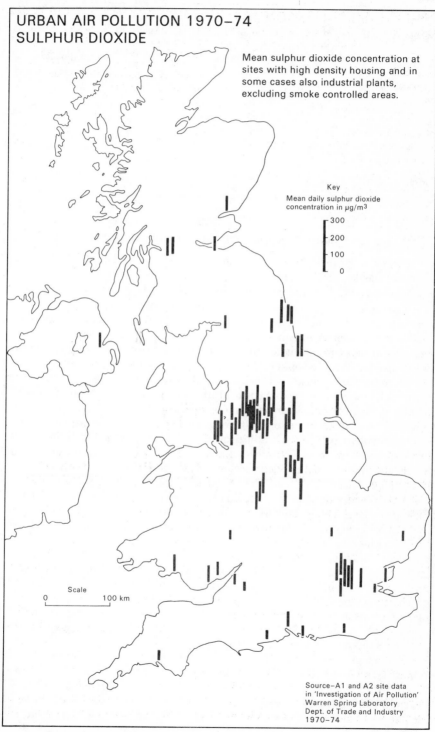

URBAN AIR POLLUTION 1970–74
SULPHUR DIOXIDE

Mean sulphur dioxide concentration at sites with high density housing and in some cases also industrial plants, excluding smoke controlled areas.

Key
Mean daily sulphur dioxide concentration in µg/m³

300
200
100
0

Scale
0   100 km

Source–A1 and A2 site data in 'Investigation of Air Pollution' Warren Spring Laboratory Dept. of Trade and Industry 1970–74

Figure 3.9   Urban air pollution, UK, 1970–4, sulphur dioxide

TABLE 3.8

Average Concentrations of Smoke and Sulphur Dioxide, UK Regions, 1973–74

Region	Smoke $\mu g/m^3$	Sulphur dioxide $\mu g/m^3$
North West	65	118
North	73	82
Yorks. and Humberside	59	106
Scotland	58	78
N Ireland	58	69
E Midlands	62	86
W Midlands	50	87
E Anglia	32	77
Greater London	32	64
South East	30	116
Wales	29	52
South West	34	64

Source: Royal Commission on Environmental Pollution: Fourth Report 1974

future problems by the siting of houses and industry but would need guidelines on air quality standards and a knowledge of present patterns of air pollution in developing areas (R. Comm. Pollution 1976A).

The concentrations of *smoke* and *sulphur dioxide* depend very much on the degree of dispersion, which varies with wind and the vertical temperature gradient. Temperature inversions prevent vertical mixing and lead to the heaviest concentrations. Certain areas may be more prone to inversion because of their topography, for example the valleys on either side of the Pennines (Garnett 1971). Siting of new factories in such areas ought to be avoided, for landscaping can only hope to control shallow radiation fogs by encouraging cold air drainage. Buffer zones around major polluting industries would improve pollution in residential areas but create economic problems as it would sterilize some high-value land and increase the distance to work (R. Comm. Pollution 1976A). It is difficult to devise generalized models since each pollution source may be affected in a different way by architecture, topography and atmospheric dispersal, but mathematical models which can predict the effects of potential industrial development could be valuable planning tools. Sophisticated models allowing for these variables could only be applied if a much clearer picture of micro and local meteorology becomes possible. The building of high stacks (MHLG 1967) can control ground level concentration even from large installations to an upper limit of 460 μg per m^3. Ground-level concentrations are inversely proportional to wind speed and the square of the effective height of emission. Low chimneys below 91 m have effluents of low buoyancy, while the high stacks which may be over 244 m in height send plumes rising to 550 m, though even this may not be high enough to penetrate high stratus cloud cover. High stacks relieve the pollution of the immediate surrounds but transport the effluent far beyond the region. Although UK emissions have been held responsible for increasing soil acidity in upland Sweden it has been argued that they have not the capacity to carry the necessary amount of sulphur and there is no evidence of the same effect in our own uplands. Transfers within the UK have been proved and recent research has shown that more sulphur dioxide may be transported away from the UK than is supposed (Garland 1975). Concentrations of sulphur dioxide on the east coast of UK suggests that easterly winds can bring pollutants from Europe (Barnes 1975). The pollution in country around Leicester can be attributed to more distant urban areas, while in Yorkshire downwind drifting has been shown to carry 50 to 60 km from the source (Gooriah 1968). Smoke has been transported 40 km from S Wales and 180 km from the W Midlands (Barnes 1975). Light winds favour drifting for the turbulence and mixing associated with strong winds leads to dispersal. There is a limit to the distance that pollutants can be carried in high concentrations, and coastal sites, for example in Norfolk, record low annual figures. Few records exist for open country and they are usually at sites where a pollution source exists or is suspected. The sites listed in table 3.9 all had some sources of pollution. Few areas of UK are completely free from smoke emissions but areas free from sulphur dioxide emissions have concentrations below 10 μg per m^3 (Barnes 1975) though a mean concentration for rural areas is probably about 40 μg per m^3 (Garland 1975). Scottish sites remote from industrial centres and Western coasts show low levels but country sites near urban conurbations can receive considerable smoke concentrations, due to drifting which has been known to raise daily values to 200 μg per m^3 at open sites 20 km east of industrial S Yorkshire. Lytham St Annes on the coast of S Lancashire had twelve days in the winter of 1962–3 with concentrations exceeding 500 μg per m^3 (table 3.9).

TABLE 3.9

Atmospheric Pollution at Selected Sites in Open Country*, 1971–4

| | Smoke concentrations in μg/m^3 per day | | | | Mean | Highest daily record |
	1971	1972	1973	1974	1971–4	1971–4
Lerwick, Shetland	1	4	3	1	2	39
Pembroke	4	NR	7	7	6	30
Stornoway, Lewis	3	4	4	2	3	58
Amroth, Pembrokeshire	3	NR	6	6	5	33
Eskdalemuir	6	8	6	5	5	40
Camborne, Cornwall	6	9	8	NR	8	122
Didcot, Berks	NR	15	14	13	14	87
Lytham St Annes	40	30	24	19	28	639
Norton, Runcorn	30	NR	28	19	26	286
Sheffield	28	26	21	16	23	286

* These sites are not entirely without sources of pollution. Only Didcot has no sources within ¼ mile.
NR = No record

Source: Warren Spring Laboratory (1971–4)

The effect of smoke control under the *Clean Air Act* (Publ. Gen. Act 1956) is difficult to assess because there has been a change in fuel since its inception, but a general reduction in pollution has occurred and the most dramatic fall has been in urban areas. By 1974 72 per cent of premises in the 'black areas' (MoF 1953) were controlled; after 1974 local authorities became responsible for future control. While in 1952 43 per cent smoke came from domestic sources industry has since been so successfully controlled that despite a reduction of 80 per cent from domestic sources in 1974 domestic sources contributed as much as 90 per cent of the total smoke emissions (R. Comm. Pollution 1976A).

Smoke control areas have generally lowered pollution levels in all urban areas. One site in Salford showed a fall of 50 per cent daily concentration of smoke and

30 per cent SO$_2$ between 1971 and 1972, due to effective control of neighbouring urban areas. Moreover, days exceeding 500 μg/m^3 smoke concentrations fell from fifty-three in 1971 to twenty-two in 1972. When this site became controlled itself after 1972 continued improvement took place though the changes were less dramatic particularly with regard to the maximum daily concentrations (table 3.10). The

TABLE 3.10

Changes in Atmospheric Pollution, Salford 1970–4

	Smoke (μg/m^3) mean winter	max. daily	Sulphur dioxide (μg/m^3) mean winter	max. daily
1970–1	414	1,779	261	898
1971–2	277	872	250	623
1972–3	241	712	203	659
1973–4	142	645	180	807

Source: Warren Spring Lab. (1971–4)

change in sulphur dioxide was much lower than that of smoke, and in fact since control in the area in 1972 maximum daily concentrations of sulphur dioxide have increased. This emphasizes that the measures designed to control smoke do not affect sulphur dioxide, which depends on the sulphur content of fuels, though recently smokeless fuels with a high sulphur content have been rejected. Nevertheless ground level sulphur dioxide has been reduced by 45 per cent from 1966 to 1976 in urban areas, but it was accompanied by a rise in SO$_2$ in rural areas (R. Comm. Pollution 1976A).

Table 3.11 shows all available sites in dense residential areas which became controlled after 1971–2. Smoke concentration fell by an average of 38 per cent, though

TABLE 3.11

Change in Mean Daily Concentrations of Smoke and Sulphur Dioxide, after Smoke Control, Selected UK Sites, 1971–4

	1971–2	Smoke (μg/m^3) Mean 1972–74 (after control)	% change	Sulphur dioxide (μg/m^3) 1971–2	Mean 1972–4	% change
Colne	58	29	−50	122	93	−24
Droylsden	68	60	−11	134	130	−3
Leeds	76	46	−39	137	118	−14
Middlesbrough	153	64	−58	112	75	−33
Oldham	73	52	−29	114	114	0
Salford	225	148	−34	212	151	−29
Southampton	35	21	−40	87	85	−2
Tynemouth	116	76	−34	98	74	−24
Wandsworth	59	35	−41	158	120	−24

Source: Warren Spring Lab. (1971–4)

without Droylsden, which is surrounded by a region of lower industrial and urban density, the average fall was 42 per cent. On the other hand, SO$_2$ showed only an average 17 per cent fall.

The effect can also be seen at a national scale in table 3.12 which shows a fall in the mean concentrations of smoke and sulphur dioxide at all available sites with

TABLE 3.12

Atmospheric Pollution of High Density Residential Areas With Extensive Built-up Areas (Excluding Sites within Smoke Control Areas), 1963–74

	Smoke concentrations μg/m³			Sulphur dioxide concentrations μg/m³		
	Mean	Std. dev.	No. of sites	Mean	Std. dev.	No. of sites
1963	210	87	72	207	89	72
1971	90	47	63	118	39	63
1972	71	34	77	112	36	77
1973	65	31	63	102	33	63
1974	55	25	44	93	32	44

Source: Calculated from site data, Warren Spring Lab. 1963–74

high density housing in extensive built-up areas. When sites came under smoke control they were excluded from the calculation. New sites were included as recording commenced. From 1963 to 1974 a distinct downward trend in smoke correlates with the increase in smoke control orders ($r = -0.96$). In 1969 there were approximately 81,341 ha under smoke control which by May 1975 had reached 31,282 ha. Smoke control of 40,000 ha has had the effect of reducing the mean daily urban pollution levels by 8.6 μg/m³ for smoke and 6.6 μg/m³ sulphur dioxide. London is currently about 93 per cent smoke-controlled which explains the low level of pollution in the unrestricted sites shown in fig. 3.8. Rapid advances are being made in areas of heavy industry. For example, Newcastle upon Tyne has controlled 63 per cent of the urban area and had hoped to achieve 100 per cent control before 1980, if finance permits.

Attempts have been made to remove sulphur dioxide from emissions but the processes developed are viable only for large installations like Battersea power station. Even here the expenditure would not relieve SE England of pollution unless similar measures were taken in neighbouring European countries. Much more success has been achieved with smoke control. Fuels have been developed to reduce smoke and their improved efficiency partly compensates for the higher cost; furthermore, grit- and dust-arresting devices are in operation. There are no technical problems in removing pollutants such as oxides of nitrogen and sulphur but the process frequently has noxious effluent and the cost is often prohibitive. Washing of gases lowers their temperature, which reduces their buoyancy. High concentrations of washed gas can be as undesirable as the untreated smoke. Thus despite the cost of approximately £1 million per 200 m of chimney, high stacks are still a better way of reducing ground level pollution.

Monitoring for international control While the policy of using high chimneys to disperse pollution has reduced ground level concentration in the UK some is spread beyond the country and this contribution to European and global environmental problems is of interest to international agencies. Six special remote sites in UK, together with a site in W Ireland and one on the east coast of England, monitor the movement of pollutants across the UK, and assess the effects on background pollution in Europe. These stations are also monitoring acidity of rain and total sulphur content. The need for coordination of effort in the UK to provide a framework for control at the national and international level has prompted the suggestion of the creation of an Air Management Group (DoE 1974B).

Already some directives have come from Europe, such as standards of bio-degradability of detergents and noise and pollution from motor vehicles.

V.4 Pollution of the Land Surface

The effects of agriculture on the land have been discussed earlier. Pesticides, herbicides and fertilizers form an important part, though less than in N America, of the total pollution of the land surface. In the UK, industrial and urban activity has created more tangible effects on the landscape. The effects of early lead and fluorspar workings have persisted in the carboniferous limestone areas. When soil is polluted from the air or by surface water it can be controlled by statutory regulations, but only recently, in 1972, has any attempt been made to check the indiscriminate dumping of toxic materials. Dumping can have an immediate danger to individuals or can represent a more widespread hazard by contaminating streams or ground water. Pollution by nuclear waste from industry is much smaller than fallout from nuclear explosions, but nevertheless important since the danger period before the complete decay may be thousands of years. For these reasons it is not surprising that the permissible levels for emissions into the Irish Sea are low, although there is some uncertainty over standards (R. Comm. Pollution 1976B). However, the disposal of the residue, which is 99.9 per cent of the total waste produced and is highly radioactive, presents a major pollution problem. This residue is stored in steel tanks, encased in 2.4 m walls of concrete, with stringent safety precautions, although this has not prevented leakages of radioactive material. Radiation is more carefully monitored than any other pollutant and in 1970–1, 28 per cent of all research expenditure was on problems of radioactivity. Increase in the development of nuclear power, which by the official strategy may mean doubling the nuclear contribution by 1980, and increasing it twenty-fold by the year 2000, greatly exacerbates the problem of radioactive waste disposal and thus is controversial (R. Comm. Pollution 1976B). Pollution by other forms of industrial waste creates problems due more to volume than to toxicity. About 50 per cent of the volume of raw material used by industry is waste and its disposal has been treated with much more apathy than if it were more highly toxic. The increase in the amount of waste will continue and, with highly sophisticated industrial techniques, more of it will be toxic. The problem is to find suitable ways of disposing of this increasing volume of urban and industrial waste. One alternative, most frequently used up to the present, is the land surface; another is the sea, with effects described in the next section.

In a recent estimate (DoE 1971) of the annual 20 million tons of waste disposed of by local authorities 72 per cent was domestic and trade refuse. However, many industrial concerns dispose of waste in other ways and no comprehensive estimate of industrial waste is possible. It is thought that about 11 million tons of toxic waste, including 4 million tons of solids, are produced annually by industry (MHLG, SDD 1970), but over 80 per cent of this toxic material is relatively inert. Local authorities dispose of 90 per cent of the refuse by direct tipping on the land, 71 per cent of this being controlled, usually because of a need for material for reclamation (fig. 3.10). Large areas have been reclaimed in this way for port facilities, for example at Southend, Liverpool and Portsmouth. At Belfast mudflats have been re-

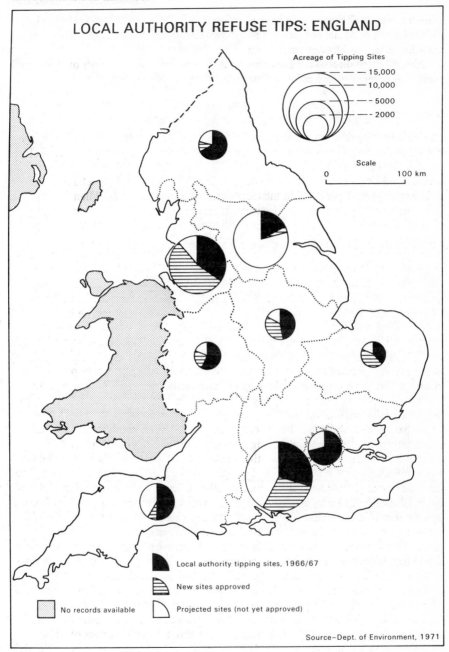

Figure 3.10   Local authority refuse tips, England, 1966—7

claimed for the expansion of aircraft works and runways. Tipping on the land requires planning permission and the *Coast Protection Act* (Publ. Gen.
Act 1949) controls tipping below the high water mark, though the harbour schemes already
completed or in progress have not caused any serious pollution of tidal waters. Tipping is cheaper than the other alternatives, pulverization, incineration or composting. Pulverization has grown in importance since 1960, but in 1973 handled only
3.7 per cent of the refuse and the existing plants can serve only small populations
of less than 50,000. Composting is not likely to be encouraged by demand from
agriculture, largely because of its low nutrient content and the possibility of toxic
elements. Its potential use is probably limited to improving marginal land.

Refuse is increasing in weight annually, though the annual increase rate of 0.7
per cent per person in the ten years 1955—65 has since decreased, largely due to the
rapid reduction in consumption of solid fuel. Since 1957 dust and cinder content
has fallen by two-thirds. Paper, plastics, packaging and non-returnable bottles have
increased rapidly and are likely to increase five times in the next ten years, so that
the volume of refuse is increasing, though it is of lower density than in the past.

It has been estimated that less than one-fifth of the excavations made by mineral
extractors annually could accommodate all the house refuse produced. Opencast
mineral workings are increasing at about 2,023 ha per annum, half of this by sand
and gravel excavators. Land made derelict by industry could be improved using
refuse as infill and reclamation of tidal mudflats is another possibility. Tipping can
create derelict land unless treated. Since 1950 8,000 ha have been reclaimed for
other uses but 2,900 ha still remain derelict and by the end of the century industry
will create a further 48,564 ha of derelict land, if annual reclamation does not increase
(Barr 1969, 200). Currently 810 ha of land is reclaimed annually, and this includes
industrial land.

One of the problems of choosing sites is the pollution hazard to ground water
resources and studies of land fill sites are in progress. Compacted refuse covered
with soil can absorb rainfall and give a low rate of percolation. For the first year
percolating water is heavily polluted but it rapidly declines to reach low levels within three years. Sand or gravel can act as a natural filter protecting ground water, but
currently research is being carried out on the movement of pollutants in the lower
greensand and plateau gravels (NERC 1976). Bacteria will die off within a few feet
of the surface, but chlorides and nitrates will persist in solution. Where the underlying rock is fissured, percolation can be very rapid, but sealing with puddled clay
can protect ground water if drains are led to filter beds or a sewer. Alternatives are
to line the base of the tip with 60—90 mm of aerated gravel or to prevent any percolation by sealing the surface but this causes rapid surface run-off. Tipping directly
into water is more of a hazard than dry tipping since de-oxygenation can occur
rapidly, allowing bacteria to produce hydrogen sulphide. Wet gravel pits require the
added expense of chlorination in hot weather; clay pits on the other hand can be
pumped dry before tipping.

Streams emanating from tips can become de-oxygenated or, more commonly,
fouled by sewage fungus. River Authorities have been responsible for all discharges
but have no powers to control dumping on the land surface. However, because of
the risks to water pollution, they have invariably been consulted.

Tipping is likely to continue as the most common method of waste disposal,
accounting for 86 per cent in 1973, but in the future, if space becomes scarce, other
methods may be developed, e.g. pyrolysis where high temperatures are used to

reduce all waste, including plastics to carbon, oil, tar and gas. The water content is reduced to one-tenth in this process. Scrap motor cars increase in numbers annually. In 1969, 13 million cars were in use and 1 million became obsolete. After compression and separation of non-ferrous material some can be sold as scrap for steel mills. A few large hammer mills do the separation of ferrous metal magnetically. To use pulverizers economically they must be working continuously, which is only possible in large conurbations. 400,000 vehicles are processed annually at a London plant, 200,000 vehicles at one in Hertfordshire and the same number at a plant in Lancashire. If used to capacity these three could convert 80 per cent of all waste vehicles into separated steel scrap, but the problem is the transporting of vehicles from other areas. Rubber tyres are discarded at the rate of 12 million per annum and, except for Merseyside which has a factory for reclaiming rubber, there is no easy method of disposal. Many London authorities, for example, will not accept them.

A recent survey of more than 1,000 firms showed that about 1.8 per cent of all industrial solid and semi-solid waste is toxic. Only 0.8 per cent is dealt with by local authorities, the rest being disposed of by individual contractors. About 75 per cent of this toxic waste is dumped on surface tips, where it creates a serious hazard to ground water. The effect of the toxic material may be to destroy normal biological activity on the surface and if it is soluble no filtering is possible in its percolation through permeable strata. More often the tips are on impermeable strata and so the percolate drains to surface streams. Guidelines on disposal of hazardous waste are being prepared for DoE. There are more cases of river pollution than ground-water pollution. Ground water under a gravel pit used for chemical waste had an oxygen demand of 4,000 mg/l and the chemicals inhibited biological oxidation. Tips have been known to pollute ground water for eighty years after all tipping ceased. In 1963 an industrial tip polluted surface water in a neighbouring farm and caused animals to die. These are extreme cases but it is common to have some phenol contamination in water supplies. Large ground-water reserves are less vulnerable because of dilution, and because of their size the authority can exercise more control over surface tipping. The greatest hazard comes from unauthorized tipping which is difficult to solve as tighter restrictions can lead to greater dangers from illegal jettisoning of material. If land sites are to be used for toxic waste, it can be kept dry, compacted and the surface sealed to prevent all percolation; another alternative is dumping at sea. Unused mines are only satisfactory if they are deep and not linked to exploitable aquifers. A large mine in the Midlands is being used in this way but attempts to use old mines elsewhere have been opposed.

V.5 Water Pollution

Much of the pollution of the land and air reaches surface streams and therefore the land use of the catchment has an important effect on the state of the river. Runoff carries fertilizer and pesticides from agricultural land and industry discharges effluents which demand oxygen and include chlorine which causes high salinity in estuaries (Volker 1974). Some water pollutants are nutrients, such as nitrates and phosphates, which cause enrichment or eutrophication and the excessive growth of fresh-water plants. These can block dams, whilst some algae produce toxic products and on dying oxygen is removed from the water. This has the same effect as excessive organic wastes from sewage which led to a lifeless Thames in the mid-nineteenth century. In England and Wales only 5 to 9 per cent of the nitrogen in rivers comes from agriculture. However, high nitrate levels due to breakdown of organic matter during mild winters and its reduced dilution in periods of low rainfall has caused concern for infant health (R. Comm. Pollution 1974). Despite the fact that consumption of nitrogenous fertilizers has doubled in ten years the level in UK rivers has not increased. By 1968–9 organochlorate pesticides replaced DDT but despite the persistence of organochlorides less than 0.05 mg/l occurred in UK rivers in 1966, well below the 1 mg/l threshold for trout. Between 1953 and 1966 the phosphate concentration doubled but this was due to sewage and effluent rather than to fertilizers. Damage to fish population may not be judged by concentrations below a lethal threshold, for lower levels may destroy food and changes in water softness could increase the toxicity of some pollutants. Salmon and trout are the most sensitive to pollution and for this reason often used to indicate levels of toxicity.

Pollution is measured in terms of biochemical oxygen demand (BOD). The *Royal Commission on Sewage Disposal* (1912) produced the standard 30 mg/l suspended solids and 20 mg/l BOD which are still accepted. However, these levels required dilution by 8 parts of water to 1 of effluent which may not be possible during dry periods in UK rivers. In SE England dilution in summer is often only 2 to 1 so that sewage outfalls have to be far enough apart to allow natural cleansing. Lower dilutions require stricter standards for sewage effluent than those of the Royal Commission.

The Irwell, Tame, Rother, Mersey, Don and Avon (Severn) have as much as half their dry season flow in the form of treated sewage effluent. Slight pollution is made harmless by dilution; increased pollution and decreased dilution can have the same effect.

In 1958, 73 per cent of rivers in England and Wales were unpolluted, that is with less than 3 mg/l BOD, but 6 per cent were grossly polluted with over 12 mg/l BOD and so de-oxygenated and without fish. From 1970 to 1972, 240 miles of heavily polluted rivers were improved so that by 1972, 77 per cent of the rivers in England and Wales were unpolluted and 3.7 per cent were grossly polluted (DoE 1974B). Improvements have been achieved only on short rivers, such as the Lea, while the rivers draining the main industrial regions, the Trent, Mersey, Ouse and its tributaries, the Tyne and Tees remain polluted. Cleaning of these rivers is possible, and a tributary of the Trent, the Derwent, once grossly polluted by the industrial effluents of Derby, is now clean enough for fish. The reorganization of 29 River Authorities and 1,400 other bodies involved in water supply and sewage treatment into 10 multi-purpose regional authorities simplifies water pollution control. Planned sewage improvements should lead to the upgrading of 45 per cent of the rivers totalling 2,800 miles and 20 per cent of the canals. The mileage of unpolluted rivers should increase to 81 per cent and grossly polluted rivers reduce to less than 1 per cent. While rivers can carry away waste and at the same time provide water for industry, it is doubtful if the standards as measured by BOD are satisfactory when the water is extracted for human consumption, for industrial effluents can contain toxic as well as oxygen-demanding elements. Further industrial development is limited by the availability of water and facilities for discharge. Effluent may be accepted by a local authority for sewage treatment if it is within the authority's capacity, or the industry may discharge into rivers with the consent of the River Authority. Industries pay the local authority for treatment either directly or through rates, but some firms may treat effluent, which if sophisticated may require high capital and running costs. The CBI estimates that industries are spending 2 to 15 per cent of their total capital investment on treatment. The expenditure will rise further with demands for higher quality effluent from River Authorities wishing to abstract public supplies from the river, but could be a serious handicap to many industries competing with European countries where the quality of effluent is less carefully controlled.

Sewage is mainly water and therefore forms a significant part of the flow of many rivers. About 14,000 Ml are discharged into sewers, about one-half from industry and the other from domestic sources. The GLC sewage works discharges 2,500 Ml/d into the Thames and its successful treatment allows the extraction of about one-third of SE England's water needs from the river.

Many sewers built during the last century no longer have the capacity to deal with modern developments. In Coventry, for example, it has been necessary to reconstruct the main sewage system. The problem is aggravated at times of heavy rain since surface runoff can augment the sewers and cause overflow, polluting streams with untreated waste. Storm-water balancing tanks are used to rectify this. Oxygen-demanding water can be readily treated. Sewage works can remove as much as 95 per cent of the oxygen-demanding and sludge-forming constituents by settlement and biological processes. In the past, sewage farms did this by spreading, but the enormous demands that this would make on land today have led to the use of biological filters and a process of activated sludge which accelerates the anaerobic process. At present about four-fifths of the population of the UK is served by such biological plants. Ammonia is oxidized to nitrates, the effluent is clear and can be discharged without seriously affecting the river, and in some cases as at Luton, the effluent is below 10 mg/l solids and 10 mg/l BOD and the river Lea can supply London with water. These high standards of treatment must be maintained both by sewage works and industry since in the upper Lea their effluents form as much as 50 per cent of the normal daily flow. However, not all sewage works are so efficient for in 1964—5, 60 per cent had effluents with averages in excess of the Royal Commission standard, which was designed for disease prevention rather than public re-use. In 1970 54 per cent of the total volume of sewage effluents entering rivers came from only 36 per cent of sewage works, so that improvements in these could substantially reduce the general levels of river pollution. If effluents are to be improved more extensive treatment must be carried out. For example pathogens are not removed, but would be destroyed naturally by bacteria. Chlorination is undesirable because the effluent contains the toxic by-products of the chemical process and the necessary bacteria would be destroyed. Conventional biological treatment only removes 37 to 46 per cent of phosphates. These together with nitrates can lead to eutrophication and some UK rivers have shown this effect in years of high sunshine. It is not a problem likely to develop in running water and no large inland water bodies receive enough effluent for the effect to be felt. However, the Irish Sea receives effluent from Lancashire as well as from Dublin and it has been suggested that eutrophic conditions will spread outwards leading to a slow deterioration, similar to what is now happening in the Baltic (O'Sullivan 1971). While 42 per cent of the nitrogen reaching the sea has its origin in agricultural land, as much as 80 per cent of the phosphates comes from domestic and industrial effluents, including 30 to 50 per cent from detergents. The appearance of synthetic detergents on the market in 1949 created a major treatment problem which led to their replacement by biologically degradable constituents in the 1960s. Organochlorides in UK rivers have reached levels in excess of concentrations reported from the USA. Most of these come from industry where they are used in mothproofing, etc. Although pesticides have generally low levels in UK water the danger is through accumulation in algae.

The **disposal of sludge** creates a greater problem than the liquid discharged. After a process of anaerobic digestion which largely destroys pathogens about one-fifth of the sludge is dumped in the sea beyond the 4.8 km limit. Manchester and London use this method, and London has a special fleet of ships. It has the advantage of economy but the effects on the sea are not certain, although it has been suggested that sludge disposal in Liverpool Bay even if increased six times would not affect marine life and would not be hazardous to health (DoE 1972A). Studies in the Firth of Clyde indicate that sludge dumping has only a local effect on 20 km^2 of the seabed (Thornton 1975). The dilution and purification processes in the sea may not be very effective in disposing of organic material when it is dumped in deep water. Below 1,000 m microbial activity is greatly reduced and dilution may put the pollutant beyond microbial attack. Two-fifths of the treated sludge is used as fertilizer, but it will not replace balanced artificial fertilizer as the total output of sludge could only supply 4.5 per cent of the nitrogen and phosphate required and it is very deficient in potash. The presence of toxic metals limits its use and in any case it can only be economically distributed within a 16 km radius of sewage works. It has been assumed that tidal estuaries have unlimited capacity to receive pollution and the practice of discharging untreated sewage and industrial effluent has continued almost unabated. The large volume of water in estuaries dilutes the effluent, and mixing by tidal movements promotes natural purification, but recently the levels of pollution have reached heights which threaten shell fisheries. Moreover tidal scour may not immediately dispose of wastes to the sea so that some potentially dangerous substances like mercury can accumulate in muds (R. Comm. Pollution 1973). It has been suggested that regional geochemical maps based on stream sediment analysis and knowledge of industrial waste disposal can be used to assess the metal status of estuaries (Thornton 1975). In 1972 only 49 per cent of all tidal estuaries were considered clean and 13 per cent were grossly polluted. Many have become the focus of industry and dense urban concentrations. The Tyne, for example, receives 168 Ml/d of sewage and 45 Ml/d of trade waste from its banks while the Severn receives waste from a population of over 1 million. At times of reduced flow the Ouse and Trent discharge water with 200 tonnes per day of effective oxygen demand which would use up oxygen from about 22,730 Ml of sea-water in the Humber. In these circumstances bacterial pollution extending far out to sea has been reported, as for example up to a distance of 8 km beyond the Tyne. The badly polluted estuaries are being cleaned up by sewage improvements costing: on Tyneside, £40 million; Teesside, £20 million; and for the GLC £100 million. In the case of the Tees domestic sewage is only a fraction of the total oxygen demand which is mainly from industry. In 1976 the two major industrial companies ICI and British Steel, had reduced their polluting discharges to one half of the 1971 amount (R. Comm. Pollution 1974). However, many estuaries like the Solent could become as heavily polluted if they continue to receive untreated effluents. New treatment works at Beckton on the Thames halved the oxygen demand between 1972 and 1975 but there is a limit to such improvements when the cost of abatement exceeds the cost of damage caused by the pollution.

The problem of discharge to the sea is not confined to estuaries, for many sewage authorities dispose of untreated sewage by discharge into the sea. A cooperative research report in 1967, however, came to the conclusion that the coastal waters of the UK showed little pollution and this was localized near outfalls from coastal industries (Woodhead 1971). Yet few existing discharge pipes extend far enough out to sea to prevent beach pollution, though with modern techniques it is now economically feasible to lay pipes 3 to 5 km out to sea. Bacterial contamination has its effect on marine life, especially shell fish, but industrial effluents have been known to kill off marine life around the outfall, the most toxic being organochlorate pesticides and polychlorinated biphenyls. Toxic materials in effluents discharged offshore come outside the scope of the *Clean Rivers (Estuaries and Tidal Waters) Act* (Publ. Gen. Act 1960) and can only be controlled through the powers of the Sea Fisheries Committee, which only apply to England and Wales.

Beyond the 4.8 km limit, there is no effective control over dumping at sea, though under the Oslo Convention the UK must record dumping in the NE Atlantic. Disposal of highly toxic materials at sea is usually in very deep water, exceeding 3,650 m beyond the continental shelf, where slow diffusion of pollutants from their containers is diluted so much that there is no danger of surface contamination. The total effect is difficult to measure, much of the research being directed towards the influence of heavy metals on ecosystems. More is known about the pollution of the Irish Sea because of the concern over effluents from the Windscale reactors, though it is said that present levels of nuclear waste reaching the sea are unlikely to have any observable effect on the natural environment. Natural runoff from mineral-rich areas like N Wales or Devon contributes to the presence of metals in coastal waters but high concentrations, for example 47.6 μg/l zinc in Liverpool Bay, which is ten times the level in the open sea, and the 4.2 μg/l cadmium level in the Bristol Channel, which is thirty to forty times that at sea (Abdullah et al 1972), can be attributed to industry. Also the North Sea has shown high cadmium levels offshore from industrial sites, such as NE England. However, these are all localized peaks and concentration falls away rapidly from the coast. The levels have not increased in the past ten years and in fact cadmium has decreased except for the local concentration off Barry in S Wales. However, the detrimental effects of heavy metal concentrations could become serious in the long-term if they accumulate in offshore sediments (Bryan 1971). Evidence of biological changes is difficult to interpret. In the 1930s nutrient salts and zooplankton declined in the English Channel seriously, reducing the regular winter herring fishing industry, but recovered again in 1965 probably due to climatic fluctuations which cause north and southward shifts of marine populations (Russell 1971). Marine biological surveillance by NERC has so far linked trends in plankton in the North Sea and the N Atlantic to climatic events. Pollution in near shore waters and estuaries seems to affect mussels but the variability between animals seems to be due to the inherent characteristics rather than pollution.

The waste disposal problems of **agriculture** have changed in character in recent years and become more serious with the growth in intensive animal farming. Since 1946 pigs have trebled and poultry doubled. Large units find it difficult to dispose of manure cheaply. Despite the obvious nutrient value for arable farming there are problems of transport and difficulties of application compared with artificial fertilizers. Access to fields is not always possible if soils are heavy and the high water content of slurries could lead to waterlogging if soil water is at or near field capacity. The bacteria present in slurry presents a health hazard especially if used to fertilize grass on dairy farms and manures from animals fed with chemicals or antibiotics could be harmful to plant growth. Poultry manure which has the highest concentration of NPK (nitrogen, phosphates, potash) of all farm animals has been dried for fertilizer as well as for animal feeding but this disposes of only a small proportion.

Some are treated by storage in ditches while oxidation takes place and then discharged to streams. Sewage works have not the capacity to deal with agricultural refuse.

Unlike radioactivity we have no clear idea of the safe level of **oil-pollution**. So far the effects have been limited to the destruction of some marine communities like shellfish and seabirds. Oil persists for fourteen months on beaches and because of some toxic and persistent constituents may enter food chains and have far-reaching effects. Since dilution of these toxins reduces landwards, the coast, which may include spawning grounds, is the most vulnerable. The Torrey Canyon disaster in 1967 was the most damaging incident in UK waters, but the immediate destruction of eggs and young fish in SW England by oil and oil removers has not had long-term effects and fishing recovered the following season. North Sea fisheries have shown increased landings over the past fifty years which suggests no detrimental effects of oil pollution but exploitation of the North Sea oil field adds a further hazard to marine life, though it is thought that even a major spill in the oilfields would not be a serious longterm threat to plankton.(R. Comm. Pollution 1974).

Thermal pollution of water can occur through the return of water from cooling systems, particularly in power stations and will increase as they reach peak capacity. The Trent has power stations generating 12,000 MW in a distance of 160 km (Hawes 1970). Temperatures of discharged water are often 10°C above river water temperature, but studies in the USA (Merriman 1970) suggest that this becomes undetectable 3 km from the outfall. Tower cooling at power stations also increases the oxygen content of the water. Studies of the effect of discharging sea-water heated 10°C above ambient temperature at 91,000 m^3 per hr have been made at Hunterston, Ayrshire. These suggest that the effect on marine life is to prolong the breeding season in the immediate vicinity of the effluent (Barnett 1971), but the overall effect in a temperate climate is very small.

Aircraft noise is localized, affecting about 2½ million residents and can be progressively reduced by lower noise limits. 8 million people are affected by unacceptable levels of traffic noise.

VI   CONSERVATION

VI.1   Nature Conservation

The conservation movement in N America was stimulated by the disastrous effects of reckless agricultural exploitation, whilst in the UK the need for conservation has become obvious due to the rapid expansion of urban and industrial life, which has depleted the natural landscapes and through its demands changed the rural agricultural scene. For this reason much of the conservation movement in the UK has been directed towards the preservation of natural habitats (Stamp 1969), but these measures may in many cases only artificially prolong the life of some rare species in danger of extinction. Although man-made, the common lands are open spaces and their preservation desirable on aesthetic grounds. True natural habitats are more difficult to preserve in the UK except in the large areas set aside by the Nature Conservancy in Scotland, the North of England and Wales. The Conservancy, established in 1949,and, since 1965, under the wing of the Natural Environment Research Council, is more concerned with management of these reserves by ecological methods than with isolating them. Most of these areas are in uplands, but none can be considered wilderness for the present condition is largely the result of man's activity (Pearsall 1950). The upland moors are largely the result of degeneration while natural fires occurred before man's occupation, their incidence being greatly increased with the use of the uplands for grazing. Burning does not seriously deplete nutrients by removing them in volatile form, but severe burning can destroy the seeds on the ground and thus slow down the rate of recolonization which is in any case a slow process on high exposed sites. Thus many areas of upland Scotland have suffered soil erosion, the degree depending on physical conditions and land-use both at the site and in other areas within the same catchment (McVean and Lockie 1969).

In the lowlands direct *changes in habitats* have been brought about by agricultural developments. Hedges have been removed in the cereal-growing area of SE and E England; in places as much as 70 per cent of the hedges have disappeared. While intensification of grassland has led to similar changes in the pastoral areas the amount of hedgerow removal is much less serious and in any case the small farms of the West, including N Ireland, have a high density of hedges. The removal of some hedges has the effect of reducing species of birds as well as insects, though if the remaining hedges are well cared for the loss could be greatly reduced. The relationship between the wild life and changes in crops is being investigated. Chemicals used on crops or as herbicides on field and road margins can have deleterious effects on wild flowers, with harmful effects to useful insects such as bees which are vital in the pollination of fruit trees. Pesticides used on or near waterways can destroy fish. Intensive rearing units for livestock have the special problem of disposal of waste, but until adequately monitored the degree of pollution can not be assessed. The drainage of the wetter lowlands and marshes, whilst creating new agricultural lands, can have a serious effect on water resources and wild life. Dredging and straightening of rivers greatly reduce the cover for birds and animals as well as fish, apart from the often permanent destruction of water plants. Forestry has also changed natural habitats on hillsides and peat bogs, while many old established woodlands have been replanted with conifers. Pure strands of spruce, when mature, have a very limited fauna except on the margins and along breaks. However, the problem is great only with the very large forest units, since small forests provide much more cover for wild life than the open moorlands and farmland they replaced. The policy of planting a variety of trees, including deciduous species, has improved the habitat of many forests though it is difficult to create variety without increasing the risks of windthrow. The planting of windbreaks for both forests and farmland is an opportunity to improve habitats.

VI.2 Land Use Conflicts

Scarcity of good quality agricultural land in the UK has aggravated land-use conflicts, for although there is a need for space to be used economally, the land is also a natural resource which will be depleted if not used properly. There is a need for effective control of future development, which has proved possible for nature reserves, but where there is economic exploitation principles of ecology are more difficult to apply. There is no overall authority responsible for resource conservation. The uplands can be used productively both for forests and for annual grazing. Planting of coniferous trees is acceptable on the acid soils but the production of acid *mor humus* by these trees can lead to degradation of soils by accelerated leaching, while deciduous trees, particularly birch, can bring nutrient salts to the surface. The application of fertilizers to make up deficiencies has had the effect of accelerating erosion of peats (Parker 1962), but the development of drainage and planting techniques for the wet moorlands has helped to check the accumulation of peat. Grazing is not without its problems for trampling can destroy soil structure and grazing by sheep has led to the spread of *nardus stricta* previously controlled by cattle. Undesirable effects of sheep grazing can only be remedied by management of the grassland using fertilizers and reseeding. Since returns for these investments depend on soil, areas of the Scottish Highlands, cultivated before the rapid shrinking of arable in the nineteenth century, are being reseeded. Immediate returns must not be the only consideration as soil improvement gives a longer term return on capital.

The uplands provide facilities for recreation which is almost impossible to evaluate in the same terms as productivity of pasture or forest (Dept. Education and Science 1966). Even more than agriculture, forest lends itself to multiple use. The setting-up of forest parks is an example of multiple use and it has been suggested that in future forests should be zoned according to the relative importance they have for timber production, pulp production, or sport and recreation (McVean and Lockie 1969). One of the aims of the new water authorities set up in 1974 is to make maximum use of water for recreation and amenity (DoE 1973B). The Nature Conservancy is attempting to solve the problem of multiple use in the uplands by constructing models to guide future decisions. However, classification of land needs to be further advanced to provide the necessary data.

VI.3 Industrial and Urban Derelict Land

In the lowlands the most serious problem has been the dereliction left by industry. The disposal of waste, destruction of the surface by extensive opencast working, slag heaps and tips have devastated an area estimated at about 101,000 ha. Despite reclamation this area is growing annually at about 1,400 ha (Barr 1969, 15), and urgently needs rehabilitation. Unlike the development of the uplands, dereliction which frequently occurs in areas of urban blight, should present a unique opportunity at least to improve the existing landscape. The question of optimum use need not arise. Although large acreages of conifers have been planted with the help of the Forestry Commission, the nature of the derelict land greatly reduces its potential for timber. Purely rural areas are also affected, such as china clay tips in Cornwall, and within national parks and areas of outstanding natural beauty there are 1,800 ha of derelict land (Oxenham 1966). Reclamation in the urban areas has been largely for housing development or industrial re-zoning and only a small proportion has been developed as open space or for recreation areas.

From a purely physical standpoint the problem of reclamation depends on the type of derelict land. Oxenham usefully differentiates between the mounds and spoilheaps, including those from collieries, quarries, a variety of industries and the opencast workings, and the pits and excavations created in the aftermath of mining. All of these have problems related to their size, shape and the composition of the waste. The number of disciplines involved in the *Swansea Valley Project* (Hilton 1967) demonstrates the extent of the physical problem of attempting to develop a large area devastated by the spoilheaps from heavy iron and steel industries. It has been suggested earlier that instead of creating new tips on fresh pieces of land the hollows left by the extractive industries could be simultaneously reclaimed. This would not always be possible, but at least some knowledge of the future of the area devastated by tipping could allow effective control over the nature of the tipping. This still does not solve the problem of the great area of existing derelict land. After infilling or levelling the composition may make landscaping difficult. For example in the Swansea project neither the zinc nor the copper waste tips had much vegetation, though steel slag could support growth and there is little knowledge of the degree of tolerance by plant species. Very often the problem is one of excessive drainage which could lead to wilting during rainless periods, rather than toxicity. Some minerals present in waste, while not preventing grass growth, could accumulate and become a hazard to grazing animals. The surface can be made acceptable by topsoiling, applying fertilizer or organic matter, and pioneer vegetation, most commonly grass, can be established. Many spoilheaps in the W Riding have been successfully planted in grass. Difficult sites have been planted using soil conditioners which create the necessary crumb structure and improve germination. Steep spoilheaps have been rapidly covered, using sets of creeping bent. Derelict land developed for playing fields requires much more careful landscaping and preparation than these efforts to reduce the ugliness of the landscape. Trees have been planted extensively in Co Durham and large schemes in Lancashire have been very successful. Rapid results, though expensive, are obtained by transplanting mature trees, using machinery. The total cost of reclaiming the 24,000 ha of what has been called 'hard core' derelict land has been estimated at £3½ million over a ten-year period (Christian 1966) and this still leaves the task of improving the landscape of a further 77,000 ha. In 1973 over 2,828 ha were reclaimed. The worst affected areas are to be restored by 1981, but areas coming under a wider definition of dereliction amounted to 60,600 ha (R. Comm. Pollution 1974).

REFERENCES

ABDULLAH, M I *et al* (1972) 'Heavy Metal Concentration in Coastal Waters', *Nature, 235*, 158—60

ABERCROMBIE, P (1945) *Greater London Plan 1944*, HMSO

AGRIC. ADVIS. UNIT (1970) *Modern Farming and the Soil*, HMSO

AGRIC. LAND SERV. (1966) 'Agricultural Land Classification', *Tech. Rep. 11*, MAFF, London

ATKINS, D H F, COX, R A and EGGLETON, A E J (1972) 'Photochemical Ozone and Sulphuric Acid Aerosol Formation in the Atmosphere over Southern England', *Nature, 235*, 372—6

BALL, D F (1971) 'The Identification and Measurement of Gaseous Pollutants', *Int. J. Environ. Stud., 14*, 267—74

BARNES, R A (1975) 'Transport of Smoke and Sulphur Dioxide into Rural Areas of England and Wales' in HEY, R D and DAVIES, T D (eds) *Science Technology and Environmental Management*, Farnborough, 165—79

BARNETT, P R O (1971) 'Some Changes in Intertidal Sand Communities due to Thermal Pollution', *Proc. R. Soc., Ser. B, 177*, 353—64

BARR, J (1969) *Derelict Britain*, London

BEAVER, S H (1968) 'Changes in Industrial Land Use 1930—67', *Inst. Br. Geogr., Spec. Publ. 1*, 89—100

BEST, R H (1968) 'Land Use and Resources', *Inst. Br. Geogr., Spec. Publ. 1*, 89–100
BIBBY, J S and MACKNEY, D (1969) 'Land Use Capability Classification', *Soil Surv. Tech. Monogr. 1*, Harpenden and Craigiebuckler
BIRSE, E L and DRY, F T (1970) *Assessment of Climatic Conditions in Scotland*, Macaulay Inst., Aberdeen
BIRSE, E L and ROBERTSON, L (1970) *Assessment of Climatic Conditions in Scotland, 2*, Soil Surv. Scotland, Craigiebuckler
BLEASDALE, J K A (1959) 'The Effects of Air Pollution on Plant Growth, in YAPP, W B (ed) *The Effects of Air Pollution on Living Material, Symp. Inst. Biol. 8*, London, 111–30
                              (1965) 'Improvement of Raingauge Networks', *Met. Mag., Lond., 94*, 137–42
BRYAN, G (1971) 'The Effects of Heavy Metals on Marine and Estuarine Organisms', *Proc. R. Soc., Ser. B, 177*, 389–410
CABORN, J M (1957) 'Shelter Belts and Microclimate', *Bull. For. Commn. Lond., 29*, 3–29
CENT. ADVIS. WATER COMM. (1959) *First Report of the Sub-committee on the Growing Demand for Water*, HMSO
CHRISTIAN, G (1966) *Tomorrow's Countryside: the Road to the Seventies*, London
CLARKE, G R (1971) *The Study of Soil in the Field*, Cambridge
CLAYDEN, B (1971) 'Soils of the Exeter District', *Mem. Soil Surv. Gt Br.*, Harpenden
COLEMAN, A (1961) 'The Second Land Use Survey', *Geogrl. J., 127*, 2, 168–80
COPPOCK, J T (1971) *An Agricultural Geography of Great Britain*, London
COX, R A (1975) 'Measurements of Atmospheric Ozone in Rural Locations' in HEY, R D and DAVIES, T D (eds) *Science Technology and Environmental Management*, Farnborough, 181–8
DAVIES, W E and TYLER, B F (1964) 'The Effect of Weather Conditions on the Growth of Lucerne' in TAYLOR, J A (ed) *Climatic Factors and Agric. Productivity, 6*, Aberystwyth, 12–18
DENMEAD, O T and SHAW, R H (1962) 'Availability of Soil Water to Plants as affected by Soil Moisture Content and Meteorological Conditions', *J. Agron., 45*, 385–90
DES (1966) *Forestry, Agriculture and the Multiple Use of Rural Land*, Rep. of the Land Use Study Group, HMSO
DEPT. EMPLOYMENT and PRODUCTIVITY (1968) *Dust and Fumes in Factory Atmospheres*, HMSO
DoE (1971) *Refuse Disposal*, HMSO
      (1972A) *Out of Sight, Out of Mind. Rep. of a Working Party on Sludge Disposal in Liverpool Bay*, HMSO, 2 vols.
      (1972B) *River Pollution Survey of England and Wales*, updated 1972, HMSO
      (1973A) *The New Water Industry: Management and Structure*, HMSO
      (1973B) *A Background to Water Reorganisation in England and Wales*, HMSO
      (1974A) *The Water Services: Economic and Financial Policies*, HMSO
      (1974B) *The Monitoring of the Environment in the UK*, Rep. by Cent. Unit Environ. Pollution, HMSO
DOUGLAS, I (1970) 'Sediment Yields from Forested and Agricultural Lands' in TAYLOR, J A (ed) *The Role of Water in Agric., 12, Aberystwyth*, 57–88
EDWARDS, K A (1970) 'Sources of Error in Agricultural Water Budgets', in TAYLOR, J A (ed) *The Role of Water in Agric., 12*, Aberystwyth, 11–23

FISHER, R A and HAGAN, R M (1965) 'Plant Water Relations, Irrigation Management and Crop Yield', *Exp. Agric., 1*, 161–77
FORESTRY COMMN. (1968) *Forest Research*, HMSO
        (1974) 'Fifty Years of Forestry Research', *Forestry Commn. Bull., 50*, HMSO
        (1975) *55th Ann. Rep. and Accounts of the Forestry Commn. for the Year Ended 31 March 1975*, HMSO
FRASER, A I (1972) 'The Effect of Climatic Factors on the Development of Plantation Structure' in TAYLOR, J A (ed) *Res. Pap. Forest Met.*, Aberyswyth, 59–74
GARLAND, J A (1975) 'Dry Deposition and the Atmospheric Cycle of Sulphur Dioxide' in HEY, R D and DAVIES, T D (eds) *Science Technology and Environmental Management*, Farnborough, 145–64
GARNETT, A (1971) 'Weather Inversions and Air Pollution', *Clean Air, 1*, 3, 16–21
GILBERT, O L (1971) 'Some Indirect Effects of Air Pollution on Bark Living Invertebrates', *J. Appl. Ecol., 8*, 1, 77–84
GLOYNE, R W (1971) 'A Note on the Average Annual Mean of Daily Earth Temperature in the UK', *Met. Mag. Lond., 100*, 1–6
GOODE, J E (1970) 'The Cumulative Effects of Irrigation on Fruit Crops' in TAYLOR, J A (ed) *The Role of Water in Agric. 12*, Aberystwyth, 161–70
GOORIAH, B D (1968) *Distribution of Pollution at some Country Sites*, Warren Spring Laboratory
GRAINGER, J (1967) 'Meteorology and Plant Physiology in Potato Blight Forecasting' in TAYLOR, J A (ed) *Weather and Agriculture*, Aberystwyth, 105–13
GRANT, S A (1969) 'Temperature and Light Factors in the Growth of Hill Pasture Species', *Hill Land Productivity, 4*, 30–4
GRAYSON, A J (1967) 'Forestry in Britain' in ASHTON, J and RODGERS, S J (eds) *Economic Change and Agriculture*, Newcastle upon Tyne, 168–89
GLC (1974) *Statistical Review of Progress and Effects of Smoke Control in London*, RM422, rev. edn., 1974
GREEN, F H W (1970A) 'Some Isopleth Maps based on Lysimeter Observations in the British Isles in 1965, 1966 and 1967', *J. Hydrol., 10*, 127–40
        (1970B) 'The Flexibility of Land Use in Relation to the Water Balance' in TAYLOR, J A (ed) *The Role of Water in Agric., 12*, Aberystwyth, 185–94
GREGORY, S (1954) 'Accumulated Temperature Maps of the British Isles', *Trans. Inst. Br. Geogr., 20*, 59–73
        (1964A) 'Some Aspects of Water Resource Development in Relation to Lancashire', *Problems of Appl. Geogr.*, Warsaw
        (1964B) 'Water Resource Exploitation, Policies and Problems', *Geogr., 49*, 310–14
HAWES, F B (1970) 'Thermal Problems "Old Hat" in Britain', *CEGB Newsletter, 83*
HAWKESWORTH, D L (1971) 'Lichens as Litmus for Air Pollution', *Int. J. Environ. Stud., 14*, 281–96
HILL, D A (1947) *The Land of Ulster 1: The Belfast Region*, Belfast HMSO
HILTON, K J (ed) (1967) *The Lower Swansea Valley Project*, London
HOGG, W H (1965A) 'Climatic Factors and Choice of Site, with Special Reference to Horticulture' in JOHNSTON, C G and SMITH, L P (eds) *The Biological Significance of Climatic Changes in Britain, Symp. Inst. Biol., 14*, London, 141–55
        (1965B) 'Measurements of the Shelter Effects of Landforms and Other

Topographical Features', *Scient. Hort., 17*, 20–30

    (1966) 'Climate and Surveys of Agricultural Land Use'', *UNESCO Natural Resources Res., 7, Agroclimatological Methods*, Reading

    (1967A) 'Meteorological Factors in Early Crop Production', *Weather, 22*, 3, 84–118

    (1967B) *The Atlas of Long-term Irrigation Needs for England and Wales*, MAFF, London

    (1967C) 'The Use of Upper Air Data in Relation to Plant Disease' in TAYLOR, J A (ed) *Weather and Agriculture*, Aberystwyth, 115–27

    (1968) 'The Analysis of Data with Particular Reference to Frost Surveys', *WMO Proc. Reg. Training Semin. in Agromet.*, Wageningen, 343–50

    (1970) 'Basic Frost Irrigation and Degree Day Data for Planning Purposes' in TAYLOR, J A (ed) *Weather Econ., 11*, Aberystwyth, 27–43

HOLMES, J W and COLVILLE, J S (1968) 'On the Water Balance of Grassland', *Int. Congr. Soil Sci., 9*, Sydney, 39–46

HORNER, R W (1971) 'The Thames Barrier Scheme', *Jl R. Soc. Arts, 5178*, 119, 369–80

HUNTER, R F and GRANT, S A (1971) 'The Effect of Altitude on Grass Growth in Eastern Scotland', *J. Appl. Ecol., 8*, 1, 1–19

HURST, C A (1964) 'Grass Growing Days' in TAYLOR, J A (ed) *Climatic Factors and Agric. Productivity, 6*, Aberystwyth, 25–9

JARVIS, M G (1973) 'Soils of the Wantage and Abingdon District', *Mem. Soil Surv. Gt. Br.*, Harpenden

JONES, G E (1972) 'An Investigation into the Possible Causes of Poor Growth in Sitka Spruce' in TAYLOR, J A (ed) *Res. Pap. in Forest Met.*, Aberystwyth, 147–55

KNOCH, K (1963) 'Die Landesklima Aufnahme, Wesen und Methodik', *Ber. dt. Wetterd., Offenbach, 85*, 12, 1–64

LAMB, H H (1965) 'Britain's Changing Climate' in JOHNSTON, C C and SMITH, L P (eds) *The Biological Significance of Climatic Changes in Britain*, London, 3–31

LAWRENCE, E N (1971) 'Recent Trends in Solar Radiation, Maximum Black-bulb and Air Temperatures in Britain', *Weather, 26*, 4, 164–72

McVEAN, D N and LOCKIE, J D (1969) *Ecology and Land Use in Upland Scotland*, Edinburgh

MERRIMAN, D (1970) 'The Calefaction of a River', *Scient. Am., 222*, 42–52

MILITARY ENGNG EXP. ESTABL. (1969) *The Prediction of Soil Water Tension from Weather Data*, MEXE Rep. 1025, Christchurch

MINIST. AGRIC. (1967) 'Potential Transpiration', *Tech. Bull., 16*, HMSO

MAFF (1974) 'Land Capability Classification', *Tech. Bull., 30*, HMSO

MINIST. FUEL and POWER (1953) *Committee on Air Pollution*, Interim Rep., Cmnd 9011, HMSO

MINIST. HOUSING and LOCAL GOVT. (1967) *Chimney Heights*, 1956 Clean Air Act Memorandum, HMSO

MINIST. HOUSING and LOCAL GOVT. and MAFF (1962) *Water Conservation: England and Wales*, Cmnd 1693, HMSO

MINIST. HOUSING and LOCAL GOVT. and SCOTT. DEV. DEPT. (1970) *Rep. of the Technical Committee on the Disposal of Toxic Solid Wastes*, HMSO

MINIST. TECHNOLOGY (1965) *The Investigation of Atmospheric Pollution 1958–63*, HMSO

NERC (1976) *Report for the Council for the period 1st April 1975 to 31st March 1976*, HMSO

NICHOLSON, M (1970) *The Environmental Revolution*, London

NE DEV. ASSN. (1950) *A Physical Land Classification of Northumberland and Durham and Part of the N Riding of Yorks.*, Newcastle upon Tyne

O'HARE, P J (1972) 'A Comparison of the Effect of Young Forest and Grassland on the Water Table in Blanket Peat' in TAYLOR, J A (ed) *Res. Pap. Forest Met.*, Aberystwyth, 126–33

O'RIORDAN, T (1970) 'Spray Irrigation and the Water Resources Act 1963', *Trans. Inst. Br. Geogr., 49*, 33–46

O'SULLIVAN, A J (1971) 'Ecological Effects of Sewage Discharge in the Marine Environment', *Proc. R. Soc., Ser. B, 177*, 331–51

OXENHAM, J R (1966) *Reclaiming Derelict Land*, London

PARKER, R E (1962) 'Factors Limiting Tree Growth on Peat Soils', *Ir. For., 19*, 1, 60–81

PEARS, N V (1972) 'Interpretation Problems in the Study of Tree Line Fluctuations' in TAYLOR, J A (ed) *Res. Pap. Forest Met.*, Aberystwyth, 31–45

PEARSALL, W M (1950) *Mountains and Moorlands*, London

PENMAN, H L (1948) 'Natural Evaporation from Open Water, Bare Soil and Grass', *Proc. R. Soc., Ser. A, 193*, 120–45

 (1950) 'Evaporation over the British Isles', *Q. Jl R. Met. Soc., 76*, 372–83

 (1962) 'Weather and Crops', *Q. Jl R. Met. Soc., 88*, 209–19

 (1968) 'Available and Accessible Water', *Proc. Ninth Int. Congr. Soil Sci.*, Adelaide, 29–37

POLLARD, E and MILLER, A (1968) 'Wind Erosion in the East Anglian Fens', *Weather, 23*, 10, 415–17

PRICKETT, C N (1970) 'Current Trends in the Use of Water' in TAYLOR, J A (ed) *The Role of Water in Agric., 12*, Aberystwyth, 101–19

PUBL. GEN. ACTS See list p. 516

PUGH, N J (1963) 'Water Supply', *Symposium on the Conservation of Water Resources in the UK*, Inst. Civil. Engrs., London, 8–14

PYATT, D G (1966) 'Soil Problems in Border Forestry', *Proc. N. England Soils Discussion Group, 2*, 43–5

REED, L E and TROTT, P E (1971) 'Continuous Measurement of Carbon Monoxide in Streets 1967–9', *Atmos. Envir., 5*, 27–39

REES, J A (1969) 'Industrial Demand for Water: a Study of South East England', *LSE Res. Monogr. 3*

ROBERTS, D G (1972) 'The Modification of Geomorphic Shelter by Shelter Belts', in TAYLOR, J A (ed) *Res. Pap. Forest Met.*, Aberystwyth, 134–46

ROBINSON, A J (1971) 'Air Pollution', *Jl R. Soc. Arts, 5180*, CXIX, 505–16

RODDA, J C (1970A) 'Definite Rainfall Measurements and their Significance for Agriculture' in TAYLOR, J A (ed) *The Role of Water in Agric., 12*, Aberystwyth, 1–10

 (1970B) 'Rainfall Excesses in the UK', *Trans. Inst. Br. Geogr., 49*, 49–70

RODE, A A (1968) 'Hydrological Profile', *Proc. Ninth Int. Congr. Soil Sci.*, Adelaide, 165–72

ROUSE, G P (1961) 'Some Effects of Rainfall on Tree Growth and Forest Fires', *Weather, 16*, 9, 304–11

ROY. COMMN. (TREATING AND DISPOSAL OF SEWAGE) 1912–13. *Eighth Report*, Cmnd 6464, HMSO

ROY. COMMN. ENVIRON. POLLUTION (1971) *First Report*, Cmnd 4585, HMSO
                                             (1972) *Second Report*, Cmnd 4894,
HMSO
                                             (1972) *Third Report*, Cmnd 5054, HMSO
                                             (1973) *Pollution in Four Industrial*
Estuaries, HMSO
                                             (1974) *Fourth Report*, Cmnd 5780,
HMSO
                                             (1976A) *Fifth Report*, Cmnd 6371,
HMSO
                                             (1976B) *Sixth Report*, Cmnd 6618,
HMSO

RUSSELL, F S et al (1971) 'Changes in the Biological Conditions in the English Channel', *Nature, 234*, 468–70

RUTTER, A J (1972) 'Evaporation from Forests' in TAYLOR, J A (ed) *Res. Pap. Forest Met.*, Aberystwyth, 75–90

RYDZ, B (1969) 'Water Conservation' in *Water Resources Committee, Assocn. of River Authorities Year Book*, London, 195–214

SCALE, R S (1975) 'Soils of the Ely District', *Mem. Soil Surv. Gt. Br.*, Harpenden

SHELLARD, H C (1959) *Averages of Accumulated Temperatures and Standard Deviation of Monthly Mean Temperatures over Britain, 1921–50*, HMSO

SMITHSON, P A (1969) 'Effects of Altitude on Rainfall in Scotland', *Weather, 24*, 9, 370–6

SPEIGHT, H (1968) 'Upland Catchment Management: a Water Resources Board View', *Upland Catchment Management Conf.*, Attingham Park Coll., Shrewsbury

STAMP, L D (1947) *The Land of Britain: Use and Misuse*, London
                  (1969) *Nature Conservation in Britain*, London

STEWART, W D P, TUCKWELL, S B and MAY, E (1975) 'Eutrophication and Algal Growth in Scottish Freshwater Lochs' in CHADWICK, M J and GOODMAN, G T (eds) *The Ecology of Resource Degradation and Renewal*, Oxford, 57–80

STILES, W and GARWOOD, E A (1964) 'Drought, Soil Water and Grass Growth' in TAYLOR, J A (ed) *Climatic Factors and Agric. Productivity, 6*, Aberystwyth, 19–24

SYMONS, L J (ed) (1963) *Land Use in N Ireland*, London

TAYLOR, J A (1964) 'Economic and Ecological Productivity under British Conditions' in TAYLOR, J A (ed) *Climatic Factors and Agric. Productivity, 6*, Aberystwyth, 1–5

THOMASSON, A J (1971) 'Soils of the Melton Mowbray District', *Mem. Soil Surv. Gt Br.*, Harpenden

THOMPSON, F L (1945) *Merseyside Plan 1944*, HMSO

THORNTHWAITE, C W and MATHER, J R (1955) 'The Water Balance', *Drexel Inst. Technol., Lab. Clim., 8*, 1, Centerton, New Jersey, 22–67

THORNTON, I (1975) 'Geochemical Parameters in the Assessment of Estuarine Pollution' in CHADWICK, M J and GOODMAN, G T (eds) *The Ecology of Resource Degradation and Renewal*, Oxford, 157–72

VOLKER, A (1974) 'Management of Water in the Coastal Zone' in FUNNELL, B M and HEY, R D *The Management of Water Resources in England and Wales*, Univ. E Anglia, 115–20

WARDLE, P A (1966) 'Land Use Policy: the Claims of Forestry on Resources and its Contributions', *Timber Grower, 19*, 18–25

    (1970) 'Weather and Risk in Forestry' in TAYLOR, J A (ed) *Weather Econ.*, Aberystwyth, 67–82

WATER RESOURCES BD. (1966) *Water Resources of the South East*, HMSO

    (1970) *Water Resources in the North*, HMSO

    (1971) *Water Resources in Wales and the Midlands*, HMSO

    (1973) *Water Resources in England and Wales*, vol 1: Report; vol 4: Appendices, HMSO

WATSON, J P and ABERCROMBIE, P (1943) *A Plan for Plymouth*, Plymouth

WILLIAMS, R J H and RICKS, G R (1975) 'Effects of Combinations of Atmospheric Pollutants upon Vegetation' in CHADWICK, M J and GOODMAN, G T (eds) *The Ecology of Resource Degradation and Renewal*, Oxford, 127–38

WILSON, C L (1970) *Man's Impact on the Global Environment*, Massachusetts Inst. Technol.

WINTER, E J, SALTER, P J and COX, R F (1970) 'Limited Irrigation in Crop Production' in TAYLOR, J A (ed) *The Role of Water in Agric., 12*, Aberystwyth, 147–60

WOODHEAD, D S (1971) 'The Biological Effect of Radioactive Waste', *Proc. R. Soc., Ser. B, 177*, 423–37

4

Power and the Industrial Structure

I   THE POWER INDUSTRIES

I.1   Significance and Structure

The fuel and power industries play a vital role in the economic, social and political life of the modern UK. The large numbers of people they employ, the dependence of industry upon adequate energy supplies and the long debates in Parliament over various aspects of energy policy, all serve to indicate their all-pervasive importance. It is hardly surprising therefore, that the geography of these industries has always been of practical relevance and concern. This becomes most obvious when the location and distribution of these industries undergoes major change. It is then that effective intervention to achieve desired spatial patterns requires proper understanding of the processes involved. This kind of regional and spatial planning is in effect geography applied. One such period of rapid change occurred in the decade 1965–75, which saw a revolution in the geography of the UK fuel and power industries unmatched since the British coalfields were first developed. The three most important factors which provoked this revolution were: the replacement of coal by oil as the most important single source of UK energy; the use of a new source of energy in the form of natural gas; and the discovery of major domestic oil and natural gas resources beneath the North Sea. By the late 1970s the resulting creation of a new geography of energy in the UK was almost complete. By then the distribution of coal production between the coalfields was vastly different to the pattern in 1960, the arrival of natural gas had swept away the 150-year old gas-making industry, most electricity was being supplied by power stations less than fifteen years old and most British oil refining capacity was little older. The purpose here is not just to describe what happened, but also to indicate the main forces generating change and shaping the results. The task is somewhat complicated by the variety of industries forming the fuel and power group, and the degree of alteration in their relative importance, and in some cases in their individual character.

In the past there was a simple distinction between the primary energy sources of coal and petroleum, and electricity and gas which were secondary sources of energy derived from the conversion of primary energy sources into more convenient forms. Since 1960 the contribution of nuclear power to electricity generation and the replacement of secondary manufactured gas by the primary fuel natural gas, has complicated the previously simple situation (fig. 4.1). It is also relevant to recognize that the coal-mining industry has had a long and influential history, whereas the other energy industries did not appear until much later in the industrialization process (Manners 1971A, 38). Despite these complexities, it is possible to identify certain major factors which explain the spatial patterns that can now be observed. In terms of industrial location theory these are transport economies, markets, political

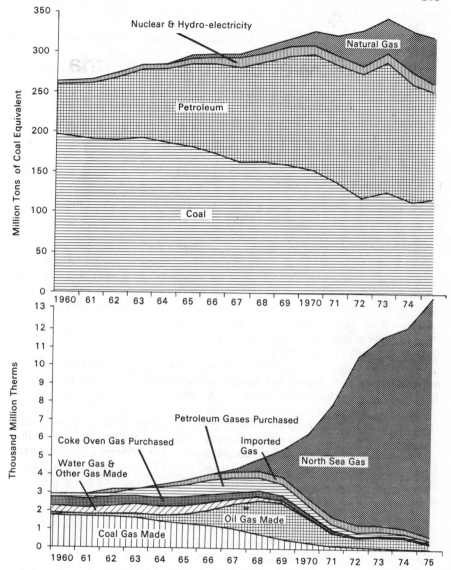

Figure 4.1a   Primary energy consumption in the UK, 1960–75

Figure 4.1b   Public supply gas sources, UK, 1960–75

factors including ownership, technology and physical geography. The importance of all of these is brought out in each of the power industries in turn.

The major primary sources of power in the UK in 1975, in order of importance, were oil, coal, natural gas, and nuclear energy. Water power made a minor contribution but with little potential for expansion. Each of these primary sources can be used direct or in modified form, but 13 per cent of the final energy consumption in

TABLE 4.1

Energy Consumption, UK, 1975

| | Million tonnes of coal equivalent | | Used by electricity industry |
	Amount	%	
Coal	120.0	37.0	74.5
Petroleum	136.5	42.0	21.8
Natural gas	55.3	17.0	3.4
Nuclear electricity	11.0	3.4	10.9
Hydro-electricity	1.9	0.6	1.9
Total	324.8	100.0	112.7

Source: Digest of Energy Statistics, (1976) HMSO

the UK in 1975 was in the converted form of electricity. Table 4.1 shows the contribution each fuel made to total energy consumption, and how much of each was used for electricity generation. A feature of the table is that in 1975 coal was still contributing over one-third of the national energy requirements, though it had held a 63 per cent share only a decade earlier. The decline in the importance of coal was part of a major shift which occurred in the UK energy budget as alternative sources were developed. Until 1960 the UK remained a two-fuel economy, dependent upon coal and oil. Prior to 1956 the coal-mining industry had found difficulty in meeting the growing fuel demands of the nation, and petroleum consumption had risen to fill the energy gap. Although declining in relative importance however, coal production was continuing to increase, reaching a peak output of 217 million tons in 1956. Subsequently coal consumption declined and petroleum consumption underwent massive expansion. In the 1960s the use of nuclear power and natural gas became significant and by 1970 they were contributing 3 per cent and 5 per cent respectively of the national energy budget. The UK had by then changed from a two-fuel, to a four-fuel economy. Coal has since continued its decline and in 1971, for the first time, oil became the most important single source of energy consumed in the UK, a position it has maintained ever since.

Within the total picture there were major changes in the way coal was used, and in the gas industry. For coal the major change was from direct consumption to indirect consumption, as sales to the electricity generating industry rose from only 26 per cent of the total in 1960, to 62 per cent in 1975 (table 4.2). For gas two successive major shifts occurred. First was the replacement of coal by oil as the primary source of fuel for gas manufacture in the 1960s. This was soon followed by the virtual disappearance of the manufactured gas industry with the completion of the natural gas trunk pipeline network in the 1970s. The growing availability of natural gas at very competitive prices affected all the fuel industries after 1970.

I.2   Coal

Coal-mining is almost the archetype primary industry. It experiences high weight loss in use since the energy it produces has little or no weight and the residue after the energy is extracted is waste. Coal production is tied to fixed locations, since the

TABLE 4.2

Coal Consumption, UK, 1950–75 (million tonnes)

		1950	1960	1970	1975
Indirect consumption	Electricity power stations	33.5	52.7	77.2	74.5
	Gas works	26.6	23.0	4.2	0.0
	Coke ovens	22.9	29.2	25.3	19.1
	Other fuel conversion Miscellaneous	3.0*	2.3	4.1	4.0
Total indirect consumption		86.1	107.2	110.9	97.7
Direct consumption	Agriculture	0.8	0.3	0.2	0.0
	Collieries	10.8	5.1	1.9	1.2
	Industry	45.3	35.4	19.6	9.6
	Rail and water transport	15.6	9.4	0.2	0.1
	Domestic	38.1	36.0	20.2	11.7
	Public services	5.8	4.1	2.9	1.8
Total direct consumption		116.5	92.5	45.8	24.4
GRAND TOTAL		202.6	199.8	156.8	122.2

* Estimated
Source: Digest of Energy Statistics (HMSO)

raw materials are available only at the coalfields. It has a high weight output per employee, and its location pattern has been considerably affected by increased economies of scale and by mechanization. More than any other fuel industry it has suffered from government policies, having had to balance direct economic profit against maximum public good in the national economy. It has also been much more affected by technological change than the other fuel industries because, being much older, it had a much greater inheritance of obsolescence. Unlike the others it has suffered continuing decline of output since 1960 and so had the unenviable task of coping with massive innovational change at a time of contraction. Being older, it had acquired a whole set of social and economic responsibilities in the coal-mining regions which coloured government decisions about its development.

In examining the main features of the geography of the industry attention is focused on the National Coal Board (NCB) deep-mining operations. Private coal-mining and open-cast mining operations are included in a final section.

Coal resources Estimates of the amount of coal available in the UK vary according to the criteria which are used. For the present we may take it that, at current production rates around 120 million tonnes a year, there is sufficient to last for at least two more centuries. How much of this will ever actually be extracted depends not so much upon the quantity available, as upon the circumstances which prevail in the future when mining decisions are made.

Traditionally the distribution of coal-mining has been shown on a map by the geological boundaries of the coalfields. Today these are somewhat misleading, since deep mining is now confined to only parts of the geological coalfields. For understanding the pattern of mining it is much more relevant to have a knowledge of the types of coal being mined in each area and of the structural features which affect mining operations. The types of coal being mined in 1968 are shown in fig. 4.2. The lower the number of a coal, the higher its quality. Certain coals are required for specific purposes: anthracite is best suited to space heating and smokeless zone use, coking coal for steel-making, steam and general coals for electricity generation. Fig. 4.2 shows that in general the higher quality specific coals commanding higher prices form a greater proportion of output in NE England, Scotland and Wales, and the lower quality general coals dominate output in the interior English coalfields.

Structural conditions vary significantly over the coalfields. The Scottish and Welsh coalfields suffer most from variation of geological conditions. Not only is there much more faulting and folding on a major and minor scale, but variations in seam thickness are much more frequent. In general, the more regular the coal seams the more amenable they are to mechanized working and automation. Clearly production control and planning is easier and more successful under uniform conditions, all these factors contributing to lower mining costs.

Added to these features is the importance of the past history of mining. Those areas with coal occurring at or close to the surface, especially near the coast, were the earliest to experience mining on an industrial scale. Such areas have the most depleted reserves, but more than that, in 1960 they had older and generally smaller collieries. In contrast, where the coal lay deepest or concealed beneath more recent rocks, coal-mining developed much later. The collieries in these areas were initially larger and laid out on more modern lines to tap seams previously unworked. In the first group are the peripheral coalfields of Scotland, Wales, the NW and NE of England. The newer areas where deep coal is worked are E Durham, the eastern areas of the Yorks., Derby. and Notts. coalfields and the Kent coalfield.

A dramatic recent illustration of the advantages to be gained in such areas is to be found in the current development of the previously unworked Selby coalfield, underlying a predominantly rural area between Selby and York. Production here from the Barnsley seam alone is planned to reach 10 million tonnes a year by 1985, and to continue at that rate well into the next century. Access to the workings will be by five vertical shafts and two inclined drifts, with a total of 50,000 tonnes of coal a day raised via the drifts. The suitable geological conditions will allow the most efficient mining techniques and organization to be used, so that only 4,000 men will be needed compared with the 20,000 required in other coalfields in 1975 to achieve the same rate of output (NCB 1975; Spooner and North 1976).

Though needing to overcome objections to coal-mining in a rural area, the extensive coalfield recently discovered beneath the Vale of Belvoir between Nottingham, Grantham and Melton Mowbray, is likely to be developed in a similar manner. The reserves of 500 million tonnes of coal occur in six seams at depths of between 400 and 850 metres beneath an area 18 km long and 19 km wide (NCB 1977).

Geographical patterns Between 1960 and 1975 the geography of coal-mining was radically transformed in response to changing economic conditions in the UK (table 4.4). Overall deep-mined coal output declined by nearly 40 per cent, but as table 4.4 shows, there were considerable differences from coalfield to coalfield. All the northern and western coalfields experienced a halving of their tonnage output, as did Kent. The lowland coalfields, which stretch from the Aire Valley in Yorkshire along the eastern flanks of the Pennines as far as Leicestershire, were much less affected. Production in Yorkshire fell by only 22 per cent and in the E Midlands by even less. As a result coal-mining has become much more concentrated geograph-

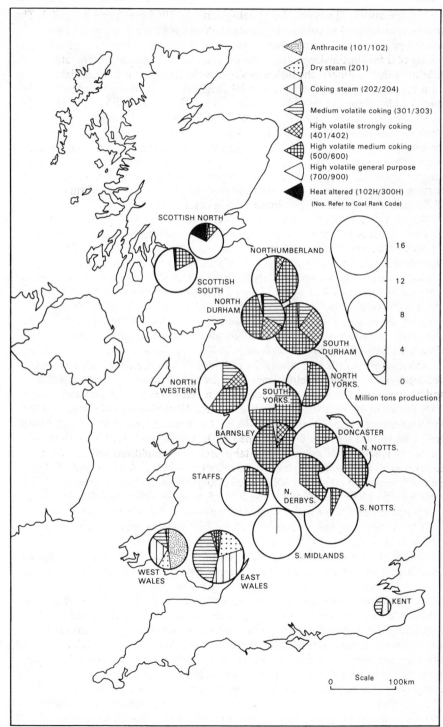

Figure 4.2   Types of coal produced, NCB Areas, 1967–8

TABLE 4.3

NCB Productivity and Production Costs by Regions, 1950 and 1960

	Productivity output per man shift		Production costs per ton saleable	
	1950 cwt (50 kg)	1960 cwt (50 kg)	1950 s/d	1960 s/d
Scottish	22.8	22.4	46/9	101/6
Northern	22.9	27.3	48/11	87/9
Durham	20.0	22.3	51/7	97/2
N Western	21.3	26.0	50/0	93/1
W Midlands	26.3	28.6	42/7	87/0
S Western	18.6	20.6	54/7	107/3
Yorkshire	26.3	31.0	42/5	76/3
E Midlands	34.5	42.1	36/6	63/5
Kent	24.8	23.3	49/4	106/7
Total (NCB)	24.2	28.0	45/5	84/5

Source: NCB

ically. The Yorks. and E Midlands coalfields, which were responsible for producing only 46 per cent of the coal in 1960, supplied 60 per cent of output in 1975. The peripheral coalfields now produce proportionally less and in the Cumbria and Somerset coalfields production has ceased.

In addition to these regional shifts there have also been substantial changes in the geography of coal-mine distribution within each coalfield. Two main features are worthy of comment. In all the coalfields there has been a tendency for mining to cease along the long-worked outcrops, and to concentrate on the deeper and concealed areas. The other feature has been the reduction in the number of collieries to a greater extent than the decline in output might lead one to expect. This occurred primarily because of the increase both in productivity and in the average size of individual collieries. The effect has been to replace a pattern of a large number of small collieries, by one which has a much smaller number of larger collieries; the distances between collieries has thus tended to increase (House and Knight 1967). These two changes mean that large areas within the geological limits of all the coalfields no longer have any collieries and are not deep-mining areas.

The forces at work There are several reasons for the geographical changes described. From nationalization of the UK coal industry (1947) to 1960 the main explanation could be found in the characteristics of the industry which the NCB inherited. At nationalization the industry was both obsolete and run-down. Profits in the inter-war period had been inadequate to allow sufficient investment to keep the industry up to date. The position had been aggravated by the subsequent six years of war, during which time capital, men and equipment were all in short supply and the industry was operated with only the minimum amount of maintenance to sustain output. The first task of the NCB was to right these inherited wrongs and bring the industry to an acceptable condition. Large sums of money had to be invested, but this could be justified only where sufficient reserves were thought to be available to give an economic return. These were located for the most part in deeper, unworked

TABLE 4.4

NCB Deep-mined Coal Production by Regions, 1950–75

	Output (million tonnes saleable coal)				%			
	1950	1960	1970*	1975	1950	1960	1970	1975
Scottish	23.3	18.0	11.5	9.7	11	10	8	8.5
Northumberland	13.4	12.2	7.0 ⎫	14.6	7	6	5 ⎫	12.7
Durham	26.7	23.1	13.8 ⎭		13	12	10 ⎭	
Yorkshire	43.0	41.0	36.4	31.9	21	22	25	27.9
E Midlands	40.5	44.3	43.5	36.9	20	24	30	32.2
NW	14.4	13.1	7.1 ⎫	12.0	7	7	5 ⎫	10.6
W Midlands	17.5	14.0	8.7 ⎭		8	8	6 ⎭	
SW	24.4	19.4	13.0	8.4	12	10	9	7.4
SE	1.7	1.5	1.1	0.7	1	1	1	0.6
UK	205.6	186.8	142.2	114.4	100	100	100	100

* Distribution between regions is estimated because of changes in regional boundaries between 1960 and 1970

Sources: Digests of Energy Statistics (HMSO), and NCB

parts of the coalfields. Until 1956 the inability of the industry to produce sufficient coal to meet domestic demand caused serious concern (Minist. Fuel and Power 1955, 10), and plans for the future were based upon a continuing need to increase output. There was no serious competition from alternative fuels, with the result that even the high-cost mines in older mining areas were maintained in production. Geographical change occurred mainly as a result of closing collieries when local coal reserves were exhausted. This situation continued from 1956 to 1960, though an industrial recession at this time hastened the closure of some collieries.

In contrast with the previous minor alterations in the patterns, the period after 1960 saw a radical transformation of the geography of British coal-mining. This was mainly in response to growing competition from alternative fuels, strongly reinforced by the changes which were taking place in the structure of the UK economy. After 1960 the heavy coal-using industries were slow-growing or in decline, whilst the expanding industrial sectors were those dependent upon oil or electricity. The resulting reduction in coal demand was accelerated by the increasingly efficient use of coal by large consumers such as the steel and electricity industries, and the conversion of traditional coal consumers to new fuels such as occurred with the dieselization of the railways. In the 1960s the main competitor for coal was fuel oil, but by 1970 the availability of cheap natural gas in large quantities offered a further threat. The response of the NCB was to switch emphasis from maximization of output, which had been the aim in the 1950s, to minimization of costs, and progressively to reduce planned output targets. Until 1960 the aim had been to maintain output at around 200 million tonnes per year, but by 1975 the target was 142 million tonnes a year and even this looked rather high (Manners 1976).

These were the factors necessitating change, but other factors influenced the geographical results. One of the most important was the increasing use of improved mining methods and techniques, for which physical conditions were much more critical. Thus much greater regularity of the coal seams in the eastern parts of the Yorks., Derby. and Notts. coalfields are better suited to mechanized working and make forward planning much more reliable. Under these conditions both higher productivity rates and greater economies of scale are easier to achieve, and production costs are lower, as is shown in table 4.5. It is here too, that general coals predominate, which are attractive to the electricity market because they command a lower price. Thus it is hardly surprising that these eastern coalfields suffered much less decline in output and as a result came to dominate UK output by the 1970s.

What is less obvious from the account so far and from the figures quoted, is why as much as one-third of UK coal output still comes from the high-cost coalfield

TABLE 4.5

NCB Deep-mined Coal Operations, 1963–4 and 1975–6

	Saleable output		Productivity OMS overall		Costs per ton saleable[†]	Number of collieries in production at end of year	
	Million tons (1 ton = 1.016 tonnes)		Cwt (50 kg)		£ p		
	1963–4	1975–6	1963–4	1975–6	1975–6	1963–4	1975–6
Scottish North	7.5	9.6	28.5	39.4	15.75	47	21
Scottish South	9.0		27.7			40	
Northumberland	11.0	14.4	32.8	38.6	17.31	35	32
N Durham	9.4		25.2			52	
S Durham	12.1		26.9			35	
N Yorkshire	10.4	8.3	38.2	51.7	14.20	30	18
Doncaster	9.8	7.9	37.2	48.4	15.56	14	10
Barnsley	11.7	7.4	36.3	45.1	15.81	36	18
S Yorkshire	11.2	7.8	34.3	43.5	16.41	22	19
N Western	12.8	11.9	30.0	44.6	17.49	42	24
Staffordshire	10.9		36.1			35	
N Derbyshire	14.6	7.8	41.9	59.2	12.77	34	12
N Notts.	11.1	10.6	49.3	57.3	13.64	12	15
S Notts.	14.0	9.6	52.9	57.9	12.86	19	12
S Midlands	11.1	8.2	43.7	58.5	13.13	17	15
E Wales	11.9	8.3	25.2	26.9	24.56	51	42
W Wales	7.6		22.1			51	
Kent	1.6	0.7	28.2	21.2	33.22	4	3
UK	187.6*	112.6*	33.4	44.8	16.07	576	241

* Columns do not add up to total because of rounding up
† Figures for 1963–4 not available

Source: NCB

areas. It is here that the market, transport economies and political factors play their part.

The market has influenced the pattern in several ways. Not all coal is alike and certain markets require specific types of coal. As a general rule the highest quality coals form a much higher proportion in the peripheral coalfields than in the east-central coalfields. High quality and high costs have in the past thus been spatially correlated. Good examples are the anthracite coals of western S Wales, and the coking coals of W Durham. As long as the markets exist for these coals, output will be maintained. The high price charged for these coals also partly compensates for their higher production costs.

Markets also help to explain continuing production in another way. Of all the sources of energy, coal is probably the most expensive to transport. In 1976 the cost of transporting coal added an average £1.80 per ton or 12 per cent to the cost of production. Distance to a certain extent thus protects the local markets of the high-cost coalfield coal from competition from coal brought in from other places (Manners 1971B, 165). This has certainly been the case in Scotland and parts of Wales, which are the remotest areas from the low-cost E Midlands and S Yorkshire coalfields. Similarly, output in NE England was higher than it would otherwise have been because of the low cost of sending coal by ship to its traditional market area of SE England.

Transport costs contributed to the increased dominance of the E Midlands and S Yorkshire coalfields. With coal production costs cheaper there, they attracted large proportions of the coal-fired electricity-generating stations built after 1950. It is cheaper to send base load electricity to markets than to send the coal and generate the electricity there. Consumption of coal for electricity-generation rose markedly 1950–75, maintaining and strengthening the position of the E Midlands and S Yorkshire coalfields. Geographically the low-cost coalfields also lie closer to the major coal consumption areas of the W Midlands and SE England. They thus benefit from lower land transport costs to these markets.

Political factors are important in explaining the maintenance of so much deep-mined output in the high-cost areas. The government has always taken account of the fact that coal is an indigenous fuel, whereas until 1970 most of the alternatives had to be imported at the cost of foreign exchange. In addition, in many parts of the coalfields, coal-mining has long been the mainstay of local communities. Reduction of output has regional social and economic repercussions of considerable significance. With these in mind, successive governments took measures to limit the rate of coal-mining decline in the 1960s and to ameliorate the local impact of colliery closures. Although this benefited all the coalfields, it is the high-cost areas that have most of the marginal units which would have gone out of production without such protection. On the national front, the government imposed a special tax on fuel oil to limit its effectiveness in competition with coal. This gave an effective price advantage to coal of 130p per tonne. In addition, permission for the import of coal was granted only under special circumstances and the conversion of coal-fired power stations to other fuels was restricted. The *Coal Industry Act* (Publ. Gen. Act 1967) went further and arranged for additional consumption of coal at power stations by means of subsidies. The extra coal used in this way amounted to some 6.6 million tonnes in 1968–9 (CEGB 1969, 3). Government financial support was also given to keep collieries open when closure would have caused local social hardship.

With the political involvement must be coupled ownership, since the coal industry has been nationalized since 1947. The geographical effect of planning and operating the industry as a whole since then has been considerable. It is this that has made rationalization and centralization possible in a way inconceivable had the coal mines remained in the hands of a large number of privately-owned companies.

Opencast and private mining The deep mines of the NCB are not the only producers of coal in the UK. Private mines still operate under licence from the Coal Board, but since 1960 their output has not exceeded 2 million tonnes a year so that their con-

tribution is insignificant in a national context. Most of the output comes from
S Wales, where it helps supplement production of high quality steam and anthracite
coals from pockets too small to make exploitation by the Coal Board worthwhile
(Marnell and Humphrys 1965, 328). Opencast mining is much more important: output in 1975 was 11 million tonnes. The mines are the responsibility of the Opencast
Executive of the NCB who contract the actual extraction out to private firms. Most
of the firms involved are well-known national construction companies, such as
Wimpey and Derek Crouch, who have the expertise and the equipment available for
the heavy earthmoving tasks involved. Opencast sites exploit mainly shallow seams
down to about 100 m, though they do extend to depths of 200 m or more at times,
and are thus normally located on the exposed coalfields, mainly along the outcrops.
Any one site is temporary, with an average working life of around five years, seldom
more than ten years. The average site covers 120 ha and produces 200,000 tonnes
of coal annually. Opencast mining has always been very profitable for the NCB and
although production has never exceeded 15 million tonnes a year, it could easily be
increased substantially. With lower costs, opencast production would make coal
much more competitive as a fuel than it is at present. One reason for restricted output is the agreement with the unions that opencast coal-mining be limited to that
necessary to supplement the deep-mined output where the latter fails to meet the
demand. Thus a large proportion of the anthracite consumed in the UK comes from
opencast sites in western S Wales. Achievement of profitable deep-mined output
there has always been difficult and opencast mining has expanded in supplementa-
tion. The present aim is to achieve and maintain opencast output at about 15 million
tonnes a year, but if controls on opencast mining were to be relaxed there is little
doubt that output by this means could expand dramatically and the geography of
coal-mining in the UK would undergo a further change.

Coal distribution A *Report of Inquiry* (1958) into coal distribution costs in GB was
able to state that 'In spite of great changes which have taken place since the 1930s
in the conditions in which the trade is carried on, the general methods of distribution and the structure of the trade do not appear to have undergone much change'
(Minist. of Power 1958, 2). Until then, with coal in short supply and government
control of the allocation of supplies, the lack of change was not all that important.
But coal distribution costs at that time were equivalent to 25 per cent of the pit
price of the coal. It was clear that under the conditions of increased competition
during the 1960s this was an area for considerable improvement. A programme to
modernize and rationalize coal distribution to cut costs was begun in the early
1960s, and was completed by 1972 (NCB 1971, 20). It was accelerated by the reorganization and rationalization of the railways, in which the concentration of
services was taking place at the same time and much more realistic charges for the
small unit load movements were beginning to be made.

   Deliveries of coal to power stations were the easiest to improve and were important since they represented nearly half the inland market. Economies of scale
were achieved by the introduction of 'merry-go-round' trains. These are trains used
exclusively between collieries and power stations, and made up of wagons which are
never uncoupled. At the power station end mechanical unloading and coal-handling
facilities make the process even cheaper, and rapid loading techniques have been
introduced at the collieries as well. In 1975 merry-go-round trains delivered 41
million tonnes of coal, 60 per cent of it loaded at rapid-loading installations. This

kind of organization, although still using discontinuous transport media, gets closest to movement by pipeline, and has cut delivered coal cost substantially. The other way in which economies of scale have been achieved is through centralization of the retail distribution depots; in 1958 there were still some 5,800 in the UK. The average annual tonnes handled per trader using these depots was 1,767 and there were 16,778 traders. Of this total, only 7,533 traders handled over 1,000 tonnes of coal a year, and on this basis could be said to be fully employed in the retail trade (Minist. Power 1958, 50). With so many depots involved, individual deliveries of coal were small and few depots justified mechanical handling facilities for unloading, storing and bagging. The trade was essentially labour-intensive. This was further encouraged at the consumer level. There was little or no encouragement of domestic consumers, especially, to provide larger storage space so that deliveries could be made in bulk. In the 1960s all this was changed. Coal distribution depots were centralized, so that by 1976 only 420 main depots remained. Each of these was designed to deal with much larger quantities of coal, with adequate ground storage to ensure continuity of supplies and with a modern efficient layout. Supplies could be delivered by the trainload, and installation of automatic handling equipment was justified by the larger quantities of coal handled. These depots were located in those centres accessible to the largest number of customers in the shortest distance. This reduced the transport element in the delivered cost of coal. The NCB played a major role in the rationalization through two wholly-owned subsidiaries and four part-owned associated companies. By 1976 one of the wholly-owned subsidiaries, National Fuel Distributors Ltd, was the largest domestic fuel retailer in the UK, with total sales exceeding 2 million tonnes. By then only 7,051 approved coal merchants remained. The problem of the small storage capacity of the domestic consumer remains. Colliery production capacity is relatively inflexible in the short-term, so that coal must be stored in sufficient quantity to meet peak demands. This is best done by the consumer, since any other solution involves strain on the transport facilities for delivery at times when bad weather makes this strain difficult to bear. A differential price was introduced to encourage this, making coal cheaper in summer and dearer in winter. This had some effect, but there are still too many domestic consumers who take delivery weekly of one or two hundred-weight (50 kg) bags and who invariably suffer in bad winters because supplies cannot be made available immediately when demand takes a sudden and massive upsurge.

Coal distribution then has experienced concentration and rationalization to take advantage of economies of scale. This has changed the location of depots, concentrating them into the largest central places and increasing the scale of individual depots. Ownership has been important in this. With one single supplier in the NCB, the improvements have been much more easily achieved than if the industry had remained split between a large number of private companies.

I.3 Oil

Before 1960 oil was still a minor source of energy in the UK. At mid-century consumption had barely reached 20 million tonnes a year and domestic refineries could process only half that amount. From 1957 consumption began to rise rapidly. A number of traditional major coal users such as the railways, were converting to oil and the fastest growing industries were those using electricity or oil as their main sources of energy. After 1960 the process accelerated as oil became more cost competitive. It already had the advantage over coal of being easier to move and store and it can be more closely controlled quantitatively and qualitatively in use. Oil consumption which had risen to 45.7 million tonnes a year by 1960, doubled to 91 million tonnes in 1970 with a corresponding increase in refinery capacity. In the early 1970s three major developments once more changed the situation. The first was the dramatic increase in the price of oil following the action of the Middle East crude oil producers from 1973. This made oil much less competitive in the UK, causing a reduction in demand which was aggravated by the onset of an economic recession. Second was the growing availability of cheaper natural gas from the North Sea gas-fields. This new fuel captured some of the markets which otherwise would undoubtedly have been supplied by oil. As a result of these two changes although oil-refining capacity expanded to 152 million tonnes a year by 1975, demand had stagnated at less than 100 million tonnes. 1975 saw the beginning of the third and even more significant development in the UK oil industry. On 11 June 1975 the first oil was brought ashore from the major British oilfields discovered beneath the North Sea, and by 1980 it is anticipated that domestic output of oil will exceed UK demand.

The expansion of consumption in the 1960s caused significant shifts to occur in the geography of the UK oil-refining industry, but by the late 1970s the more recent changes had achieved only limited geographical impact. This was for three main reasons: the availability of a considerable surplus of refinery capacity whose location had been determined under earlier conditions; the long lead time between the initial decision to build a new refinery and its completion; and the limited amount of oil which was coming ashore from the North Sea by 1977. The first of these make it likely that the geographical distribution of the UK oil-refining industry will not significantly alter in response to the changed circumstances until the end of the 1980s.

Oil resources Britain has been an oil producer for a very long time. Oil was being extracted from the oil shales found west of Edinburgh in the early nineteenth century, and in the twentieth century small quantities of oil have long been produced from the oil wells of Dorset and the E Midlands. It was not until the 1960s, however, that the major domestic oilfields lying beneath the North Sea were discovered, and it was not until the late 1970s that production from these fields began to contribute a major proportion of British oil needs.

Seismic prospecting for oil and gas in the North Sea began in the early 1960s and full-scale exploration in 1964. By the end of 1975 115 exploration or appraisal wells had been drilled, and commercial oil production had begun from the Argyll and Forties fields. By then the geography of the North Sea oil resources was becoming clear. Plans already published indicate the main lines of likely development of these resources through to the 1980s, but the account here is concerned with the patterns that actually exist rather than with those anticipated.

By the end of 1975 proven recoverable reserves of oil in the British sector of the North Sea amounted to around 1,625 million tonnes, located in fifteen major commercial oilfields, with an ultimate potential reserve variously estimated at between 4,060 and 5,080 million tonnes. Odell and Rosing (1974) suggest that the potential recoverable reserves are likely to be very much more than this. Even taking conservative estimates the reserves are likely to be able to meet most UK demands until the first decades of the next century. In addition, the considerable oil reserves found

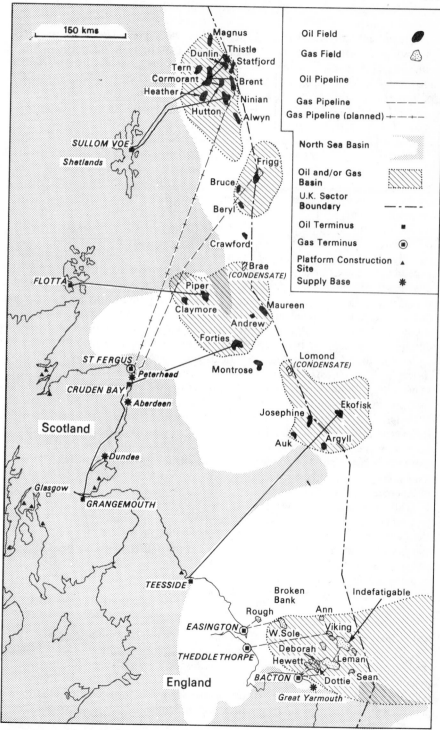

Figure 4.3   North sea oil and gas fields in the UK sector and pipelines to the UK, 1975

in the Norwegian sectors of the North Sea are also likely to be drawn upon by the British industry.

The oilfields discovered are geologically complex and occur in two distinct provinces in the northern part of the North Sea Basin (fig. 4.3). In the northern province most of the oil is found in Jurassic deposits, while in the more southerly province, which includes the Montrose and Forties fields, the oil-bearing rocks are of Tertiary age (Rosing 1976). The oil-bearing strata lie at depths down to 3,658 m or more below the sea bed, which is itself 91–121 m below sea level. Present technology limits offshore drilling to water depths of less than 183 m though work is being done to try to extend this. In the northern North Sea severe weather, with winds of up to 130 knots and 30 m waves, makes operations and maintenance of the oil rigs both hazardous and expensive. The oil-bearing strata extend into the Norwegian sector of the North Sea and because a deep undersea trench lies off the Norwegian coast to the east, much of this oil is expected to be piped to terminals on the UK mainland. The British government leases areas in the UK sector to companies for exploration purposes and not only controls the level of taxation on any oil produced, but through the government-owned British National Oil Corporation participates in development. How much of the oil will eventually be extracted will depend upon the financial return on the capital investment necessary and upon the relative attractiveness of the financial returns in the British sector compared with those from oilfields elsewhere. The high cost involved in the North Sea development means that, to be exploited, an oilfield must have large reserves to ensure that an adequate return on investment can be obtained, and already a number of the smaller oilfields discovered have been declared non-commercial because of this.

Most of the oil from the North Sea fields will be moved to shore by the pipelines shown in fig. 4.3. Costs are such that the underwater pipelines will be kept as short as possible, with much of the oil redistributed from the terminals by tankers. This means that the impact of the North Sea oil developments on land is concentrated at a few terminals and servicing ports. The greatest impact has been at Aberdeen which is the centre of North Sea oil operations in the UK (ch. I.V.2, Scotland). Again, because of the location of the oilfields it is Scotland that will derive most benefit from this activity, and the only pipeline so far planned to move North Sea oil on land already supplies the Grangemouth refinery from the Cruden Bay terminal north of Aberdeen.

While most interest and effort up to 1975 had been concentrated in the North Sea, oil and gas fields may also exist beneath the seas to the west of the UK from the Celtic Sea to north of the Hebrides. So far drilling in the UK sector of the southern Celtic Sea has produced no significant finds, though gas has been found in the Irish sector to the west. The potential here is thought to be much less, but if commercial oilfields are discovered the obvious base for operations in the south is the major oil-refining port of Milford Haven.

Oil refining The more than threefold increase in British oil-refining capacity, 1960–75, brought about several spatial changes of geographical significance, as seen in table 4.6. The most striking feature was the spread of oil-refining into three new regions in the 1960s; these had acquired 18 per cent of the British capacity by 1975. Most of this change was at the expense of the North West, which failed to grow at a sufficient rate to maintain its position, and of Scotland, both of which became

TABLE 4.6

Regional Distribution of Crude Oil Distillation Capacity, UK, 1950–75

	Million tonnes per annum at end of year			
	1950	1960	1970	1975
SE	3.0	30.8	44.3	49.0
W Midlands				
NW	3.3	7.6	13.3	20.7
Scotland	0.8	3.6	9.4	9.3
North			10.4	10.9
Yorks. and Humberside			11.0	13.4
E Midlands				
E Anglia				
SW				
Wales	2.6	7.8	24.2	43.8
N Ireland			1.5	1.5
Total	9.8	49.9	114.1	148.8

Source: Digests of Energy Statistics (HMSO)

relatively less important. Despite these changes, 36 per cent of the oil-refining capacity remained concentrated in the SE of England (fig. 4.4).

The other feature of geographical interest was the increase in average size of refineries. In 1950 the largest could process only 2.6 million tonnes of crude oil a year. By 1975 there were five with capacities of over ten million tonnes a year, i.e. individually greater than the national refining capacity twenty years earlier, and fifteen others were larger than the largest in 1950 (table 4.7). Over 95 per cent of the refinery capacity was concentrated in these giant units, half of it in the five largest. Clearly the pattern and landscape impact of these was much different from that which would have resulted if refineries had remained individually small.

Market attraction played a dominant role in the location of oil-refining in the UK. With little weight loss in processing there is no heavy penalty incurred through carrying the raw material to market for refining. Moreover, with virtually all the crude oil arriving from offshore, there is no attraction to a raw material site within Britain. Most refinery capacity is therefore located at an import point as close as possible to the market. Other locations have been chosen only where special factors operate and the exploitation of North Sea oil shows little sign of altering this situation. The largest market for refinery products has always been SE England, with Greater London having the largest single concentration of demand. It is hardly surprising therefore that the Thames Estuary has attracted the largest concentration of oil-refining or that, together with Fawley on Southampton Water, this south-east corner of the UK in 1975 had over one-third UK oil-refinery capacity. These refineries were well-situated to serve, in addition, not only the inland markets of the Midlands, but also the smaller regional markets accessible by coastal vessels serving depots along the North Sea shores. The opposite end of the axial belt of industry and population in Britain reaches the sea in the NW region, which in 1975 had a further 14 per cent of the national refining-capacity. With nearly 50 per cent of oil-refining taking place in these two areas, the other regional outputs are much smaller.

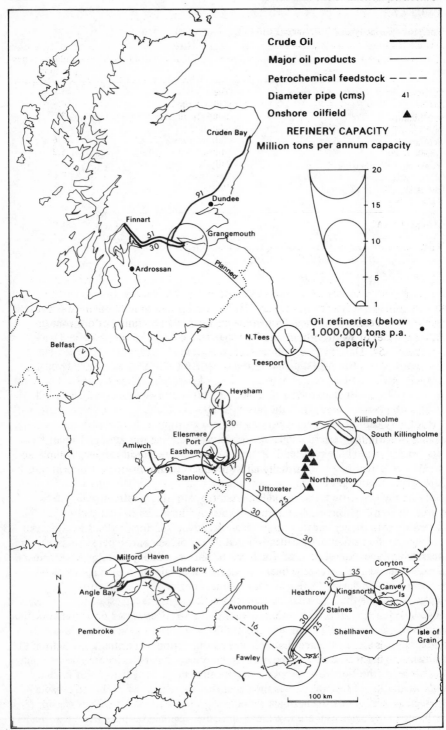

Figure 4.4   Oil-refinery capacity and oil pipelines, UK, 1975

TABLE 4.7

Distillation Capacity of Oil Refineries UK 1975[1]

	Million tonnes per annum		Million tonnes per annum
Coryton	8.7	Teesport	5.9
Eastham	0.7	Killingholme	4.4
Fawley	19.2	South Killingholme	8.9
Isle of Grain	10.7	Llandarcy	8.2
Shellhaven	10.3	Milford Haven (Esso)	15.6
Ellesmere Port	1.4	Milford Haven (Gulf)	5.2
Heysham	0.7	Milford Haven (Amoco)	5.0
Stanlow	18.5	Pembroke	9.5
Grangemouth	8.6	Belfast	1.5
North Tees	5.0		
GRAND TOTAL			148.0

[1] Refineries with a capacity of less than 0.5 million tonnes per annum are excluded
Source: Digest of Energy Statistics (HMSO)

Nevertheless the industrial regions of C Scotland and S Wales both acquired the first British crude oil refineries in the early 1920s. Grangemouth in Scotland was chosen because of an earlier historical base in the extraction and refining of oil from the local oil shales of West Lothian; the Pumpherston refinery on the shalefield was closed in 1964. Llandarcy, near Swansea, serves its local industrial area plus the Severn estuary and accessible areas of the south-west Midlands as well. Two regions which might have been expected to acquire crude oil-refining earlier were Humberside, to serve the markets of the W Riding industrial complex, and the NE. But it was not until after 1960 that local demand in these areas was sufficiently large to justify local oil-refining, to compete with refinery products brought from elsewhere, or that other inducements to develop locally were sufficiently strong. The same is true on a lesser scale of N Ireland. Relatively isolated, the small refinery completed there in 1962 is able to sell virtually all its products within the local markets, mostly in close proximity to Belfast.

While market attractions have dominated the oil-refinery distribution pattern, government inducements and transport economies have also played their part. Government influence showed up particularly strongly in the 1960s, when most of the expansion of oil-refining capacity in the UK took place in the development areas. This was because the grants and tax incentives available gave the development areas a considerable advantage over other parts of Britain for projects such as oil refineries, in which very large capital investment is involved. The government used its IDC controls over industrial location to the same end. The strength of this government influence is indicated by the fact that six new refineries and 65 per cent of the new refinery capacity completed in the 1960s were located in the development areas. There is some evidence that political consideration had influenced location decisions earlier than this. Llandarcy oil refinery in S Wales was located on what was thought to be a strategically safe site in the 1920s. Similarly, the only refinery built during the Second World War was sited at Heysham in N Lancashire with strategic considerations uppermost.

Transport economies have exercised a locational influence in several ways. All the crude oil refineries in the UK were located, at least initially, on sites easily accessible from oil tanker berths. Coastal locations not only minimize the transport cost of the crude oil, but also allow the distribution of refined products by coastal vessel wherever possible. The location of oil refineries within the UK has been considerably influenced by the increasing size of the tankers used to transport the oil to Britain (ch. 5.V.2). These have allowed a continuing reduction in shipping costs and therefore in the delivered price of the crude oil. In 1951 most of the ships in use were less than 20,000 deadweight tons and the largest was only 50,000 dwt. By 1961 the largest ships were over 100,000 dwt, and a decade later a 250,000 dwt tanker had discharged its cargo at Milford Haven in S Wales. In 1970 the total daily costs of a 200,000 dwt tanker per thousand tons were only 80 per cent of those of a 90,000 dwt tanker and less than 50 per cent of those of a 25,000 dwt tanker (Hallett and Randall 1970, 29). But in the UK the larger the tanker, the smaller the number of deep-water anchorages capable of accommodating such ships. To take advantage of supertanker economies, refineries either have to locate at these deep-water sites, or be linked to these terminals by pipelines. Both developments have occurred in the UK. The three terminals capable of taking supertankers of over 100,000 dwt in 1975 were at Finnart on Loch Long, western Scotland, Milford Haven in S Wales and the Rhos terminal, Anglesey. The first was built in 1951 to serve the long-established Grangemouth refinery by pipeline, whilst Milford Haven acts in both capacities. The availability of the deep water there attracted four large refineries with a combined capacity of 35 million tonnes by 1975. In addition there is a pipeline to Llandarcy near Swansea where direct imports to the 8 million tonne refinery via the nearby Swansea docks had been limited to the use of 20,000 dwt ships. The North West region overcame the shortcomings of its limited depth anchorages by establishing terminals progressively further away, linked to the refineries by pipeline. Thus in 1954 a special oil dock was completed at Bromborough capable of taking 32,000 dwt ships; this soon proved inadequate and a jetty was built at Tranmere Port which could take 65,000 dwt ships. By 1970 this too was proving too small and in 1975 a deep water oil terminal was completed in Anglesey to serve the NW. This comprises a mooring buoy capable of handling 300,000 ton tankers, with the oil transferred to an onshore tank farm before being piped to Stanlow. In this way the changes in transport, and especially the increased size of bulk oil carriers, attracted developments to the west coast with its deep water and shorter haulages from extra-European oilfields, counteracting to some extent the market attraction of the east of Britain commented upon earlier.

Improved technology and technical considerations have also played a part in the changing picture. Until 1950 the main consumer demand was for the light products produced from crude oil, principally for road vehicle consumption. When these were extracted, large quantities of heavier products remained which were difficult to sell. In this situation there were advantages in refining the crude oil near to the oil wells. The problem was eased by the development of the cracking process, by which some of the heavier oil is broken down to provide a bigger yield of light products, but there is a limit to how much of this can be done and it is expensive. The real solution came with the expansion of markets for the heavier products as well. Fuel oil in particular became much more competitive with coal in the UK after 1956, and in the 1960s the growing British petrochemical industries came to use increasing quantities of the heavy residual materials produced. As a result, today 95 per cent of the crude oil received at a UK refinery normally ends up as saleable products, with half of the rest being consumed by the refinery for its operation. This reduction in the weight loss has made the market location much more attractive, so that whereas in 1950 UK domestic refinery capacity was only 50 per cent of refined product needs, in 1976 domestic refinery capacity was well in excess of demand.

The geography of oil-refining in the UK then can be understood in these terms. From 1960 to 1973 government influence, transport economies and physical geography have all favoured the location of new refinery capacity in the west and north of the UK. Market attractions favoured locations in the South East in particular, and encouraged the building of small refineries near the major regional concentrations of industry and population. The arrival of North Sea oil has now altered the situation, but with so much capital already invested in existing refineries with long useful lives and with present capacity likely to meet any increase in demand until the early 1980s, this will not be reflected in any significant change in the geography of UK oil-refining before about 1990. By then additional refineries can be expected to have been added in NE England and Scotland.

Distribution and refinery products Deliveries of petroleum products for inland consumption in the UK in 1970 totalled over 96 million tonnes, having more than doubled from 1960. Consumption continued to increase, reaching a peak of 100 million tonnes in 1973, but fell to only 83 million tonnes in 1975 as a result of increased cost and an economic recession. Fuel oil consumption in 1975 constituted 44 per cent of the total, motor spirits 19 per cent and gas/diesel oil a further 22 per cent. Fuel oil consumption amounted to 36.5 million tonnes, distributed as shown in table 4.8. Regional deliveries of fuel oil, excluding that used by refineries and for electricity generation, are shown in table 4.9. The SE accounted for 21 per cent of the consumption with the W Midlands and NW England taking a further 23 per cent between them.

For distribution, oil products move in increasingly smaller quantities until the final consumers are reached. Because of economies of scale, and especially the large proportion of total costs that are taken up by terminal costs of loading and unloading, the aim is to retain cheaper bulk movement as far as possible. The cheapest means of movement are by water and by pipeline, and both are used in Britain in addition to road and rail. Deliveries are usually made direct to customers located within about 96 km of a refinery. For bulk consumers with rail facilities these deliveries are made by the trainload. Where justified by large continuous demand, oil pipelines are used (Simpson 1966, 127). For example, pipelines carry refined products from Stanlow to the Manchester area, from Fawley to Staines and Heathrow airport, and from Llandarcy to the giant Port Talbot steelworks. The oil pipeline network in Britain (ch. 5, p. 429) has grown as individual markets have expanded sufficiently to consume continuous flows of oil products. In 1969 a 394 km pipeline was opened, feeding refined products to N London and the Midlands from refineries and installations on the Thames and Mersey, and another was completed in 1973, from Milford Haven to the Midlands and Manchester. These were in addition to the various specialized pipelines carrying petrochemical feedstock from some refineries to petrochemical complexes. Since 1969 the tonnage of refined petroleum products transferred by pipeline in the UK has exceeded that going by rail. For other consumers delivery is normally by road, but since road transport is the most expensive per tonne-km, bulk oil depots are established to serve customers beyond the refinery supply area. Here physical geography plays a

TABLE 4.8

Fuel-oil Consumption, UK, 1970, 1973 and 1975 (thousand tonnes)

	1970	1973	1975
Steel industry	5,079	4,433	2,951
Chemical industry, including petrochemicals	2,407	3,650	2,711
Other manufacturing industries	12,103	10,455	8,325
Gas-making	185	173	122
Electricity generation	11,904	16,580	13,130
Other public utilities	149	54	49
Non-manufacturing industries	2,065	1,612	992
Non-industrial central heating	4,179	2,722	2,249
Petroleum industry (mainly refinery consumption)	6,534	7,558	6,553
Total	44,608	47,240	37,084

Source: Digest of Energy Statistics (HMSO)

part. The UK has a long coastline compared with area, and all but a very few of the oil refineries are on coastal sites. In addition, few industrial markets in Britain are more than 96 km from navigable water. Depots can thus be sited close to markets, yet be supplied by cheap water transport. As a result, coastwise traffic in refined products in 1975 amounted to 26 million tonnes, with a further 6 million tonnes transferred by inland waterway (Dept. Energy 1976, 79). In the past oil was competitive at coastal locations, but as inland markets have grown and as more pipelines become economic, the cost of oil at inland sites will be reduced, making it more competitive with other fuels.

TABLE 4.9

Inland Deliveries of Fuel-oil, UK Regions, 1970 and 1974 (Excluding deliveries for refinery fuel, gas-making and electricity generation) in thousand tonnes

	1970	1974
South East	5,782	4,319
West Midlands	2,152	1,212
North West	4,168	3,588
Scotland	2,879	3,013
North	2,470	1,376
Yorks. and Humberside	2,639	1,926
East Midlands	1,051	781
East Anglia	364	386
South West	1,352	925
Wales	2,930	2,434
N Ireland	701	839
Total	26,492	20,803

Source: Digests of Energy Statistics (HMSO)

I.4   Gas

Public supply of gas in the UK dates from 1807, but until 1920 it was used mainly for lighting. After that electricity rapidly captured the lighting market and by 1945 gas was being used principally for heating. Between 1945 and 1975 the gas industry was radically transformed by two developments, with most of the changes occurring after 1965. By 1975 the industry had little in common with what can only be described as its technological predecessor, which had remained dominant until the late 1960s.

The first major transformation followed the nationalization of the industry in 1949. At that time there were 991 undertakings supplying gas in GB, one-third of them belonging to local authorities. Under the 1948 Act the undertakings were grouped into twelve Area Gas Boards, and a major programme of rationalization was undertaken to improve the quality and efficiency of the service; at the same time production and distribution facilities were modernized. Gas was being produced from 1,050 separate gas works, with over 97 per cent of the raw materials being coal or coke. By 1963 the number of works had been reduced to only 307, though production capacity was 30 per cent more than in 1949. In addition to the gas being made in its own works, the Gas Board bought 20 per cent of its gas supplies from outside sources, mainly coke ovens and the steel industry, and from oil refineries.

Before 1960 gas sales were rising much more slowly than sales of electricity. A major reason for this was the faster rise in the price of gas coal, than in the price of the general coals upon which the electricity supply industry depended.

The second transformation was brought about by the change in source of gas used (table 4.10; fig. 4.1b). As late as 1960 over 90 per cent of the gas available was produced from coal or coke. By 1965 coal was supplying only 70 per cent of the gas, with petroleum refinery gas supplying 25 per cent. But 1964 had seen the first commercial bulk deliveries of natural gas from the Sahara to the UK and in 1965 the first productive natural gas well was discovered in the North Sea. By 1975 natural gas accounted for 97 per cent of total UK gas supplies and the British public supply gas industry had become essentially a wholesaler rather than a manufacturer as before (table 4.11). The first pipeline to pump the gas ashore from the North Sea was completed to Easington, Humberside in 1967, and since then additional pipelines have been laid to terminals at Bacton, Norfolk; Theddlethorpe, Lincolnshire; and St Fergus, Grampian. In 1975 proven gas reserves amounted to 8,495 Mm^3 and the total possible reserves are thought to exceed 14,158 Mm^3. The proven reserves could support production at about 140 Mm^3 a day by 1980 with a further 28 Mm^3 available from the Norwegian section of the Frigg field. If further commercial discoveries are made, as seems likely, this level of production would be increased and maintained at a higher level until the 1990s; otherwise production will slowly decline from 1980. The gas being used in 1975 came from fields in the southern North Sea within 161 km of the coast. Further north the basins contain both oil and gas and are located beneath deeper parts of the area further from land. The latest gas pipeline linking the joint British/Norwegian Frigg gas field with the St Fergus terminal north of Aberdeen, came into use in 1976, with a further pipeline from the Shetland basin to the same terminal to be built by 1980.

Although offering the advantages over coal of control of temperature to a fine degree and of not needing customer storage, gas did suffer some disadvantages compared with electricity. For industry it was essentially a supplier of energy in bulk, and did not compete with electricity for the small power market for machinery or lighting. In the domestic market electricity had the major advantage that virtually every house in the UK already used it for lighting purposes. Gas supply had to be provided specially as a separate additional service, and was essentially competing for

TABLE 4.10

Primary Fuel Input used in the Gas Industry, UK, 1960, 1970 and 1975

| | Million tonnes of coal or coal equivalent | | |
	1960	1970	1975
Coal	22.9	4.2	0.1
Petroleum	1.4	6.2	0.8
Petroleum gases	0.5	1.5	0.2
Natural gas	0	10.5	54.9
Total	24.8	22.4	56.0

Source: Digests of Energy Statistics (HMSO)

the space-heating market. But it was not until the early 1960s that domestic central heating became a commonplace in new housing in the UK, or that the move away from coal as a general industrial fuel gave gas a better chance to compete for industrial space-heating. It was for these reasons that in 1960 gas sales were very little more than they had been in 1950. The 1960s saw a much more rapid expansion, mainly through aggressive and successful sales campaigns in the domestic heating market. Central heating systems were rapidly replacing open coal fires, and the flexibility of control, cleanliness, constant supply on tap without storage and relative cheapness, made gas a strong competitor as the alternative fuel. Its use in industry also grew, and in the late 1960s sales to all markets benefited from the increasing availability of cheaper natural gas. By 1970 gas sales, measured in millions of therms, had more than doubled in ten years and they more than doubled again to 1975, with all the increase supplied by natural gas (table 4.12).

Geographical patterns In the first decade after nationalization in 1949 there were two important changes in the geography of the gas industry. The first was in the actual production facilities, the second in the development of regional gas grids, both inter-related. The pattern of production changed in the first decade through the closure of two-thirds of the plants inherited at nationalization. Production was concentrated wherever possible on larger, more modern units and by 1960 seventy-

TABLE 4.11

Net Total Gas Available for UK Consumption, both Public Supply and Other, 1960, 1970 and 1975

| | million therms | | |
	1960	1970	1975
Town gas	2,696	4,297	717
Coke oven and blast furnace gas	2,740	2,238	1,759
Petroleum gas	867	1,334	1,702
Natural gas	15	1,557	12,568
Total available	6,318	9,426	16,746

Source: Digests of Energy Statistics (HMSO)

TABLE 4.12

Sales of Gas by Gas Boards, UK, 1960, 1970 and 1975

| | million therms | | |
	1960	1970	1975
Domestic	1,279	3,522	5,869
Industrial	858	1,472	5,870
Commercial	405	685	1,171
Public administration	42	68 ⎫	
Public lighting	24	3 ⎭	171
Total supplied	2,608	5,750	13,081

Source: Digests of Energy Statistics (HMSO)

one of these were producing 71 per cent of the nation's gas (Gas Council 1960, 62). As a rule it was the smaller local works that were closed, so that production was increasingly centralized in the larger population centres in each Gas Board area. The closures were hastened by the purchase of increasing quantities of gas from products outside the industry. Up to 1960 the main external source was coke-oven gas from the steel industry in particular, though oil refinery 'tail gases' had also begun to be used.

These developments were facilitated by changes in the distribution system. Prior to nationalization each gas works supplied its own area through a discrete distribution system. Integration or even inter-connection of these local networks was virtually absent except around G London. In 1949 the new Gas Boards immediately set about developing regional gas grids for their own areas. Between 1949 and 1957 the length of mains in use rose from 119,735 km to 145,404 km, most of which were developed for the integration of works and formerly separate discrete distribution systems rather than as the result of extending the urban areas served (Manners, 1959, 156). This allowed concentration of production on the larger more efficient works, and made possible the more widespread use of gas from coke ovens and oil refineries. Not all areas were able to benefit from these advantages at that time. It was not economic to extend the gas grids to replace small gas works serving isolated markets. This was especially true in Wales and Scotland, where small gas works maintained a higher proportion of output.

In the early 1960s it was anticipated that supplies of gas made from coal, whether in gas works or from coke ovens, would in future form a decreasing proportion of public supply. The main alternative possibilities then being actively pursued were the making of gas from oil, and the importation of natural gas from N Africa. At the same time a methane gas grid was developed to distribute imported natural gas from the import point at Canvey Island, east of London. This was in effect the beginning of a national gas grid which had been proposed by the Gas Council (1958, 7) and which was the next logical step in the evolution of the public supply industry. The discovery of large quantities of North Sea gas in the mid-1960s necessitated a reappraisal. Plans for increasing gas-making capacity were shelved, and the implementation of a national gas grid for the distribution of the new supplies was given priority. By 1975 the number of gas works in production was down to fifty, dis-

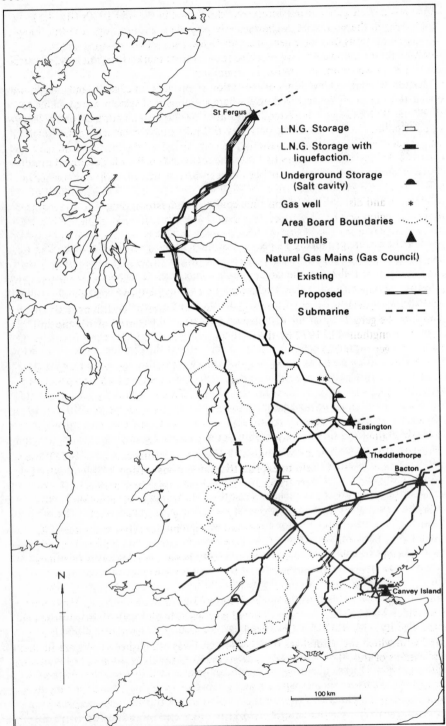

Figure 4.5   National natural gas grid, UK, 1975

and a new natural gas transmission system developed in the mid-1970s (fig. 4.5).

Changes in the sources of gas have clearly played an important part in the changing spatial patterns that have been described. The form of the changes and the resulting pattern, however, owe much to four factors: markets, technology, political control and ownership, and transport economies.

Rationalization achieved by concentration of production capacity in larger, more efficient units, could be achieved only where an integrated system was available to distribute their products; both required central ownership and control for implementation. Nationalization is not the only way this might have been achieved, though in retrospect it is unlikely that any alternative centralization of control would have occurred. In the first period, up to 1960, the regional Gas Boards developed in isolation. As late as 1964 movement of gas between Boards was virtually non-existent, and the national gas grid was still to be implemented (fig. 4.7). The geography of production and distribution at this time could be understood only if it is recognized that each region was isolated, operating almost as a self-sufficient island. This was the next stage on from the pattern of local isolation which had prevailed in 1949 (fig. 4.6). This regional heritage of the early 1960s was still obvious in 1970, but by then central authority was already asserting itself more strongly, aided by the appearance of North Sea gas and the development of the associated national gas network for its transmission. By 1975 the public supply gas industry had acquired a more rational pattern, related not to regional but to national conditions. This latest change in the geography of the industry was facilitated by central ownership and control, strengthened in 1972 by the setting up of the British Gas Corporation with much stronger central authority.

The part played by transport economies is becoming increasingly important as the industry becomes fully adjusted to the loss of its manufacturing operations and to its new function as simply a distributor. In the post-war period gas transport costs rose much more slowly than transport costs for other forms of energy. As a result it became cheaper to transport gas by pipe than to transport coal overground. This contributed to the closure of small works and to the development of large gas works able to take advantage of economies of scale in getting coal delivered. These transport economies also help to explain the way rationalization of the industry led, wherever possible, to a concentration of gas-making capacity at or near sources of raw materials, that is to say on the coalfields and near major oil refineries.

Pipelines, however, are competitive only with a high load factor (ch. 5.VI.2). This is because 75 to 80 per cent of the cost of pipeline transport is capital cost, which has to be borne regardless of the quantity of material being moved. In addition there are considerable economies of scale in using larger diameter pipes (Manners 1971A, 119). These economic aspects of transport have become even more important with the coming of natural gas. This has more than double the calorific value of manufactured gas, and so effectively doubles the fuel value capacity of pipes which hitherto carried manufactured gas. There is thus little to be surprised at in the alacrity with which the Gas Board in the UK took to natural gas or in the speed with which the natural gas transmission grid was established. There are further implications of this, though, stemming from the need for the natural gas transmission grid to be operated at a high load factor to be efficient. Unfortunately gas demands fluctuate seasonally, and if pipelines capable of meeting peak demands are laid, they would operate well below capacity for much of the time. The obvious solution is to have storage facilities near the markets to meet peak demands (fig. 4.5), with the

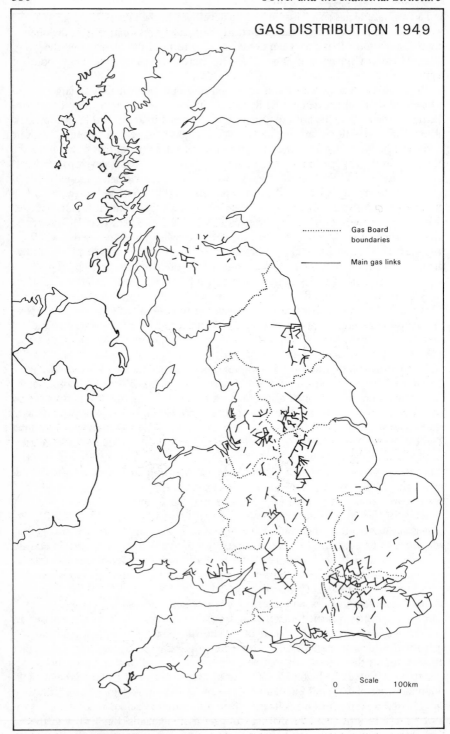

Figure 4.6   Gas distribution, UK, 1949

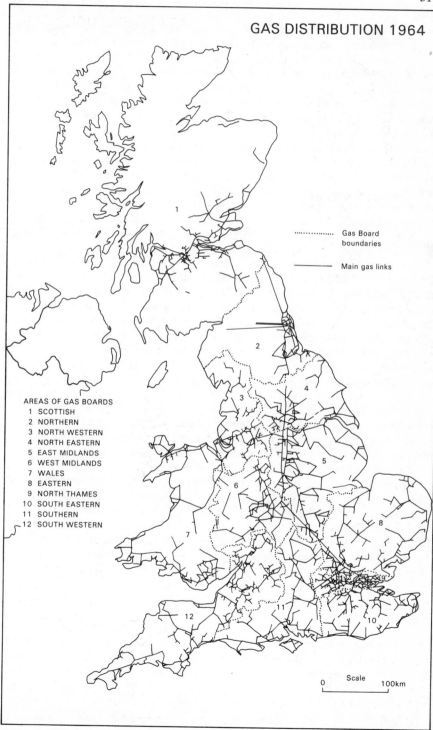

Figure 4.7   Gas distribution, UK, 1964

pipelines capable of meeting base and middle load demands. A supplementary technique is to have an interruptible supply contract with large industrial consumers, for which they receive special rates. Both methods are being used in Britain.

The location patterns of the public supply gas industry have always been strongly influenced by the pattern of demand. Until 1949 the whole industry was essentially market-oriented. By then, wherever demand was sufficient gas works had been established, each with a discrete local distribution network, unconnected with its neighbours. In this situation obviously each local area had to have its own gas-making works. Locational choice was limited. Nationalization however, brought with it rationalization, and more especially the development of regional gas grids, with the result that within each region, production capacity could be concentrated near the major markets. Only where an area was too isolated, and had too small a market to justify the cost of extending the regional grid to it, were alternatives tried. Thus tanker or bottle gas is distributed in parts of Wales, and where coal-based production is very expensive butane/air installations have been tried. It has been suggested, however, that in such areas it is a waste of financial resources for the two industries of gas and electricity to compete, and that the market should simply be left to electricity, which has to penetrate such areas anyway to provide lighting (Manners 1970). It is not difficult to see that the next logical development would have been the concentration of production at the best national sites, with a national gas transmission grid to ensure adequate distribution to all regions. But the need for such a development was overtaken by the discovery and rapid switch to North Sea gas, requiring a natural gas transmission grid. This too was influenced in its pattern by the geography of the market. Allowing for the sources of supply being off the east coast of Britain, the pattern of the grid coincides closely with other national network patterns of motorways, trunk railways, and the electricity supergrid, and for the same reasons. They all conform to the pattern of maximum demand. It has been pointed out that over 70 per cent of the gas sales in Britain were made in a belt 56 km wide each side of a straight line joining London and Manchester. In 1975 the gas regions with sales in excess of 1,000 million therms in descending order of magnitude were North Western, E Midlands, W Midlands and N Thames.

Technology has played only a relatively minor role in the present geography of the public supply gas industry, though it had its effect earlier. Shortages and the cost of coking coal in the 1950s led the industry to seek alternative sources of gas. The cheapest Lurgi coal gasification process needed a coalfield location and plants were built in Scotland and the W Midlands. A gas-from-oil process, developed in the late 1950s, proved very attractive commercially and plants were built near oil refineries, as at Shellhaven and Llandarcy. In addition, pipeline transport costs were also reduced through technological improvements, which made the development of regional and national gas grids more attractive. Techniques for underground storage of gas have also helped in the use of natural gas, though without specific geographical effects.

The most important single fact in understanding the geography of the contemporary gas industry is the changeover since 1965 from its being a producer of secondary energy, to being a distribution industry of a primary fuel. Even in the late 1970s, however, the existing pattern still bore evidence of pre-1965 development.

I.5 Electricity

The first public supply of electricity in the UK dates from 1881. From its earliest days the industry has been subject to some degree of public control. In 1926 the government set up the Central Electricity Board to construct and operate a national grid inter-connecting individual power stations. In the succeeding twenty years this resulted in generation and transmission being increasingly coordinated. In 1948 all municipal and private undertakings, other than those in N Ireland, were nationalized. The generation of electricity in England and Wales was put in the hands of the Central Electricity Generating Board (CEGB), who were made responsible for transmitting the electricity they produced in bulk to the twelve separate Area Electricity Boards. The Area Boards were made responsible for the distribution and selling of the electricity to consumers in their own areas. In Scotland, the North of Scotland Hydro Electric Board and the South of Scotland Electricity Board both generate and distribute electricity. In N Ireland a joint electricity authority was set up in 1967 to coordinate electricity generation. The electricity is sold in bulk to the Belfast Corporation, the Londonderry Corporation and the Electricity Board for N Ireland, who distribute it to consumers in their own areas.

TABLE 4.13

Fuel Input in the Electricity Industry, UK, 1950–75

| | Million tonnes of coal or coal equivalent | | | | |
	1950*	1960	1970	1973	1975
Coal, coke and breeze	33.1	53.5	77.2	76.9	74.6
Oil	1.5	9.3	21.4	28.8	21.8
Natural gas	–	–	0.2	1.1	3.4
Nuclear power	–	0.9	9.5	10.0	10.9
Hydro electricity	0.8	1.7	2.3	2.0	1.9
Net imports of electricity	–	–	0.3	–	–
Total all fuels	35.4	65.4	110.9	118.8	112.6

* Figures are approximate
Source: Digest of Energy Statistics (HMSO)

Between 1945 and 1975 the electricity industry experienced three important changes affecting its geography. On nationalization in 1948 the first change was to centralized control and ownership. This had its main impact on the pattern of electricity distribution, since electricity generation had been publicly coordinated since 1926. The second change was the increasing use of fuels other than coal for electricity generation (table 4.13). In 1950, except for hydro-electricity generation in N Scotland, virtually the only source of electricity was from coal-fired power stations. But by 1960 oil had come to supply nearly 20 per cent of the primary fuel used for electricity generation, and small quantities of electricity were becoming available from nuclear power stations. In the 1960s oil maintained its share, but nuclear power grew in importance, and by the end of the decade was supplying nearly 10 per cent of the electricity used. At the beginning of the 1970s natural gas also began to be used to fire power stations, and subsequently increased its contribution. Despite this increasing use of new fuels, coal continued to hold pride of place. Until 1973 coal was becoming *proportionately* less important, but increasing *tonnages* of coal were used, as growth in demand for electricity absorbed more than the output contributed by other fuels. Since 1973, however, electricity demand has fallen slightly and it is coal consumption that has borne the brunt of the resulting decline in demand for fuel. These developments have altered the pattern of public supply generation stations, since the locational considerations which apply differ between the different fuels. The third major change was the rapid growth in the amount of electricity used in Britain up to 1973. At nationalization output capacity was 11.8 thousand megawatts (MW) and sales amounted to 38,821 million kilowatt hours (kWh). Subsequent growth is shown in table 4.14, where it can be seen that output capacity and sales more than doubled between 1950 and 1960, and doubled again between 1960 and 1975. In achieving this success, electricity had several basic advantages over other power sources. The first was its virtual universal availability, since its use for lighting means that nearly all potential customers are already linked

TABLE 4.14

Output, Capacity and Sales of Public Supply Electricity, UK, 1950–75

	1950	1960	1970	1975
Number of generating stations at end of year	338	319	289	262
Plant capacity at end of year (GW)	15.1	31.9	60.5	72.4
Total sales to consumers (GWh)	45,912	102,363	193,907	217,500

Source: Digest of Energy Statistics (HMSO)

into the distribution system. The availability of electricity at the turn of a switch also means that it is more convenient than coal or oil, where supplies have to be ordered and stocks maintained, and where appliances have to be serviced more frequently. Massive investment, to meet the continual increases in demand, allowed much more rapid modification of the geographical patterns of the industry than would have occurred had demand risen only slowly.

There are two ways in which the geography of the public supply electricity industry has changed since 1960. The first is in the distribution of production facilities, and the second is in the development of a national transmission grid for the movement of electricity in bulk. Change did take place earlier following nationalization, as shown in table 4.15. In 1950 nearly 60 per cent of British electricity production was situated within the axial belt of England stretching from Thameside through to Merseyside. Power stations at that time were located mainly in and around the major urban consuming markets. Most were small, but the eighty-seven of 50 MW capacity or more generated 90 per cent of the electricity. Coal contributed over 95 per cent of the fuel used. By 1960 as a result of different rates of growth in installed capacity in the different regions of the UK the axial belt was providing only 48 per cent of output, while the E Midlands and Yorkshire had increased their share to 26 per cent. Output had doubled but the number of power stations had fallen, indicating a massive increase in the individual generating capacities of the newer stations being built.

The biggest changes occurred in the succeeding fifteen years, with much of the development taking place in the decade 1965–75. At the regional level there was a shift in location of production away from markets, with new capacity being developed close to coal supplies and especially near the cheap coal sources of the east central coalfields. There was a shift too in fuel sources, with cheap fuel oil being attractive from 1960 to 1973, cheap natural gas becoming available from 1965 and with nuclear-powered stations being completed. As a result of these shifts, by 1975 coal was providing only two-thirds of the fuel used by the industry, with oil contributing 19 per cent, nuclear energy 10 per cent and natural gas 3 per cent.

Despite the doubling of generating capacity between 1950 and 1960 and a doubling again between 1960 and 1975, the number of power stations underwent continuous decline (table 4.14). This was one indication of the increase in station size. In 1950 the largest were rated at less than 200 MW capacity. In 1963 the first 550 MW generating unit was commissioned at High Marnham; in 1968 the first 2,000 MW stations were brought into operation at West Burton and Ferrybridge; in 1975 there were ten sites with over 2,000 MW capacity and at one of these, Drax in Yorkshire, two generating sets, each with a capacity of 660 MW, were in operation. The rate at which these changes took place was facilitated by the rapid increases in demand which occurred up until 1973, allowing the building of new stations using the latest technology at a more rapid rate than would otherwise have been possible. It also meant that the distribution of stations adjusted more rapidly to the changing situation than would have occurred had demand risen only slowly. Paradoxically, the much slower rate of growth after 1973, also hastened change through more rapid closure of older less efficient stations than would have occurred otherwise. Thus in 1975 a programme of closures was announced whereby, by 1978, 22 of the 161 stations operating in England and Wales in 1975 were to cease operations. The importance of minimizing generating costs, which played a vital role in all the changes, is indicated by the fact that in 1975 nearly 69 per cent of the electricity generated for public supply in England and Wales came from the twenty oil and coal fired stations with the highest thermal efficiency, plus the eight nuclear-powered stations.

Distribution These production changes required considerable adaptation in the electricity distribution system. When the industry was nationalized the distribution systems within the individual regions were already fairly well integrated. In addition, a 132 kV grid was available for the transfer of limited amounts of electricity between regions. This grid was not designed to carry current in bulk over any great distances, however, and its inadequacy had become apparent with the heavy demands made on it during the Second World War. It was decided therefore to install a 275 kV grid to provide greater transmission capacity and allow freer choice in the best location for new power stations. By 1960, 1,046 km of this new supergrid had been completed. In the early 1960s it was decided to increase the capacity for transfers, and to minimize the number of environment-intruding transmission lines by developing a 400 kV grid. Starting in 1965 most of this was created by upgrading the 275 kV grid. By 1975 there were 4,697 kms of 400 kV grid, and 2,117 kms of 275 kV grid in the UK, none of which had existed twenty years earlier (fig. 4.9). These developments made the UK system the largest integrated power network in the world (COI 1971, 265). Effectively what had been a set of separate regional supply systems was converted into a single system centred on a metropolitan structured core in the

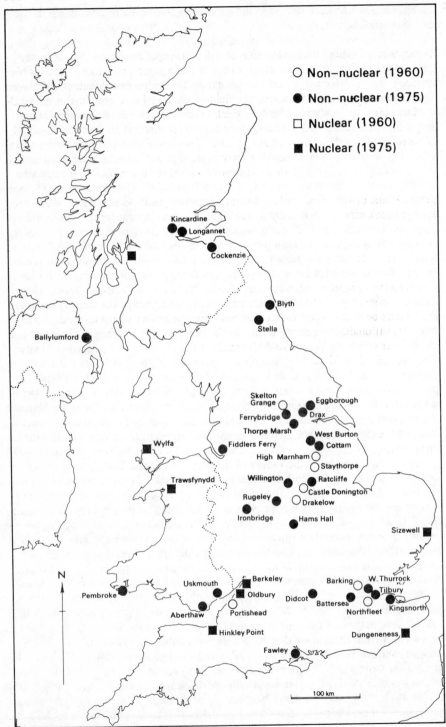

Figure 4.8   Electricity generating stations over 500 MW capacity, UK, 1960 and 1975

central UK, with links to outlying city structural systems, such as those of NE
England and C Scotland.

Generation Although the explanation of the location of electricity generation is
more complex than in the case of the other fuel and power industries, it is possible
to recognize the more important factors involved. Transport economies have played
a very important part in explaining the changes since 1945. At the time of nationalization, electricity generation was essentially market-oriented. At first sight this is
surprising, since transmission of base load electricity was then competitive with all
other forms of land transport of energy over distances of about 80 km. It was more
efficient therefore to locate base load power stations at the fuel supply and transmit
the electricity to markets, than to put power stations at the market and carry coal
supplies to them. In practice this had not occurred before 1948 because generating
plant became obsolete so quickly. Technical improvements to make new plant more
efficient took effect very rapidly as new plant was continually being built to meet
the growth of demand. As a result, any one generator did not contribute to base
load electricity supply for more than a few years. For the rest of its useful life it
was used to meet middle and peak load demand. But it was not economic to transmit middle and peak load electricity over any distance. In this situation even base
load stations were located near to markets, in the certain knowledge that the short-
term loss of having them there would be offset by the gains in the longer-term when
they would be suppliers of middle and peak load electricity only (Manners 1971A,
161−2). Nationalization changed this. In the late 1940s it was thought unlikely that
any further substantial gains would be made in the efficiency of generating plants.
To achieve further economies the industry now turned to minimization of transport
costs and it was decided to build large new stations to meet base load demands
nearer to the fuel sources, which at this time meant the coalfields. The most attractive for this purpose were those of S Yorkshire and the E Midlands which produced
the cheapest coal in Britain and were closest to the south of England and S Lancashire, where electricity demand was growing fast and already exceeded local generating capacity. These inland coalfields also had cooling water for power stations
readily available nearby in the valleys of the Aire, Calder and Trent Rivers. It was
for this reason that the S Yorkshire and E Midlands areas acquired such a large proportion of the new electricity generation capacity built in the 1950s. At the same
time, however, coal-fired power stations were also being built at some market locations. These were where the market lay close to a coalfield that could supply the
fuel, or where coal could be supplied cheaply by water transport. Middle and peak
load stations using coal were also built close to markets. In those cases it was
cheaper to take coal to them than to provide and maintain the extra transmission
capacity necessary if they were to be located elsewhere.

These trends in coal-fired power station location were continued in the 1960s, but
by then the use of oil and nuclear energy was also becoming significant. Most of the
new oil-fired stations were built in areas where transport costs made coal more
expensive. Within these areas they have been built either near the major oil refineries, as at Milford Haven, or on sites easily served by cheap water transport, as at
Plymouth. Transport costs are much less important in the location of nuclear power
stations, which are used almost exclusively to supply base load electricity; fuel
transport costs are a minor element in their operation.

From what has been said already it is clear that *market attractions* play an im-

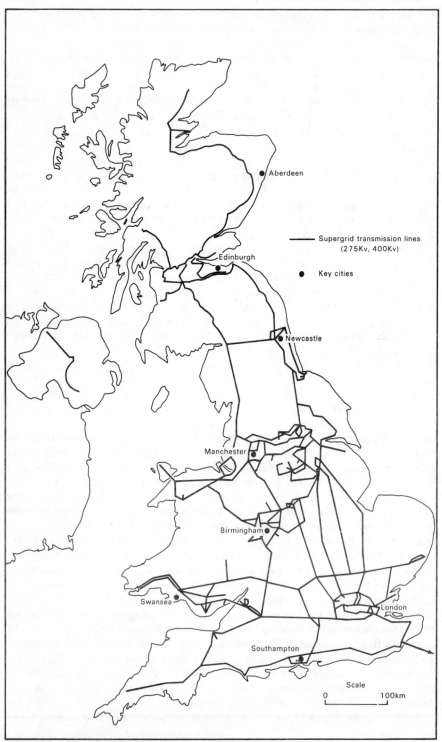

Figure 4.9   Electricity grid, UK, 1972

TABLE 4.15

Electricity Supply and Consumption by Generating Regions, GB, 1950–75

	1950		1960			1975*	
Division	TWh sent out	TWh received	TWh sent out	TWh received	Division	TWh sent out	TWh received
London	9.1	5.2	11.7	8.8			15.6
S Eastern	2.2	2.6	5.4	6.5	SE	40.5	14.0
Eastern	2.6	4.3	6.6	10.1			21.9
S Western	1.9	1.6	4.1	3.9			10.1
Southern	1.5	2.8	5.4	8.5	SW	37.1	19.4
S Wales	2.8	2.8	6.7	6.0			9.8
Midlands	5.8	5.2	9.2	11.0	Midlands	58.6	20.3
E Midlands	3.5	3.9	14.3	8.4			17.7
N Western	8.7	8.3	14.9	15.5	NW	21.6	29.3
N Wales	0.1	0.6	1.2	1.7			2.7
Yorkshire	6.1	5.1	15.0	11.0	NE	46.9	20.1
N Eastern	2.9	3.2	8.6	6.1			11.7
S Scotland	3.4	3.8	6.4	6.4		16.8	17.1
N Scotland	1.3	0.7	2.4	2.3		7.6	7.1
Great Britain	51.9	50.1	111.9	106.2		229.1	216.8

TWh = terawatt hours (thousand million kWh)
* Minor boundary changes mean the figures for 1975 are not strictly comparable with earlier years
Source: Digest of Energy Statistics (HMSO)

portant part in the pattern of power station distribution in Britain. Table 4.15 shows that most market areas supply 90 per cent or more of their electricity requirements themselves, irrespective of whether or not they have their own fuel supplies of oil or coal. The areas with a surplus of these fuels take advantage of their location on the coalfields, or in proximity to oil refineries, to a much lesser extent than is sometimes assumed. In 1948 the industry was even more strongly market-oriented, both at the regional and the national levels. Subsequently, although base load stations were increasingly located closer to their fuel sources, installed capacity also increased at the market. For coal-fired stations this was mainly, but not exclusively, to meet peak load demand, as in the London region. The new oil-powered stations were fortunate in that they could usually obtain their fuel oil from refineries located close to where the electricity was to be sold. They therefore show much greater market orientation than other forms of generation. For nuclear power, until the late 1960s, the stations were all located in areas deficient in coal, i.e. that were importing electricity from surplus areas. They were attracted to areas where transport costs made coal-fired electricity generation more expensive. In the late 1960s, however, proposals were made to locate some new nuclear stations in S Wales and the NE. As these were areas with high coal production costs, this indicated a new trend in nuclear station location. Intra-regionally, urban areas still prefer not to have nuclear power stations too close, and so siting factors have pushed them away from optimum locations vis-à-vis the regional market. In the late 1970s, serious reservations about the environmental hazards associated with nuclear power stations made further expansion of nuclear electricity generation unlikely until the late 1980s at the earliest.

Technological development has influenced the patterns in several ways. It was mentioned earlier that in 1947 it was thought the peak of efficiency of stations was very near and this was reflected in a pull to the coalfields. In fact this was not borne out in practice (Manners 1971A, 166). Further improvements occurred which tended to reduce the attractions of the coalfield sites in the longer-term, as explained earlier. Offsetting this to a certain extent were the economies of scale achieved, from less than 200 MW capacity in 1950 to 2,000 MW capacity twenty years later. The 2,000 MW stations generated base load electricity and were made possible by the availability of the grid by which their product could be distributed to wherever it was needed, since local demand could not consume all their output. Such developments reflect back on transport economies, since the larger the blocks of energy transmitted the cheaper the transport per unit becomes, and the larger the station the more efficiently it should operate in terms of thermal efficiency. It is technological developments also that have made nuclear power usable for electricity generation. The effect of this has been to locate more capacity nearer to markets than might otherwise have happened if coal and oil had remained the sole fuel sources. Nuclear power has heavy capital costs, making it much more suitable for base load supplies. This strengthens the attractions of locations away from cheap coal areas which were originally also base-load oriented. The first nuclear power stations to supply electricity commercially to the supergrid, were Bradwell in Essex and Berkeley on the Severn estuary in 1962. The first is located in the heavy electricity-importing areas of the Eastern Region; the second is close, in grid terms, to the heavy demands of the W and SW Midlands. Hinkley Point and Oldbury in the lower Severn estuary reinforced this pattern in the mid-1960s, and Trawsfynydd and Wylfa (1971) on Anglesey helped to supply the Merseyside area. In Scotland, Hunterston in Ayrshire is suitably placed to supply the Clydeside conurbation which has been a deficit area for electricity since the 1950s (Hauser 1971).

Finally, government involvement has played a role in location throughout the development of the electricity industry. To the control provided in the setting up of the Central Electricity Board in 1926 was added public ownership in 1948. The centralization of ownership gave freedom for the national organization of the industry not fully possible under the mixed ownership which existed previously. From 1948 planning was able to take advantage of national rather than just intra-regional locational advantages. It was this central planning of the industry on a national scale which allowed concentration of production on the cheap coalfields, and of nuclear and oil-fired power stations at the nationally advantageous places. Apart from centralizing ownership, the government also indirectly influenced location through its fuel policy. Sensitive to the social and economic problems associated with the coal industry, in 1961 a fuel-oil tax was imposed, aimed at limiting the competition of oil with coal. The effect was to encourage dependence on coal, and to attract power station capacity to where coal was available at an acceptable price. The government also influenced the pattern by financing the basic research necessary to make nuclear electricity generation a commercial possibility. Fierce arguments rage over the true cost of the electricity produced (Posner 1973, 89–105). It can be made to look dearer or cheaper than electricity from coal-fired stations, depending upon whether the government-financed research and development costs are included or excluded in the calculation. Either way it seems unlikely that nuclear power would have been supplying 11 per cent of the electricity used in the UK in 1975 if government sponsorship of the development had not been on such a massive scale. This 11 per cent would have had to come from other sources and stations located differently to the nuclear power stations in 1975.

Distribution The development of the fully integrated distribution grid in the UK reflects all the factors mentioned. Central control was essential for the full development of a national grid and this was contributed by the nationalization of the industry. Transport economies determined the grid pattern since, as was pointed out earlier, high voltage lines are justifiable only where bulk movements are to be handled. They became necessary with the central decision to concentrate production in certain areas, from which large surpluses would have to be transferred. Markets also played their part in the grid pattern, as can be seen from fig. 4.9. The high density areas of the grid are to be found within the largest consumption areas in what is now the metropolitan core of Britain, linking it with surplus production centres like the E Midlands. Technology has not really influenced the location pattern of the grid, except in so far as development of higher voltage lines has minimized the number of transmission lines that would otherwise have been necessary.

II INDUSTRIAL STRUCTURE

II.1 Introduction and Method

The distribution of manufacturing and services in the UK is never constant. The patterns are continuously changing to meet new needs and circumstances, but in the longer term the *rate* of change fluctuates. Periods of slow growth or even stagnation are separated by periods when rapid development takes place. 1960–73 belongs in the latter category, while it is now becoming clear that 1973 saw the beginning of a phase of stagnation.

The major patterns inherited in 1960 were surprisingly similar to those in existence fifty years earlier. The economic uncertainties of the 1920s and 1930s had inhibited development, while from 1939 to 1945 all effort had been directed to meeting the needs of total war. The subsequent decade was essentially a time when the necessary foundations for later development were laid down. Thus the geographical distributions of 1960 were ill-adapted to the prevailing conditions. Rapid change in the subsequent thirteen years led to the emergence of new patterns, more in keeping with the needs of the last part of the twentieth century. The speed of change was facilitated by continuing economic growth which allowed considerable capital investment, and by expectations that the growth and accompanying increases in personal affluence would continue for the foreseeable future. From 1973, however, the situation was fundamentally altered in two ways. Energy costs rose steeply following action by world oil-producing nations, sharpening awareness of the significance of spatial distributions of manufacturing and services through an increase in the cost of overcoming distance. Secondly, the UK economy stagnated. The accompanying fall in public and private investment, limited the rate of spatial alteration. Change in this new situation was predominantly by redistribution, with the gains of one area being the losses of another. By the end of 1976 the political implications of the new conditions were being reflected in changes in the increasingly influential government spatial policies.

Throughout the period since 1960 the same factors and processes have been at work reshaping the spatial patterns, though their impact was varied over time and has been influenced by the inherited distributions on which they acted. In examining the changes, this chapter works from the whole to the parts. The first section sets the overall scene, by showing how the structural changes which have occurred within and between the manufacturing and service sectors have geographical implications. The second and third sections look separately at manufacturing and services respectively, to show what factors have been responsible for spatial changes.

Employment figures are used throughout to measure the distribution of economic activity, because of their suitability for most geographic purposes. The spatial association between changes in economic activity, as indicated by employment, and the effects of those changes, is normally very strong. This is because most people in the UK live within the region in which they work. When other measures are used, such as output, productive capacity or investment, the spatial association between the change and its effects is much less strong. For example, increase in output at a particular factory, without an increase in employment or wages, might have no effect whatsoever on the locality in which the factory is situated. Any increase in profits might accrue to shareholders living in a different region, or even nation, and any increased demand for such things as transport or equipment might be met by firms based elsewhere. An increase in *employment* at that same factory, however, could be reflected through increased demands, both economic and social, in the local area where the workers would live. Employment figures have additional advantages in being more readily available over the period studied, both for the nation as a whole and for the various regions, without the problems of inflation which bedevil monetary measures, or of comparability if measures of quantitative output are used for manufacturing and services. This is not to say that employment statistics have no faults: they have. Methods of collection have varied over time, changes in definition have occurred, and labour varies in quality and composition, if only because male and female, adults and youths, are all included under the one heading. But for the present purpose employment figures are the best available. In Britain employment is classified according to economic activity into twenty-seven industry orders using the Standard Industrial Classification (SIC) (CSO 1968). Employment in manufacturing industry is classified into orders III to XIX inclusive, and that in services into orders XX to XXVII inclusive; orders I and II cover the primary activities of mining and agriculture (fig. 1.2).

II.2 Structural Change

Chapter 2 described the relatively slow growth of the labour force in the UK in the period between 1945 and 1975. Despite this slow growth employment structure changed substantially. In keeping with a trend common to all the advanced nations of the world, there was a continuing increase in the proportion employed in the service sector, with corresponding decreases in the proportion employed in primary industries, and to a lesser extent in manufacturing. These trends are plotted in fig. 4.10, which shows their persistence throughout the period since 1950. Services expanded rapidly in the 1950s and by 1976 were employing over 64 per cent of the

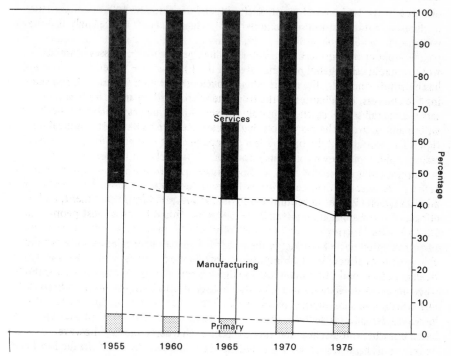

Figure 4.10   Employees in employment: primary manufacturing and service sectors, UK, 1955–75

nation's workforce. Manufacturing employment also grew until 1966, though much more slowly, and the number of employees subsequently declined. Even these figures underestimate the shift towards service activity that was taking place in the employment structure of the UK. This is because in most manufacturing industries fewer and fewer people were engaged in actual production, and an increasing proportion were in white-collar jobs. By 1976 fewer than three-quarters of manufacturing employees were classed as operatives. Statistics related to the actual job done, as opposed to the industry within which a person is employed, are published in occupation tables in the decennial census reports (Minist. Labour 1961). These show that since 1950 all manufacturing industries have had an increase in the proportion of their employees engaged in clerical and allied occupations, irrespective of whether the total employment in an industry increased or declined.

These are the sectoral structural changes which occurred, but within each sector it is possible to recognize shifts in the same direction which confirm a general pattern and which, it will be shown later, have considerable geographical importance. These trends are best understood by recognizing that the orders of the SIC can be arranged along a continuum, starting with heavy industry at one end, ranging through light industry to central services, and finishing with consumer contact services. The heavy industries are those making capital goods or producer goods such as iron and steel or ships. Light industry extends from the making of components out of some of the products of heavy industry, to the manufacture or assembly of final consumer goods. Such industries include both durable consumer products such as television sets, and perishables such as fresh food products or newspapers. Central services are those such as bank or insurance company headquarters, while consumer contact services are those where face-to-face exchanges are usual, such as retail shopping and medical care.

Traditionally, British geographers have concentrated their attention upon the heavy industries, with consumer goods production receiving much less study and service industries neglected. Historically there were good reasons for this. In the past, when geography was confined to the study of man's relationship with his environment, especially with his physical environment, it was in the heavy industries that such relationships seemed most obvious. These were also the dominant industries in the UK economy in terms of both employment and tonnage output. Pragmatically it was, and is, easier to study heavy industry. Statistics were and are more readily available in a more suitable form, and the number of production units involved is generally smaller and/or more areally restricted in distribution. The textile and tinplate industries afford good examples. But this emphasis by geographers on the heavy industries has outlasted the conditions which gave rise to it. Geography has expanded to become much more concerned with understanding the spatial structure of society, than just with man–land relationships. At the same time the heavy industries have lost their dominance, declining in manpower and relative importance as other industries have grown. Among the goods-producing industries, light manufacturing is now far more important in terms of net output and employment. But the production industries as a group have been overtaken anyway by the service industries, which have for long employed more people than manufacturing in the UK, as shown in fig. 4.10. By 1976 there were over 14 million people employed in the service sector, compared with only 7 million in manufacturing and less than 1 million in primary production. The significance of these trends is that the light industries, which form an increasing proportion of manufacturing, have different locational requirements from the heavy industries, which have experienced relative and absolute decline (Warren 1973). Particularly important for the location of light manufacturing is accessibility to markets. Markets are normally associated with people, and most people are now employed in services rather than in production industries. The location pattern of services is thus of major importance in understanding the economic geography of the UK. It is the geographical implications of these trends, and the factors influencing the changing patterns that are discussed in the following two sections.

III   MANUFACTURING

III.1   Regional Change

Changes in the distribution of manufacturing in Britain have occurred both between regions and within regions since 1950. At the regional level there were the shifts described in ch. 2, while within individual industries there have been adjustments in location which have often been intra-regional.

Much of the change in the regional distribution of manufacturing in the UK has occurred because of the structural differences in employment between the various regions. Those with a high proportion of growing industries, and few industries in

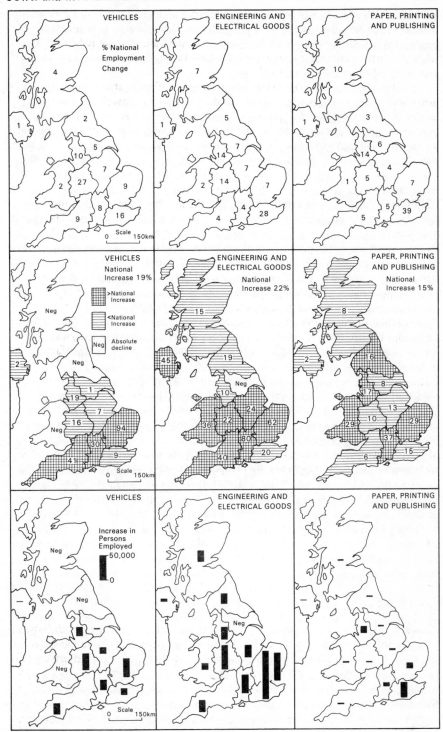

Figure 4.11   Three major growth industries, UK, 1951–61

decline, have acquired an increasing proportion of the nation's total manufacturing labour force, while regions with an opposite structure have ended up with a smaller proportion. Studies of the growth industries of the 1950s, showed that there were marked disparities in their regional distribution (Humphrys 1962, Smith 1965). It was further shown that the national growth industries which were identified had different growth rates in each of the Standard Regions then in use. The pattern is shown on fig. 4.11. There it can be seen that over 50 per cent of jobs in the three industries with the fastest employment growth, was to be found in just three regions: London and the SE, the Midlands, and the NW. The peripheral regions of Scotland, Wales and N England, which had high percentages of declining industries, did not have more than 15 per cent of the employment in each of the growth industries to share between them. Even this understated the effect of structural differences. This is indicated in the second row of maps where the growth rates of the three industries in each region are mapped. These show that there were wide variations around the national rate in each case, and that in some regions the national growth industries actually underwent decline. The bottom row of maps shows the absolute increases in employment in the three industries. The striking feature here is that in two of the growth industries the London and SE region had about double the amount of the next largest regional increase shown. In the other industry, vehicles, the three peripheral regions of Scotland, Wales and N England had declining employment in what was a national growth industry.

The effect of these differences in growth on the location of manufacturing in the UK in the 1950s was being reinforced by the pattern of industries experiencing decline or only slow growth. The heaviest declines were taking place in textiles, shipbuilding and marine engineering, and the clothing and footwear group, while slow growth was occurring in the metal industries. Most of these were heavily concentrated in regions other than those shown earlier to have concentrations of growth. Further corroboration of these structural effects on the pattern of manufacturing growth come from studies in greater detail, using sub-divisions of the industry orders. These showed, for example, that the greater part of the difference between manufacturing change in the UK and that in Scotland was accounted for by the structural factor, and that for SE England, structural factors accounted for over two-thirds of that region's above average growth performance. The below average growth in Wales and N England was also shown to be largely accounted for by structural differences (McCrone 1969, 173–4).

Similar analysis of changes in the 1960s is hampered because employment statistics comparable over the whole decade are not available. Those published for 1965 and 1969 are on the same basis, but even here interpretation of the changes during this period is complicated because the late 1960s was a time of employment decline in the UK. It was also a period of vigorous application of the distribution of industry policy, which encouraged the location of manufacturing growth in the development areas. Despite these shortcomings some comment can be made on the changes in the three manufacturing groups with the largest increases in employment between 1965 and 1969. These were Other Manufacturing (order XVI), Engineering and Electrical Goods (order VI) and Paper, Printing and Publishing (order XVI). The patterns are shown in fig. 4.12. In each growth industry the SE and the E and W Midlands together had over 50 per cent of the national employment in 1970. With this in mind the figures indicate how government measures to aid the development areas helped Wales in particular to attract an unequal share of the new employ-

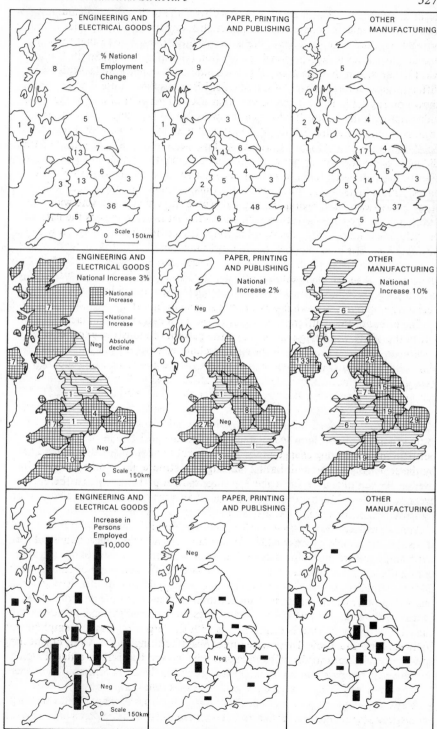

Figure 4.12   Three major growth industries, UK, 1965–9

ment in the growth industries, and restricted the rate of growth in the W Midlands and the SE. But it is striking how E Anglia appears among the three regions with the fastest growth in each case, and the SW in two out of three of these growth industries. Both are adjacent to the SE region and undoubtedly benefited from firms moving as short a distance as possible from areas of restricted development in the Midlands and the SE. When figures for absolute growth are examined, it can be seen that 40 per cent of the new jobs in the engineering group and in other manufacturing, and half the new jobs in the paper, printing and publishing group, were located in those regions south-east of a line drawn from the Humber to the Severn. The pattern of concentration of manufacturing growth in the southern regions of Britain during the 1950s was thus no more than modified by the strong government action to influence the distribution of industry in the 1960s (figs. 4.14a and b).

Statistics published in 1976 revealed that the redistribution trends of the 1965–9 period were continued between 1971 and 1975, but with one significant difference. No manufacturing industry experienced national employment growth over this more recent period. Thus it is the regional changes in the three industries with the smallest percentage declines in employment between 1971 and 1975, that are shown on the maps in fig. 4.13. These show that despite overall decline three regions, Yorks. and Humberside, Wales and the SW, experienced growth of all three industries. The SE suffered the highest absolute declines and the W Midlands stagnated. These redistribution trends support the view that the southernmost of the areas receiving government aid for industrial development (fig. 1.4) are now more attractive for manufacturing than the SE and W Midlands. They also indicate the importance of government policies in limiting the impact of the recession of the 1970s upon some of the DAs, though further analysis is needed to support these tentative conclusions.

III.2 Productivity

Structural differences between regions further contributed to spatial change, by variation in the impact of manpower productivity improvements. In the UK as a whole, the largest increase in actual numbers employed after 1945 occurred in the newer, lighter industries, while older, heavier industries had much smaller increases, or in some cases actually underwent decline. Some of the largest increases in employment took place in industries where only modest increases of output occurred, while some of the industries with little or no employment growth achieved considerable output expansion. The explanation for this lies in productivity differences between various industries, and the improvements in productivity over the period 1945–70. Smith (1949) pointed out that the further along the production chain an industry lay, the more labour-intensive it could be expected to be and the less important were raw materials in determining its location. He illustrated his point by showing that in 1935 the weight of materials used per operative per year was 1,762 tonnes in blast furnaces, 157 tonnes in steel-works and rolling mills, and only 9 tonnes in mechanical engineering shops (Smith 1949, 374). This holds true for most manufacturing, with fewer people needed to manufacture a ton of flour from wheat compared with the number needed to make a ton of bread from flour, or per ton of nylon fibre compared with a ton of nylon shirts.

Although the Census of Production no longer provides tonnage figures for various industries, some indication of the extent of these differences between heavy and

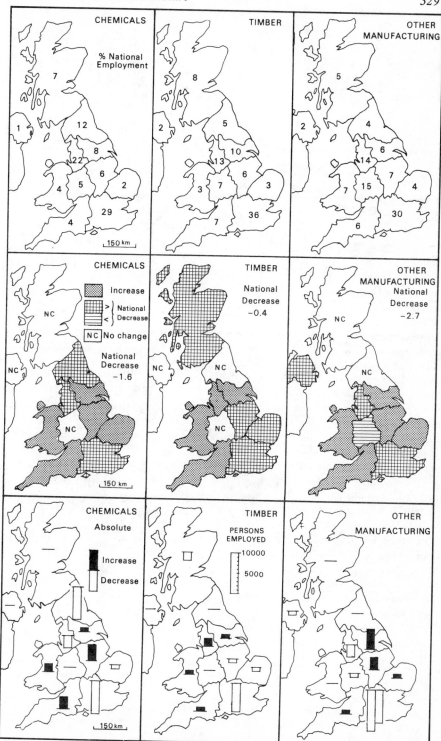

Figure 4.13   Three major growth industries, UK, 1971–5

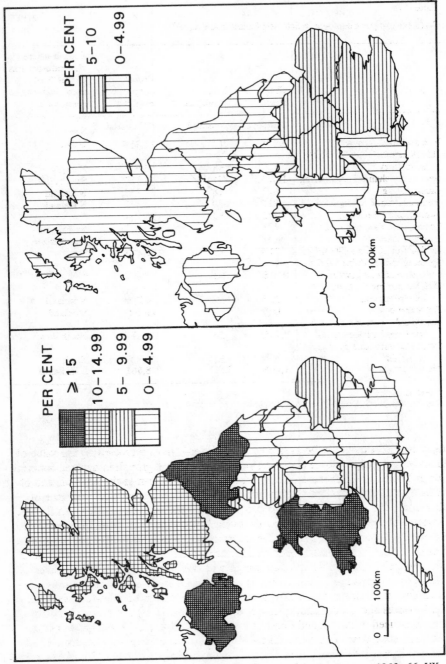

Figure 4.14a   Manufacturing employment deriving from inter-regional moves, 1953–66, UK regions

Figure 4.14b   Manufacturing employment in moves from a region 1953–66, as per cent manufacturing employment in each UK region, 1966

Table 4.16

Gross Output per Employee in Selected Industries, UK, 1974

	Gross output	Total employment	Gross output per employee	Region where this industry was largest % of manufacturing employment
	£ million	thousand	£ thousand	
Iron and steel (general)	3,474	242	14,355	Wales
Miscellaneous (non-electrical) machinery	665	88	7,557	E Anglia
General mechanical engineering	1,070	171	6,257	South East
Grain milling	672	18	37,333	N Ireland
Bread and flour confectionery	813	140	5,807	N Ireland
Sugar (mainly refining)	392	13	30,154	*
Cocoa, chocolate and sugar confectionery	775	74	10,473	Yorks. and Humberside
Production of man-made fibres	715	45	15,889	*
Spinning and doubling on the cotton and flex systems	476	62	7,677	*
Overalls and men's shirts, underwear etc.	235	50	4,700	N Ireland
Paper and board	1,008	63	16,000	Scotland
Cardboard boxes cartons and fibreboard packing cases	759	73	10,397	North West
Synthetic resins and plastics materials	1,192	52	22,923	North
Plastics products	1,048	121	8,661	E Midlands

* Not available
Source: Census of Production (HMSO 1974)

light manufacturing, can be gained by using instead the figures showing the value of gross output per employee (table 4.16). These show that growth in demand for consumer goods generates more employment per unit of output at the finishing end of industry than in the primary manufacturing stages. The geographical relevance of this is that the major concentrations of primary manufacturing industries in the UK were established early in the industrial revolution, and their location changed little between 1900 and 1945. These palaeotechnic industries were mostly heavy weight-loss or bulk-reduction industries, and so were initially strongly attracted to those places which had available adequate supplies of raw materials and fuel and water. Thus primary iron and steel production was concentrated on the western and northern coalfields, textile-making located along the eastern and western flanks of the Pennines and in Scotland, brickmaking on the coalfields, and heavy chemicals were produced in the NE and Cheshire and linked with the coke and gas works on the coalfields. Most of these areas had previously been only sparsely inhabited and the new industries dominated the local economies (Rawstron 1964). Moreover, each region tended to specialize. While these developments were taking place there was little alteration in the distribution pattern of lighter manufacturing. This remained concentrated in central and southern lowland Britain, where it had been located previously, and where the largest concentrations of the population and hence of consumer demand remained. The only other manufacturing that was attracted to the heavy industrial areas was usually either directly dependent, such as textile machinery manufacture in Lancashire and wagon works in Wales and Scotland, or served the local markets, making such things as confectionery or milk products. The survival of these patterns until 1945 influenced subsequent development. Productivity differences meant that increases in output generated most employment in the central and southern parts of the economy where the light manufacturing was concentrated. Much less employment generation accompanied increases in output in the peripheral regions, because of the dominance there of heavy industries with their higher gross output per man.

This was not the only way productivity made a contribution to the changing geography of manufacturing. Continuing improvements in manpower productivity have affected employment in the older heavy industries in particular. They suffered not only from having been developed much earlier, but also from the inadequate investment in modernization in the 1920s and 1930s. Thus they inherited per capita output rates well below what had been shown to be possible in other parts of the world. Newer industries were less affected, since they already incorporated much more advanced technology in their initial development, and so already had higher rates of output per man. All the heavy industries, however, both old and new, had higher manpower productivity figures than most light manufacturing. This meant that small percentage improvements in productivity in the heavy industries could cope with much larger increases in demand without increased employment than was the case in the rest of manufacturing. For most light manufacturing, rapid growth in demand contributed substantial growth in jobs. The effect of percentage productivity improvements in restricting employment growth were thus much greater in areas of heavy industry concentration than in areas with concentrations of light manufacturing. In fact in some of the heavy industries the manpower productivity increases outstripped the rate of increase of demand for their products, so that they had to reduce employment even as production went up. Classic examples occurred in the S Wales steel industry. At Port Talbot, for example, steelmaking capacity was increased from 3.0 to 3.4 million ingot tonnes a year between 1968 and 1972, while the labour force was reduced by over 30 per cent from 18,000 to 12,500. Even in the newer heavy chemical industry ICI doubled the value of its output at Billingham between 1946 and 1959, while reducing its labour force from 15,000 to 14,800. A further effect of productivity differences was that where new primary processing industries were developed, their high productivities and capital-intensive nature meant that they required fewer employees. Though spectacular in terms of output or capital cost, such industrial developments generated fewer direct jobs in the peripheral regions, where they were often located, than the processing of their output generated in industries further along the production line towards the final consumer.

Finally, productivity differences between various industries were contributing to the different rates of manufacturing employment growth of the various regions through the process of structural change. This was particularly true in the peripheral regions, where the decline in jobs was in such labour-intensive industries as shipbuilding, cotton and linen textiles. The new growth that did take place in these regions was frequently of capital intensive industries which were the growth industries of the mid-twentieth century: steel strip mills and oil refineries in Wales and Scotland, synthetic textiles and petrochemicals in Wales, electronics in Scotland, motor vehicle industries in Wales and Scotland. As a result there were insufficient new jobs available to employ all the available labour. In Wales, for example, textile manufacture, mainly man-made fibres, which was expanding, had a net output per employee of £2,132, while railway carriages and wagon and train manufacture, which was contracting, had a net output per employee of only £1,380. Substantiating these comments are those statistics which indicate that, until the late 1960s, the peripheral regions of the UK had employment growth which was further behind the national average than their rate of growth of output. This showed that these regions were achieving a more rapid improvement of productivity than the country as a whole. Wales and N Ireland had above average rates of productivity growth in the 1950s and 1960s; Scotland achieved improvements roughly equal to the UK average in the 1950s, but in the 1960s her annual growth of productivity was 3.6 per cent compared with 3.1 per cent for the nation as a whole (McCrone 1969, 160). In this situation these regions needed a higher rate of growth of *output* than the national average to achieve a rate of *employment* growth equal to the national average.

III.3 Market Influences

The last section indicated that the slow growth and declining industries were concentrated where they were mainly for historic reasons. But this does not explain why the industries with more rapid employment growth were so unevenly distributed. The major factor in this was, undoubtedly, the distribution of the market in the UK. It has been suggested that under contemporary economic conditions a market location is now the 'norm' for modern industry. Locations other than at the market need to be explained by factors which prevent market location, or by lower costs elsewhere which outweigh the market attractions. Clark (1966) produced a map showing the geography of the market in Britain in 1960 (fig. 4.15). It is based on his concept of economic potential, which he defines as the sum of incomes in areas adjacent to a particular geographical point divided by their distances from that point. The higher the economic potential the greater the power to attract economic activity. Fig. 4.15 corresponds fairly closely to the pattern of regional economic growth in the UK discussed earlier. The reasons for this are not difficult to find. A number of manufacturing industries are essentially consumer-oriented, either because of the perishability of their product, for example the making of fresh bread and the manufacture of local or regional newspapers; or because of the need for personal consumer contact as in custom tailoring; or because of bulk gains or low value of the product as in the example of soft drinks manufacture or made-up boxes. Such industries are distributed roughly according to population, with the largest numbers employed where there are the largest population concentrations and/or market potential. These industries will grow fastest where population growth is strongest. In the UK the largest markets and the greatest increases in population were coincident between 1945 and 1975. They are found in the area reaching from London through the Midlands to the Lancashire industrial region. Other regions with smaller populations, and with much slower-growing populations (fig. 2.5), clearly will not have benefited to the same extent from development of these industries. A further stimulus in the central areas of the economy was the faster growth of service employments described later. With the service sector expanding more rapidly than manufacturing, this helped to stimulate consumer demand still further

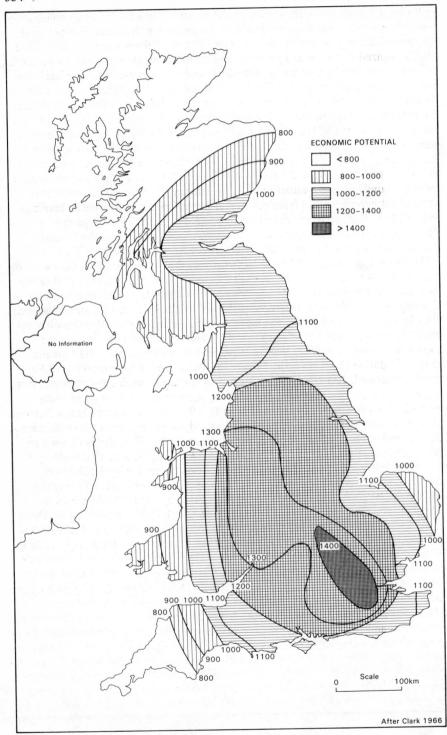

Figure 4.15   Economic potential, GB, 1960 (after Clark)

in the large population centres, adding to their attractions for the consumer-oriented industries. In this sense service industry development can be thought of as stimulating manufacturing expansion. Beyond these factors of sheer size and growth, it is also recognized that large and growing markets more readily generate new industries, attract new industries that started elsewhere, and in both cases are more likely to nurture them successfully (Hall 1962, 168; Rawstron 1964, 315; McCrone 1969, 57). Apart from sheer size various factors help to explain this. Labour in sufficient quantity and of appropriate quality is likely to be more readily available in the larger centres of economic activity than elsewhere. Factory buildings, especially small units, are usually available in larger numbers for rent or purchase. External economies are also more likely to be obtained from such things as greater ease of contact with consumers and with other industries supplying components or services, from the familiarity with initiative by local industry, from discussion with like-minded entrepreneurs, and from the greater pool of existing experience. Investigation of the linkages between manufacturers and their suppliers and markets, is furthering understanding of the way external economies influence the location decisions to create the spatial patterns of manufacturing (Hamilton 1974).

In the case of London Hall (1962) also argued that the operative factors were the same in the twentieth century as in the nineteenth. The difference was that in the nineteenth century the major heavy industries found even greater advantages in locating close to their raw material sources and especially close to their fuel supplies, than by locating in previously developed manufacturing centres. This situation explained the spectacular growth of the coalfield economies in particular. In the twentieth century raw material attractions became less important, and a greater range of industries have developed where the attractions of large markets, real or merely perceived, have been able to exert their influence much more strongly. It is these newer industries that were attracted to, and grew more strongly in, close proximity to the major markets in Britain. By 1945 London was the major focus of attraction, with the largest concentration not only of people, but of manufacturing and of market potential as well. Further centres were the W Midlands focused on Birmingham, and the Merseyside—Manchester—W Riding areas further north.

The peripheral regions suffered relative disadvantage in having much lower market potential because of smaller populations and lower incomes (Coates and Rawstron 1971). Most of them suffered two other important disadvantages in addition. The first was a net outward migration of population, stemming largely from the fact that in these regions major industries were contracting. Their market potential was thus declining, either absolutely or relatively, or was thought to be so. Secondly, the heavy industries were themselves experiencing a change in the kinds of manufactured goods they needed. This kind of change was often one where in addition to, or instead of, using products of local industries which had grown up to serve them, they turned to the products of the newer industries. An extreme example is the coal-mining industry. After nationalization, two results of the capital investment and modernization programme were the changeover of all collieries from steam-driven winding engines to electric winding, and the replacement of trams for underground haulage by conveyor belt systems wherever possible. The old components had often been made in or near the mining areas. The new components were more likely to be produced elsewhere in Britain. Thus the older heavy industrial areas not only did not have the characteristics which encouraged growth of the light industries, but the heavy industries themselves stimulated the output of newer industries often located in other regions.

Discussion of market influences has so far been mainly concerned with the markets for finished products. The market for manufactured goods, however, is not only, or even mainly, with the final consumer. In the production process many manufacturers never sell anything direct to the final consumer. They make parts or assemble components which are then sent on to another manufacturer who carries the process one stage further, and so on until the final product is put together. The most familiar example of this is the motorcar, which is assembled from the products of a wide range of manufacturers. Many of the components seen in the finished car carry names other than that of the company making the final assembly, e.g. Lucas, Dunlop, Triplex. The metal-based industries indulge in particularly heavy inter-trading of this kind, which contributes to spatial association of these industries within certain areas of preference. It is because of this factor that industry aiming to produce semi-manufactures for other industries generally prefers to locate close to where the market is largest and most varied. In Britain this is within or close to the polygon bounded by a line joining London—Southampton—Bristol—Birmingham—Liverpool—Sheffield—Leicester—London, that is, the area now thought of as metropolitan Britain.

Apart from the national impact of these factors influencing the distribution of manufacturing between regions, they also had an intra-regional impact. Those newer industries developed to serve mainly the markets of the region in which they were located, also tended to follow the national pattern at the lower scale. Within regions they congregated in the larger central places where the regional market was concentrated, or from which it was most accessible.

Given the pattern of economic potential and the attractions of the major growing market regions, it might seem surprising that there was as much expansion of manufacturing employment, especially light manufacturing employment, in the other regions. Two main factors account for this growth. The first was the development of manufacturing serving mainly or exclusively local and regional demands, and the second was the effect of government policy. Industry serving regional or local markets was stimulated by the growing affluence which affected all parts of the UK. This was offset, to a certain extent, by the decline of working population and higher unemployment rates in some of the regions, as for instance in parts of Scotland and N Ireland. In the late 1960s the effects of economies of scale in some of these industries, discussed later, also eroded part of this growth by shifting location to areas with higher economic potential. Between 1945 and 1970, however, these locally-oriented industries did contribute to the expansion of consumer goods production even in areas with relatively low economic potential. Good examples include some food industries such as brewing and soft drinks, stationery printing, packaging materials, and the making of building industry components such as doors and window frames, building blocks and concrete mixing. All these were noticeably at the consumer goods end of the continuum. A prominent feature of the location of these industries was their tendency to congregate in the larger central places within the smaller regions. They were exhibiting the characteristics of the national pattern within their regions, by locating in the areas with the highest regional economic potential. Edinburgh in Scotland, Cardiff and Swansea in Wales, Belfast in N Ireland, Tyneside in the Northern region, and Bristol and Plymouth in the SW, all provide examples of this trend.

Government policy had a different effect (ch. 1.III). Since 1934 a major aim in regional planning has been the deliberate encouragement of manufacturing expansion in the regions of slow growth or decline, and the movement of manufacturing out of the regions of overgrowth especially in the SE and the W Midlands (fig. 1.4). This policy has had a major impact in stimulating new manufacturing growth in the development areas of the UK. For many manufacturing industries certain conditions in the areas of high economic potential were conducive or even essential to their *initial* development. But once established there were no good economic reasons why many of them could not then be transferred, or have their expansion transferred, to other regions and flourish successfully (Rawstron 1964, 315). This was confirmed by Luttrell, who concluded that the majority of British industry could operate successfully in any of the major industrial centres of Britain (Luttrell 1962, 347–8). According to traditional location theory, the main disadvantage of such moves would arise from added transport costs. In practice these have been shown to be a relatively unimportant part of total costs in many British industries. The Toothill Committee found the effect of transport costs on firms which chose to locate in Scotland, for example, to be less than two per cent (Scottish Council 1961, 72–5), a figure they considered to be insignificant. Chisholm (1966) argued that such transport effects as did exist were diminishing quite rapidly. He further pointed out that uniform delivered prices were quoted for any location in Britain for many components or part manufactures used in production, and that in fact uniform delivered prices are more usual than unusual. Evidence to support this contention was drawn from a whole range of industries, including car electric equipment, semi-manufactured copper and copper-based alloys, chemical fertilizers and pneumatic tyres. Apart from transport costs, other detailed studies have indicated that in the clothing and radio industries, firms which have opened branch factories in development areas have not suffered substantial transport cost disadvantages compared with the branch they might instead have opened in London. In fact, overall, the advantage was slightly with the provincial plant (Hall 1962, 169). Empirical evidence of the flourishing of so many new manufacturing industries in the DAs would seem to bear out these findings. A word of caution is necessary, merely to point out that there are industries where these conditions do not apply; notably the consumer contact industries mentioned earlier, and some of the heavy industries where raw material costs loom large or the product has low value per unit bulk, on which transport costs bear especially heavily. In addition, disproportionate rises in fuel costs since 1973 have increased the significance of distance.

III.4 Government Policy

Government policies to influence the geography of manufacturing industry in Britain, have now been applied for over forty years. The effects have been substantial, though just how substantial is difficult to establish with any precision. This is partly because it is difficult to disentangle the effects of government policy from changes which would have occurred without it. The evolution of government action since 1934 is described in ch. 1.III, from which it can be concluded that government policy has been *a* major factor if not *the* major factor in the changes in the *regional* distribution of manufacturing since 1945. The greatest effects have been in stimulating manufacturing development in the peripheral regions which previously had the smallest manufacturing employment. For the growing regions of the SE, E Anglia, and the W Midlands, however, inter-regional manufacturing moves originating there represented less than 8 per cent of their 1966 manufacturing employment, which did help constrain the regions' growth, but clearly only to a relatively minor extent.

III.5 Economies of Scale: Internal

Economies of scale played a particularly important part in the changing location of manufacturing after 1960. This was mainly through changing the inherited pattern within, rather than between, regions. The pattern of production inherited in 1945 was essentially one of small-scale units. Even in iron and steel-making, no works had a capacity of more than one million ingot tonnes a year. Textile manufacture was in a large number of small mills; although there were some large car works, most motorcar manufacture was in small factories, with output measured in hundreds rather than thousands of cars a year. In food production, for example, small family bakers still dominated bread output, and the few large breweries produced a small proportion of total output. One of the geographical implications of this state of affairs was that much more locational dispersion was possible. For a given output there were a large number of works and these could be, and usually were, widely dispersed. Being small there were a myriad places which had sufficient labour to meet their needs. Where such small factories employed several hundred people, they dominated the economy of the small places in which they were located.

Well before 1945 it had been recognized that there were economic advantages to be gained in many industries from large-scale operations. But achievement of these economies was usually by replacement of men by machines in order to obtain higher productivity, and usually also meant larger premises to cope with expanded output. Both required the investment of capital, which had been in short supply for much of the previous twenty-five years, and there were other inhibiting factors like the fragmented ownership discussed below. As a result, by 1945 all too few industries were taking advantage of the economies of scale thought to be available. Some increases in size of unit began to appear by 1955, but it was not until later that substantial changes occurred. This is brought out in table 4.17 where employment per establishment is plotted. In some cases growth was achieved by expanding output on existing sites, in others by building new green-field factories. Some industries had both. Until 1973, growth in the economy allowed these changes to be achieved by the large new units meeting the increased demand, while old factories continued in operation. In many cases, however, centralization occurred, with many smaller older units being closed down as output was concentrated in a few new larger factories, and this became more common when the economy stagnated after 1973. Classic examples occurred in the iron and steel and tinplate industries in S Wales (figs. 4.16a and b) (Humphrys 1972, 117–27). Some industries which were virtually new could start operating at the scale suited to contemporary conditions. This was particularly true of consumer durable manufacture, such as the production of washing machines or television sets, and of such new industries as plastics and electronic equipment. The geographical effect of these changes was to reduce the total number of works needed for a given output. Where an old-established industry was involved this usually caused local changes only, though in some cases an entire industry was lost from a region. Output became concentrated into fewer but larger-scale production units. The effect of implementing changes to achieve these economies of scale normally meant increases in labour productivity, so that employment might be reduced even though output had increased. Good examples of these trends come

Power and the Industrial Structure 339

TABLE 4.17

Manufacturing Employment by Establishment Size, UK, 1947–72: Percentage Distribution of Employees in Manufacturing Industries in Establishments Employing more than Ten Persons

Size group of establishment	% total employees				
	1947	1955	1963	1968	1972
11–24	4.0	3.4	4.8	4.4 ⎫	
25–49	6.9	6.6	4.5 ⎫	11.3 ⎬	20.0
50–99	10.5	9.7	8.2 ⎭	⎭	
11–99	21.4	19.7	17.5	15.7	20.0
100–249	18.7	17.3	20.2* ⎫	37.0 ⎱	32.2
250–499	15.6	15.0	11.4† ⎭		
500–999	13.9	14.6	14.0	14.0	14.9
100–999	48.2	46.9	45.6	51.0	47.1
1,000–1,999	12.3	12.8	13.7	NA	NA
2,000–4,999	11.4	12.3	13.2	NA	NA
5,000 and over	6.7	8.3	10.0	NA	NA
1,000 and over	30.4	33.4	36.0	33.3	32.9
	100.0	100.0			

* Estimated, Census of Production, 1963
Source: Annual Abstracts of Statistics and Census of Production (HMSO)

from the flour-milling industry. Where an old geographical pattern has been modified, certain trends can be identified. Usually the larger newer works are located near a major urban centre, with the closures taking place in the smaller towns where the smaller, older works were located. Centralization has both geographical and economic connotations. Because of increasing scale of operations the larger works or factories require better facilities for movement of materials and goods in bulk. They also need a large labour supply. This means locating in a large urban centre or at a point with a large enough journey to work hinterland to generate the quantity and quality of labour required. In spatial terms the location requirements are now more specific and limiting. There are a smaller number of locations likely to be able to meet them; indeed many of the smaller, older centres do not meet these requirements. But extension of the journey to work, by use of the private motorcar, has meant that the former production centres could often be within travelling distance of the location of the large new works or factory where production has been centralized. A further implication of the increased economies of scale is that of local diversification. With the average size of works increasing, a local economy is much more likely to be dominated by an industry than previously. Factories employing more than 4,000–5,000 are now fairly commonplace. Even in 1963 nearly 10 per cent of the employees in manufacturing were employed in establishments of over 5,000 employees. Two such factories could employ all the manufacturing workers in a town of 40,000 people, since the labour force of such a town would be around 20,000 of whom roughly half could be expected to be in services (fig. 4.17).

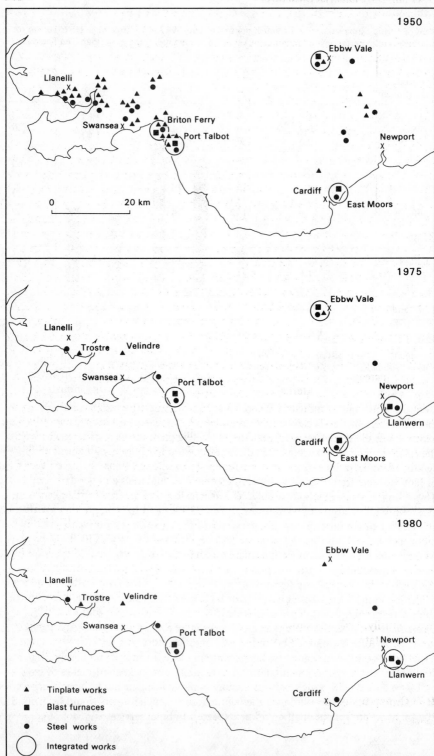

Figure 4.16a, b, c   S Wales. Iron, steel and tinplate industry, rationalization, 1950—80

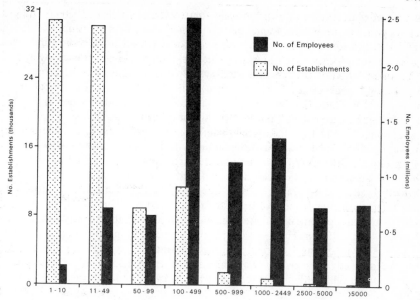

Figure 4.17   Employees and establishments, by establishment size, UK, 1963

III.6 Economies of Scale: External

The above discussion has been confined to internal economies of scale and the effects of increasing the scale of production in a single unit. There are also advantages to be gained from external economies of scale in manufacturing industry, which have helped create new spatial patterns of industry in the UK. For small factories there are external economies of scale to be obtained by clustering. In this way some of the services needed can be jointly financed, while others can be more easily provided. As important has been the fact that the development of clustered factories on estates makes industry more manageable for planners. Such estates are also cheaper to develop, an important consideration where publicly financed or privately financed estates are set up in advance of occupancy. Industrial estates became a familiar feature of the British industrial landscape after 1945, whereas previously they had been an exception. Here again it was the large industrial estates which could benefit most, and these have to be located near large centres, or at accessible journey-to-work points for sizeable numbers of people (Florence 1962).

The basic importance of economies of scale, then, has been the alteration of inherited patterns, the smaller urban places losing manufacturing jobs which have been centralized into large units located in the larger towns. New manufacturing industry has taken advantage of economies of scale by setting up large establishments initially. Smaller factories have been involved by being clustered together on industrial estates, whereas they would have been dispersed under previously prevailing conditions. Examples of these changes can be found in every region of the UK.

III.7 Ownership and Control

Contributory factors, allowing the centralization to achieve economies of scale to take place, were changes in ownership and control. Hamilton (1967, 364; 1974, 32–41) has pointed out how locational decisions are affected by ownership, with individual, and corporate ownership differing from each other and from state organizations in their location decisions. In particular, the private entrepreneur works within the context of satisfying his needs, usually from a single establishment. The corporation is generally aiming to optimize economic returns from a number of establishments. State organizations often have to operate within the constraint of contributing to national or regional economic needs as well as, or instead of, achieving economic returns from a particular operation. In 1945 the individual entrepreneur was common in UK manufacturing industry and many companies owned just one or two factories. Any one industry had a large number of controlling interests. This made agreement on rationalization and centralization of operations much more difficult. Individual entrepreneurs were frequently more concerned with protecting their interests as they perceived them, and the interests of their factory and workmen, than in any potential increase in economic returns. Subsequently the situation changed. Until 1955 the changes were relatively small and mainly of two kinds. The first was state involvement: directly through nationalization, as in the steel industry, and indirectly by such means as allocation of defence contracts or state aid, as in aircraft and shipbuilding. The second change was that much of the manufacturing growth was in new industries with strong corporate management. Multi-national corporations became much more familiar in the UK and decisions were being taken on a large scale. Initially there was little geographical change as a result of these ownership and control developments. For the large new industries this was a time of expansion anyway, which limited the need for centralization. In the 1960s, however, there were obvious gains to be had by rationalization and concentration of production at a smaller number of larger factories. A spate of company mergers and amalgamations, and of large companies buying small companies occurred, and some small companies simply went out of business in face of strong competition. As a result, many industries ended up with control centred in a small number of hands (table 4.18).

The need for such developments to make industry more efficient and competitive was recognized by the government in 1966, when they set up the *Industrial Reorganization Corporation*. Until it was abolished in 1971, this body gave financial aid to industries to encourage centralization and rationalization. Following the General Election of February 1974, public involvement in British industry once more increased. This was partly because of the political commitment of the new government, but it was facilitated by the serious financial difficulties of some major companies during the post-1973 economic recession. The *Industry Act* (Publ. Gen. Act 1975) aimed to help regenerate British industry by the development of new institutions. Thus the National Enterprise Board (1972) was set up to take initiatives in stimulating development in key sectors of the British economy, with the appropriate functions of the Board in Scotland and Wales carried out by the Scottish Development Agency (1975) and the Welsh Development Agency (1976). While similar to the Industrial Reorganization Corporation, the NEB can also take shareholdings in companies, and has the power to initiate new ventures and join with private companies in joint developments. It had vested in it existing government shareholdings in such companies as Rolls-Royce (1971) Ltd, International Computers (Holdings) Ltd, Nuclear Enterprises Ltd, and Norton-Villiers-Triumph Ltd. Under the *Industry Act*, public ownership is to be extended through community

TABLE 4.18

Concentration of Sales of Selected Products by Larger Firms, GB, 1958 and 1963

Standard industrial classification, minimum list heading	Product or group of products	Number of enterprises	% total sales 1958	1963	Number of enterprises in 1958 with same concentration ratio as 1963
211 (part of)	White flour for bread-making	5	71.5	79.2	over 10
212	Bread sold in loaves or in rolls	5	31.5	71.4	over 10
	Flour confectionery	5	26.7	51.0	over 10
277 (1)	Polishes	5	67.1	79.6	9
352	Watches and clocks and parts thereof	5	72.7	80.8	9
364 (part of)	Television receiving sets complete	5	52.7	81.6	over 10
383 (part of)	Aircraft complete, new and reconditioned and air frames	5	86.6	98.0	over 10
384	Locomotives, complete	5	80.9	93.0	10
411	Man-made fibres	7	not available	100	not available
450 (part of)	Men's, youths' and boys' footwear	5	22.2	30.3	9

Source: Census of Production (HMSO 1963)

ownership of development land, the British National Oil Corporation, the nationalization of the shipbuilding and aerospace industries, and extension of public ownership from the existing bases in road haulage, construction, ports and cargo handling. Beyond this, a system of planning agreements with major firms is to be instituted following economic analyses of various aspects of vital industries by the *National Economic Development Council.* The significance of these developments is that state ownership or involvement may result in different location and investment decisions from those of individual entrepreneurs or private corporations. Moreover, one of the main stated aims of the *Industry Act* was to promote industrial efficiency and thus international competitiveness. This will inevitably mean some rationalization, with reduction in the number of operating units in existing industries and concentration of production at a smaller number of factories. The geographical outcome of such changes could occur without ownership and control changes, though it would take longer and a different form, or the industries might die before the necessary improvements were achieved.

In addition to these organizational changes, new trends in the spatial distribution of UK manufacturing became apparent in the first half of the 1970s. In the nation as a whole manufacturing employment fell by 6.8 per cent between 1971 and 1975, but the job losses were very unevenly distributed. The sharpest decline took place in the SE region, which had 12 per cent fewer people employed in manufacturing in 1975 than in 1971. Three other regions, the W Midlands, the NW and N Ireland, declined by more than the national rate. The other regions had lower rates of decline and one, E Anglia, achieved an increase of 4.2 per cent. As a result of these changes, the peripheral regions of the UK increased their share of national manufacturing employment (table 4.19), reversing the dominant trend of the previous half century. Redistribution has also occurred within regions. An increasing proportion of manufacturing employment is locating near the outer edges of cities and conurbations. This has been caused partly by industrial expansion in peripheral locations and partly because of job losses nearer the city centres.

It appears that several factors have contributed to these new trends. One is that improvements in communications and transport (ch. 5) have made urbanization economies, i.e. those gained by spatial clustering of different industries, available over a much wider area within Britain. Companies serving national markets (section III.3) thus have greater flexibility in choosing a manufacturing location. In this situation other factors have come to play a larger part in the choice, so that the inducements to locate in a DA have become relatively more important. This is supported by the findings of North (1974, 235) in his study of the UK plastics industry, and would help explain the relative success of the SW and Wales in employment changes in the 1971–75 period (Humphrys 1976). Other factors have affected the redistribution of industry within city regions. Undoubtedly one major influence has been the extensive redevelopment which is a feature of the downtown area of every British city. In the process large areas with older, cheaper industrial premises have been cleared. Such premises were often seedbeds for new industrial development by small businesses with high risk and limited capital resources. Industries previously established in these city regions often find that costs in the redeveloped areas are too expensive for them even if such areas continue to be zoned for industry. Those serving national markets may even move to a DA if not already in one, while local and regional serving industries will move to industrial estates located near the urban

TABLE 4.19

Changing Regional Distribution of Manufacturing Employment, UK, 1971–75

Standard Region	Manufacturing employment 1971	Share of national total	Manufacturing employment 1975	Share of national total	Employment change 1971–75
	000's	%		%	%
South East	2,173	26.9	1,913	25.5	−12.0
W Midlands	1,104	13.7	1,021	13.6	−7.5
North West	1,131	14.0	1,042	13.9	−7.9
E Anglia	190	2.4	198	2.7	+4.2
E Midlands	618	7.7	593	7.9	−4.0
Yorks. & Humberside	777	9.7	733	9.8	−5.7
South West	439	5.5	427	5.7	−2.7
Wales	324	4.0	317	4.2	−2.2
Northern	461	5.7	454	6.1	−1.5
Scotland	669	8.3	637	8.5	−4.8
N Ireland	170	2.1	154	2.1	−9.4
UK	8,056	100	7,489	100	−7.0

Source: Dept. of Employment

periphery. Downtown areas thus become de-industrialized. Examples of such shifts can be found in every large British city, but they appear to have had the greatest impact in London and Birmingham. There, by the mid-1970s loss of manufacturing jobs in inner cities had resulted in some having higher rates of unemployment than the DAs. This situation raised questions about planning policies for the distribution of economic activity, and caused some government action to alleviate the problems.

IV   SERVICES

IV.1   Significance

Since at least as early as 1950 the service sector in Britain (orders XVII–XVIV 1958 SIC; XX–XXVII 1968 SIC) has employed more people than primary production and manufacturing combined. Between 1950 and 1976 this dominance was strengthened as employment in services grew by 40 per cent while that in manufacturing and in primary activities declined (fig. 4.10). Since employment in large part determines the location of the population, and most employment in Britain is in services, it follows that the pattern of service employment is today of fundamental importance in the human geography and planning of the country. This is most obvious in those areas where service employment *growth* is located, since this normally accompanies, or is caused by, population expansion. This in turn stimulates spatially associated economic, social and physical demands for such things as shops, schools and housing. Beyond this, the distribution of the service jobs has considerable significance for manufacturing. It was argued earlier that an important influence on the distribution of manufacturing, especially of light manufacturing, was the location of the market. When discussed in general terms the market means purchasing power, which in turn goes with jobs. Since most people in Britain work in services, it follows that they are an important element in determining where the consumer market is, thus influencing the location of manufacturing. Here a precautionary note must be introduced since this is one of the situations where differences within the employment figures are significant. The majority of the workers in services are women, and much of the expansion that has taken place has occurred by an increase in female participation in the labour force (table 4.20). The relevance of this is that wage rates in services in general are lower than in manufacturing or primary industries, and wage rates for females have tended to be lower than for males in Britain in the past (COI 1976, 337).

IV.2   Flexibility of Location

Studies by economic geographers to explain these patterns of service location have been very limited in the past. One of the reasons for this was the false assumption, made not only by geographers but also by others such as economists and planners, that the location of services will coincide with the location of the primary and secondary industries, which directly and indirectly controls the demand for them. While there is some validity in this assumption at the national level, at the regional, and more particularly at the intra-regional level, there are too many exceptions involving a large number of employees for it to be even a working rule. In elaborating

TABLE 4.20

Increase in the Number of Employees, UK, 1950–75* (in thousands)

Employment sector	1950			1960			1970			1975		
	Men	Women	Total	Men	Women	Total	Men	Women	Total	Men	Women	Total
Primary	1,626	135	1,761	1,308	117	1,424	744	92	836	637	116	753
Manufacturing	5,677	2,872	8,549	6,013	2,933	8,947	6,274	2,802	9,075	5,262	2,226	7,488
Service	6,694	4,116	10,810	7,354	4,977	12,331	7,586	5,948	13,535	7,633	6,832	14,465
Grand total	13,997	7,123	21,120	14,675	8,027	22,702	14,604	8,842	23,446	13,532	9,174	22,706

* Because of changes in definition and methods of compilation, the figures for each sector are not strictly comparable over time and are given to indicate the main trends only.

Source: Dept. of Employment

this it is necessary to distinguish clearly between ubiquitous and flexible services, a distinction which is fundamental to any understanding of the changes and trends in the geography of services in Britain.

Ubiquitous services are those which depend upon direct consumer contact, and are, therefore, located within the immediate vicinity of the populations they serve. Good examples of ubiquitous services are general practitioners, hairdressers, opticians and laundrettes. Other things being equal, it can be expected that the distribution of these services will be closely correlated with the distribution of population. *Flexible* services on the other hand are those which do not need direct consumer contact, so that they are much more flexible in their choice of location. Examples of such services include head offices of building societies, national libraries, or electricity board headquarters. For these the choice of location is spatially circumscribed only by national or regional boundaries. The ubiquitous and flexible services thus described are, of course, the extremes of what in fact is a continuum grading from extreme flexibility. This continuum is best illustrated by reference to the education service in the UK. It is generally accepted that primary schools need to be located as close as possible to the homes of the children attending them. To minimize the movement of pupils, such schools are normally provided within the neighbourhood which they serve. At the next higher stage in education, junior comprehensive schools are fewer in number than the primary schools. They have larger enrolments and on average are further from pupils' homes, but still normally within the local community they serve. The senior comprehensive schools are fewer in number again, and so on average are still further away from pupils' homes, serving perhaps several communities. At the next level a further education college will usually have a much wider catchment area, and a college for the training of teachers will draw on a wider catchment still. Finally, a university or medical school can be built almost anywhere in the UK and will still attract students. In this context the university would seem to have complete flexibility in its choice of location. The example of the education service illustrates the whole range of location types in the services, from those governed by the need for close consumer contact, to those facing problems of having their location choice governed not so much by proximity to consumers as by other factors.

In practice this range of locational type is comparable with that found in manufacturing. Those manufacturing industries requiring close customer contact, such as jobbing printers, or which involve high bulk gain or whose products have high perishability, such as soft drink manufacture or bread baking, have a ubiquitous distribution. At the other end of the range those industries involving high weight loss or which use a high proportion of low-value raw materials, tend to locate at their raw material sources, or where the raw materials are imported, and are not governed by customer locations to the same degree, e.g. oil-refining, flour-milling or steel-making. It follows from this that far from the distribution of many services being controlled by the distribution of the population, they are much more akin to manufacturing in being influenced by other locational requirements.

In looking at the distribution of service employment in the UK, the distinction between ubiquitous and flexible services is important for two reasons. The first is that the flexible services tend to have grown more rapidly since 1960, and secondly, the degree of flexibility of most services has been increasing. The more rapid growth of the flexible services has been less significant in absolute numbers but nonetheless the trend was an important one.

IV.3 Changing Location

With considerable freedom from locating close to consumers, much of the growth of the most flexible services in fact took place in SE England, especially in and around London (Manners 1963). By 1964, for example, of the seventy-six main government research establishments fifty-nine were in SE England (Hammond 1967). Government office activities appeared to be even more attracted to the London region, with 71 per cent of all headquarters staff in the non-industrial Civil Service in SE England in 1972. In those cases where there were constraints to locate within particular regions, then the locations chosen were similar to the national pattern, that is, there was a marked preference to be in or near the regional capital (Humphrys 1972, 138–50). Thus half the 1961 office rateable value in England and Wales outside the SE, was located in a handful of regional cities: Manchester, Birmingham, Liverpool, Leeds, Newcastle, Bristol and Cardiff (Buswell and Lewis 1970). In the case of Scotland, Wales and N Ireland the similarity to the national pattern was even greater, in that the capitals in each case happen to be in the south-east of their territories. Although reasons can be suggested for this uneven distribution, such as availability of better communications or supporting services, or that this allows central government offices to be close together in the provincial capitals, none of these in the last resort is conclusive. There is little evidence to suggest, for example, that the Aluminium Research Association laboratories could not function just as successfully closer to major aluminium working centres in Scotland or Wales rather than in Oxford (Wright 1967). Similarly, the development of three university-level institutions in Cardiff, the University College of S Wales and Monmouthshire, the University of Wales Institute of Science and Technology, and the University of Wales School of Medicine, was a matter of inertia and historical accident rather than positive locational forces determining the choice (Coates and Rawstron 1971, 180).

While the increasing concentration of the growth of flexible services in the capital cities in particular, was bringing about changes in the distribution pattern, there were other changes of equal importance that were making possible the rearrangement of existing service provision. For many services there was an observable trend towards increased flexibility in location. This had repercussions mostly at the intra-regional rather than the inter-regional level, but it was nonetheless important because of that. The main contributory factors to increasing flexibility were changes in organization, increasing opportunities to take advantage of economies of scale and the increasing mobility of the service consumers.

IV.4 Organization and Control

Prior to 1945 many of the service industries were under the control of local government, or, in the commercial sector, were in the hands of a multitude of small companies, or of individuals who had limited means at their disposal and limited aims. Good examples of these conditions could be found in the environmental services of gas, electricity and water, in personal services such as medicine and education and in commercial services such as cinemas, retail distribution and dry-cleaning. The effect of this kind of control was that services were very dispersed. In the public sector, local authorities usually operated as if their areas were islands. For example, each local authority that provided a gas supply service in its area would normally have a gas-making plant and a full range of necessary administrative and maintenance staff (Ordnance Survey 1951). Similarly in the private sector many grocers owned and operated just one shop, and would adapt and accept reduced profits to stay in business at a place when commercial principles might indicate that the location had outlived its usefulness. Many of the services then had an organization and a location pattern that had grown up in a previous period and was suited to earlier conditions.

IV.5 Public Sector Developments

The inhibiting influence of small-scale organization on change was drastically reduced after 1945. Major changes came about in several of the services through nationalization. In some cases the effect of this was to transfer a service from the private to the public sector, as happened with the railways. In other cases, where both local authorities and private companies were involved, such as gas and electricity distribution, nationalization imposed uniform public sector control. The effect in either case was to replace diverse and variously organized systems of small-scale operations by large-scale integrated organization. The resulting centralization of control created the necessary conditions for rationalization to take place. The immediate spatial impact was in fact relatively limited. The lack of capital in a country still recovering from six years of war, and the need to gain operating experience, delayed change. The full effects did not really make themselves felt until after 1955, and it was only in the 1960s that the new patterns began to dominate. The basic change was that the newly nationalized services were no longer constrained by area or regional boundaries, imposed from outside, in their decisions on location of their activities. At the same time any duplication resulting from the previous multiplicity of ownership could be eliminated. Thus the gas and electricity boards were able to create their own patterns. They established their own regions, within each of which there was a central headquarters with a hierarchy of district and area offices below that. These replaced the mixture of local authority and private undertaking offices which had existed previously in so many parts of Britain. The result of this rationalization process, however, was to reduce employment and to centralize activities in the most suitable locations, reducing the number of places from which services operated. In the health services the changes in the pattern of hospital provision were detailed in a Hospital Plan (NHS 1962). There the same trend was observable (fig. 4.18). The aim of the plan was to achieve uniformly adequate hospital provision over the whole of the UK, in place of the considerable variation in hospital bed availability which had arisen prior to nationalization. The location of the new and replacement hospitals could now be determined, not as previously, on the basis of availability of local funds or adequacy of local organization but on the basis of proper distribution.

After 1945, partly as a result of nationalization and the extension of public ownership, and partly by expansion and extension of previously existing government services, public control of the service sector grew to substantial proportions. In 1975 of the total employment in services of 14.5 million people, 6.3 million were working in such public sector services as gas, electricity and water supply, road and rail transport, health, education and government. Beyond this direct employment, indirect control was especially strong in the construction industry which in 1975 had a workforce of 1.3 million. 45 per cent of the construction industry output was for public authorities, and government decisions on such things as availability of housing improvement grants considerably influenced the demand for the services of

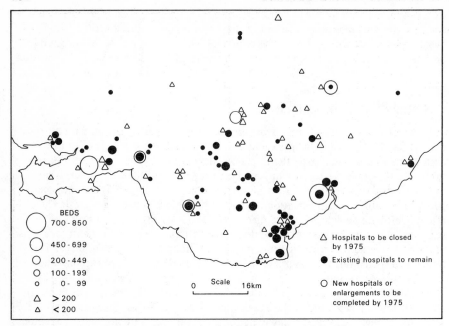

Figure 4.18   Plan for hospital development, industrial S Wales, 1961—80

small local building firms. The implication of such extensive public ownership and influence in the service sector is that the government now has considerable control over employment in services, and especially over its location, if it decides to exercise it. As a corollary, government, both local and national, had assumed considerable responsibility for ensuring a proper distribution pattern of service jobs and for the results of any changes initiated by policy decisions.

IV.6 Private Ownership and Control

In the private sector similar trends are readily identifiable, though with greater multiplicity of ownership and considerable inertia the effects have generally been more limited. Most people are familiar with the changes which have occurred in the retail trade, especially in the ownership and organization of food and clothing shops (Hall, Knapp and Winsten 1961; Thorpe 1968). In most British town centres, locally-owned foodshops have given way to those owned by large grocery chains, so that by 1975 just six major grocery chains accounted for one-third of the £7,500 million spent in grocers'. A similar process has taken place in mens' tailors, womens' clothing, and shoe provision. As early as 1961 nearly one-half of all speciality shoe shops in Britain were multiples, with even higher proportions in mens' outwear, retailing and radio and television shops. Furniture, electrical appliances and stationers are other examples. The geographical effect is that the controlling companies maintain operations only where an adequate return is earned on the capital invested. If sales or earnings drop below what is considered acceptable, then a store is closed. This is in contrast with the small individual shop owner, who would often accept a

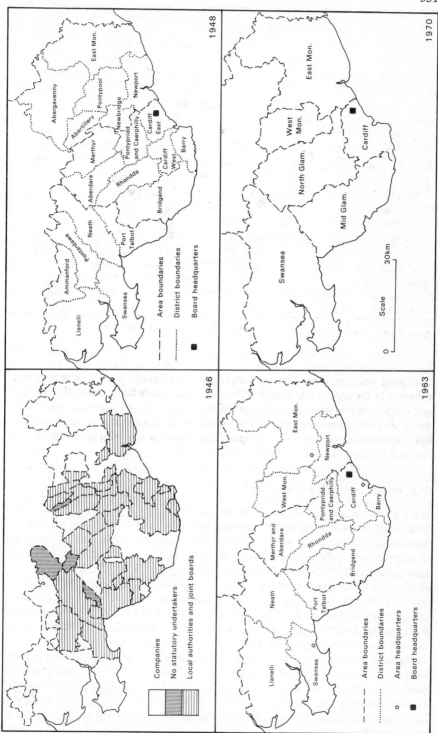

Figure 4.19 S Wales Electricity Board. Rationalization of administrative areas, industrial S Wales, 1946–70

lower income or make other adjustments to maintain his shop, since it is the only one he has (Scott 1970, 26). With larger organizations there is better chance too of locational investigation before a new store is opened, to ensure as far as possible that the right choice has been made (Scott 1970, 42). This again contrasts with the private shop owner, who is more likely to be influenced by personal rather than commercial considerations. Again the greater financial resources and better management make the larger organizations very competitive, so that they can often capture sales from small shop owners if they are in competition for a limited market. Finally, rationalization occurs not only as a result of the above trends but also through mergers and takeovers with one large organization combining with another. Where both have outlets close together in a shopping centre, there is a likelihood that only one will survive. Many of these developments in the private sector took place in the 1960s, which allowed rationalization and centralization to be taken advantage of to an increasing extent in the 1970s.

The service least affected by these tendencies was order XX, construction. About 40 per cent of the employees in this order are engaged in building maintenance, which offers little chance for rationalization and is ubiquitous in distribution. Moreover, nearly one-quarter of the 66,000 firms in this activity are one-man businesses. Roughly 20 per cent of the 1.3 million operatives are engaged by local authorities, which again limits rationalization. However, two relevant trends have become apparent. The first is the reduction of on-site work in new construction. This is especially noticeable in house-building, where increasingly such items as doors, windows and even roof structures, plumbing items, and concrete, are delivered to the site having been manufactured elsewhere. While pre-fabrication of complete dwelling units has not yet become popular in the UK, pre-fabrication of many components for assembly and installation by construction workers on site is now commonplace. The second trend was the development of major companies operating nationally or internationally. By 1970 there were over 220 firms, each with over 600 employees (COI 1976, 246). Many of these had developed permanent central offices where much of the preparation work, such as design and administration, could be centralized.

IV.7 Increased Mobility

A factor affecting the location of services at the intra-regional level was the change in the field of transport. Public road transport in many areas was improved by the provision of faster and more comfortable services, while prior to the oil price increases since 1973 the cost of travel became much less of a burden as average income per employee increased. Greater affluence over this same period also resulted in many more people having their own means of transport, in the form of a private car (table 5.1). This reduced the problems of distance quite considerably. Technical improvements both in vehicles and in road quality contributed to the same end. Empirical evidence for this, not surprisingly, suggests that households with cars tend to rely less on local centres, and travel greater distances to a wider variety of centres than households without cars (Scott 1970, 61).

The resulting greater mobility has received most attention because of the greater distances people were prepared to travel to work (ch. 2.IV.5), but there was an equally important impact on the journey to services. Because it became financially less of a burden and physically less of a strain, people not only could, but did, travel greater distances to obtain the services they required. This in turn relieved the services of the need to be within such close proximity of the population they aimed to serve, and allowed them much greater latitude in their choice of location. In this way many services have become more flexible in their location choice.

IV.8 Economies of Scale

The changes in organization and transport discussed so far were important because they altered the basis on which locational decisions were made. Their greatest impact was probably achieved because they allowed advantage to be taken of the increasing economies of scale available in the service sector. When the distances people are prepared to travel are relatively short, then it is necessary to have a large number of service points close to the population being served. This was the position in the UK in the period before 1950. It was encouraged by the form of ownership and control, which favoured the retention of a wide distribution of service points in both the public and the private service sectors. But a wide distribution also meant small individual units, whether offices or shops. Changes in the constraints described above, however, made it possible to alter the pattern so that any one place served a much wider area. The advantage of this was that each operational unit could be larger, and through economies of scale, more economically efficient. Technological advance made such developments even more desirable. For example, the financial cost of providing expensive office or medical equipment can only be justified where there is sufficient demand to keep such equipment economically occupied. The greater the turnover of the office or hospital, the greater the demand is likely to be, while offices or hospitals with small turnovers might be below the threshold size at which investment in the facilities is considered justifiable. The effects of taking advantage of such economies of scale became increasingly apparent in the UK in the 1960s, although the process had begun much earlier. In the public services it could be seen in the 1961 Hospital Plan, where the underlying principle was one of closure of small hospitals and their replacement by fewer but larger hospitals at suitable central locations (fig. 4.18). Similarly in the gas and electricity services administrative work was concentrated into fewer centres. In the case of these utilities the process proceeded by stages with the effects of the initial rationalization being relatively slight, but subsequent change was achieved by progressive increases in the size of the administrative areas and consequent reduction in their number, and in the number of area offices and of such things as stores and maintenance service depots.

The same trends were evident in the *transport services*, and even in railways which was one of the services to suffer major decline. The rationalization of the railways which took place after 1963 was based on the proposals in the Beeching Plan (Min. of Transport 1963). This had shown that 50 per cent of the stations provided only 1 per cent of the passenger receipts, and that there were many places where lines were unnecessarily duplicated. The proposed solution to the problem was the concentration of activities on the most-used facilities which could be shown to be paying their way. The effect of implementing this proposal was the withdrawal of services from areas which generated the lowest traffic income, generally areas with small dispersed populations, and improvement of services where traffic was greatest, usually between areas of dense population. Here again, even in decline, economies of scale played a major part in reforming the geographical pattern. Servicing, maintenance and goods depots were concentrated to achieve greater efficiency, and the number of passenger stations reduced, with consequent increasing intensity of use of those that remained.

In the private sector the largest employment group is Retail and Wholesale Distribution. This group employs one in five of all the employees in the service sector, and one in ten of the total insured labour force. Scott commented on the 'pronounced dis-economies of small-scale' in retailing (Scott 1970, 9). This was substantiated in the UK after 1960 by the rapid increase in the number of large stores for shopping and especially by the proliferation of supermarkets, defined as self-service shops with a minimum of 186 m^2 of selling area. There were 870 supermarkets in 1961. By 1971 the number had risen to 4,800 and they were handling nearly one-third of all retail food sales. At the same time all the major categories of shops in the clothing and footwear trades in the UK experienced decline in the number of separate establishments, largely owing to the growth of multiple ownership and the increasing size of stores. Similarly, in the grocery trade turnover expanded by 23.7 per cent between 1961 and 1966, and by 37 per cent between 1966 and 1971. Under previous conditions this expansion would have resulted in a proliferation of small shops with a dispersed pattern. What actually happened was that the number of establishments in the grocery trade fell by 15.9 per cent, 1961–6, and by 12.8 per cent, 1966–71. Turnover per establishment was rising rapidly during this time, going up from £15,016 in 1961 to £23,566 in 1966 and to £37,121 in 1971. Further development of these trends in the form of hypermarkets, defined as stores with over 4,645 m^2 selling area, has been inhibited by local authority refusal to grant planning permission for their construction. By the end of 1976 only 4 had been built in the UK, at Irlam, Lancashire, Eastleigh, Hampshire, Telford (Salop) and Caerphilly, Mid-Glamorgan, in contrast with the large numbers operating in France and Germany (Parker 1975). The fear is that such large developments would have a detrimental effect upon shopping facilities in their vicinity, but the continuing pressure of applications for planning permission for hypermarket construction (Dawson 1976) make it almost certain that they will become a more familiar part of the geography of retailing in future.

The geographical impact of these trends has been quite marked, though in some areas of the UK the effects in some services have been masked by the effects of the considerable local economic growth that has occurred. But basically there was a tendency for scale of operations to increase in all services. This happened either by increasing the average size of individual establishments, by closing small units and opening larger new ones as in the case of hospitals, schools and in the retail trade, or by increasing the size of existing individual establishments as happened with the universities. Most of these changes involve geographical change, either through the centralization of a scattered distribution of establishments into a smaller number of places, or by a certain limited number of places growing relatively faster than others causing redistribution. Whatever the method by which the changes occurred a definite geographical trend can be identified. In general it is that the higher order centres in any particular area or region tended to gain, while the losses were concentrated in the smaller centres which stagnated or declined.

This conforms with the hierarchy arrangement put forward in Christaller's *Central Place Theory* (Berry 1967, 59–73). The theory shows how, under idealized conditions, services in greatest day-to-day demand are located in the smallest service centres, which serve very limited surrounding market areas. Since everyone living in the theoretical landscape would need to be served by a centre, every part of the landscape would be in a market area. In an idealized landscape these market areas would be hexagon-shaped for maximum efficiency. The smallest service centres and their associated market areas or hinterlands would lie within the hinterland of a larger service centre, which would provide those services less frequently demanded: a specialized delicatessen shop rather than a general grocers, the area headquarters of a bank rather than a branch bank. Each higher order centre would thus serve a wider area than the lower order centres in its hinterland. These higher order centres and their hinterlands would in turn lie within the hinterland of a still higher order centre providing services even less frequently demanded, or which control a number of lower order services. This is where the wholesale grocer or the regional head-quarters of the bank would be located. There is therefore, a hierarchy of service centres, with the next higher order service centre having all the functions of the lower order centres below it, but with additional superior functions which they do not have (Scott 1970, 16); see also ch. 6.III.2).

The relevance of this theory for the changing pattern of service employment in Britain is that the trends described have all tended to make the higher order centres more attractive relative to the lower order centres (Westaway 1974). Greater mobility and willingness to travel further has meant that services can locate further away from their customers. Changes in organization and control described earlier have allowed advantage to be taken of this much more readily, a trend encouraged by the economies of scale available when services are concentrated in fewer larger units. The underlying geographical trend has been a shift of service activity away from the smallest, lowest order centres, to the smaller number of next higher order service centres. The latter have in this way grown at the expense of the former. These geographical shifts are most obvious in the public sector services, where stronger central control has facilitated rationalization. The replacement of smaller hospitals by fewer larger units, or the development of giant comprehensive schools in place of the much smaller secondary schools are good examples. In the private sector, the reduction in the number of small independent grocers, or of bread and confectionery shops, and their replacement by supermarkets, shows the same process at work. The effects of these trends are offset in some areas because growth of population or purchasing power may allow a service centre to maintain itself. The corollary is that the effects are best seen in areas where the population is in decline or static. In such areas the population declines are accelerated in the smaller places by the removal of service employment, which may be in small numbers in absolute terms but which made a significant contribution to the local economy.

IV.9 Flexible Services Location

Having explained the geographical shifts which have occurred, it is also important to point out that for many of the more flexible services there seem to be no good economic or commercial reasons to justify the concentration of many of the jobs involved into the highest order centres. Gottmann (1970) has suggested some factors which might explain the need for some services to cluster, but Rhodes and Khan (1971, 27) found among executives who were responsible for location decisions 'an obsession with psychological and environmental factors' at the expense of financial consideration. From the present state of knowledge in this field (Goddard 1975), there appear to be no good reasons why much of the routine clerical work involved with the accounting side of the electricity and gas boards, for example, could not be located elsewhere within the administrative boundaries of the areas they serve than in the largest city, which is where they are usually centred today. The location of the routine administration of county councils, or national government departments could similarly be shifted. At the national level, recognition that this could be done, and needed to be done, arose mainly from the development of office space and employment in London (Daniels 1975). 80 per cent of the office space in England and Wales for which planning permission was given between 1945 and 1962 was located in London (Wright 1967, 221). Moreover in the central areas of London, where more than half the employment increase in the conurbation was concentrated between 1945 and 1963, two-thirds of the increase occurred in office jobs, and these trends continued in the 1960s. Between 1964 and 1967 there was a net increase of 1.8 million m^2 of office floorspace in the SE planning region alone. This represented 56 per cent of the total growth of office floorspace in England and Wales during that period (Daniels 1969). Westaway (1974) showed that head offices of the 1,000 largest companies in the UK are predominantly in London, and that between 1969 and 1972 the number of head offices in London increased by 30, while all other large cities recorded declines. Hall (1966) pointed out that projections for employment growth in the London region over the period 1961–81 showed that two-thirds, or about 750,000 jobs, would be in office employment. He further concluded that: 'The real answer to the question of London's future, then, hinges on the economics of office location' (ch. 1.V.5). Even in 1966 the SE region had 49 per cent of the four million office workers in England and Wales, as against only 36 per cent of the economically-active population. This expansion was a major cause of the overgrowth of London and the SE region in the period up to 1970. It was clear that some of this office employment could be located elsewhere and still be economically viable, and so efforts were made to redistribute this growth. For the private sector the quasi-independent Location of Offices Bureau (1964) was established to persuade offices to move out of C London and Office Development Permits were introduced by the government to control new office building. This action resulted in some offices being dispersed mainly to the outskirts of London or to other parts of SE England. Thus 84 per cent of office moves organized by the LOB between 1967 and 1974 were within the SE region, though in the year ending March 1975 this figure had fallen to 70 per cent.

In the public sector, the *Flemming Report* (1963, not published) suggested dispersal of some government work, and the *Hardman Report* (Civil Service Dept. 1973) made more detailed suggestions for various government departments. Acting on these recommendations, central government set an example by locating employment-generating office developments of their own in other regions. Amongst others, the National Savings Bank headquarters was located in Glasgow, the Business Statistics Office in Newport, Gwent, and the Driver and Vehicle Licensing Centre in Swansea, W Glamorgan. In addition, it was planned to move 31,000 central government jobs from the London area between 1975 and 1984. Since 1960 the possibilities of influencing the location of flexible service employment have been explored and the significance of such employment in planning regional development is now widely recognized. Though both the policies adopted and their effects have been criticized, by 1975 it was clear that the proper planning of the location of economic activity in the UK would in future result in more of the flexible service activities being distributed to the Development Areas, in the same way as the location of 'footloose' manufacturing industry had been influenced during the previous thirty years. What was also becoming apparent by the mid-1970s, however, was that in the DAs these services were clustering in or near the largest centres, creating a concentrated decentralization pattern. This should make it easier for *regional* services to be shifted away from such centres, to help achieve the proper distribution of employment which is one of the aims of government regional policy.

REFERENCES

BERRY, B J L (1967) *Geography of Market Centres and Retail Distribution*, Englewood Cliffs

BUSWELL, R J and LEWIS, E W (1970) 'The Geographical Distribution of Industrial Research Activity in the UK', *Reg. Stud., 4*, 297—306

CEGB (1969) *Annual Rep. and Accounts 1968—9*, HMSO

COI (1976) *Britain 1976*, London

CSO (1968) *Standard Industrial Classification*, 3rd. edn., HMSO

CHISHOLM, M (1966) *Geography and Economics*, London

CIVIL SERV. DEPT. (1973) *Dispersal of Government Work from London* (Hardman Report), Cmnd 5322, HMSO

CLARK, C (1966) 'Industrial Location and Economic Potential', *Lloyds Bank Rev., 82*, 1—17

COATES, B E and RAWSTRON, E M (1971) *Regional Variations in Britain*, London

DANIELS, P W (1969) 'Office Decentralisation from London: Policy and Practice', *Reg. Stud., 3*, 171—8

(1975) *Offices: an Urban Regional Study*, Oxford

DAWSON, J A (1976) 'Lack of Decision Retards Retailing Investment', *Geogrl. Mag. Lond., 48*, 759—60

DEPT. ENERGY (1976) *Digest of Energy Statistics 1976*, HMSO

DEPT. TRADE and INDUSTRY (1971) *Census of Distribution and Other Services Report 1966*, vol 2, HMSO

(1972) *Census of Distribution and Other Services Report 1961*, Supplement, HMSO

FLORENCE, P S (1962) *Post-War Investment, Location and Size of Plant*, Cambridge

GAS COUN. (1958) *Annual Rep. and Accounts 1957—8*, HMSO

(1960) *Annual Rep. and Accounts 1959—60*, HMSO

GEORGE, K D (1960) 'Economics of Nuclear and Conventional Coal-fired Stations in the UK', *Oxford Econ. Pap., 12*, 3, 295—309

GODDARD, J B (1975) *Office Location in Urban and Regional Development*, Oxford

GOTTMANN, J (1970) 'Urban Centrality and the Interweaving of Quaternary Activity', *Ekistics, 29*, 322—31

HALL, M, KNAPP, J and WINSTEN, C (1961) *Distribution in GB and N America*, Oxford

HALL, P G (1962) *The Industries of London since 1861*, London

(1966) *World Cities*, London

HALLETT, G and RANDALL, P (1970) *Maritime Industry and Port Development in S Wales*, Cardiff

HAMILTON, F E I (1967) 'Models of Industrial Location' in CHORLEY, R J and
   HAGGETT, P (eds) *Models in Geography*, London, 361–424
                     (1974) *Spatial Perspectives on Industrial Organisation and
   Decision Making* London
HAMMOND, E (1967) 'Dispersal of Government Offices', *Urban Stud., 4*,
   258–75
HAUSER, D P (1971) 'System Costs and the Location of new Generating Plants in
   England and Wales', *Trans. Inst. Br. Geogr., 54*, 101–21
HOUSE, J W and KNIGHT, E M (1967) *Pit Closure and the Community*, Newcastle
   upon Tyne
HOWARD, R S (1968) *The Movement of Manufacturing Industry in the UK 1945–
   65*, HMSO
HUMPHRYS, G (1962) 'Growth Industries and the Regional Economies of Britain',
   District Bank Rev., 144, 35–56
                     (1972) *Industrial Britain: South Wales*, Newton Abbot
                     (1976) 'Industrial Change: Lessons from South Wales', *Geogr., 61*,
   246–54
LUTTRELL, W F (1962) *Factory Location and Industrial Movement*, 2 vols,
   London
McCRONE, G (1969) *Regional Policy in Britain*, London
MANNERS, G (1959) 'Recent Changes in the British Gas Industry', *Trans. Inst. Br.
   Geogr., 26*, 153–68
                     (1963) 'Service Industries and Regional Economic Growth', *Tn
   Plann. Rev., 33*, 293–303
                     (1970) 'The 1970s Power Game', *Geogrl. Mag. London., 42*, 442–9
                     (1971A) 'Some Economic and Spatial Characteristics of the British
   Energy Market' in CHISHOLM, M and MANNERS, G (eds) *Spatial Policy Prob-
   lems of the British Economy*, Cambridge, 146–79
                     (1971B) *The Geography of Energy*, 2nd edn, London
                     (1976) 'The Changing Energy Situation in Britain', *Geogr., 61*,
   221–31
MARNELL, M J and HUMPHRYS, G (1965) 'Private Coal Mining in S. Wales',
   Geogrl. Rev., 55, 328–38
MINIST. FUEL and POWER (1955) *Programme for Nuclear Power*, Cmnd 9389
   HMSO
MINIST. LABOUR (1961) 'Occupational Changes 1951–61', *Manpower Stud., 6*,
   HMSO
MINIST. POWER (1958) *Report of the Committee of Inquiry into Coal Distribu-
   tion Costs in GB*, Cmnd 446 HMSO
                     (1967) *Fuel Policy*, Cmnd 3438 HMSO
MINIST. TECHNOLOGY (1975) *Digest of Energy Statistics 1974*, HMSO
MINIST. TRANSPORT (1963) *The Reshaping of British Railways*, HMSO
NCB (1971) *Annual Rep. and Accounts 1970–1*, vol 1, HMSO
   (1975) *Annual Rep. and Accounts 1974–5*, vol 1, HMSO
   (1977) 'The Vale of Belvoir', *Coal News, 187*
NAT. HEALTH SERV. (1962) *A Hospital Plan for England and Wales*, London
NORTH, D J (1974) 'The Process of Locational Change in Different Manufacturing
   Organisations' in HAMILTON, F E I (ed) *Spatial Perspectives on Industrial Or-
   ganisation and Decision Making*, London

ODELL, P R and ROSING, K E (1974) 'Weighing up the North Sea Wealth', *Geogrl. Mag, Lond., 47*, 150–5

ORDNANCE SURV. (1951) *Map of GB: Gas and Coke 1949*, 2 sheets, Scale 1:625,000

PARKER, A J (1975) 'Hypermarkets: the Changing Pattern of Retailing', *Geogr., 60*, 120–4

POSNER, M V (1973) *Fuel Policy: A Study in Applied Economics*, London

POWELL, A G (1960–1) 'The Recent Development of Greater London', *Advmt Sci., 17*, 76–86

PUBL. GEN. ACTS See list p. 516

RAWSTRON, E M (1964) 'Industry' in WATSON, J W and SISSONS, J B (eds) *The British Isles: a Systematic Geography*, London, 297–318

RHODES, J and KHAN, A (1971) *Office Dispersal and Regional Policy*, Cambridge

ROSING, K E (1976) 'Oil and Gas: Beneath the North Sea', *Geogrl. Mag., Lond., 48*, 758–9

SCOTT, P (1970) *Geography and Retailing*, London

SCOTT. COUN. (1961) *Report of the Committee of Enquiry on the Scottish Economy*, Edinburgh

SIMPSON, E S (1966) *Coal and Power Industries in Post-War Britain*, London

SMITH, D M (1965) 'Recent Change in the Regional Pattern of British Industry', *Tijdschr. econ. soc. Geogr., 56*, 133–45

SMITH, W (1949) *An Economic Geography of GB*, London

SPOONER, D and NORTH, J (1976) 'Yorkshire Coal Crop from Selby Farmland', *Geogrl. Mag., Lond., 48*, 554–8

THORPE, D (1968) 'The Main Shopping Centres of GB in 1961. Their Location and Structural Characteristics', *Urban Stud., 5*, 165–206

WARREN, K (1973) 'The Location of British Heavy Industry — Problems and Policies', *Geogrl. J., 139*, 76–83

WESTAWAY, J (1974) 'The Spatial Hierarchy of Business Organisations and its Implications for the British Urban System', *Reg. Stud., 8*, 145–55

WRIGHT, M (1967) 'Provincial Office Development', *Urban Stud., 4*, 218–57

5

Transport

I   INTRODUCTION: SOME THEORETICAL AND EMPIRICAL BACKGROUND

I.1   Transport Systems

Transport is a quantifiable means of interaction, potentially a measure of the 'differences between different areas', and it is important to an understanding of most economic, social and political distributions. Even today, however, traffic-flow statistics for the UK are inadequate, and moving back in time any precision in measurement is very soon lost. Nonetheless it is important to appreciate the influence at any stage of contemporary modes of transport upon the patterns of economic activity and to acknowledge the legacy of this influence in the present landscape. The present transport system is the result of a long evolution continually modified by changing demands and developing technology. It was an evolution with overlapping phases of dominance: of coastal shipping and inland waterways in the eighteenth century, of the railway throughout much of the nineteenth and of road transport in the third-quarter of the twentieth century. The accumulation of modes and networks with few attempts at conscious integration has been well documented (Smith 1949; Savage 1966; Dyos and Aldcroft 1969). No considera-tion of present-day transport in the UK begins with a *tabula rasa*. Thus in road transport, for example, it is a tribute to its adaptability that it could begin its modern rise to dominance without major initial investment, but it must face the major problems caused by high density operation on a road network still largely attuned to a horse-and-carriage age (Paterson 1972).

The development of transport networks has been continuously influenced by considerations of physical environment, notably by relief (Appleton 1962). More important, however, have been the influences of *dimensions* and *insularity*, reflected primarily in the limitation of the distances over which the systems could develop and work out a *modus vivendi*. These characteristics impart to UK trans-port a measure of distinctiveness, especially by comparison with other European systems. The critical influence in all transport development is need. Capital invest-ment and operational viability rest ultimately on demand, usually economic but potentially strategic or social. Regrettably it is a demand often viewed in isolation and with an imperfect appraisal of the economic and technical characteristics of the available media and of their suitability to meet the needs in question.

The matching of the demand for transport with the available facilities has usually been made in terms of costs but this has been modified in some degree. For a growing majority of UK industries, for example, transport costs are now of limited importance (Brown 1969). It has been estimated that the share of transport in the total costs of producing and distributing is 9 per cent although there are very considerable variations according to the type of industry (Edwards and

Bayliss 1971). It is broadly true that as the pace and level of economic development increase then transport costs become less important and concern for the
quality of the service increases (Owen 1964). Certainly it is becoming more
common to consider goods transport as the *logistic* or *physical distribution* aspect
of an industrial activity rather than as a discrete element of the tertiary sector, and
transport costs will be subsumed within some form of the total cost concept (ch. 4
III.3). All these issues are reflected in the developing transport system of the UK
and not least in the fact that it is clear that the larger portion of transport costs
now relate to the movement of people and not of goods (Chisholm and Manners
1971, 240).

There has been a gradual change in emphasis in the forces moulding the
transport system. Increasingly technological achievement has made it possible to
overcome any physical environmental problems, but to do so at a cost. Thus in
transport developments, as in so much of economic development, the point at
issue is not whether it is technically possible but whether it is economically
feasible. Moreover at the level of capital provision commonly required for transport development, economic feasibility tends to be interpreted largely in terms of
whether the development is considered to be politically desirable. The same may
be true of the maintenance, by subsidy, of existing facilities. The transport system
thus tends to reflect the volume and nature of demand assessed in terms of the
economic and technical characteristics of the available transport media, but
viewed in the light of the existing socio-political order. An explanation of the
development of the transport system must consider in particular technological
change and public policy.

I.2   Transport Development 1950–75

Marshall wrote in 1890 of the development of transport as 'the dominant economic
fact of our own age' (Marshall, 1890, 718–19). He wrote in a different age but the
growth and elaboration of transport has continued unabated. His statement might
be considered equally apt today. Notwithstanding the important achievements of
earlier times it is probable that the transport developments of the last twenty-five
years will ensure that this period emerges as one of major and accelerated change.
An important aspect of such contemporary change is that several transport media
are involved and are increasingly integrated by these changes. As vehicles become
more sophisticated and expensive and individual transport media more specialized,
ideally they should cooperate to provide the most economical overall system. Such
cooperation may be achieved through *coordination* – agreement between the media
to improve interchanges and to eliminate duplicate services – or through *integration*, which involves the systematic replanning of the transport of an area or route
so as to use each medium to best advantage. Integrated systems are often planned by
teams responsible to the community rather than to an individual medium. Since
coordination and integration are easier to plan than to achieve, theory is often
many years in advance of practice. It is a further general characteristic of recent
change that it has tended to an increased measure of concentration of activity
within each medium, that is, to the more intensive use of some parts of the system.
Also changed is the relative importance of the various media within the total
system. This change is related first to technological advances and, secondly, to
changing demand for transport.

Technological advances are concerned primarily with an increase in load capacity in several sections of the total system. Some developments relate to the vehicles in use, for example the increased size and specialization of merchant vessels (ch. 5.VI.1), and the increased capacity of aircraft highlighted by the first commercial flight of the Jumbo Jet in January 1970. Load capacity is also a function of speed and efficiency. Commercial aircraft speed has increased greatly over this period and the railway saw important changes in traction with the final replacement of steam by diesel in August 1968, the development of some mainline electrification, and the introduction of the High Speed Train in October 1976. There were also notable increases in the number of carriers, for example, of merchant vessels, especially tankers, and outstandingly a five-fold increase in private motor cars. Developments in networks and in terminals were often no less important to advances in transport. In this the extension and elaboration of seaport and airport layouts and facilities have been important. There can be no doubt, however, that the most striking and novel achievement of the period since the Second World War has been the slow and as yet limited construction of a motorway system following the first short section (the Preston by-pass) in December 1958 and the initial 88.5 km section of the M1 in November 1959 (table 5.1). One important aspect of

TABLE 5.1

Roads and Vehicles, UK, 1951–74

	1951	1961	1971	1975
Motorway km	–	218	1,356	2,132
Trunk roads (incl. motorway), km	13,829	14,225	15,277	16,032
Trunk road expenditure (£'000)	8,524	52,778	306,973	384,762
Vehicles in use:				
Cars ('000)	2,433	6,144	12,358	14,095
Goods vehicles ('000)	955	1,491	1,660	1,829
New registrations: (GB only)				
Cars ('000)	136	743	1,302	1,180
Goods vehicles ('000)	85	220	234	222

Source: Basic Road Statistics, Br. Road Fed. (1972) *Ann. Abstract of Statistics*, 1976, HMSO

technological change, belonging mainly to the 1960s, and indeed mainly post-1965, has been the development of unit-load goods traffic, which has transgressed the divisions between the media more effectively than ever before and assuredly to more lasting effect (ch. 5.VI.1).

The *change in demand* for transport was engendered by the continuation of the inter-war trends resulting from the secular decline of heavy industry and the rise of consumer goods and service industries within a more prosperous and mobile society. Increased car ownership, in particular, placed sections of the system under severe strain, as for example the urban road network and the public transport services in both urban and rural areas. Indeed the increasing dominance of road transport is the most striking characteristic of the inland transport scene in the period since 1950. As noted earlier, both vehicle numbers and improvements to the road system contributed to this and it became clear that the inter-city motorway programme was likely to be one of the more influential forces shaping the economic

geography of the UK in the next decade (Chisholm and Manners 1971, 5). Such
road developments placed the rail system under severe competitive pressure as
also, to a much more limited extent, did the increased volume of domestic air
traffic, notably for passenger traffic on Anglo–Scottish services. The railways did
not succumb without rearguard actions. Like the canals at an earlier time (the
canal network of approx. 6,485 km at a maximum (R. Commn. Canals and Waterways 1909) is now reduced to 544 km of commercially-used route) the railways
drastically reduced their network. By 1975 the UK rail network had been reduced
by 13,676 km since 1951, with less than half of the route kilometrage of 1951
still available for passenger working (table 5.2). Moreover British Rail attempted to

TABLE 5.2

Rail Network, UK, 1938–75

Route open to traffic (km)	1938	1951	1955	1961	1965	1967	1970	1975
GB	32,191	31,145	30,669	29,555	24,056	21,193	18,984	18,114
N Ireland	852	769	614	477	326	326	326	326
UK	33,044	31,914	31,283	30,032	24,382	21,519	19,310	18,440

Source: Annual Abstract of Statistics, CSO; *Committee of Inquiry into Internal Transport*
(Irish Stationery Office, 1957); British Rail Board *Ann. Rep. & Accts. 1975*

concentrate its efforts upon the traffic and length of haul which were judged to be
its most effective operations.

Table 5.3 summarizes the changing volume of traffic and the changing relative
importance of the media between 1953 and 1974. Within this period the total
tonne-km of railway goods traffic increased by 65 per cent, but traffic on the roads
by 183 per cent. The total passenger kilometrage increased by 139 per cent in
1953–73, but there was a more than five-fold increase in private road transport
during the same period, followed by a decline after 1973. By 1975, 65 per cent of
goods traffic and 92 per cent of passenger traffic was on the roads. Rail tonne-km
declined until 1967 (22,101 million tonne-km), and has since fluctuated. The long-
standing tradition of coastwise traffic reached a post-war maximum in 1966
(25,338 million tonne-km). Inland waterways, pipeline and domestic air transport
make relatively small contributions to UK traffic totals although their absolute
increases in traffic are impressive. The increased volume and changing composition
of UK traffic has posed particular problems of coordination and rationalization,
some of which are discussed in ch. 5.VI.

I.3   Transport Policies

(for references to all Acts see 'Public General Acts', p. 516)

Transport is so all pervading and the influences of transport are so widespread
that 'almost every transport decision is a public issue' (Munby 1968, 7). Moreover
'transport gives the government powers of positive planning unrivalled in any
other field' (Patmore, 1972, 50–61). It is perhaps then surprising that while there

TABLE 5.3

Goods and Estimated Passenger Traffic, GB, 1953–74

Goods traffic	Thousand million tonne-km					Per cent				
	1953	1960	1965	1970	1974	1953	1960	1965	1970	1974
Total	84.6	99.8	120.4	136.1	139.7	100	100	100	100	100
Road	32.2	48.3	68.7	83.0	91.4	38.0	51.3	57.2	60.9	65.3
Rail	37.3	30.4	25.1	26.7	24.4	44.0	31.9	20.9	19.9	17.5
Coastal shipping	14.6	19.4	25.0	23.1	20.7	17.4	16.2	20.7	17.0	14.8
Inland waterways	0.3	0.3	0.1	0.1	0.1	0.4	0.3	0.1	0.1	0.1
Pipelines	0.1	0.3	1.3	2.9	3.5	0.2	0.3	1.1	2.1	2.5

Passenger traffic	Thousand million passenger-km					Per cent				
	1953	1960	1965	1970	1974	1953	1960	1965	1970	1974
Total	188.4	255.1	332.5	408.2	443.0	100	100	100	100	100
Road										
Private transport	67.7	143.8	232.8	315.6	350.0	35.9	56.2	69.9	77.2	79.5
Public service vehicle	81.5	70.6	63.0	54.8	55.0	43.3	27.7	18.9	13.4	12.0
Rail	38.7	39.9	35.0	35.7	36.0	20.6	15.7	10.5	8.7	8.0
Air	0.3	0.8	1.6	1.9	2.4	0.2	0.3	0.5	0.5	0.5

NB Excludes traffic in N Ireland except (i) petroleum moved by sea; (ii) air passenger traffic to and from GB
Source: Annual Abstracts of Statistics, CSO

is a long history of government involvement it can rarely be accurately described as a widespread or positive influence upon UK transport. Historically the role of government was more that of a regulator than an initiator (Owen 1964, 33). In the nineteenth century local authorities' responsibilities for the roads were widened and local public corporations assumed responsibility for most ports and for urban passenger transport. The private development of the inland waterways and notably of the railways was curbed only by regulations relating to safety, to the possible abuse of monopoly and to the protection of the financial interests of the traders (Sharp 1965). Government policies have been directed most frequently towards the attempted solution of some specific transport problem rather than demonstrating any firm attachment to principle or to a national perspective. The *Ministry of Transport*, established in 1919, heralded much fuller and direct government concern. The ensuing years have produced a large volume of legislation mainly aimed, as Gwilliam (1964) points out, at tackling conflicts between rail and road, between private and public carriers, and doctrinaire conflicts over ownership.

For the most part government policy did not provide a context for the development of an effective national network in any medium and least of all for any coordination in an integrated plan. Coordination was considered by the *Royal Commission on Transport* (1930) but was not implemented except to a limited extent in the *London Passenger Transport Board* (1933) and, indirectly, in the obvious concern of the legislation to influence the competitive relationships of rail and road. After 1930 this was largely a matter of restricting the capacity of developing road transport by the *Road Traffic Act* (1930) (licensing public services coaches) and the *Road and Rail Act* (1933) (licensing road goods vehicles). On the other hand the *Trunk Roads Act* (1936), making a basic network eligible for Treasury support, could only improve the roads' attraction. In any event, in a sharply changing transport demand situation, no moves towards a supposedly *fair basis* for competition could significantly affect the declining status of the railway. However unrealistically, the railways did tend to attribute their plight to the continuing influence of policies which left their common carrier obligations and their distinctive rate structure unchanged.

It remained true that charges were not comparable on rail and road and the failure to ensure the choice of the cheapest medium was a main reason for the limited achievements of the *Transport Act* (1947), which was the first explicit attempt at a comprehensive view of the national system. The newly created *British Transport Commission (BTC)* acquired all railways, inland waterways and road haulage undertakings except those operating within 40 km of their base. The required provision of an *adequate* service seemingly envisaged the support of some unremunerative services by a process of cross-subsidization (Gwilliam, 1964, 96). An important continuing aspect introduced by the 1947 Act was the ability of transport undertakings to negotiate Treasury grants via the Minister of Transport, although the level of this support has varied with government attitudes and reflected the advances and recessions of the economy. With a pendulum-like swing the *Transport Act* (1953) began demolition of the monopoly. Road haulage was removed from the BTC, with the exception of 7,000 lorries retained by British Road Services. In striving to replace inland transport on a competitive basis the Act abolished some of the railways' restrictive obligations although its freedom in charging remained in practice incomplete. Most importantly, the 1953 Act facilitated competition between road and rail at a time when changing transport demands markedly favoured road transport rather than the railway service then available. The result was not surprisingly a growing contrast in the share of inland transport handled by the two media and it was in the aftermath of the 1953 Act that the Beeching retrenchment proposals for the railways were worked out and progressively implemented in the early 1960s (MoT 1963B).

The statutory framework for the 1960s, at least until 1968, was mainly provided by four Acts: The *Road Traffic Act* (1960) was a consolidating Act incorporating little change; the *Civil Aviation (Licensing) Act* (1960) allowed BEA's monopoly of major internal air routes to be challenged; the *Transport Act* (1962) reorganized the nationalized undertakings and, while removing further restrictions from rail operation and also giving a measure of protection to coastal shipping (from the railway), the Act says very little in general about the relationships between the media; the *Pipeline Act* (1962) (in direct contrast to the approach in the *Civil Aviation and Transport Acts*) assumed that pipelines are a natural monopoly to be protected against duplication and excess capacity (Gwilliam, 1964, 224–32).

The *Transport Act* (1968) embodied several signal advances, some of which have survived subsequent changes of government. Container traffic on road and rail was integrated in the *National Freight Corporation* (NFC). Perhaps even more significant, in principle, the Minister of Transport was empowered to subsidize named transport services (road and rail) which were making a financial loss, but were considered to be socially necessary to retain population or to encourage new industries in Development Areas. The 1968 Act also provided for *Passenger Transport Authorities* (PTAs), subsequently established in the metropolitan counties of the W Midlands, Merseyside, Greater Manchester, W Yorkshire and Tyne and Wear, also in the Glasgow area of Strathclyde, on the 1933 model of the London Passenger Transport Board. It should be noted that an important aspect of the 1968 Act, the quantity licensing provision which was intended to direct all goods traffic over distances in excess of 160 km and in vehicles of over 16 tons on to the railway, has not been implemented.

The 1968 Act ushered in a period of substantial agreement on transport policy between the major political parties. There is no doubt that the political pendulum of the previous twenty-three years had had a seriously debilitating effect on the transport system. It was a major inhibition and frustration to the operation and staffing of transport undertakings that in general terms almost fourteen years was spent mainly in waiting for new legislation or reorganizing to meet the requirements of the latest statute. The transport provisions of the *Local Government Act* (1972) and the *Railways Act* (1974) attracted more general political party support. Indeed the Railways Act (ch. 5.II.3) was drafted by the Conservatives and passed during the subsequent Labour administration as the fourth post-war attempt to secure a viable financial structure for British Rail.

Although progress towards the long-term objectives of transport policy was slow, substantial uniformity in methods of appraising investment had been achieved by the early 1970s. These methods are discussed in DoE 1976A (vol II Paper 5) and Starkie (1973). Briefly, *financial appraisal* based on the assessment of discounted cash flows is used where investments and returns can be expressed in monetary terms. This applies when considering railway inter-city passenger and inter-regional freight investment and also the operations of the *British Waterways Board*, the *National Bus Company* and the *National Freight Corporation*. **Cost benefit analysis (COBA)** is used where the values of time, peace and quiet, death by accident, or any other factors which have no money equivalent are being considered. It is therefore relevant to trunk and local road programmes, rural railway closures and the planning of journeys to work. The COBA computer package enables complex cost and benefit sequences to be compared. Common evaluation by one or other of these methods facilitates submission of investment programmes from government departments, local authorities and nationalized transport industries to the Public Expenditure Survey Committee.

Common structures for local transport planning have been introduced in recent years. The complementary planning of transport and land use was encouraged by the incorporation of the former MoT within the DoE from 1970–76. The provisions of the *Town and Country Planning Act* (1968) and the *Local Government Acts, England and Wales* (1972) and *Scotland* (1973) required local authorities to relate local transport policies to their structure plans and to consult with both DoE and the relevant nationalized transport industries.

It sometimes seems that the real commitment of a government to its policies may be measured through its expenditure on them. Certainly it is instructive to view expenditure as a key to policy thinking and achievement. This information has been brought together, in broad terms, in the *Public Expenditure Survey* (Treasury 1975) and is also reproduced in DoE 1976A and 1976B. Expenditure on surface transport in GB, including the capital expenditure of the nationalized transport industries, has more than kept pace with public expenditure as a whole. In terms of constant prices, subsidies to surface transport in GB more than doubled between 1968–9 and 1975–6 while investment in public transport rose by 150 per cent. Government investment in transport, measured at constant prices, rose to a peak in the financial year 1975–6 and is planned to decline to its 1970–1 level by 1979–80. This decline is due to several reductions in future public expenditure made since 1973 as a result of Britain's economic problems.

It can be estimated from public expenditure figures that about one-third of expenditure on surface transport is directed to inter-city and inter-regional transport and the remainder to essentially local transport needs. As a proportion of total expenditure, the trunk road programme fell from 22 per cent to 16 per cent between 1970–1 and 1975–6 and is planned to continue at about this proportion during the next four years. Investment by British Rail, on the other hand, plus central and local government subsidies to rail, amounted to 13 per cent of the surface transport budget in 1970–1 but now form 20 per cent and may reach 22 per cent by 1979–80. The railways are currently carrying 8 per cent of passenger km and 18 per cent of freight km, user expenditure on railways has fallen to a mere 4.5 per cent of the total user expenditure on surface transport. As these proportions are not expected to alter much within the next few years, it is clear that current government expenditure on the railways is related to factors other than their current economic performance. It is also relevant to the future use of road and rail transport that while retail prices in general rose by 93 per cent from 1970–5 during the early stages of inflation, the estimated costs of running a car rose by 105 per cent, bus fares by 110 per cent and rail fares by 138 per cent.

The rapid expansion of traffic, especially road traffic, received a sharp jolt late in 1973 when the price of oil doubled, leading to a rapid increase in the running costs of vehicles. More important effects were felt more gradually as government attempts to arrest the ensuing inflation included increasingly severe cuts in the programme of future public investment in transport. The first casualties were the proposed sea- and airport at Maplin and the Channel tunnel, soon followed by reductions in the length and capacity of the planned network of trunk roads. It was of long-term significance that the investment policies of individual transport media and of government at all levels had been based on the forward projection of the rapidly rising traffic trends of the late 1960s. When it was generally agreed that these trends were likely to be modified to an unknown degree, under the influence of higher fuel costs and the falling exchange value of the £, it became more difficult to assess the demand for individual investments. Thus by 1975 a major national debate on future transport policy was under way.

Considering the complexity of the issues and the number and variety of deeply-entrenched vested interest groups, it is not surprising that successive governments made slow progress in the formulation of a general transport policy to meet the changed conditions of the 1970s. The possibilities of making expensive additions, or even changes, to the existing networks, melted away under the baleful inflation which developed after 1973. Although major policy pronouncements were repeatedly postponed a consultative document on transport policy (DoE 1967A) was eventually issued in order to clarify the issues under public discussion.

The transport policies so far discussed, seek to improve the economic efficiency of transport media, acting individually or together, as measured by the local or national community. Another approach to transport policy, increasingly heard in the debates of the 1970s, is the measurement of the value of a transport service by social or political criteria. These may include the saving of fossil or imported fuel, the reduction of environmental pollution, the creation or preservation of employment or consideration of the special needs of old, poor or isolated members of the community (Indep. Commn. on Transport 1974) (DoE 1976A). Many such discussions include proposals to increase the share of inter-city traffic carried by the railways.

The activities of 'environmental' pressure groups became increasingly significant in many western countries during the 1970s. The novelty of their arguments was reinforced by a skilful dramatization of issues in order to obtain maximum exposure on televised news programmes. There were growing fears that irreplaceable natural resources were being used up too rapidly in the developed world and that the atmosphere was being polluted by emissions from motor vehicle and aircraft engines (ch. 3.V.2–3). Many people who were worried about global pollution were anxious to challenge the assumptions underlying the prediction of future traffic trends in the UK and, at local level, supported local interest groups concerned with the preservation of recreational activities (usually identified with the maintenance of existing land uses and landscapes) and of peace and quiet around their homes. Delays and changes in the provision of new transport facilities brought about by pressure groups are detailed further in II.2 and II.3 below.

The adherence of the UK to the EEC in 1973 has had little effect on transport policy to date. European Transport Commission policies have been regulatory rather than innovative. The Commission attempts to harmonize the transport regulations of member countries in order to remove obstacles to the free operation of the market. The underlying philosophy of the transport policy of the original six members (Despicht 1969; Gwilliam and Mackie 1975) encouraged competition between media and a charging system which bore a reasonable relationship to the distance travelled. British practice has been markedly different in detail to that of the Community in the past but both sets of policies have tended to restrain the economic forces of change within the transport industry and so to maintain existing services and spatial relationships.

II   INLAND TRANSPORT BETWEEN CITIES AND REGIONS

II.1   Traffic Flows

Transport in the UK is characterized by short journeys. The majority of journeys are local, inter-city distances are short even by European standards, and few journeys to and from ports exceed 160 km. Of the 55 million inhabitants of the UK, 32 millions (58 per cent) live in the so-called axial belt 400 km long and 120 km broad extending from Kent to Lancashire but occupying less than one-fifth of the UK land space. A further 7 million people live in S Wales, Avon, Hampshire, Humberside and N Lancashire, on the periphery of the axial belt and within 160 km of at least two of its conurbations. Freight flow data, collected by the MoT in 1964, have been analysed by Chisholm and O'Sullivan (1973). From their tabulations it is possible to calculate that the axial belt generated 59 per cent of the originating traffic of GB and received 57 per cent. A further 14 per cent originated and 14 per cent terminated in the peripheral areas listed above. It is not, therefore, surprising to find that the mean freight haul was only 60 km and the mean road freight haul 51 km.

Since 1970 there has been no increase in the amount of freight carried in GB and only a relatively small shift from rail to road-borne freight. No significant further increase in the volume of goods transported is expected during the next decade (DoE 1976A, vol 2, Paper 7). The increase in tonne-km is due to small increases in average journey length. The average length of road freight haulage, which was 43 km in 1965 and 52 km in 1974, is expected to extend to perhaps 65 km in 1985. The average rail haul, which rose from 107 km in 1965 to 137 km in 1974, is not expected to increase further. The average freight haul on the inland waterways had fallen to 19 km by 1974 (DoE 1976B). In general terms the traffic flows of the UK form three distinctive but inter-connected systems: first, the flow of raw materials and passengers from abroad and the return movements of passengers and manufactured products through the ports and airports; secondly, the flow of freight and passengers between the major conurbations and regions within the UK; and thirdly, local movements of people and goods to and from work, school and shops; also the collection and distribution of freight within towns, between neighbouring towns and in rural areas.

The majority of traffic movements can be assigned to one of these broad categories (in fact the vast majority of movements are local) but the detailed picture contains many complications. Passengers and goods may pass from local origins to distant destinations without passing through regional interchange points or using major through-routeways. Seaports, which specialize in international traffic, also handle coal and oil-products moving from one part of the UK to another. The transport system of N Ireland is a discrete sub-system of that of the UK, only making connection with British transport through sea and airports, but it has strong historical ties and contemporary land links with the transport system of the Irish Republic.

These and many other complexities do not invalidate a general analysis of UK traffic flows at international, inter-regional and local levels. The urbanization of the country has led to growing concentration of population in conurbations and large towns, separated by rural areas of much lower population density. Many of the changes in transport geography during the post-war period have resulted from increasing concentrations of traffic passing through a limited number of nodes. Each mode of transport has attempted to adjust to these developments but has been hampered by the legacy of its past, when traffic flows were more diffuse and did not fit so clearly into the broad flow systems described above. To change the pattern of the network has not only required capital investment beyond the resources of the transport industries themselves but has required changes of attitude among management, trades unions, government and the general public, the abandonment of long-established services and widespread redundancy in employment. This section is concerned with the effect of these changes on the pattern of transport networks, but continual reference must be made to the institutional frameworks and economic circumstances within which they have occurred.

The period from 1870 to 1950 was one of relative stability for transport networks within the UK. The roads had been asphalted in the early twentieth century but the pressures generated by the steady increase in road traffic had not yet led to major changes in route network. The density of the transport network was lowest in the uplands of the Atlantic Face of Britain where few canals were found and railways and some roads were single track. The UK network was distinguished from that of European neighbours by its high capacity in regions of moderate population density 250–1, 300 per km^2 where most railways were double-tracked. The heavy traffic flows generated in areas of high population density within the axial belt were accommodated by a large number of alternative routes and nodes of medium-capacity rather than by a few high-capacity routes. There were no motorways in 1950 and only one 74 km high-capacity inland waterway, the Manchester Ship Canal.

The Irish transport system evolved when the island was part of the UK but the establishment of a 1.6 m gauge on the Irish railways in 1846 precluded the subsequent development of train ferries and the through-working of rail wagons between Ireland and Britain. The county boundaries which were hastily chosen in 1921 to form the boundary between the Irish Free State and the UK bore no relation to the road and rail networks of the island. The intricate net of country roads crossed by the sinuous boundary has been a source of political and military embarrassment to both governments. The 1921 Treaty would have preserved the unity of the Irish railway system under the jurisdiction of the Council of Ireland. Attempts to develop the Council were suspended in 1925 and rejected by the N Ireland electorate in 1973 (ch. 1.IV). The Great Northern Railway from Dublin to Belfast and to Londonderry was partitioned in 1958. The *Transport Act, N Ireland* (1948) contained provisions for the nationalization of the transport system similar to those of the British *Transport Act* (1947).

Fig. 5.1 (adapted from maps 8 and 9, *British Railways Board* 1965) shows the general pattern of inter-regional inland traffic flows in GB in the 1960s (Ministry of Transport 1966A). As the data on which fig. 5.1 is based relate to weight and not value, fuel- and ore-traffic play an important role. Thus the average freight flow between adjacent conurbations or regions was of the order of 7.6 million tonnes, but this was exceeded in flows to or from all coalfield areas. The average

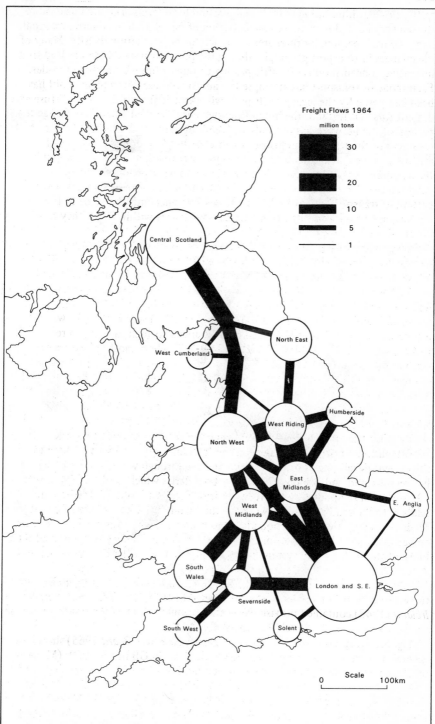

Figure 5.1   Major inter-regional freight flows, GB, 1964

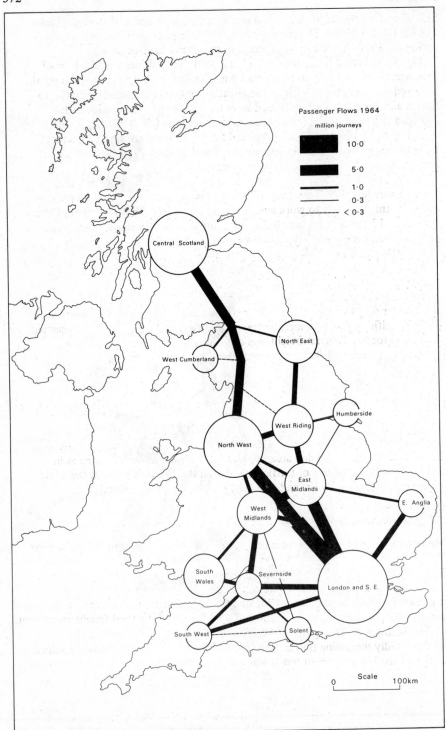

Figure 5.2   Major inter-regional passenger flows, GB, 1964

haul of coal on the railways in 1974 was 94 km, and of iron and steel products 118 km (DoE 1976B). The construction of four large coastal iron ore terminals during the 1970s has led to a reduction of the inland haulage of ore.

Fig. 5.2 (adapted from maps 10, 11, 12 BRB 1965) shows that the flow of passengers is much more evenly spread than the flow of freight, but it should also be noted that passenger traffic in the Greater London area, including traffic to Sussex and Kent, has been excluded from the inter-regional map although it provided one-third of the railway passenger mileage in GB. While fig. 5.1 may record up to 80 per cent of inter-regional freight movements, fig. 5.2 does not show passenger movements by private car. These formed 79 per cent of all journey-km in 1974 (apart from short journeys on foot).

In 1972 (DoE 1975) 25 per cent of all trips (excluding walks of less than 1.6 km) were less than 3 km long, 67 per cent were under 8 km and 85 per cent under 16 km. Journeys to work and to school accounted for 36 per cent of these trips: only 12 per cent represented holiday and pleasure journeys which might have involved travel away from the local area. Evidence from surveys in the Lake District (Mansfield 1969) suggests that day pleasure trips average 71 km.

These patterns of traffic flow are fairly long-standing. Sherrington (1928) showed, for instance, that in 1865 the average annual flow of mineral traffic was 3,788 tonnes per route km, but that the railways of Scotland and NE England carried over 6,314 tonnes of minerals per route km and those of the northern English coalfields 4,419 tonnes, whereas the railways of E and S England carried under 630 tonnes. General freight was more evenly distributed among the companies, averaging 1,893 tonnes per route km, but ranging from 5,683 on the Lancashire and Yorkshire Railway, to 3,150 on the Midland, Great Northern, Great Central and South Eastern Railways, and 1,260 tonnes per route km on most other railway companies. Average passenger flow per route km was 11,835, ranging from 31,950 on the railways linking London with the South West to 28,400 on the Lancashire and Yorkshire system, with a minimum of 5,917 in SW Scotland. On the best available estimate, the proportion of British passenger traffic in the Greater London area appears to have been about the same as in 1965. Changes in patterns of traffic flow during the 1960s and 1970s therefore must be seen as marking the end of a long period of relative geographical stability.

II.2   Trunk Road Development

Modern road transport for passengers and freight began to develop after the First World War. It soon outpaced the capacity of the roads which could be used as inter-city routeways, fulfilled almost all new transport needs and captured some traffic from the railways and inland waterways. The number of private cars reached 1 million in 1930, 10 million in 1961 and 14 million in 1974. The roads were then carrying 92 per cent of passenger km and 65 per cent of the total freight movement.

The Ministry of Transport has been faced with the task of adapting the roads to this rapidly increasing traffic. Shortage of investment capital imposed a selective policy of road improvement but it was not until the 1960s that adequate information on traffic flows became available and rational prediction models were developed.

Many roads of all classes have been improved to higher capacity by widening and realignment, for the increasing flow of traffic creates more and more 'bottlenecks' where the flow of traffic exceeds the capacity of the road to carry it except at greatly reduced speeds. County road authorities in particular have sought to eliminate the worst stretches of overcrowded road, which have high accident rates, but the removal of individual bottlenecks by road widening often merely creates another bottleneck further along the road. This is particularly likely if expenditure on road-widening schemes does not keep up with the overall growth of traffic in the area.

A network of Trunk roads, for which the Ministry of Transport (and not the local authorities) was responsible, was established in 1936 and extended in 1938. In 1974, 5 per cent of the total road network in GB was classified as Trunk road, and 10 per cent as Principal road. In N Ireland 3 per cent of the network is classified as Trunk and 7 per cent as Principal road.

The improvement of classified and trunk roads made slow progress before 1955. Dyos and Aldcroft (1969) pointed out that total road kilometrage grew by only 4 per cent between 1899 and 1936. It grew by a further 5 per cent 1936—55, and by 14 per cent between 1955 and 1974. British roads remain among the most crowded in the world with 124 vehicles per km of road in 1974, compared to 103 per km in W Germany.

The need for selective investment in the road network became more apparent as more detailed road censuses were taken. In 1964 the Trunk roads in GB were carrying 2 million vehicle-km per road km, the classified roads 600,000 and the unclassified roads only 100,000. Thus 1 per cent of the total road length carried 25 per cent of the traffic, with an average flow of 15,000 vehicles per day. A further 9 per cent of the road length carried a further 40 per cent of the traffic, and the remaining 35 per cent of the traffic was spread over 90 per cent of the road mileage, half of which was only carrying 500 vehicles per day, a figure well within the capacity of a two-lane road.

Post-1955 The British Motorway plan (H of C 1957) comprised 1,600 km of motorway and a further 1,600 km of dual carriageway route to be completed by the early 1970s. These routes were designed primarily for the benefit of internal freight traffic, linking the main industrial areas by the shortest feasible network. As pointed out by Appleton (1962), London was linked to four conurbations by only one motorway as far as Watford Gap, where the Leeds (M1) and Carlisle (M6) roads diverged. A similar situation had lasted on the railways only from 1847 to 1860. There were no direct links from the urban periphery of tidewater conurbations to their docks and no motorways were planned to Harwich, the Channel ports or Southampton, despite the increasing orientation of British overseas trade towards the European continent. There was no specific provision of motorways on routes linking conurbations with scenically attractive areas which carried heavy private car traffic, despite many examples of such roads in N America. Some of the most overcrowded and dangerous roads in the country led into Devon and Cornwall and the Lake District, as holidaymakers deserted the express train in favour of their own cars for annual holidays and weekend outings.

An important feature of the road construction programme after 1955 was the replacement of estuarine ferries by bridges and tunnels. In a major bridge-building programme, costing £82 million, nine high-level bridges and four tunnels were built. The completion of the Humber Bridge is expected in 1979 but schemes for a barrage carrying a high-capacity road across Morecambe Bay have been dropped in favour of the upgrading of road access to W Cumberland across the Lake District (A66).

As the tide of post-war prosperity and reconstruction began to ebb during the later 1950s, the 'depressed areas' of the 1930s began to re-emerge as shoals and islands of unemployment and deprivation in the economic geography of the country. Road schemes in these Development Areas, recommended in *White Papers*, including the *Hailsham Report* on the NE (Secretary of State, 1963) and the equivalent study of C Scotland (Scottish Development Dept. 1963), were accelerated. Later they were exempted from the capital spending cuts of the late 1960s. Such road schemes are intended to facilitate the concentration of investment *within* Assisted Areas, alleviating unemployment by enabling longer journeys to work in the short term and the redistribution of population in the long term (Gwilliam 1964, 169–81).

Public Investment In 1938–9 £1.5 million was spent on new construction and major improvement of Trunk roads and £8.8 million on class I roads. By 1947–8 these expenditures had fallen to £1.0 million and £1.6 million respectively, only 4 per cent of the total spending on public roads in GB in that year. From 1949–54 major improvement and new construction expenditure on Trunk roads remained at just under £2 million per annum but rose on class I roads to £4 million. After 1954 expenditure on major improvement rose rapidly: on Trunk roads to £12 million in 1957, £32 million in 1958, £68 million in 1962 and £417 million in 1973–4. By 1973 expenditure on new construction and major improvements on all roads was £538 million, representing 57 per cent of the total expenditure on roads. The share of this expenditure devoted to Trunk roads rose from 9 per cent in 1938 to 26 per cent in 1973. New construction included the extensive provision of dual carriageways between towns and the separation of fast and slow traffic on hills by the provision of three lanes.

The British motorway building programme has been more modest than those of her European neighbours. In 1973 the UK had 1,754 km of motorway compared with 5,258 km in W Germany, 5,090 km in Italy and 2,041 km in France. In historical perspective the first fifteen years of railway building (1830–45) produced over 3,200 km of line.

Network planning While the first 1,600 km of motorway were under construction, new methods of trunk-route network planning were developed which were as significant to the future geography of the UK as the motorways themselves. The *National Motorway Plan* of the mid-1950s and the roads built in development areas in the early 1960s relied, like the proposals of the inter-war period, on rather generalized traffic data and on the belief that road construction is generally beneficial to industrial development. After the completion in 1959 of the main section of the London to Birmingham motorway it was possible to study the effects of the new trunk routes on traffic flows in their vicinity, and to begin to estimate the amount of new traffic generated by the motorway and the amount diverted from earlier roads (Beesley, Coburn and Reynolds, 1959). The Ministry of Transport developed its research organization, collected more traffic data, began to use more sophisticated prediction models of car ownership (Wagle 1968, 44–99; Tanner 1963, 276–84), and also took into account proposals of the regional Economic Planning Councils for the development of New Towns and the prospective location of other major traffic-generating installations, such as green-field industrial plant, seaports and airports. Reynolds (1960), Dawson (1968) and Gwilliam and Mackie (1975) describe transport planning criteria in more detail.

The new road plans were suggested in a *Green Paper* (MoT 1969A) and proposed in *White Papers* (MoT 1970; Scottish Office 1969; Welsh Office 1967). The 1969 strategy routes gave a more even areal coverage of Britain but the 1970 proposals were more closely related to existing and prospective traffic flow, giving a more extensive network of high-capacity roads, i.e. 3,200 km of motorway and 2,400 km of dual carriageway by 1982, thus bringing every town of over 80,000 people within 16 km of a high-capacity road. By 1976 only nine such towns (Aberdeen, Cambridge, Norwich, Swansea, Grimsby, and the resorts of Bourne-mouth, Worthing, Brighton and Torbay) were more than 16 km from the high-capacity network; Brighton and Torbay were, however, 22 km away.

While the objective of 5,500 km of high-capacity road remains, it may not now be reached before the 1990s and will have a smaller motorway component than was originally planned. Priority in building will be given to urban bypass stretches and other routes carrying heavy freight traffic.

Investment in roads continued to expand until 1973, when oil-producing countries began to raise the price of petroleum, thereby drawing attention to UK dependence on oil imports and providing justification for successive governments to pay particular attention to the road programme when cutting investment budgets. The programme was cut four times in 1973—4, reducing its share of the total investment in transport from 48 per cent in the early 1970s to 35 per cent in plans for the mid-1970s. The government has not cancelled contracts for roadwork in progress but has delayed the start of new road schemes (MoT 1970). More detailed planning and consultation procedures and changes in local government responsibility for transport make it likely that tactical and regional considerations will play a larger role in road planning in the late 1970s and 1980s at the expense of strategic and national considerations. Changes in the planning structure, financial stringencies and a growth in public awareness of environmental issues, have all weakened the national drive to build new trunk roads.

The 'demand' for trunk roads is derived from current predictions of the future volume of traffic and its directions of flow. These are based on expected trends of population change, GDP per head and the cost of motoring. Forecasts in current use in the Dept. of Transport (DoE 1976A; Tanner 1974) suggest that car owner-ship will rise steadily from the present figure of 4.0 persons per car to 2.3 persons per car in the years 2000 or 2010 and will then stabilize. Since private car traffic contributes 80 per cent of the vehicle kilometrage on British roads and this ratio is not expected to change in the future, the volume of car traffic dominates the thinking of traffic planners. Trunk roads, including motorways, carry 25 per cent of private car vehicle km and 41 per cent of the vehicle km of lorries over 1.5 tonnes. The volume of freight on British roads is expected to return to the 1973 level of 91,600 million tonne-km before 1980 and then to rise to 120,000 million tonne-km by 1985. This may not necessarily entail more lorries on the roads: the lorry fleet is expected to include larger vehicles travelling longer average distances.

While increased traffic may damage the environment through greater congestion, new trunk roads can make drastic alterations in the visual landscape and carve up formerly peaceful rural tracts. The solution to this dilemma of the 1970s may be found in more detailed and sophisticated planning, engineering design, and consultation, but each of these elements will add significantly to the total cost of each road. The preservation and perhaps even the conservation of the British landscape during the last quarter of the twentieth-century threatens to cost more than the British economy can afford.

By the late 1960s the detailed planning of high-capacity roads involved elaborate studies of the system, carried out by regional Road Construction Units of the DoE, and a high degree of public participation. Normally a regional origin and destination survey, extrapolated by forecasts of future traffic flow, was followed by studies seeking to accommodate the maximum satisfaction of road freight and passenger 'desire lines' with the minimum addition to the existing network, and thereafter by evaluations of construction costs, compensation payments, and assessments of damage to the visual landscape. Final decisions on the route were taken after a public enquiry to which all interested groups and individuals were invited. This planning process is enlightened in that it brings the technical skills of planners and the democratic process into full play, but it cannot provide quick decisions. At planning enquiries, local hostility to the routes of new roads grew rapidly during the 1970s, in volume, technical sophistication and legal expertise. By 1976 several motorway enquiries were disrupted by objectors. When objectors gained the right to question the national trunk road programme at local enquiries planning procedures for specific routes were seriously delayed.

During the long gestation period of several high-capacity roads, reductions in finance for the road programme have so retarded schemes that they have been superseded by new evaluations of traffic need. Similarly, the arguments of pressure groups, even though failing to convince the Minister making the final decision, have on occasion imposed such delays as have led to the indefinite postponement of the project. Changes of government in 1964, 1968 and 1974 provided the opportunity for reassessment of some projects but the differences in the road policies of the Conservative and Labour parties, when in office, should not be exaggerated. Each inherited a substantial commitment to road construction in progress and has followed policies very similar to those of other 'western' governments. In the UK, as abroad, enthusiasm for road construction in the 1950s and 1960s gave way to a concern in the 1970s for the parallel development of other transport media. Although geographical criteria were prominent in the motorway plans of 1957 and 1970 (MoT 1970), an explanatory analysis of what has actually been built requires detailed historical study of the state of public opinion, as perceived by governments, and of national financial constraints during the time each road project was under investigation. Paradoxically, the sophisticated, sensitive and expensive planning mechanism of the 1970s, because of its inherent need for time, may result in a road network which fails to reflect the application of a recognizable set of national planning criteria. Fig. 5.3 shows the pattern of high-capacity roads in 1975.

II.3 The Modernization of the Railway System

Although the railway was invented in the UK, the British Isles do not provide ideal operating conditions for it. Modern railways work most efficiently, relative to other transport modes, when they carry full trainloads over distances of 240 km or more and large regular flows of passengers over distances of 160–640 km. The population of Britain is too concentrated and the population of Ireland too sparse

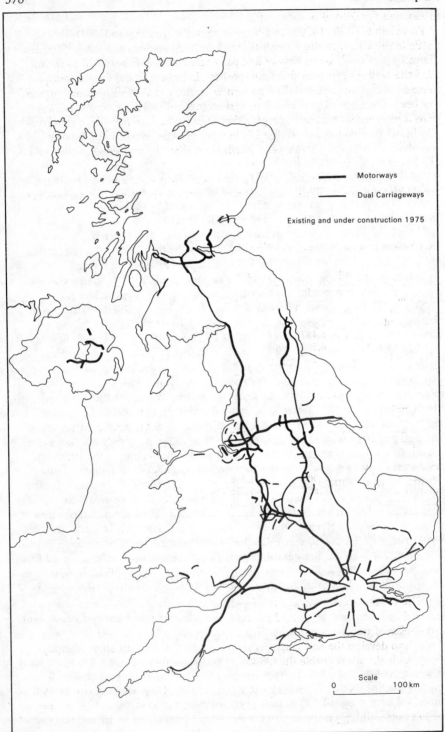

Figure 5.3   Motorways and dual carriageways, UK, 1975

to generate a great deal of such traffic.

From about 1850–1920 railways monopolized both long- and short-distance traffic in the UK, requiring a dense network of lines, stations and sidings, and also a large fleet of small goods wagons and passenger coaches. From 1920 to about 1955 the railways lost their dominant position in passenger and freight transport to road vehicles but retained their pattern of services, their fleet of steam engines, coaches and wagons and almost all their route network. During the last twenty years it has been increasingly accepted that railways have an important role to play in the transport system of the UK in three main areas: the long distance movement of bulk freight; inter-city passenger traffic; the journey to work in the larger conurbations.

Table 5.4 shows the decline in the relative share of freight and passenger traffic carried by the railways during the post-war period. As traffic fell the railways have

TABLE 5.4

The Changing Railway System, GB, 1950–74

	1950	1974	1974 as % of 1950
Route km	31,690	18,532	58
of which electrified	2,090	3,903	187
Stations	8,487	3,038	36
for passengers	6,500	2,620	40
for freight	6,595	511	8
Staff	606,000	219,000	36
Locomotives	19,736	3,941	20
Freight wagons	1,122,215	244,000	22
Freight wagon capacity (tonnes)	14,648,000	4,674,000	32
Passenger coaches	42,218	20,814	49
Passenger seats	2,506,000	1,106,000	44
Passenger km	32,464,800	36,035,160	111
Freight tonne km	35,615,215	24,136,600	68

Source: Ann. Abstract of Statistics. These figures include London Transport railways but exclude railways in N Ireland.

become overequipped and overmanned. By 1962, for instance, they accounted for 80 per cent of the total road and rail freight vehicle capacity (Deakin and Seward 1969) but only carried 32 per cent of the freight tonne km and 17 per cent of the value of transported freight. This created a difficult economic environment in which to develop the new concepts and to install the radically changed equipment which alone will enable the railway to play a useful part in the UK transport system of the future. The economic and technical metamorphosis of the railway is more fully discussed in Aldcroft (1968); Dyos and Aldcroft (1969); Pollins (1971); Thomson and Hunter (1973); Bagwell (1974); Barker and Savage (1974) and Pryke and Dodgson (1976).

For successive railway administrations the over-riding problems have been to pay wages and other current expenses while simultaneously finding capital for the further mechanization of the system: to develop a new railway while still operating an old one. Two aspects of subsidiary economic importance but considerable geographical interest, namely the diminishing size of the railway network and changes in accessibility brought about by new services, are illustrated in figs. 5.4 and 5.5.

Since the development of road transport during the 1920s the railways have found it difficult to attract new traffic or to benefit from changing patterns of industrial location. Freight carried by the railways fell from 310 million tonnes in 1928 to 178 million tonnes in 1975 although tonne-kms did not fall so steeply. The railways found it less easy to retain the wagon-load traffic of small- and medium-sized manufacturers who often rated reliability, speed and security above cost of transport (Deakin and Seward 1969; Wallace 1974, 25–43). Surveys conducted in the W Midlands in 1953 (Walters 1968) confirmed earlier findings (Walker 1947) that the service provided by road transport was considered superior to that of rail in terms of reliability, less damage in transit and also speed. The decline in the production and use of coal and the rationalization of the steel industry have reduced the coal and ore traffic, both staples of railway freight transport. Coal traffic fell from 223 million tonnes in 1913 (61 per cent of tonnage forwarded) to 98 million tonnes in 1975 (55 per cent of tonnage forwarded). Other freight amounted to 141 million tonnes in 1913 and 90 million tonnes in 1975. Although steel traffic is declining, the railways have developed a significant traffic in petroleum products (17 million tonnes) and building materials. Rail revenue is becoming increasingly dependent on a relatively small number of large firms, including nationalized industries and multinational corporations. In 1971 75 per cent of railway freight revenue was derived from 300 customers, including 50 per cent from 30 firms only (Pryke and Dodgson 1976). The private car created a new dimension in passenger travel and railway passenger journeys fell from 2,064 million in 1919 to 733 million in 1974.

In the face of these trends the railways have sought national support for ambitious programmes of modernization to increase the capacity of the network. After catching up on capital investment, which had been largely suspended during the Second World War, the railways planned a major national scheme of modernization which was to take place from 1954–69 (British Transport Commn. 1955). The rapid replacement of steam by diesel engines enabled a general acceleration of passenger services and improvements in their punctuality. The older freight wagons and passenger coaches have been replaced by much more effectively utilized vehicles. In particular, the development of centralized signalling and the computer monitoring of wagon movements (TOPS, completed in 1975) have improved the efficiency of service.

Inter-war electrification was confined to London and south coast commuter services, to three lines radiating from Manchester, and to the Tyneside suburban service. The first electrification scheme primarily designed for freight was completed from Wath and Sheffield to Manchester via the rebuilt Woodhead tunnel, in order to facilitate the flow of coal from S Yorkshire to NW England. One of the main axes of the system, the route from London to the W Midlands, Manchester and Merseyside, was electrified in 1966, and in 1974, electrification was extended along this route to Glasgow, thus linking five of the seven largest

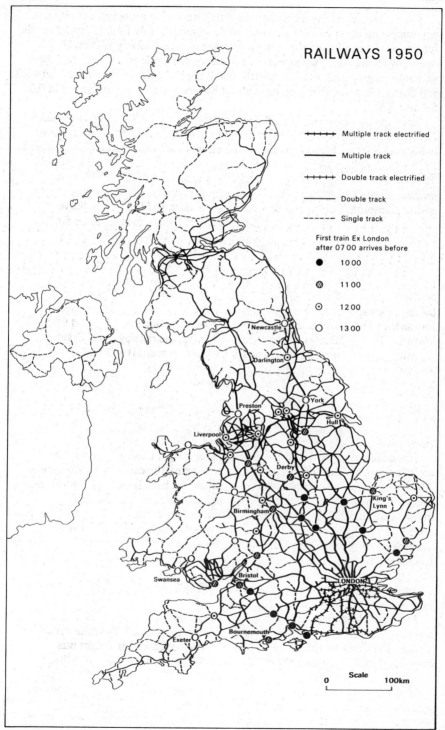

Figure 5.4   Railway network, UK, 1950

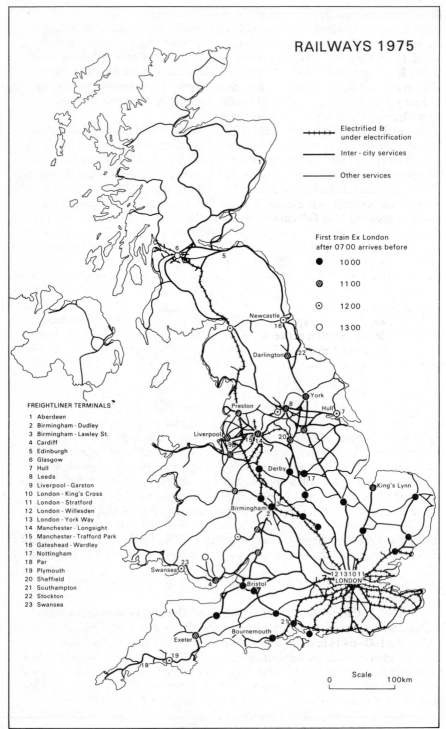

RAILWAYS 1975

├┼┼┼┼┤ Electrified &
          under electrification

───── Inter - city services

───── Other services

First train Ex London
after 07 00 arrives before

● 10 00

◍ 11 00

◉ 12 00

○ 13 00

1

6   5

Newcastle
16

Darlington ◍ 22

York ◍
Preston   8
Liverpool   Hull ● 7
            9◍5 14
            ◍15   20◍
                         Derby ●
                         17 ●
                               King's Lynn ●
            ◍
Birmingham ● 3
            2
            ◉

Swansea ◉ 23

4

Bristol

12 13 10 11
LONDON

21

Bournemouth ●

Exeter ○

18 ○   19 ○

FREIGHTLINER TERMINALS

1   Aberdeen
2   Birmingham - Dudley
3   Birmingham - Lawley St.
4   Cardiff
5   Edinburgh
6   Glasgow
7   Hull
8   Leeds
9   Liverpool - Garston
10 London - King's Cross
11 London - Stratford
12 London - Willesden
13 London - York Way
14 Manchester - Longsight
15 Manchester - Trafford Park
16 Gateshead - Wardley
17 Nottingham
18 Par
19 Plymouth
20 Sheffield
21 Southampton
22 Stockton
23 Swansea

Scale
0   100km

Figure 5.5   Railway network, UK, 1975

British conurbations. This operation also involved extensive resignalling, the institution of centralized traffic control and virtually the complete rebuilding of the section from London to Crewe — one of the busiest railway routes in the world. In SE England electrification was extended to the Channel Ports in 1962 and to Bournemouth in 1967. Electrification has been extended northwards to Hitchin and has begun on the London–Bedford line. The railways have played a major role in the reorganization of public transport on Clydeside by the electrification of 208 km focusing on Glasgow.

The modernization of many main lines during the 1960s allowed British Rail to take the initiative in the land movement of the large modern *containers* which began to arrive at British ports, initially from America. The containers were loaded on to trains travelling at high speed on standard daily schedules. The first of these services was launched between London and Glasgow in 1959 and later 'Freightliner' services were extended to provincial centres (fig. 5.5) and to the new container berths at Felixstowe, Harwich, Tilbury, Fishguard and Holyhead. Inland customs depots were set up in each of the conurbations. Development was slower than had been hoped. Thomson and Hunter (1973) suggested that the efficiency of the rail freightliner only overtakes that of door-to-door road transport at about 240 km and that the economic collecting radius of a freightliner terminal is about 16 km. This puts only about 5 per cent of all traffic within the freightliner range in Britain.

The railways partially replaced their declining coal traffic with oil products, whose traffic was doubled between 1963 and 1966, possibly forestalling a more extensive network of pipelines. The coal traffic itself was rationalized. Many power stations and steel works were adapted to take permanently-coupled 'merry-go-round' trains operating from the larger collieries (ch. 4.I.5). The rail haul of domestic coal was concentrated at central depots. 'Company' trains provided regular transport between different branches of the same firms, notably the major car companies, or between producers and whosesalers, as in the case of whisky or beer. Accessibility to the dispersed factories of some firms has improved greatly since the 1950s and so have some long-distance services to ports. Inter-city passenger trains run faster and at more regular intervals. Further improvements in railway passenger speed will accompany the introduction of the High Speed Train (HST) which has a top speed of 200 kph. This conventional train began service between London and South Wales in 1976, and is expected to link the main British conurbations by 1981, including services on the Newcastle–Bristol axis. During the 1980s the Advanced Passenger Train (APT) will be introduced. The APT is a lightweight train of radically new design which will operate at 234 kph on conventional track. The Hovertrain, a tracked hovercraft designed to link the conurbations on a new reserved track at speeds of 400 kph during the 1990s, was cancelled in 1972.

Even before the introduction of the HST, British railways were competing successfully with buses on the motorways and with domestic airlines over distances within the 160–640 km range wherever speed had been increased through electrification or other modernization measures. The European railways have had similar success with Trans-European Express (TEE) services. Both British Rail and TEE services stood to benefit by direct linkage which would provide rail services between Manchester, Birmingham, London, Brussels and Paris at city centre to city centre timings shorter than the current journey times by air. The Dover Strait was first surveyed for a tunnel in 1836. Enabling bills for its construction were passed in 1875 but the project was stopped by the British government in 1882. A revival of interest in the late 1960s led to a new Anglo—French treaty (1973) for the joint construction of a rail tunnel from Folkestone to Calais. A new railway, built to the continental loading-gauge, was to link the Channel tunnel with west London. The project was, however, cancelled in 1975 as one of a series of cuts in public expenditure, so the railways were again excluded from the large cross-channel inter-city traffic market.

Within Britain, improvements in accessibility by rail have been more marked along the Dover—London—Liverpool axis than elsewhere on the network. The high capacity road network (fig. 5.3) on the other hand, with its twin motorway circuits (M1—M4—M5—M6:M1—M6—M62) and spurs radiating from the conurbations has improved the speed and convenience of road transport throughout the country, since most journeys between regional centres are already partially or wholly served by motorway and/or dual-carriageway routes. Railways will need a long period of investment in capacity and speed before they can develop new traffic in a variety of directions.

All W European railway systems have required extensive financial aid from their governments in order to bridge wide gaps between revenues and costs during the modernization of inter-city services. The British government has shown a continuing concern over the operation of rural and urban local railway services. Before considering the development of government policy towards the railways it is important to make a rough and ready allocation of the UK railway network to its main functions. London could be linked to each of the main conurbations of GB and to the short-sea ports for Ireland, France and the Netherlands by a minimum route network of about 1,600 km. A network which provided minimum links between the conurbations and penetrated outlying regions such as SW England and NE Scotland, would need to be at least 2,800 km but 70 per cent of the British population would live within five miles of it (Fullerton 1975). Further extensions of the minimum network would be necessary to allow access to mines, quarries and industrial plant in order to cater for inter-regional movements of bulk freight. The official map of inter-city passenger services (British Rail 1976) shows a network of 6,050 km but this figure includes about 800 km of route to south coast towns and a further 800 km in Cornwall, W Wales and the Scottish Highlands. A British Rail study in 1970 is generally believed (Pryke and Dodgson 1976) to have identified an inter-city 'core' passenger network of 3,400 km, an inter-regional network for existing trainload and wagonload traffic of 8,000 km and a commuter network for London and SE England of 2,400 km.

The existence in Britain of a railway network of 37,000 km in 1921, slimmed to 28,300 km by 1963, can be explained by four main historical factors. First, was the real need during the nineteenth century for improved transport between coal-fields, ports and factories, city centres and dormitory suburbs, and between the main population centres. Secondly, companies frequently built lines in anticipation of needs which were not subsequently justified by the traffic generated. Thirdly, the competitive structure of the railway industry in its early years led to duplication of routes in order to share potential traffic with rival companies or to forestall their access to particular markets. Fourthly, the technical advantages of the railway over other forms of transport for all purposes led to its ubiquitous coverage of the UK. The extensive use of small private wagons, especially the ten-tonne coal wagon, required a high ratio of track to traffic, especially in the numerous marshalling yards.

The *modernization report* (BTC 1955) marked a high point of optimism concerning the future role of the railways in the British transport pattern. It was issued in a year which some economists now see as a turning point of British economic fortunes, between the period of post-war reconstruction and economic expansion and the first of many cuts in public investment which began in 1956 (MoT 1959).

The railways had paid their way until 1952 but by 1962 working expenses exceeded receipts by £100 million. These financial problems led to a reappraisal of the **modernization report** (MoT 1959) and a financial reconstruction of the railways in 1960 (MoT 1960). Many experts now accepted that capital expenditure under the modernization report could not achieve revenues sufficient to offset the downward trend in many traditional traffics.

The *Beeching Report* (MoT 1963B) broke new ground in that it was based on an analysis of costs and revenues of different types of railway service and enough data was published to show in general terms how the financial balance of these services was reflected in the profitability of different parts of the network. Although the *Beeching Report* did not hazard a guess as to how much of the railway network could ultimately be made to pay, it put forward proposals for shaping the system to provide rail transport for that part of the national pattern favourable to railways.

In 1962 half the railway route-km carried only 5 per cent of the freight tonne-km and only 4 per cent of the total passenger km. This route kilometrage earned £20 million, but cost £40 million to operate. Of the 4,300 passenger stations on the British railway system, the 95 busiest yielded 48 per cent of total passenger receipts but the 3,000 least-used stations produced only 6 per cent of the receipts. Passenger and freight revenue supported each other to viable levels on about 14,000 km of the railway network. A further survey (BRB 1965) suggested the abandonment of duplicated routes between conurbations and cities and, on the basis of forecast traffic flows for 1984, recommended a further reduction of the network to 4,800 km.

In N Ireland, the *Benson Report* (Govt. N Ireland 1963) traced the decline of the railway network in the six counties from 1,930 km in 1914 to 475 km in 1962, and suggested its further reduction to 120 km as a commuter service from C Belfast to Larne, Bangor, Portadown (for Craigavon New Town). The line from Portadown to the border was to be retained for as long as CIE wished to retain a through rail service from Dublin to Belfast. In the Irish Republic a reduction of railway route km from 3,060 km to 1,360 km was recommended in 1957 (Govt. of Ireland 1957) and was subsequently achieved.

In Britain, closures under the *Beeching Plan* were relatively slow and in 1966, when there were still 22,000 km in operation, the government agreed with the BRB that the network should be stabilized at 17,700 km (MoT 1967A), including the main inter-city routes, major feeder lines to them, intensive passenger commuter services and rural services 'essential to the life of remote areas'. A further 4,000 km, although not recommended for future development, might be maintained for specialized freight services. Under the *Transport Act* (1968) (MoT 1966B, 1967B, 1967C, 1967D), the government undertook to subsidize specified passenger railway services on an annual or short-term basis. Under the *Local Government Act* (1972) the English metropolitan counties, through their *Passenger Transport*

Authorities, are able to purchase or subsidize rail services within their boundaries in pursuit of integrated local transport schemes. The counties of England and Wales and the regions of Scotland are empowered to subsidize rail services in order that those parts of the network which serve local needs may be, if necessary, retained at local cost.

The subsidies which supported the extensive rural and urban railway networks in Britain were intended to cover a six-year period until the railways could reach a level of profitability which would enable some or most of these services to be retained. The 1968 Act included a financial and organizational restructuring of British Railways which, it was hoped, would allow modernization to take place sufficiently rapidly to maintain existing traffic and generate new traffic. These hopes were not realized, partly owing to delays in the introduction of some new services, partly to reduced activity among some of the railway's best industrial customers, but chiefly due to the increasing dominance of railway finances by the annual wage bill. Labour costs constituted 65 per cent of total costs in 1974 and wages were rising faster than the workforce could be reduced. British Rail made a loss in 1971, and by 1972 many traffics had resumed their downward trend. In that year the DoE, the Railways Board and the railway unions separately reconsidered the future role of the railways. The DoE, after reviewing alternative networks of 14,000, 7,000 or 5,000 km respectively, appear to have agreed with British Rail (MoT 1973) that 'in conventional commercial terms there is no viable railway network and any significantly smaller network would require greater financial support than the present day railway.'

The *Railways Act* (1974) withdrew subsidies to specific services in favour of a general subsidy to the whole rail passenger operation, including those costs shared with freight transport, for a five-year period. Within this period further investment and reform of services was to take place while the network of routes was substantially maintained. Under this Act two-thirds of the total subsidies available for inland surface transport were given to British Rail by 1976. Although the railway carried only 8 per cent of the total passenger mileage in Britain in 1974, passenger fares were only contributing about one-third of the factor cost of rail passenger transport. These large subsidies were not sufficient to prevent a rapid rise in passenger fares during the severe inflation of the mid-1970s which caused a slight decline in the patronage of inter-city routes.

Since railway passenger and goods traffic is not expected to increase significantly during the next decade (DoE, 1976A) a further restructuring of the finances and, perhaps, the network of British Rail seems likely during the late 1970s.

III   LOCAL TRANSPORT

The growth in car ownership from one car per 21 people in 1951 to one per 4 people in 1974 has had an even greater impact on local than on inter-city transport. Travel opportunities have been revolutionized for car owners and drivers, but only 55 per cent of the households in Britain had the regular use of a car in 1974 (ranging regionally from 43 per cent in the N Region to 63 per cent in E Anglia) and only 63 per cent of the adults had a driving licence. The remainder of the adults, and also older children going to school, rely on public transport services which have been reduced in speed and frequency as the private car fleet has grown, and can no longer operate without private subsidy. The mobility gap between those who can drive whenever they wish and people with limited or no access to cars, is becoming steadily more important as services concentrate. Schools, hospitals, administrative offices and shopping centres are becoming larger and more widely spaced with substantial potential economies of scale. The car owner can circulate freely between these facilities and enjoy the benefits of centralization. People without a car, or the exclusive use of one, may find access limited and time-consuming. Only the most careful joint planning of the sites of new services and the public transport network can reduce the mobility gap.

III.1 The Coordination of Urban Transport Systems

Before the First World War the larger towns of the UK had municipal tramway networks which were supplemented in the conurbations by local railway services. London and Glasgow had underground railway systems as well. Between the wars buses replaced trams and, outside London, fewer people used railways for short journeys. In the large towns the dense network of the municipal services was heavily used and fares were low. Smaller towns were served by the regional bus companies established after the *Road Traffic Act* (1930). In these companies town fares subsidized rural routes.

These urban bus services attained their maximum development in 1953. In 1955 (DoE 1973B) the estimated passenger kilometrage in private cars exceeded that in buses for the first time and from then onwards the speed, reliability and frequency of buses, and also the ratio of revenues to costs (of which wages comprised 71 per cent), steadily declined. Fares rose faster than average prices. Between 1963 and 1973 passenger journeys on buses fell by 33 per cent but vehicle km fell by only 10 per cent and the number of vehicles by 4 per cent. Calculations in the late 1960s (Hillman, Henderson and Whalley 1973) showed that even on short journeys of less than 6.5 km, door-to-door trips took twice as long by bus as by car and that bus journey times have lengthened by about one-fifth during the 1960s as a result of road congestion and one-man operation.

As major traffic pressures built up during the late 1950s, plans were made for increased investment in urban roads. These included the construction of circumferential bypasses, the widening of radials and the diversion of traffic through residential streets (Mossé 1974). Forecasts suggested that increased traffic could be accommodated for several decades by road improvements, but traffic in GB grew much faster than had been foreseen and rapidly occupied the new roads to the limits of their design capacity. To accommodate further traffic growth it would have been necessary to build large-scale urban motorway networks on the N American model, but UK cities lacked the space and the resources for such schemes and their planners appreciated that motorways which are built to serve existing traffic also generate much new traffic as people adapt their lives to wider travel opportunities (Schaeffer and Sclar 1975). Towns sought to revalue their existing transport systems using concepts like total social cost (C D Foster 1963). An assessment of the total social cost of a traffic management scheme attempts to balance the obvious benefits to users against the often indirect damage to the interests of non-users and to the environment in general.

The *Buchanan Report* (Buchanan 1963) had considerable influence on urban planning in the UK (ch. 6.IV.1). It proposed a sophisticated approach to urban traffic problems, related to the size of individual towns and the layout of their existing streets. Attention should be given to the 'primary distributors', major roads which carried traffic into and around towns, in the hope of creating pedestrian precincts and low density traffic zones between them. Where the volume of traffic reached a point when the primary distributors and their extensive interchanges became so large as to dominate the visual environment and displace large numbers of dwelling houses, schemes for the restricting of traffic by limiting parking, licensing or road pricing should be considered. Accessibility must be balanced with environmental preservation when the environmental deterioration caused by enlarging the major roads was no longer acceptable. Public transport systems would then have to play an increasing part in moving people to work and to shop. The Report recommended planned coordination between transport systems, developed through the medium of a statutory development plan which took into account predictions of size and direction of traffic flows.

The expertize in the formulation of combined traffic and land-use surveys, which had been accumulated in studies of the N American conurbations during the 1950s by several firms of international consultants, began to be applied to British cities, with the firm backing of the Ministry of Transport (DoE 1972; Starkie 1976). These surveys involved the recognition and analysis of traffic flow systems and the motivations which lay behind them. They used newly-developed computing techniques to develop and to choose between complex solutions to the problems of future traffic movement. The separate planning of transport and land use was increasingly seen to be unproductive as highway engineers and town planners were drawn into closer association (C D Foster 1974, 166–91). In 1962 the *London Traffic Survey* was begun. This has developed under the GLC as a permanent *London Transportation Study* (GLC, 1969; Collins and Pharaoh 1974; Foster, Bayliss and Blake 1970; Ridley and Tresidder 1970). Similar studies, supported financially by the MoT, began in the other conurbations and large towns in the UK in 1964. These studies are listed in Starkie (1973 and 1976). They depended on the extensive collection of data on the vehicular movement of people and goods. This data was analysed using traffic models and vehicle growth forecasts in order to predict traffic growth and change over a period of ten to twenty years. Alternative strategies, with different combinations of new road building and public transport provision, chould then be formulated and subjected to cost-benefit study (Solesbury and Townsend 1970; Wilson et al 1969). Traffic management is now seen as much in terms of protecting the existing urban environment as in circulating more cars through the streets.

The traffic studies, first published during the early 1970s, recommended considerable capital expenditure on new roads. but while the studies were being prepared the growth of traffic persuaded growing numbers of the articulate public to believe that investment in public transport would offer better relief for traffic congestion. As the first sections of urban motorway networks were being built and road costs and housing dislocation were much more apparent than the benefits of traffic relief, elected councillors and MPs were made aware of public disquiet. The government response (DoE 1972) was to extend compensation in the *Land Compensation Act* (1973). This measure increased the cost of new motorways and the likelihood of legal delays. New arrangements were also made for the consultation of the public before motorway schemes were started (DoE 1973C): in 1975 the role of public enquiries was extended. This combination of rising costs, delays and the prospect of severe cuts in public expenditure led many towns to abandon large sections of their planned road network and face the prospect of increased traffic congestion during the 1980s.

The *Transport Act* (1968) introduced the first government grants for public transport and made provision for the establishment of Passenger Transport Authorities (PTAs) in the conurbations. Under the *Local Government Act* (1972) metropolitan counties control transport in their areas, operating through PTAs. The national government gives substantial grants to the PTAs for infra-structure, railways, bus lanes and the building of transport interchanges so that all modes may be used in combination. The metropolitan counties can choose the level of support they are prepared to give to British Rail services and can determine the fares. Outside the GLC area, services on about 1,600 km of railway route, carrying about 8 per cent of the railway passenger kilometrage, are subject to PTA policies. On Tyneside a new 54 km 'Metro' light railway system is under construction which will incorporate both underground lines and suburban surface railway lines which had first been electrified in 1907. Together with London Transport, PTAs serve 37 per cent of the UK population. In other towns, the shire county authorities are required to develop public transport and may receive government grants for this purpose.

Central government grants for specific transport projects and services were replaced in 1975 by Transport Supplementary Grants and Rate Support Grants to each county and Scottish region. For the first time the counties are wholly responsible for both land use and transport planning and the pattern of local investment and service does not depend on policies determined at national level. Counties can also decide on the balance of expenditure between capital investment and subsidies to current transport services within their areas. The size of the government grant to each county depends on its population, existing commitments to transport and national constraints on public spending.

The grants are awarded on the submission of an annual county Transport Policy and Programme to the DoE. This programme must include a ten to fifteen-year transport strategy which takes into account the plans of the DoE, the National Bus Company, British Rail and other national operators for inter-city and rural transport links within the county. County transport policy programmes must be related to their structure plans but must also use nationally comparable methods of policy analysis and evaluation. When awarding grants the government will naturally look most favourably on county schemes which are aligned with current national transport policies.

Within five years the interest of the local council in transport was thus expanded from the ownership of a local bus service at most to responsibility for the planning of a co-ordinated transport service and, in metropolitan counties, for the operation of an integrated transport system. Local transport investment, predominantly urban, now accounts for 44 per cent of the national transport budget. In the Transport Policy Programmes for 1975–6, 90 per cent of the grants available for public transport were awarded to the metropolitan counties. This money was equally divided between investment and the support of current services and between railway and bus transport. The shire counties of England and Wales devoted 95 per cent of their Transport Grants to roads, fairly evenly dividing the funds between construction and maintenance.

It will be some years before the benefits of this radical reorganization will be apparent, since it will be necessary to replace gradually the vehicles and inter-changes inherited from the former separate transport organizations. The new system should enable the costs and benefits of each service to be assessed as a basis for a rational decision between alternative investment schemes.

There is considerable variation from town to town in the amount and kind of transport investment which has actually taken place since 1955. Traffic management schemes are almost universal. The planning and building of a stretch of urban motorway or a new railway/bus station may take ten years but planners, politicians and the articulate public can change their minds within a matter of months. There was a rather rapid disillusionment with the attempt to accommodate growing traffic on urban motorways during the early 1970s at the very time when motorways planned about 1960 were being opened (Independent Commn. on Transport 1974). The new enthusiasm for large investment in public transport systems which replaced the desire for motorways unfortunately coincided with a national economic crisis which led to the curtailing or postponement of many road and passenger transport schemes.

With the largest population and most complex bus, railway and underground system, London has the largest schemes and the highest proportion (54 per cent) of journeys to work on public transport. Improved underground services include the Victoria line, the first new underground line since 1907, planned in 1949 and opened in 1969; and the Fleet line, approved in 1971 with a 100 per cent government subsidy for its central London traverse. At that time London Transport Executive planned to spend £500 million at current prices on extending and renewing its underground railways and £200 million on buses and their routeways. British Rail had a £220 million investment plan to improve its surface commuter services up to 1980. These public transport services link the suburbs with the central shop and office areas. The number of journeys from one suburb to another by express buses, delivery vans and private cars grows as the city centre loses population and there is a limited decentralization of offices. To serve this traffic and to link the national motorways with the port and airports of London and the short sea crossings to Europe three concentric motorway routes totalling 248 km were proposed in 1967. The cost of £850 million would have roughly equalled the cost of investment proposals for public transport over the same period. The ringway proposals were based on detailed analysis of traffic flows and trends but met with mounting public opposition. In 1971 the London Labour party carried out their election promise to abandon the scheme.

Similar schemes on a smaller scale have been proposed and opposed in the other British conurbations. Differing approaches by local councils and their planners and traffic engineers, changes in political control and in the date of initial plans, are likely to bring about a situation in which the British conurbations will look less like each other as the century advances, as each imposes a different balance between private and public transport on an already varied urban or physical morphology. Thus Clydeside already had 32 km of motorway when the PTA was established but little road building has taken place in Edinburgh. In Newcastle the central area was replanned before the traffic and land-use study took place but the PTA was established before the urban motorway was built. Nottingham is hoping to develop a system of traffic management which encourages the motorist to park as he approaches the city centre but imposes progressive constraints on further movement.

Almost all urban transport investment is restricted to transport modes which were invented by the end of the nineteenth century. There is considerable experimentation in mini-vehicles for individuals, maxi-taxis available on request, moving pavements, light elevated busways and central control of traffic. It is difficult to see how further growth in the traditional transport vehicle fleets can be accommodated in many British regional capitals for much more than a further decade.

III.2 The Changing Pattern of Rural Transport

Rural transport is defined here in its widest sense as local transport outside towns. The rural railways were built in the mid-nineteenth century and rural bus services established in the 1920s. Further development of private car ownership during the 1920s created a total supply of transport well in excess of the ability of rural populations to pay for it.

The rural transport situation varies with rural settlement geography and four characteristic patterns may be distinguished:

Areas within 80 km of conurbations with population densities of over 100 persons per km^2. In S England and in rural areas within 30 km of conurbations and coalfields in the rest of the UK, the rural population has been swelled by an adventitious population of retired people and commuters who own at least one car per family, who enjoy higher average incomes than those working in local agriculture and other rural industries, and wish to combine the advantages of rural life with access to urban facilities.

Prosperous agricultural areas with population densities of over 100 persons per km^2 and a village settlement pattern with most people living in communities of 3,000 or over. Many coalfield areas conform to this pattern. Such areas lent themselves to bus transport and had inherited rail services from the nineteenth century.

Areas of dispersed rural settlement in hamlets, as in SW England, the Welsh Borders and N Ireland, or in strings of valley-bottom houses separated by uninhabited interfluves as in C Wales or the Pennine Dales.

The NW Highlands and Islands of Scotland with a total population of 420,000 present the special problem of linear coastal settlements separated from each other by seas and from C Scotland by extensive tracts of uninhabited upland. There is a considerable literature on the transport problems of the NW Highlands (Scottish Dept. Agriculture 1967; Munby 1954; Turnock 1965; Scottish Office 1964; HIDB 1957; Thomson and Grimble 1968; O'Dell 1966). Since 1745 successive UK governments have provided, or paid for, roads, canals, harbours and railways in this area. Payments for postal services have effectively subsidized the operation of MacBraynes bus and steamship services. Air services to the islands have been cross-subsidized by BEA.

The need for rural transport has grown steadily since the Second World War. As employment in agriculture and mining has declined the medium-sized towns have increasingly supplied employment for rural inhabitants. Economies of scale in medicine and education have favoured the development of the relatively large district general hospital of 800–1,000 beds and the secondary school of 500–1,000 pupils (ch. 4.IV.5). Primary schools, maternity and geriatric hospitals are more frequently dispersed, but if the rural population wish to participate in rising national standards of living and welfare they are increasingly forced to travel to urban service centres in order to obtain these benefits. The introduction or retention of manufacturing or mining industry in rural areas has frequently required road improvements or the extension or maintenance of rail services.

The pattern of rural transport from the 1920s to the 1950s was of road and railway passenger services supported by cross-subsidization from urban and inter-urban services. Many road freight services were provided by manufacturers operating their own vehicles under C licences or by wholesale and retail companies whose transport operations were inseparable from the rest of their business. The *Transport Act* (1947) enabled British Road Services to cross-subsidize rural routes if they so wished. Thus the supply of the commodity needs of the rural population, the sale of farm products and the movement of fertilizers could be accommodated in the private sector of the road transport system relatively easily. The pattern of bus routes about 1950 was analysed by Green (1950, 1951).

Car ownership is normally higher in rural than in other areas. In 1952, for instance, when there were 16 people per private car in GB, there were 10–12 in the counties of Mid-Wales, and in 1971 when there were 4.7 people to the car in GB some rural areas had reached levels of 3.6 (MoT 1963A; Council for Wales 1972; Thomas 1963). Swedish studies have suggested that when car ownership passes the level of one car per 7 people public transport begins to have economic difficulties. This figure was reached in some rural areas in 1960, in GB in 1963 and in N Ireland in 1965. Pilot studies of transport in rural areas of Devon and W Suffolk (DoE 1971 A and B), demonstrated the unsuitability of train and bus services for meeting irregular and scattered demand. Only 3 per cent of journeys made by people who owned cars were on public transport; three-quarters of all households had one car; in one-third of households at least two people had full use of a car. As many journeys were made in the form of 'lifts' as on stage bus services. The level of car ownership among men was double that for women, three times as high among the upper two social classes as in the lowest two classes, and three times as high among the under 45s as among the over 65s. The actual numbers of people relying solely on public transport, non-driving mothers with young children, the elderly and handicapped, had become relatively small, their needs being largely catered for by lifts. Only 6 per cent of all trips took place on public transport, including 7 per cent of journeys to work and 13 per cent of shopping trips. Half the population never used public transport.

The concept of total social cost assumes that certain levels of welfare must be available to all members of the rural community. It is then possible to consider to what extent a concentration of transport on a limited number of routes or modes will provide access to minimum welfare, or whether subsidies will be necessary in order to maintain the rural population in their present geographical distribution.

The Devon and Suffolk studies showed that the purposes of rural journeys were fairly evenly divided between shopping and business (25 per cent), leisure (24 per cent), work (22 per cent), and school (18 per cent). The remainder of the journeys did not fit these classifications but it seems apparent that between a half and three-quarters of journeys are to a larger urban centre.

These findings clearly call into doubt the future role of rural railway and conventional bus services. Transport facilities often outlast their need and the withdrawal of public transport has lagged several years behind the growth in car ownership. Rural rail lines began to be abandoned in the 1920s and by 1952 the Minister of Transport had announced that railways were no longer obliged to retain uneconomic stations or branches; however, the rate of closure up to 1962 was slow (Patmore 1966).

The publication of the *Beeching Report* (MoT 1963B) led to a notable public outcry over the proposed closure of rural rail lines, although there were few suggestions as to how the rural railway services might be made economically viable. The subsequent closure of many lines took place under the provisions of the *Transport Act* (1962) necessitating public enquiries, discussions with Transport Users' Consultative Councils and, after the *Transport Act* (1968), with Regional Economic Planning councils. Closures rose from a rate of 2 per cent per annum of the existing route km between 1958 and 1962, to 8 per cent per annum between 1965 and 1968, but fell away to 2 per cent per annum in 1969 and 1970 (Aldcroft 1968). The route km had fallen by 34 per cent in nine years but remained half as large again as that recommended by the 1963 Report and four times as large as that recommended by the 1965 Report (BRB 1965). Among railway lines to be maintained in the 1966 'Network for Development' were included 'services which, although they may never pay their way commercially, have an economic or a social value to the community as a whole which outweighs their money costs. These include . . . some rural services where alternatives would be impracticable or excessively costly.' (MoT 1967A).

Although the 1963 Beeching proposal of 12,000 km and the 1965 proposal of 4,800 km was extended to 17,500 km in 1966, there are differences in the shape of the network. Several routes recommended for retention in 1963 have been closed while many recommended for closure have been retained. These variations show how appreciations of the relative value of specific railway lines have changed within the BR administration as its accounting procedures become more sophisticated, and they also show the effects of local pressure. Such services operate on about 8,000 km. Half the route km of British Rail, therefore, carried 6 per cent of railway passenger km.

It is government policy (DoE 1976A) to devote the relatively small funds made available to shire counties for Transport Policy Programmes to the maintenance of a skeleton service of rural bus routes.

The decline in profitability of rural bus services came later than that of the railways and was more complex in its effects. Besides the regional bus companies, formed under the *Road Traffic Act* (1930), there were a large number of small operators who provided stage carriage, coach and charter services between villages and market towns until the late 1950s. Television dealt a fatal blow to most of these local companies by reducing the demand for evening coach trips to urban cinemas (Snaith, Robinson and Minnear 1957), since contract work accounted for 50—65 per cent of their gross revenue. The viability of small firms was further weakened by rising costs of petrol, replacement vehicles and more stringent safety standards. During the 1960s, as their urban routes became less economic, the regional bus companies found cross-subsidization of their rural routes less viable. They ceased to take over the routes of small operators when the latter suspended services and increasingly sought permission from the MoT to abandon routes or to reduce or 'rationalize' services.

The number of passenger journeys on rural buses rose from 5.7 million in 1950 to 6.0 million in 1955 but then began to decline slowly to 3.7 million in

1970, by which time half the kms run by the National Bus Company failed to cover costs. Rural bus services were particularly affected by inflation since wages formed up to 60 per cent of operating costs and operational economies by the reduction in kms or frequency of service may do nothing to lower wage, depreciation and terminal costs. On the Western National services, for instance, which cover a large sector of rural SW England, the number of passengers halved between 1955 and 1970, but the vehicle mileage only fell by 20 per cent (DoE 1971 A and B).

The National Bus Company and Scottish Bus Group, established under the *Transport Act* (1968) to run inter-urban-rural services, saw their initial profits become a combined loss of £9.9 million by 1970. In the same year the Highland, Island and coastal services of Caledonian MacBrayne lost £405,000.

The National Bus Company therefore proposed withdrawal of unremunerative bus services unless local authorities were prepared to grant-aid them under the provisions of the 1968 Act. The government subsidizes fuel costs and is pledged to contribute half of the cost of new buses until 1980.

The *Jack Committee* (MoT 1963A) considered that the concentration of school, post, parcels and other luggage transport on to one vehicle would offer only limited solutions in rural areas. Further studies produced little action until the amendment of the vehicle licensing regulations under the *1968 Transport Act* enabled mini-buses to be run by private individuals for public carriage. Dial-a-bus schemes by which potential customers book seats on a vehicle or divert it from its standard route if they require a service are now in an experimental stage. Some rural communities own mini-buses which are operated by volunteer drivers as a social service.

The statutory obligation of local education authorities to provide bus or taxi services for children living more than two miles from a scheduled service to school was extended under the *Transport Act* (1968) to allow school buses, which already accounted for 60 per cent of all bus journeys in the rural areas studied in 1971, to be used by other passengers. The Post Office may carry passengers on mail services and four such services are now in operation. Private hire operators may be allowed to pick up separate fares en route: works' contract buses were carrying 6 per cent of journeys to work, as many as on public buses, in Devon and Suffolk (DoE 1971 A and B).

Since 1968, railways have been the main beneficiaries of subsidy to rural transport. In 1970, for instance, £30 million was paid to railways for services outside the conurbations, although they were estimated (RDC Assn. 1971) to be carrying only 19 per cent of the annual passenger mileage. Local buses only received £1 million, shared by government and local authorities. The *Railways Act* (1974) replaced specific grants by a general grant to the railways, but it is government policy to maintain the present size of the network. Rural trains, which cost four to five times as much to run as rural buses, are thus preserved – the only element in the local transport system outside the financial responsibility of county authorities. It remains to be seen whether the different counties will feel able to increase subsidies to rural bus services and how they will weigh the needs of their rural populations against those of their urban populations in their transport policies. Although ways are now being sought, under the pressure of rising costs, to meet the need of those rural inhabitants without access to private car transport in one way or another, a strict operation of tests of economic viability at any time in the near future would virtually eliminate public rail and road transport services from the rural areas of the UK. (Bracey 1970; Ramblers' Assn. 1971; Clout 1972; Hibbs 1972; Whitby et al 1974; and Pulling and Speakman 1974).

IV AIR TRANSPORT

IV.1 Traffic

This section concentrates on the role of air transport within the UK, including traffic to the Isle of Man and the Channel Islands. Internal air transport began on an experimental basis during the 1920s and the pattern of present services traces its origin to 1932. Dyos and Aldcroft (1969) give a history of inter-war domestic aviation and show that almost all the routes in current use (with the exception of London—Manchester) were in operation before the Second World War, and that the number of passengers carried reached a peak in 1937 of 161,000.

Air services were fully resumed in 1946 and domestic passenger km doubled every four years from 1946 to 1974, when a small decline was registered as a result of the fuel crisis. Table 5.5 shows that over 8 million passengers were carried and

TABLE 5.5

Air Traffic, UK, 1946 and 1974

Domestic flights	1946	1974
Aircraft km flown (million)	8.7	46.8
Passengers carried (million)	0.4	8.4
Passenger km (million)	48.4	2,254.0
Freight tonne-km (million)	0.1	22.4
Foreign flights		
Passengers carried (million)	0.2	28.3
% of total passengers	45	63
Freight handled (thousand tonnes)	3.7	241.4
% of total freight	81	78
% Overseas journeys by air	1960	1974
Total	47	67
Irish Republic	34	50
Europe	46	63
N America	74	99
Other continents	47	96

Source: Ann. Abstract of Statistics, Transport Statistics GB 1964—74

2,254 million passenger km were flown on domestic routes in 1974. The size of the UK tends to restrict the average length of flight, which was only 283 km. This distance is less than the most economic flying sector of most medium-range modern aircraft, and contributes to the problems of air-passenger transport in competition with land transport in GB. The average distance between airports which serve the conurbations and major cities of the UK is 262 km and the average distance between adjacent major airports is only 160 km.

Fig. 5.6 shows the main domestic routes and table 5.6 illustrates the two main types of service within the UK: routes between the four London airports of

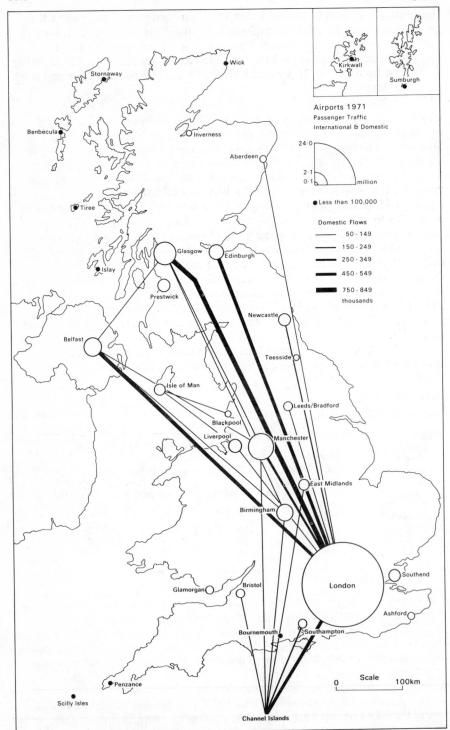

Figure 5.6   Airports and domestic air traffic, UK, 1971

Heathrow, Gatwick, Stansted and Luton and the more distant cities of the UK accounted for half the domestic traffic in 1975–6 (22 per cent from Glasgow and Edinburgh, 8 per cent from Belfast, 7 per cent from Manchester). Short sea crossings, including London–Belfast, accounted for 44 per cent of traffic, including 17 per cent from Belfast, 21 per cent from the Channel Islands and 7 per cent from the Isle of Man.

The Highlands and Islands services of British Airways form an essentially separate network, linking Glasgow, Edinburgh and Aberdeen with Campbeltown, Inverness and Wick, also the island airports of Islay, Tiree Barra, Benbecula, Stornoway, Kirkwall and Sumburgh. Like other rural transport services, these links are cross-subsidized within BA and provide, among other things, direct access to the business centres and medical services of the mainland cities. A helicopter service provides a similar link between the Scilly Islands and Penzance.

Of the 43 million passengers using UK airports in 1975 30 million (70 per cent) were flying to or from foreign airports. Of the passengers leaving the UK, 30 per cent were bound for the adjacent countries of France, Germany, the Irish Republic and the Low Countries, 32 per cent for more distant European countries (Spain, Italy, Switzerland and Scandinavia) and 14 per cent for N America. Table 5.5 shows the extent to which air transport had captured the overseas traffic on these services. In 1960 the near neighbours had accounted for 57 per cent of the air traffic, the more distant European countries 19 per cent and N America 13 per cent. The growth of traffic to Spain by 1,400 per cent in thirteen years accounts for most of these differences.

Table 5.5 shows that the growth in air freight transport since the Second World War has been twice as rapid as that of passenger traffic, and that the growth

TABLE 5.6

Domestic Air Passenger Traffic, UK, 1975–6

Airport	Monthly av. of domestic traffic May 1975–April 1976 (thousands)	Per cent distribution 1975		
		London	Belfast, I. of Man, Channel Is.	British mainland
London area	341		28	72
Glasgow	118	63	10	27
Belfast	91	47	4	49
Manchester	69	56	30	14
Edinburgh	65	75	3	22
Newcastle	30	86	14	
Birmingham	27	17	57	26
Southampton	26		94	6
Liverpool	22	42	58	
Leeds/Bradford	20	63	31	6
E Midlands	19		78	22

Derived from *Civil Aviation Authority Monthly Statistics, 1975–6*

of foreign freight traffic has been greater than that of domestic freight, which amounted to only 22 per cent of the total in 1974. London Heathrow is the third port of the UK in terms of the value of the goods which pass through it. **The**

London airports and Southend handled 75 per cent of all air freight in 1973, followed by Manchester and Liverpool (9 per cent), Glasgow and Prestwick (5 per cent), Belfast (3 per cent) and the Channel Islands (2 per cent).

IV.2 The Location and Development of Airports

Although several UK airports have the technical capability to handle the largest inter-continental aircraft, London dominates the international air traffic of the UK. There are only a small number of inter-continental scheduled flights from other airports and one-third of the domestic air passenger traffic of the UK is travelling to or from foreign airports via London (DoT 1975). The dominance of the London airports in UK air traffic depends on several factors. London is a world business centre, the largest British conurbation and the chief single focus of land communications in GB. In the early, formative years of air transport, London generated most of the official passenger and mail traffic which then formed a major component of airline business, and became the headquarters of the national and most of the charter and private airline companies. Although business passengers are not so numerous as leisure passengers, who comprised 75 per cent of the passengers at London airports in 1972, their journeys are not seasonal and form the base load of regular demand for air transport. Leisure travel, on the other hand, is expected to grow to 80 per cent of the total of British traffic by the end of the century and the number of foreign visitors is expected to grow markedly. At the present time almost all foreign tourists visit London and 85 per cent go nowhere else in Britain.

The *Roskill Report* (Dept. of Trade and Industry 1971) on the third London airport lists income, family composition and age as the chief factors affecting people's choice of air travel for holidays. Sealy (1967 A and B) pointed out that the rapidly growing leisure air travel is strongly related to discretionary income, i.e. the amount of money available after basic needs for food, housing, clothing and taxation have been met. This discretionary income is higher in the South East and rises, as a proportion of total income, ahead of that of the other regions, so that apart from the fact that European travel is marginally cheaper from the SE than from more distant regions, the amount of money available for it is greater and therefore the SE generates more leisure travel. The proportion of retired people is also greater in the SE than in other regions.

London (Heathrow) was built as a national airport from 1943–54 and London (Gatwick) was developed in 1955 (Sealy 1955). The predicted increase in air traffic, when applied to contemporary routes in the late 1950s, suggested that a third international airport would be needed in SE England during the 1970s. The years 1961–74 were spent in a search for an agreed site for this airport. Stansted was chosen in 1961 on relatively simple criteria but local opposition forced the government to appoint the Roskill Commission (Dept. of Trade and Industry 1971). Although limited in its brief to the location of a third *London* airport the seven volumes of evidence and analysis include valuable cost benefit studies (App. 15 and 20) and gravity models (App. 17–19). The government rejected the majority view of the Commission and chose a site at Maplin on the Essex coast. In 1974, after receiving revised predictions of future capacity at Heathrow and Gatwick due to the introduction of jumbo jets (which had been developed and come into service while the government was taking advice) the government abandoned the Maplin project (J G U Adams 1970, 1971; Hall 1971; Mishan

1970).

The latest forecasts (DoT 1975), based on the likelihood of a more even spread of demand at Gatwick and Luton, steeper increases in fuel costs and passenger fares, and also a slower rate of growth of British incomes, lead the government to suggest that an 'incremental' policy of progressive addition to the terminal and apron facilities at the four London airports will satisfy demand until the 1990s without a new airport, new runways or the imposed diversion of traffic from the SE airports.

The distribution pattern of provincial airports is inherited from the 1930s, when accessibility by surface transport was relatively restricted. Airports were then generally located within twenty to forty minutes of major railway stations by airport bus. The trunk road network and faster inter-city rail services of the 1970s would, in theory, enable both current and potential traffic to be handled to a smaller number of airports, each large enough to attract a wider variety of services than are now operated. Many provincial airports are now eccentrically located in terms of the load centre of their present traffic, and in some cases their sites restrict present traffic or its predicted growth. Prestwick, for example is 45 km west of Glasgow airport and Edinburgh airport only 65 km by motorway to the east. On or near the M62 motorway lie the airports for Manchester and Liverpool to the west and Leeds/Bradford to the east.

A national airports plan was foreshadowed in 1945 (Min. of Civil Aviation 1945) but government policy, expressed in the *Civil Aviation Act* (Min. of Civil Aviation, 1961; Sealy 1976, 40—54) has been to encourage local authorities to take the initiative in developing new airport facilities in their areas. Almost all provincial airports have required subsidies from their local authorities and most domestic air routes have been cross-subsidized from international services by air transport companies. Local authorities have lacked the resources to make investments in airports other than piecemeal improvements to satisfy conservative, short-run traffic forecasts. Few regional airports generate enough passengers from their own areas or attract sufficient passengers from other regions to support a wide range of services. Although half of the passengers between regional and foreign airports fly via London (DoT 1975), there is only limited demand for flights between specific regional and foreign destinations. British Airways and other companies are, however, experimenting with a number of direct flights from provincial cities to major European airports such as Amsterdam, Frankfurt and Paris. It is difficult to see how the 80 per cent of London airport passengers with origins or destinations within SE England could be persuaded to use more distant provincial airports.

The widely held view that investment in airports and air services can play an important role in regional economic development was accepted by the *Edwards Committee* (Comm. of Inquiry into Civil Air Transport, 1969) although they called for further research into the matter. The government has admitted that too much attention may have been paid to the views of the air transport industry during the search for London's third airport in the 1960s. Proposals from the British Airports Authority (which owns the London airports, except Luton, and the major Scottish airports) to the Edwards Committee offer an hierarchical plan which would have regional implications. They suggested (a) that major international and domestic services should operate from London, Manchester and Glasgow; (b) that a further seven regional airports should have links to the major UK airports and to some European destinations; (c) six provincial airports should have domestic feeder services and summer flights to Europe and the British islands; (d) a larger number of local airports should be developed for business flights, small feeder services and air taxis. Such a policy might enable the major airports at least to reach viable thresholds for a range of international services as demand grows during the remainder of this century.

As the prospects for the development of short- or vertical take-off and landing aircraft (STOL or VTOL) appear to be small before the 1990s (DTI 1971, 18.5, 19), air routes within Britain may be subject to increased competition from high speed trains. The numbers of passengers to Ireland and Europe may increase markedly, but in the absence to date of a national policy to meet the air transport needs of the UK it is doubtful whether the degree of concentration of traffic at specific airports will be very different in the year 2000 from the pattern of the late 1930s. This is because of investments having been made at each stage by a large number of authorities each with relatively small resources in this, the most capital intensive and commercially regulated of all transport modes.

V   SEAPORTS AND WATER TRANSPORT

V.1   The Hierarchy of Seaports

With the exception of the English Midlands all of the main UK concentrations of industrial urbanism are directly connected in some measure with seaport functions. The status and functions of the major ports are of fundamental importance to the UK economy, so heavily dependent as it is upon overseas trading and industrial production. These seaports are major transport nodes, the points of interchange between sea and land transport, sometimes points of break of bulk but increasingly for non-bulk cargoes, the pivot of a through-transport link. These seaports are also almost invariably important industrial centres, perhaps industrial *complexes* in the sense of inter-related industrial production, for which the seaport location is, or has been, crucial. Some industry, however, is related to the needs of the population grouping itself and the central place functions, the regional or metropolitan role, which the settlement has come to support.

The distribution and hierarchy of major seaports is always related to some extent to the physical environmental basis for port development (Jones 1931; Bird 1963). The potential of both water site and land site influence port develop- ment and indeed these influences have been reasserted, albeit indirectly, as the requirements of modern vessels and of port industries have become more exacting. Indirectly reasserted, because clearly these are not rigidly limiting influences but advantages to be utilized or disadvantages to be overcome and appear accordingly in the cost-benefit analysis of port development. Thus port growth and development may be influenced by the physical conditions of *site* but are commonly influenced more fundamentally by the economic conditions of *situation* – the potential to develop hinterlands and forelands (Elliott 1966, 1969). The hierarchy of seaports emerges from a continual reappraisal of physical and economic circum- stances. For most major seaports this is a long and complex historical process, very often given its initial stimulus by a conscious declaration of intent, a political act in the granting of trading and market privileges or in the declaration of a sphere of interest (Bird 1971). Once firmly established the commitment and complex inter-relationships of land, labour and capital in a major port are such that momentum and/or inertia ensure that 'there is not a rapid fluctuation in the relative status of these major ports' (Bird 1963, 23). This remains, certainly in the short-term, a valid, suitably qualified generalization but the contemporary reappraisal in terms of the striking technological developments in transport within recent decades has significantly modified the rank-order of the major UK seaports and will continue, perhaps increasingly, to do so.

Unfortunately there is no simple definitive method of establishing a *hierarchy* of seaports. The two most generally acceptable indices, although each has limitations, are the Net Registered Tonnage (NRT) of vessels and the value of cargo handled. The NRT of vessels *arriving* (or *departing*) with cargo and in ballast provides a measure of all traffic using a port. This does not reflect precisely the cargo handled as, quite apart from the unspecified tonnage in ballast, the figures do not recognize that some vessels will discharge only a part-cargo. Note also that it may be considered that NRT figures are in any event restricted, perhaps increasingly so, in their ability to reflect the trade and traffic of a port for two reasons. First, the NRT figures may be greatly inflated by a limited number of calls by massive bulk-carriers, especially super-tankers. Secondly, the much greater efficiency in break-bulk cargo handling following from unit-load cargo, and especially from containerization and cellular vessels, means that the volume of cargo handled may increase significantly without a concomitant increase in NRT. Since neither of these issues affects all ports equally the rank-order may change and certainly NRT figures cannot be so appropriately used, as commonly in the past, to suggest secular trends in port development. The value of cargo handled provides a more uniformly consistent measure at a given time although trends are impaired by the rise and fall of prices and in the long-term by the change in value of money. The use of value figures clearly accentuates the status of the main break-bulk cargo ports. Conversely, NRT figures cause the bulk ports, or the bulk elements of any port, to be overstressed. Compare, for example, the rankings in the first instance of Hull and in the second of Milford Haven. What is a 'major' port? Any classification inevitably is questionable in some respects. The category may involve a measure of sophistication, commercial status and associated population concentration, but on the basis of traffic and trade which identify the hierarchies there is no assurance that this is the case. The buoy at Amlwch (Anglesey) and the terminal at Sullom Voe (Shetland) can be expected to follow the example of Milford Haven and stand high in some rank orders of the 1980s. A comparison of the rankings by NRT and by value, together with some analysis of goods other than fuels, gives the most acceptable approach to a hierarchy of seaports (tables 5.7 and 5.8).

NRT figures are subdivided between coastwise and foreign but value figures are available for foreign trade only (NPC). In a British context, although it was not so in the past, coastwise trade now rarely makes a main contribution to the status of major ports. Only in the case of Belfast, a reflection of the distinctive economic relationship between N Ireland and the rest of the UK, does NRT coastwise comprise as much as 70 per cent of the total NRT. For Swansea petroleum products and for the Tyne the remnant of the formerly large coastwise coal trade ensure that coastwise NRT is commonly about one-half of each port's total. For the Clyde about 30 per cent coastwise NRT includes the Irish trade and the particular requirements of the Highlands and Islands. In general the major ports are also major coastwise ports but apart from these particular examples coastwise

TABLE 5.7

The Hierarchy of UK Ports (Rank Order 1–15), by Value of Foreign Trade; Exports (including exports of imported merchandize) and Imports, Annual Averages for the Three-year Periods, 1936–8; 1958–60; 1968–70

1936–8

	£ million total	% UK total
1 London	556.2	37.8
2 Liverpool	320.1	21.8
3 Hull	89.1	6.1
4 Southampton	66.7	4.5
5 Manchester	62.9	4.3
6 Glasgow	60.3	4.1
7 Bristol	31.5	2.1
8 Newcastle	28.6	1.9
9 Harwich	27.4	1.9
10 Swansea	21.3	1.5
11 Grimsby	19.0	1.3
12 Leith	16.7	1.1
13 Cardiff	15.6	1.1
14 Goole	14.4	1.0
15 Belfast	13.9	0.9
		91.4
Total UK	1,469.9	

1958–60

	£ million total	% UK total
1 London	2,605.6	36.2
2 Liverpool	1,656.5	23.0
3 Hull	411.0	5.7
4 Manchester	386.6	5.4
5 Southampton	310.5	4.3
6 Glasgow	295.2	4.1
7 Bristol	194.5	2.7
8 Harwich	124.7	1.7
9 Swansea	112.1	1.6
10 Dover	109.8	1.5
11 Newcastle	106.6	1.5
12 Middlesbrough	83.8	1.2
13 Grimsby	71.2	1.0
14 Belfast	66.7	0.9
15 Goole	66.5	0.9
		91.7
Total UK	7,192.5	

1968–70

	Exports	£ million imports	Total	% UK total
1 London	2,069.7	2,003.4	4,073.1	30.8
2 Liverpool	1,137.8	1,029.3	2,167.1	16.4
3 Hull	390.7	385.3	776.0	5.9
4 Harwich	382.2	337.5	719.7	5.4
5 Southampton	271.6	333.9	605.5	4.6
6 Manchester	207.7	368.7	576.4	4.4
7 Felixstowe	216.1	233.5	449.6	3.4
8 Dover	177.1	197.9	375.0	2.8
9 Clyde	174.7	198.4	373.1	2.8
10 Grimsby	117.2	234.2	351.4	2.6
11 Forth	151.3	130.2	281.5	2.1
12 Bristol	45.2	230.7	275.9	2.1
13 Tees	108.5	152.0	260.5	2.0
14 Milford Haven	37.7	165.9	203.6	1.5
15 Swansea	60.9	88.4	149.3	1.1
				87.9
Total UK	6,124.8	7,104.1	13,228.9	

NB Glasgow (Clyde 1968 onwards) includes Greenock. Grimsby includes Immingham, and Forth (from 1968 onwards) includes Leith, Granton, Grangemouth, Burntisland, Kirkcaldy and Methil. Tees (1968–70) incorporates Middlesbrough.

Sources: Annual Statement of Trade of the United Kingdom, vol. IV, Supplement (1938 and 1962); Digest of Port Statistics, (1969–71 inclusive); J H Bird, The Major Seaports of the United Kingdom (1963)

TABLE 5.8

The Hierarchy of UK Ports (Rank Order 1–15), by Net Registered Tonnage (NRT) of Vessels arriving with Cargo and in Ballast in Foreign and Coastwise Trade, Annual Averages for the Three-year Periods, 1936–8; 1958–60; 1968–70

1936–8	NRT thousand tons	%UK total	1958–60	NRT thousand tons	%UK total	1968–70	NRT thousand tons			%UK total
							Foreign	Coast	Total	
1 London	30,965	16.7	1 London	42,279	20.1	1 London	35,773	7,957	43,730	17.1
2 Liverpool	17,467	9.4	2 Southampton	24,816	11.8	2 Southampton	19,566	6,270	25,836	10.1
3 Southampton	13,366	7.2	3 Liverpool	19,743	9.4	3 Liverpool	16,043	5,548	21,591	8.5
4 Glasgow	9,899	5.4	4 Glasgow	9,499	4.5	4 Milford Haven	12,667	3,677	16,344	6.4
5 Newcastle	9,066	4.9	5 Manchester	8,118	3.9	5 Dover	12,587	257	12,844	5.0
6 Belfast	7,561	4.1	6 Newcastle	7,555	3.6	6 Glasgow	7,708	3,156	10,864	4.3
7 Cardiff	7,269	3.9	7 Belfast	7,448	3.5	7 Belfast	2,424	7,269	9,693	3.8
8 Hull	6,178	3.3	8 Bristol	6,017	2.9	8 Middlesbrough	6,758	1,576	8,334	3.3
9 Plymouth	5,908	3.2	9 Hull	5,919	2.8	9 Harwich	8,202	111	8,313	3.3
10 Manchester	3,941	2.1	10 Dover	5,694	2.7	10 Grimsby	5,906	1,997	7,903	3.1
11 Bristol	3,782	2.0	11 Middlesbrough	5,090	2.4	11 Hull	5,373	1,011	6,384	2.5
12 Swansea	3,464	1.9	12 Swansea	4,977	2.4	12 Tyne	2,817	3,042	5,859	2.3
13 Middlesbrough	3,135	1.7	13 Harwich	3,736	1.8	13 Manchester	5,571	275	5,846	2.3
14 Newport	2,344	1.3	14 Cardiff	3,336	1.6	14 Bristol	3,015	1,732	4,747	1.9
15 Grimsby	1,969	1.1	15 Grimsby	3,008	1.4	15 Swansea	1,876	2,381	4,257	1.7
		68.2			74.8					75.6
Total UK	184,900		Total UK	210,314		Total UK	173,263	81,745	255,008	

NB Glasgow includes Greenock and Grimsby includes Immingham. Tyne (1968–70) is comparable to Newcastle in earlier periods

Sources: *Board of Trade Journal* (1938–9 and 1958–61); NPC, *Digest of Port Statistics* (1969–71 inclusive); J H Bird, *The Major Seaports of the United Kingdom* (1963)

traffic is of limited relative importance. Thus London is the leading coastwise port by NRT, exceeding Belfast, although coastwise tonnage comprises only about 18 per cent of the total NRT of London. However not all major ports have an important coastwise component. It is insignificant at Dover and Harwich reflecting the distinctive packet-boat/ferry-style functions and the lack of the time-honoured traditional basis which is a feature of some coastwise trade; it is unimportant for reasons of access at Manchester and limited in volume at Hull, as other Humber ports have more importantly assumed this role. In contrast to the relative concentration of foreign trade the very nature of coastwise trade, its structure and operation, means that a large number of ports are significantly involved (48 handling over 100,000 NRT 1970) and the major ports handled only 57 per cent of the total coastwise NRT.

A comparison of the rank-order of the fifteen leading ports by total NRT with a rank-order according to value of foreign trade (in each case on the basis of annual average figures, 1968–70 as comparable figures are no longer published by the NPC) confirms the pre-eminence of London as the leading UK port and clearly identifies the *major* ports in that thirteen ports appear in both rank-orders. Belfast and Tyne occur only in the NRT ranking and Felixstowe and the Forth occur only in the ranking by value. Such discrepancies now or at earlier times may be due to a combination of reasons, for example, the inclusion in the NRT of a considerable coastwise element (Belfast, Tyne); the fact that the value figures refer to Customs ports or a group of such ports which may cover an extensive area (Forth – although this is now one Port Authority); or to the very nature of an important element of the cargo, for example, high bulk, low unit-value (Tyne coal) or vice versa (Felixstowe container traffic). There is no particularly clear reason why fifteen ports should be listed in each ranking. A critical break has often seemed to appear at different times somewhere between eleventh and fifteenth in both NRT and value rankings. An extension to fifteen ports in each ranking, involving in total seventeen individual ports, gives a basic distribution of the main port activity of the UK (figs. 5.7 and 5.8). Perhaps the only area which may seem undervalued in this distribution is S Wales and specifically by the omission of Cardiff. This distribution of major ports represents a considerable measure of concentration which is more pronounced in terms of value of cargo than in NRT, since the necessity to keep land transport costs to a minimum ensures that a larger number and a more widespread distribution of ports are importantly involved in handling cargoes of low value per unit weight. In the value rank-order the two leading ports (London and Liverpool) handle 47 per cent of the total, four ports (Hull and Harwich added) handle 59 per cent and the fifteen major ports comprise 88 per cent of the total UK foreign trade by value. Four ports (London, Southampton, Liverpool, Milford Haven) handle 42 per cent of the total foreign and coastwise NRT and the fifteen major ports by NRT comprise 76 per cent of the UK total.

A further partial measure of the status of ports may be gained in terms of the tonnage of goods handled. In such an analysis the greatest single distorting factor is petroleum traffic (table 5.11). A ranking by tonnage of goods *other than fuels*, although still including other major bulk commodities such as iron ore, perhaps provides a more effective indication of varied economic activities and multifarious port functions (table 5.10). Only Newport, due to the iron ore trade, is added to the major ports identified in the earlier rank-orders. This hierarchy shows an even less pronounced concentration of trading and indeed it is an important feature of

TABLE 5.9

The Hierarchy of UK Ports (Rank Order 1–15) by Tonnage of Goods, other than Fuels, in Foreign and Coastwise Trade 1965, 1972–74

Thousand gross tonnes	1965	Coast	1974 Foreign	Total	1972–74 Average total	%UK total	1965–74 Index of change 1965 = 100
1 London	20,266	1,621	16,366	17,987	18,310	15.1	88.8
2 Liverpool	15,515	674	9,521	10,195	10,863	9.0	65.7
3 Tees	7,339	904	9,413	10,317	9,121	7.5	140.6
4 Immingham	3,082	292	9,375	9,667	7,842	6.5	313.7
5 Manchester	5,832	582	4,978	5,560	5,768	4.8	95.3
6 Clyde	6,104	562	4,725	5,287	5,488	4.5	86.6
7 Forth	3,444	615	3,568	4,183	4,078	3.4	121.5
8 Hull	4,621	153	4,176	4,329	4,071	3.4	93.7
9 Newport	3,706	2	3,058	3,060	3,878	3.2	82.6
10 Southampton	1,304	50	3,640	3,690	3,318	2.7	283.0
11 Felixstowe	442	19	3,421	3,440	3,023	2.5	778.3
12 Bristol	3,805	95	2,842	2,937	2,993	2.5	77.2
13 Dover	823	54	3,038	3,092	2,672	2.2	375.7
14 Harwich	584	—	2,580	2,580	2,437	2.0	441.8
15 Tyne	2,402	115	1,045	1,160	1,879	1.5	48.3
						(70.8)	
Others	19,681	7,138	28,434	35,572	35,459	29.2	180.7
Total GB	100,394	12,876	110,180	123,056	121,200	100.0	122.6

NB Immingham includes Grimsby

Source: N. Ports Council (1974) *Digest of Statistics* vol 1

TABLE 5.10

Major Bulk Cargoes, Leading UK Ports, 1974

Petroleum (total traffic)

Port	Petroleum traffic (million tonnes)	% total petroleum traffic	Total traffic of port (million tonnes)	Petroleum as % of total
Milford Haven	59.5	26.3	59.5	100.0
London	24.6	10.9	46.2	53.2
Southampton	23.7	10.5	27.5	86.2
Medway	22.5	9.9	24.6	91.5
Liverpool	17.0	7.5	27.8	61.2
Tees	14.7	6.5	25.0	58.8
Immingham	11.9	5.2	22.1	53.8
Clyde	11.8	5.2	17.4	67.8
Manchester	10.8	4.8 (86.8)	16.3	66.3
Others	30.0	13.2	101.3	29.6
Total GB	226.5	100.0	367.7	61.6

Ores and scrap (foreign imports)

Port	Ores and scrap (million tonnes)	% total ores and scrap	Total foreign imports of port (million tonnes)	Ores as % of total
Tees	5.4	23.3	20.0	27.0
Immingham	4.9	21.1	18.4	26.6
Port Talbot	3.4	14.7	3.8	89.5
Clyde	2.4	10.3	14.4	16.7
Newport	2.0	8.6	3.7	54.1
Liverpool	2.0	8.6	25.3	7.9
Cardiff	0.9	3.9 (90.5)	2.5	36.0
Others	2.2	9.5	123.0	1.8
Total GB	23.2	100.0	211.1	11.0

NB Immingham includes Grimsby
Source: N Ports Council (1974). *Digest of Port Statistics vol 1*

this distribution that almost 30 per cent of the goods in question is handled by
'other ports'. This analysis underlines also the growing status of the east and south
coast ports, although London has not held its own, and the uncertain status of
some long-established ports, especially in the west. Indeed the ports which have
grown rapidly have tended to be the traditionally less important ones, for example,
Southampton, the Tees, Immingham and Dover. Part cause and part effect of this
is the fact that the traditional major ports are now undoubtedly those with the
pronounced problems of excess area, obsolete facilities and surplus manpower.
Large sections of the older ports have been closed. Three dock systems within the
Port of London Authority have been closed within the last ten years and similar

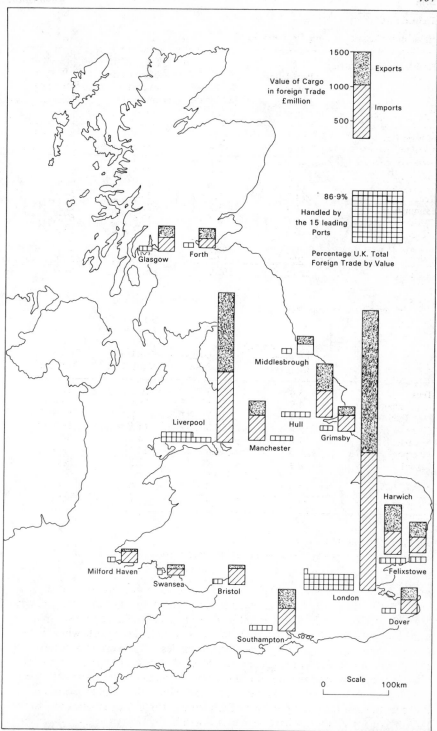

Figure 5.7   Hierarchy of ports (rank order 1–15), by value of foreign trade, UK, 1968–70

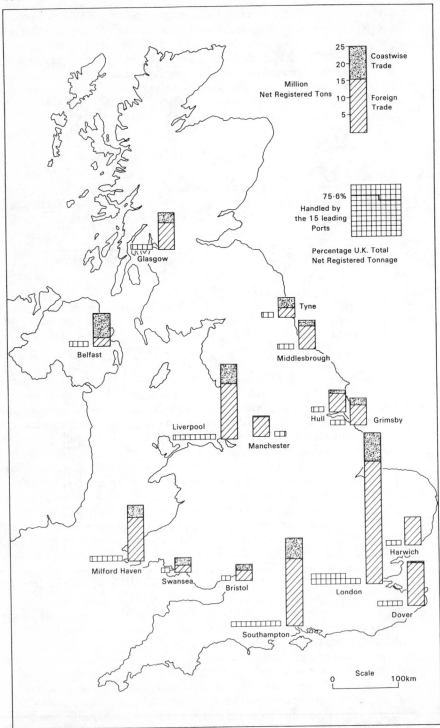

Figure 5.8   Hierarchy of ports (rank order 1–15), by net registered tonnage of vessels, UK,
1968–70

closures have occurred in Liverpool, Hull, Glasgow and on the Tyne (N Ports Council 1976). The present hierarchy retains the signs of a long evolution but it also reflects the impact of recent technological developments in transport and changing patterns of trade. Such developments have provided new opportunities, which are available and implemented to varying degrees, to modify the hierarchy of ports. The opportunities are broadly two-fold; first, to develop the port's function of cargo-handling and, secondly, to enhance the port as a centre of industrial investment.

V.2   Seaports and Cargo-handling

One of the most striking economic developments of the post-Second World War period, a result of increased economic interdependence, has been the very rapid growth in the tonnage of international sea-borne cargo. The pre-war maximum, following the trough of the depression, was not greatly changed from that of 1929. In the post-war recovery a similar level was again reached in 1949 (about 490 million tonnes) and then within twenty years there was a remarkable four-fold increase. The vast rise in cargo has been outstandingly of bulk cargoes. Of the world total cargo handled in 1972 of 2,830 million tonnes, more than half (1,640 million tonnes) was of oil and more than 75 per cent of the total weight was of oil and dry bulk cargoes (i.e. of oil and of iron-ore, grain, sugar, coal, fertilizers and so on). Total tonnage has continued to increase to 3,248 million tonnes in 1974, but in a changed fuel situation tanker cargo declined from 58 to 43 per cent of the total between 1972 and 1974 (Gen. Council of British Shipping 1976). The secular trend in cargo-handling at UK ports differed only in detail. It is true that the total of 82.6 million tonnes in 1948 was 30 million tonnes less than a decade earlier, due to the radical and irretrievable decline in coal exports, but thereafter the growth rate was close to that of world trade as a whole with a total of 270 million tonnes of foreign cargo in 1974. The expanded UK trade moreover was structured similarly to the international trade with crude oil imports as the main growth point.

The general structure of sea-borne cargo is basically a response to the changing pattern of world trading and, in particular, to the changes in this pattern which relate to Europe's needs for energy and raw material resources in the economic development of the post-war period. Important major flows have developed, often over long distances, linking the areas of economically advanced industrial urbanism in north-west Europe (and also in north-east USA and Japan) with mineral primary producers. These are often asymmetrical trade flows and the probability of sailing one direction in ballast, a reflection not only of the areas linked but also perhaps of the specialized vessels involved, has required the economies which large vessels allow.

A rapid growth of new tonnage and an increased size of vessel were the most general developments in maritime transport inter-related with the expanding and changing pattern of trade. These were often developments involving specialized and faster vessels and perhaps incorporating more advanced cargo-handling techniques. The increased size of vessel has been most obvious in the development of massive bulk-carriers to handle the greatly increased volume of movement of oil and to a lesser extent of ores. There are important general economies related to size of vessel but the main concern in this present context is that increased size has made vessels more discriminating and demanding in terms of their depth

requirements and the facilities they need (Hunter and Wilson 1969). Port costs in
terms of dredging, facilities and installations rise with increasing ship size and may
at some stage offset the economies of larger vessels. The increase in tanker size has
meant that fewer ports are involved in handling the imports of crude oil and more
oil is being moved by pipeline. Four oil terminals, Forth (Hound Point 98 ft, 30 m
depth), Clyde (Finnart, 95 ft, 29 m depth), Milford Haven (68–70 ft, 20–21 m
depth) and Humber (Immingham 68 ft, 20 m depth) can handle tankers in the
250,000–275,000 dwt range or above fully laden. They were joined in 1976 by
the new Shell facility, a single buoy 3 kilometres off the north-west coast of
Anglesey at Amlwch which is capable of handling a vessel of 700,000 dwt. There
are five other terminals (Thames, Southampton Water, Medway, Mersey and Tees)
which offer depths of 45 ft (13.7 m) or over. It is a distinctive and important
characteristic of oil cargoes that a variety of berthing systems, for example, using
jetties or hose, may potentially be used. The Flotta (Orkney) terminal uses the deep
water of the wartime anchorage of Scapa Flow to provide two single-point mooring
towers (200,000 dwt range) as well as a conventional berth for tankers and gas
carriers. Four ports handle more than half of the total petroleum traffic (57.6 per
cent), Milford Haven (26.3 per cent, 1974), London (10.9 per cent), Southampton
(10.5 per cent) and Medway (9.9 per cent). In fact since the Second World War oil
has been a significant item in the trade of most major UK ports and its distinctiveness is shown more obviously where it comprises a high proportion of total trade
(Milford Haven virtually 100 per cent, Southampton 86.2 per cent, Medway 91.5
per cent) and/or when it is linked to refinery capacity (see table 5.11 and ch. 5.V.3).
An important element, about one-third, of all sea-borne petroleum movements is
in coastwise trade, a result of the transfer of crude stocks and of the distribution
of refined products. In this connection it may be noted that on present projections
by 1980 Sullom Voe (Shetland), at jetties able to take vessels of up to 300,000
dwt, will be handling more oil traffic than any other British port and presumably,
at least initially, it will be mainly coastwise.

Iron-ore vessels are less demanding in terms of depth but they do require conventional berths with specialized handling equipment. Until 1969, when the new
facilities at Port Talbot came into operation, the Tyne with 30 ft (9.1 m) LWOST
and able to handle vessels of 37,000 dwt provided the deepest available ore-berth.
Port Talbot with a tidal harbour (29 ft, 8.8 m, tidal range) is now able to handle
vessels of more than 100,000 dwt. More recently, important additions to such
deep-water facilities able to handle the largest ore-carriers in common use have
been made on the Humber (Immingham 1972, 65,000–70,000 dwt); on the Tees
(Redcar 1973, 120,000–150,000 dwt) and on the Clyde (Hunterston 1977, over
130 ft, 40 m, depth, and potentially able to handle vessels of 350,000 dwt). The
23.2 million tonnes of ores and scrap imported in the foreign trade in 1974
showed a similar measure of port concentration to the petroleum traffic and
indeed a more pronounced concentration if estuarial groupings are considered
(table 5.11). Of the total imports, 60.8 per cent is handled in the three estuaries
(Severn, Tees and Clyde) associated importantly with the steel industry and 27.2
per cent of the total is handled by S Wales ports. The ore trade is focused mainly
on the leading industrial seaports (see ch. 5.V.3) although it has been in the past,
and is likely to be increasingly in the future, influenced by available depths of
water and the available or projected handling facilities. The rapid rise in
importance of Immingham as an ore importer is related to the expansion of the

British Steel Corporation's activities at Scunthorpe (Anchor scheme). Ores are not a main item of most major ports' trade as is petroleum and the three S Wales ports (Port Talbot, Cardiff and Newport) are distinctive in the high proportion of ores in their total foreign imports.

None of the other bulk cargoes are of comparable volume or have shown a similar rate of increase in traffic in recent years. The coastwise coal trade of 5.2 million tonnes in 1974 is very largely the lingering special relationship between the ports of NE England and the Thames. Coal has never regained its pre-Second World War importance in the foreign export trade and a volume of 4 million tons in 1974 (mainly from Immingham and S Swansea) was surpassed by exports of chemicals (6.1 million tonnes – Tees, Liverpool, Manchester) and crude fertilizers and crude minerals (5.1 million tonnes – Fowey and Par). The most significant of the bulk imports were unmilled cereals (6.3 million tonnes – notably London and Liverpool); timber (5.9 million tonnes – London and Hull) and crude fertilizers and crude minerals (5.3 million tonnes – Immingham and Manchester). The remaining main bulk import trades were, perhaps surprisingly, coal with 3.7 million tonnes (especially at Port Talbot); pulp and waste paper (2.8 million tonnes – London and Manchester) and sugar (2.8 million tonnes – London, Liverpool and Clyde). Most of such bulk imports are related to industry within the ports.

Important though the developments associated with bulk handling have been, there is no doubt that in the long-term the development of various forms of unit-load handling has more revolutionary and widespread implications for both trade and seaports. The general results of unit-load cargo have been discussed elsewhere (ch. 5.I.2 and 5.VI.1). More specifically in relation to ports, the developments concern the spread of handling techniques and specialist vessels which are transforming the mode and pattern of general-cargo movement with important effects on traditional port functions. Unit-load refers to a variety of forms used to *consolidate* general cargo and has its full expression in containerization. Often initially unit-load was associated with roll-on operation (where the road vehicle is carried on the vessel) and this is still favoured for some traffic and for particular routes. More importantly unit-load relates to various forms of palletization and particularly to the use of the standard metal container. It involves, in varied measure, the use of special cranage and of converted or specially-designed vessels. Not all operators are convinced that full containerization should be developed wherever possible. It is pointed out that palletization requires less costly equipment on both ship and berth. There is, of course, no dispute that unit-load, of whatever kind, reduces handling costs and thus in respect of through-transport costs the greatest gains are achieved on short-sea routes where terminal charges form a greater proportion of the total. It was on the short-sea routes to Europe that the new techniques were first developed by UK shippers but they have had an increasingly widespread effect on the hierarchy and functions of UK ports and thus the location of unit-load facilities has been very important in the growth and development of ports within the last decade (McKinsey & Co 1966; Little 1967, 70).

The development of unit-load facilities has taken place in the piecemeal unplanned and potentially wasteful fashion which has characterized so much of British transport history. There was very little government influence and no positive planning and control over the proliferation of unit-load facilities (ch. 5.V.4).

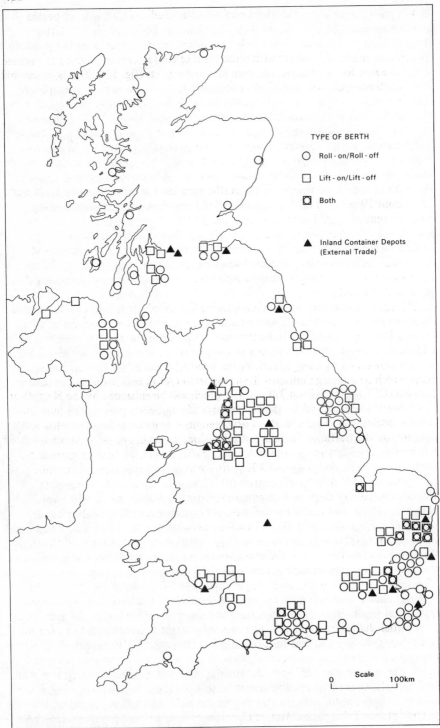

TYPE OF BERTH

○ Roll - on/Roll - off

□ Lift - on/Lift - off

◻ Both

▲ Inland Container Depots
   (External Trade)

Scale

0   100km

Figure 5.9   Unit transport berths and inland container depots, UK, 1974

In 1962 there were 21 berths which could be classified as unit transport berths and this number had increased to 91 by 1969 and to 166 in 1975. This latter figure may in part reflect a fuller collection of information than in earlier years. In fact roll-on or lift-on facilities with some form of container crane tended to become a *sine qua non* for most ports, not even just major ports (fig. 5.9). This is far removed from the theoretical concept of the way in which these new handling techniques should concentrate general cargo handling. The diversity of uses possible with roll-on facilities and the moderate size of ships employed in trade with Europe have enabled a large number of ports to grow, and to do so without related investment proportionate to the amount of cargo handled, precisely because of the low-cost high-throughput possibilities of the system. The initial development and the widespread distribution were related mainly to the near-sea trade (for definition see N Ports Council Digest). Some of the berths were used in more than one trade but only about 10 per cent of the berths handled some deep-sea trade (comprising 24.2 per cent of loaded units, foreign trade 1974). The largest number were concerned with the short-sea (17.6 per cent of loaded units) and near-sea (58.2 per cent) trades, and particularly with traffic to France, Belgium, Netherlands and W Germany. Coastwise movement of unit-loads has an important role in Scotland notably in the Highlands and Islands, and it is also a component of the strong flow, part coastwise and part foreign, across the Irish Sea (almost one quarter of the total loaded-units in foreign and coastwise trade). Of course not all of these berths were handling standard-sized containers with transporter cranes from cellular vessels. This was more likely to be the case in the deep-sea trade but even here only a limited, although growing, amount of concentration of traffic has occurred. It does appear that a focusing of activity has been achieved in the UK–Australia trade which Associated Container Transportation (ACT) and Overseas Containers Limited (OCL) operate from Tilbury and which will be enhanced by the Northfleet Hope development whereby a deepwater riverside container port will be built outside the enclosed docks. Similarly, a new container terminal at Southampton will concentrate the traffic of the South African Conference in one port. No such accord has been reached in terms of the N Atlantic traffic in which a large number of UK ports vie for trade. At least seven UK ports are significantly involved in unit-load transport on the N Atlantic (Grangemouth, Greenock, Liverpool, Manchester, Felixstowe, Tilbury and Southampton) suggesting a clear excess of tonnage capacity. In unit-load traffic overall there are certain areas of concentration, for example, the importance of Dover in roll-on activity, but the six leading ports, each handling over 100,000 loaded units in 1974, handled only 60 per cent of the traffic. The remaining 40 per cent of the units, which in fact involved almost one-half of the tonnage of goods handled in unit load (15.2 million tonnes from a total of 30.6 million tonnes), were handled by no less than fifty-three ports (table 5.11).

One of the important implications of unit transport berths is that some of the traditional functions in handling, sorting and distribution are lost to the port. It is an essential characteristic of unit-load operation that the berth should be used for trans-shipment only and that Inland Container Depots (ICDs) are established to perform all other functions including Customs. Fifteen ICDs have been built and operate on a 'common user' basis although in most instances involving British Rail (fig. 5.9). There is no compelling reason why ICDs should be near the ports. It is in retrospect perhaps unfortunate that two of the earliest and most publicized ICDs at Orsett (near Tilbury) and Aintree (Liverpool) should have been so near the port

TABLE 5.11

Container and Roll-on Traffic, Leading UK Ports, 1969–74

Port	(1,000 loaded units) Foreign traffic			% UK total 1974	Total traffic 1974		Million tonnes of goods	% total goods *
	1969	1971	1974		Wheeled	Container		
London	93	219	266	13.2	1	265	3.0	16.7
Dover	80	124	244	12.1	237	7	2.9	93.8
Southampton	52	96	230	11.4	52	178	2.9	78.6
Felixstowe	91	122	206	10.2	77	129	2.9	84.3
Liverpool	128	186	140	7.0	26	147	1.5	14.7
Hull	72	71	125	6.2	50	75	2.2	50.8
				(60.1)				
Others	432	541	805	39.9	435	734	15.2	18.9
Total GB	948	1,359	2,016	100.0	878	1,535	30.6	24.9

NB Total goods is 'goods other than fuels' in foreign and coastwise trade.
Source: N Ports Council (1974) *Digest of Port Statistics vol. 1*

area in each case as to provoke industrial unrest by the apparent usurpment of what is traditionally considered to be dockers' work.

V.3 Seaports and Industry

The link between seaports and industrial development was forged in early medieval times in areas on or near the coalfields and was well established on many British estuaries by the mid-eighteenth century. There are traditional and continuing influences which promote industry in and around port areas. The attractions of a port location include: the cheap assembly of varied raw materials, especially those of high bulk and low value per unit weight, which in the past were unable to stand the costs of inland transport; the ability to utilize direct water access as in shipbuilding and repairing, or merely in the shipment of the end product; the ability to develop associated industries, cognate or ancillary to the main undertakings, and thus contribute to the inter-related complex of industrial production which is characteristic of most major ports (Elliott 1962).

The secular decline of some heavy industries, especially in this context coal, shipbuilding and to a lesser extent textiles, allied with the depression of the 1930s obviously influenced ports and the level of port industries. On the other hand, the move of the iron and steel industry to the coast was one of the most important changes in economic patterns in the UK within this century and, progressively, particularly within the last twenty-five years, the development of the oil and petrochemical industries has markedly enhanced the significance of tide-water sites. Indeed, the recent past has seen a powerful restatement of the assets of port locations for industrial development. There is no doubt, for example, that the greatly increased size of vessel markedly enhances the asset of low-assembly costs for raw materials. It is true that not all ports can take advantage of these possibilities since clearly the requirements of such vessels are more exacting and equally the industries may be more discriminating in their locations. Clearly physical environmental considerations have been reasserted in port growth and development, and outstandingly in the growth of industry within ports. This is a matter of both land-site and water-site. Major modern industrial development in ports requires extensive areas of level land or perhaps the ability to reclaim such land. The handling of the massive bulk-carriers requires considerable depths of water, preferably at all states of the tide. In recent years it might be considered that deep water, in the right place, is one of the scarcest industrial resources. The Upper Clyde and the Tyne epitomize the industrial ports of the mid-nineteenth century associated with the inter-relationship of coal and cheap water transport which produced a distinctive, specialized and vulnerable industrial structure. Their inadequacy has been increasingly apparent since the Second World War and the industrial future may lie with the Humber, the Tees and Severnside.

Undoubtedly the economic and technical changes of the period since 1945 (chs. 1.I.1 and 4.I) have been conducive to major industrial development in seaport locations. It would appear, however, that the attitude of British port authorities to industrial growth has not undergone an equally felicitous transformation. With the notable exception of the Manchester Ship Canal Co, no British major port has pursued industry in a methodical and sustained fashion. British ports have suffered from a lack of local interest in them as poles of attraction for industry. This lack of interest is the more surprising in view of the preoccupation with regional development since the war and the role which estuaries can play within this. Many British major ports are Trust ports (G Adams 1973) in which the controlling bodies are dominated by port-users whose main concern has been to keep port charges low and uniform rather than to develop an adventurous and adaptable commercial policy. It is true that continental rivals of the UK have been aided by local and central government subsidies, but they have also pursued much more enterprising and flexible development policies that very clearly demonstrate the new potential for industrial investment characteristic of port locations in recent years. These ports show equally that a main emphasis in that growth has lain with the oil-refinery industry and associated petrochemical developments, and to a lesser extent with the development of the steel industry. Significantly perhaps, neither of these industries is inevitably tied to port locations. The fact that in the recent past they have been attracted overwhelmingly to coastal sites may serve to stress the particular contemporary assets offered by such locations. Moreover, these industries are of particular importance in that either or both may form the focus for an industrial complex of inter-related industries.

Major demands for large acreages of level land with deep-water access have been made by the oil industry (ch. 4.I.3). Direct water access is not inescapable for either refinery capacity or any associated petrochemical developments but the balance of locational advantages has tended to retain such industrial growth on coastal locations and may well continue to do so. UK refinery capacity in 1974 stood at 145 million tonnes (about 2.5 million tonnes of crude oil was refined in Britain in 1947) with notable concentrations on the Thames Estuary, at Milford Haven and on Southampton Water. The oil industry has certainly focused attention on deep-water access but recent developments have shown also the potential of new pipelines to reaffirm established locations at Stanlow and Grangemouth. It is noticeable that a variety of other issues may influence proposed developments. Such developments may, for example, be a part of comprehensive development proposals, they may be influenced by environmental issues or their location may be affected by nearness to the oil resources. Development plans, including the oil industry as a main element within them, have been proposed for the Clyde and notably for the Hunterston site where they are linked in the first instance with an iron-ore quay, a steel works and an additional power station. Thus far, however, only the iron-ore quay is established. A wide-ranging development plan, within which the oil industry has some part, is a proposal for Foulness which could provide the first custom-built industrial port. A further proposal for the Clyde, the Murco refinery planned for Bishopton, 16 km from Glasgow, was in 1970 the first major economic development in Scotland to be rejected at the planning stage, mainly on the environmental argument of the potential threat of air pollution. Environmentalist pressure groups also succeeded in impeding but not preventing the commencement of an off-shore terminal and on-shore storage for oil on Anglesey to feed the large and expanding refinery on the Mersey at Stanlow. Although seemingly an unlikely consideration when a commodity so eminently transportable as oil is involved, there is no doubt that the location of oil resources has importantly influenced developments on the east coast of Great Britain in the recent past (fig. 4.3). The working of British Petroleum's Forties field, 177 km east of Aberdeen will, in time, increase considerably the throughput of the Grangemouth refinery to which oil is being sent by sea- and land-pipe, and a new *island* terminal has been constructed downstream of the Forth Bridges to handle the export of surplus crude and perhaps of petroleum products. Again explicable mainly in terms of relative position, the Philips' Ekofisk petroleum field, on the Norwegian continental shelf but separated from the mainland by the major gash of the Norwegian Trench, is sending the oil westward by undersea pipeline to the nearest effective British estuary, the Tees. It is estimated that this will more than double the crude oil (c. 15 million tonnes) previously handled by Teesside refineries.

According to the extent of processing of the petroleum feedstocks and natural gas, petrochemical production may take place within the refinery or on a separate, often adjacent, site. The refinery might commonly produce raw materials (for example naphtha) and intermediates (for example propylene). Finished products such as plastics would be more commonly produced on a separate site and this need not be adjacent to the refinery. Petrochemical feedstock pipelines link ICI Wilton to Runcorn and the Stanlow refinery (125 km) with off-shoots to Partington (near Manchester) and Fleetwood. Fawley is linked by a similar pipeline to the petrochemical developments at Severnside (70 km). Whether within refineries or not, petrochemical industries have in recent years made a major contribution to industrial investment in ports and have grown at an appreciably faster rate than the national economy. These are highly capital-intensive industries but nonetheless petrochemical development greatly increases employment as compared with the oil refinery alone.

Also of increasing importance in focusing industrial investment in seaport locations in the period since the Second World War has been the steel industry The British steel industry has come to rely increasingly upon imported ores. Measured by iron content, imports comprised about 91 per cent of the ores used in 1974 compared with about one-half in the immediate post-war years. Indeed total ore imports into the UK increased from 5 million tonnes in 1945 to 21.7 million tonnes in 1973. Since commonly more than half the cost of steel is accounted for by the delivered cost of production materials it is not surprising that there has been an increased emphasis upon seaport locations. The assets of such locations were enhanced by the increased size of ore-carrier developed although this was a development of which the British steel industry was very slow to take advantage.

With a dispersed and fragmented pattern of production, a legacy from the nineteenth century, the British steel industry has been increasingly conscious in the post-war period of its limitations in equipment and size of plant compared with its continental rivals. A programme of rationalization has aimed to concentrate production and, especially in recent years, to concentrate it in modern Basic Oxygen Steelmaking (BOS) plants. In this, the established coastal locations play a major part, notably S Wales (exemplified by the Llanwern works at Newport and the new dock and BOS developments at Port Talbot) and the S Teesside group (Lackenby, Redcar).

Not surprisingly, some of the most notable recent developments of industry in seaports have related to the increasing assets of the cheap assembly of raw materials made possible by the increased size of bulk carrier. Although the size of production unit involved may not seem to have fully exploited the advantages of bulk carriage, three new aluminium smelters came into production in 1970–1 at Holyhead (Rio Tinto Zinc), at Lynemouth near Blyth (Alcan) and at Invergordon (British Aluminium). Both Holyhead and Invergordon can handle vessels of 50,000 dwt and the 22,500 dwt possible at Blyth is quite adequate to the capacity of the nearby plant. The scale of vessel in use in recent years has also stimulated development in the handling of grain and in flour-milling, one of the range of food industries, sugar-refining is another, processing imported raw materials. Recent developments at London, Liverpool and Glasgow to handle the larger vessels of 50,000–60,000 dwt which may now be used in the grain trade have reaffirmed flour-milling as a port activity and in the case of Tilbury have attracted one large new flour mill.

The MIDA concept Although the very varied port industries demonstrate differing measures of inter-relationship and differing degrees of dependence upon the trading functions of the port, these industries do show a common reliance upon the basic infra-structure of the surrounding area and more specifically a reliance upon the port facilities and the navigable channel of the port. In 1967 the UK government commissioned an enquiry into sites suitable for maritime industrial development. This was not published but was broadly interpreted in the National Ports Council's *Progress Report* (1969); see also Preston and Rees (1970). The Report notes that size of ship and the extent to which direct water access is critical are problems of varying degree according to the particular requirements of specific industries. It is clear also that the search for potential industrial sites is made more difficult by the fact that most obvious sites are already in use while others are remote and/or have a high amenity value (Hallett and Randall 1970). The criteria suggested for suitable sites provide an interesting comment on the present inter-relationships of ports and industry and upon the potential pattern of future activity. It is suggested that MIDA (Maritime Industrial Development Areas) require first, to be near to deep water (now seen as 50–60 ft, 15–18.5 m) mean high water neaps without excessive dredging); secondly, to have a minimum of 2,200 ha level land, although this may be obtainable if necessary by reclamation; and thirdly, to be near main population concentrations and have good transport links inland. Only three sites were considered to meet all these requirements: Humberside, Thames–Medway and Cardiff–Newport. Eight further sites met some of the requirements and were considered possible MIDAs: Cromarty Firth, Firth of Tay, Clyde Estuary, Upper Firth of Forth, Tees Estuary, Lune Estuary, The Wash and Weston Super Mare–Clevedon (fig. 5.10). In fact no such major developments have ensued. It may well be that the emphasis laid upon long-term views and optimum solutions, involving expensive investment projects unlikely to be implemented in the immediate future, has impeded development which might perhaps have proceeded had attention been given to less ambitious projects using existing facilities. As Hallett and Randall (1970, 108) conclude, decisions on the location of maritime industry have frequently been determined on a too restricted basis which frustrates the type of coordinated development which in the long run would be desirable from the viewpoint of both industrial efficiency and amenity. The inter-relationships of seaports and industries are, however, only one sphere of activity which may suggest that the broad *strategic* decisions on infrastructure have not received the attention they deserve in national policy-making. The immediacy of the demand for oil-rig construction has led to the development of limited and specialized MIDAs, on the Clyde and notably on the east coast of Britain at Nigg Bay (Easter Ross); Methil (Fife) and on the Tees. Such development proposals have often provoked environmentalist opposition, sometimes protracted and successful as at Drumbuie (Wester Ross). There are eleven sites in Scotland and there has been an increasingly formalized governmental aim of preventing widespread proliferation of sites, especially in areas of scenic interest. Although it may be clearly unlikely that a very limited number of sites would effectively meet the needs of varied maritime-related activities and the particular choice may seem to undervalue the UK distribution of population and economic activity, the Report of the *National Ports Council* (1973) suggested that the forseeable demand for MIDAs could be accommodated at three sites: the Tees, Cromarty Firth and on the Clyde (Hunterston). A government decision in 1976 to permit the development of a refinery at Nigg, contrary to the recommendation of the public enquiry, acknowledged the probably detrimental environmental effects but clearly saw the proposal as appropriate to the plan for Cromarty Firth to be an area of substantial industrial growth.

V.4 The Changing Status and Functions of Seaports

The outstanding technological developments in transport in the last decade, gradually achieving their full potential, were the catalyst in the changing status and functions of ports. Important developments have occurred already but, in general, it is true to say that the initiative still lies firmly with the ports, and that major changes must ensue if the full advantages of modern transport are to be reaped. In the recent past, UK ports have not been noted for providing facilities in advance of a demand and this has sometimes led to the criticism of port authorities as providing too little and too late.

Port developments are basically related to changes in the volume and pattern of trading and the effects which these changes produce in port facilities and in the structure and operation of the merchant fleet. In more specific detail, the changes in ports relate to the inter-relationships between land and sea transport. In the past, the high costs of inland transport, and also the small size of vessels in use, produced a dispersed pattern of ports. Inland transport costs may still be relatively important, often as an expression of time delays, and there is, in a general sense admittedly, some tendency to use the nearest port; ports too develop some measure of monopoly hinterland (Martech Consultants 1966). However, developments in inland transport have allowed widespread accessibility and lower costs so that, in theory, the possibilities of competition between ports, for containerized general cargo for example, are greatly enhanced. On the one hand it might be considered that these recent developments suggest the retention of a dispersed pattern of ports, but such a pattern could be uneconomic and inhibit ports from taking full advantage of the technological possibilities of efficient and effective operation. Moreover, it has been true in recent years that, because of its striking technological advances, the more compelling component of the sea and land transport relationship has been sea transport. This certainly would suggest a concentration of activity. Ports can now be technically more efficient and handle much greater volumes of cargo, theoretically reducing shipping costs through the use of large vessels. Such economies may then be more important than inland transport costs. However, while in the recent past it would seem that sea transport has been able, in some measure, to shape port developments and land transport networks to meet its needs, it is as well to remember that since the volume of goods in foreign trade is so small a proportion (about 10 per cent) of the total goods moved in the UK, the needs of foreign trade are unlikely to dominate inland transport developments.

Port developments have occurred and will continue to take place within certain broad limits related to physical conditions and to economic and political influences upon port operation and administration. That is, port developments continue to be influenced by considerations of *site* and of *situation*. Neither are static influences and require to be reappraised continually in the light of technical and economic changes. At most levels of operation the increased size of vessel has meant that depth limitations have had some influence on port development. Clearly, however, this has been rigorous only in the case of the exacting requirements of tanker operation and only a small proportion of the world's merchant tonnage is ever likely to be of the massive dimensions of the VLCC (very large crude carrier). The most appropriate size of vessel and the ultimate limits of vessel size will vary in different trades. Also the rate and extent of the acceptability and operation of larger vessels may vary from trade to trade. All such issues influence the extent to which depth is an important guiding factor in port development. The insularity of the UK and the number and variety of the physical sites thus provided may be seen as a major asset and one which would seem to encourage the continuation of a dispersed pattern of port activity. Note also that any limitations in this respect of the UK ports may be less obvious and less restrictive if the trade route links areas of less sophisticated port facilities; for effective operation a similar level of facilities must be available at *both* ends of the maritime route. In terms of site, particularly if the industrial potential of the port is involved but also for container operations, the nature and extent of the suitable land-site may be of as great importance as the depth of the navigable channel. Despite these variously qualified comments it may well be that physical environmental conditions of site, in so far as they affect the status of UK ports, have been reassessed rather more rigorously and to greater effect than have the economic issues of situation. In this there is a considerable measure of inertia. The commercial connections of an established port are not readily set aside. There must be a considerable momentum in the traffic flows of major UK ports outlined by Bird (1969, 284–302), although hinterlands and forelands are being reshaped in terms of the new potentials of both land and sea transport. Equally they are continuing to be shaped by particular initiatives of port authorities, by the actions of trading companies and shipowners and perhaps, almost indirectly, by public policy.

Investment At least in theory, investment decisions may be seen as subsuming in varying measure a wide range of physical, technical, economic and political influences upon port development. Many UK ports are being faced with difficult investment decisions and, at the level of capital provision required, it seems probable that everywhere, although in varying degree, the government will be increasingly involved, if only in an attempt to avoid uneconomic duplication and ensure the best use of scarce resources within a national framework. In fact, as yet, the UK government's direct involvement has been very limited. Concern over the lack of investment in British ports was one reason for the establishment of the *Committee of Inquiry* (MoT 1962); and its Report did stimulate the level of investment. In 1964, £20 million was invested and in six years from 1965–70 a total of £245 million was invested in UK ports with about one-third occurring in the nationally-owned ports. However, UK port investment has declined in real terms in the last decade and compares very unfavourably with expenditure in other areas of transport (1975 £56 million; £26 million at 1965 prices). It is of course true that

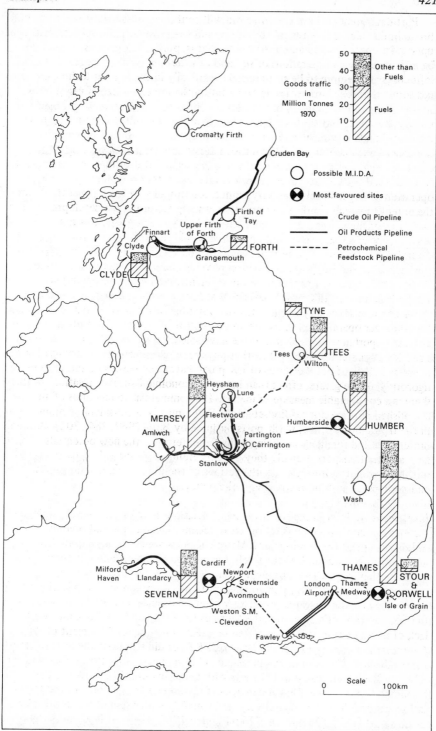

Figure 5.10   Main estuaries and MIDA sites, UK, 1974

users providing their own facilities can make an important contribution (1975 £21 million). This was still not high by NW European standards. Largely because of the make-up of the controlling boards of most British ports, the investment record in the recent past has not been good, but although doubts have been expressed about the level of managerial skills and their competence to pursue the required aggressive and forward-looking policy it would be a mistake to regard the amount of investment in the ports as an index of their efficiency. The recent financial problems of the Mersey Docks and Harbour Board underline a more widespread problem.

Clearly there is competition for investment or for government approval of investment plans which will achieve the differentiation between port facilities and schedules; that is, the difference in the *services* upon which competition between ports is based. Although there has been central control over major investment, in fact, with few exceptions, the tendency has been to encourage *all* ports. There has been no overall national plan clearly defined but nonetheless the status of ports is changing. Such changes are continually underway as the ports react variously to the new possibilities of growth and development. Thus the Tees, with developing chemical, steel and oil industries associated with major reclamation schemes, typifies the impact of the new industrial potential in ports. Felixstowe exemplifies the impact of the new transport technology in cargo-handling, having increased its trade from about 59,000 tonnes in the 1950s to 3.4 million tonnes in 1974. Felixstowe and Harwich together are now listed by the NPC for statistical purposes among the estuarial groupings as the Stour and Orwell estuary (the Haven Ports). It is as yet uncertain to what extent such changes involve an overall concentration of activity and a refining of the pattern of ports in the UK. It may be that developments will produce dissimilar results in differing regional areas. The rate and diversity of growth of industrial port activities on Teesside in the last twenty years has certainly markedly changed the relative importance of the ports of NE England. The Tees has now outstripped all rivals. The Tyne has limited prospects and is likely to be shorn further of its bulk trades. The Wear and Blyth have no certain long-term viability and the small coal ports such as Amble and Seaham Harbour have no long-term future. On the other hand, the growth of short-sea trading has revitalized some of the small ports of E Anglia, which have increased their proportionate share of UK foreign trade. The concentration of activity has been pursued more markedly in respect of bulk cargoes and industrial activity rather than in relation to general cargo-handling. Moreover, in the recent past, the flow of general cargo at the major terminals has sometimes seemed particularly vulnerable to industrial disputes. In some measure at least, overmanning and unreliability have tarnished the reputations of the large traditional ports. This has encouraged small ports which, without the bitter legacy of the past, may be well suited to the development of new patterns of trade and perhaps can operate without the burdens of the heavy costs of development land and of traffic congestion in the conurbations. Some such ports operate outside the *National Dock Labour Scheme* but this is a wider issue not related solely to small ports. A recent survey (NPC 1973) stated that the non-scheme ports offer pay and conditions which are 'reasonably comparable'. The report concludes that the recent trends in traffic (non-scheme ports handled about 20 per cent of port traffic in 1971 and their share had increased 1965—71) are not a simple matter of transfers from scheme to non-scheme ports. This is undoubtedly so; in particular, location in terms of the currently expanding trade flows is important, but it will not go unremarked that

Felixstowe, Dover and British Rail (including the port of Harwich), three of the five main non-scheme operating authorities, are among those major ports which have grown most forcefully in recent years (see table 5.10).

Change is clearly occurring although it may be questioned to what extent it is a directed and planned process. The planning procedure available to the government is in essence a negative one. The government has power to withhold investment approval under Section 9 of the *Harbours Act* (1964) for projects costing £1 million and over, and therefore it is very difficult for the *National Ports Council* in its capacity as counsellor to the Minister of Transport to envisage and maintain a coherent plan. Very often developments have been approved (as most proposals have been) as economically appropriate to individual ports but it is at least doubtful if they were in the overall best interests of the nation. It was, however, on the latter grounds that the proposal to develop at Portbury (Bristol) was refused and the reasons for the Minister's decision produced a good analysis of the wider implications of an individual port's development (MoT 1966C). The case for a planned approach to port development would seem a strong one. However, it is certainly valid to ask what kind of a dock system would have been inherited if our predecessors had had the benefits now available to us of a highly introspective economic theory with which to quench their vigorous acts of expansion on a speculative basis (Wilson 1965, 90). It is at least possible that the rate of change will be slower and certainly less ruthless as government policy and public inquiry replace commercial initiative and this may not always be in the best national interest. The planned approach may be considered to be essential, however, insofar as the implications of MIDAs go far beyond the port requirements, and must involve government in considering the potential for the port as an instrument in both regional and national planning (Jurgenson 1971). Moreover, there is no doubt that in the reshaping of the pattern of port activity there will be great redundancies of labour, services and equipment, and that the UK ports are faced in effect with a problem similar in kind, if not in scale, to the rationalization process which faced the NCB after 1948. Significant progress has been made in tackling overmanning. For example, the number of UK registered dock workers ('permanent men') was reduced from 51,646 in 1969 to 34,582 in 1974. In a wider sphere, in the port transport industry as a whole, employment was reduced by over 40,000 within the same period. Equipping the UK ports for the last quarter of the twentieth-century may well be an exciting and challenging process but it will certainly be a painful one which requires a carefully planned and almost certainly governmental approach. There is also the quite basic general point that modern port technology is such that competition could be wasteful of capital resources. Given such technology ports are *natural* monopolies and quite positive national control should be exercised over their investment activities (Garnett 1970; Klaasen and Vanhove 1971).

It seems too often the case that an individual port development is viewed in relation to its investment profitability and too rarely placed in a context aimed at minimizing the costs of the complete door-to-door transport system for flows of imports and exports for *the country as a whole*. Again, while not gainsaying the necessity for a national approach, it is sometimes questioned whether this is strictly an economic issue at all. Ports, it is said, should be constructed as a matter of policy and justified not in economic terms but in terms of the extent to which they are used. It is as yet too early to see the full implications of the impact of the contemporary revolution in transport technology upon the pattern of port activity, but it is likely that in the long evolution of seaports the 1970s may well appear as a period during which major decisions of long-term significance were taken.

V.5   Inland Waterways

The Inland waterways of the UK now perform a very limited transport function (0.1 per cent of total UK freight tonne-km) with most of the commercial traffic on rivers where the navigable channel has been regulated and locked. It is no longer appropriate to identify an inland waterways *network* for traffic purposes. The relevant stretches of waterway are in small separate sections mainly linked to major estuaries. The role of the waterways is now very largely that of a feeder to and from selected ports. The waterways demonstrate, in extreme form as far as transport is concerned, the focusing of activity upon restricted stretches of the traditionally available pattern.

The UK has never provided favourable conditions for the development of inland water transport. Even before the railway provided overwhelming competition, the effectiveness of coastal shipping in serving centres of population and industry, mainly located on tidewater, limited inland water transport. Equally fundamental, in most areas the relief of the country and especially the short distances involved are not conducive to efficient operation of this transport form. Historically the piecemeal development of canals with varying widths and capacities, and with fragmented ownership, did not encourage the functioning of a network over the longest possible distances. There has been also a secular decline in demand, quickening in the period since the Second World War, for the type of services which the inland waterways can supply. Watts (1967) pointed out that it is not common in the UK for distances to be long enough and for vessels to be large enough to counteract the disadvantages of high terminal charges. The present commercially-operated stretches of waterway reflect these circumstances. The preferred distances are rarely available but the most effective waterways are those which are able to use the larger vessels and to do so with *direct* loading from ship or factory, thus keeping terminal costs as low as possible. The traditional categories of waterway are narrow and wide (or broad) but since 1965 the British Waterways Board has recognized a two-fold division into 'commercial waterways', totalling about 547 km and 'other waterways' with very limited traffic and with functions relating to water supply and/or especially recreation and thus of no direct relevance in this context. The commercial stretches are: the Weaver navigation, related especially to canal-side industry; the Lea navigation and the lower Grand Union system, both concerned with distribution from the Port of London; the Severn system linking the Port of Bristol with the W Midlands; and the most extensive system, radiating from the Humber and including the Aire and Calder, the Sheffield and the S Yorkshire canals where the main traffic is coal, together with the Trent navigation from the sea to Nottingham, notably carrying petroleum inland.

These commercial waterways handle about 95 per cent of the traffic. The total of 3.9 million tonnes in 1974 was perhaps unduly low, being affected by external factors such as the three-day working week and industrial disputes, but even the 1973 total was less than half that of 1953. There is no doubt about the secular decline in tonnage handled and in tonne-km, especially in the 1960s (table 5.12).

The average length of haul (table 5.13) is now even less than the 27 km of 1953 which was already too low for effective inland waterways operation (BTC

TABLE 5.12

Traffic British Waterways Board, 1953–74

	Million tonnes	Million tonne-km		Million tonnes	Million tonne-km
1953	10.4	301.2	1965	8.6	216.4
1955	10.7	300.2	1967	7.2	160.9
1957	10.0	286.4	1969	6.8	140.0
1959	9.1	267.7	1971	5.4	99.7
1961	9.4	267.5	1973	4.9	89.8
1963	9.2	242.0	1974	3.8	73.1

Sources: BTC, Annual Report 1962 (London 1963); *BWB Annual Report* (1963 to date)

TABLE 5.13

Average Length of Haul, BWB, 1964–74 (km)

	1964	1969	1974
Coal, coke and patent fuel	18	17	14
Liquids in bulk	38	29	24
General merchandize	25	20	19
All freight	25	21	19
Freight conveyed by BWB fleet	64	48	40

Source: DoE (1976)

1955). The traffic in 1973 was 68 per cent bulk fuels, being 43 per cent coal and coke, and 25 per cent liquids. The remainder of the cargo, classified as general merchandize, was largely grains, oil-seeds and timber (table 5.14). Recent government attitudes and policies towards the waterways reflect, in general terms, the transport situation. The enquiries of 1955 and 1958 were still looking to commercial possibilities with a fairly widespread network and with an air of expectancy and development (BTC 1955; MoT and Civil Aviation 1958).

TABLE 5.14

Traffic Composition, BWB, 1973

Commercial waterways	1,000 tonnes	% total	1,000 tonne-km	% total
Coal, coke and patent fuel	2,067	42.7	24,687	27.8
Liquids in bulk	1,241	25.6	31,926	36.0
General merchandize	1,536	31.7	32,319	36.2
Total	4,844	100.0	88,932	100.0
Other waterways total	144		844	
Total traffic	4,988		89,776	

Source: BWB (1974) *Annual Report 1973*

The reports of the 1960s made, from a transport viewpoint, a much more realistic appraisal of the prospects of commercial operation in limited separate systems and did so with an air of retrenchment and abandonment (BWB 1964). They led, however, to financial support for the Waterways Board's total commitment, although aimed especially at its non-commercial, cruising network. The grant-in-aid in 1974 was £6 million (table 5.18). The proposals, for implementation in 1974, which seemed to demote the transport function in an administrative framework which envisaged control of waterways by ten regional authorities based particularly on catchment and water-supply areas, were not implemented and the integrity of BWB now seems secure.

The still considerable dependence upon coal traffic is not reassuring for the future of the waterways. In 1971 the gas industry decided to terminate gas-coal movement by waterways because of the progress with North Sea gas and this meant a loss of about 246,000 tonnes of traffic. Also, the liquids are threatened by pipeline competition – as has already occurred on the Severn system north of Worcester. A main positive development was the Board's introduction in 1971 of a push-tow fleet and its involvement in a BACAT (barge aboard catamaran) service begun in 1974 to link the W Riding and the Rhine. Such developments, essentially similar to LASH (ch. 5.VI.1), may perhaps have revitalized some limited sections of waterway with suitable capacity as the traffic between continental Europe and British east coast ports increased. By reason of trade union opposition, however, the BACAT service was abandoned at the end of 1975. An indication of revitalization is the planned improvement of the Sheffield and S Yorks. Navigation, which received parliamentary approval in 1974, and which will allow barges of 700 tonnes to the outskirts of Rotherham and 400 tonnes to Rotherham itself, compared with a present limitation to 90 tonnes. In the changed fuel situation it will be reaffirmed that waterways are much more efficient in terms of fuel use per tonne-km than other inland transport forms and that the commercial waterway network is clearly under-utilized. There will be no radical reappraisal but in particular areas waterways may make a useful contribution. An interesting proposal, still under investigation, involves the improvement of the lower section of the Grand Union Canal to enable commercial freight operation and relieve road congestion in London by giving access from the docks to a new trans-shipment depot west of the conurbation with access to the M1 and M4 motorways (BWB 1974).

VI   RETROSPECT AND PROSPECT: SOME DEVELOPMENTS AND PROBLEMS

VI.1 The Transport Revolution

Technological developments have played an important role in changing transport patterns in the UK in the recent past. Within the last decade it has become commonplace to refer to a transport revolution in goods transport. Changes have been very rapid and although there were precursors (e.g. the LMS Railway Co. was first to use containers in 1926 and they were used by the Ford Motor Co. to ship from Dagenham to Amsterdam in the 1930s) the main expression of the developments has been within the last ten years and the full implications are yet to be experienced. The revolution refers particularly to the changes in bulk movement and to the progressive spread of unit-load transport in increasingly integrated systems.

Important developments in bulk-handling, with widespread implications (ch. 5.V.2 and 5.V.3), concern the greatly increased *size of vessel*. Both construction costs per tonne and operating costs per tonne decrease as the dwt of the vessel increases and operating costs do so at a faster rate so that the largest vessels are most effectively and efficiently used over long distances. More specifically and in detail the advantages vary according to the type of vessel (Hallett and Randall 1970; McFadzean 1968; Hunter and Wilson 1969; Goss and Jones 1972; Hunter 1974). Oil tankers have demonstrated the most striking rise in total tonnage and in size of vessel. In 1950 only 5 per cent of the world's tanker tonnage was of vessels over 20,000 dwt, in 1969 more than 19 per cent was of vessels of over 100,000 dwt and by 1974 36 per cent was of vessels of over 200,000 dwt. Although some larger vessels are already in operation (by 1974 some thirty-four tankers of over 275,000 dwt had been built and many more were on order), it is doubtful if any main economies are to be gained by tankers of over 250,000 dwt. In the case of specialized ore-carriers the main advantages have been reaped by the time the size of vessel has reached 90,000 dwt and they may remain predominantly at about 100,000 dwt although some combined function carriers (especially the OBOs, Ore/Bulk/Oil) are operating at more than twice this size. In any event, apart from the economies of scale becoming less apparent after a certain point, there are other even less advantageous aspects of operating very large vessels which may curb the size to which they will commonly develop. Quite specifically in the case of oil-tankers the hazards of potential pollution and destructive explosions, although clearly not restricted to super tankers, are of greater impact the larger the vessel and the greater the capital risk. Doubts from these sources about supertankers are reinforced by the increased insurance premiums which have been charged following pollution claims and tanker explosions. For the tanker of 250,000 dwt insurance premiums form more than half the running costs.

A more recent and as yet restricted development which increases the flexibility and adaptability of bulk movement is the LASH (Lighter Aboard Ship) technique. In this a mother-ship carries barges (a vessel with 73 of 400 tonnes each is in service on the N Atlantic and one of 18 x 140 tonnes on the short-sea route to Europe) which are handled by the ship's own gear and proceed independently as required at the assembly and dispersal ports. Obviously this is a system which is most effective if there is an extensive and efficient inland waterway network at one or both ends of the trade route. In an elementary sense this is an intermodal system. Of much greater importance to the development of intermodal transport and central to the *transport revolution* is the container or some less formal type of unit-load transport. The tonnage of goods handled by UK ports in unit-load has increased very rapidly from 3.5 million tonnes in 1965 to 12.7 million tonnes in 1969 and 30.6 million tonnes in 1974 when it comprised one-quarter of all goods '*other than fuels*'. Commonly in the past each element of a transport chain has been concerned almost solely with its own sphere of activity although it has long been true that developments in one link of the chain tend to have implications and to promote change elsewhere. Containers presuppose a through-transport system. It was necessary that one element amongst those involved should have an overall view and take the initiative in imposing the system. For the most part this has been done by the ship-owners and appropriately so because of their pivotal position and capital resources. Nonetheless a major part of the working-out of the system, and very often its chance of success, rests with the land-based components.

An investigation of total transport costs for non-bulk cargoes from inland point to inland point between N America and W Europe suggested that 62 per cent of total cost related to sea freight of which about half was the cost of loading and discharging, 28 per cent to inland freight and 10 per cent to port charges and dues (OECD 1968). Containerization is already modifying this costing. It would appear that the ports have the most to gain and certainly in the maritime section of the trade route the results of unit-load operations can be pronounced. A considerable increase in tonnage can be handled over a single berth. Although estimates vary a total of about 100,000 tonnes per annum over the conventional berth is considered to be increased about five times by roll-on operations and by at least ten times by full containerization (Little 1967). It also follows that there is a considerable decrease in the number of vessels required for a particular traffic, that there is a decline in the requirement for port labour, that the costs of general cargo handling may well be decreased (and reflected in lower charges at least on short-sea routes where conference agreements are not involved), and that finally a speedier and more efficient service will be provided. In short, this is one of the best indications that merchant shipping has become, and seaports *must* become, increasingly capital-intensive. Although containerization has been widely developed it is not without opponents in some circumstances and certainly not without problems. The costs of conversion from conventional operation to palletization are relatively small when compared with a fully containerized system and thus palletization may be preferable on lower density routes and on shorter routes (Turner 1969). Moreover a greater proportion of general cargo can be palletized than containerized. An average load is pallet-sized (1 – 1.5 tonnes) and only 4 per cent of non-bulk dry cargo consignments weigh 10 tonnes or more (about 10 tonnes being the preferred full – 9 m – container-load). Equally basically, effective container operation requires comparable facilities and access inland for containers at *both* ends of the trade route and outstandingly it requires a suitable *two-way flow* of cargo (at present about one-third of all containers travel empty).

Containerization has not only given reality to a through-transport system between sea and land transport but also has potentially made feasible a much greater integration between rail and road transport. Containers are not new to the railway but the main development followed the Beeching proposals with the formation of the Freightliner system. The first Freightliner ran from London to Glasgow in November 1965. The Freightliner system in external trade linking the regions with Inland Container Depots (ICDs) and the ports has been referred to earlier (ch. 5.V.2). A largely separate network, necessary as the ICDs involve HM Customs and the goods are in bond, handles inland trade with twenty-three Freightliner terminals sharing between them about thirty-two two-way services linking the main centres of population (Johnson, Garnett et al 1970). Road transport of containers is involved at the terminals and is directly in competition for container traffic over the shorter distances. Even in the limited period to date there has been some readjustment in the competitive relationship between rail and road, although Freightliner has not as yet developed as British Rail forecast. It clearly shares some of the same problems discussed in terms of maritime container routes. There is, however, some evidence of integration in, for example, the road hauliers' use of Freightliner for the trunk haul operation. Air transport is not excluded from the transport revolution or from intermodal developments but air freight, especially domestically, has relatively a very small volume. Specialized freighters have increased in speed and capacity. However, while standard containers are handled, more common is the pallet-style *igloo* shaped to the cross-section of the fuselage for easy and efficient loading.

VI.2 Pipeline Development

Although an inconspicuous, indeed usually concealed, element of the transport system, pipelines have been extended rapidly in the last decade, mainly in relation to the transport of energy. The separateness and exclusiveness of the pipeline network is to some extent deceptive. From tanker to pipeline is clearly intermodal transport and there is competition between pipeline and coastal shipping and more directly between the pipeline and the railway. Pipelines undoubtedly have an increasing role in UK transport, but it must be noted that this is a role limited not only by the particular characteristics of the pipeline as a transport medium but also quite specifically limited by the size and shape of the country. The dimensions of the UK are such that the main asset of pipelines, bulk movement over long distances, cannot be fully exploited. Moreover, since there are no inland refineries, tankers can commonly provide equally cheap movement of oil, and so traditionally there have been few demands for crude oil pipelines.

Any pipeline has certain specific characteristics and a distinctive competitive potential. Both influence the involvement of pipelines in the total transport system. Most obviously pipelines are a restricted medium because of the rigidity of the route and especially in the limited range of commodities which can be transported, mainly oil, gas and some solids as slurry. Pipes are able to handle greater gradients than any other media but although they involve continuous movement at a constant rate they are invariably slow, perhaps 5–8 kmph. Pipelines are a high-capacity medium and to operate effectively need a consistent even demand (since unlike other media capital costs completely dominate pipeline transport) and preferably a high level of demand (since with increased diameter, capacity increases at a faster rate than costs) (Manners 1962, 154–63). Pipelines have the asset of potential use

TABLE 5.15

Pipelines: Oil and Petroleum, UK, 1964–74

Overland length of line, weight moved	1964	1968	1971	1974
Length of line (km)	819	1,513	1,702	2,613
Tonne/km moved (millions)	1,123	2,368	3,311	3,568

NB Excludes pipes of less than 50 km length
Source: DoE (1976)

for large-volume storage, and have a very low labour requirement. Pipeline transport costs, when appropriate comparisons are possible, are usually assessed at about equivalent to those of water transport and thus perhaps, in comparable situations, no more than one-quarter the cost of rail transport. Pipes may offer increasing competition to the railway for the movement of coal or ore as slurry, although the limited distances involved and the fact that a railway hungry for traffic will often be available must limit development.

A remnant of the extensive wartime network to supply airfields is still in use but the effective present-day pipeline network is almost entirely a product of the 1960s. Developments after the *Pipeline Act* (1962) (applicable to all pipelines over 16 km in length) took advantage of a much simplified, although still strictly controlled, procedure which previously required a private Bill in Parliament. There are three short stretches conveying gaseous oxygen and one moving chalk slurry for the Portland Cement Co. from Dunstable quarries to Rugby but most pipelines are in two broad categories: oil, indeed mainly oil products, and gas (Foster 1969). With water transport so all-embracing there has usually been little demand for crude oil pipelines. The first in the UK linked the incomparable depth advantages of Finnart on Loch Long with Grangemouth refinery in 1951 (with a new pipe in 1969). In 1975 the same refinery was linked by 208 km of pipe to Cruden Bay, the landfall of the BP Forties field and also to the new Hound Point terminal on the Forth (figs. 4.4 and 5.10). Further lengths of crude oil pipeline have been laid to feed refineries at Llandarcy (1960), Heysham (1967) and Stanlow (1976), where depth limitations prevent the use of large tankers. Overland crude oil pipelines in 1976 had an aggregate length of 640 km. The development of North Sea oil, at distances of 160 km offshore, had added a new dimension to crude oil pipelines with undersea pipes. Such pipelines, completed or well advanced, include in addition to the Forties to Cruden Bay link: Ekofisk (1975) to Teesside, Piper (1976) and Claymore to Flotta, and Brent and Ninian to Sullom Voe. The petroleum products pipelines, the main network, include stretches of the wartime network, notably, for example, linking the Isle of Grain refinery to Walton-on-Thames (and subsequently to London Airport [Heathrow]), and linking Stourport to Reading. The developments of the 1960s were essentially of similar links to meet the needs of transport and industry, for example the pipeline from Fawley to Staines and London Airport in 1963, the Thames and Mersey link with short Midlands offshoots completed in 1969, and the longest development (481 km) linking Milford Haven to Manchester, Birmingham and Nottingham (1973). Petrochemical feedstock pipelines linked Fawley to Severnside (1962) and interconnected two further main concentrations of the petrochemical industry, the Tees (Wilton), and Lancashire and Cheshire (Fleetwood, Partington, Runcorn and Stanlow) by 1968.

Oil pipelines may seem largely removed from the intermodal transport system but clearly competitive situations can arise. It is less easy to envisage such situations in respect of natural gas. However, that there can be some link with other transport media is shown by the first main length of the present natural gas pipeline system completed in 1962 from Canvey Island (Thames) to Leeds to carry Algerian methane gas brought as a refrigerated liquid by tanker. The situation was soon to be transformed by North Sea gas. In 1967 the West Sole well was linked to Easington (near Hull) and to Sheffield and the Leeds pipeline. The following year the Leman, Hewett and Indefatigable fields feeding to the coast at Bacton (Norfolk) were joined to the distribution grid at Rugby. The grid continues to spread into North and South Wales, into the South West peninsula and into eastern Scotland, then arcing west ultimately to end near Glasgow (Glenmavis). Gas from the Frigg field (352 km NE of Aberdeen) will come ashore at St Fergus near Peterhead and work is in progress on the pipelines, which will be needed by 1978, to link the old and the new natural gas supplies at Bathgate (ch. 4.I.4). The dimensions over which pipelines can operate have been stretched into the North Sea by gas and by oil. It is possible, although unlikely, that the distance restraints of insularity could be removed by under-Channel links. Nonetheless pipelines are not without the potential to re-shape some economic distributions and could certainly do so to the detriment of industrial seaports, although perhaps in most instances the advantages of the coastal site would continue to prevail.

VI.3 Complementary or Competitive Transport Media?

The UK transport situation has been always basically competitive; the media compete for traffic and thus none of them works to capacity. The costs involved, in fact the costs of having a choice of modes, are considered justified by the efficiency which the competitive situation is thought to promote. Theoretically, in this context, no control is needed to ensure that each medium operates in the most appropriate sphere. Alternatively it may be argued that the excess capacity could be avoided by rigorous planning of networks and of modal choice, embodying, for example, a decision that all heavy traffic will go by rail. Such an approach may attempt to ensure that each medium handles the traffic for which it is technically and economically most suited, but it fails to cater for a choice which is related not so much to costs as to the quality of service, which may indeed be unfavourably affected by such plans. This approach might well also prove unduly rigid, inimical to technological change, and not necessarily more efficient than a competitively based one. It would aim 'to ensure that the required transport services are provided with the minimum call on the real resources of the nation' (Gwilliam 1964, 214). The position of the transport system at any given time on the continuum between competitive and complementary extremes has tended in the period since the Second World War to be a political issue reflected in policies (ch. 5.I.3). On balance, and over a much longer period, the prevailing view has been that competition is necessary but there has invariably been a failure to pursue comparability of charges to ensure effective competition and informed choice. A basic issue in the approach to transport is often the provision of so-called *essential services*. A failure to provide such services may be adjudged to occur with either broad approach but the decision deliberately and directly to subsidize particular groups or areas is more likely to occur following a political decision aimed at a complementary approach.

The general spheres of operation of the different transport media are fairly well-established. Water transport (together with pipelines) and air transport lie at opposite ends of both cost and speed scales. While they may intrude competitively into the middle-ground in particular circumstances, this area is pre-eminently that in which the inter-relationship of rail and road has produced the most intractable transport problems of the last fifty years. It is realistic to reaffirm at the outset that since 1945 the dominance of road transport in the UK has been confirmed largely by reason of its increased economy and reliability, its ability to provide low volume transport and especially because it provides the quality of service in demand (Owen 1964, 99). There is, of course, some measure of interdependence between road and rail in the extent to which the road still serves as a feeder to the rail network. Road transport from rail terminals is not infrequently a potent cause of inner-urban congestion. It may seem also on occasions that the competition is more apparent than real. Rail freight is in some measure distinctive, a high

TABLE 5.16

British Rail: Freight moved, Average Length of Haul, 1964–74

	Freight moved (Million tonne/km)		Average length of haul (km)	
	1964	1974	1964	1974
Coal, coke	12,215	8,282	82	94
Iron and steel	5,332	3,648	114	118
Other train/wagon-load traffic	7,976	9,703	181	194
All commodities	25,523	21,633	106	128

Source: DoE (1976)

proportion being coal, iron ore and other minerals which form a very small part of road freight. Even more obviously than in the past, rail is now the transport medium of the heavy industries. To that extent its declining freight traffic is related more to changes in the national structure of industry and in the particular transport needs of heavy industry rather than to any switches in modal choice. Of course there is no doubt that the rail lost some of its most lucrative traffic to road transport in the 1930s but in the 1950s, when road freight first achieved clear dominance, modal changes of freight were not an important issue. The respective roles of rail and road have been more clearly defined in the period since 1950. However, in recent years the attempt of the railway to regain lost traffic by Freightliner operation has again widened the scope of effective competition, although it seems unlikely to affect importantly the growth of road traffic. The freight moved by train in 1974 is atypical due to industrial disputes but does show a 22 per cent increase in 'other traffic' in the preceding decade (table 5.16). In part confirming a modal split by the nature of the commodity, Edwards and Bayliss (1971) found that, while there was no conclusive influence upon choice between rail and road haulier, consignment weight was most important in explaining the distribution of traffic between these two modes. They note also, however, that 'ready availability and speed' were considered important and both increased the probability of carriage by road haulier. If the modal choice included the firm's own transport then length of haul was very clearly the main explanatory factor. There is equally evidence of a generalized split between rail and road based mainly on their most effective operating distances. Gwilliam in 1964 gave the average rail haul as about 113 km and the average road haul as about 40 km (Gwilliam 1964, 123 et seq). The average rail haul has been increased for all types of operation since 1964 but so, much more strikingly, has the road freight haul lengthened. It is estimated that at about 242 km the *direct* costs of road and of rail Freightliner are equal and that rail offers a slight saving over this distance. It is true that 70 per cent of the traffic of British Road Services is over distances of less than 242 km and this compares very closely with an estimate of 73 per cent for all road goods transport in 1974 (table 5.17). Nevertheless when 17 per cent of all road goods movement and 22 per cent of goods moved specifically by public road haulage is over distances in excess of 320 km it is clear that the modal split is being progressively blurred. (Johnson, Garnett et al 1970; Transport Holding Co. 1968).

The competitive basis between rail and road is continually changing. After the Second World War the railway was poorly equipped to meet intensified road

TABLE 5.17

Road Goods Traffic: Goods moved, by Length of Haul and Mode of Working, 1974

	(Thousand million tonne/kms) Mainly public haulage	Mainly own account	All goods	% All goods
Less than 40 km	8.1	8.0	16.2	18.0
41–80	7.7	7.8	15.5	17.2
81–160	10.7	7.6	18.3	20.4
161–240	11.1	4.4	15.5	17.2
241–322	7.5	1.9	9.4	10.5
Over 322	12.4	2.6	15.0	16.7
All distances	57.5	32.3	89.9	100.0

Source: DoE (1976)

competition, one aspect of the declining demand for its services which by the mid-1950s had seriously impaired BR's financial position. British Rail's subsequent retrenchment and reorganization has once more improved its competitive position although difficult problems remain. A main reason for BR's financial problems is usually said to be the failure to reduce the labour force sufficiently and to use those employed in the most efficient manner (Pryke and Dodgson 1976). Even by the mid-1970s some estimates suggest that the excess labour is 50,000–60,000. There is some evidence from the 1960s of increased tonnages of freight and of increases in the average length of haul, but these developments may not significantly affect the long-term trends. Minerals, especially utilizing the 'merry-go-round' continuous flow technique, and other 'whole-train' loads are the growth area for rail freight. As an example of the former, experimental running of 100-tonne wagons was begun in 1974 in trains with a pay-load of 2,000 tonnes, the largest in BR's history, carrying imported iron ore from Port Talbot to Newport. Also in 1974 the second of two 'Fletliner' schemes was agreed between BR and the London Brick Company. These services transport Fletton Bricks from near Bedford to London and to Liverpool–Manchester with a joint capacity to replace sixty heavy road vehicle movements per day. Although such developments are clearly encouraging for the railway, not even a vast expansion of railway freight would now impair the dominance of road transport. Electrification has undoubtedly strengthened the passenger-carrying role of the railway and traffic in 1974 was at the highest level for ten years. This growth is at least in part in competition with air transport, which the railway would now claim to have counteracted at distances of less than 400 km. This may be modified further by the work on the Advanced Passenger Train (APT), to be capable of 250 kph on existing tracks. This was to operate a London–Glasgow service in 1978, but a maximum speed schedule is not now expected before the 1980s.

No development by the railway, except perhaps in particular circumstances in urban areas (e.g. the Tyne–Wear PTE's Metro) can hope to compete with the personal transport of the private car, especially with the owner's usually quite unrealistic costing of the car as, in effect, do-it-yourself transport. The attraction of the private car has been importantly enhanced now that the motorways allow sustained speed, but so also have the advantages of the long-distance bus. The cost advantage of the inter-urban bus is reasonably accurately reflected in the price per mile paid by passengers which is about half that of the train. The bus journey, however, typically takes about 50 per cent longer than an express train on the same route. Road transport is the only transport form at present subject to direct legislation within the EEC although there is a declaration of intent to *harmonize* the various media. The competitive position of road transport in the UK is likely to be influenced by regulations controlling driving hours and daily km run. Such regulations have applied to international journeys since January 1973, but vigorous lobbying has successfully deferred their application to domestic journeys. An increase in the maximum weight of road goods vehicles is also in prospect following the confirmation of the UK's entry into the EEC.

Transport policies have contributed to the changing relationships between the media, although rarely positively and comprehensively facing the problems. The *Transport Act* (1968) provided a more effective base than previously available from which to achieve an effective coexistence. In a sense it contributed something to both the complementary and competitive approaches. In the rural areas, where bus services have been in decline since the early 1950s, any unprofitable routes considered to be socially necessary can be submitted to the local authority as candidates for subsidy before being withdrawn. Local authorities, however, are not eager to take up opportunities for subsidy although they have increasingly done so. The bus companies have been ordered to operate profitably so cuts and changes in services will be made and it is likely that public road transport will quickly become worse. However, in some areas a combination of postal services and bus services is increasingly accepted by local authorities faced with the provision of public transport for sparsely populated areas. One of the features of the early days of the postal service was that the mail coach carried passengers. Following the first experiment in Montgomeryshire in 1967, there are now fifty post-buses operating, thirty of them in Scotland. British Rail was similarly empowered so that, especially in the peripheries of the network which are still under threat, named services could be offered to the central government for direct subsidy. Such grants for social reasons totalled £136 million in 1974 (table 5.18).

TABLE 5.18

Transport Subsidies, 1969–74

(£ million)	1969	1970	1971	1972	1973	1974
British Rail Unremunerative passenger services grant	71	61	65	58	74	136
Road passenger transport – Local authorities subsidies	1	4	6	9	12	40
BWB – Grant-in-aid	2	2	2	3	4	6

Source: DoE (1976)

In theory both public road transport and British Rail should be able to operate more effectively and competitively as a result of these developments, but the Act does not ensure that the competition is any more nearly on a basis of true costs. It would be unwise to assume that if any action follows from the Consultation Document (DoE 1976A) it would be likely to lead quickly to a radically reformulated confrontation between road and rail. The document does consider that road freight transport does not pay its way and looks to increased taxation. It suggests further that British Rail's inter-city and London and south-east suburban passenger services should cover costs by 1981. This could only be achieved by major fare increases. Having earlier stated a need to assess the environmental effects of policy, in considering the critical issue of a possible switch of goods traffic to rail the Report fails to note that while it is true a major increase in rail freight would have little impact on total road freight, it could lead to a much greater proportional decrease in long-distance freight in large lorries and have a considerable environmental benefit.

VI.4 The Rationalization of the Ports

If the ports of the UK are to take full advantage, both in cargo handling and in industrial investment, of the technological advances in maritime transport and if also they are to compete more effectively with the ports of the north-west European interface especially from within the EEC, then a rationalization of facilities is an urgent need (NPC 1974). Such a move raises difficult decisions of investment, of choice of sites and of integration. As has been shown to have occurred, or to be necessary, in so much of UK transport, a more intense use and development of selected sections of the system is required.

The traditional problems of a port authority in seeking to initiate major capital schemes are markedly exacerbated by the present tempo of technological change in transport. A new vessel can be built within a year and the conversion of a vessel carried through in half of this time. However, to plan, build and equip a dock may take at least three years. There is, moreover, the perpetual problem that the infra-structure of a port is much longer-lasting than the life of a merchant vessel. Major mechanical equipment such as cranes and loading bridges may be written-off within twenty-five years but for quay walls and port works a period of fifty years would be more normal. It is clearly unlikely that a period of fifty years' calm will be available to port authorities to accommodate this rate of depreciation. For both these reasons the port authority must not only attempt to forecast future developments but also provide a design which is sufficiently flexible to meet unforeseen changes. Informed and planned choice of sites for development is therefore critical and this is difficult to envisage without positive government oversight, especially since government will undoubtedly be involved in the provision of capital. In contrast to the Belgian and French governments' practice of paying respectively 100 per cent and 80 per cent of port infra-structure costs, the UK government's contribution has been limited to 20 per cent of certain restricted types of port investment. This low level of direct government financial involvement has sometimes been considered a disadvantage of the UK ports compared to their continental rivals and notably, for example, with Antwerp and Rotterdam which have demonstrated so forcibly the benefits of a vigorous planned investment policy (Takel 1974; NPC 1976).

The choice of sites to be emphasized raises many problems. There is no lack of candidates. In terms of industrial development the government enquiry (ch. 5.V.3), although acknowledging other influences, paid most attention to the physical characteristics of the sites. In fact it must always be acknowledged that the established major ports with possibilities of reclamation near the sea or off-shore, will have a real and justifiable advantage. New deep-water locations to meet the exacting requirements of modern vessels are unlikely and will certainly be few and specialized. Does this mean that the list of proposed MIDA sites can be sifted and sorted; and that perhaps (in terms of their site, situation and current achievement) the Thames–Medway, Humber and Tees have a distinctive potential for industrial development possibly allowing a special place for the Cardiff–Newport location to meet the unlikely event that the depth limitation of the English Channel will ever become a serious inhibiting influence? In cargo-handling the commercial initiative of ports has given a more positive lead to influence developments and concentrate activity. This is seen clearly in the case of Southampton. Atlantic Container Lines' decision to base its transatlantic operations in the port, followed by Southampton's nomination by ACT, OCL and the Ben Line as the premier port for the Far East, its choice by the African Conference Lines and Elders' and Fyffes' decision to group all their banana and cargo operations in the port, are of main importance to the future development of Southampton. Similarly, a measure of increasing concentration has occurred through British Rail's decision to concentrate its container movements to the continent through Harwich and those to Ireland through Holyhead. These commercial initiatives require, of course, the cooperation of the port authority and ultimately, as major finance is almost invariably involved, the imprimature of public policy through the approval of the Minister of Transport.

One important development, in part government-stimulated and in essence no more than a restatement of a long-standing feature of British port activity, has been the attention given to estuarial groupings. The *Rochdale Report* (MoT 1962) focused ideas of reorganization upon the estuaries and subsequently the National Ports Council recommended amalgamations. Between 1966 and 1968 reconstituted authorities on the Clyde, Tees and Forth assumed such comprehensive estuarial responsibilities and the new Port of Tyne Authority was a similar, although incomplete, reorganization (British Railways Board Dunston Staiths remained independent). In a more limited sense, in those areas where several major undertakings are operated by the British Transport Docks Board, e.g. the Severn, the Humber and Southampton Water, more formal and more positive cooperation has enhanced the estuarial focus. The Ministry of Transport working documents which served as a basis for consultation leading up to the White Paper, *The Reorganization of the Ports* (MoT 1969B), proposed the development of eight regional port authorities with wide independence. However it had begun to seem that this suggestion was unlikely to be implemented even before the entire proposals, which were in effect a ground-plan for nationalization, were put aside at the change of government in 1970. In a more comprehensive nationalization proposal, made in 1974 as a basis for discussion, all commercial ports, not just the larger ports, were included. Many of the port authorities, for example the Public Trusts, would remain and merely be licensed by a National Ports Authority which would direct strategy. Given Britain's preoccupation with regional development since 1945, albeit with sporadic enthusiasm, it is strange that the ports have not played a more positive role. It has long seemed likely that the most appropriate development would be to create some formal link between the estuarial ports and the authorities concerned with regional development in their area. It seemed possible that the schemes for the reorganization of Local Government Areas would provide a renewed opportunity for such associations. In fact such potential remains fairly limited although importantly it includes two major expanding estuaries in Teesside (Cleveland County) and Humberside.

Apart from integrating the port activities fully with a developing regional economy the aim of these estuarial amalgamations is to rationalize the services and in so doing to specialize and to concentrate activities in a smaller number of ports to enable the full advantages of the technological advances in both land and sea transport to be achieved. Some concentration of activity is seen as critical to the achievement of an acceptable efficiency. A smaller number of ports is required to exploit the possibilities of larger vessels and of modern cargo handling. Views are divided on the measure of concentration required. The present dispersed pattern follows from the aggregate of commercial decisions and reflects a proven demand. Only a few small ports have closed since the Second World War although very few ports have been consistently successful financially. It is suggested that the physical and economic geography of the UK makes for a dispersed rather than a concentrated pattern of ports. Moreover, this may be particularly appropriate when so much traffic is across the North Sea and deep-sea trade is a continuously declining proportion, likely to be no more than a third of British exports in 1985 (NPC 1976). Within the limits of clearly uneconomic duplication of facilities it may be argued that the UK has a considerable asset in being able to sustain, and indeed develop, a dispersed pattern of port activity. The extent to which this has occurred is surely one reason why the UK has no Rotterdam although this is also a reflection of the vastly greater population and market represented by NW Europe compared with the UK. It follows equally from technological change that trans-shipment as a port operation will grow in importance. Some ports will require to settle for a function as *feeder* ports rather than as *pivot* ports in a reshaped trading pattern. Trans-shipment must now be viewed in a wider context than the UK. Trans-shipment of UK cargoes in European ports does not involve an important proportion of UK trade overall, but it is significant in particular trades, especially import trades and notably grain. Although apparently an emotive issue it must be kept in perspective. Obviously it affects only deep-sea trade and indeed to the extent that British cargo is trans-shipped the UK is sharing the situation in a large part of continental Europe (NPC 1976). It is sometimes suggested that if an adequate concentration cannot be achieved otherwise, then it might be necessary statutorily to designate ports or estuaries to handle particular geographical trading areas and in this way to concentrate traffic. In whatever way concentration is achieved there are clearly political problems to be faced at both the regional and national levels in the selection of a limited number of favoured ports. That some measure of concentration of activity might be appropriate to the rigours of competition within the EEC is perhaps suggested by the fact that the UK has about fifteen major ports while Germany, Belgium and the Netherlands have about three each. It is true that within a little more than 160 km there are the ports of Dunkirk, Zeebrugge, Ghent, Antwerp, Rotterdam and Amsterdam. However, while their hinterlands are not constrained by international boundaries, these ports remain nationally administered. On this basis the UK may be seen as oversupplied to serve a much less populous and productive hinterland than north-west Europe. It is interesting, finally, to note that within the EEC port policy is likely to remain under national jurisdiction and will not come under the Common Market Transport Policy, at least for some time (Powrie 1975).

REFERENCES

ADAMS, G (1973) *The Organisation of the British Port Transport Industry*, NPC, London
ADAMS, J G U (1970) 'Westminster, the Fourth London Airport?', *Area, 3*, 1–9
          (1971) 'London's Third Airport', *Geogrl J.*, *137*, 468–505
ALDCROFT, D H (1968) *British Railways in Transition*, London
APPLETON, J H (1962) *The Geography of Communications in GB*, London
BAGWELL, P S (1974) *The Transport Revolution from 1770*, London
BARKER, T C and SAVAGE, C I (1974) *An Economic History of Transport in Britain*, London
BEESLEY, M E, COBURN, T M and REYNOLDS, D J (1959) 'The London–Birmingham Motorway, Traffic and Economics', *Road Res. Lab. Tech. Pap. 40*, HMSO
BIRD, J H (1963) *The Major Seaports of the UK*, London
          (1969) 'Traffic Flows to and from British Seaports', *Geogr.*, *54*, 284–302
          (1971) *Seaports and Seaport Terminals*, London
BRACEY, H E (1970) *People and the Countryside*, London
BRIT. RAILWAYS BD. (1965) *The Development of the Major Railway Trunk Routes*, HMSO
BRIT. TRANSPORT COMMN. (1955) *Canals and Inland Waterways*, London
          (1955) *The Modernisation and Reequipment of British Railways*, HMSO
BRIT. WATERWAYS BD. (1964) *The Future of the Waterways*, HMSO
          (1965) *The Facts about the Waterways*, HMSO
          (1974) *Ann. Rep. and Accounts*, HMSO
BROWN, A J (1969) 'Regional Economics with Special Reference to the UK', *Econ. J.*, *79*, 759–96
BUCHANAN, C D (1963) *Traffic in Towns*, HMSO
CHISHOLM, M (1970) 'Forecasting the Generation of Freight Traffic in GB' in CHISHOLM, M et al (eds) *Regional Forecasting*, Colston Research Soc., *22*, 431–42
CHISHOLM, M and MANNERS, G (eds) (1971) *Spatial Policy Problems of the British Economy*, Cambridge
CHISHOLM, M and O'SULLIVAN, P (1973) *Freight Flows and Spatial Aspects of the British Economy*, Cambridge
CIV. AVIATION AUTH. (1970) *Passengers at London's Airports*, HMSO
          (1972) *Airport Planning – an Approach on a National Basis*, HMSO
CLOUT, H D (1972) *Rural Geography – an Introductory Survey*, London
COLLINS, M F and PHARAOH, T M (1974) *Transport Organisation in a Great City – The Case of London*, London
COMM. INQUIRY INTO CIV. AIR TRANSPORT (1969) *British Air Transport in the Seventies* (Edwards Rep.), Cmnd 4018 HMSO
COUNC. WALES and MON. (1972) *Report on the Rural Transport Problem in Wales*, Cmnd 1821 HMSO
DAWSON, R F F (1968) 'The Economic Assessment of Road Improvement Schemes', *Road Res. Lab. Tech. Pap. 48*, HMSO

DEAKIN, R M and SEWARD, T (1969) 'Productivity in Transport', *Cambridge Dept. Appl. Econ. Occ. Pap. 17*, Cambridge

DoE (1971A) *Study of Rural Transport in Devon*, HMSO

(1971B) *Study of Rural Transport in W Suffolk*, HMSO

(1972) *New Roads in Towns – Report of the Urban Motorways Committee*, HMSO

(1973A) *Urban Transport Planning – Government Observations on the Second Report of the Expenditure Committee*, Cmnd 5366 HMSO

(1973B) *Passenger Transport Statistics*, HMSO

(1973C) *Participation in Road Planning*, HMSO

(1975) *National Travel Survey 1972–3*, HMSO

(1976A) *Transport Policy: Consultation Document*, 2 vols, HMSO

(1976B) *Transport Statistics Great Britain 1964–74*, HMSO

DEPT. TRADE (1975) *Airport Strategy for GB*: Part 1 *The London Area*; Part 2 (1976) *The Regional Airports*, HMSO

DEPT. TRADE and INDUSTRY (1971) *Rep. of the Commn. on the Third London Airport* (Roskill Commn.), HMSO

DESPICHT, N (1969) *The Transport Policy of the European Communities*, London

DYOS, H J and ALDCROFT, D H (1969) *British Transport – an Economic Survey from the Seventeenth Century to the Twentieth*, Leicester

EDWARDS, S L and BAYLISS, B T (1971) *Operating Costs in Road Freight Transport*, DoE

ELLIOTT, N R (1962) 'Tyneside, a Study in the Development of an Industrial Seaport', *Tijdsch. econ. soc. Geogr.*, *53*, 225–37 and 263–72

(1966) 'The Functional Approach in Port Studies' in HOUSE, J W (ed) *Northern Geographical Essays*, Univ. Newcastle upon Tyne, 102–18

(1969) 'Hinterland and Foreland as Illustrated by the Port of Tyne', *Trans. Inst. Br. Geogr.*, *47*, 153–70

FOSTER, C D (1963) *The Transport Problem*, London

(1974) 'Transport and the Urban Environment' in ROTHENBERG, J G and HEGGIE, I G *Transport and the Urban Environment*, London, 166–91

FOSTER, C D, BAYLISS, B T and BLAKE, J L (1970) 'Comments on the London Transportation Study', *Reg. Stud.*, *4*, 63–83

FOSTER, R T (1969) 'Pipeline Development in the UK', *Geogr.*, *54*, 204–11

FULLERTON, B (1975) *The Development of British Transport Networks*, Oxford

GARNETT, H C (1970) 'Competition between Ports and Investment Planning', *Scott. J. Pol. Econ.*, *17*, 411–19

GEN. COUNC. BRIT. SHIPPING (1976) *British Shipping Statistics 1975*, London

GORDON, I R and EDWARDS, S L (1973) 'Holiday Trip Generation', *J. Transport and Econ. Policy*, 7, 153–68

GOSS, R O and JONES, C D (1972) 'Economics of Size and Dry Bulk Carriers', *Govt. Econ. Serv. Occ. Pap. 2*, London

GOVT. OF IRELAND (1957) *Report of the Committee of Inquiry into Internal Transport*, Dublin

GOVT. N IRELAND (1963) *N. Ireland Railways*, Cmnd 458 Belfast HMSO

GLC (1969) *Greater London Development Plan*, London

GREEN, F H W (1950) 'Urban Hinterlands in England and Wales – Analysis of Bus Services', *Geogrl. J.*, *116*, 64–88

(1951) 'Bus Services in the British Isles', *Geogrl. Rev.*, *41*, 645–55

GWILLIAM, K M (1964) *Transport and Public Policy*, London

GWILLIAM, K M and MACKIE, P J (1975) *Economics and Transport Policy*, London

HALL, P G (1971) 'The Roskill Argument: an Analysis', *New Society, 17*, 145–8

HALL, P G and SMITH, E (1976) *Making Better Use of Rail Ways*, Reading

HALLETT, G and RANDALL, P (1970) *Maritime Industry and Port Development in S. Wales*, Univ. Coll. Cardiff

HIBBS, J (1972) 'Maintaining Transport in Rural Areas', *J. Transport & Econ. Policy, 6*, 10–22

HIGHLANDS and ISLANDS DEV. BD. (1957 onwards) *Ann. Rep.*, Inverness

HILLMAN, M, HENDERSON, I and WHALLEY, A (1973) *Personal Mobility and Transport Policy*, London

HOUSE OF COMMONS (1952) *Hansard*, vol 501, col 490
                                        (1955) *Hansard*, vol 536, col 1095

HUNTER, E and WILSON, T B (1969) 'The Increasing Size of Tankers, Bulk Carriers and Containerships with some Implications for Port Authorities', *Res. & Tech. Bull.*, NPC, *5*, 180–224

HUNTER, T (1974) 'Recent Trends in Sizes and Dimensions of Tankers', *NPC Bulletin, 6*, 20–8

INDEPENDENT COMMN. ON TRANSPORT (1974) *Changing Directions*, London

JOHNSON, K M, GARNETT, H C et al (1970) *Final Report on Containerisation*, Univ. Glasgow & Strathclyde

JONES, L R (1931) *The Geography of London River*, London

JURGENSON, H (1971) 'The Regional Impact of Port Investments and its Consideration in Port Investment Policy' in REGUL, R (ed) *The Future of the European Ports*, Bruges, vol 2, 576–602

KLAASSEN, L H and VANHOVE, N (1971) 'Macro-economic Evaluation of Port Investment' in REGUL, R (ed) *The Future of European Ports*, Bruges, vol 2, 521–74

LITTLE, A D (1967) *Containerisation on the North Atlantic: a Port to Port Analysis*, NPC, London
                        (1970) *Transshipment in the Seventies – a Study of Container Transport*, NPC, London

McFADZEAN, F S (1968) 'The Economics of Large Tankers', *Strathclyde Lecture, March 1968*, Shell Int. Petroleum Co. Ltd., London

McKINSEY and CO. INC. (1966, 1967) *Containerisation: the Key to Low-Cost Transportation*, Rep. to Brit. Transport Docks Bd., London

MANNERS, G (1962) 'The Pipeline Revolution', *Geogr., 47*, 154–63

MANSFIELD, N W (1969) 'Recreational Trip Generation', *J. Transport & Econ. Policy, 3*, 152–64

MARSHALL, A (1890) *Principles of Economics*, London

MARTECH CONSULTANTS LTD. (1966) *Britain's Foreign Trade: a summary of the Report prepared for the Port of London Authority covering Britain's Overseas Trade*, London

MINIST. CIV. AVIATION (1945) *British Air Services*, Cmnd 6712, HMSO
                                    (1953) *London's Airports*, Cmnd 8902 HMSO
                                    (1961) *Civil Aerodromes and Air Navigational Services*,
        Cmnd 1437 HMSO

MINIST. TRANSPORT (1959) *Reappraisal of the Plan for the Modernisation and Reequipment of British Railways*, Cmnd 813 HMSO
    (1960) *Reorganisation of the Nationalised Transport Undertakings*, Cmnd 1248 HMSO
    (1961) *Report on Rural Bus Services*, HMSO
    (1962) *Report of the committee of Inquiry into the Major Seaports of GB* (Rochdale Report), Cmnd 1824 HMSO
    (1963A) *Rural Transport Surveys*, HMSO
    (1963B) *The Reshaping of British Railways* (Beeching Report), HMSO
    (1966A) *Survey of Road Goods Transport 1962, Final Results and Geographical Analysis*, HMSO
    (1966B) *Transport Policy*, Cmnd 3057 HMSO
    (1966C) *Portbury: Reasons for the Minister's Decision not to Authorise the Construction of a New Dock at Portbury, Bristol*, HMSO
    (1967A) *British Railways Network for Development*, HMSO
    (1967B) *Public Transport and Traffic*, Cmnd 3481 HMSO
    (1967C) *Railway Policy*, Cmnd 3439 HMSO
    (1967D) *The Transport of Freight*, Cmnd 3470 HMSO
    (1969A) *Roads for the Future, a New Interurban Plan*, HMSO
    (1969B) *The Reorganisation of the Ports*, Cmnd 3903 HMSO
    (1970) *Roads for the Future, the New Interurban Plan for England*, Cmnd 4369 HMSO
    (1973) *Annual Rep. and Accounts*, HMSO
    (1975) *Annual Rep. and Accounts*, HMSO
MINIST. TRANSPORT and CIV. AVIATION (1958) *Report of the Committee of Inquiry into Inland Waterways*, Cmnd 486 HMSO
MISHAN, E J (1970) 'What is Wrong with Roskill?', *J. Transport & Econ. Policy*, 4, 221–34
MOSSÉ, R (1974) 'An Introduction to Urban Transportation Problems' in ROTHENBERG, J G and HEGGIE, I G, *Transport and the Urban Environment*, London
MUNBY, D L (1954) 'Transport Costs in the North of Scotland', *Scott. J. Pol. Econ.*, 1, 75–95
    (1968) *Transport, Selected Readings*, London
NAT. PORTS COUNC. (annually) *Digest of Port Statistics*, London
    (1969) *Port Progress Report*, London
    (1973) *Survey of Non-Scheme Ports and Wharves*, Final Report, London
    (1974) *Comparison of the Costs of Continental and British Ports*, London
    (1976) 'Port Perspectives 1976', *NPC Bull.*, 9
O'DELL, A C (1966) Highlands and Islands Developments, *Scott. Geogr. Mag.*, 82, 8–16
OECD (1968) *Ocean Freight Rates as Part of Total Transport Costs*, HMSO
OWEN, W (1964) *Strategy for Mobility*, The Brookings Institution, Washington

PATERSON, J H (1972) *Land, Work and Resources*, London
PATMORE, J A (1966) 'The Contraction of the Network of Railway Passenger
    Services in England and Wales 1936–62', *Trans. Inst. Br. Geogr.*, *38*, 105–19
            (1972) 'New Directions for Transport' in CHISHOLM, M (ed)
    Resources for Britain's Future, London, 50–61
POLLINS, H (1971) *Britain's Railways – an Industrial History*, Newton Abbot
POWRIE, P J (1975) 'The Community and the Ports', *NPC Bull.*, *7*, 3–17
PRESTON, M H and REES, R (1970) *Maritime Industrial Areas: a Preliminary
    Report*, NPC, London
PRYKE, R J and DODGSON, J (1976) *The Rail Problem*, London
PUBL. GEN. ACTS See list p. 516
PULLING, L and SPEAKMAN, C (1974) 'The Impact on Rural Life of Declining
    Public Transport Services for Communities and Individuals' in INDEPENDENT
    COMMN. ON TRANSPORT *Changing Directions*, London
RAMBLERS ASSOCN. (1971) *Rural Transport in Crisis*, London
REYNOLDS, D J (1960) 'The Assessment of Priority for Road Improvements',
    Road Res. Lab. Tech. Pap. 48, HMSO
RIDLEY, T M and TRESIDDER, J O (1970) 'The London Transportation Study
    and Beyond', *Reg. Stud.*, *4*, 1, 63–83
ROYAL COMMN. CANALS and WATERWAYS (1909) *Report*, Cmnd 4979
    HMSO
ROYAL COMMN. TRANSPORT (1930) *Final Report*, Cmnd 3751, HMSO
RURAL DISTRICT COUNC. ASSOCN. (1971) *Rural Transport, What Future
    Now?*, London
SAVAGE, C I (1966) *An Economic History of Transport*, London
SCHAEFFER, K H and SCLAR, E (1975) *Access for All*, London
SCOTT. DEPT. AGRIC. (1967) *Report of the Highland Transport Board on
    Highland Transport Services*, Edinburgh HMSO
SCOTT. DEV. DEPT. (1963) *Central Scotland, a Programme for Development and
    Growth*, Cmnd 2188 Edinburgh HMSO
SCOTT. OFF. (1964) *A Programme of Highland Development*, Cmnd 7976
    Edinburgh HMSO
            (1969) *Scottish Roads in the 1970s*, Cmnd 3953 Edinburgh HMSO
SEALY, K R (1955) 'London's Airports and the Geography of Airport Location',
    Geogr., *40*, 255–65
            (1967A) 'Stanstead and Airport Planning', *Geogrl. J.*, *133*, 350–4
            (1967B) 'The Siting and Development of British Airports', *Geogrl. J.*,
    133, 148–78
            (1976) 'Airport Planning and Airport Strategy', *Theory and Practice
    in Geography*, Oxford
SEC. STATE IND., TRADE and REG. DEV. (1963) *The North East: a Programme
    for Regional Development and Growth*, Cmnd 2206 HMSO
SHARP, C (1965) *The Problem of Transport*, Oxford
SHERRINGTON, C E R (1928) *The Economics of Rail Transport in GB*,
    London
SMITH, W (1949) *An Economic Geography of GB*, London
SNAITH, W R, ROBINSON, S E and MENNEAR, D (1957) *The Rural Transport
    Problem in Mid-Northumberland*, Northumd. Rural Community Counc.,
    Newcastle upon Tyne

SOLESBURY, W and TOWNSEND, A (1970) 'Transportation Studies and British Planning Practice', *Tn Plann. Rev.*, *41*, 63–80

STARKIE, D N M (1973) 'Transportation Planning and Public Policy' in DIAMOND, D and McCLOUGHLIN, J B (eds) *Progress in Planning*, London, *1*, 313–91

(1976) *Transportation Planning, Policy and Analysis*, Oxford

TAAFE, E J (1956) 'Air Transport and United States Urban Distribution', *Geogrl. Rev.*, *46*, 219–39

(1962) 'The Urban Hierarchy, an Air Passenger Definition', *Econ. Geogr.*, *38*, 1–14

TAKEL, E E (1974) *Industrial Port Development*, Bristol

TANNER, J C (1963) 'Car and Motorcycle Ownership in the Counties of GB, 1960', *Jl. R. Statist. Soc.*, Ser. *A*, *126*, 276–84

(1974) 'Forecasts of Vehicles and Traffic in Great Britain, 1974 Revision', *Traffic and Road Res. Lab., LR 650*

THOMAS, D St J (1963) *The Rural Transport Problem*, London

THOMSON, D C and GRIMBLE, L (1968) *The Future of the Highlands*, London

THOMSON, A W J and HUNTER, L C (1973) *The Nationalized Transport Industries*, London

TRANSPORT HOLDING CO. (1968) *Ann. Rep.*, London

TREASURY (1975) *Public Expenditure Survey, 1969–79*, Cmnd 5879 HMSO

TURNER, N I (1969) 'For and Against: Containers, Pallets and Roll-on, Roll-off', *Dock and Harbour Auth.*, *49*, 389–90

TURNOCK, D (1965) 'Hebridean Car Ferries', *Geogr.*, *50*, 347–8

(1970) *Patterns of Highland Development*, London

WAGLE, B V (1968) 'A Statistical Analysis of Car Ownership in GB and a Forecast for 1975', *J. Inst. Petrol.*, *54*, 44–9

WALKER, G (1947) *Road and Rail*, London

WALLACE, I (1974) 'The Relationship between Freight Transport Organisation and Industrial Linkage in Britain', *Trans. Inst. Br. Geogr.*, *62*, 25–43

WALTERS, A A (1968) *Integration in Freight Transport*, London

WATTS, H D (1967) 'The Inland Waterways of the UK', *Econ. Geogr.*, *43*, 303–13

WELSH OFF. (1967) *Wales, The Way Ahead*, Cmnd 3334 Cardiff HMSO

WHITBY, M C et al (1974) *Rural Resource Development*, London

WILSON, A G et al (1969) 'The Calibration and Testing of the SELNEC Transport Model', *Reg. Stud.*, *3*, 337–50

WILSON, G A (1965) 'The Effect on Land Transport Systems of Ports and Water Transport', *Dock & Harbour Auth.*, *46*, 537, 89–96

6

The Urban System

I   INTRODUCTION

The UK is one of the most highly urbanized nations, in which the urban settlements collectively compose an extremely complex structure or system, in the sense that the hundreds of urban centres that comprise it are given a unity and coherence by their inter-connection and inter-dependence. This system of cities, towns and villages, because of its long settlement history, its rapid industrialization in the nineteenth century, and the massive impact of social, economic and technological change in the twentieth century, presents elements of both continuity and change. The social life of the nation is largely conducted through its urban centres, which are also the essential foci that articulate its economic endeavours. Significant regional variations in the between-town comparisons or within-town differences, contribute a further element of diversity (Carter 1965; McWilliam 1975). This great complexity and variety of the urban system creates considerable difficulty for any description and explanation.

The approach here is to stress the mechanisms or processes which, through time, have been responsible for creating the distribution of the varied towns and cities of today's urban system. This makes it possible to convey both a general understanding and an explanation of particular cases. Most attention is given to large cities rather than small towns, since not only are the former socially and economically dominant but they most appropriately typify the British urban system, dominated as it is by the Victorian city created in the last century and somewhat modified in this.

The city or town can be defined in two rather different ways. In a purely physical sense an urban place means an area of buildings designed for specialized functions, while in a functional sense an urban place is one that performs urban activities, manufacturing, commerce and administration. The people who perform these activities are urban and the area in which they live as well as work would also be defined as urban in consequence. Until almost the end of the nineteenth century these two definitions, physical and functional, coincided; increasingly in modern times they do not. The distinction between settlement form and settlement function is reflected in this chapter in the separate accounts or urban structure (section II) and urban function (section III). Section IV discusses the way in which the UK, since 1945, has attempted to engineer urban change in the public interest to overcome particular problems, largely legacies from the nineteenth century.

I.1   Definitions

Urbanization is a multi-faceted phenomenon and it is difficult to give a concise definition of an urban place by a single criterion, in spite of the everyday use of terms such as metropolis, city or town. In the UK settlements called urban clearly possess all the significant physical and functional attributes regarded internationally as pertaining to an 'urban' place, and such a multi-criteria definition includes almost all the nucleated settlements. The seven criteria most used are (1) population size (exceeding a minimum usually of the order of 1,000 to 2,500) and population density (the minimum figure varies greatly because of the influence of arbitrary boundary definition); (2) marked spatial differentiation of land uses, giving rise to functional areas; (3) density of development, usually measured as a ratio between the floor-space provided in such buildings as houses, factories, offices, schools, etc. and their site area; (4) the great intensity of the network of purpose-built transport and communication facilities; (5) the occupational structure of the inhabitants, characterized by a few farmers, fishermen and foresters and a high proportion of service workers (normally in Britain the dominant group, and in many towns over 50 per cent of the total work-force); (6) the existence of a legal or civic identity, usually conferring limited rights and responsibilities of administration and government; and (7) impersonal relationships characterizing much face-to-face contact of the inhabitants, e.g. people met at work are usually different from those met while engaged in other activities, and during each day everyone expects to have contact with many people who will be total strangers.

Faced with obvious measurement difficulties, boundary problems in applying these criteria and the near impossibility of combining them, official definitions, not surprisingly, have usually been based on criterion (6) which provides a precise limit, normally an administrative boundary. Though convenient to the data-gatherer, this practice creates major difficulties for the analysis and description of urban systems. The actual boundaries are not located consistently, frequently reflecting property boundaries fixed in the distant past, and thus making inter-urban comparisons (especially of density) very difficult to interpret. The boundary represents the granting of chartered rights by an often lengthy and cumbersome legal process, originally by the monarch or feudal lord in the middle ages or subsequently by Parliament, or its appointed agency such as the Local Boundary Commission of the 1950s. There is thus a marked tendency for the official designation and delimitation of a town to lag in time behind the actual physical reality. From the 1880s until the 1972 reform of local government (ch. 1.IV.3), the resistance by the largely rural counties to the areal extension of towns and cities resulted in large-scale under-bounding: that is, the administratively defined urban place was considerably smaller in extent than the actual pattern of 'bricks and mortar'. Population living in these physical extensions of the city, adjacent to but beyond the city limits, were not included in the population of the city, and, depending on the status of the administrative unit in which they lived, may not even have been included as urban population. This difficulty of under-bounding associated with the official definition can be seen from the fact that in the decade 1951—61 the rural districts of England and Wales increased in population more than twice as fast as the urban areas, and in the decade 1961—71 seven times as fast as the urban areas. The explanation of this paradox is, of course, that rural districts were increasingly invaded by suburban development as the expansion of towns crossed administrative boundaries. The third major difficulty is that comparability through time is very difficult to establish because of the instability of the spatial units consequent on the slow but steady adaptation of boundaries, sometimes resulting in the disappearance or appearance of entire areas.

Between 1951 and 1961 there was a net gain of twenty-eight new urban areas in the census.

Nevertheless, in 1971, despite the certainty of substantial underestimating, the censuses of population for England and Wales, Scotland and N Ireland recorded an urban population (i.e. residents in administrative areas described as urban) of 43,084,000, equivalent to 77.8 per cent of the total UK population (table 2.3). In England, Wales and N Ireland, this urban population comprised the residents of county, municipal, and London boroughs and urban districts, while in Scotland cities, large and small burghs and selected districts of county were included. In the 1981 census for England, Wales and Scotland these definitions will have to be revised in the light of the local government structure that now exists. As a comparison with this official measure of urbanization it should be noted that less than 2 per cent (1.7) of the employed population work in agriculture, fishing or forestry, which suggests an 'urban' work force of 98 per cent of the total.

There are two main ways of assessing the reality of urbanization in the UK: first, by the use of specific criteria to establish the extent of the *continuously built-up area* and, secondly, to attempt to establish a *functional* concept in contrast to this more obvious physical concept. Following suggestions by Geddes (1915) and later by Fawcett (1932), the 1951 Census of Population identified seven conurbations, which it defined in the following terms:

> 'a local authority should be considered for inclusion in a conurbation to whose focal centre it was strongly attached as a centre for work, shopping, higher education, sports or entertainment, and consideration should be given to population density' (GRO 1956).

Although based primarily on physical aspects, there is a clear attempt to recognize functional elements by the concern shown for ideas of association, interdependence and circulation, and, despite criticisms of the intuitive process of deciding which local authority areas to include (Self 1957; Carter 1972), they bear a close resemblance to the Metropolitan Counties established in 1974.

Metropolitan Areas

The functional definition of urban areas in Britain has not yet been formally accepted by the Census authorities (as it has in the USA), but all individual studies have in common an underlying *metropolitan* concept of urbanization. Economic activity is very heavily concentrated in a small number of large towns and cities which, as a consequence, exert a powerful influence on the daily pattern of life over a surrounding area extending well beyond their own administrative boundaries. Economic activity and the settlement pattern combine to create these concentrations of people, goods, information and movement, now found all over the industrial world. With only minor variation they are composed of an urban core with a high density of population, and especially of employment, surrounded by rings in which the density of population and employment decline with increasing distance from the core, until a wholly rural area is encountered. At this point the interest of the local population in the jobs, services and facilities of the now distant urban core is so low that no real relationship can be said to exist. Defined by this social and economic 'watershed' is an entity whose cohesion derives from the social and economic interaction that exists and operates within it. It is these city-focused areas to which the title city-region has been given by several authors (Diamond and Edwards 1975; R. Commn. Local Govt. 1969; Wise 1966).

The most thorough application of the concept in Britain is represented by the devising and delimitation of 'Standard Metropolitan Labour Areas' (SMLA) and 'Metropolitan Economic Labour Areas' (MELA) (Hall et al 1973) in a study of post-war urban growth in England and Wales. In this study, Hall translates the American Standard Metropolitan Statistical Area into a British setting, using census of population statistics because reasonably comparable data on residence, employment and journey to work are available over a long period. He argues:

'There is a certain logic in relying upon them: together, they present an integrated picture of the two most important within-place activities in most people's lives, in terms of the time devoted to them, together with a between-place function that relates them together. More than this, they focus on those relationships likely to be of great importance in the study of urban growth processes: the job, the home, and the journey between the two. If one is seeking a logically-based geographical framework for a functional urban area, within which to study the physical facts of urban growth, a metropolitan area defined in these terms seems the most promising one.'

Whatever their name – city-region, metropolitan region or SMLA – these areas are essentially employment cores and their commuting hinterlands. The major definitional difficulties associated with them are two-fold: How should the core be defined – in land use or employment terms, with a minimum density or not – and, secondly, what should be the cut-off value for the outer edge of the commuting zone? Hall's SMLAs extend outwards from the core, defined as a local authority with an employment density of over twelve employees per ha or a total employment of over 20,000, to include all areas from which more than 15 per cent of the economically active population commute to the core. The employment core and commuting hinterland must have a total population of 70,000 persons or more. The fact that these statistical criteria must be applied to local authority areas to compile the SMLAs introduces an unavoidably capricious element; the overall similarity of the different investigations is revealed in table 6.1.

An accurate and standardized definition of urban places is ultimately linked to the spatial quality of the basic data. The replacement of the present highly variable system of local authority areas by standard quadrat units based on the national grid is being experimented with by the General Register Office, using 1971 census data. Meanwhile one must remain aware of the limitations of current data, and appreciate the range of scale at which the geographical analysis of urban Britain is conducted. Thus studies of physical urbanization based on land use can be either at the inter-urban scale, as in an analysis of the amount of urban land in each economic region, or at the intra-urban scale, as in a study of the internal differentiation of land uses in one city. Equally, studies of functional urbanization can be either inter-city in scale, as in regional migration analysis, or intra-city in scale, as in town traffic-flow studies. The fundamental geographical significance of this scale difference was captured in Berry's (1964) plea for 'geographers to examine each city as a system with a system of cities'.

TABLE 6.1

Some Metropolitan Definitions in England and Wales

Author and name	Date of definition data	No.	Largest (000s)		Smallest (000s)	
1. Schnore (Metropolitan Area)	1951	52	London	10,283	Gloucester	104
2. Hall et al (SMLA)	1966	100	London	9,157	Stafford	66
3. Drewett et al (SMLA)	1966	115	London*	8,837	Ellesmere Port*	62
4. Diamond (Metropolitan Region)	1966	50	London*	12,811	Carlisle*	101
5. Senior (City Region)	various	35**	London***	7,380	Carlisle***	157

*   population at 1971
**   Wales excluded
*** population at 1969
Sources: 1 *Econ. Geogr.*, (1962) *38* 215–33
                2 *The Containment of Urban England*, vol I, 151
                3 *British Cities* (1976), DoE
                4 *Business in Britain: a management planning atlas*
                5 *Roy. Commn. on Local Govt. in England*, vol.II, Cmnd 4040, I

I.2   Urbanization in Britain

Both the sequence of events that comprise British urban history and the diverse topographical conditions, together with evolving social structure, through their endless interaction with each other create jointly a context which has given the process of urbanization its character in Britain. Whether the town arose or expanded, as elsewhere, to fulfil a defence role, a socio-political role in organizing society, a trade role or an industrial or mining role, it is the subtle and diverse influence of a combination of time, place, and culture that fashioned the outcome at both the intra-urban and the inter-urban scales. Indeed, it is difficult to imagine in just how many different ways our island coastline, with its positive and negative aspects, and the domination in politics since Cromwell's time by the merchant class not the aristocracy, has influenced both the distribution of towns and their morphology. A different but vivid contemporary example is surely the immense effort made by civic authorities in Britain since 1955 to modernize their town centres (section IV) rather than follow the American example of abandoning them to decay as decentralization proceeds. The examples could be multiplied endlessly, since it would be no great exaggeration to say that the whole of the nation's history could be discovered from a careful investigation of the present urban system.

Even more than the countryside towns present palimpsests which record the past activities of society in the contemporary scene. In any town with a long history an imprint is left on the urban morphology by the organization and aims of past society and the functioning of past technology. Often the successive phases of history result in concentric rings of development only partly obliterating the contribution of earlier periods. Saxon, if not Roman, sites, adapted to Norman usage and medieval growth, followed sometimes by eighteenth-century development in the grand manner and frequently by nineteenth-century factory-cum-housing development, ringed by inter-war and post-war housing estates, tell a common story and describe a frequent pattern. Sometimes the evidence is clear in an entire district of a town, sometimes only faint traces remain in the survival of an individual building or in the alignment of the street pattern.

Just as form is a rough record of past activities at the intra-urban scale, so is the distribution of settlements a record at the inter-urban scale. The market squares in the frequent minor town centres on any main road in Lowland England are a forceful reminder that the last thing a medieval borough wanted was a by-pass. Without its castle towns and English bastides, Wales would be virtually devoid of urban centres, and in parts of C Scotland, Lancashire and Durham a very distinctive mining settlement pattern continues to exist after the end of local coal production. Not all towns can have their location accounted for in such practical terms: Harewood, Milton Abbas, Fochabers and Inverary are all where they are because it suited their aristocratic founders that it should be so. Each replaced an older settlement that did not suit the owner's taste or fancy.

The early establishment of strong central government in England and Wales had particular significance in creating an urban personality so different from that of nearby France. It not only encouraged the establishment of towns but it discouraged the renewal of early medieval town walls, and many pre-Victorian towns which arose with the development of trade, handicraft industries or early mining were never walled. This allowed England to develop a low density (usually two-storey) terrace or cottage housing style which has led today to the vast tracts of semi-detached suburban villas with garden plots at back and front, which continental Europeans regard as quintessentially English. It was during the vast urban expansion in the mid-nineteenth century that this English trait became so obvious, in contrast to the Scottish fashion of building four-storey blocks of flats, still referred to today (in the original French) as tenements.

Two reasons help to explain why this accretionary characteristic developed so strongly in British towns. The durability of the urban fabric is not itself sufficient explanation, though clearly relevant; the more fundamental cause is the nature of private rights in property. At least since the Domesday Book, the thorough and accurate recording of the ownership of land has meant that property boundaries, once established, are extremely difficult to alter, and especially so if alteration of a street alignment is a likely consequence. Thus in the town centre, where economic pressure for change is often greatest, the town plan, because of the density of the street network, is most resistant to change. Buildings which can be adapted and even replaced entirely are less resistant to change, and land use (or more strictly floor use) is the most adaptable element in the townscape. Thus strong private rights in property have stimulated growth by peripheral expansion and have required Parliament's permission when exceptionally the society has wished to over-ride these rights, as for railway construction or, after 1947, for comprehensive slum clearance. Nor should it be forgotten that the contemporary method for managing this balance between peripheral growth and internal restructuring, namely town planning, has elaborate legal and administrative procedures designed expressly to protect legitimate individual rights in property.

The second reason for the built-up area in both its functional organization and its physical townscape to become an accumulated record of social and economic development is that any existing town has great attractions for new development because of its many existing facilities and services. Rather than start from scratch, advantage was usually taken of the nodality and the labour supply of a pre-existing settlement. Thus, given the very widespread distribution of towns throughout the UK by the end of the eighteenth century (including market towns, small industrial centres, fishing and commercial ports, coastal and inland spas), there was a strong tendency throughout the industrial revolution and since for factories and houses to be attached to existing towns, even if this profoundly altered their functional and morphological character. Only the street pattern indicates today where the pre-industrial town was located in Birmingham or Glasgow or Newcastle, which were all sizeable centres by 1750. The major exceptions to this general principle were towns located on new sites to serve as ports (e.g. Middlesbrough), mining settlements (e.g. Coatbridge) or resorts (e.g. Skegness); the pull of the natural resource to be exploited outweighed any disadvantages, and often the original layout was conceived and designed as a New Town (Bell and Bell 1972). It is interesting to note, however, that of the official New Towns started since 1946, only three (Aycliffe, Peterlee and Glenrothes) can really be regarded as 'green-field' sites with populations at the date of designation of less than 1,000, and that the most recent are more accurately des-described as town expansions (section IV, p. 493).

The single most important conclusion to be drawn from this discussion of the nature of urbanization in Britain is the great importance of past events for an explanation of the present situation. A graphic illustration of this was given when Sir Halford Mackinder (1919) said,

> 'There is one thing that can be said with certainty and it is that the geographical circumstances which in the past have conduced to the growth of the city, would not in this twentieth century suffice to create anew in this locality a great centre of activity, if for any reason, whether of military defeat or economic strife, Glasgow were now to cease to flourish.'

The numerous urban problems that claim so much attention and generate so much discussion today necessarily have their roots in the evolution of the urban system and owe their existence to an inheritance from the past. Further, all the possible solutions, social, economic, spatial or technological, or more likely some combination of these, must be compatible with the existing urban system, whose diversity, spatial spread and socio-economic importance is now the major influence on its own future development. Both change and resistance to change are simultaneously fundamental features of the British urban system.

I.3   An Overview

The urban population is resident in certainly more than 1,200 urban places in the UK, varying greatly in size and distributed in an irregular pattern, despite the existence of apparent similarity in some instances — Oxford and Cambridge, Southport and Eastbourne, Darlington and Crewe, Leicester and Nottingham, Ely and Wells. The average density of urban places is considerable and the actual distance between any centre and the nearest centre of equal or greater importance is usually not more than an hour or two's journey at the most. There are multiple, high capacity connections between all the centres, road, rail and telecommunication links, and each town is therefore deeply embedded in the national system and is frequently, rapidly and substantially influenced by, and in turn influences, what happens in other towns. There is little isolation, and overwhelming integration in the British urban system. Although the townscape is dominated by Victorian and post-Victorian buildings, especially in the largest centres there still remain hundreds of smaller towns with significant pre-Victorian elements which add significantly to their individuality. Again, although very few inhabited areas are more than 30 km from a town of 10,000 persons or more, the vast majority of the nation's population live within 50 km of the dozen largest centres.

London is not only the capital, the largest and the most important centre of all, but has been the primate city for a very long time indeed. It is the only member of the British urban system which can truly be called a world metropolis, and while this brings benefit to the nation and to Londoners, there are immense problems of management and planning in maintaining the diverse facilities that will allow it to continue in this role. As an illustration, the Church authorities have recently sought professional advice to devise a pedestrian flow arrangement which can cope with the four million annual visitors that Westminster Abbey now attracts!

A list of major provincial centres always includes Birmingham, Manchester, Liverpool, Leeds, Glasgow and Newcastle upon Tyne, and many authorities have included Edinburgh, Bristol and Nottingham, and some Sheffield, Leicester, Belfast and Cardiff. The character of the regions dominated by these major cities differs and is reflected clearly in the number, function and spatial pattern of the urban centres. Lancashire's cotton towns are never confused with the Black Country centres, which are as different again from the outer metropolitan area centres that ring London from Southend in the east to Reading and Guildford.

At the lower end of the size range are more than 300 towns with fewer than 10,000 persons which again show marked regional variations (Best and Rodgers 1973). Interestingly, although average population size was the same, the average urban area (housing, schools, industry, and public open space) is 29 ha per 1,000 people in centres in the Highland Zone (essentially north and west Britain) compared to as much as 39 ha per 1,000 in the Lowland Zone. Thus in the south and east of Britain on average each 100 people consume one ha more of urban land than people living in the north and west.

In the face of this contrast between world metropolis and overgrown village the least misleading generalization is the Standard Metropolitan Labour Area. Fig. 6.1 shows the pattern of SMLAs in the UK, 128 in all in 1971, accounting for just over 80 per cent of the total population. If the boundaries of these SMLAs are extended to include all local authority areas sending commuters to the 128 urban cores (thus forming what Hall calls MELAs), then some 97 per cent of the UK population is included, and half of this was accounted for by the core areas. Some indication of the dynamism of this sub-system is indicated in fig. 6.2, which shows the changing order of all SMLAs ranked according to population in 1951, 1961 and 1971. The authors of the study note that 'the most striking feature is the continuity of change between the two decades' (DoE 1976).

Examination of the pattern of growth and decline in employment and population within these SMLAs led Hall to suggest a four-stage model of British urban development in which most centres are now in stage three, but a few of the bigger metropolitan areas have reached the later stage (Hall 1971). In the first stage of the model, some time in the nineteenth century, both people and jobs concentrated in the cores of the metropolitan area; the ring was strictly non-existent, and the area later to be incorporated in the ring was rural, in both a functional and a physical sense, and it lost population to the town.

In the second stage, roughly 1900–50, because of greater mobility and the

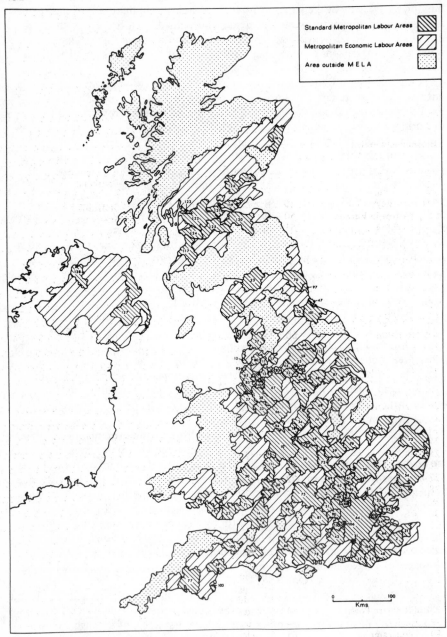

Figure 6.1   Metropolitan structure, UK, 1971
              Standard Metropolitan Labour Areas: 1 Aldershot, 2 . . . 128 Londonderry (see
              table p. 453 for full list)
              Source: *British Cities: Urban Population and Employment Trends 1951–71*, 1976
              Res. Rep. *10*, DoE

England and Wales

1	Aldershot	46	Harrogate	91	Southampton
2	Ashford	47	Hartlepool	92	Southend
3	Aylesbury	48	Hastings	93	Southport
4	Barnsley	49	Hemel Hempstead	94	Stafford
5	Barrow-in-Furness	50	Hereford	95	Stevenage
6	Basildon	51	High Wycombe	96	Stoke
7	Basingstoke	52	Huddersfield	97	Sunderland
8	Bath	53	Hull	98	Swansea
9	Bedford	54	Ipswich	99	Swindon
10	Birmingham	55	Kidderminster	100	Taunton
11	Blackburn	56	King's Lynn	101	Teeside
12	Blackpool	57	Lancaster	102	Thurrock
13	Bolton	58	Leeds	103	Torquay
14	Bournemouth	59	Leicester	104	Tunbridge Wells
15	Brighton	60	Leigh	105	Wakefield
16	Bristol	61	Letchworth	106	Walton & Weybridge
17	Burnley	62	Lincoln	107	Warrington
18	Burton-on-Trent	63	Liverpool	108	Watford
19	Bury	64	London	109	Wigan
20	Cambridge	65	Luton	110	Woking
21	Canterbury	66	Maidstone	111	Worcester
22	Cardiff	67	Manchester	112	Workington
23	Carlisle	68	Mansfield	113	Worthing
24	Chatham	69	Milton Keynes	114	Yeovil
25	Chelmsford	70	Newcastle	115	York
26	Cheltenham	71	Newport		
27	Chester	72	Northampton		
28	Colchester	73	Norwich	**Scotland**	
29	Corby	74	Nottingham		
30	Coventry	75	Oxford	116	Aberdeen
31	Crawley	76	Peterborough	117	Ayr
32	Crewe	77	Plymouth	118	Dundee
33	Darlington	78	Portsmouth	119	Dunfermline
34	Derby	79	Port Talbot	120	Edinburgh
35	Dewsbury	80	Preston	121	Falkirk
36	Doncaster	81	Reading	122	Glasgow
37	Eastbourne	82	Rhondda	123	Greenock
38	Ellesmere Port	83	Rochdale	124	Kilmarnock
39	Exeter	84	St Albans	125	Motherwell
40	Gloucester	85	St Helens	126	Perth
41	Great Yarmouth	86	Salisbury		
42	Grimsby	87	Scunthorpe		
43	Guildford	88	Sheffield	**Northern Ireland**	
44	Halifax	89	Shrewsbury		
45	Harlow	90	Slough	127	Belfast
				128	Londonderry

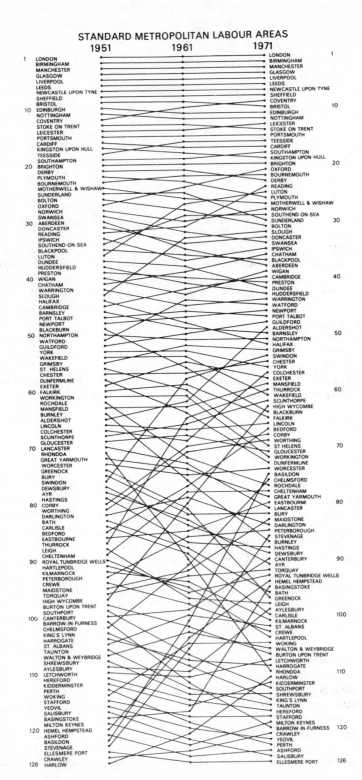

Figure 6.2   Standard Metropolitan Labour Areas, UK, rank order, 1951–71
Source: as fig. 6.1

spread of home ownership; population began to migrate from the core to the sub-urban periphery. But the population of the core continued to rise, though at a slower rate than in the ring. Only in the biggest cities, before 1939, did slum clearance contribute to an actual decline in population in the core. Office and retail employment increased at the centre more rapidly than new factory building at the periphery.

In the third stage, typical of larger metropolitan areas since 1951 but above all since 1961, there was marked actual decline in population, largely arising from inner city redevelopment for commercial and slum clearance purposes. Though there were continuing increases in office and other service employment at the core, these were outweighed by the effects of redevelopment and above all by the rapid growth of local service employment (plus perhaps some decentralized factory employment) in the suburbs.

The fourth stage has so far been reached only by London, and perhaps by Manchester, during the 1960s. Necessarily, it applies only to very large metropolitan areas which stand at the centre of a system of metropolitan areas. In this stage, decentralization both of people and of jobs continues a stage further; the metropolitan area as a whole tends to lose both people and employment to other metropolitan areas.

It was to cope with the consequences of these changes in the urban system that town and country planning was effectively begun in 1947. Over the last thirty years it has had an increasingly important impact on the internal structure of the cities, their rates of growth and decline and their functional role. In a few cases it has even been primarily responsible for the birth of new urban centres and the death of others.

II INTERNAL URBAN STRUCTURE

Even small towns can have an elaborate and varied internal structure, as the studies of Aberystwyth, Alnwick and St Albans (Carter 1958; Conzen 1960; Thurston 1953) have clearly shown. In the larger cities where the effects of the patterning processes are often more readily detectable because of their greater spatial extent, simple descriptions of distinctive localities and activities have entered into everyday language — docklands, West end, inner city, town centre, rush hour, bank holiday. Varying combinations of three key components of the urban structure produce this patterning (variously termed landscape region [Jones], urban region [Smailes], townscape [Carter]), which geographers have attempted to identify in their studies. These three principal components: (a) the town plan, including the street network and property ownerships; (b) the actual buildings and other built structures, with their varying ages, architectural styles and construction materials; and (c) the uses to which the land and floor-space is put — possess many attributes. There is an almost infinite number of possible ways of using them in combination to delimit distinctive localities and rhythms within the built-up area that contribute to an understanding of the way the city works. The numerous criteria reflect the subtlety and complexity of urban structure, which is further complicated by its atomistic and dynamic nature. Every household, firm and organization has an impact on the urban structure and although a change in an individual relationship frequently has no significant effect, the consequences of multiple changes can be very dramatic, as, for example, when all the bus drivers refuse to work or a major factory ceases production. In-

frequent and unwanted as these events are, they demonstrate clearly the high degree
of perpetual inter-dependence (or inter-action) of people, structures and activities
within the city. The internal structure of the city is thus a continually altering
pageant with literally thousands of actors. Many of the inter-actions making up the
almost endless chains of cause and effect that create and modify the urban structure
are poorly understood at present, and consequently accounts of the internal structure of the British city can give only a rather limited, simplified and static picture
of the reality. Here we examine first the kinds of process-creating urban structure,
and then describe the resulting patterns of land use.

II.1   Process

Although it is useful to regard the inter-actions that create urban structure in the
UK as belonging to one of four major kinds of process – physical, economic, social
(private), and community (public) – the reality is that at any point in time all the
processes are at work. Their individual impacts, however, have not remained constant through time, and there seems considerable evidence to suggest that the 'community' process is perhaps now the dominant one; certainly it has never been as
powerful in any previous era.

The **physical** process of urban growth can take three spatial forms, each of which
has a clearly different impact on urban structure. It can give rise to peripheral expansion and most commonly does. It can also give rise to infilling – that is,
additional urban structure without expansion of the urban area as a whole. Thirdly,
it can give rise to replacement – that is, demolition followed by new construction,
which, depending on whether the density of development is greater or less than that
it replaces, may or may not imply further expansion overall; or it may give rise to
a combination of all three.

Although present in the middle ages peripheral expansion was clearly secondary
to infilling simply because the limited means of transport available put a very high
premium on accessibility to the market square. In this way the narrow street front-
ages with land extending back at right angles from the street gave rise to the burgage
plot, whose outlines still dominate the town plans dating from before about 1800.
On this type of town plan (looking much like an urban version of open-field strips)
the growth process (Conzen 1960) was one of steady infilling by 'backland' development. It was the combined effects of the rapid growth in population and the improvements in local transport that gave peripheral growth its great opportunity from
the end of the eighteenth century. Except where physical conditions made it difficult or dangerous to do so, as on land along rivers liable to occasional flooding, expansion occurred in all directions around either the pre-existing settlement or the
newly-established mine, factory, mill or other place of employment.

The scale and nature of peripheral expansion since 1800 has been and remains
the dominating element of the British townscape. Coupled with outward growth
was a generally uneven pace of expansion, which helps to give British cities their
characteristic concentric rings of distinctive development, especially clearly seen in
the pattern of residential land use. So abrupt was the change from boom to slump
in Victorian times and so lengthy the two world-war periods that between the end
of one era of expansion and the beginning of the next some change in social
attitudes, in transport technology, or in building style arose to differentiate clearly
the one from the other. In the nineteenth century it was the change in building

materials (in Glasgow, for example, from grey carboniferous sandstone to pink old red sandstone in 1870, and to brick after 1900), coupled with the impact of bye-law regulations; in the twentieth century it has been more a product of fashion, of layout and house-type.

Two other characteristic features of the British townscape are associated with the process of peripheral growth. The distribution of institutional land uses such as cemeteries, convents and priories and later hospitals, universities and other land-extensive activities have been shown by Whitehand (1972) frequently to represent a relict fringe-belt marking a previous period of standstill in the expansion of the city. In this century the fringe-belt has achieved its ultimate form as the statutorily designated green-belt. In the outward spread of development a substantial number of villages and small towns have become engulfed, but because of their nodality and pre-existing functions have often developed as local service and community centres. Rasmussen (1951) regards this feature of urban structure as particularly English and has described it for the early growth of London:

> 'around every little village the buildings crystallized into a borough so that London became a greater and still greater accumulation of towns, an immense colony of dwellings where the people still live in their own houses in small communities with local governments [he was writing in 1934], just as they had done in the middle ages'.

Very large tracts of our cities were built in a great hurry within a relatively few years, as was the case in all the industrial cities of the nineteenth century with only minor variations in timing, so that 120–150 years later, all these extensive areas require either rehabilitation or redevelopment. Thus a wave of slum clearance and redevelopment, begun in the mid-1950s, now characterizes much of the inner core-city zone but with very different layout, house-type and land-use patterns (section IV.2). The replacement process has not been limited to public slum clearance schemes, even though some of the earliest of these were in the 1870s in Glasgow and London, where overcrowding of the late medieval town produced a severe health hazard for the rest of the city's inhabitants. Redevelopment of individual plots has been and remains characteristic of town and city centres. The need for extensive, (i.e. multi-plot) replacement as a consequence of wartime bomb damage in Exeter, Coventry, Bristol, London and Plymouth provided an opportunity to re-structure the street pattern and alter individual property ownerships on a scale that normal urban growth and decay could never provide. The overall success of these early town centre redevelopment schemes led to the idea being widely copied in hundreds of other towns and cities throughout the 1960s, spurred on as they were by increasing traffic congestion and the threat of major decentralization of retailing.

The **economic** process of urban growth refers to the competition of different users for scarce space endowed with urban facilities. Explaining the pattern of land values in American cities, Hurd (1924) described the process as one in which, 'since value depends on economic rent and rent on location, and location on convenience, and convenience on nearness, we may eliminate the intermediate steps and say that value depends on nearness'. Thus, it is argued that the use which can extract the greatest return from the site because of its particular nearness or accessibility requirements will become the occupier of the site, and in this process the city structure will evolve towards a most efficient land-use pattern. Although there are important reasons why towns in the UK responded to this free market process with less emphasis and in differing ways from towns in the USA, there can be little doubt that it has had a major impact. The highest land values are associated with central areas and in particular with retailing and commercial offices, the former requiring accessibility to the customer potential represented by the metropolitan population and the latter requiring close proximity to other offices to facilitate the face-to-face contact which is such a feature of this activity (Goddard 1975). As a detailed study of land uses in central Glasgow in 1958 (Diamond 1962) has shown, however, the pattern of land uses seems remarkably finely adjusted to the pattern of accessibility created by mass public transport. In smaller centres where the railway did not arrive at the existing town centre (usually the medieval market place) the new accessibility pattern often brought substantial changes in the distribution of activities within the town, even on occasions transferring the central area to the vicinity of the railway station.

The locational pattern of industry within British cities is also heavily influenced by the pattern of accessibility created for the movement of goods and raw materials. The ring of mixed industrial uses which typically surrounded the central area but has today often almost vanished as a result of post-1945 decentralization, acquired marked radial rather than zonal extensions, as first canals, then railways and then inter-war major road improvements produced linear accessibility patterns. In London (fig. 4B), Birmingham (the Tame Valley), Glasgow (along the Forth—Clyde canal and river Clyde), Belfast and many other cities, these marked radial or sector patterns were reinforced by the influence of rivers, especially where these could be modified to provide port functions. As the use of trucks and the ownership of cars has increased, the locational influence of accessibility has become more diffuse. As a result other influences, often with greater social or cultural content, have had greater impact. Thus, although the pattern of functional areas created in the nineteenth century by the differing accessibility requirements of various urban functions has lost its original rationale, the pattern is perpetuated by other location factors. Inter-firm linkages, associated with component assembly manufacturing, and the public control of industrial land use by the establishment of industrial estates and the preparation of development plans under the 1947 *Town and Country Planning Act* (Publ. Gen. Act 1947) are probably the two most influential.

Households, firms and many other organizations make many of their locational decisions in a manner in which individual taste, social custom and habit play a major part, thus creating powerful **social** processes which give pattern to the urban structure. Because many of these decisions are made almost intuitively, without exhaustive analysis of the possible alternatives, they are difficult to trace by social survey and consequently they tend to be inferred from maps showing uneven distribution of the social characteristics of urban residents. Given that residential land use is by far the largest single use of land in urban areas, these patterns often tend to dominate geographical interpretations of urban structure. It is well to remember, however, in a period of social mobility and considerable social change, that the apparently orderly social geography displayed in the results of various methods for delimiting urban sub-areas may result less from like individuals making similar choices than from the nature of the census data commonly employed and the aggregate scale of the analysis.

The patterning of residential areas by social choice seems to reflect three closely interlocking aspects of people's life-style: the desire to have as neighbours people with similar attitudes and behaviour; the attempt to choose a convenient location for the household's major activities; and the ability to choose to live in a particular type of dwelling associated with a particular kind of local environment. What makes these aspirations so powerful in fashioning city structure is their high degree of association. Income, occupation, education, social class of close relatives, household size and family stage have all been used as criteria to measure differentiation of residential areas. Migration history, too, is an immensely powerful influence when it results in a large minority group whose race, nationality or religion give it a social distinctiveness. Social segregation is thus a multi-faceted phenomenon which although present in all towns, can take different forms. The intensity of segregation – a concept very difficult to establish quantitatively – varies through time, not just with the degree of dynamism in the local economy, but also in times of social stress when the clustering of the minority is accentuated in the search for a sense of security, as recent events in Belfast and Londonderry have tragically demonstrated (Poole and Boal 1973).

Segregation in residential areas The spatial sorting of residential areas has now been investigated in several studies in Britain by various forms of multi-variate analysis, and sufficient similarity in the results suggests that three major dimensions exist. The first is **socio-economic status**, which is most obviously measured by occupation or by what the census calls socio-economic group, which is a simplified classification of occupations. Social status is a somewhat subtle attribute of people and in the development of British society (Halsey 1972) has undergone change, particularly since 1945. Robson (1975) has made the interesting suggestion that as the education, income, and occupation changes have led to a blurring of social distinctions there has been as a consequence a tendency for social segregation to become more marked. Certainly it is difficult to find the present-day equivalents of the nineteenth-century examples of small-scale mixing of different social classes, as in the mews flats that lay behind the grand terrace houses of the upper middle class. A study of Crawley (Heraud 1960) showed that although the extent of social segregation was less than in other towns, as might be expected from a balanced population policy (section IV), there was clear evidence that 'a large number of families move from district to district . . . thus Langley Green was developing into a working class area and Tilgate was becoming predominantly middle class'. Heraud emphasized that such segregation was occurring not only because of individual choices made by those who moved, but by the change in Development Corporation policy in the middle 1950s to allow substantial private housing development. Further, middle-class families were over-represented in a growing movement to the surrounding small towns and villages with a much more marked rural or countryside atmosphere. In the early stages of such a trend – Pahl (1965) has described the process in detail for Hertfordshire villages in the London green-belt – the result must be a considerable decline in segregation as the newcomers mix with the existing population.

More generally, sociological studies suggest that as greater income equality has emerged between the manual and white-collar jobs and car ownership has as a consequence become very widespread, general lifestyle differences have remained. Type of leisure activities and degree of activity within the kinship network have remained distinctive, and are strong determinants of the locational element in residential site selection.

A second major dimension of social segregation in UK cities is associated with the **age structure** of the population. While one expects very marked differences in

family size and household composition between one area and another in Belfast,
associated with marked religious segregation (Jones 1960), or in cities with substantial recent overseas migrants, it is rather more surprising that this feature of segregation is in fact widespread in British towns. The study by Westergaard (1964) of the
outer suburbs of London revealed a pattern of age-structure types which are widely
typical. The explanation of such segregation is that at different stages of its life-
cycle a family or household has very different needs in size of dwelling (i.e. number
of rooms) and access to particular facilities. Families with young children will value
access to play-space, schools, clinics, swimming baths and so forth, and single person
households will have an entirely different set of accessibility requirements. When this
tendency is coupled with the uneven spatial distribution of house sizes that exists in
any town as a result of its social and economic history, the patterning becomes com-
prehensible, especially where privately-owned houses are concerned. Since 1945,
however, most local authority housing allocation schemes have used some kind of
points system to give priority to families with children. In Glasgow, for example,
where such a scheme operates for a very large council house waiting list, the result
has been that the percentage of families with children increases progressively from
the inner city through the inter-war suburbs to a maximum in the post-war
municipal estates. Variations in the scale and age of the municipal housing stock
create variations between authorities, but, given the self-contained nature of this
stock as a housing market, extreme over- and under-crowding are often found within
public sector housing.

    In an attempt to improve efficiency in the use of the stock of dwellings as well
as to increase tenant satisfaction, authorities have arranged various schemes for the
exchange of houses. A recent study (Bird and Whitbread 1975) of tenants' requests
to be transferred showed that in Greater London and Newcastle upon Tyne about
one in five tenants wished to transfer but that only 3 per cent are moved each year.
Although size, amenity and location were all reasons for tenants requesting a move,
the result was 'queues of households for the dwellings with certain attractive
features as well as queues to leave dwellings of less popular types (flats) or in less
desirable locations'. Contrasting patterns of desired movement were revealed by the
mapping of tenants' requests to move, with a strong decentralizing pattern in
London compared with inter-suburban movement in Newcastle together with a
noticeable backflow into the city centre (fig. 6.3). Yet the strong tendency for intra-
urban migration to show a marked radial pattern, as described in Hoyt's well-known
sector theory of urban growth, was evident and appears to be identical with the
other examples of this process, including the movement of religious minorities
(Jews in Belfast and Glasgow) and industries (in Greater London). The desire to
retain reasonable access to employment, friends and relatives, which appears to explain this, underlines the powerful patterning influence of radial transport routes in
large urban areas.

    The outstanding example, however, of life-cycle influencing residential site selec-
tion is the decision of elderly couples to move to a small house without stairs in a
pleasant town beside the sea (fig. 6.3b). So powerful is this preference that it has
created a recognizable inter-regional migration flow and produced a distinctive
category of towns with very special social services and urban facilities (section III.3).

    The third dimension consistently revealed in the analyses of urban structure in
Britain is the nature of the **housing market** (table 2.19). Two features are of particular significance. The first is the virtual elimination of the private landlord and

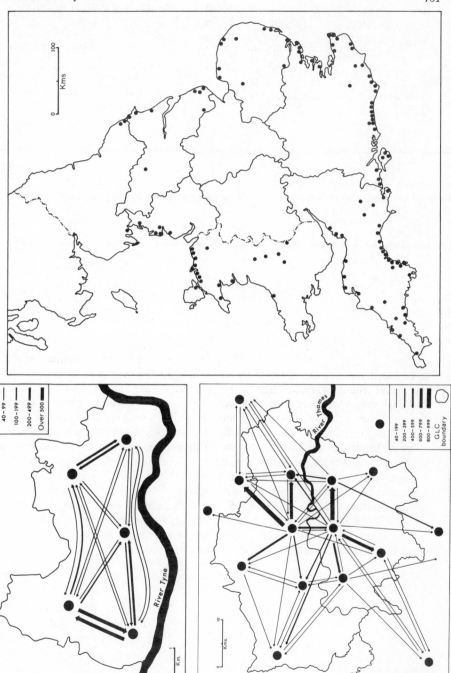

Figure 6.3   Residential migration: (A) Pattern of council house transfers in Newcastle upon
Tyne and London; (B) Retirement towns in England and Wales (20 per cent or
more of population of pensionable age)

houses to rent, and the second the high degree of self-containment of the owner-occupied and public-rented sectors. The explanation for both these features lies in a complex social history (Cullingworth 1965, Donnison 1969), but their importance to urban structure in Britain is substantial in several ways (Pritchard 1976). Condition and amenity vary considerably between these types. Generally, public housing provides better physical amenities than do either privately-rented or owner-occupied houses at comparable expenditure, and thus qualification for housing tenure by type rather than income is the determinant of housing standard. Consequently, once a household finds accommodation in a public sector dwelling, it is usually reluctant to change to another tenure type. The number of local authority houses per 100 persons is substantially higher in Scotland (53) than in England and Wales (28), where it does vary considerably between towns, e.g. Bournemouth (3), Sheffield (13). The filtering effect of new house construction is equally affected by this crucial public—private dichotomy. Since the local authorities responsible for the provision of public housing have to determine their policy in relation to the needs of their own area rather than some socio-geographic entity, such as the city region, there has been considerable impact on the distribution and density of housing. This can be explained only in terms of the multitude of local authorities responsible for providing public sector houses.

The seven 'housing classes' that Rex (1968) sees as the outcome of political and market forces operating on an historically determined housing supply situation, are essentially a tenure and age-of-dwelling combination. The three ways of life that result he describes as 'the rich settle in the classy inner suburbs, the white-collar people aided by mortgages live further out in suburbs of semi-detached dwellings and finally, the working classes, having attained a measure of power in the town hall, have their own suburbs built for them'. Thus in competing for scarce housing people are distinguished from one another by their strength in the system of housing allocation — from the strongest (class 1) to the weakest (class 7), in the following terms:

Class 1   the Owners of large houses in desirable areas
    2   the Mortgage payers in the process of acquiring whole houses in desirable areas
    3   Council tenants in Council-built houses
    4   Council tenants in slum houses awaiting demolition
    5   Tenants of private house owners, usually in the inner city
    6   House-owners who must take in lodgers to meet loan repayments
    7   lodgers in rooms.

Such housing classes will also tend to have a 'definite territorial distribution in the city depending largely on the age and size of dwellings' as was confirmed in the study of Sparkbrook in Birmingham (Rex and Moore 1967). Clearly the hierarchy of status areas assumes that the owner-occupied house in the suburbs is an aspiration common to all groups. Areas of 'gentrification' or the invasion of traditional working-class areas by middle and upper income groups, as Hamnett's (1973) study of inner London shows, are characterized by Georgian and Victorian terraced housing of three stories, adjacent to existing high-status areas and easily accessible to central London, so giving them a distinctive spatial pattern with a rationale fully compatible with Rex's thesis and reinforced by the vagaries of government policy over improvement grants (i.e. financial assistance to owners for the installation of basic amenities).

This late 1960s phenomenon also demonstrates how the rules applied by the insurance companies, building societies, and local authorities in respect of housing finance to families, coupled with the pattern of the housing stock, affects the residential distribution of socio-economic groups (Williams 1976). Gentrification thus appears as the combined outcome of life-style preferences, character of the housing stock, occupational credit-worthiness and government policy.

The substantial immigration from West Africa, India, Pakistan and the West Indies during the late 1950s and early 1960s had led to marked concentrations of coloured population within some major cities (ch. 2.II.6). In addition to the socio-economic status and tenure factors in these circumstances there is often a racial prejudice element as well, which sharpens the pattern of segregation (Jones 1967).

Public interest planning The fourth major process involved in structuring urban areas in the UK, with many distinctively British features, concerns the various constraints which are imposed on development or change in the name of the *community* for its supposed benefit. In the contemporary interventionist age the cumulative effect of such regulations and controls is enormous, and there are now so many different organizations involved in recommending, implementing or policing aspects of life in British towns that it is questionable if all are necessary. Fundamentally, the nature of the city itself has been the cause. Given the great density of people and structures and their need for common facilities and services, the community in all urban areas has throughout history imposed restrictions on the freedom of individuals, to prevent catastrophe or chaos. Conflagration and epidemic were the catastrophes most feared in the Middle Ages and led to early regulations about construction materials, disposal of waste and the establishment of special organizations such as the fire brigade or Dean of Guild. Pollution control through smoke abatement zones or parking restrictions to keep traffic moving are not just twentieth-century ideas: both were tried in medieval London. Realistically, it has been noted that 'urban civilisation is a matter of discipline and drains'. Thus, while the positive externalities found in cities are often regarded as the major reason for urban growth, these have in fact been accompanied by negative externalities which require concerted public action if they are to be ameliorated. In Britain today environmental regulations are devised and enforced by a considerable variety of official organizations and institutions, among which the local authority is the most influential. The Medical Officer of Health is responsible for declaring buildings unfit for habitation and so for identifying sub-standard housing; the Environmental Health Officer (in Scotland the Sanitary Inspector) is responsible for ensuring the standard of hygiene throughout the food trade, including all who manufacture, distribute and retail food; the police are responsible for traffic control; and the city planning officer is responsible for creating plans which will lead to an improvement in the quality of life; as the chief planner for London put it, by 'promoting the desirable, assimilating the inevitable and forestalling the objectionable' (Collins 1951).

The powers of the town planning authorities since 1947 typify best the way in which urban structure is extremely powerfully influenced by community needs and desires. Up to 1974 (1975 in Scotland) the County Boroughs and Counties were the planning authorities responsible for (a) making a Development Plan, essentially a map of the desired future land-use pattern and for (b) granting or refusing planning permission largely according to whether or not the application conformed to the Development Plan. Thus it was hoped that by sanctioning only those kinds of change that were thought desirable from an overall community viewpoint it would be possible to achieve the greatest advantages and least inconvenience for both the individual and society as a whole. It would resolve conflicts over the use of land in an orderly manner and help to turn into physical reality the hopes of society for the kind of built environment it wanted. Simultaneously with the reorganization of local government the major reforms contained in the 1968 *Town and Country Planning Act* (1969 in Scotland) were finally implemented, superseding the old-style Development Plan by a new-style Structure Plan – a document setting out broad policy concerned with social, economic and physical factors so far as they are subject to town planning control or influences – together with Local Plans of various kinds. The evolution of the nature and method of British town planning since 1947 is too large a topic to include here (Cullingworth 1974; Evans 1974; Solesbury 1974), but the essential features that have influenced the urban system in diverse and significant ways must be noted, despite the real and considerable difficulties of any evaluation of the impact of town planning on urban structure (Diamond 1975).

Unlike its predecessors the 1947 Act, which laid the foundation of town-planning practice, was both spatially and functionally comprehensive in its coverage; the entire country was covered and the definition of development was all-embracing: 'The carrying out of building, engineering, mining or other operation in, on, over or under the land, or the making of any material change in the use of any building or other land'. With such a wide definition it is not surprising that on average 400,000 planning applications were decided annually, and of these 38 per cent were for residential development, 14 per cent for domestic garages, and 5 per cent each for shops and factories, while changes of use accounted for 12 per cent. Refusals have averaged about 15 per cent and applicants appealed against the refusals in only one-quarter of the cases. As a measure of total impact, however, these data are severely limited, since no one can estimate the deterrent effect of the system in general and the publication of Development Plans in particular. Despite the great powers of the town planners, which have decisively influenced what kind of houses are available and in which areas they are found, because the British planning system is fundamentally a method of land-use control it is inevitably at the mercy of powerful social and economic forces which operate indirectly on the land-use system. The plans that town planners make are not all fulfilled, and, although the land owner as an influence has greatly declined in significance, this does not by any means appear true of the developer, as Marriott (1967) has shown for offices and Craven (1969) for housing. Although the 'coal-face' of town planning is the local authority planning department, it must be understood that a powerful, if delicate, control of its activities is exercised by central government, which ensures that similar standards apply throughout the UK. Especially significant in all kinds of public development (schools, hospitals, libraries and leisure facilities, as well as roads, water supply and sewage, and all local authority housing) are the various financial arrangements between local and central government. As a consequence of the decline in the share of local authority expenditure covered by rates, the central government's influence has grown, and thus the level and volume of Treasury money made available through ordinary housing subsidies, high flat subsidies, improvement grants, transport subsidies and reclamation grants, etc, has increasingly influenced the kind and rate of urban growth (Levin 1976).

Recent legislation has emphasized the role of plans as the policy element in administrative systems focused on the management of change, and has thus drawn attention to the *aims* of town planning and consequently to the significance of these goals for any explanation of the development of urban areas in Britain over the last thirty years. An early aim of town planners was to create the City Beautiful by achieving and maintaining a high standard of visual beauty. Planning authorities in Britain have the right to refuse permission, for example, for development (in the 1947 Act sense of the word) of a proposed commercial office block that would spoil the skyline or obscure the silhouette of a famous historical building; or of a suburban house which is judged out of character with the rest of the neighbourhood; or of an application to alter the external appearance of an existing building which is judged to be an essential element in an architectural composition of historical importance and visual quality. The rationale for giving the community the right to impose its wishes in these various ways on individual members of society clearly stems from a belief that the quality of life in towns depends in part on a townscape that contributes visual satisfaction to its citizens.

Development control, however, has more than visual beauty as its aim. The health and safety of residents in a town is as much a conscious objective of town planners today as it was when cholera and tuberculosis were real threats. The City Safe and Convenient is today most vividly illustrated by the proposals planners produce to allow people as pedestrians to survive alongside the growing flood of vehicles. Whether it is a town-centre redevelopment scheme incorporating the segregation of pedestrians from vehicles by construction of a shopping precinct (only the twentieth-century version of the medieval market square), or a Radburn design for the layout of a new residential area, or the location of primary schools within a neighbourhood unit so that young children may reach school without crossing any main road, the objective is clearly safety for citizens in the same way as the daylight standards, sunlight standards, overcrowding standards and building codes, first used at the beginning of the century. During the 1950s, before traffic problems came to dominate the planning scene, an improvement to the health and safety of citizens was sought by detailed proposals concerning the future use of land in each part of the town. Planners sought to keep apart incompatible uses such as noxious industry and housing, and to structure the land-use pattern in such a way that environmental quality and convenience to local facilities, as well as health and safety, were all achieved to a higher standard. The clearest evidence of the impact of planning standards on the land-use pattern of cities is the fact that in the New Towns started in the 1950s, largely on green-field sites, the land-use map that appeared was radically different from that in existing towns.

During the 1960s national economic difficulties, very substantial demographic growth, and a deepening understanding of just how outworn and outmoded most of Britain's major industrial cities were, led to the development of a new emphasis in the work of town planners. Questions began to arise about the optimum size of a city, the most efficient use of scarce national resources for new schools, new sewage works and, most expensive of all, new high-capacity, high-speed urban roads. Threshold analysis (Hughes and Kozlowski 1968) was used to examine current and potential capacity for further expansion of existing settlements, and plans were produced based on the argument that it was more efficient to expand this settlement rather than that one. Plans appeared arguing that one spatial structure in the region rather than another was both more conducive to economic growth and minimized the cost of public sector infra-structure (such items as new airports, container depots and inter-city communications). Growth-points or growth-zones were designated and public sector investment of a wide variety, including notably several New Towns, was concentrated in a limited number of locations. The City Efficient ideal thus made an impact not only on the internal structure of the city but also at the regional scale, where it caused the rates of growth of towns to be different because planners seeking national efficiency influenced the spatial distribution of most government investment and even much private investment.

The fourth and final stage in the evolution of town-planning aims, currently proceeding, and therefore is not as clearly identified as the earlier stages. Town planning is increasingly being regarded not only as a method for improving the quality of life for all, but of doing so particularly for the less well off and more disadvantaged groups. The City Just concept asks planners to realize that every plan changes the spatial distribution of facilities in towns and cities and asks them to ensure that those with poor housing, bad schools, little open space, no convenient shops, poor accessibility to employment opportunities, or some combination of these, are benefited more than others.

The distribution of the costs and benefits of particular planning policies falls unequally on different groups in the society. Public perception of this really seemed to grow out of the practice of building urban motorways through tracts of very poor quality housing because the land was least expensive in such areas. Whatever the benefits of such improvements are, they did not accrue to those people who had their homes demolished and thus were forced to change their place of residence, since they were overwhelmingly non-car owners. It may over-simplify a complex social change to say that this led in turn to an increasing demand by the public to be consulted about planning policies.

It is perhaps most important of all to realize that these stages in the evolution of town-planning aims have been additive, with each new aim complementing those already in use, rather than competing with them or being seen as a replacement or alternative. Thus the quality of life that town planners are seeking to realize will be found in the city that is at one and the same time beautiful, safe and convenient, efficient and just. This Utopia is not expected by the town planner to occur tomorrow, but it does define the direction in which he is seeking to go. It informs his choice of tools and helps to explain why, despite the mistakes, frustrations, delay and interference with private rights that are apparently an inseparable part of British planning, the activity continues. A discussion of the way in which these aims and methods of town planning have influenced the existing urban system is contained in section IV of this chapter.

Other kinds of organizations apart from governmental or quasi-governmental ones are also capable of influencing urban structure. In fact, interest groups of a great variety of kinds play roles of varying significance. It is curious, as Barker (1975) has commented that 'just as British town and country planners had about finished establishing themselves as a proper profession, equipped to operate the world's most advanced system of statutory land-use controls for the benefit of all, the tendency for private citizens to form themselves into groups concerned with planning issues was also rising rapidly'. In addition, however, to over 1,100 amenity societies in 1974 there are others ranging from the local Chamber of Trade to the neighbourhood community action group and from tenants' associations to ratepayers' groups. How effectively they influence planning is really known only for a small number of case studies (Gregory 1971), but clearly the potential is substantial and seems likely to increase (Simmie 1974).

II.2 Pattern

The above discussion of the various kinds of process which generate the internal structure of the city and give it a distinctive patterning suggests that although an endless variety of combinations will arise in different towns, there is nevertheless enough universality to allow the description of a typical or average case. Such an epitome is most unlikely ever to be found in reality but it provides a norm against which the actual pattern of existing cities may be viewed, to gain an understanding of deviations from a general theory as they develop under the time and space circumstances of particular places.

The British town or city can be thought of as possessing a particular pattern of internal structure resulting from the super-imposition of *three patterned spaces* (fig. 6.4), themselves the result of a combination of processes. The 'physical space' pattern reveals the pre-Victorian nucleus surrounded by a continuous and compact ring of nineteenth-century development, itself surrounded by an even broader ring of twentieth-century expansion involving the engulfing of two minor centres. The tendency to a star-shaped form was more pronounced at the end of the nineteenth century than now. Basically the pattern is distinctly zonal: the outcome of growth by peripheral expansion and economic competition for space, influenced by a radial transport network of limited density. The 'social space pattern' combines both zonal and sectoral patterns. The three sectors represent the status differences generated by social class segregation, while the concentric zones indicate both the family-cycle process and the impact of the housing market with its tenure divisions. These are the three dimensions that have emerged most frequently and most strongly from the factorial ecology studies in Britain.

Several points can be noted. The inner zone of the high-status sector consists largely of privately-rented housing in which elderly households of lower middle class status dominate (1). Students and young professionals also live here in small flats and 'bedsit' conversions. The main exception is a small area of privately-owned houses (1a), a residential pocket of large Victorian or Edwardian terraces recently expanded through 'gentrification' (1b). In the low-status zone the privately-rented houses contain the immigrant community (3a); the medium-status zone retains traditional working-class families with few children in houses nearing the end of their life (3). The remainder of the inner zone consists of redeveloped slum clearance areas (2). Council housing outside the inner zone is most widely distributed in the low status sector occupying most of the middle (5) and outer zone (6), while in the inner zone high-rise flats have replaced Victorian working-class housing (2). The middle zone in the medium- and high-class sectors consists of inter-war owner-occupied houses, in which most families are now without children (4). Post-war semi-detached and detached owner-occupied houses occupy the outer zone of the high status sector (7). Professional people with young families and large mortgages are the typical household in this category. The two engulfed villages present a contrast, since that located in the high-status sector has been invaded by high-income residents who, from the late 1920s, have steadily displaced the original population of farm-workers and have then either modernized the old cottage-style buildings or built modern replicas in 'stockbroker tudor' fashion. The low status sector village (8) has a mixed pattern, since it has attracted both middle-income and working-class population because of the early railway connection to the city and the consequent industrial development.

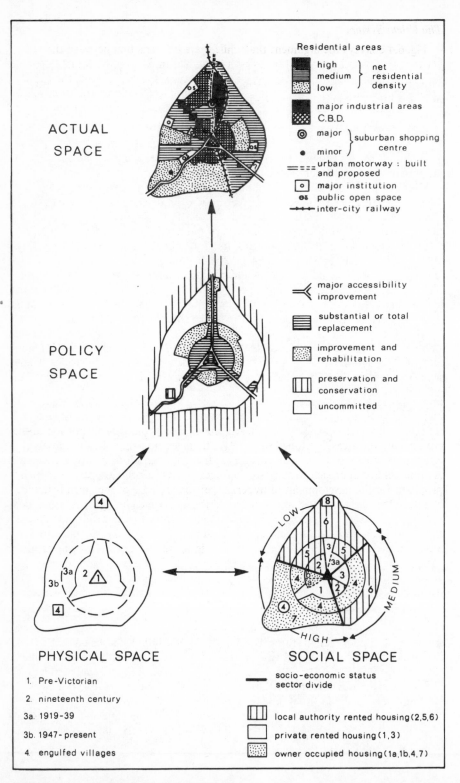

Residential areas

high ⎫
medium ⎬ net residential density
low ⎭

major industrial areas
C.B.D.
⊚ major ⎫ suburban shopping centre
• minor ⎭
≡≡≡≡ urban motorway : built and proposed
⊡ major institution
⊛ public open space
┼┼┼ inter-city railway

ACTUAL SPACE

POLICY SPACE

⟨ major accessibility improvement
▤ substantial or total replacement
▨ improvement and rehabilitation
▥ preservation and conservation
□ uncommitted

PHYSICAL SPACE

1. Pre-Victorian
2. nineteenth century
3a. 1919-39
3b. 1947- present
4. engulfed villages

SOCIAL SPACE

—— socio-economic status sector divide

▥ local authority rented housing (2,5,6)
□ private rented housing (1,3)
▨ owner occupied housing (1a,1b,4,7)

Figure 6.4   Internal structure of the British city

Fig. 6.4 conveys the argument that while there is interaction between the patterns of physical and social space both have their impact on the actual city structure 'filtered' by the presence of 'policy space'. Policy space represents the impact of the urban managers (i.e. the planners) in response to community politics. It is a curious blend of professional planners' ideology and the distribution of power among the main groups in the city. Thus a combination of the planners' wish to improve accessibility and reduce congestion, combined with pressure from car-owners and the business community, has resulted in policy proposals for a high-capacity inner ring road on the edge of the central business district linked to motorway-standard radial roads to connect the town to the region. Essentially planners attempt to manage the internal city system by influencing the rate of change (section II.1), and so the policy space can be categorized as in fig. 6.4 in terms of the degree of change which the city has adopted as its policy and expressed in its statutory planning documents. Areas with change kept to the minimum possible, by strict preservation policies, include the urban fringe (with its designated green belt) and selected historic buildings in the town centre, either 'listed' individually or contained within a designated conservation area. Areas where radical change is being positively promoted also include the city centre (e.g. a new shopping precinct by the local authority in partnership with commercial property developers), together with most of the area built in the nineteenth century where a programme of comprehensive redevelopment, already partly complete, will result in the disappearance of sub-standard houses and the typically mixed industrial and residential land use, and in a marked improvement in the provision of public services, such as schools and parks. Surrounding the zone of radical and immediate change is an area proposed for gradual change, largely through a process of housing and local environmental improvement through the designation of General Improvement Areas and local plans involving only limited redevelopment. For a considerable portion of the city, mainly the areas developed since 1945, there are no firm policy proposals either to stimulate or to restrain changes, as there appear to be few major problems. A rather ad hoc approach to suggested changes in these areas is adopted, in which proposals for the development of hypermarkets on the edge of the green belt will be refused on the grounds that it is incompatible with green-belt purposes and likely to be harmful to the existing pattern of shopping, especially the major new shopping centre being built in the city centre. The possibility of establishing an industrial estate on the site of the now disused city refuse dump will, however, be investigated with vigour, for although not an ideal site, it would, if successful, help to offset the gradual decline in employment in the city's traditional industries. At the same time it would improve the balance between jobs and residence within the city, which until now has meant substantial commuting flows from the east and south through the city centre to the employment concentrations in the north-east sector.

As a consequence of the combination of physical space with social space and the superimposition of policy space on both, a generalized urban structure purporting to be the typical British city emerges and is shown at the top of fig. 6.4 in terms of major land-use categories. Even this simplified presentation underlines how varied the internal structure of British cities can be, and why it is more helpful in attempting to understand such variety and complexity to emphasize process rather than pattern, function rather than form. Although a relationship always exists between form and function, its precise nature is often forbiddingly difficult to determine.

Characteristic features The British city clearly conforms to Dickinson's (1947) dictum that the structure of the modern city tends to be a broad zonal arrangement around the city centre, and this tendency although only one among several, is the most important one. Essentially, the concentric rings represent in plan a cone of development whose peak is the city centre and from which the *density* declines gradually as distance from the centre increases. Innumerable criteria have been used in Britain to identify this basic structural feature: population density (with the Central Business District devoid of residential population a volcano-like profile emerges), floor-space density, land value, traffic-trip generation, employment density, etc., all of them widely depicted in the basic urban geography textbooks (fig. 6.4). More surprising and still largely unexplained, is the way in which the density gradient appears in many other distributions of phenomena in the city. Recent studies of medical geography in British cities (Bagley 1965; Castle and Gittus 1957) have shown that infant mortality, schizophrenia, and other illnesses often have this pattern, and from a few largely unpublished studies of minor crime, traffic offences, educational attainment and fertility, a similar picture emerges. Understandably, it is difficult to trace the complex associations involved, and even more difficult to begin to identify cause. In a recent review of the relationships between housing, health, and environment in cities, Martin (1967) concluded that 'the evidence shows the clear association of health with socio-economic conditions, over-crowding and air pollution — when these are eliminated the influence of other factors is slight'. Advances in medical treatment have eliminated some classical environmental diseases, such as tuberculosis, but some commentators have remarked that others, such as attempted suicide, appear to take their place. Even if the cause is not identified the correlation in spatial distributions between bad health, poor housing, low educational attainment and other social pathologies suggests that there are still several facets of city structure to be explored.

The density gradient in most British cities has been levelling off for several decades as a consequence of both private decisions to migrate from the inner higher-density zones to lower-density outer zones, and of public policies, especially those affecting the density of residential areas after redevelopment and those attempting to disperse industry away from locations close to the central area. In SE England this tendency for central densities to decline while the peripheral zones increase, extends to over 65 km round London.

The various aspects of London's urban structure shown in figs. 6.5 and 6.6 have been selected to show how the key features of British urban structure can be identified in the capital. Fig. 6.5B, showing the predominant non-residential land uses provides several illustrations of the way in which the zonal, radial and nucleated patterns predicted by the ecological theories of Burgess, Hoyt and Harris and Ullman are additive, as well as showing the degree to which functional areas show up at this scale of generalization. Note too the strong association between the industrial and the transport patterns, especially in the inner areas, and the very widespread distribution of all public buildings (including health and education), thus emphasizing their relationship to residential areas. Other patterns less obviously discernible are the major suburban centres with their commercial land-use concentration and some new largely fragmented fringe belts of open space, vacant land and institutional land use. The actual distribution of land uses is given in table 6.2.

The central area (or CBD) is clearly distinguished on fig. 6.5B by the dominance of commercial land uses, despite its relatively small size. In 1966 this compact, high-

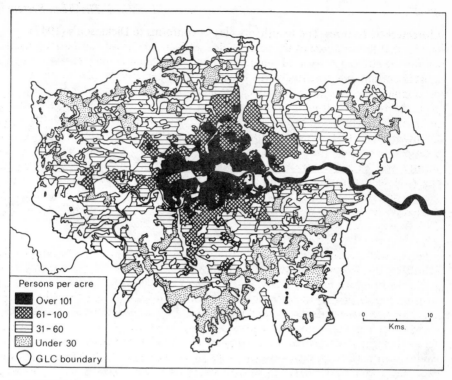

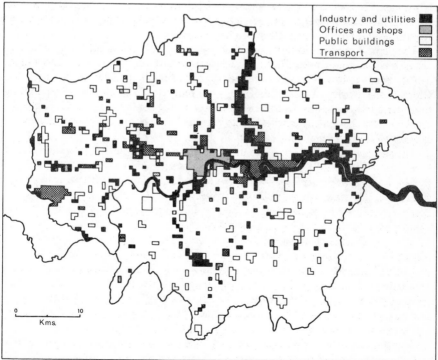

Figure 6.5   The patterns of land use in London: (A) Residential density; (B) Predominantly non-residential land use
Source: *Rep. of Studies*, GLC, 1969

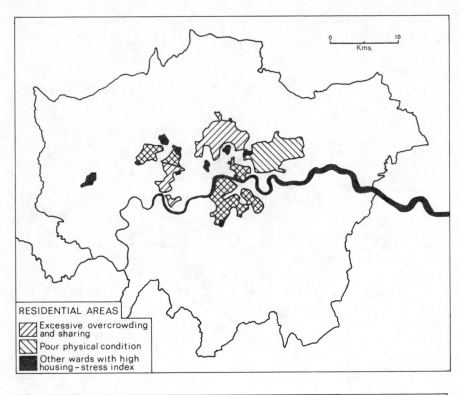

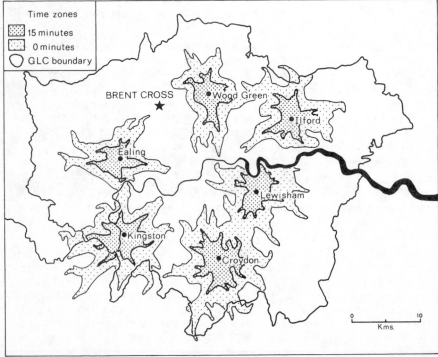

Figure 6.6   London: (A) Housing stress areas; (B) Accessibility to major shopping centres
Source: *Rep. of Studies*, GLC, 1969

density area, known throughout the world, contained 30 per cent of the total employment, 60.4 per cent of all the office floor-space, 25 per cent of all the commercial floor-space and even 10 per cent of all the industrial floor-space in Greater London. Together with the presence of famous and historic buildings, notable public institutions like the University of London or museums, its major public open spaces, and even pockets of specialized residential use (including luxury hotels, student hostels, embassies, council flats and privately-owned charity accommodation), it has a powerfully distinct character of its own. The detailed studies of central areas throughout Britain (notably, for example, Glasgow (Diamond 1962) and Cardiff (Carter and Rowley 1966)) have confirmed what has been even more obvious in London (Goddard 1970), that there is an intricate patterning of functions associated with the great competition for land, and often very considerable levels of congestion. It has been shown how variations in the composition of office employment between different districts is closely associated with variations in the scale and type of retail shopping outside the primary retail zones.

TABLE 6.2

Distribution of Land Uses, Greater London, 1966

Use	Greater London %	Built-up area (excluding green belt) %	Inner London %
Residential	33.4	42.2	36.3
Open areas	29.6	16.3	15.2
Roads	10.9	12.8	16.9
Transport	4.5	5.7	5.2
Vacant land[1]	5.0	4.8	3.6
Education	3.4	3.7	3.1
Public buildings	2.4	2.5	3.7
Industry	2.0	2.5	2.7
Utilities	2.2	2.3	1.6
Water	1.9	2.3	4.7
Commerce	1.5	1.8	2.3
Offices	0.9	1.2	2.1
Health	1.0	1.0	1.3
Shops	0.8	0.9	1.3
Minerals	0.5	–	–
	100.0 (161,795 ha)	100.0 (125,103 ha)	100.0 (30,872 ha)

[1] includes buildings under construction and unoccupied
Source: GLC *Land Use Survey* (1966)

Surrounding the central area of British cities is what has now come to be called the inner city, in contrast to the outer or suburban zone. As table 6.2 shows, there is proportionately less residential land and more road space than in the city as a whole, but its distinctive character in Britain arises from the age of the buildings and the mixture of land uses. Despite the steady decentralization of industry from these areas in the major cities and conurbations since 1945, the presence of factories and warehouses among pockets of densely developed housing remains characteristic of areas not yet reached by the redevelopment programmes of the city planners.

Industry is housed typically in old, small, often multi-storeyed properties, which is why the still considerable concentration of industry found in London in a wide band along the northern edges of the central area is not identifiable in fig. 6.5B. This description of a townscape in Belfast could be applied widely: 'against a setting of mills and smoke, stacks and gantries, are set the endless rows of countless small, identical, workers' houses which the last century has bequeathed to this. On the whole, conditions are mean, cramped and crowded. Every corner has its shop, every vista has its factory, and every alley-way is a playground for scores of children' (Jones 1950, 123).

The mixed land-use pattern is only part of the reason why the inner city is best known today for its bad housing conditions. The internal facilities of the houses and their external environment have been wholly outmoded by rising aspirations and modern standards. Coupled with the simple fact of age and lack of maintenance, this has created areas where the density of people per room exceeds one; where the net residential density usually exceeds 370 persons per ha; where the proportion of houses without baths, indoor toilets and hot running water exceeds 50 per cent of the total; where the structural condition is such that a 10–20-year life is all that is expected; where the schools have inadequate play space; where public parks and playgrounds are very few; and where factories and traffic intrude noise, dirt and danger. These are physical attributes which slum clearance can correct (section IV). The shortage of housing and the operation of the housing market, however, have created a multiple-occupancy problem, so that the residential areas that are over-crowded when measured by the proportion of families sharing kitchens almost co-incides with these worn-out areas – as shown in fig. 6.6A. Not surprisingly, there-fore, the inner city is also characterized by less social stability. In Inner London a survey showed that 20 per cent of households were actively seeking to move, com-pared to 9 per cent for London as a whole.

The outer or suburban zone is typically a contrast – lower net residential densities, a much more segregated land-use pattern and considerably more open space. The correlation between the decline in residential densities (fig. 6.5A) and the rise in levels of car-ownership expresses well the different life-style of this zone. Although there are contrasts between inter-war and post-war development, between council houses and owner-occupied areas, these are clearly less significant than those between inner and outer metropolis. Almost without exception among urban studies the division of the outer-zone into sub-areas follows a sectoral pattern reflecting, especially in the conurbations, the fact that residents from one sector (e.g. south-east or north-west) rarely, if ever, visit the other sectors. Journeys to the centre for employment, shopping and entertainment are common, but lateral movement is both difficult and normally undesired. This is particularly well illustrated by the pattern of accessibility to major suburban shopping centres in London (figs. 6.6B) and is not only widely repeated in other cities but also sought by the planners to assist in the development of community and in the efficient provision of public services in urban areas where the residential densities are at their lowest.

Variations in site conditions can be an important reason why the simplistic geo-metry of zones and sectors is not more obvious as a result of physical growth and functional change. Furthermore, the way in which topography has affected urban structure has altered through time, as changing technology has both created fresh problems and provided new opportunities. Thus London and Glasgow among many other cities grew up at convenient and feasible river crossing-points, which provided them with great nodality. As ship technology altered both began to provide docks, and in Glasgow the River Clyde was deepened from an average of 2.4 m in 1758 to 12.1 m in 1958. In Manchester, where this was not possible, an artificial river was created. Subsequently, as the port function has migrated downstream to deeper water and modern facilities, these largely relict features have become obstacles to easy vehicular movement, necessitating an enormous investment in bridges and tunnels in the post-1945 era. The most striking case of the changing value of topography in the urban context are the defensive sites. Edinburgh and Stirling sited on dramatic 'crag and tail' formations, Durham and Shrewsbury within their incised meanders and Guildford on its ridge top commanding the gap, have all had their growth patterns very substantially influenced by conspicuous local relief. Although the impact of site is often regarded as most powerful in the earliest stages of the growth of the town there are many examples of its continuing influence. The direction of spread of central business districts has often encountered the 'barrier' effect of a river and although the metropolitan accessibility of north Lambeth and Southwark in London, much of Gateshead in Newcastle, and the south bank of the Clyde in Glasgow, is as great as that on the immediately opposite bank, only fringe central areas have developed. In London this has allowed the planned development of a public entertainment complex, 'the South Bank', with amazing metropolitan centrality at relatively low cost.

Altitude in urban areas has frequently been associated with social status because of its amenity quality: the opportunity for views, greater freedom from pollution, and distance from railways and industrial land in the valley bottoms. Thus in the west-end residential area of Glasgow the existence of an irregular drumlin field has produced a parallel complex 'social topography'. On the top of each drumlin are large Victorian villas (often now converted to use as a specialized college or small private school) surrounded by fine terraces on the upper slopes (still occupied by the middle class) and in turn surrounded by intensive tenement development, with industry and transport in the intervening hollows and on the adjacent flood plain. There is thus a precise inverse relationship between altitude and net residential density. In York and Chester sentiment and the tourist value of the city walls reflect an indirect influence of topography, repeated in St Albans, where the combination of flood plain, Roman remains and cathedral has effectively blocked an entire quadrant of the town's site from urban encroachment. More obviously and more unusually the pattern of growth of Peterlee New Town is almost wholly related to the rate at which settlement and subsidence occur in areas recently mined for coal. These examples illustrate the role of site, but because its influence is always exerted through social and economic processes, making some possibilities attractive and others merely costly, it is easily included in a process-dominated explanation of city structure.

III   URBAN FUNCTIONS

The irregular distribution of towns and cities within Britain and their already noted diversity of size and internal structure is probably more closely related to their functional attributes than to any other possible cause. Despite this there has been little systematic analysis of the functional roles of the settlements comprising the urban system and their associated features. The present distribution of settlements of different size is the outcome of three major phases of urban growth (section 1.2), each with a distinctive economic rationale, which has imparted massive change to the relative significance of individual settlements.

Before the industrial period (Dickinson 1947) the country was peppered with closely-spaced small towns. Their genesis and growth, closely influenced by geographical and historical factors, derived from their capacity to serve as trading centres for the agricultural population living within a short radius around them. Poor transport confined their areas of influence, usually to within 6–8 km miles radius, the limits of a day's journey, there and back, for human beings and livestock on their own feet.

Bringing new sources of power and cheaper, more effective, transport, the industrial revolution led to the growth of much larger towns. Some of these, like Nottingham or Leicester, were old-established towns, well placed to take advantage of the new industrial processes. But many were a new kind of specialist industrial town: cotton and woollen textile towns in the Pennine foothills of Lancashire and Yorkshire; some Black Country centres turning out coal, brass and iron; places like Jarrow and Hebburn lining the Tyne, living by exporting coal and building ships. Such industrial towns had almost no connection with the rural populations around them. Hastily built, their housing usually of low standard, poorly provided with shops and urban amenities, they grew to a large extent by attracting rural migrants seeking employment. They had few services to offer people still living in the surrounding rural areas. Robson (1973, 38) has examined the pattern of growth in the nineteenth century and comments on the changes in rank order of the twenty-five largest towns in England and Wales as follows:

'London, the largest town in 1801, retained its rank throughout the whole period, Manchester and Salford, starting in the second rank, had fallen to third place by the end of the period at the expense of Liverpool which had moved from third to second. Birmingham retained its rank of fourth throughout the whole period. All of these larger places, indeed, show relatively little change in their rank orders over the whole period. On the other hand, with the smaller places there is a tendency for increasingly large fluctuations to occur at smaller city sizes. Some places move rapidly up the rank hierarchy: Exeter, for example, began at 20th position and had fallen to 65th by 1911, even though its fall was halted briefly in the period 1821–41. Other places show more fluctuating fortunes: Coventry, which began in 19th position, had fallen to 48th by 1881, but climbed back to 33rd by 1911.'

At present, too, there are major economic differences between one city and another. Some, with above average number of growth industries, are expanding physically and demographically. Having recruited and raised more than their share of young, mobile and successful people, they provide more emigrants (Fielding 1972). Others grow at a slower rate and some are declining rapidly, even when defined on a functional, not physical, basis. Long-term economic change has tipped the scales against Liverpool, Glasgow and Newcastle. London aspires to a world role, while some regional centres like Bristol, Southampton, Reading, Leicester, Oxford and Luton were among the fastest growing places (defined on a Standard Metropolitan Labour Area basis) between 1961 and 1971.

The combination of massive dispersal of population from large and medium-sized cities with the growth of employment in services throughout this century, and spectacularly since 1945, has altered the functional rationale of many towns and cities in only a twenty-year period. The increasing economic significance of information flows rather than the flows of goods and the increasing scale of business enterprises have been suggested as the underlying causes of economic growth in the urban system in what is coming to be called the post-industrial era (Goddard 1970).

III.1 Hinterlands

Although the essence of the modern town is that it provides specialized services, and the vast majority of the population of the UK live within easy access of a town, the territorial extent of the area over which specific towns exert their influence (i.e. the hinterland) is varied and notoriously difficult to delimit. Each centrally located facility, be it a department store, cinema or livestock market, has its own tributary area and the generalization of these to form a single hinterland must be highly subjective (Carter 1965, ch. 6). Consequently, studies examining the extent of urban spheres of influence have preferred to select a single criterion and apply it nationally, as was done in defining SMLAs. The first attempt to delimit such hinterland areas for the whole country (Green 1950) was a contribution to the new development plans under the 1947 Act. The allocation of land in town centres for commercial business and leisure uses could have been highly unrealistic without regard to the total populations using them. Green (1950) devised a method of analysing bus services in order to define urban centres and their hinterland areas. The existence of a bus route indicated a public demand, and the centres to which the routes led were those to which most people wished to go. Centres were defined as places with some 'magnetism' for buses, in that at least one service from smaller places terminated there, and in most cases it was easy to draw limits within which each centre was more accessible to the surrounding local population than any other centre. Green's published studies distinguished about 950 centres in GB each with a surrounding 'sphere of influence'. Such centres were the kind to which people would mostly go for weekly shopping and other frequently recurring needs. The growth of private car ownership and the associated decline of rural bus services since 1955 has not drastically altered the situation, since the same route network is used, and although a car journey is quicker the relative accessibility of one place to another remains the same.

Around all sizeable towns there is a rather sharp gradient from an inner zone, throughout which the town is supreme and unchallenged, to an outer zone within which the urban and rural inhabitants habitually use more than one centre to obtain a considerable range of services. Beyond this again there is often a fringe area within which some city centre services are used sometimes. Less important centres, however, have only small hinterland inner zones, or may lack them altogether, experiencing competition from other centres throughout their sphere of influence. It is within the conurbations, however, that the degree of overlapping of service centre hinterlands is most pronounced (Lomas 1964). Elsewhere the pattern is less complex and broadly approximates to the nested hierarchy predicted by central place theory. Several small towns with their limited hinterlands (e.g. Honiton, Chard, Bridgwater) lie within the larger hinterland of a more important town (Taunton), itself one of several such towns within the hinterland of an even more important place (Bristol).

Although the evidence is incomplete, it appears that for major shopping, entertainment, and many professional services, the population has increasingly relied on the larger urban centres, which have as a consequence increased their dominance over their hinterlands. The growth of employment in city centres has heavily reinforced this trend. It is not surprising, therefore, that it was the emergence of these large, powerful community-of-interest areas, city regions as they are often termed, that underlay much of the demand for local government reorganization in the 1960s (ch. 1.IV.3). This new scale of social organization was made possible by the motor vehicle, made necessary by the large threshold populations required by theatres, hospitals and other specialized services, and is defined by the distances people are prepared to travel by car, bus or works' coach in order to benefit from the wider choice of jobs, durable goods, entertainments and other services. According to Senior (Roy. Commn. Local Govt. 1969, II, 46), only one million people live in the peripheral parts of England still beyond the range of effective access to any centre offering city level opportunities. Commuting hinterlands are discussed in ch. 2.IV.5.

III.2 Hierarchy

Almost as elusive to establish as the limits of an urban hinterland is the actual hierarchical rank of the urban centre containing the facilities and providing the services. Despite the real technical and data difficulties, urban centres in Britain certainly differ significantly in their importance (measured by many very different indices). Confirmation of this intuitive assessment abounds: almost all organizations and services covering the national territory show some hierarchical structuring, viz: universities/colleges/secondary schools/primary schools, or morning newspapers/ evening papers/weekly newspapers, etc.

In the geographical literature the prevalence of retail sales data to establish the hierarchy is more a reflection of data availability than anything else. Although the various studies are not strictly comparable, it is of interest to compare a sample, particularly for the top of the hierarchy, where the actual number of centres is not great. Table 6.3 shows that although there are the expected variations, the similarities are much more striking than the differences.

The dynamics of the urban system is a major reason for the differing results of the investigations. Some centres, such as the early post-war New Towns, are attracting services and functions and consequently climbing up the hierarchy, while others are making the opposite journey. Smith (1968) has examined the changes in status over the period 1938–65 in a study which uses over thirty-five indicators of status ranging from a principal orchestra (the rarest) to banks open daily (the most ubiquitous). Of his 606 centres he estimates that 138 show a rise in status and 78 a decline, corresponding broadly to what one would expect in a period of growing population. He found, however, considerable regional variations in the pattern of change: rises were concentrated in the SW, SE, E Anglia and the E Midlands, with the notable exception of most coastal centres which lost status. The NE and the W Riding contained a notable concentration of declining status centres. Apart from the stability of most centres two further points of interest emerge. Where population was static or declining over a region, it was the larger centres that showed improvement, and where expanding regions established new small and medium-sized centres these generally looked very similar to the long-established centres of similar size. Recent studies, however, of the way businesses have been concentrating their head offices in major cities, so that the key control functions can have maximum accessibility to specialized information, suggest that the growing dominance of the high-order centre

TABLE 6.3

Identification of the Urban Hierarchy in England, 1944–71

	1	2	3	4
Author	Smailes	Carruthers	Smith	Drewett et al
Date	1944	1961	1965	1971
No. of levels identified	6	3	4	n.a.
No. of centres in system	606	240	735	115

Top 15 centres in descending order of importance

	1	2	3	4
1	Manchester	Manchester	Manchester	Birmingham
2	Liverpool	Birmingham	Birmingham	Manchester
3	Birmingham	Liverpool	Liverpool	Liverpool
4	Newcastle	Leeds	Leeds	Leeds
5	Bristol	Newcastle	Newcastle	Newcastle
6	Leeds	Nottingham	Sheffield	Sheffield
7	Nottingham	Leicester	Bristol	Coventry
8	Sheffield	Sheffield	Nottingham	Bristol
9	Bradford	Bristol	Leicester	Nottingham
10	Hull	Hull	Hull	Leicester
11	Plymouth	Bradford	Southampton	Stoke
12	Southampton	Wolverhampton	Plymouth	Portsmouth
13	Leicester	Coventry	Coventry	Teesside
14	Norwich	Plymouth	Norwich	Southampton
15	Brighton (?)	Southampton	Bradford	Hull

The solid line indicates where each author identifies a major break in hierarchical status.

Sources:
Col. 1 Smailes, A E (1944) 'The Urban Hierarchy in England and Wales', *Geogr., 29* 41–51. The rank orders are interpreted from the table given on p. 50.
Col. 2 Carruthers, W I (1967) 'Major Shopping Centres in England and Wales 1961', *Reg. Stud., 1*, 65–81.
Col. 3 Smith, R D P (1968) 'The Changing Urban Hierarchy', *Reg. Stud., 2*, 1–19.
Col. 4 These SMLAs ranked only in terms of their 1971 populations, are taken from fig. 6.2 for comparison purposes only.

will continue unless public policies attempt to alter the trend (Westaway 1974).

Even if structural changes were not occurring and creating change in the urban system, reflected in changes in rank in the urban hierarchy, the movement of population itself would cause change, since many of the functions performed relate closely to size of hinterland population served. In a quite real sense each centre is competing with the other centres of similar rank for customers, and this process of spatial competition results in a remarkably even spread of centres (fig. 6.7, Thorpe 1968).

III.3 Classification

The functional role of a town or city is generally regarded as its single most significant attribute, capable not only of explaining why, where and when it was established and its subsequent history of growth and decline, but also its present socio-political structure. Although every urban centre is in a very real sense unique, there are many similarities among urban centres over a wide range of attributes. Not

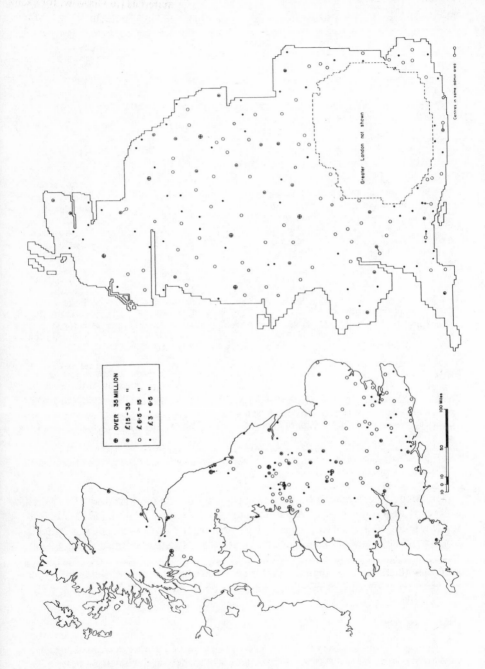

Figure 6.7   Shopping hierarchy, GB, 1961
             The location of main shopping centres by volume of retail sales in 1961. Area in
             the population cartogram is proportional to the number of people resident
             Source: *Urban Stud.* (1968), *5*, 176−7

surprisingly, this has led to attempts to classify centres in such a way as to maximize the homeogeneity within each group and minimize the differences between the groups. The value of such a grouping procedure for public policy is clear. Many of the problems needing attention in Southport must have their identical counterparts in Eastbourne (Armen 1972); and conversely, if it is true that Merseyside is the most distinctive of all provincial conurbations, then perhaps it merits special attention.

There are two important general points to remember when examining city classifications in Britain. First, much of the economic activity of any city is identical with that in all other cities in the national system; for example, almost all the local public and private services. Then ideally any comparative approach should exclude these common elements. More often than not data difficulties prevent this, and the distinctions between city types are as a consequence somewhat blurred. The second issue is more specifically British. Because of the highly integrated character of the British urban system, it is somewhat unreal to think of each town having its own mini-version of the national economy. What is required conceptually is data on the volume, value and direction of flow of the goods and services imported and exported by each urban centre or city region. In the absence of this kind of data such studies as exist have used a very wide range of characteristics in the hope that some will act as proxies for the non-existent data.

Moser and Scott (1961) in their study of 157 local authority areas with populations greater than 50,000 in 1951, used sixty variables arranged in eight groups: population size and structure (7), population change (8), housing and households (15), economic (10), social class (10), voting behaviour (7), health (7) and education (2). Because many of the towns had similar rank in the array on each of several different criteria, principal components analysis was employed to discover how much variation could be explained by a small number of basic dimensions. The results were remarkable: only four dimensions accounted for over 60 per cent of the co-variance of the variables. The four dimensions were labelled as: social class, growth patterns 1931–51, growth patterns 1951–8, and overcrowding. The towns were then classified by a grouping technique applied to their position in the 'space' defined by the four major dimensions. Subsequently, Andrews (1971) has revised the classification. Most of the fourteen clusters can be labelled by economic descriptions. Thus a group (cluster 8) comprising Worthing, Hove, Hastings, Eastbourne, Bournemouth, Torquay, Harrogate and Brighton, are clearly 'resorts'. Another group – Liverpool, Newcastle upon Tyne, Gateshead, South Shields and Sunderland – are port and industrial centres in NE England (except Liverpool). The other clusters can be similarly labelled, but with more difficulty.

More recently Armen (1972) has classified 100 cities in England with over 50,000 people using 130 variables selected to reflect people characteristics, place characteristics and activity characteristics, as of 1966. He produced an hierarchical classification in which 3 basic types divide in 8 sub-groups and these into 23 clusters. Again, functional labels fit the groupings at all three levels.

100 Cities

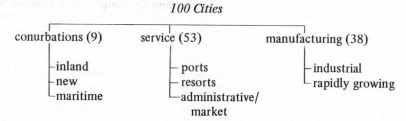

One cluster within the industrial sub-group is composed of Preston, Doncaster, Rugby, Darlington, Crewe, Swindon, all 'railway' towns. Another cluster within the administrative/market centre sub-group is composed of Exeter, Carlisle, Worcester, Peterborough, Chelmsford, Shrewsbury, St Albans, Guildford, Chester and York — all market and cathedral towns. In this classification Eastbourne, Southport, Hastings/Bexhill and Worthing form a 'coastal retirement' cluster, while Harrogate is grouped with Windsor/Slough, Tunbridge Wells and Maidstone as 'inland retirement' centres. Since Armen uses the continuously built-up area to define his centres, Gateshead is included within Tyneside, a maritime conurbation; while Sunderland is found with Swansea, Hull, Barrow-in-Furness and the Hartlepools as a 'medium port'. Encouragingly, the highest within-cluster similarity is found in the group composed of Basildon, Hemel Hempstead, Harlow, Crawley and Stevenage, all New Towns near London with very similar starting dates in the early 1950s. The use of a wide range of variables has the advantage of allowing similarity in many different aspects to influence the grouping procedures, which in turn makes for better descriptions. The 'ports' sub-group, for example, are similar to one another in the predominance of unskilled labour in their work-force, the high rate of unemployment, high density of population, poor housing, presence of consulates, hotels and boarding houses, dancing and night clubs, cinema and bingo halls, slipper baths and betting offices, pubs, cafes and a host of other characteristics. Surprises are possible too: Portsmouth and Yarmouth in the same cluster as Bournemouth and Brighton, and Bath in the same one as Reading. Nevertheless, the ease of attaching labels and the broad correspondence with other classifications suggests that this picture of 100 cities (fig. 6.8) reasonably represents the pattern of urban ways of life in modern Britain.

IV   PLANNING AND THE URBAN SYSTEM

Town and regional planning in Britain has had an extensive and pervasive influence on the nature of the urban system. Although the roots of planning go back to the early years of this century there is little doubt that the passing of the *Town and Country Planning Act* (1947) led to a level of town planning activity that unquestionably justifies its inclusion among the major influences on the British settlement pattern. To the traditional geographical factors of site, situation, morphology and function, used in urban geography, must now be added town planning. Indeed, since the impact of town planning on the pattern and functioning of towns in Britain has been cumulative, the total effect, after thirty years of intensive professional activity, is now very substantial indeed. Perhaps it is because it has been a cumulative process that it has tended to be overlooked by geographers. Not until 1973 was the first major assessment of this era of 'town planning control' published by a geographer (Hall et al 1973). Further, the current trend seems clearly to indicate that the influence of planners will grow rather than decline over the coming decades, e.g. the extension of local authority planning powers embodied in the *Community Land Act* (1975), though as was pointed out in section II, the aspects of the urban system over which their growing influence will be exercised will probably continue to shift and change as it did from 1945 to 1975.

After the Second World War there was not only widespread agreement about planners' aims but also the opportunity of reconstruction in the extensively war-

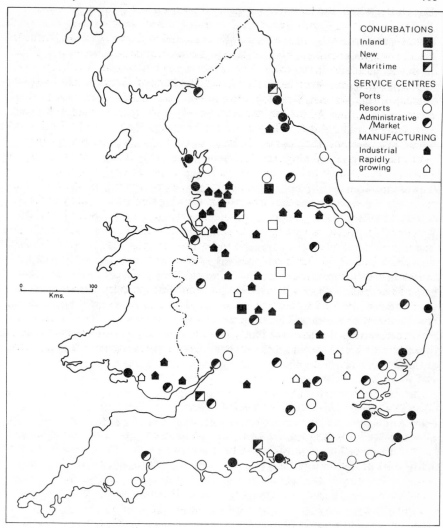

Figure 6.8   Functional city types

damaged cities, such as Coventry, Plymouth, Clydebank, Bristol and London. This combination of general purpose and specific opportunity provided an early test for the newly-passed planning legislation, which by demonstrating the applicability of its methods, helped it gain general acceptance from the population. The early New Towns and the reconstruction schemes together provided a powerful example to planners working in the major conurbations as to the kind of new urban development that was possible. For ten years after the war the impact was mainly visible in the character of the major peripheral extensions undertaken by the largest urban authorities, such as Birmingham, Liverpool and Glasgow. After 1955, when the central government began to encourage local authorities to undertake large-scale slum clearance, the same ideology influenced the character of the redevelopment schemes.

Perhaps the most significant impact of the 1947 Act on the urban structure of Britain has, however, not been through positive proposals for change, but through the operation of the development control responsibilities of local planning authorities. In essence the 1947 Act permitted no development, defined in a very comprehensive way, without permission from the local planning authority, and, as was pointed out in section II, this involved the handling of hundreds of thousands of development applications from both large and small land and property owners. Just how much contribution to the visual quality, safety and convenience, efficiency and social justice of our cities today has been imparted by this control process is impossible to say in precise terms. No one doubts that were it not for development control, the green belts round the major cities would have long since disappeared, but in the complex environment of an existing city the overall impact over a period of years is beyond the possibility of careful measurement. Its potential effect is, however, surely enormous, for it applies not only to minor changes in land use, as from garden use to garage, but also to a major urban improvement, such as converting a now unused railway station into a major new commercial centre with offices, shops and entertainment facilities. In addition to the actual applications accepted, modified or refused, there must also remain an unknown number of applicants who were deterred from making an application, largely because they judged it would not prove acceptable. Although, therefore, no measurement of the impact of development control on the structure of the British city is possible, its cumulative effect over the years since 1947 must be very considerable. Both positive and negative aspects of the town and country planning system have influenced the British urban system.

Before examining the three major types of impact one over-riding general characteristic must be noted. The essential mechanism of the British planning system is control of land use or floor use. This is clearly a sensible choice for a country which introduced planning only after a period of rapid urbanization and when facing a period of much more modest growth, requiring substantial restructuring of the existing urban fabric. Because of this essentially physical basis, however, the process of town and country planning is frequently at the mercy of strong social and economic forces, which operate indirectly on the land-use pattern. The changes in the social and economic structure of Britain since 1945, such as the population boom in the 1960s; the greatly increased number of households reflecting earlier marriage and smaller families; the increased participation of women in the labour force; the rise in real income and associated shifts in aspiration (e.g. the fantastic growth in the demand for leisure facilities); and the accompanying technological changes, especially in transport, have combined to change dramatically the context in which planning operates (table 1.1). Early post-war planning was based largely on the Abercrombie model: an approximately circular shape with concentric rings of development, including the green belt as a limit to suburban sprawl. This physical design was matched by a social policy born of the English view that big cities are bad. A near-universal aim was the dispersal of people, to be achieved through density control in the centre and the creation of new or expanded satellite settlements beyond the green belt. Conservation groups, agriculture and the slum dweller appeared as joint beneficiaries, forming a powerful concensus.

The post-war years saw planning strongly affect the course of urban development as the professionals produced statutorily-backed plans for the whole country. Legislation provided power for their implementation. But since the mid-1950s social and economic change has quickened, and this has itself considerably affected urban growth and structure. New towns have been established, other towns dramatically enlarged, redevelopment and traffic planning have radically altered the internal structure of most cities, and amenity planning has heavily affected the countryside and coastline. Nevertheless, the housing shortage remains a crucial political issue, regional differentials persist, and for many the quality of urban life is still far short of the desired standard. The Abercrombie model is no longer thought adequate, but as yet no alternative has emerged from the confusion (Donnison 1972). The confusion arises from the rapid and radical alteration in planning methods and purposes in the ten years from about 1964. Structure planning is broad rather than narrow in its concerns, is flexible and orientated towards process rather than to formulating a rigid end-state framework. As the link between budgets and plans has begun to be forged so political choice and values have become increasingly central to its vision.

Against this background it seems sensible to examine the impact of planning under three major headings: (a) urban form (the general structure of urban areas); (b) urban renewal (the changing internal structure); and (c) settlement strategies (the location, size and role of urban centres), each an area of considerable debate and effort within planning in the post-war period.

IV.1 Urban Form

The general character of British industrial towns has felt the impact of planners seeking the goals discussed in section II.1 in two main ways: through their efforts to reduce densities, and their attempts to rationalize the land-use pattern. In both of these objectives the efforts of the planners have been parallelled by similar market trends occasioned by the weakening ties between home and workplace, and changing patterns of industrial location. Nevertheless, some idea of the likely extent of the planning influence can be obtained from examining the intentions of the planners. Table 6.4 compares the actual (1955) land-use budget in a sample of existing towns with the proposals for the New Towns. It clearly shows the extent to which planners were hoping to reduce the overall average density, by 4 ha for every 1,000 of the urban population in existing towns. The early New Town planners were aiming at a lower density (23.1 compared to 21.6 ha per 1,000 population), which by the early 1960s had fallen even further, as the later New Town master plans show. In 1970 the Milton Keynes master plan was advocating 35.4 ha acres per 1,000 people, an increase in space of over 100 per cent on the actual situation in 1955. 70 per cent of the increased land need for existing towns is accounted for by residential and educational space, clearly revealing the planners' social aims. A comparison of the proposals for existing cities with those for the later New Towns shows that of the overall increase in land need in the New Towns of 2.8 ha per 1,000 people, 1.8 ha is accounted for by residential and open space use and a further 1.4 ha by industrial use, suggesting that public policy rather than market trends is the major influence. Another sample survey, again in 1955, but of 185 small towns with an average population of 30,000, revealed an existing overall density of 29 ha per 1,000 people and proposals by their planning authorities to increase this to 32.5 ha when the development plan is fulfilled. This makes an interesting comparison with the plan for Milton Keynes, which could thus be fairly described as a major new city (target

population 250,000), planned at an average density somewhat lower than that proposed for much smaller towns fifteen years earlier.

The twenty-nine New Towns in Britain, together with Craigavon, Londonderry
and Antrim—Ballymena in N Ireland, designated since 1946, demonstrate through
their distinctive urban forms the way in which planners have been influencing urban
structure (ch. 2.IV.6). Londonderry and Antrim-Ballymena should strictly be
excluded as they are characteristically 'expanded' towns, and their forms and
densities are rather those of traditional urban centres. Although more obvious in a
New Town (and green-field) setting the same kind of influence is operating in the
existing cities, though understandably in a slower and more complicated manner.
Diversity of urban form, however, exists even among the new towns. Champion
(1970) comments:

> 'neither individually nor collectively are the new towns following a consistent
> density policy. Instead, the space standards for each use would seem to be
> selected independently on their own merits in relation to overall town design and
> to special features of the site. Thus the high average densities proposed for new
> housing at Cumbernauld, Newton Aycliffe, Runcorn, and Skelmersdale reflect
> the importance attached to pedestrian accessibility to service centres and park-
> land. With open space, the differences between towns derive largely from the
> very unequal land provision for informal recreation and visual amenity, which in
> its turn seems to depend on the strength of local pressures on rural land resources
> and on the availability of physically suitable land'.

The explanation of this diversity is partly revealed in fig. 6.9, which shows that
the New Towns may be grouped into two main categories according to their date of
designation. Between 1946 and 1950 fourteen were started, mostly on 'green-field'
sites and with target populations which even by 1974 did not exceed 100,000. Between 1961 and 1970 another fourteen were started, mostly with substantial
populations living within the designated area at the time of designation and with
target populations often over 200,000, and in the largest, central Lancashire,
approximately 430,000. This contrast between the 1950s and the 1960s reflects the
major change in the mix of goals the planners sought (section II.1), as they adapted to
the changing social and economic context in which they had to work.

In the 1950s considerations of social balance, community participation and
proximity to work led to the adoption of the guidance of the Reith Committee on
New Towns (1946) so that very similar urban forms emerged for all the New Towns.
A town centre surrounded by four or five physically separate neighbourhood units
and usually two or three peripheral industrial estates were the basic components.
The major peripheral expansions of the conurbation cities (often similar in scale to
a New Town) and the GLC's out-county estates had a similar physical form and in
them the major commercial focus was often termed a township centre. By the mid-
1960s, these plans were being criticized as inflexible, over-centralized, and with too
rigidly segregated concentrations of different activities. The new plans spoke of
choice, flexibility, efficiency and mobility as the important objectives, and in
contrast to the earlier period a variety of urban forms was proposed.

Rationalization of the land-use pattern became a matter of traffic planning
(ch. 5.III.1), the dispersal of high intensity, trip-generating activities replacing the
segregation of land uses for social and environmental purposes. It was the steep rise
in family car ownership that was, of course, mainly responsible. The new plans had

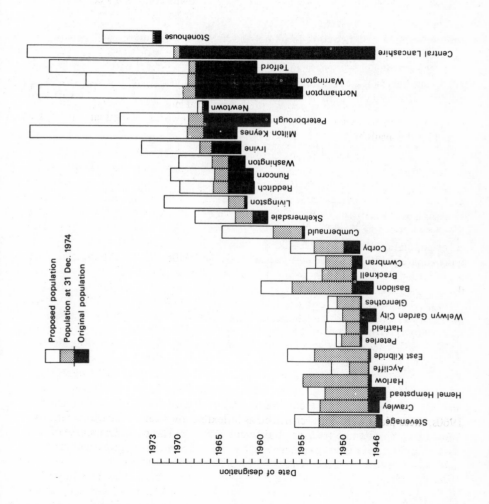

Figure 6.9   New Towns, 1975

to provide for the impact not only on the physical fabric but, equally important, on the changing social habits. Buchanan's (1963) concept of a hierarchy of road networks (primary district and local distributors, and access roads) forms the framework for all the post-Cumbernauld New Town master plans. It was elaborated fully in his study in 1967 for the progressive development on a 'directional grid' of both Portsmouth and Southampton to create a new Solent City of 1,750,000. The most important routes would connect to the national road grid; at right angles to them other routes would connect to the most important structural elements within the city region; again at right angles lesser routes would connect communities of 90,000 people. The next series would be local distributors, followed by smaller community routes leading into residential areas, and eventually a system of footpaths. Within the hierarchy of the six major types of routeways there would be many different modes of transport. Principles of separation, free flow and linkage between the different zones of activity would be adopted in a logical manner. The most important roads, and so on down the chain to the security of the footpath for the mother walking with her child to school and local shop. His urban facilities are grouped on alternative routes which he calls 'spines of activity'.

In the existing cities, where adaptation of the existing street pattern is both costly and very slow, decentralization of some central area functions was increasingly adopted as a policy to help overcome congestion and peak-hour chaos. Typical was

TABLE 6.4

Urban Land-use Budgets: Actual and Planned

	ha per 1,000 population					
	Residential	Industrial	Educational	Open Space	Other	Total
Existing large towns[1]	7.7	1.4	0.4	3.2	4.6	17.4
Proposed large towns[2]	9.5	2.3	1.4	4.2	4.6	21.6
Early new towns[2]	11.7	2.3	2.0	4.4	3.0	23.2
Later new towns[3]	8.7	3.4	2.0	6.9	3.6	24.5
Milton Keynes	16.1	3.2	1.4	4.8	9.7	35.4

[1] A sample of 79 towns whose average size was 160,000
[2] The first 12 New Towns in England and Wales – see fig. 6.9
[3] Includes Livingston, Redditch, Runcorn, Skelmersdale, Washington and expansions of Basildon, Stevenage, Cumbernauld and Glenrothes.
Sources: Best, R (1964) *Land for New Towns*; Llewelyn-Davies, et al (1970) *The Plan for Milton Keynes* p. 22; and *Rep. of the Minist. of Housing and Local Govt.* 1958 (1959), Cmnd 737, HMSO, App. XII.

the suggestion in the *Greater London Development Plan* (1969) that six of the larger suburban centres (Croydon, Ealing, Ilford, Kingston, Lewisham and Wood Green) should be designated as major strategic centres to cater for substantial expansion of their shopping, office, entertainment and public-transport interchange functions and so take pressure off the Central Business District (fig. 6.5A).

IV.2 Urban Renewal

While the New Town planners were more or less successfully inventing the city of the future, the vast majority of planning effort has gone into the herculean task of managing the upgrading and restructuring of the existing urban centres, particularly the conurbations with their massive environmental problems. Although individual property and land owners have participated extensively in urban renewal in a general sense (although always with permission of the local planning authority), it is the major improvement schemes initiated by the local authority that have had the most visible effect on the internal geography of the city.

Until the mid-1950s policy was directed to providing additional houses, schools and factories by peripheral expansion. Outside the major reconstruction schemes renewal was primarily by small-scale clearance but increasingly this piecemeal approach was found defective. A comprehensive approach was required which aimed at improving all aspects of the urban fabric. It involved not only replacement of slum houses, but selective rehabilitation and conservation, a clean air programme, remodelling of the street pattern, drastic alteration to the shopping facilities, new educational and recreational facilities and concern for local employment opportunities. Essentially this was a campaign to provide twentieth-century facilities in our nineteenth-century cities. While recognizing the need to accommodate some market trends (e.g. providing shops that would be rented by private traders), all the major decisions affecting these policies were made by the local planning authority albeit with the necessity for central government approval. The location, size and timing of redevelopment, as well as the mix and intensity of replacement land uses, can be understood only in the light of local planning policy within a broad national context of recommended standards (such as net residential density, etc.) and subsidies (such as the clearance grant, high flat subsidy, improvement grant, etc.).

The 1947 Act had acknowledged the necessity for tackling redevelopment comprehensively in order to overcome the difficulty of the multiplicity of ownerships and the physical limitations of out-of-date street patterns, by empowering local authorities to define as an

> 'area of comprehensive development' 'any area which in the opinion of the local planning authority should be developed or redeveloped as a whole, for any one or more of the following purposes, that is to say, for the purpose of dealing satisfactorily with extensive war damage or conditions of bad layout or obsolete development, or for the purpose of providing for the relocation of population or industry or the replacement of open space in the course of development or redevelopment of any other area or for any other purpose specified in the plan'.

This legislation and the accompanying powers for compulsory purchase have provided the basis for the designation of thousands of CDAs (Comprehensive Development Areas) in British cities, ranging from schemes covering 526 ha in Stepney-Poplar to as small as 4 ha or even less. Though the CDA plan is promoted by the local planning authority, it need not itself undertake the actual development.

In those CDAs involving city centre land and activities, the local authority usually enters into partnership with a private development company, which obtains a long-term lease on the site from the local authority, which remains landlord, and the developer then builds the offices and shops while the local authority undertakes the road improvements, new bus station, etc. In the middle 1960s there were over 400 town or city centre redevelopment schemes either approved or waiting approval from the Minister. Many of these are now partially or fully complete although others have failed to get off the ground. Guidance provided by the then Ministry (Housing and Local Govt. 1963) gives some idea of likely spatial and functional effects of these schemes. The town centre map, showing in outline the local authority's proposals for the future development of the town centre, was to be based on research which paid attention to:

Land use: density and amount of floor space.
Property values: with particular attention to the comparative costs of acquisition in different parts of the town centre, and sites whose values could be significantly increased by redevelopment or improvement.
Town character: distinguishing features and buildings worth preserving, needing improvement, and ripe for development.
Pedestrian movement: main pedestrian flows and meeting places within the centre, with reference to congestion, adequacy of pavements, safety and conflict with vehicular traffic.
Vehicular movement: volume and direction of flow at different times, origin and destination; service access; public transport.
Parking: amount, location, duration and trends, related as far as possible to particular parts and functions of the town centre.

A further inescapable conclusion is that some of the changes in the urban hierarchy must owe their existence to the energy and initiative of local planning departments as much as to inherent advantages derived from an historical role.

Extensive areas of mixed housing, industrial and commercial development of mid- or late Victorian age, have been demolished in the inner area of British cities under the CDA procedure since 1955 (fig. 6.10). The scale of activity can be judged from the results now visible in Newcastle, Sheffield, Liverpool and so on. In Glasgow, a 1957 plan identified twenty-nine CDAs with an average density at the time of 990 persons per ha of housing land and involving one-third of the city's housing stock and approximately 300,000 persons. Clearly, redevelopment on this scale presents both opportunities and problems, each with considerable significance for the geography of the city. To set against the undeniable benefits of improved housing and environmental conditions such as safety, more open space, and car parking provision, are costs of various kinds.

First, uncertainty and then dislocation, which may particularly affect the small business man. Social disorganization can occur as family and neighbour relationships are irreparably broken, and economic relationships, too, are severed; employers lose their workers, shopkeepers see the numbers of their customers decline rapidly. Cheap industrial premises, which the inner city has traditionally provided, vanish, and new firms may have greatly increased difficulty in getting established. Some of these problems have been ameliorated by public policy, such as the attempt by Glasgow and Birmingham to provide new low-cost premises for small firms with extensive inter-firm linkages.

The dominating outcome is the drop in density of population, and the decline in the intensity of development generally. In Birmingham the first three post-war schemes yielded a 30 per cent overspill and in Glasgow 60 per cent, despite redevelopment at a net residential density of 370 persons per ha. The land uses which consistently increased their share of the total were school and public open space. The new residential areas incorporate the neighbourhood design principle, involving the provision of local facilities and some variant of the Radburn principle of

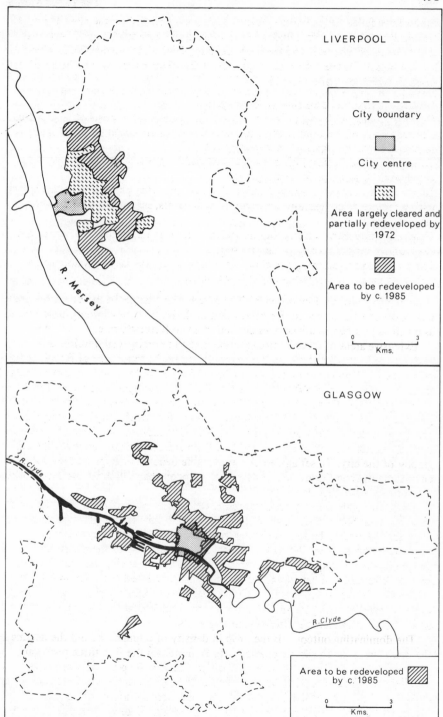

Figure 6.10   Comprehensive redevelopment: Liverpool and Glasgow
Source: City Planning Depts., Liverpool and Glasgow

pedestrian-vehicle segregation.

Even if there had been neither pressure for commercial expansion nor slum clearance, the impact of the car would have made comprehensive development an essential tool for urban renewal. The fact is, however, that many CDAs have been designed to achieve all three purposes simultaneously — commercial expansion, slum clearance and replacement, and improved accessibility. The problem of actually accommodating the car in a physical fabric largely built to accommodate public transport has influenced the form of redevelopment in two major ways in addition to the decentralization policies already referred to. In his *Traffic in Towns* (1963) Buchanan linked his concept of a hierarchy of roads to that of environmental areas. These were not 'precincts', in the sense of freedom from traffic; rather they were the rooms of a town, 'areas or groups of buildings and other development in which daily life is carried on, and where, as a consequence, it is logical that the maintenance of a good environment is of great importance'. These areas may be busy, of mixed uses, and very different environmental standards might obtain, but the basic idea for traffic flow was exclusion of extraneous traffic, 'no drifts of traffic filtering through without business in the area'. Almost every town and city, too, now shows some attempt to segregate pedestrians and vehicles — in the major shopping areas by closing streets or constructing precincts, and even by multi-level development, as in the Bull Ring in Birmingham; and increasingly in new residential development. Since the early 1970s public policy has begun to alter so as to give public transport, through traffic management, a more significant role in the pattern of movement within the major cities. Exactly what the impact of this on the urban land-use pattern will be is as uncertain as whether or not the population will come to accept it.

Public policy initiatives designed to facilitate urban renewal are not limited to the three discussed here, though they are the major ones from a geographical standpoint. A fuller account would have to include the now much wider range of interventionist policies involved. These would include the planning authorities' powers to designate a General Improvement Area within which the aim is to help and persuade owners to improve their properties and the external environment with financial assistance, the Community Development Projects sponsored by the Home Office urban programme and the Educational Priority Areas of the Dept of Education, as well as employment and training programmes by the Dept of Employment and the activities of the Race and Community Relations Commissions. Physical change is no longer seen as the only way to restructure our cities; what the Dept of Environment (1973; 1977) called the 'total approach' is more eloquently put by Donnison (1972, 24):

> 'It would help people if the rungs in the ladders of opportunity were set close to each other, economically, spatially and culturally. People move most easily to a *slightly* more expensive house, *close* to their previous home. More important still, the different ladders which people mount must be set close to each other: it will be easier to get that more expensive house if there are better paid jobs within reach, and easier to get the jobs if there are opportunities for a better education and further training. Conversely, it will be easier for people to stick at their education (or persuade their children to do so) if it promises a better job, it will be easier to stick at the job if it offers more money, and the money will be worth more if it could secure a better home for the worker — or something else which his family really wants.'

IV.3 Settlement Strategies

Chapter I has referred to the work of the Regional Economic Planning Councils, and other chapters to some of the consequences for employment and industry respectively. Here it is intended to refer briefly to the way regional planning affects the national urban system (Bourne 1975). Regional planning is the focus of two rather different but closely related functions, both aimed at increasing the national welfare. The first is a mainly economic exercise concerned with the broad distribution of the nation's resources, including population, which seeks both efficient allocation and reduced regional disparities. In contrast, the second function is the devising and implementing of regional strategies for physical development to ensure an efficient and convenient settlement pattern, and is consequently mainly concerned with land-use needs and locational appraisal. Clearly, the two are closely related – the *inter*-regional balance being influenced by and influencing the *intra*-regional pattern. Thus New Towns and expanded towns appear in this dual role, as instruments both for implementing a regional strategy and for influencing the balance of social and economic opportunity between regions.

Since the revival of government interest in regional planning in 1964, it has had an increasingly close relationship with the urban system. This has arisen as it was appreciated that the social aims being sought through a programme of planned dispersal involving overspill from the conurbations to new and expanded towns, could also be a major tool in achieving important economic goals.

In almost all aspects of new town development the 1960s contrast markedly with the earlier period (ch. 2.IV.6). Indeed it is those aspects which differ most – purpose, size and location – that have the closest connection with regional planning. During the 1960s half of the newly-designated New Towns were located in the development areas, the conurbations in the North West and W Midlands were provided with 'overspill' New Towns, and the scale and phasing of the New Town programme in the South East was discussed in the light of its possible effects on other aspects of the government's then reviving regional policies. The average target population was increased substantially as the social and economic consequences of a 60,000 target population came to be appreciated and because several of the designated sites included well-established towns. Five of the New Towns had populations in excess of 70,000 (C Lancashire, Northampton, Peterborough, Telford, Warrington) at the time of designation, and these, together with Milton Keynes, all have target populations for the early 1990s of 200,000 or more.

The development of these changes can be observed: from the designation of Skelmersdale as the first 'overspill' New Town for Liverpool in 1961, which was granted DA status although located outside the officially defined development area; through the discussion stimulated by the publication of the government's appraisal of population growth in the South East and its proposals for three new cities and six major expansions; to the recent designation of an area (Central Lancashire New Town) including nearly 250,000 persons in Preston, Leyland and Chorley, with a target population of about half a million by the end of the century.

Among the causes of the government's revived interest in regional planning was paradoxically the experience of most of the first wave of New Towns. Glenrothes is probably the most striking instance, located as it was in a rather remote place, 48 km from Edinburgh and 40 km from Dundee by road and ferry across the Firths, solely to be close to the proposed new colliery. Just as Glenrothes began in 1958 to develop as an industrial growth point with the attraction of an American electronics firm, so the industrial success (in spite of rather than because of regional planning) of many of the early New Towns drew attention to their potential as a likely effective tool for implementing regional policy.

Like Glenrothes, the other early New Towns could offer a quality of local environment, physically and socially, coupled with improving communications and a growing local labour supply, that appeared to constitute the conditions required to generate employment growth. This success was especially marked in Scotland and the North East where the almost full employment of E Kilbride, Cumbernauld, Glenrothes and Aycliffe contrasted with the dismal situation in other parts of these regions. The industrial success demonstrated the feasibility of an urban growth-point strategy, and its capability to establish self-sustaining centres of economic growth, while at the same time minimizing public-sector infra-structure costs (especially new and improved transport facilities), providing as wide a choice of opportunities as possible, given the rising threshold levels of viability for most service industries, and continuing the overspill programme.

The strategy, however, also revealed a possible conflict between the 'overspill' and 'growth-point' or 'counter magnet' roles. The former emphasizes quick action, often therefore necessarily close to the congested metropolis with the possibility of commuting, while the latter requires a balanced development at a greater distance from the metropolis. No greater contrast with the first wave exists than in the discussion of local labour markets, for as *The Strategic Plan for the South East* (SE Jt. Planning Team 1970) showed, this problem, if not fully resolved, is being debated and examined and not ignored, as was the case in the 1950s.

Hall et al (1973) have recently described five case studies of the interaction between urban development and regional planning and, in explaining the marked differences between them, suggests that local government arrangements were a crucial factor. In C Scotland the relationship between regional planning and urban policy is in its most advanced form. It is possible that the severity of the challenge of the social and urban problems, as well as the regional economic difficulties, has generated this level of response, greatly aided by the existence of an effective 'regional' authority (in GB terms) – the Scottish Office.

After designating the only New Town to be built in the UK between 1951 and 1960, Cumbernauld (1955) with the novel arrangement that 80 per cent of its immigrant population must come from the City of Glasgow, the Secretary of State proceeded to designate Livingston in 1961. This proposal contained a number of noteworthy innovations of significance to regional planning and economic development.

Although essentially an 'overspill' New Town for Glasgow the location chosen was considerably nearer to Edinburgh than to Glasgow. Thus for the first time overspill was being used to achieve a redistribution of population not merely within, as previously, but *between* major city regions. It had growth point and rehabilitation aims as well, however, as the draft designation order points out:

'a New Town here would offer the possibility not merely of helping solve Glasgow's housing problem but also of using "overspill" constructively to create a new focus of industrial activity in the central belt of Scotland, linking the West with the centres of expansion in the Forth Basin, and at the same time revitalising with modern industries an area hitherto over-dependent on coal and shale'.

Clearly, Telford is a direct descendant of these ideas.

It was recognized that the development of Livingston and the surrounding small towns as a growth point would require an attempt to identify its particular economic strengths and weaknesses, and thus the designation order referred to 'a comprehensive regional scheme of development'. The resulting *Lothians Regional Survey and Plan* (Robertson et al 1966) included economic analysis of the labour market, public sector investment, industrial prospects, etc., as well as what would today be called a sub-regional structure plan. One consequence was the government's ready acceptance that the target population of the New Town should be increased from 70,000 to 100,000 and that of the whole sub-region to 250,000 because of the marked economic and social advantages expected to accrue from this increased scale of development.

These ideas were carried further in the *White Paper* (Scottish Devel. Dept. 1963) and extended to the entire area from Dundee to Ayr, a distance of almost 160 km. In addition to a framework of transport and infra-structure, including new motorways, airport and port development, railway modernization and a water grid, it identified eight growth points, of which four were existing New Town sites and a fifth, Irvine, was proposed and later designated (in 1966). The Grangemouth—Falkirk area, also identified as a growth point, was already a town expansion scheme (Robertson *et al* 1968). This total effort of planned intervention included comprehensive redevelopment, town expansion, the establishment of four new universities (making seven in all in C Scotland), the operation of growth area working parties jointly manned by local and central government officials, and the improvement of regional industrial incentives (e.g. the granting of SDA status to Livingston and Glenrothes New Towns). This action is effecting a remarkable redistribution of the population, restructuring of the economic base, and reconstruction of its largely outworn infra-structure. The economic and social advantages originally sought within a concentrated high density city are now being sought within a broad urbanized zone extending for 160 km; economies of scale and linkage, pools of skilled labour, proximity to large consumer markets, choice in educational, technical, and vocational opportunities, can, it is believed, be more efficiently provided in this polynucleated urban form not fundamentally very different from Ebenezer Howard's (1898) idea of 'social cities'. He proposed multi-centred city regions with 250,000 people in each.

The future settlement pattern in C Scotland is no longer obscure, but is beginning to emerge from planned development and even to dominate the regional landscape. It is now clear that a series of decisions concerning the location, sequence and scale of New Town development will make the whole pattern of life in C Scotland by 1980 radically different from that in the period 1945—65. In essence it can be described as the planned integration of three city regions, those of Glasgow, Edinburgh and Dundee. Although a large extension of the built-up area has been required, this has been done in such a manner that it enhances the prospects of future economic growth and ensures a satisfactory quality of local environment. This clearly meets the aims of both the intra- and the inter-regional facets of regional planning.

Nor is the Scottish case unique. Broadly similar changes in the location and roles of towns under the impact of regional planning are emerging in the NW, with three new towns in the belt between Manchester and Liverpool, and in the NE. In Co. Durham, in addition to the development of New Towns the planners have attempted since the mid-1950s to rationalize the entire settlement system by providing a detailed classification of all existing settlements in terms of their growth potential. The six types of settlement are: (1) major expansion is expected; (2) further development should be limited to what is appropriate to the settlement's character but will be considerable; (3) some development will occur but should be limited in scale; (4) no great changes are expected and any development should be closely related to the present size, character and function of the settlement; (5) no development should be allowed, but settlement will continue to exist for a long time; and (6) no new development is allowed to occur and clearance of old houses is proceeding rapidly. It must be said, however, that the designation of a village for 'no development' inevitably produced the strongest possible local political reaction, one of the earliest and most positive indications of public interest in planning.

To conclude. Even if planning is often a largely invisible bureaucratic process, interwoven with other causes and effects in the urban system, somewhat slow-moving in realizing its aims and with a flexible attitude to them, its diverse influence on the British urban system has grown over the last thirty years, and without an assessment of it we shall be missing a large and increasing part of the explanation why our cities are what they are today and will become tomorrow.

REFERENCES

ANDREWS, H F (1971) 'A Cluster Analysis of British Towns', *Urban Stud.*, *8*, 271–84
ARMEN, G (1972) 'A Classification of Cities and City Regions in England and Wales, 1966', *Reg. Stud.*, *6*, 149–82
BAGLEY, C (1965) 'Juvenile Delinquency in Exeter: an Ecological and Comparative Study', *Urban Stud.*, *2*, 33–50
BARKER, A (1975) 'Studying Amenity Societies', *Tn Ctry Plann.*, *43*, 302–4
BELL, C and BELL, R (1972) *City Fathers*, Harmondsworth
BERRY, B J L (1964) 'Cities as Systems within Systems of Cities', *Pap. Reg. Sci. Assocn.*, *13*, 147–63
BEST, R H and RODGERS, A W (1973) *The Urban Countryside*, London
BIRD, H and WHITBREAD, M (1975) 'Council House Transfers and Exchanges', *New Society*, *33*, 671, 359–61
BOURNE, L S (1975) *Urban Systems: Strategies for Regulation*, Oxford
BUCHANAN, C D (1963) *Traffic in Towns*, HMSO
CARTER, H (1958) 'Aberystwyth: the Modern Development of a Medieval Castle Town in Wales', *Trans. Inst. Br. Geogr.*, *25*, 239–53
            (1965) *The Towns of Wales*, Cardiff
            (1972) *The Study of Urban Geography*, London
CARTER, H and ROWLEY, G (1966) 'The Central Business District of Cardiff', *Trans. Inst. Br. Geogr.*, *38*, 119–34
CASTLE, I M and GITTUS, E (1957) 'The Distribution of Social Defects in Liverpool', *Sociol. Rev.*, *5*, 43–64
CHAMPION, A G (1970) 'Recent Trends in New Town Densities', *Tn Ctry Plann.*, *38*, 5, 252–4
COLLINS, B J (1951) *Development Plans Explained*, HMSO
CONZEN, M R G (1960) 'Alnwick, Northumberland: A Study in Town Plan Analysis', *Inst. Br. Geogr. Publ. 27*, London

CRAVEN, E (1969) 'Private Residential Expansion in Kent', *Urban Stud.*, *6*, 1–16

CULLINGWORTH, J B (1965) *English Housing Trends*, London

(1974) *Town and Country Planning in Britain*, London

DoE (1973) *Making Towns Better: The Sunderland Study; the Rotherham Study; the Oldham Study*, HMSO

(1976) 'British Cities: Urban Population and Employment Trends 1951–71', *Res. Rep. 10*, HMSO

(1977) *Inner Area Studies: Liverpool, Birmingham and Lambeth*, HMSO

DIAMOND, D R (1962) 'The Central Business District of Glasgow' in NORBURG, K (ed) *Proc. IGU Symp. in Urban Geogr., Lund 1960*, Gleerup, Lund

(1975) 'Planning the Urban Environment', *Geogr.*, *60*, 189–93

DIAMOND, D R and EDWARDS, R (1975) *Business in Britain: a Management Planning Atlas*, London

DICKINSON, R E (1947) *City, Region and Regionalism*, London

DONNISON, D V (1969) *The Government of Housing*, Harmondsworth

(1972) 'Ideas for Town Planners', *Three Banks Rev.*, *96*, 3–27

EVANS, H (1974) *The New Citizen's Guide to Town and Country Planning*, for TCPA, London

FAWCETT, C B (1932) 'Distribution of the Urban Population in GB', *Geogrl. J.*, *79*, 100–16

FIELDING, A J (1972) 'Internal Migration in England and Wales', *Univ. Working Pap. 14*, Centre for Environ. Stud., London

GEDDES, P (1915) *Cities in Evolution*, London

GEN. REGISTER OFF. (1956) *Census 1951, England and Wales: Report on Greater London and Five Other Conurbations*, HMSO

GODDARD, J B (1970) 'Functional Regions within the City Centre', *Trans. Inst. Br. Geogr.*, *49*, 161–82

(1975) 'Office Location in Urban and Regional Development', *Theory and Practice in Geography*, Oxford

GLC (1969) *Greater London Development Plan*, London

GREEN, F H W (1950) 'Urban Hinterlands in England and Wales: An Analysis of Bus Services', *Geogrl. J.*, *116*, 64–88

GREGORY, R (1971) *The Price of Amenity*, London

HALL, P G (1971) 'The Spatial Structure of Metropolitan England and Wales' in CHISHOLM, M and MANNERS, G (eds) *Spatial Policy Problems of the British Economy*, Cambridge, 96–125

HALL, P G et al (1973) *The Containment of Urban England*, 2 vols, London. For problems of definition see particularly vol 1, 42–68 and 117–40

HALSEY, A H (ed) (1972) *Trends in British Society since 1900*, London

HAMNETT, C (1973) 'Improvement Grants as an Indicator of Gentrification in Inner London', *Area*, *5*, 252–61

HERAUD, B J (1968) 'Social Class and the New Towns', *Urban Stud.*, *5*, 33–58

HOWARD, E (1898) *Garden Cities of Tomorrow, a Peaceful Path to Real Reform*, London

HUGHES, A J and KOZLOWSKI, J (1968) 'Threshold Analysis – an Economic Tool for Town and Regional Planning', *Urban Stud.*, *5*, 132–43

HURD, R M (1924) *Principles of City Land Values*, New York

JONES, A (1960) *A Social Geography of Belfast*, London

JONES, P N (1967) *The Segregation of Immigrant Communities in the City of Birmingham 1961*, Hull
LEVIN, P H (1976) *Government and the Planning Process*, London
LOMAS, G (1964) 'Population Changes and Functional Regions', *J Tn Plann. Inst., London, 50*, 21–31
MARRIOTT, O (1967) *The Property Boom*, London
MARTIN, A E (1967) 'Environment, Housing and Health', *Urban Stud., 4*, 1–21
McWILLIAM, C (1975) *Scottish Townscape*, London
MIN. HOUSING and LOCAL GOVT. and MIN. of TRANSPORT (1963) *Town Centres: Current Practice*, HMSO
MOSER, G A and SCOTT, W (1961) *British Towns: a Statistical Study of their Social and Economic Differences*, Edinburgh
PAHL, R E (1965) *Urbs in Rure*, London
POOLE, M A and BOAL, F W (1973) 'Religious Residential Segregation in Belfast in mid-1969: a Multi-level Analysis' in CLARK, B D and GLEAVE, M B (eds) *Social Patterns in Cities*, Inst. Br. Geogr., London
PRITCHARD, R M (1976) *Housing and the Spatial Structure of the City*, Cambridge
RASMUSSEN, S E (1951) *Towns and Buildings*, Liverpool
REX, J A (1968) 'The Sociology of a Zone of Transition' in PAHL, R E (ed) *Readings in Urban Sociology*, Oxford, 211–31
REX, J A and MOORE, R (1967) *Race, Community and Conflict*, London
ROBERTSON, D J, JOHNSON-MARSHALL, P E A and MATTHEW, Sir R H
    (1966) *Lothians. Regional Survey and Plan*, 2 vols, Edinburgh HMSO
    (1968) *Grangemouth/Falkirk Regional Survey and Plan*, 2 vols, Edinburgh HMSO
ROBSON, B T (1973) *Urban Growth: an Approach*, London
            (1975) 'Urban Social Areas', *Theory and Practice in Geography*, Oxford
ROYAL COMMN. LOCAL GOVT. 1966–9 (1969) Vol II, *Memorandum of Dissent (D. Senior)*, Cmnd 4040 HMSO
SCOTTISH DEVELOPMENT DEPT. (1963) *Central Scotland: a Programme for Development and Growth*, Cmnd 2188 Edinburgh, HMSO
SELF, P J O (1957) *Cities in Flood*, London
SIMMIE, J (1974) *Citizens in Conflict*, London
SMITH, R D P (1968) 'The Changing Urban Hierarchy', *Reg. Stud., 2*, 1–19
SOLESBURY, W (1974) *Policy in Urban Planning*, Oxford
SE JOINT PLANNING TEAM (1970) *Strategic Plan for the SE*, HMSO
THORPE, D (1968) 'The Main Shopping Centres of GB in 1961. Their Location and Structural Characteristics', *Urban Stud., 5*, 165–206
THURSTON, H S (1953) 'The Urban Regions of St Albans', *Trans. Inst. Br. Geogr., 19*, 107–21
WESTAWAY, J (1974) 'The Spatial Hierarchy of Business Organisations and its Implications for the British Urban System', *Reg. Stud., 8*, 145–55
WESTERGAARD, J H (1964) 'The Structure of Greater London' in CENTRE FOR URBAN STUD. *London: Aspects of Change*, London
WHITEHAND, J W R (1972) 'Building Cycles and the Spatial Pattern of Urban Growth, *Trans. Inst. Br. Geogr., 56*, 39–56
WILLIAMS, P R (1976) 'The Role of Institutions in the Inner London Housing Market: the Case of Islington', *Trans. Inst. Br. Geogr., New Ser. 1*, 72–82
WISE, M J (1966) 'The City Region', *Advmt Sci., 23*, 571–4

7

In Conclusion

I   An Assessment

This geographical interpretation of the economic, social or political conditions affecting and affected by the UK space since 1945 has been concerned with the changing balance of forces, the spectrum of trends, the ensuing problems, and the shifting public and private policy mix over three decades. Even in terms of public policy, overall coherence of spatial objectives has been lacking, much has been piecemeal in character, and indeed public recognition of the importance of a spatial perspective in national affairs has been both tardy and grudging. This situation has scarcely been helped by the lack of sophistication in regional or other spatial analytical methods in all social sciences until very recent years. The persistent lack of adequate and comparable regional data is only now being remedied, and that only partially.

National needs The needs are thus for clearer and more comprehensive spatial management objectives, to be operated through the regional and/or urban networks, and with an ordered sequence of priorities for the use and safeguarding of natural resources, including land, distribution or deployment of people and work, harnessing and harmonizing of energy sources and industrial strength, with full exploitation of the potential offered by the great increases in mobility of people and commodities. There is no optimal geographical solution to the arrangement of the UK space but the range of options urgently needs to be more fully and clearly defined at both national and regional levels. Increasingly in a democratic society, and almost as a counterweight to the centralizing tendencies of a complex urban and industrial economy, there is a rising emphasis upon nations and economic regions as the first-stage breakdown of the UK, and a viable level for enhanced decision-taking. Indeed the conferment of powers and channelling of initiatives at this regional level may ultimately contain the key to the hitherto elusive problem of growth without inflation in the post-war UK.

The economic and social record of the UK since 1945 has been steady rather than spectacular, lacking in 'economic miracles', but with general forward momentum until the early 1970s, albeit by any criterion somewhat slowly and irregularly. By the time of entry to the EEC the UK had achieved a major post-war transformation, a redefined and reduced world role. What is henceforth economically and socially possible in UK planning, what can be afforded and what is seen to be desirable, will need to take a wide range of EEC perspectives into account, though not exclusively so. The difficulties in balancing internal UK forces with externalities in an interpretation of post-war changes in the UK space have become apparent in succeeding chapters. The externalities are likely to be even more important in the future, but the problems of public management of economy and society are not likely to become less by virtue of an increase to the European-scale perspective in the short-term.

Planning problems Problems facing UK planners are substantial and complex. Though the projection of population from the mid-1970s is now more modest (section III) there will still be a sizeable increase and it may accelerate towards the end of the present century. The distribution of the industrial and urban population continues to reflect an Industrial Revolution heritage, changed in degree rather than kind in the twentieth century. Physical planning in the UK has made giant strides since 1945 but coherent regional planning is still in its infancy, both conceptually and in reality on the ground. The debate on optimum population size is mounting, to rival that on the possibilities and risks of unrestrained economic growth. Arguments for greater social justice command increasingly wide assent and the need for greater decentralization in decision-taking is the more stridently proclaimed as economic and administrative forces seem to favour ever more rationalization and concentration, to achieve economies of scale and of unit costs.

Confident forward projections for the UK space are hard to justify, except in very general terms, in face of the complexities and uncertainties of both the immediate and the longer-term future. Furthermore the ability to predict ahead varies with the discipline being used: reliable manpower forecasts rarely go beyond a few years, land allocations in physical planning up to fifteen years, and broad regional strategies may set up speculative options to the end of the century. Predictions will also be conditioned by political beliefs and intentions, by an assessment of the likely and desirable courses of changes in economy and society, as well as in polity.

Balance of forces At the base of all forecasting, in the light of the evidence of this book, lies the prime need to *evaluate and rank the forces which are tending to polarize, centralize or concentrate, on the one hand, and those which are tending in the opposite direction to disaggregate, disperse or breakdown concentration or congestion.* The aggregating forces have been strongly and increasingly detected through the chapters of this book, notably the range of market forces leading to concentration at fewer, larger sites in: energy output, manufacturing or commercial plants or firms, transport nodes, major recreation centres or water storage sites. To these forces the centralizing tendencies in government, banking, insurance and finance may be added, in the search for administrative efficiency or convenience. Spatially interpreted, these forces tend to the strengthening of the centre against the periphery, of more affluent against less prosperous regions; in short the growth regions against the development regions (see ch. 1.V.1).

On the other side of the argument, and together these forces may prove to be increasingly decisive, must be listed: the desirability of greater regional balance in the economy and society of the UK, for the satisfaction of component national and regional aspirations, but also from the commonsense points of view of reducing congestion in growth regions, diminishing the sources of inflationary pressure there and spreading social justice and better prospects for economic growth throughout the

UK space. Regional policies by successive UK governments have recognized the validity of this thinking, but the means provided have not yet permitted the desirable ends to be realized. Keeble's (1976) postulation of a 'periphery-centre' reversal of the traditional centripetal polarization in UK industrial location seems optimistically premature.

The mid-1970s Since the first edition of this book (1973) economic prospects for the UK have deteriorated sharply, at least for the short-term. Though the causes of this recession are variously attributed, and externalities have not been without their influence, the deepest genesis lies surely within the economy, society and polity of the UK. The pursuit of a sustainable momentum of economic growth, at full potential rate without an unacceptable level of inflation or serious damage to the balance of payments, has been the theoretical cornerstone of national investment strategy for the past three decades. Only thus could higher living standards, fuller and better social provision, and the promotion of full employment be both attained and maintained. In no other way might social justice be advanced for deprived groups, but also for localities, cities and regions in the UK space.

By any objective assessment the truth is that economic growth during the early 1970s has been slow overall, fitful in its incidence, and by 1975 was in secular reverse. The spatial impact of this increasingly undesirable state of affairs has been uneven, but to the traditional structural and locational problems of the assisted areas have now been added the sharp deterioration in social conditions in many inner cities, and the emergence of serious pockets of local unemployment in hitherto affluent regions of Britain. Coventry and inner London vie with Gateshead, Lanarkshire and Belfast for the sympathy of the nation, and for priority aid from governments. British Leyland, Chrysler (UK) and Rolls-Royce have been recent supplicants for public largesse, much more so than any textile or shipbuilding firm.

Diagnosis of our many ills indicts countless culprits: governments, for their doctrinaire views, their inability to manage the national economy, and their lack of a clear, coherent and inter-related public investment strategy, whose priorities might match the capacity of the nation to finance them adequately in time and in place; entrepreneurs, for their unwillingness to invest, modernize, rationalize, and for inefficiencies of management; organized labour, for its traditional attitudes, practices and low productivity; the general public, for its false priorities within savings and consumption, and for an ingrained demand for greater welfare and a fuller 'social wage' than the flagging Gross Domestic Product can reasonably provide.

Prescriptions for the patient are equally legion, from the doctrinaire to the pragmatic, from the grand design to the empirical, from the moral to the political. It is becoming increasingly clear that there can be no single universal 'solution' to our national problems, to be planned for, optimized, promoted and monitored until realized. Indeed, the growing revulsion against most forms of planning is a disturbing thought to those who see as the greatest need the creation of ever more complex and sophisticated operational models to programme and control our collective futures. In the undoubted diversity in human conditions and aspirations in the UK lies both the greatest constraint for the planner, and yet, at the same time, the greatest potential for generating and accommodating to change. In all this the geographer has one of the most important roles in the assessment and interpretation of the variegated urban and regional kaleidoscope of modern Britain.

II The Regional Problem

Speaking of the regional *problem* rather than accentuating regional *potential* is a
fair comment on a state of affairs which has persisted in spite of three decades of
varied government aid policies. Such regional problems are common to all developed
economies and their origins lie in the fundamental inequalities of resource endow-
ment, including natural and human resources, together with the attributes of location. Such seemingly inexorable geographical logic has been modified through time
by changing technology, and variations in investment, supply and demand. Resources have been revalued and fresh, mobile resources may have been introduced,
but some of the underlying realities have proved remarkably enduring.

Since the economic depression of the early 1930s governments have been persistently and increasingly involved in policies of economic and social aid for regions,
successively defined as distressed, development or assisted areas (ch. 1.III). Though
the policy mix has been varied through three decades and measures have rarely been
consistently implemented, there has been general political assent to the promotion
of full employment, the pursuit of greater equality in living standards, growth prospects, and betterment of the 'living environment'; reduction in the levels of inter-
regional net migration has been an additional purpose on occasion. Progress towards
all of these objectives, can be demonstrated, for some areas and at certain periods.
What is not clear is how and when, if at all, the objectives may be finally achieved
and what part public policy (whether UK or EEC) must continue to play, for how
long, and at what cost? More specifically, to what extent is the attempt to solve
problems at the *regional* scale likely to be, or already in effect is, at the expense of
aggregate national well-being.

These questions have not been answered effectively in either public or academic
debate, and it is not hard to see why. It is difficult enough to trace the multiplier
effects of particular ministerial policies at the regional level, even more to evaluate
what might have happened without such policies, or by a different mix in time and
space. It is virtually in the realms of pure conjecture what might have been the outcome of different policies. The most important question of all, indeed, may be what
effect certain public policies can have, in any case, upon a complex market situation
in which externalities seem to be increasingly dominant. No one has ventured to
look so far ahead as to envisage a time when regional policies may no longer be
necessary, given the eventual achievement of sufficient equality between British
regions. Perhaps this is because, like the poor, regions will always be with us. Their
built-in geographical diversities can be modified but not fundamentally changed, and
the pursuit of equality is really the never-ending quest for equity, or social justice,
not so easily, if ever, satisfied.

In the mid-1970s the *regional debate* (ch. 1.III) was becoming more sharply
polarized, among both academics and public policy managers. There is, moreover, a
burgeoning political dimension to the debate, among nationalists and regionalists at
home and among the nation-states at the level of the EEC. Not surprisingly, the
mainsprings of difference are between those living and working in the assisted areas
and those in more affluent regions. A second major distinction is between those
who are insistent upon the economic logic behind policies and their impact, and
those who are prepared to weight social benefit variables elastically, even electorally.
Ironically, the most reliable assessment of regional policy prospects at the present is
that characteristically Scottish verdict — 'not proven'. Furthermore, and paradox-

ically at a time when theoreticians are proclaiming, ever more stridently, that the regional problem is but the varied expression of a national problem, the groundswell of political opinion is increasingly insistent upon devolution and decentralization, upon regional control over regional destinies (ch. 1.IV).

The regional-national debate now has a further national-supra-national dimension (ch. 1.III). At the present stage of regional policy-making in the EEC it is right to think of its Regional Development Fund as supplementary to national measures, rather than the first step towards more radically different 'market' policies. The definition of new categories for regional aid (Commission of the European Communities 1975) appeared to threaten only the intermediate areas of UK policy, by classing them with other central areas. Given the political balance of forces within the EEC it seems unlikely that the present UK assisted areas policies will be dismantled or very much modified, even after the transitional period of British integration into the EEC (1975–8).

From the mid-1970s it is not readily possible to look ahead clearly and confidently. The general ferment of regionalism is towards devolution and decentralization, and it is gaining ground. Accommodation is being sought for the political wishes of the Scots, Welsh and Ulstermen (ch. 1.IV) but seems unlikely for the English regions, at least in the short-term. The national economic situation more and more resembles that of a siege economy, and policies, even regional policies, have to be trimmed, if not slimmed. Ch. 1.V surveyed the problems and aspirations of the UK regions, formulated through regional strategy proposals. Though these may be non-standardized, inadequately inter-related, and even at times internally inconsistent, they reflect the first stirrings of the regional voice. As and when this voice is given further utterance through representative regional institutions popularly elected, regional strategies will pass from being claims and counter-claims for scarce national resources, to the role of manifestos for self-determined regional actions. In the interim they continue to be the framework for structure plans, once the strategy has been approved by the minister. This should not be allowed to disguise the fact that the recognition and accommodation of regional aspirations, and their harmonization with national or European objectives continues to be perhaps the greatest problem and challenge UK governments are likely to meet in the immediately foreseeable future.

III Population Trends and Prospects

The stagnation and possible fall in population numbers expected from pre-1939 trends, especially the level of births, have not transpired (ch. 2). Higher birth-rates than were anticipated prevailed from the mid-1950s to the late 1960s, due in part to earlier and more universal marriage and to increased illegitimacy rates, together with a further reduction in infant mortality and general death-rate. Reflected in a gradual increase in expectation of life, these have led to higher natural growth rates than were forecast by the *Royal Commission on Population* (1949). Net immigration gains from overseas in the late 1950s and early 1960s, together with the natural increase from this relatively youthful population, have further assisted a steady increase in numbers in the UK. Estimation of future population levels on the basis of past and current trends is a hazardous business for they depend on assumptions which may be quickly invalidated by changing social and economic circumstances. Successive revisions of population estimates for 1990 led, for example, to estimates varying between 53 million (based on 1955 assumptions) and 67 million (1964-based); these wide differences are due largely to alternative assumptions concerning birth-rate.

Whatever their precise level, however, all estimates from the mid-1950s agree in predicting growth into the 1990s and it is unlikely that the recent downturn in birth-rate will change this trend. If continued into the 1980s, as seems likely, it would certainly reduce the relatively modest growth rates of some 0.7 per cent per annum that were made on the basis of the 'moderate' 1968-based estimate to less than 0.2 per cent per annum by the 1974-based projection. In any case many people now challenge the ability or desirability of growth in such a populous and, in some urbanized industrial regions, already over-crowded country. Hence, in the last few years, the debate has been joined over what is regarded as an optimum population for the UK, a debate which reflects a growing awareness of the significance of population trends and distribution for all aspects of national life – demographic (Population Investigation Commn. 1970), social, economic and environmental (Taylor 1970).

An optimum population is not capable of a single, precise definition since it depends upon many variables, each of which is dynamic: population, resources, land, the level of expectations, and consumption. The first official investigation considered these problems in an appropriately wide context, and gathered evidence from a very wide range of viewpoints (House of Commons 1971), but did not emerge with any general consensus, though it did make a number of recommendations which amounted to a possible population policy for the UK.

It would be foolish to speculate over precise future population totals in view of the fluctuating trends in population of the last thirty years. This underlines the need for flexibility in economic and social policies related to population. But it is possible to indicate the sort of problems which must be taken into account in any analysis of the spatial and environmental implications of population. In terms of food and natural resources the UK would certainly be regarded as over-populated already, if we depended upon indigenous supplies alone, for we do not support anything like our present population. Indeed a suggested maximum of 40 million people, made some years ago by the then President of the British Association (Hutchinson 1966), is not unrealistic in this context. However, neither on the basis of present population trends, nor of any envisaged, is such a target likely to provide the basis of a practical policy, at least in the foreseeable future.

Population is, moreover, potentially an economic asset, both now and in the future, arguably the most important which the UK, as a technologically-advanced society, possesses. Over the past two centuries a numerous, vigorous and inventive people have proved capable of enlarging the economic capacity and population potential of our islands at a rising standard of living for an increasing proportion of our people. They may be capable of doing so into the future, though certainly not at the rate which characterized rapid nineteenth-century growth. However, decreasing demand for manpower, in terms of numbers, as against skills, which has already been reflected in at least some of the structural component of unemployment in the past few years, sheds doubt on our capacity to absorb the potentially larger labour force even in the 1980s.

One of the most powerful factors behind the growing concern over population growth in the UK, as in other parts of the developed world, has been an increased awareness of the enormous environmental impact of a large and closely-packed population in a modern industrial and urbanized society. Pressures on basic resources such as land and water, as well as on food and raw materials, are reflected in growing problems of over-use, e.g. for recreation, and problems of waste disposal, both human (sewage) and non-recoverable (such as plastics or poisonous chemicals), and in problems of excessive pollution of air, water and, in places, also land (ch. 3.V).

While undoubtedly many such difficulties are due to misuse of the environment and past irresponsibility by industry, commerce and private individuals, they are exacerbated by high population numbers and concentrations. Loss of land to building and communications is not likely to pose insurmountable problems over the next thirty years, not least because of the slowing down in housing and road-building programmes, but it will undoubtedly add to pressures which are already severe in some large urban areas. It may well be that some more stringent curbs will need to be introduced on further industrial, commercial, housing and transportation growth in some over-congested regions. There will also have to be a more positive approach to the problem of urban decay, with its associated complex problems of social and economic blight.

Seen thus, one critical aspect of UK population problems, now and in the future, is that concerning regional distribution and trends. The UK could probably have accommodated the population of up to 80 million forecast in the mid-1960s for the second quarter of next century. The present slow growth rates will produce at most some 58 million people by the first decade of the twenty-first century. Yet even modest growth will require a more satisfactory regional and intra-regional balance of population in relation to land, resources and communications than that of the present day. In this context population policy is not a separate target for national planning but rather a key aspect for regional planning policy. Any major problem of regional planning today illustrates this point: the dispersal of homes and people from overcrowded cities; the location of employment in both industry and services; the provision of adequate transportation; access to land for recreation; environmental control and restoration.

Without appropriate and integrated regional planning policies, especially for land use and industry, it will be impossible to relieve population pressure in the over-crowded areas. Yet in some of the less prosperous regions additional jobs, homes and people could be easily accommodated. It is unlikely that left alone or subjected to the limited and intermittent regional planning policies of the past three decades trends will differ greatly from those of the post-war period, although in *all* regions growth will be less than forecast in the late-1960s, particularly in the South East. Nevertheless, the *pattern* of change (fig. 7.1) is likely to be similar to that of 1961–9 (fig. 2.5). Migration gains are likely to be mainly in the arc from the South East through the Midlands, but the greatest increases are still likely to occur in the environmentally vulnerable area between London and Birmingham, and, to a lesser extent, between the W Midlands and NW England. If a British megalopolis stretching from Greater London is to be avoided, more people must be retained in, and indeed must be attracted to, the hitherto less prosperous regions, some of which have more land for housing and industry and most of which are nearer to good recreational areas on the coast, in highlands and in national parks. In such areas investment in urban renewal could be an act of population policy as well as of economic, social and regional planning. But to retain or attract population there and redress the imbalance of the last seventy years, capital will be needed to rectify the many deficiencies in housing, education and amenities – social as well as physical – in the inner city and in the older industrial regions.

If we do not fully utilize the resources of the whole of our islands, further population increases will inevitably bring greater and perhaps intolerable pressures to the present overcrowded regions. In recommending that a special government office should be set up to deal with these problems a Select Committee (House of Commons 1971) urged that it should take account not only of population but also of 'such major issues as food supplies, natural resources, economic growth and the environment'. In appointing in December 1973 a Minister with special responsibility for population questions, government showed itself responsive to such advice. However, as birthrate has continued to fall in the 1970s, so the concern for policies to limit population growth seems to have diminished. Little had been done to extend the anti-natalist policy implicit in the two Private Members' Bills which led to *Family Planning* and *Abortion Acts* of 1967 (Publ. Gen. Acts 1967) before the declining births of the 1970s were leading some to question not only whether such policy was desirable, but whether they may be replaced by pro-natalist policies in the 1980s (Brooks 1975; Buxton and Craven 1976). Despite a considerable increase in the numbers of women of marriageable age in the 1980s, a product of the 'baby boom' of the early-to-mid-1960s, the situation in which in most households both husband and wife work, the changed role and status of women in society and a developing concern for the effects of population pressure may all contribute to fewer births in the late 1980s and 90s than were forecast a few years ago. Such rapid changes in population structure and trends call for greater flexibility in social and economic policy, and in public investment, a question recently considered in a government Central Policy Review Staff report (Cabinet Office 1975).

While recent population forecasts might seem to deny it, the UK undoubtedly has a population/resources problem, the outcome of which will be a key factor in the social, economic and regional geography of the UK in the late twentieth century. The deterioration in the UK's economic situation in the 1970s is bound to slow down the rate of change over the next twenty or thirty years. Population numbers would already appear to have begun to adjust to the changed situation. But regional and local imbalances, both economic and social, still exist and are reflected in many aspects of population behaviour. Despite the shortage of public funds, it is important that flexible and effective policies designed to alleviate inequalities within the UK population should continue to receive attention.

IV Environment and Land Use

Environmental management will become increasingly important as pressures for space increase with the need to optimize the available resources in the interests of all land users. The apparent conflicts between these users are no doubt a result of lack of liaison hitherto rather than intention and can only be adequately resolved by adopting conservation or management policies which take all potential users into consideration. While short-term decisions may be satisfactorily made by subjective means, in the long-term it would appear necessary to have complex models where evaluation of land-use policies can be fully tested. For this, continued data collection and research into the relationships between land use and environment is an urgent need. However, there is clearly a dilemma, for land use requires field observation and is therefore both costly and slow and the more detail required the longer it will take. Stamp's land-use survey was kept simple and was thus completed within a short time. The more detailed second land-use survey is of necessity a much slower operation and its value as an inventory on which to base planning decisions is thereby greatly reduced, particularly on a regional or national scale.

Land classifications have a similar problem but the complexity of the environment makes it essential for the classification to consider the potential user of the map so that no universally satisfactory classification can be produced. Because of the variety of users more classifications are needed in the future, a task facilitated by data storage and retrieval systems, though the problem of interpretation of environmental factors for specific purposes remains. Modelling of land-use systems, at present being developed for uplands where the conflicts between agriculture, forest, urban water-supply and recreation are relatively simple, must be extended to include the much more complex problems of the heavily populated lowlands.

Many aspects of *measurement of the physical environment* can be improved and in particular, the closing of the wide gap between the macro-climatic scale of standard meteorological records, which exist over a long period of time, and the micro-climates which so clearly affect human activity. The development of studies of local climates must again be problem-orientated. This, however, involves the isolation of the parameters important to production, particularly the commercial yields and potentials of living things such as agricultural plants and forest trees. Equally important to production are the physical conditions permitting work to be carried out, e.g. in certain farming operations water may be critical, or in building operations wind and temperature could be limiting. The accurate prediction of these conditions will enable industry or agriculture to project production and to make more efficient use of human resources. However this will only be possible by improvements in the long-term forecasting of these parameters.

Environmental pollution will change in its nature and effects so that continual monitoring is necessary. Water pollution and land pollution will become a matter of river-basin management and can be more effectively controlled under the administrative reorganization carried through in 1974 in England and Wales. Conservation must imply continuance, though not necessarily maximization of production, rather than just preservation, so that here too industrial and agricultural land use must be evaluated in terms of the long-term effects on the environment. On occasion there may be a major conflict between the desire to attract industry (or allow it to grow) and priorities in conservation. Studies of industrial and urban pollution must not remain a UK problem in isolation. Entry into Europe brings with it an opportunity to achieve a measure of environmental control over the atmosphere and the seas of Europe, notably the North Sea, which could not be envisaged before.

It is as yet too early to state with confidence that environmental constraints will eventually set limits to economic growth, but it is already clear that increasing numbers of citizens are prepared to evaluate, take into account, and even give precedence to environmental implications arising from excessive preoccupation with growth.

V   Distribution of Economic Activity

It is becoming increasingly apparent that the evolution of the economic patterns in the UK since 1945 fall into three main periods: 1945–60, 1960–73 and post-1973.

The period **1945–60** was essentially one of adjustment following the disruption

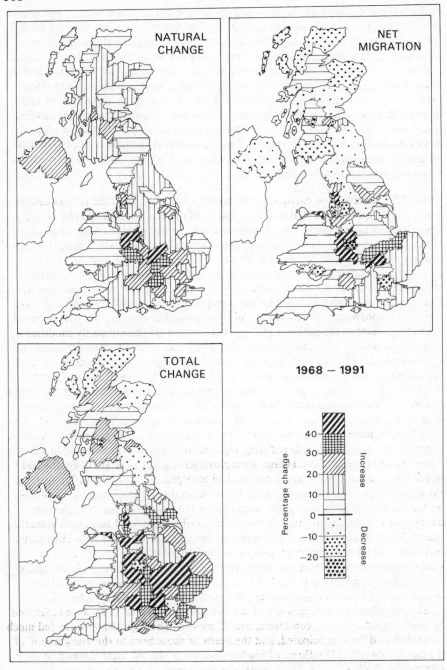

Figure 7.1   Projected regional population changes, UK, 1968–91

of the Second World War (Chisholm 1974). Maximization of production was at a premium and some of the growth in employment that resulted was diverted to the DAs by government action. However, by the end of this period the distribution of economic activity remained familiar. Traditional industries such as cotton in Lancashire, wool in Yorkshire, shipbuilding in N Ireland and coal and steel in S Wales and the North East, had further declined but still dominated those regions to a surprising extent. In the service sector the foundations for subsequent change had been laid by centralization of control, through nationalization of electricity and gas distribution, health and transport, but by 1960 shortages of capital for the necessary investment limited the geographical impact. Personal mobility was still restricted by low private car ownership rates which inhibited the locational flexibility of services and to a lesser extent manufacturing.

1960–73 This situation changed in the period 1960–73, when the factors described in ch. 4 were most influential in the evolution of the economic geography of the UK. The structure of the economy altered substantially, with dramatic declines in the importance of the traditional 'heavy' industries, including coal-mining, textiles, shipbuilding, metal-making, and a substantial increase in the proportion of the labour force in services. There was continued centralization of control in industry, allowing rationalization and increasing size of units to achieve economies of scale. The effective economic distance between major centres was reduced, through road transport improvement in particular. All these tended to increase the attractions of market locations at the national and regional levels, a trend only partly modified by government action, which influenced some of the more flexible manufacturing and service activities to expand in the DAs. Within individual regions the same trends, and especially the growth of private car ownership and affluence, allowed greater flexibility of locational choice, with manufacturing and services now able to disperse farther out from main centres. As the traditional industries declined, in regions of former dominance they lost their premier positions to growing light industries, especially engineeering, which was attracted to the DAs by regional incentives. The effect of this restructuring, in reducing regional differences, was reflected in the convergence of regional percentage unemployment figures after 1970. By the end of the period a new geographical pattern had emerged, substantially different from the inherited patterns still apparent in 1960. Natural gas and oil became more important than coal in the energy patterns, services location became an important determinant of the distribution of the market, influencing local and regional market-oriented manufacturing if not that serving national markets, while individual factories became larger and smaller factories clustered together on industrial estates. Decanting of manufacturing, and later services, employment from the larger cities to the urban periphery or to the DAs, created problems for the inner-city. This period then was one of major changes in the economic geography of the UK.

The considerable developments of the two periods prior to 1973 were facilitated by, and dependent upon, continuing overall growth. The population expanded much more than had been anticipated, and the needs of those born in the 'baby boom' of the late 1940s (ch. 2.I) influenced market demand in the UK right through to their maturity in the late 1960s. Many industries and almost all services planned their developments to meet continued increases in demand. At the same time the government was concerned with controlling growth, guiding it away from overgrowth areas into areas of need as recommended by the *Barlow Commission Report* (R. Commn.

Indus. Popul. 1940). Even in 1970 the economic sections of regional plans were still concerned with influencing the location of expected growth to achieve desired spatial distributions (ch. 1.V). At the national scale, development of the estuarine areas of Humberside, Severnside and Tayside, and of New Towns and even of a New City at Milton Keynes to cope with projected population growth, were expected to have a major impact on the distribution of economic activity in the UK.

The mid-1970s It is the change from this state of actual and anticipated growth, to a situation of actual and anticipated non-growth, that distinguishes the third period which began in 1973. Information about this changed situation is still becoming available and too short a time has elapsed for the implications to be properly evaluated or for the duration of the non-growth situation to be predicted. What evidence there is, however, does give some basis for comment (Eversley 1975). The number of people in employment has fallen since 1973 and unemployment has risen. Public investment has been postponed and plans revised. With the market stagnant, private investment in manufacturing and office development has markedly declined. Contributing to this non-growth state was the rise in oil prices, following the action of the Middle East producers in 1973. This had the effect of increasing the cost of transport, reversing the trend of the 1960s. Birth-rates have continued to fall and by 1975 were barely keeping pace with deaths and net emigration from England and Wales. Demand for major development in the estuarine areas to cope with major national population growth to the end of the century has evaporated, while New Towns have to re-examine their position. Present trends indicate that some of the proposals which emerged in response to anticipated growth were as much as decades premature. In the new circumstances the amount of change to be expected in the distribution of economic activity in the UK is very much less than occurred in the 1960s, since lack of investment will severely limit alteration of patterns of activity.

The most obvious exception is the development of the North Sea oil resources. Much of the impact so far has been concentrated in E Scotland, with industrial C Scotland also benefiting (Dept. of Industry 1975A). Industrial development in the form of petrochemical plants is expected to be located mainly in NE England and E Scotland. Elsewhere what changes do occur will continue the trends described in ch. 4, though clearly at a very much slower rate. Improved efficiency will remain at a premium, with rationalization and economies of scale still being one source of improvement, thus continuing to alter distribution patterns. The best example, already announced, is the programme for steel industry development through to the 1980s: to reorganize the geographical pattern of the industry and to aim to maintain output while substantially reducing the labour force and the number of steelmaking plants (British Steel Corp 1973). One difference from the earlier periods, however, is likely to be in the field of government distribution of industry policies (Chisholm 1976). In order to achieve stated aims it will no longer be possible to divert *some* of the growth occurring in one region to another so that both grow — as was attempted in the past. In a situation of national non-growth, one region can grow only if another is in decline. Redistribution to prevent decline will be possible only by taking away any growth which one region might have and transferring it to a region where contraction is occurring. Such a policy, which requires fossilization of the distribution of economic activity, is unlikely to be acceptable politically. Moreover, parts of former source areas of growth, such as the W Midlands and the SE, have already begun pressing their own cases for needing help (Falk and Martinos 1975).

The best example is the inner cities from which industries have moved elsewhere, especially to the metropolitan fringes. Their economic decline has left local problems equal in some cases to those more familiar from the DAs (Gripaios 1976). In the new situation intra-regional problems such as this are expected to attract far more attention, and to influence government action on the distribution of economic activity as much as on inter-regional problems.

These comments leave little doubt that the considerable changes in the patterns of economic activity within the UK Space between 1945 and 1973 (ch. 4) were much greater than the differences which can be expected to occur in the foreseeable future. The Victorian mould of Britain's economy and geography, which survived to 1945 and to a considerable extent even to 1960, was at last structurally adapted to the needs of the late twentieth century. The changes now likely are expected to consolidate and further develop the patterns which have emerged, modified by the development of offshore fuel resources and in the longer-term by changes in government policies influencing the distribution of economic activity.

VI Transport

The outstanding period of transport development, beginning soon after the Second World War, is not yet complete. Some developments are yet to be fully implemented and further important technological advances have not been used commercially. If the technological possibilities are to be fully exploited then certain recent features of the UK transport systems will be accentuated in the years ahead. There will be a further concentration of activity into a limited number of nodes such as certain of the major ports and an increased intensity of working in limited sections of the transport networks, as has so obviously taken place in rail and inland waterways transport. Transport also will continue to become increasingly capital-intensive and within the next decade both the railways and, outstandingly, the ports will face difficult problems of labour redundancy. The systems will continue to be shaped mainly by demand. It will be a demand which increasingly involves the quality of service and thus presumably, in inland transport, reinforces the dominance of road transport. However it is likely that transport, and road transport in particular, will be subject to environmentalist pressure groups and arguments about the 'quality of life' which may well influence the relationships of road and rail media over long hauls and the status of the road within urban areas.

The immediate future is likely to see a fuller development of inter-modal transport and this will assuredly be an influence upon the investment decisions to be made concerning motorway mileage and the rationalization of the ports. The development of the Advanced Passenger Train (APT) and of vertical take-off and landing aircraft (VTOL) promises more radical change. On present showing the APT is the firmer and more immediate prospect. It may well equalize the distance over which the railway is competitive for passengers with air transport to include the Anglo-Scottish services. Later the VTOL aircraft may cause a reversion to the present competitive limits of about 400 km. However, while there are clearly technological advances to bring to fruition, it may be that after a period dominated by technological issues the transport systems to the end of the century will be influenced notably by the reassessments of scale and of space relationships which follow from membership of the EEC. In some respects the insularity and limited dimensions which have been a feature of UK transport will be modified. More immediately, the activities of a wider community will inevitably thicken the transport concentration in SE England, accentuate the problem of circumnavigating London, or perhaps lead to an increasing volume of traffic avoiding the problem by using E Anglian ports. Indeed, in general, it seems likely that the eastern seaboard of Britain will assume a relative importance unapproached since the advent of transoceanic trade.

By the end of 1975 it was clear that British Rail, like other large firms in the UK, would soon have to reduce its services, its payroll and/or its investment programme, since annual increases in the level of government financial support could no longer be expected. The widening gap between railway income and expenditure led to a revival of interest in the more radical changes in the railway system which had been proposed since 1945. The conversion of some or all railways to limited access roads, originally mooted in 1955 (Lloyd 1955) was considered in an unpublished study of several railway routes in E London and Essex. Press reports of originally confidential discussions between the W German government and the Federal Railways concerning the reduction of the German network from 28,960 km to 14,480, 9,650, or even 6,435 km, reminded British observers of similar proposals in the Beeching Plan (Min. of Transport 1963). During the 1950s and 1960s recommendations for changes in the railway network had been published in some detail and subjected to reasoned argument. In the mid-1970s governments, apparently fearing public discussion of alternative future networks for the railways, created a climate of hostility and distrust in advance of new statements on transport policy.

The real difficulties attending such a policy may be illustrated from air transport. Formulation of national airport policy awaits a study of provincial airports but a review of the situation in SE England (Dept of Industry 1975B) forecast a slower growth of traffic up to 1990 than had been envisaged before the fuel crisis. The predicted numbers of air passengers in the London area in 1990 lay between 67–107 million. The Report suggested that most of this range of traffic could be accommodated by extending the facilities of Heathrow, Gatwick, Luton and Stansted airports. If the highest predicted traffic figures were, however, reached in 1990, it would have been necessary to start building a new airport in 1978. In the uncertainties of the mid-1970s, therefore, it is seldom possible to forecast with sufficient certainty the need for a transport facility within the time needed to build it.

VII The Urban System

Any forecast of probable changes in the British urban system over the next twenty or so years is more than usually difficult to make in the mid-1970s. Substantial uncertainty surrounds several of the major influences. Official population forecasts now predict a net addition substantially less than that forecast in the late 1960s (section 7.III). The rapid and substantial increase in the real cost of petrol is beginning to alter mobility patterns and if it continues commuting and leisure may be substantially affected. In contrast to these trends, which would tend to slow down the rate of decentralization, there are others which might accelerate it. New and improving telecommunications technology could make dispersal more possible, while the pressure from families in the inner-city areas of the conurbations for more space and improved living conditions will see traditional physical planning policies continued, favouring further decentralization. In political terms, however, the problems of the inner cities (not least those of C London) led in 1976 to pressures for reversal of the decentralization policies for overspill which had characterized spatial planning since 1945. At the same time, the programmes for New Town expansion came under equally critical review.

The scale and the strength of the decentralization pressure in individual towns, cities and SMLAs will depend to a large degree on the regional economic dimension. New cores for emerging metropolitan areas will arise, if employment decentralization from the conurbations continues despite the national economic difficulties. Increasing metropolitanization of free-standing towns will occur in some localities in response to changing economic opportunities, as North Sea oil has already demonstrated in Scotland. Regional policy and transportation investment will continue to remain significant background influences under the control of central government. In general the role of cities in steering the pattern of regional growth and decline seems likely to obtain greater recognition and consequently regional policy will probably come to have a more explicitly urban character.

It is possible therefore that the period 1975–2000 will not see changes in the British urban system as great as those in the period 1950–75. Almost certainly the city-region or metropolitan area will continue to be the dominant settlement type. By the year 2000, however, continued expansion among the adjacent and overlapping metropolitan areas from Southampton and Southend to Lancaster and Leeds, whether planned as in the case of Northampton, Milton Keynes, Warrington and Swindon, for example, or otherwise, will have begun to create a megalopolitan structure in which the complexity of inter-city and intra-city movements makes the definition of individual metropolitan areas less useful. The outstanding feature of this highly inter-locked urban system will be the intensity and diversity of the communication channels for people, goods, and particularly information (Cowan et al 1969).

Both the major urbanized zones beyond this megalopolitan heartland, the North East and C Scotland will also be characterized by megalopolitan features, as the planned integration of the city regions (Glasgow–Edinburgh–Dundee and Newcastle–Teesside) is achieved. Elsewhere, rural zones providing essentially either recreation or agriculture will exist with minor centres and the exceptional freestanding city region, e.g. Aberdeen and Plymouth.

The most uncertain question of all is whether local, regional, and national planning processes are capable of managing the continuing evolution of the urban system in a fashion that brings widespread public support. Without a deep and continuing commitment to intervention in the public interest, the influencing of the diverse private interests in a populous, developed and metropolitanized nation is impossible.

VIII A Final Note

A mid-1970s postscript must necessarily be somewhat less optimistic than one of even a few years ago (Hudson Institute 1974). Preoccupation with serious and deep-seated structural economic problems in the UK implies a halt in, if not a reversal of, the dramatic trends of growth and change since 1945 (Leicester 1972). Membership of the EEC, confirmed in 1973, may well provide the expected economic benefits from the larger market in due course, but of this there are few short-term indications. Such enhanced growth momentum may, however, be the opportune if not the only means of completing the structural reform of the UK economy and society started a few decades ago.

The problems endemic in slow growth or in the steady-state society require sensitive planning measures, the more difficult in that they must now also carry conviction with sectional interests, as well as with the public. The continuing distribution, or redistribution, of national wealth among classes and regions is central to public policies, but to be implemented needs sufficient sustained economic growth. Whether to promote growth, to stabilize, or to accept a measured decline, the mobilization of regional and national forces on the grand scale is an urgent task. The verdict of this book is that such a mobilization is technically and geographically feasible and indeed that it is overdue. Careful public management and monitoring of the economy will continue to be essential, but such deliberate public intervention should take more fully into account for the future the variegated characteristics, the many constraints, but especially the infinitely greater potentials which have been shown to be inherent in the complex geographical character of UK space.

REFERENCES

BRIT. STEEL CORPN. (1973) *Ten-year Development Strategy*, London
BROOKS, E (1973) *This Crowded Kingdom: An Essay on Population Pressure*, London
BUXTON, M and CRAVEN, E (eds) (1976) *The Uncertain Future*, Centre for Stud. in Soc. Pol., London
CABINET OFF., CENT. POLICY REV. STAFF (1975) *Joint Framework for Social Policies*, HMSO
CHISHOLM, M D I (1974) 'Regional Policies for the 1970s', *Geogrl. J, 140*, 215–31
          (1976) 'Regional Policies in an Era of Slow Population Growth and Higher Unemployment', *Reg. Stud., 10*, 201–13
COMMN. EUROPEAN COMMUNITIES (1975) *General Regional Aid Systems*, COM (75) 77, Brussels
COWAN, P et al (1969) 'Developing Patterns of Urbanisation', *Urban Stud., 6*, 279–453
DEPT. INDUSTRY (1975A) 'Oil-related Developments in Scotland', *Scott. Econ. Bull., 7*, 8–13
          (1975B) *Airport Strategy for Great Britain. Pt. 1 The London Area. A Consultation Document*, HMSO
EVERSLEY, D (1975) *Planning without Growth*, London
FALK, N and MARTINOS, H (1975) *Inner City*, London
GRIPAIOS, C (1976) 'A new Employment Policy for London?', *Nat. Westminster Bank Q. Rev.*, August, 37–45
HOUSE OF COMMONS (1971) 'Population of the UK', *First Report of the Select Comm. on Sci. & Technol.*, HMSO
HUDSON INST. (1974) *The UK in 1980?*, London
HUTCHINSON, Sir J (1966) 'Land and Human Populations', *Advmt Sci., 23*, 111, 241–54
KEEBLE, D (1976) *Industrial Location and Planning in the UK*, London
LEICESTER, C (1972) *Britain 2001 AD*, HMSO
LLOYD, T I (1955) 'Potentialities of the British Railway System as a Reserve Roadways System', *Proc. Inst. Civil Engrs., 4*, 1, 732–88

MIN. of TRANSPORT (1963) *The Reshaping of British Railways* (Beeching Rep.), HMSO
POPULATION INVESTIGATION COMMN. LSE (1970) *Towards a Population Policy for the UK*, London
PUBL. GEN. ACTS See list p. 516
ROY. COMMN. DISTRIBUTION OF THE INDUS. POPULATION (1940) (Barlow) *Rep.*, Cmnd 6153 HMSO
ROY. COMMN. POPULATION (1949) *Rep.*, Cmnd 7695 HMSO
TAYLOR, L R (ed) (1970) 'The Optimum Population for Britain', *Inst. Biol. Symp.*, *19*, London

Public General Acts

Index

For authors see the references for each chapter. Italicized references indicate figures in the text.